THE HOLOCAUST

Containing an almost entirely new selection of texts, this second edition of *The Holocaust: Origins, Implementation, Aftermath* presents a critical and important study of the Holocaust. Many of the pieces challenge conventional analyses and preconceived notions about the Holocaust, whether regarding genocidal precedents and the centrality of anti-Semitism, the relationship between ideological motivation and economic calculations, or the timing of the decision on the Final Solution.

Starting with the background of the Holocaust and focusing on colonial violence, anti-Semitism and scientific racism as being at the root of the Final Solution, the book then examines the context of the decision to unleash the genocide of the Jews. Several powerful texts then provide readers with a close look at the psychology of a perpetrator, the fate of the victims – with a particular emphasis on the role of gender and the murder of children – and the impossible choices made by Jewish leaders, educators, and men recruited into the Nazi extermination apparatus. Finally, there is an analysis of survivors' testimonies and the creation of an early historical record, and an inquiry into postwar tribunals and the development of international justice and legislation with a view to the larger phenomenon of modern genocide before and after the Holocaust.

Complete with an introduction that summarises the state of the field, this book contains major reinterpretations by leading Holocaust authors along with key texts on testimony, memory, and justice after the catastrophe. With brief discussions placing each essay in historical and scholarly context, this carefully selected compilation is an ideal introduction to the topic and essential reading for all students of the Holocaust.

Omer Bartov is the John P. Birkelund Distinguished Professor of European History and Professor of History and German Studies at Brown University and has written on the Holocaust, Nazi Germany and modern genocide. His books include *Erased: Vanishing Traces of Jewish Galicia in Present-Day Ukraine* (2007), *Germany's War and the Holocaust: Disputed Histories* (2003) and *Mirrors of Destruction: War, Genocide and Modern Identity* (2000).

REWRITING HISTORIES
Edited by Jack R. Censer

PRAISE FOR THIS BOOK

"In this sophisticated anthology, Omer Bartov has assembled an outstanding sampling of research literature illustrating some of the most fruitful new directions in studying the Holocaust that have emerged during the last decade. These academic writings are supplemented with important primary sources illustrating many of the problems of interpretation with which contemporary scholars are grappling. *The Holocaust* offers students a fine introduction to a complex subject."

David Engel, *New York University, USA*

"…outstanding. Professor Bartov has selected instructive, clearly written articles of the highest quality by leading scholars in Third Reich and Holocaust Studies that deftly combine historiography, narrative and argument. This volume will engage university students and generate important discussions."

Paul E. Kerry, *Brigham Young University, USA*

THE HOLOCAUST

Origins, Implementation, Aftermath

Second Edition

Edited by
Omer Bartov

Routledge
Taylor & Francis Group

LONDON AND NEW YORK

First published 2015
by Routledge
2 Park Square, Milton Park, Abingdon, Oxon OX14 4RN

and by Routledge
711 Third Avenue, New York, NY 10017

Routledge is an imprint of the Taylor & Francis Group, an informa business

British Library Cataloguing-in-Publication Data
A catalogue record for this book is available from the British Library

Library of Congress Cataloging-in-Publication Data
The Holocaust: origins, implementation, aftermath / edited by Omer Bartov. – Second edition.
    pages cm – (Rewriting histories)
    Includes bibliographical references and index.
    1. Holocaust, Jewish (1939–45).   2. Holocaust, Jewish
(1939–45)—Causes.   3. Holocaust, Jewish (1939–45)—Influence.
4. Germany—History—1933–45.   5. Germany—Ethnic relations—
History—20th century.   I. Bartov, Omer, editor.
    D804.3.H6478   2015
    940.53′18—dc23

                                                          2014024268

ISBN: 978–0–415–77850–3 (hbk)
ISBN: 978–0–415–77851–0 (pbk)

Typeset in Goudy
by RefineCatch Limited, Bungay, Suffolk

To Shira and Rom, for always drawing me out from
my chamber of horrors.

CONTENTS

CONTENTS

Appendices

SERIES EDITOR'S PREFACE

Rewriting history, or revisionism, has always followed closely in the wake of history writing. In their efforts to re-evaluate the past, professional as well as amateur scholars have followed many approaches, most commonly as empiricists, uncovering new information to challenge earlier accounts. Historians have also revised previous versions by adopting new perspectives, usually fortified by new research, which overturn received views.

Even though rewriting is constantly taking place, historians' attitudes towards using new interpretations have been anything but settled. For most, the validity of revisionism lies in providing a stronger, more convincing account that better captures the objective truth of the matter. Although such historians might agree that we never finally arrive at the "truth," they believe it exists and over time may be better approximated. At the other extreme stand scholars who believe that each generation or even each cultural group or subgroup necessarily regards the past differently, each creating for itself a more usable history. Although these latter scholars do not reject the possibility of demonstrating empirically that some contentions are better than others, they focus upon generating new views based upon different life experiences. Different truths exist for different groups. Surely such an understanding, by emphasizing subjectivity, further encourages rewriting history. Between these two groups are those historians who wish to borrow from both sides. This third group, while accepting that every congeries of individuals sees matters differently, still wishes somewhat contradictorily to fashion a broader history that incorporates both of these particular visions. Revisionists who stress empiricism fall into the first of the three camps, while others spread out across the board.

Today the rewriting of history seems to have accelerated to a blinding speed as a consequence of the evolution of revisionism. A variety of approaches has emerged. A major factor in this process has been the enormous increase in the number of researchers. This explosion has reinforced and enabled the retesting of many assertions. Significant ideological shifts have also played a major part in the growth of revisionism. First, the crisis of Marxism, culminating in the events in Eastern Europe in 1989, has given rise to doubts about explicitly Marxist accounts. Such doubts have spilled over into the entire field of social history which has been a dominant subfield of the discipline for several decades. Focusing on society and its class divisions implied that these are the most important elements in historical analysis. Because Marxism was built on the same claim, the whole basis of social history has been questioned, despite the very many studies that directly had little to do with Marxism. Disillusionment with social history simultaneously opened the door to cultural and linguistic approaches largely developed in anthropology and literature. Multiculturalism and feminism further generated revisionism. By claiming that scholars had, wittingly or not, operated from a white European/American male point of view, newer researchers argued that other approaches had been neglected or misunderstood. Not surprisingly, these last historians are the most likely to envision each subgroup rewriting its own usable history, while other scholars incline towards revisionism as part of the search for some stable truth.

Rewriting Histories will make these new approaches available to the student population. Often new scholarly debates take place in the scattered issues of journals which are sometimes difficult to find. Furthermore, in these first interactions, historians tend to address one another, leaving out the evidence that would make their arguments more accessible to the uninitiated. This series of books collects in one place a strong group of the major articles in selected fields, adding notes and introductions conducive to improved understanding. Editors select articles containing substantial historical data, so that students – at least those who approach the subject as an objective phenomenon – can advance not only their comprehension of debated points but also their grasp of substantive aspects of the subject

Studying the Holocaust of the Nazi era continues to expand. Public, scholarly, and student interest has increased for many reasons, including a renewed focus on World War II, the persistence of mass destruction in societies around the globe, and the efforts of groups to raise consciousness in order to try to avoid future genocidal outbreaks. Moreover, the Holocaust, even as it inspires horror, also raises extremely difficult questions on many moral issues.

This volume excels at capturing the flood of information and interpretations that have replaced previous explanations that relied only on one single cause or another. This book adds perspective by bringing in the other holocausts before and after World War II, whose addition makes one rethink how and why such terrible events occurred. The new research also deepens our specific understanding of how what transpired in Central Europe depended on a dreadful confluence of factors. In addition, this volume makes sense of how death and work camps fitted together in the Nazi plan. As one final example of this book's value, it is worth noting that several chapters put individuals caught in the Holocaust under the microscope, thus revealing the complexities of response. Clearly, the time has already arrived to reconsider the rewriting of this history.

ACKNOWLEDGEMENTS

I would like to thank my research assistant Stephanie Williams for her invaluable help in the preparation of this volume, as well as Amy Welmers and the rest of the staff at Routledge for their efficiency, professionalism, and patience, without which this book would have never seen the light of day.

All articles and extracts in this volume (except the Introduction) have already been published. We would like to thank the following copyright holders for permission to reproduce their work.

Introduction   Written for this volume by Omer Bartov.

Chapter 1   Reprinted from " 'One of these races has got to go . . .':
                Colonialism and Genocide" by Cathie Carmichael in *Genocide
                Before the Holocaust* (New Haven: Yale University Press, 2009),
                pp. 56–70. Reprinted with the permission of the publisher.

Figure 1.1   "Comrade Lenin cleanses the earth of the unclean." Soviet
                poster designed by Mikhail Cheremnykh and Viktor Deni,
                November 1920. © C. and M. History Pictures / Alamy

Chapter 2   Excerpt from *Nazi Anti-Semitism: From Prejudice to the Holocaust*
                – Copyright © 2000, 2004 by Editions du Seuil. English transla-
                tion © 2005 by The New Press. Reprinted by permission of The
                New Press. www.thenewpress.com.

Chapter 3   Reprinted from *Racial Science in Hitler's New Europe, 1938–1945*
                edited by Anton Weiss-Wendt and Rory Yeomans by permis-
                sion of the University of Nebraska Press. Copyright 2013 of the
                Board of Regents of the University of Nebraska.

Chapter 4   Reprinted from "Camps and Ghettos," by Wolf Gruner in *Jewish
                Forced Labor Under the Nazis* (Cambridge University Press,
                2006), pp. 177–95. Reprinted with the permission of Cambridge
                University Press.

Chapter 5   Reprinted from "The Holocaust and the Concentration Camps," by Dieter Pohl in *Concentration Camps in Nazi Germany*, ed. Jane Caplan et al. (New York: Routledge, 2010), pp. 149–66. Reprinted with the permission of the publisher.

Chapter 6   Reprinted from "Conclusion" by Peter Longerich in *Holocaust: The Nazi Persecution and Murder of the Jews* (New York: Oxford University Press, 2010), pp. 422–35. Reprinted with the permission of the publisher.

Chapter 7   Reprinted with the permission of Simon & Schuster Publishing Group from the Free Press edition of *"The Good Old Days": The Holocaust as Seen by its Perpetrators and Bystanders*, edited by Ernest Klee, Willi Dressen, and Volker Riess. Foreword by Hugh Trevor-Roper. Copyright © 1988 by S. Verlag GmbH. Translation copyright © 1991 by Deborah Burnstone. All rights reserved.

Chapter 8   Reprinted from "Keeping Calm and Weathering the Storm: Jewish Women's Responses to Daily Life in Nazi Germany, 1933–39" by Marion Kaplan in *Women in the Holocaust*, ed. Dalia Ofer et al. (New Haven: Yale University Press, 1999), pp. 39–54. Reprinted with the permission of the publisher.

Chapter 9   "Give Me Your Children" reprinted by permission of the publisher from *Ghettostadt: Łódź and the Making of a Nazi City* by Gordon J. Horwitz, pp. 192–231, Cambridge, Mass.: The Belknap Press of Harvard University Press, Copyright © 2008 by the President and Fellows of Harvard College.

Chapter 10   Reprinted from *Ghetto Diary* by Janusz Korczak (New Haven: Yale University Press, 2003), pp. 100–115. Reprinted with the permission of the publisher.

Chapter 11   Reprinted from " 'And it was something we didn't talk about': Rape of Jewish Women during the Holocaust" by Helene J. Sinnreich in *Holocaust Studies* (14/2) (2008): 1–22. Reprinted with the permission of the publisher.

Chapter 12   Reprinted from "Between Sanity and Insanity: Spheres of Everyday Life in the Auschwitz-Birkenau *Sonderkommando*" by Gideon Greif in *Gray Zones: Ambiguity and Compromise in the Holocaust and its Aftermath*, ed. Jonathan Petropoulos and John K. Roth (New York: Berghahn Books, 2005), pp. 37–60. Reprinted with the permission of the publisher.

Chapter 13   Reprinted from "Wartime Lies and Other Testimonies: Jewish-Christian Relations in Buczacz, 1939–44" by Omer Bartov in

East European Politics and Societies 25(3), 2011, pp. 486–511. Reprinted with the permission of the publisher.

Chapter 14   Reprinted from *"Khurbn Forshung* – Jewish Historical Commissions in Europe, 1943–49" by Laura Jockusch in the *Simon Dubnow Institute Yearbook* 6, 2007, pp. 441–73. Reprinted with the permission of the publisher.

Chapter 15   Reprinted from "Semantics of Extermination: The Use of the New Term of Genocide in the Nuremberg Trials and the Genesis of a Master Narrative" by Alexa Stiller in *Reassessing the Nuremberg Military Tribunals: Transitional Justice, Trial Narratives, and Historiography*, eds. Kim C. Priemel and Alexa Stiller (New York: Berghahn Books, 2012), pp. 104–33. Reprinted with the permission of the publisher.

Chapter 16   Reprinted from "Theorizing Destruction: Reflections on the State of Comparative Genocide Theory" by Maureen S. Hiebert in *Genocide Studies and Prevention* {3/3} (2008): 309–39. Reprinted with permission from University of Toronto Press (www.utpjournals.com).

INTRODUCTION

Omer Bartov

In the decade and a half since the publication of this volume's first edition, scholarship on the Holocaust has gone through a major transformation. Not only has the sheer number of books and articles on the genocide of the Jews greatly increased, but we have also witnessed a significant shift in areas of interest, modes of interpretation, research methodologies, and historical contextualization.[1] The current edition attempts to reflect these new trends in the historiography and to provide readers with a selection of innovative, succinct, well-researched and elegantly argued contributions to the on-going quest to reconstruct, analyze, and understand one of the most tragic events in modern history.

Because of the magnitude of new work on the Holocaust, this edition is in fact an entirely new book, containing only one chapter that was included in the original edition, a chilling extract from the diary of an SS perpetrator. This is not to say that the original chapters of the first edition are no longer relevant or useful; indeed, one can profitably use both editions side-by-side in order to gain greater insight both into the event itself and the manner in which its historiography has progressed. But in order to include the most recent research in a single volume it was deemed necessary to rethink the book as a whole rather than replace only some of the chapters. I hope that students of this period will find that the new edition piques their curiosity and motivates them to delve into the rich and complex literature on the Holocaust of which this volume can only provide a mere glimpse. For each of the chapters included here can be a gateway to many more articles and books, and was chosen with a mind to provoking readers into rethinking what they believe they know and seeking answers to new questions.

Most of the old controversies over the nature and historical context of the Holocaust have been left out of this volume, while new and more urgent issues are given much greater space. In the early postwar decades several interpretive models tried to grapple with the sheer enormity of World War II and the Holocaust, the titanic forces summoned by such regimes as Nazi Germany and Soviet Russia, and the deeper historical roots of this explosion of utterly unprecedented destruction. Several influential political thinkers such as Hannah

Arendt argued that what distinguished the twentieth century was the emergence of totalitarianism, whose ability to mobilize society and suppress the individual was matched only by its capacity for undermining the accomplishments
of Humanism and the Enlightenment and destroying both peoples and cultures
in the name of utopian ideologies.[2] Others preferred to focus on fascism and
Nazism as radical nationalist ideologies that disdained the notion of a shared
humanity and sacralized race and nation, blood and soil, promising a bright
future to their national or racial kin and dooming the rest of mankind to subjugation and genocide.[3]

In both interpretations, the Holocaust was the outcome of much larger
historical forces and political systems violently striving to establish hegemony
in their own societies and beyond. But it was not entirely clear from these
models why the Nazis specifically targeted the Jews for extinction. Here two
other models were suggested. One interpretation postulated the central role of
anti-Semitism – which had already played a significant part in Arendt's analysis
of totalitarianism – in the implementation of the Holocaust, arguing that
Europe's deeply-rooted anti-Jewish traditions and the eventual rise of a new and
much more extreme anti-Semitic discourse constituted the single most important cause of the "final solution."[4] Another interpretation explained Germany's
turn to Nazism by reference to the new nation state's historical *Sonderweg*, or
special path, which was said to have diverted it from creating a liberal middle
class and to have facilitated the rise of extremist political forces vulnerable to
militarism, xenophobia, racism, and anti-Semitism.[5]

These debates are long behind us. Interestingly, while they provided many
insights into European history, and often referred to the Holocaust as the ultimate and most radical outcome of the political systems or historical forces they
interpreted, the scholars engaged in this work rarely added much to our specific
knowledge or even understanding of the Holocaust. As research on the "final
solution" began accumulating in the 1970s and 1980s, two new schools of interpretation emerged, which, even though they can be traced back to the previous
models, were more specifically focused on Nazi Germany and the "final solution." The "intentionalists," who had a fair amount in common with certain
interpretations of fascism and anti-Semitism, argued that the Holocaust was the
outcome of a plan long in the making by Hitler and his subsequent Nazi regime
to exterminate the Jews of Europe.[6] The "functionalists," who can in certain
ways be related to the totalitarian and *Sonderweg* schools, saw the Holocaust as
the outcome of a structure of government that pitted competing agencies and
organizations against each other in an on-going process of "cumulative radicalization" as they sought to win favor with a weak but extremist dictator.[7] The
Holocaust was, then, the result of either a German obsession with the Jews
epitomized by a homicidal Führer; or the eventual systematization of a series of
decisions made by middle-ranking officials "on the ground," who applied the
most radical solutions to the self-imposed problem of conquering a "living
space" populated by unwanted races.

2

As the chapters in this volume demonstrate, this debate, too, has largely been settled, even though it has left its traces in more current interpretations of the causes and implementation of the "final solution." From this perspective, it was a productive controversy. But as research on the Holocaust expanded, the intentionalist and functionalist models were also shown to have been far too simplistic and, in some ways, to have channeled historical inquiry to rather narrow paths and restricted thinking. Many of the questions asked today by scholars about both the context and the content of the Holocaust were previously either not raised or insufficiently researched. It is to these issues that we now turn.

For several decades, the history of the Holocaust was being written in isolation from that of other modern genocides. Although the United Nations Genocide Convention of 1948 was greatly influenced by the events of World War II and the mass murder of the Jews, there was generally very little scholarship on genocide until the 1980s. By then the historiography of the Holocaust was already expanding. But especially since the 1990s, not least because of the genocides in the former Yugoslavia and Rwanda, many political scientists, sociologists, historians, and others, have begun turning their attention to the phenomenon of genocide. For this purpose, the existing scholarship on the Holocaust was extremely useful. At the same time, scholars of the Holocaust became aware that beyond the immediate historical context of the event, that is, its roots in German history, the history of European anti-Semitism, and the emergence of scientific racism, it also had to be seen within the framework of prior genocidal events.[8]

That analyses of the Holocaust and of other genocides were mutually supportive is, of course, hardly surprising, in view of the fact that the "final solution" was one of several genocides in the twentieth century, albeit a particularly extreme case with a number of distinguishing features. To be sure, there were voices that claimed that the Holocaust was unique, and therefore could not be compared with any other historical event, but those rarely came from scholars and diminished over time, as the extent and horror of other genocides became more widely known.[9] There were and are also some who argue that the focus on the Holocaust had diverted attention from other genocides; but here too, cooperation between those who investigate distinct cases of genocide and those who work in a comparative framework has been more important than polemics over the relationship between genocide and the Holocaust.[10]

Cathie Carmichael's chapter illustrates the value of learning about the larger historical context of the Holocaust. As she notes, the extraordinary brutality of several colonial regimes, such as Belgian King Leopold's rule in the Congo, which caused the death of up to ten million Africans, and the genocide declared and perpetrated by the German military in quelling the rebellion of the Herero in German Southwest Africa in 1904, clearly heralded a new type of violence exercised by Europeans over colonized peoples whether for the purpose of economic gain or in order to establish settler colonies.[11] Similarly, the state-organized mass deportation, massacres, and genocide of the Armenian population in the Ottoman Empire by the government and its agencies in 1915, coming in the wake of massive massacres of civilian populations in the late nineteenth century and during the Balkan Wars of 1912–13, indicated the new urge to ruthlessly remove or murder ethnic groups deemed alien or enemy populations especially under cover of war.[12] But Carmichael also shows that these very same events were accompanied by a growing discourse in Europe and the United States on human and minority rights and the need for international law and institutions that would prevent or punish such policies. This "prelude" to the Holocaust is crucial to our understanding of both what the Nazis believed they could do and had learned from previous events, and of the eventual responses to the Holocaust. After all, Raphael Lemkin, the man who coined the word "genocide" and played a key role in bringing about the UN Genocide Convention, had begun thinking about this issue when he learned about the Armenian genocide while studying law in the 1920s. It was that "crime without a name" that he sought to identify, define, and ban.[13]

There was also, of course, a more specific context to the Holocaust, but one that, at the same time, did have deep roots in Christian Europe. To be sure, even as anti-Semitism, in the words of Shulamit Volkov, became a "cultural code" among Central Europe's right wing and conservative circles in particular, not all Europeans, and certainly not all Germans, adopted the kind of "eliminationist anti-Semitism" suggested by Daniel Jonah Goldhagen.[14] The paradox is, in fact, that even as Jews were becoming more integrated within European society, anti-Semitism was also becoming more "*Salonfähig*," or acceptable in polite society. This was not necessarily a vehement and aggressive, or even entirely exclusive anti-Semitism, but a set of ideas, expressions, mannerisms and attitudes about and toward Jews that set them apart from non-Jews. It was a sentiment that could gradually dissipate and disappear, or could be mobilized and radicalized.[15] As Philippe Burrin shows in his chapter, it was thanks to Adolf Hitler's accession to power that his version of anti-Semitism – an extreme, violent, and potentially genocidal ideological stance – gradually transformed the endemic sentiments of many Germans into an active, as well as politically beneficial view. Hitler's charisma, his early diplomatic and economic successes, his ability to spread his message of hatred and racism through the media, schools, legislation and political rhetoric, played a crucial part in this transformation.[16] From this perspective, Hitler's worldview, according to which the "removal" of the Jews was a precondition for the accomplishment of a utopian *Volksgemeinschaft* (racial community) inhabiting its exclusive *Lebensraum* (living space), epitomized what Saul Friedländer has called "redemptive anti-Semitism," and must be included in any explanation of why Germans behaved as they did during the Holocaust.[17]

Another crucial component of the march to genocide by the Nazi regime was scientific racism. This, too, was hardly a Nazi invention. An offshoot of the theory of evolution, and influenced by categorizations of human groups according to the families of languages, eugenics asserted that humankind was made up of distinct racial groups, some more developed from and therefore superior to others, and that mixing them, or allowing the mentally and physically handicapped within them to multiply, would degrade the superior races, postulated as Indo-European, Caucasian, Aryan, Nordic, Germanic, or simply German.[18] In a racial hierarchy where Aryans were on top and Africans and Aborigines at the bottom, the Slavs and the Jews came to play a special role. The Slavs, because they populated the lands seen as Germany's past and future living space, and, following the establishment of the Soviet Union, were said to be ruled by Judeo-Bolshevism. The Jews, because they were in a sense the obverse side of the Aryans, an anti-race, which both maintained its own racial purity and miraculously also managed to contaminate all other races, while striving to take over the world, not heroically like the Aryans, but as parasites living off the accomplishments of others.[19]

In the case of the Jews, then, anti-Semitism and scientific racism could complement and radicalize each other, providing the former with scientific sanction and the latter with demonic imagery. Once Hitler came to power, the scientists, geographers, historians, and anthropologists who favored the ideas and implications of scientific racism were quickly catapulted into positions of power and influence.[20] And, as Isabel Heinemann shows in her chapter, once the war broke out, theories and ideas could be quickly translated into policy driven both by faith in the scientific truth of these notions and by opportunism and careerism.[21] As Himmler's SS set about implementing the General Plan East, which called for the expulsion of Poles and Jews from occupied Polish territory meant for settlement by ethnic Germans, Nazi racial specialists were given the task of selecting those of the Polish population who were "racially fit" for Germanization, while the vast majority were to be "removed."[22] It is important to understand here that first, the scientific community played a key role in this process of transforming the entire demography of Eastern Europe; and second that this vast undertaking formed a crucial link between population policies, ethnic cleansing, and genocide. In other words, that the demographic upheaval in Poland created the momentum for the "final solution." Since Jews, unlike Poles, could not undergo any racial screening, being by definition "racially unfit," they became targets for total removal; and since they belonged to a particularly malign racial category, the next step of removing them through mass murder came ever closer once the notion of "unwanted populations" was made into state policy.

But the Jews were also targeted by specific policies, which were not simply the by-product of larger plans and policies by the Third Reich. Jews had been subjected to discriminatory directives and regulations since the early months of Nazi rule; were deprived of their citizenship by the Nuremberg Laws of 1935; were increasingly marginalized within German society by the loss of their occupations and property; were restricted in their movement, residence, schooling, health and leisure facilities, and so forth, and finally, having become largely socially dead, were physically assaulted in the massive pogrom of November 1938.[23] German Jews were also used for forced labor, a practice that was then extended to the Jews of Poland after the country was occupied by the Germans. By 1940 much of Polish Jewry under German rule had been ghettoized, not least in such major population concentrations as Warsaw and Łódź. Enclosing the Jews in ghettos was a transitional step by the Nazi authorities, designed to concentrate the Jews in several areas so as to be able to then "solve the problem" of their presence in a manner that had apparently not yet been determined – deportation, expulsion, resettlement, or, as would happen a couple of years later, mass murder.[24]

Yet as Wolf Gruner suggests in his chapter, the idea of meanwhile employing the Jews in forced labor to the benefit of the Reich was not a haphazard measure resulting from the high death rate caused by famine and epidemics in the ghettos, but rather the continuation of a policy begun in the 1930s of making maximum use of the Jews as long as the order to remove them had not been given. This was all the more so in Łódź, renamed Litzmannstadt by the Germans, which was the most populous city in the territory of Poland annexed by the Reich, and yet contained one of the largest and longest surviving ghettos. The reason the ghetto remained in existence as late as August 1944 was that it had become economically indispensable, or at least valuable enough to keep it going – with the exception of the many who could not work, such as the elderly, the sick and the children. Hence the Jews worked for the Germans to stay alive, and the Germans kept them alive as long as they could work for them, or until ordered to send them to their death. This had the added advantage of providing the perpetrators with the argument that they killed only those who could not work, and thus that there was nothing economically irrational in genocide. On the contrary, only "useless mouths to feed" were done away with, while the strong, who were gradually reduced to the same state by malnutrition and abuse, would be kept alive just as long as they were productive.[25]

Beyond the ghettos there were the camps. Here it is important to distinguish between the concentration camps, first built in Germany in the 1930s, and then expanded into a vast network throughout Europe during the war, and the six extermination camps, operating altogether from late 1941 to late 1944, of which four – Chełmno, Sobibór, Treblinka, and Bełżec, were strictly mass killing facilities, while Majdanek and the enormous complex of Auschwitz combined gassing installations with incarceration and forced labor. The concentration camps served many purposes: incarceration and reeducation, punishment and forced labor, as well as being the sites of numerous and often extraordinarily brutal killings of inmates, as, for instance, in the notorious camp of Mauthausen; but they were not created with the purpose of immediate killing of transports as were the extermination camps. It should also be stressed that the majority of the inmates in the concentration camps were non-Jews, although the majority of those who died in them were. Conversely, most of the people who arrived at extermination camps were Jews, as were most of the victims. Hence, what has come down to us as the "concentrationary universe," was not built primarily for Jews.[26]

In the 1930s the inmates of the early concentration camps were political opponents such as communists, socialists, and trade unionists; homosexual men; the so-called work-shy, and habitual criminals.[27] Jews reached these camps in large numbers only after the November 1938 pogrom, but most of them were released on condition that they leave Germany. The complex of camps and sub-camps that kept expanding in German-occupied Europe during the war also initially had little to do with Jews, who were first targeted for murder by the *Einsatzgruppen*, the murder squads of the SS, and then sent to the extermination camps. Only in 1943, after most of the Jewish victims of the Holocaust had already been killed, and as shortage of labor combined with the beginning of a slow German retreat from the east, did Jews begin to appear in large numbers in concentration camps as slave labor, while in other cases Jewish forced labor camps were transformed into concentration camps. Here once again the distorted connection between labor and extermination becomes apparent: while the Nazis performed *Vernichtung durch Arbeit*, or extermination through work, the Jews hoped to work in order to avoid extermination. Finally, as the inmates of these camps were sent on death marches back to Germany just ahead of the advancing Red Army in late 1944 and the early months of 1945, they filled the concentration camps that were liberated shortly thereafter by the Western Allies; but they had not been there for most of the war, and were so weak and diseased that they kept dying for weeks after they gained their freedom.[28]

When and how was the decision made to exterminate all the Jews of Europe? This question has haunted scholars for decades, and they may never reach full consensus. One significant problem has been that no specific order by Hitler to carry out the "final solution" was ever found, most probably because he never issued one in the first place, preferring to provide oral instructions.[29] Another has been a matter of definition: what was meant by such terms as "final solution" or "resettlement" and did their meaning change over time? Historians have also asked whether we can date the decision to the start of mass killings of Jews in the Soviet Union in summer 1941, to the beginning of the construction of extermination camps in late fall and winter of that year, or to the setting into operation of the entire complex of extermination camps and the beginning of deportations across Europe in spring and summer 1942? Finally, and taking us back in part to the intentionalists–functionalist debate, while a number scholars argue that Hitler had intended to exterminate the Jews all along and was only waiting for the opportune moment – be it the "euphoria of victory" in fall 1941 or the sense of urgency produced by the Soviet counter-offensive and the entry of the United States into the war in December – others suggest that Hitler and Himmler only focused their minds on a continent-wide genocide in the early months of 1942, as they cobbled together a series of actions already taking place in the east into what became a systematic, state-directed policy.[30]

In his chapter, Peter Longerich suggests that in a certain sense both arguments are correct. To his mind, what he calls *Judenpolitik* – Nazi Jewish policy – was a central factor of Third Reich politics from the very start, dictating or influencing many of the regime's decisions as well as serving to justify its growing encroachment on people's private lives. At the same time, as a policy intended to remove the Jews from Germany, *Judenpolitik* failed, since hundreds of thousands of Jews were still under German rule on the eve of the war, and their numbers increased exponentially with the invasion of Poland.[31] By now *Judenpolitik* meant the deportation or ethnic cleansing of the Jews, sending them to a reservation in Eastern Poland or shipping them off to Madagascar. This thinking, argues Longerich, persisted into the early months of fighting in the Soviet Union and was reflected in the language of the Wannsee Conference of January 20, 1942. At this meeting Reinhard Heydrich, Himmler's right hand man who had just been put in charge of the "final solution," spoke of sending the Jews in vast columns to the east to do forced labor.[32] But at about the same time a new way of "solving" the self-imposed problem of occupying millions of Jews was being devised with the construction of the extermination camps. Once these facilities became operational, and deportation trains started rolling toward them from all corners of Europe, the "final solution" came to mean mass murder, and "resettlement" signified deportations to the extermination camps. From this point on, *Judenpolitik* also became a major factor in the Reich's wartime policies, including, as Longerich stresses, its relations with allies and collaborators.

The Holocaust was a vast undertaking, whose implementation required hundreds of thousands of officials of all ranks and specialization. But closer to the ground, at the point where the perpetrator encounters his victim, things were both much simpler and far more complex. They were simpler because here we find policemen and SS officials who were charged with the task of organizing the murder of specific Jewish communities. While mass killing may have been psychologically difficult for some of them, by and large they managed their tasks efficiently, and, as we find from their own letters, diaries, and testimonies, they often also had a rather good time in those towns where they were the masters of life and death.[33] Yet this is also what makes things more difficult for us to understand. Had the men in charge of local killings been merely faceless sadists and murderers, we might more easily dismiss them as an entirely different species of humanity that has nothing in common with us. But of course, while they often were sadistic and certainly were murderers, these men were also human, with urges, even feelings and emotions, not unlike those of others, even their victims.[34] Indeed, in the encounter between killers and victims there were moments of mutual recognition, even though they invariably ended up in murder.[35] For that reason our own encounter with the perpetrators is also fraught. The excerpt from Felix Landau's diary is included here not in order to evoke sympathy for a man who was engaged in the murder of the Jews of Drohobycz, an East Galician town with a large, vibrant, and creative

community. It is included to remind us that the men who implemented genocide were in fact part of humanity and that precisely for that reason we all share
in the crimes they committed and cannot assign them to anything that is
outside the sphere of human responsibility without slipping into their own
distorted view of mankind. The horrors perpetrated by Landau and others of his
ilk were one potential outcome of individual behavior, group socialization, and
cultural formation that we can recognize as not vastly different from our own. It
is for that reason that these men are so terrifying.[36]

Landau's diary exposes to us the normality of genocide and the ability of
the perpetrator to separate between sentimental love and a human urge for
warmth and passion, and the cold "work" of killing other human beings.
Apparently a loving father, Landau commissioned the local Jewish writer and
artist, Bruno Schulz, now celebrated in Poland as one of its greatest modernist
authors, to paint murals in his child's bedroom. It is almost as if the expression-
ist world of Schulz's interwar paintings and stories had turned into reality, a
fantasy that ended with the nonchalant shooting of Schulz by another SS-man
on the street.[37] But the horror of Drohobycz, the sinister, twisted links between
love and murder, must not distract us from other instances in which families
struggled to maintain a semblance of normality in a world that had quite
suddenly transformed into a Hobbesian universe, held at bay only by family ties
and devotion. As Marion Kaplan shows in her chapter, Jews finding themselves
under Nazi rule in Germany sought ways to contend with this new reality, as
their previous lives of integration within German society were ruthlessly overturned, replaced by social isolation, unemployment, harassment, and
marginalization.[38]

Long before the killing began, but very much in line with Longerich's view of
Judenpolitik being part-and-parcel of the Nazi state, it was primarily German
Jewish women who sought to maintain their families in the face of increasingly
unfavorable odds. With their husbands often unemployed or reduced to less
desirable occupations, their children pushed out of regular schools and
threatened on the streets, and their own previous social ties with local
communities disintegrating, Jewish women were confronted with the immense
challenge of keeping their families together as well as often joining the workforce even as they tried to leave the country despite endless bureaucratic
obstacles. The sad part of this story is that by the time the options for immigration had drastically diminished following the outbreak of war, the remaining
Jews in Germany were disproportionately elderly and female. As would be seen
later on in the Holocaust, gender mattered a great deal even under conditions
in which Jews were targeted irrespective of their sex.[39]

Age mattered even more, certainly in the case of children, who were, in fact,
far more likely to become victims than adults. To be sure, the Kindertransport
program shipped about 10,000 Jewish children from Germany, Austria,
Czechoslovakia, and Poland to Britain between late November 1938 and the
outbreak of war.[40] But with the incarceration of Jews in ghettos, and especially

once the deportations to extermination camps began, children were the easiest and, in the view of the Nazis, the most logical target, being useless consumers of food who could not contribute to the German war effort. Often the fate of children and women was linked. On the selection ramp in Auschwitz-Birkenau young women who refused to give up their children were sent with them to the gas chambers. In ghettos, women often deprived themselves of nutrition so as to feed their children. In hideouts throughout Eastern Europe, in forest and town "bunkers" and family camps in remote areas, women were considered responsible for their children in ways that men were not. In some cases women were not allowed to enter hideouts with babies who might expose the bunker with their cries; in other cases mothers were forced or chose to abandon their children or even smothered them when they cried during a roundup.[41]

Perhaps the single most troubling story about the fate of children in the Holocaust involves Łódź Ghetto leader Chaim Rumkowski's call to the Jews to give up their children in order to save the rest of the population. The order was given by the Germans, but transmitted by Rumkowski and implemented by the Jewish police, later "assisted" by the Germans. It is an unimaginable moment, an illustration of the moral depravity of which possibly only Nazism was capable, but also of its polluting effects on everyone that came into contact with it. The moral question – should some be sacrificed so that others may survive – should never have been raised in the first place, certainly not in the case of children, the most innocent victims of all. But in compelling the Jews to resolve it, in whichever way, the Nazis accomplished more than their goal of murdering the Jews after first using their labor to wage war; they also tainted their victims with their own evil. And, as Gordon Horwitz powerfully shows, the slaughter of Jewish children was, as so much else in the Nazi universe, the dark side of a future utopia, where Aryan children would be given everything denied the Jews: fresh air, good food, athletic activities, loving teachers, education, and joy, and ultimately, life itself.[42]

But the Nazis never succeeded in tearing apart the moral fabric of all their victims, perhaps not even most. In the combined effort to accomplish both the sheer murder of a people and to crush its spirit – in fact, the attempt to transform its soul to resemble that of Nazism – physical extinction was more easily achieved than moral dissolution. Those who faced up to the evil were few, as they always are, but their acts resonated far and wide, well beyond their own expectations and with much greater meaning than they might have intended. Some were driven by a lifetime of dedication to a moral cause, others acted on the spur of the moment. Some rose up and fought a hopeless fight; others simply refused to give up their humanity, to surrender to the exterminatory logic of the perpetrators, and to abandon the innocents in their charge. Their choices, however insignificant at a time of vast destruction, when human life was utterly worthless, negated the seemingly irrepressible course of history. In retrospect we may even say that they won in that extraordinarily unequal battle. But the price, of course, was too great to bear, or to repair.

One rebel was Mordechai Anielewicz, the young man who headed the Warsaw Ghetto uprising in April 1943. As he and his fellow rebels knew, their actions were both utterly hopeless and of great historical significance. They brought hope and pride to millions of Jews and demonstrated to the world that one could in fact resist the Germans and win a moral victory over them even in death. The uprising was also the outcome of circumstances: most of the ghetto inmate population of 300,000 had already been murdered in Treblinka and there was no question that the rest faced a similar fate. It was better, then, to go down fighting that to "march like sheep to the slaughter," as Aba Kovner, another Jewish partisan, had already said more than two years earlier.[43]

But there was another way of marching to the slaughter; not like sheep, but with pride, dignity, and a clear sense of moral right, dedication, and love, so powerful that it has created a beam of light that will always emanate even from that heart of darkness, from the very sites of the *Umschlagplatz*, the train to Treblinka, the gas chambers. This was Janusz Korczak's way and his march to the train ahead of the children of his orphanage in August 1942. Korczak was not a saint, as we can see from the diary excerpts included here. He was a man who had dedicated himself to pedagogy and to children, especially orphans, and who believed in the power of love to make children into decent human beings. He was, in the deepest sense, a humanitarian, who could glean, or at least guess and hope for, the human soul of even his own perpetrators. He was not naïve, and understood perfectly well the relentless logic of the murder machine, just as he perceived the constant bickering, denunciation, maneuvering for a better position, and sheer corruption of so many ghetto inmates. But for him the act of marching ahead of his children to the train appears to have also been a natural act that did not entail any radical decision. His place was with them. The contrast between this moment and Rumkowski's speech could not be greater.[44]

Yet we cannot allow ourselves to find comfort in such acts as Anielewicz's uprising or Korczak's sacrifice. We must also look directly into that black hole of violence and depravity that was the Holocaust. Some aspects of that universe are particularly disruptive of the moral universe in which we would all prefer to reside, and have consequently often been ignored or denied. This is especially the case with sexual violence and collaboration. Rape has been a constant companion of war since the beginning of time and was often considered – mostly by male observers – to be a natural outcome of violent confrontation between armed opponents. In fact, rape was never merely another expression of male violence but was also used as a weapon of war, collective punishment, and destruction of ethnic groups. In more recent times, as wars have generally targeted civilians on a much greater scale, and have often also been associated with ethnic cleansing and genocide, mass rape has become a lamentably frequent phenomenon, often under-reported by victims fearful of harming their reputation and shrugged off by military men and male politicians as an unavoidable attribute of war. It was only in the wake of such horrendous use of mass rape during the genocides in Bosnia and Rwanda that it finally came to be considered as a crime against humanity under international law.[45]

In the case of World War II, mass rape is most often associated with the conduct of the Red Army as it fought its way into Germany in the last months of the war.[46] Sexual violence by the German military and police apparatus has often been seen as a marginal phenomenon precisely because of the racist nature of Nazi ideology, which forbade sex between Aryans and such inferior races as Slavs and Jews.[47] This also played into the general argument of older, and mostly male Holocaust scholars, according to which there was no room to make distinctions of gender among the victims since Jews were targeted as a group.[48] But as Helene Sinnreich shows conclusively in her chapter, sexual violence against Jewish women by the perpetrators was widespread, especially in the many areas where local commanders and units could act as they pleased.[49] That such sexual abuse was often followed by murder might have made the former appear less tragic, and certainly played a role in the general silence around this issue. But another reason was the suspicion among postwar communities that women who had survived the Holocaust must have used sex as a means of survival.[50] This pernicious argument, partly no doubt made by men who felt guilty for being unable to help women, enhanced the general reluctance of victims to relate their experiences.[51] And yet, as we now know, this was one more important distinction between men and women. For while there was in fact also sexual abuse of men, it appears by all accounts that Jewish women were far more vulnerable to sexual violence, and were largely reduced to silence about these experiences for decades thereafter, with all the harmful effects of suppressing such traumas, more recently shown also in the cases of Bosnia and Rwanda, and perhaps even more alarmingly in the on-going epidemic of sexual violence in the Democratic Republic of Congo.[52]

The most disturbing and morally ambiguous case of Jewish collaboration in the Holocaust is that of the *Sonderkommandos*, the teams of mostly young Jewish men who were selected by the SS to carry out the "dirty work" in the gassing and crematoria facilities in Auschwitz-Birkenau, as well as in Sobibór and Treblinka. The "ravens" of Auschwitz, as they were called, would bring the Jews to the undressing rooms, push them into the gas chambers, then take out their bodies and cremate them.[53] It is almost impossible to understand what these young men went through during the months, in some cases years, in which they worked within the heart of the industrial murder complex created by the Nazis. But Gideon Greif has ventured into this perilous territory, and on the basis of diaries, testimonies, and interviews, has analyzed the mentality of those who lived in, and operated, what was ultimately the core of the Nazi exterminationist essence.[54] Greif does not judge the men who, like Rumkowski though in a very different manner, epitomized what Primo Levi has termed the "gray zone." Instead, he demonstrates how even in the "anus mundi" that was Auschwitz, men could create a normal universe of sorts. Moreover, those very individuals, whom one might see as perhaps embodying the ultimate degradation of the victims by their perpetrators, also rose up against the system, in the only rebellion that ever occurred in Auschwitz (as well as in Sobibór and Treblinka), and even as most of them died, they also destroyed part of the killing apparatus that they had previously operated so efficiently.[55]

Greif's reliance on survivors' testimonies is essential to his attempt to understand the daily life of the *Sonderkommando*. It is but one example of the extraordinary benefit that we can derive from using accounts by the victims of genocide. Yet, as argued in my own contribution to this volume, historians have often shied away from such subjective accounts given at a chronological remove from the events they recount.[56] The result has often been that the Holocaust was largely reconstructed from the perspective of the perpetrators, who created a rich deposit of official documentation that has all the appearance, although often only the appearance, of accuracy and objectivity. Once we do examine events on the ground not only through such official documentation but also from the perspective of those whom the perpetrators had tried to hunt down and murder, our view of the entire event changes quite dramatically. This is not only because we understand better the experience of the victims when told by them, but also because we realize that much of what the perpetrators often missed or ignored was central to the daily lives, as well as the victimization or survival of the Jews. When we focus, as this chapter does, on a single location, and try to carefully reconstruct the event of genocide there, we quickly discover that this was not only an encounter between killers and their targets, but also what I have called a "communal massacre," where the entire population of the town and surrounding villages took part in the murder and plunder of their Jewish neighbors.[57] Furthermore, it becomes clear that in such regions as Eastern Galicia, quite apart from the German genocide of the Jews, there was also a vicious interethnic conflict between Poles and Ukrainians, in which the Germans took little interest but which nevertheless projected also onto the fate of the Jews by brutalizing the entire population. This means that the presumed third category of individuals in the Holocaust – or, for that matter, any other genocide – called "bystanders," never really existed, since everyone was involved in one way or another, whether they killed or were killed, rescued or denounced, lost everything they owned or profited from their neighbors' murder.[58]

This kind of reconstruction relies on individual accounts by people who were there at the time, as well as on official documentation. While historians took several decades to understand the value of such materials, their collection began even before the war ended, with precisely the goal of writing the history of the event, as well as of using such evidence in order to prosecute and punish the murderers. But as Laura Jockusch shows in her chapter, this massive effort to collect and record the events of the Holocaust was largely forgotten, to the extent that many historians have insisted that the first two postwar decades were a period of silence.[59] In fact, several groups of historians and other scholars, as well as many dedicated laypersons, founded centers of documentation and testimony collection as soon as the territories in which they resided were liberated. One of the most important was the Central Jewish Historical Commission in Poland, which collected over 7,000 testimonies of survivors between 1944–47; others included the Center for Jewish Documentation in Paris, which amassed large numbers of documents, and Simon Wiesenthal's Jewish Historical Documentation in Vienna.[60] Many additional efforts of documentation were carried out in the displaced persons (DP) camps in Germany, Austria and Italy.[61] To be sure, the goal of using this documentation in order to write a complete history of the Holocaust was not accomplished by these organizations. This was not only because they could not reconcile their different views about the nature of documentation or the use to which it should be put, but also because of lack of funding and the rapidly shifting interest from recording the past to ensuring the future both of the DP camp inmates and of the Jewish State struggling at that time for its existence. But the documents and testimonies collected at that time have served as a crucial basis for subsequent histories, and are still being profitably tapped by a new generation of historians who have recognized their value.[62]

This brings us to the beginning. For in writing the history of the Holocaust one major question has always been the context within which it occurred. For many Jews this was a context of prewar anti-Semitism, exclusion, and violence, not only in Germany and Austria but especially also in Eastern Europe, in such countries as Poland, Hungary, Romania, and Lithuania.[63] But there was another context, both historical and judicial, which was that of genocide. Coined, as noted above, by Raphael Lemkin in his 1944 study of German-occupied Europe, the term did not gain clear judicial status and a stable definition until the Genocide Convention of 1948.[64] But as Alexa Stiller notes in her chapter, the term was in fact used already during the International Military Tribunal (IMT) of 1945–46, and even more extensively by the United States Nuremberg Military Tribunals (NMT) of 1946–49.[65] And yet, even as genocide was invoked, its meaning was gradually altered, shifting from a broader interpretation that included ethnic cleansing and biological policies of racial selection of the kind described by Heinemann, to the specific case of the genocide of the Jews, that is, a Nazi policy whose stated intent was to murder an entire people. This shift was partly reflected also in the final definition of genocide by the UN, although that definition left room also for the kind of cultural genocide entailed in the kidnapping of children, as had happened in Poland.

There were certainly political reasons for this shift, in that a broader definition of genocide would have included such a wide range of perpetrators and complicit parties that resurrecting Germany might have been deemed impossible just as the beginning of the Cold War made it appear an urgent necessity. But it also revealed the tension between viewing the Jews as the primary, most extreme victims of the Nazis, and subsuming the "final solution" under a much larger umbrella of Nazi policies and crimes. In a wider sense, this contestation of meanings pointed to the subsequent argument between those who saw the Holocaust as a genocide sui generis, of a magnitude and extremity unsurpassed before and after, and others who perceived it as only one case in a series of modern genocides, all containing distinct but also common features, which could be traced back to the late nineteenth century and had continued long after the Nazi camps were transformed into sites of commemoration.[66]

The larger and more important context of these debates is the phenomenon of modern genocide and its recent scrutiny by an increasing number of scholars from a variety of fields and disciplines.[67] Genocide is not a common phenomenon and is consequently always perceived as extraordinary, singular, and rare. When it happens, there tends to be a general sense of shock by all those who perceive it. It seems to reveal something about human culture, society, and nature that we refuse to believe and are repeatedly astonished to discover. But while it is not a common phenomenon, genocide does happen again and again, and all the vows made to prevent its recurrence and to punish the culprits do not seem to have much effect. The slogan plastered on endless monuments in scores of countries and languages after the Holocaust, "never again," seems absurd, unless it merely meant to say that the "final solution" – a historical event that by its very nature is firmly lodged in the past – should never happen again.

In her chapter, Maureen Hiebert carefully analyzes the different approaches to studying, interpreting, and analyzing genocide.[68] That such a rich field has developed in the last couple of decades indicates the general recognition that this is an aspect of human civilization, as well as human psychology, that needs to be better explored. It also demonstrates that in the seven decades since the Nuremberg Tribunal, we have not succeeded in limiting the spread of this scourge, which in 1992 also returned to Europe. Students of the Holocaust are sometimes blamed for investigating a past event of mass murder rather than turning their attention to the repeated manifestations of inhumanity in the present. But as historians we can say that such complex events as genocide, of which the Holocaust was a particularly extreme and multifaceted example, must be studied carefully and at some distance in time, in order to understand both its particular features and those that it shares with the phenomenon of genocide more generally. This book is meant to help its readers begin this difficult but necessary exploration.

Notes

1 There has also been a vast expansion in the scholarship on the Holocaust and its aftermath in Eastern Europe. See, e.g., Jan T. Gross, *Neighbors: The Destruction of the Jewish Community in Jedwabne, Poland* (Princeton, NJ.: Princeton University Press, 2001); Gross, *Fear: Anti-Semitism in Poland After Auschwitz: An Essay in Historical Interpretation* (New York: Random House, 2006); Shimon Redlich, *Together and Apart in Brzeżany: Poles, Jews, and Ukrainians, 1919–1945* (Bloomington: Indiana University Press, 2002); Redlich, *Life in Transit: Jews in Postwar Lodz, 1945–1950* (Brighton, Mass.: Academic Studies Press, 2010); Gunnar S. Paulsson, *Secret City: The Hidden Jews of Warsaw, 1940–1945* (New Haven: Yale University Press, 2002);

Ray Brandon and Wendy Lower, eds., *The Shoah in Ukraine: History, Testimony, Memorialization* (Bloomington: Indiana University Press, 2008); Timothy Snyder, *Bloodlands: Europe between Hitler and Stalin* (New York: Basic Books, 2010); John-Paul Himka and Joanna B. Michlic, eds., *Bringing the Dark Past to Light: The Reception of the Holocaust in Postcommunist Europe* (Lincoln: University of Nebraska Press, 2013). For the larger context, see Omer Bartov and Eric D. Weitz, eds., *Shatterzone of Empires: Coexistence and Violence in the German, Habsburg, Russian, and Ottoman Borderlands* (Bloomington: Indiana University Press, 2013). For conceptualizing the geography of the Holocaust, see Omer Bartov, "Eastern Europe as the Site of Genocide," *The Journal of Modern History*, 80(3) (September 2008): 557–93.

2   Hannah Arendt, *The Origins of Totalitarianism*, new ed. (New York: Harcourt, Brace & World, 1966); Carl J. Friedrich and Zbigniew Brzezinski, *Totalitarian Dictatorship and Autocracy* (Cambridge: Harvard University Press, 1956); Abbott Gleason, *Totalitarianism: The Inner History of the Cold War* (New York: Oxford University Press, 1995).

3   See, for example, Eugen Weber, *Varieties of Fascism: Doctrines of Revolution in the Twentieth Century* (Princeton, NJ: Van Nostrand, 1964); Ernst Nolte, *Three Faces of Fascism: Action Française, Italian Fascism, National Socialism*, trans. Leila Vennewitz (New York: New American Library, 1969); Walter Laqueur, *Fascism: A Reader's Guide: Analyses, Interpretations, Bibliography* (Berkeley: University of California Press, 1976); Emilio Gentile, *The Sacralization of Politics in Fascist Italy* (Cambridge, Mass.: Harvard University Press, 1996); Stanley G. Payne, *Fascism: Comparison and Definition* (Madison, Wis.: University of Wisconsin Press, 1980); Ian Kershaw, *The Nazi Dictatorship: Problems and Perspectives of Interpretation*, 4th ed. (London: Arnold, 2000).

4   See, for example, Léon Poliakov, *Harvest of Hate: The Nazi Program for the Destruction of the Jews of Europe* (Westport, Conn.: Greenwood Press, 1971); Lucy S. Dawidowicz, *The War against the Jews, 1933–1945* (New York: Bantam Books, 1976).

5   See, for example, Hans Ulrich Wehler, *The German Empire, 1871–1918*, trans. Kim Traynor (Leamington Spa, UK: Berg Publishers, 1985), and the response by David Blackbourn and Geoff Eley in *The Peculiarities of German History: Bourgeois Society and Politics in Nineteenth-Century Germany* (New York: Oxford University Press, 1984).

6   See, for example, Gerald Fleming, *Hitler and the Final Solution* (Berkeley: University of California Press, 1984); Eberhard Jäckel, *Hitler's World View: A Blueprint for Power*, trans. Herbert Arnold (Cambridge, Mass.: Harvard University Press, 1981)

7   See, paradigmatically, Hans Mommsen, "The Realization of the Unthinkable: The 'Final Solution of the Jewish Problem' in the Third Reich," in Mommsen, *From Weimar to Auschwitz: Essays in German History* (Princeton, N.J.: Princeton University Press, 1991), 224–53; Martin Broszat, "Hitler and the Genesis of the 'Final Solution': An Assessment of David Irving's Theses," *Yad Vashem Studies* 13 (1979): 61–98.

8   For further background and citations, see Omer Bartov, "Genocide and the Holocaust: Arguments over History and Politics," in *Lessons and Legacies*, vol. XI, ed. Karl Schleunes and Hilary Earl (Evanston: Northwestern University Press, 5–28).

9   One holdout among scholars is the ongoing project by Steven T. Katz, *The Holocaust in Historical Context*, Vol. 1: *The Holocaust and Mass Death Before the Modern Age* (New York: Oxford University Press, 1994), who has ironically produced a vast trove of information on other genocides. Coming from precisely the opposite direction is Mark Levene, *Genocide in the Age of the Nation State* (London: I.B. Tauris, 2005).

10 See, for example, Donald Bloxham, "Holocaust Studies and Genocide Studies: Past, Present, and Future," in *Genocide Matters: Ongoing Issues and Emerging Perspectives*,

ed. Joyce Apsel and Ernesto Verdeja (New York: Routledge, 2013), 59–81; A. Dirk Moses, "The Holocaust and World History: Raphael Lemkin and Comparative Methodology," in *The Holocaust and Historical Methodology*, ed. Dan Stone (New York: Berghahn Books, 2012), 272–89; Moses, "Revisiting a Founding Assumption of Genocide Studies," *Genocide Studies and Prevention* 6(3) (2011): 287–300; Moses, "Conceptual Blockages and Definitional Dilemmas in the 'Racial Century': Genocides of Indigenous Peoples and the Holocaust," *Patterns of Prejudice* {36/4} (2002): 7–36.

11 See also Adam Hochschild, *King Leopold's Ghost: A Story of Greed, Terror, and Heroism in Colonial Africa* (Boston: Houghton Mifflin, 1999); Isabel V. Hull, *Absolute Destruction: Military Culture and the Practices of War in Imperial Germany* (Ithaca: Cornell University Press, 2005).

12 See also Taner Akçam, *The Young Turks' Crime against Humanity: The Armenian Genocide and Ethnic Cleansing in the Ottoman Empire* (Princeton, N.J.: Princeton University Press, 2012).

13 Raphael Lemkin, *Totally Unofficial: The Autobiography of Raphael Lemkin*, ed. Donna-Lee Frieze (New Haven: Yale University Press, 2013).

14 Shulamit Volkov, *Germans, Jews, and Antisemites: Trials in Emancipation* (New York: Cambridge University Press, 2006); Daniel Jonah Goldhagen, *Hitler's Willing Executioners: Ordinary Germans and the Holocaust* (New York: Alfred A. Knopf, 1996).

15 See, for example, Peter G. J. Pulzer, *The Rise of Political Anti-Semitism in Germany and Austria*, rev. ed. (Cambridge, Mass.: Harvard University Press, 1988).

16 See also Ian Kershaw, *The "Hitler Myth": Image and Reality in the Third Reich* (Oxford: Clarendon Press, 1987).

17 Saul Friedländer, *Nazi Germany and the Jews*, Vol. 1: *The Years of Persecution, 1933–1939* (New York: HarperCollins, 1997).

18 See, for example, Michael Burleigh, *Death and Deliverance: "Euthanasia" in Germany c. 1900–1945* (New York: Cambridge University Press, 1994); George L. Mosse, *Toward the Final Solution: A History of European Racism* (Madison, Wis.: University of Wisconsin Press, 1985); Paul Weindling, *Health, Race, and German Politics between National Unification and Nazism, 1870–1945* (New York: Cambridge University Press, 1989).

19 John Connelly, "Nazis and Slavs: From Racial Theory to Racist Practice," *Central European History*, 32 (1) (1999): 1–33; John Connelly, "Gypsies, Homosexuals, and Slavs," in *The Oxford Handbook of Holocaust Studies*, ed. Peter Hayes and John K. Roth (New York: Oxford University Press, 2010), 274–92.

20 Robert Jay Lifton, *The Nazi Doctors: Medical Killing and the Psychology of Genocide* (New York: Basic Books, 1986); Robert Proctor, *Racial Hygiene: Medicine Under the Nazis* (Cambridge, Mass.: Harvard University Press, 1988); Michael H. Kater, *Doctors Under Hitler* (Chapel Hill: University of North Carolina Press, 1989); Henry Friedlander, *The Origins of Nazi Genocide: From Euthanasia to the Final Solution* (Chapel Hill, NC: University of North Carolina Press, 1995).

21 See also Michael Burleigh, *Germany Turns Eastwards: A Study of Ostforschung in the Third Reich* (New York: Cambridge University Press, 1988); Götz Aly and Susanne Heim, *Architects of Annihilation: Auschwitz and the Logic of Destruction*, trans. A. G. Blunden (Princeton, NJ: Princeton University Press, 2002).

22 See also Catherine Epstein, *Model Nazi: Arthur Greiser and the Occupation of Western Poland* (New York: Oxford University Press, 2010).

23 Karl A. Schleunes, *The Twisted Road to Auschwitz: Nazi Policy Toward German Jews, 1933–1939* (Urbana: University of Illinois Press, 1970).

24 Christopher R. Browning, *The Path to Genocide: Essays On Launching the Final Solution* (New York: Cambridge University Press, 1992).

25 For the debate over the economic rationality of the Holocaust or the "primacy of politics" in the Third Reich, see, for example, Tim Mason, "The Primacy of Politics: Politics and Economics in National Socialist Germany," in Mason, *Nazism, Fascism and the Working Class*, ed. Jane Caplan (New York: Cambridge University Press, 1995), 53–76; Ulrich Herbert, "Labour and Extermination: Economic Interest and the Primacy of Weltanschauung in National Socialism," *Past and Present* 138 (1993): 144–95; Götz Aly, *Hitler's Beneficiaries: Plunder, Race War, and the Nazi Welfare State*, trans. Jefferson Chase (New York: Metropolitan, 2007).

26 The term comes from the influential book by David Rousset, *L'univers concentration-naire* (Paris: Éditions du Pavois, 1946). See also Samuel Moyn, "From l'Univers concentrationnaire to the Jewish Genocide: Pierre Vidal-Naquet and the Treblinka Controversy," in *After the Deluge: New Perspectives on the Intellectual and Cultural History of Postwar France*, ed. Bourg, Julian (Lanham, MD: Lexington Books, 2004), 277–99.

27 See also Ulrich Herbert, Karin Orth, and Christoph Dieckmann, eds., *Die Nationalsozialistischen Konzentrationslager: Entwicklung und Struktur* (Göttingen: Wallstein, 1998); Nikolaus Wachsmann, *Hitler's Prisons: Legal Terror in Nazi Germany* (New Haven: Yale University Press, 2004).

28 Daniel Blatman, *The Death Marches: The Final Phase of Nazi Genocide* (Cambridge, Mass.: Harvard University Press, 2011); Jon Bridgman and Richard H. Jones, *The End of the Holocaust: The Liberation of the Camps* (Portland, Or.: Areopagitica Press, 1990); Joanne Reilly, *Belsen: The Liberation of a Concentration Camp* (London: Routledge, 1998).

29 Peter Longerich, *The Unwritten Order: Hitler's Role in the Final Solution* (Stroud, UK: Tempus, 2005). See also Ian Kershaw, "Hitler's Role in the 'Final Solution,'" in Kershaw, *Hitler, the Germans, and the Final Solution* (Jerusalem: International Institute for Holocaust Research, Yad Vashem, 2008), 89–116.

30 See, for example, Christopher R. Browning and Jürgen Matthäus, *The Origins of the Final Solution: The Evolution of Nazi Jewish Policy, September 1939–March 1942* (Lincoln: University of Nebraska Press, 2004); Mark Roseman, *The Wannsee Conference and the Final Solution: A Reconsideration* (New York: Metropolitan Books, 2002); Christian Gerlach, "The Wannsee Conference, the Fate of German Jews, and Hitler's Decision in Principle to Exterminate all European Jews," in *The Holocaust: Origins, Implementation, Aftermath*, ed. Omer Bartov (London: Routledge, 2000), 106–61; Richard Breitman, *The Architect of Genocide: Himmler and the Final Solution* (New York: Knopf, 1991).

31 See also Uwe Dietrich Adam, *Judenpolitik im Dritten Reich* (Düsseldorf: Droste Verlag, 1972).

32 See also Robert Gerwarth, *Hitler's Hangman: The Life of Heydrich* (New Haven: Yale University Press, 2011); Peter Longerich, *Heinrich Himmler*, trans. Jeremy Noakes and Lesley Sharpe (New York: Oxford University Press, 2012).

33 Ernst Klee, et al., eds., *"The Good Old Days": The Holocaust As Seen By Its Perpetrators and Bystanders* (New York: Free Press, 1991); Christopher R. Browning, *Ordinary Men: Reserve Police Battalion 101 and the Final Solution in Poland* (New York: Aaron Asher Books, 1992); Omer Bartov, "Genocide in a Multiethnic Town: Event, Origins, Aftermath," in *Totalitarian Dictatorship: New Histories*, ed. Daniela Baratieri, et al. (London: Routledge, 2014), 212–31.

34 On the view created of German perpetrators as sadistic louts entirely different from conventional German society, see Rebecca Wittmann, *Beyond Justice: The Auschwitz Trial* (Cambridge, Mass.: Harvard University Press, 2005); Devin O. Pendas, *The Frankfurt Auschwitz Trial, 1963–1965: Genocide, History, and the Limits of the Law* (New York: Cambridge University Press, 2006).

35 Omer Bartov, "Interethnic Relations in the Holocaust as seen through Postwar Testimonies: Buczacz, East Galicia, 1941–44," in *Lessons and Legacies*: Vol. VII: *From Generation to Generation*, ed. Doris L. Bergen (Evanston, IL: Northwestern University Press, 2008), 101–24.

36 For other perpetrators ruminating about their deeds, see Gitta Sereny, *Into That Darkness: An Examination of Conscience* (New York: Vintage Books, 1983); Rudolf Höss, *Death Dealer: The Memoirs of the SS Kommandant at Auschwitz*, ed. Steven Paskuly, trans. Andrew Pollinger (Buffalo, NY: Prometheus Books, 1992).

37 See Jerzy Ficowski, *Regions of the Great Heresy: Bruno Schulz, a Biographical Portrait*, trans. and ed. Theodosia S. Robertson (New York: W.W. Norton, 2003); Henryk Grynberg, *Drohobycz, Drohobycz and Other Stories: True Tales From the Holocaust and Life After*, trans. Alicia Nitecki, ed. Theodosia S. Robertson (New York: Penguin Books, 2002).

38 The most remarkable diary of that time is Victor Klemperer, *I Will Bear Witness: A Diary of the Nazi Years 1933–1945*, 2 vols., trans. Martin Chalmers (New York: Random House, 1998–1998).

39 See also Dalia Ofer and Lenore J Weitzman, eds., *Women in the Holocaust* (New Haven: Yale University Press), 1998, pt. 1.

40 Judith Tydor Baumel-Schwartz, *Never Look Back: The Jewish Refugee Children in Great Britain, 1938–1945* (West Lafayette, Ind.: Purdue University Press, 2012).

41 Natalia Aleksiun, "Gender and the Daily Lives of Jews in Hiding in Eastern Galicia," *Nashim* (forthcoming).

42 See also Lucjan Dobroszycki, ed., *The Chronicle of the Łódź Ghetto, 1941–1944*, trans. Richard Lourie, et al. (New Haven: Yale University Press, 1984); Alan Adelson and Robert Lapides, eds., *Łódź Ghetto: Inside a Community under Siege* (New York: Viking, 1989); Adelson, ed., *The Diary of Dawid Sierakowiak: Five Notebooks from the Łódź Ghetto*, trans. Kamil Turowski (New York: Oxford University Press, 1996); Oskar Rosenfeld, *In the Beginning Was the Ghetto: Notebooks from Łódź*, ed. Hanno Loewy (Evanston: Northwestern University Press, 2002); Josef Zelkowicz, *In Those Terrible Days: Writings from the Lodz Ghetto*, ed. Michal Unger (Jerusalem: Yad Vashem, 2002); Isaiah Trunk, *Łódź Ghetto: A History*, trans. Robert Moses Shapiro (Bloomington: Indiana University Press, 2006).

43 Simha Rotem, *Memoirs of a Warsaw Ghetto Fighter: The Past Within Me*, trans. and ed. Barbara Harshav (New Haven: Yale University Press, 1994); Israel Gutman, *The Jews of Warsaw, 1939–1943: Ghetto, Underground, Revolt*, trans. Ina Friedman (Bloomington: Indiana University Press, 1982); Philip Friedman, *Martyrs and Fighters: The Epic of the Warsaw Ghetto* (New York: F.A. Praeger, 1954); Dina Porat, *The Fall of a Sparrow: The Life and Times of Abba Kovner*, trans. and ed. Elizabeth Yuval (Stanford, Calif.: Stanford University Press, 2010); Abba Kovner, *Scrolls of Testimony*, trans. Edward A. Levenston (Philadelphia: Jewish Publication Society, 2001).

44 See also Betty Jean Lifton, *The King of Children: A Biography of Janusz Korczak* (New York: Farrar, Straus and Giroux, 1988).

45 See, for example, Beverly Allen, *Rape Warfare: The Hidden Genocide in Bosnia-Herzegovina and Croatia* (Minneapolis: University of Minnesota Press, 1996); Sandra Chu and Anne-Marie de Brouwer, eds., *The Men Who Killed Me: Rwandan Survivors of Sexual Violence* (Vancouver: Douglas & McIntyre, 2009); Elisa von Joeden-Forgey, "Gender and Genocide," in *Oxford Handbook of Genocide Studies*, 61–80; Roger W. Smith, "Genocide and the Politics of Rape," in Apsel, *Genocide Matters*, 82–105.

46 Atina Grossmann, "A Question of Silence: The Rape of German Women by Occupation Soldiers," *October* 72 (1995): 43–63.

47 For sexual crimes in war, the military, and the camps, see David Raub Snyder, *Sex Crimes Under the Wehrmacht* (Lincoln, Neb.: University of Nebraska Press, 2007);

Dagmar Herzog, ed., *Brutality and Desire: War and Sexuality in Europe's Twentieth Century* (New York: Palgrave Macmillan, 2009); Monika J. Flaschka, "Race, Rape and Gender in Nazi-Occupied Territories" (Ph.D. dissertation, Kent State University, 2009).

48 Joan Ringelheim, "Women and the Holocaust: A Reconsideration of Research," *Signs* {10/4} (1985): 741–61.

49 See also Sonja M. Hedgepeth and Rochelle G. Saidel, eds., *Sexual Violence against Jewish Women During the Holocaust* (Hanover, NH: Brandeis University Press, 2010); Alana Fangrad, "Wartime Rape and Sexual Violence: An Examination of the Perpetrators, Motivations, and Functions of Sexual Violence against Jewish Women during the Holocaust" (Masters Thesis, University of Western Ontario, 2013).

50 On this suspicion and its effects in Israel, see Omer Bartov, "Kitsch and Sadism in Ka-Tzetnik's Other Planet: Israeli Youth Imagine the Holocaust," *Jewish Social Studies* (spring 1997): 42–76.

51 For the revenge taken out on French women by the men of the Résistance for what was called "horizontal collaboration" with the Germans, see Alain Brossat, *Les Tondues: Un Carnaval Moche* (Levallois-Perret: Editions Manya, 1992).

52 On female and male prostitution and sexual abuse in concentration camps, see Robert Sommer, *Das KZ-Bordell: Sexuelle Zwangsarbeit in Nationalsozialistischen Konzentrationslagern* (Paderborn: Schöningh, 2009); Sommer, "Pipel: Homosexual Exploitation of Young Men and Women in Nazi Concentration Camps," paper delivered at "Lessons and Legacies XI," Boca Raton, November 2010. See also Ka-Tzetnik (Yehiel Dinur), *They Called Him Piepl*, 2nd ed. (Tel Aviv: Am Hasefer, 1962, in Hebrew). On the DRC, see, for example, Kirsten Johnson, et al. "Association of Sexual Violence and Human Rights Violations With Physical and Mental Health in Territories of the Eastern Democratic Republic of the Congo," *JAMA – Journal of the American Medical Association* 304 (5) (2010): 553–62; Susan A. Bartels et al., "Research Patterns of sexual violence in Eastern Democratic Republic of Congo: reports from survivors presenting to Panzi Hospital in 2006," *Conflict and Health* {4/9} (2010): www.biomedcentral.com/content/pdf/1752-1505-4-9.pdf (accessed June 10, 2014); Joanne Csete, Juliane Kippenberg, and Human Rights Watch, *The War Within the War: Sexual Violence against Women and Girls in Eastern Congo* (New York: Human Rights Watch, 2002).

53 Primo Levi, "The Gray Zone," in Levi, *The Drowned and the Saved*, trans. Raymond Rosenthal (New York: Summit Books, 1988), 36–69, discusses these men at length and refers to them by that name.

54 See also Gid'on Graif, *We Wept Without Tears: Testimonies of the Jewish Sonderkommando From Auschwitz* (New Haven, Conn.: Yale University Press, 2005).

55 Other accounts of Sonderkommando personnel include Filip Müller, with Helmut Freitag, *Eyewitness Auschwitz: Three Years in the Gas Chambers*, ed. and trans. Susanne Flatauer (New York: Stein and Day, 1979); Nyiszli, Miklós, *Auschwitz, a Doctor's Eyewitness Account*, trans. Tibère Kremer and Richard Seaver (New York: Fell, 1960).

56 For a recent attempt to overcome this predilection, see Christopher R. Browning, *Remembering Survival: Inside a Nazi Slave-labor Camp* (New York: W.W. Norton, 2010), and Browning, *Collected Memories: Holocaust History and Postwar Testimony* (Madison: University of Wisconsin Press, 2003). See also Annette Wieviorka, *The Era of the Witness*, trans. Jared Stark (Ithaca, NY: Cornell University Press, 2006).

57 This chapter presents part of my book, *The Voice of Your Brother's Blood: Buczacz, Biography of a Town* (New York: Simon and Shuster, forthcoming).

58 For the larger context of these events in the borderlands of Poland and Ukraine, see, for example, Karel Berkhoff, *Harvest of Despair: Life and Death in Ukraine Under Nazi Rule* (Cambridge, Mass.: Harvard University Press, 2004); Alexander V. Prusin, *The Lands Between: Conflict in the East European Borderlands, 1870–1992* (New York: Oxford University Press, 2010); Timothy Snyder, "The Causes of Ukrainian-Polish

Ethnic Cleansing, 1943," *Past and Present* 179 (2003): 197–234; Snyder, " 'To Resolve the Ukrainian Problem Once and for All': The Ethnic Cleansing of Ukrainians in Poland, 1943–47," *Journal of Cold War Studies* 1 (2) (1999): 86–120; Elazar Barkan, et al., eds., *Shared History, Divided Memory: Jews and Others in Soviet-occupied Poland, 1939–1941* (Leipzig: Simon-Dubnow-Institut für Jüdische Geschichte und Kultur, 2007).

59 See further in Laura Jockusch, *Collect and Record!: Jewish Holocaust Documentation in Early Postwar Europe* (New York: Oxford University Press, 2012); David Cesarani and Eric J. Sundquist, eds., *After the Holocaust: Challenging the Myth of Silence* (London: Routledge, 2012).

60 Natalia Aleksiun, "The Central Jewish Historical Commission in Poland, 1944–47," in *Polin*, Vol. 22: *Making Holocaust Memory*, ed. Gabriel N. Finder, et al., (Oxford: The Littman Library of Jewish Civilization, 2008), 74–97; Laura Jockusch, "Breaking the Silence: The Centre de Documentation Juive Contemporaine in Paris and the writing of Holocaust history in liberated France," in Cesarani, *After the Holocaust*, 67–81; Tom Segev, *Simon Wiesenthal: The Life and Legends* (New York: Doubleday, 2010).

61 Atina Grossmann, *Jews, Germans, and Allies: Close Encounters in Occupied Germany* (Princeton, NJ: Princeton University Press, 2007); Zeev W. Mankowitz, *Life between Memory and Hope: The Survivors of the Holocaust in Occupied Germany* (New York: Cambridge University Press, 2002).

62 For another immensely important collection of documents, see Samuel D. Kassow, *Who Will Write Our History? Emanuel Ringelblum, the Warsaw Ghetto, and the Oyneg Shabes Archive* (Bloomington: Indiana University Press, 2007).

63 For a view of anti-Semitism as the leitmotif of Jewish history, see, e.g., Robert S. Wistrich, *Anti-Semitism: The Longest Hatred* (New York: Pantheon Books, 1991); and with more focus on the twentieth century and the Holocaust, see Peter Murray Baumgarten, et al., eds., *Varieties of Anti-Semitism: History, Ideology, Discourse* (Newark: University of Delaware Press, 2009).

64 Raphael Lemkin, *Axis Rule in Occupied Europe: Laws of Occupation, Analysis of Government, Proposals for Redress* (Washington, DC: Carnegie endowment for international peace, Division of international law, 1944).

65 See also Michael R. Marrus, ed., *The Nuremberg War Crimes Trial, 1945–46: A Documentary History* (Boston: Bedford Books, 1997); Donald Bloxham, *Genocide on Trial: War Crimes Trials and the Formation of Holocaust History and Memory* (New York: Oxford University Press, 2001).

66 See, for example, Alan S. Rosenbaum, ed., *Is the Holocaust Unique? Perspectives On Comparative Genocide*, 3rd ed. (Boulder, CO: Westview Press, 2009).

67 To cite just a few examples: Leo Kuper, *Genocide: Its Political Use in the Twentieth Century* (New Haven: Yale University Press, 1981); Eric D. Weitz, *A Century of Genocide: Utopias of Race and Nation* (Princeton, NJ: Princeton University Press, 2003); Benjamin A. Valentino, *Final Solutions: Mass Killing and Genocide in the Twentieth Century* (Ithaca, NY: Cornell University Press, 2004); Ben Kiernan, *Blood and Soil: A World History of Genocide and Extermination From Sparta to Darfur* (New Haven: Yale University Press, 2007); Jacques Sémelin, *Purify and Destroy: The Political Uses of Massacre and Genocide* (New York: Columbia University Press, 2007); Christian Gerlach, *Extremely Violent Societies: Mass Violence in the Twentieth Century* (New York: Cambridge University Press, 2010).

68 Recent collections of essays on the topic include Apsel, *Genocide Matters*; René Lemarchand, ed., *Forgotten Genocides: Oblivion, Denial, and Memory* (Philadelphia: University of Pennsylvania Press, 2011); Samuel Totten and Paul R. Bartrop, eds., *The Genocide Studies Reader* (New York: Routledge, 2009); Robert Gellately and Ben Kiernan, eds., *The Specter of Genocide: Mass Murder in Historical Perspective* (New York: Cambridge University Press, 2003).

Part I

ORIGINS
Racism and anti-Semitism

1

"ONE OF THESE RACES HAS GOT TO GO . . ."

Colonialism and genocide

Cathie Carmichael

The Holocaust was neither the first genocide of the modern era nor the last. It was preceded by an array of massacres, ethnic cleansing operations, deportations, and targeted exterminations of entire groups of people based on their identification by the perpetrators as inferior, primitive, dangerous, obstacles to economic development or to civilization, or simply superfluous and utterly dispensable. As Cathy Carmichael succinctly demonstrates in her chapter, the discourse of purging and eradication picked up pace in the latter part of the nineteenth century as a result of a combination of ruthless colonialism by the Western powers and scientific theories about race as a defining characteristic of human groups and a means to rank them higher or lower on the evolutionary scale. Wielding superior military might and organizational skills, and sanctioned by ostensibly incontrovertible scientific theories, Western powers set about exploiting the populations of their colonies with the goal of extracting maximum economic benefits from them under the guise of bringing them culture and civilization. The most blatant example of this dark moment in human history was Belgian King Leopold's private empire in the Congo, where up to ten million Africans died between 1885–1908.

Yet, as Adam Hochschild demonstrated in his study King Leopold's Ghost, and as Carmichael argues more generally about this period, it was also the realization that Europeans had created what Joseph Conrad had famously called "the heart of darkness" in Africa that mobilized early humanitarian forces to put a stop to these practices of mass murder. This movement, which gathered momentum in response to the massacres in the Balkan Wars of 1912–13, the genocide of the Armenians in the Ottoman Empire during World War I, and the mass pogroms of Jewish populations in Poland and Ukraine during and in the immediate aftermath of the war and the Russian Revolution, eventually played a role in the creation of the League of Nations and subsequently the United Nations. But even as this list suggests, humanitarian rhetoric and legislation were hardly sufficient in stemming the growing tide of violence against civilian populations, both in the colonies and in Europe itself.

Two crucial links are suggested by Carmichael's chapter, which in many ways will be the leitmotifs of this volume. One is the relationship between the extraordinary, indeed unprecedented violence perpetrated by humans upon humans in the course of the twentieth century, and the growing body of legislation, as well as institutions, created in order to reestablish fundamental human rights and to prevent, combat, and punish genocide and other crimes against humanity. The second is the link between the genocides and other mass crimes that preceded the Nazi regime, and the Holocaust. As Carmichael indicates, several scholars have argued that one can find a variety of strands leading from such cases as the genocide of the Herero and Nama in German southwest Africa (today's Namibia) in 1904, the genocide of the Armenians, and the "final solution of the Jewish question" by the Nazis. Others insist that while the context noted above is indeed crucial to our understanding of some of the roots of the Holocaust, there are other more specific contexts that need to be taken into account, not least of which is the particular place of Jews within European culture and society, as well as the distinctive nature of Nazi ideology and policies.

In recent years scholars have begun to focus on the wider context of the Holocaust, examining the 'archaeology of genocide' as a phenomenon.[1] Dan Stone has argued that 'scholars now feel [it] incumbent upon themselves . . . to provide a historical framework for understanding genocide that situates it into the broadest developments of world history and human behaviour'.[2] Approaching these events as part of history makes far clearer what Yehuda Bauer has called the 'dialectic nature between the particularism and universalism of the horror'.[3] To some extent, the moral decline in European politics and the growth of eliminationist ideas was encouraged by imperialism. Hannah Arendt believed that fascism had represented an extreme outgrowth of nineteenth-century imperialist aspirations and racism.[4]

The expansion of the European powers between the early modern period and the nineteenth century cost millions of lives. Mark Levene has emphasized the 'fatal nexus between the Anglo-American drive to rapid state building and genocide'.[5] While some Americans were ethnically cleansed for their land, others were simply attacked or captured and worked until they died. Here the motive for expropriation was central. Evgenii Preobrazhensky and Nikolaï Bukharin attacked colonialism as a practice wherein 'the loathsome and sanguinary aspects of capitalism were . . . displayed with exceptional clearness'.[6] The transatlantic slave trade was genocidal in its consequences: of the 12 million taken from Africa, perhaps 1.5 million died en route. The trade cut the survivors off from their lands of origins and gave them an existence in which many died prematurely from diseases in trading ports or simply from sheer exhaustion. An estimated death rate of 130 per thousand per annum means in effect that slaves were being worked to death.[7] In the decades between the 1880s and the First World War, the 'Scramble for Africa' developed into genocide. In 1924, a young radical, Ho Chi Minh, addressed the Communist International in Moscow, imploring his comrades to develop a theory of colonialism that took into account the mass slaughters which had taken place in the preceding decades:

> In the Belgian Congo the population fell from 25 million in 1891 to 8.5 million by 1911. Densely populated and prosperous regions along rivers were turned into deserts within a mere fifteen years. Ravaged oases and villages were strewn with bleached bones. The plight of the survivors was atrocious. The peasants were robbed of their tiny plots of land, the artisans lost their crafts and the herdsmen their cattle. The Matabeles were cattle-breeders: before the arrival of the British they had 200,000 head of cattle. Two years later only 40,900 were left. The Hereros had 90,000 head of cattle. Within twelve years the German colonists had robbed them of half that number.[8]

Outrage at genocide and other extreme abuses of human rights was one of the intellectual building-blocks that led to the creation of the League of Nations and its successor, the United Nations, as well as such pressure groups as the Congo Reform Association, created in 1906 to combat the abuses of the Belgian King Leopold's regime, or Pro Arménia, a French pressure group which supported the Armenians after the Hamidian massacres. Humanist concerns led to a series of conventions in The Hague and Geneva from the late nineteenth century onwards, all aimed at curtailing violent, abusive behaviour and amending international law accordingly. But, at the same time, in the nineteenth and early twentieth centuries those anxious to protect human rights faced another, stronger adversary namely that of the real-life narrative of struggles between races and the inevitable extermination of the 'weakest'.[9] This narrative was to remain dominant in much of Europe until the late 1940s. It permeated European life at every level, and thus put whole groups outside of what Christopher Browning has called the 'circle of human obligation and responsibility'[10] or, worse still, it helped to present the removal of certain people in terms of a social necessity or good. The German Admiral Hans Humann justified the Ittihad persecution of the Armenians in terms of nature: 'Armenians and Turks cannot live together in this country. . . . One of these races has got to go. The weaker nation must succumb.'[11]

As with the Hamidian massacres, Dreyfus and the increasingly violent tone of literature, the abuses of imperialism created a human rights consciousness which was an intellectual antithesis to eliminationist discourses. The novelist Mark Twain wrote a condemnation of Belgian abuses in the Congo in the form of a 'soliloquy' by King Leopold, who he held responsible.[12] Forming the Congo Reform Association with Edmund Dene Morel and the Irish writer Roger Casement, the writer Arthur Conan Doyle set down an enraged protest, the *Crime of the Congo* in 1909:

> There are many of us in England who consider the crime which has been wrought in the Congo lands by King Leopold of Belgium and his followers, to be the greatest which has ever been known in human annals. . . . There have been massacres of populations like that of the South Americans by the Spaniard, or of subject nations by the Turks. But never before has there been such a mixture of wholesale expropriation and wholesale massacre all done under an odious guise of philanthropy, and with the lowest commercial motives as a reason. It is this sordid cause and the unctuous hypocrisy which makes this crime unparalleled in its horror.[13]

The aim of the Congo Reform Association was to shame. As Morel later argued in his book *The Black Man's Burden*, 'truth' was the 'stalking horse of oppression and injustice'.[14]

As far as the Marxist left of that time is concerned, it is problematic to present it as formed of wholehearted supporters of human rights. Contemporary scholars are still drawn to the writings of Marxists to conceptualize genocide and the destruction of communities: Mark Levene to the developmental theories of Immanuel Wallerstein[15] and Dirk Moses to Walter Benjamin's notion of 'anamnestic solidarity'[16] with the victims of violence. Many Marxists of the period under consideration were great humanists, and it is explicit within the theory of dialectical materialism that an end to oppression will emancipate humanity. In Italy, Antonio Gramsci also spoke out against the killing of Armenians in the Ottoman Empire,[17] initiating a debate among his comrades about the moral implications of distance. In Serbia, the Marxists Svetozar Marković and Dimitrije Tucović went against the prevailing nationalist grain and supported Albanian rights.[18] At the age of twenty-five, Rosa Luxemburg had tried to get the German Social Democrats, via their newspaper *Vorwärts*, to support the Armenians after the Hamidian massacres. She was rebuffed by Wilhelm Liebknecht who displayed the characteristic obsession of the German left with tsarist abuses of power[19] (to the detriment of their analysis of other political problems). Liebknecht believed that, as a Jew from Poland, Rosa Luxemburg 'would perhaps find a more fruitful field if she occupied herself with the Russian atrocities in Poland, and in Russia itself'.[20]

Among the left-wing in Germany, there was deep concern for the fate of Africans in colonial Namibia and compassion for the Jewish victims of the pogroms. The First World War and the subsequent Bolshevik revolution divided Marxists and, as Geoff Eley has argued, much that was valuable in socialism was lost during the Soviet domination of the Communist International from 1919 to 1943.[21] When Fitzroy Maclean encountered communists in the 1930s in Russia, he remembered 'their terror of responsibility . . . reluctance to think for themselves [and] blind unquestioning obedience',[22] conformist qualities that became one of the central themes of Alfred Andersch's celebrated novel about communism and the moral compromises involved in Stalinism and popular front politics in the 1930s and 1940s: *Sansibar, oder, Der letze Grund*.[23]

The Bolsheviks in power, with a few notable exceptions, had much less of a humanist approach to social change. They had also absorbed the prevailing *zeitgeist* of an apocalyptic world divided between opposing forces. In December 1917, Vladimir Lenin had written about 'cleansing the Russian land of all vermin, of scoundrel fleas, the bedbug rich and so on'.[24] In a famous civil war poster, he was depicted brushing away an Orthodox priest, two monarchs and a fat capitalist. (Fig. 1.1). Curiously, the Russian verb 'to cleanse' is etymologically the same as the Croatian and Serbian word (*očistiti*), which Vuk Karadžić used to describe the killing of Muslims in Belgrade in 1806.[25] In a speech made in Nova Gradiška in June 1941, the Ustaša Minister Milovan Žanić stated: 'This must be the land of the Croats and no one else and there are no methods that we Ustaše will not use to make this land truly Croat, and cleanse it (*očistimo*) of the Serbs who have menaced us for centuries.'[26] At the beginning of 1917, Austrian diplomatic papers referred to the cleansing of Christians (*von christlichen Elementen gesäubert*);[27] the term is also found in the Lepsius correspondence, where it describes the plight of the Armenians.[28]

Figure 1.1 'Comrade Lenin cleanses the earth of the unclean.' Soviet poster designed by Mikhail Cheremnykh and Viktor Deni, November 1920.

Is the repetitive use of the term 'to cleanse' in relation to the removal of a population just a semantic coincidence? Given that the Bolshevik revolution led to the exodus of many groups from Russia and that their victory in the civil war gave them a licence to kill their few remaining political opponents in Tambov in 1920 and in Kronstadt in 1921, it could be argued that the consequence of their revolution was the 'cleansing' of certain elements from the former Romanov monarchy. During the collectivization drive, many more people, classified somewhat subjectively as rich capitalist peasants or kulaks, were slaughtered by the state if they failed to deliver their property to the collective. The communist regime tried to destroy the traditional farming of most of the Soviet Union and many died as a direct result of government policy, the initiatives of fanatics, local ineptitude and inaccuracies in the command economy. Many Ukrainians believe that this amounted to genocide against them and their way of life. If we look at the United Nations' definition of genocide, which is extremely comprehensive, these events should be included, as Raphael Lemkin himself concluded.[29] Rudi Rummel has called this type of event 'death by government'. He notes: 'Power was nearly absolute . . . classes – bourgeoisie, priests, landlords, the rich and officers and officials of the previous regime – were sinful, enemies of the Good. Capitalists of their offspring were especially evil. The verdict for such class membership was often death.'[30] That the communists after 1917 had become so dislocated from their humanist roots should not in itself obscure the fact that there was an elective affinity between the left and humanism.

Those who protested against the persecution of individuals on the basis of ethnicity, religion or race were a diverse but significant constituency, most marked perhaps by their individualism and education. Sigmund Freud famously remarked to Albert Einstein in 1932 that 'whatever makes for cultural development is working also against war'.[31] The philosopher Richard Rorty concluded that an education which promotes empathy for the 'other', sentiment and relativism would produce a tolerant society as well as the preservation of individual human rights: 'That sort of education gets people of different kinds sufficiently well acquainted with one another that they are less tempted to think of those different from themselves as only quasi-human. The goal of this sort of manipulation of sentiment is to expand the reference of the terms "our kind of people".'[32] What perhaps is also important is a sense of spiritual independence. The remarkable small town of Le Chambon-sur-Lignon in the French Auvergne region sheltered and saved thousands of Jews during the Vichy occupation and elimination. What made this town – and others nearby, which assisted them in the struggle – so remarkable? Perhaps its was the minister André Trocmé, his wife Magda and his assistant Edouard Theis, but perhaps also a Huguenot tradition which had lasted for centuries despite persecution by the French state – which meant, in effect, that a form of spiritual independence had been preserved.[33]

Violence against ethnic minorities often provoked what Rosa Luxemburg called a 'gnawing sense of responsibility for social injustice'[34] or what Lynn

Hunt has more recently described as 'feelings, convictions, and actions of multitudes of individuals who demand responses that accord with their inner sense of outrage'.[35] In 1861, Alexander Herzen protested about the persecution (*gonenie*) of Muslim Tatars from the Crimea in the pages of his journal *Kolokol*, one of the earliest newspapers set up with the purpose of raising an alarm,[36] in this case about the status quo in tsarist Russia.[37] Leo Tolstoy wrote to the governor of Kishinev:

> Profoundly shocked by the atrocities committed [in your town] . . . we extend our heartfelt sympathy to the innocent victims of mob savagery and express our horror at acts of cruelty perpetrated by Russians, our scorn and disgust with all who have driven the people to such a pass and have allowed this dreadful crime to be committed.[38]

He had such a huge moral impact on generations of Russians that students wore black arm bands after the announcement of his death. For Vladimir Lenin, his writing had made a 'remarkably powerful, forthright and sincere protest against social falsehood and hypocrisy'.[39] Tolstoy's daughter tried to help Turkish prisoners of war during the Russian occupation:

> After six weeks of this, Countess Alexandra . . . came to Van and took off our hands the care of our 'guests', though they remained on our premises. She was a young woman, simple, sensible, and lovable. . . . When her funds gave out and no more were forthcoming and her Russian helpers fell ill, she succeeded where we had failed and induced the General to send the Turks out into the country with provision for their safety and sustenance.[40]

In France, horror at the Hamidian massacres of Armenians and at the Dreyfus case brought together a remarkable number of artistic and other personalities. Emile Gallé, one of the most important art nouveau designers in glass, designed *Le Sang d'Arménie* (*The Blood of Armenia*) in 1900. Those who were pro Arménia included Jean Jaurès, Georges Clémenceau and Anatole France,[41] who were also committed Dreyfusards.[42] In April 1916, Anatole France helped to organize a meeting in the Sorbonne in 'homage' to Armenia and to condemn the role of the Turks and their allies, the Germans, during the war.[43] As eliminationism was developing, another philosophical current, which might be called a human rights consciousness, was also growing slowly. 'The term "intellectual" as a description of a distinct group of people enters the French language in the latter half of the 1890s. With the Dreyfus Affair, it achieved common currency, being used immediately as a term of abuse by the Right.'[44] In Britain, the Bulgarian horrors of the 1870s had, according to the politician and biographer of Gladstone, Roy Jenkins, 'left a permanent imprint on the line divide in British politics'.[45]

Eliminationist ideas evolved at a time when the lives of colonial peoples had been sacrificed and squandered. There were, of course, many individuals directly linked to colonial atrocities who were also involved in the politics and practice of genocide in Europe. Eugen Fischer, Hermann Göring and Franz Ritter von Epp have been identified as 'human conduits for the flow of ideas and methods between the colony and Nazi Germany'.[46] Jürgen Zimmerer has argued that there was a fundamental link between colonial practices, including mass killings of Africans in the first decade of the twentieth century in Namibia by German colonists, and the way in which Jews were treated by the Third Reich.[47] If people could be killed because they were in the way, being regarded as inferior or as an obstacle to German expansion and hegemony in Africa, then why not also in eastern Europe? Dominik Schaller argued that there was a link between the Armenian genocide and the Holocaust in terms of the impact of the events of 1915 on the central European psyche and consciousness.[48] In both cases the link was not only at the level of actual people being implicated in these events, but also in terms of the ideological and moral effect that they had on the times in which these people lived. As the Roman historian Tacitus observed in his *Annals*, 'what is this day supported by precedents will hereafter become a precedent'.[49] Winston Churchill 'repeatedly used the example of the Greek-Turkish transfer of populations mandated by Lausanne as a legitimate precedent for removing the Germans'[50] from eastern Europe; they could then go on to inhabit homes in West Germany vacated by dead soldiers and civilians.

Paul Rohrbach (1869–1956) also stands out as a key figure in the intellectual development of European racist thought and imperialism. Rohrbach's academic and applied interest in regions which were to become zones of conflict and ultimately genocide (German South-West Africa, the Ottoman Empire and the Ukraine) was, to say the very least, unfortunate. Helmut Walser Smith has argued that his writings, particularly *Der Deutsche Gedanke in der Welt*,[51] 'allow us to trace the deeper logic of eliminationist racism in Wilhelmine Germany on the eve of the war'. At the very least he represents, as Dominik Schaller has suggested, an intellectual continuity of the German *Weltpolitik* between the first decade of the twentieth century and the Second World War.[52] To what extent could his imperialist writings have contributed to the creation of these genocidal situations in three parts of the world?

Rohrbach, a Baltic German by origin, was a prolific writer, traveller and political activist. His work was popular and his books were short, polemical and accessible, full of mantras and potential slogans. Munroe Smith observed in 1917 that 'popularizers' (and in this he included Rohrbach) 'do more than "solid" writers to mould opinion. [Before the war] . . . at the beer tables German civilians were annexing little neighbours and dividing great empire.'[53] Rohrbach's early theological training meant that he 'infused the vulgar world of imperialism and economic competition with . . . elevated meaning',[54] writing in his autobiography that theology could be used as a guide through challenges raised by society.[55] In his 1912 book *Der Deutsche Gedanke in der Welt*, he argued that Germans should set a moral standard in world politics, coining a phrase which is almost Lutheran in its prosaic weight: 'Wie unser Volk, so unsere Regierung' ('As our people are, so our rule will be' – namely, fair and just).[56] Because Germans had a moral duty to act in a particular way and to set an example to the world, Rohrbach had also publicly disapproved of the Kaiser visiting the harem of the Ottoman sultan in 1895.[57] For him, as for many German idealists before him and for the Russian slavophiles, Anglo-Saxon civilization was morally corrupted by materialism,[58] and he believed that Germans would inject much needed Kultur to counteract this tendency.[59]

Rohrbach was already well travelled when he took up a post as commissioner for population in German South-West Africa. Describing his career there, Michael Mann has suggested that, '[i]n the most elevated world historical terms, he endorsed complete expropriation, forcing officials into near-slave-labor conditions'. But, as Mann continues: 'He was not contemplating eliminating them. Nor was any official.'[60] It is true that, in his writings on Africa, Rohrbach does not appear to be as extreme as his colleague, General von Trotha, and he cannot be classified as a simple 'eliminationist', but his standard of 'ethics' left little room for native rights. In common with many of his contemporaries, including the anthropologist Eugen Fischer, he considered miscegenation between Africans and Europeans to be morally undesirable.[61] He considered the preservation of black tribes in South Africa to be a 'false philanthropy' if it happened at the expense of white European peoples, however loosely that might be interpreted.[62] Rohrbach wrote as if the future of Africa 'was evolutionary destiny'[63] and as if white people had the right to determine the future of black Africans.

Paul Rohrbach's most controversial role is probably in the Near East, with his work on the expansion of German influence in Ottoman Turkey. Although not himself an eliminationist, he represents a direct link between imperialism and the break-up of both Ottoman and Romanov power. In his pamphlet Die Bagdadbahn, Rohrbach had noted the economic potential of the region which would be enjoined with the railway, particularly with regard to petroleum.[64] He also saw the Ottoman Empire as the place to drive a wedge between Russian, French and British overseas interests.[65] For Rohrbach, Egypt was Britain's colonial weak link. If Britain lost control here, it would loose control of the Suez Canal and thereby the colonies in India and Asia.[66] He envisaged that the economic building up of the region would be necessary in order to settle Armenians (and other suitably hardworking groups) in Mesopotamia along the railway route. Germans would not settle there because of the climate.[67]

As a historian and traveller, Rohrbach knew better than most contemporaries the extent to which Armenians had suffered. He toured the eastern part of Turkey in 1901 and included several sympathetic photographs of Armenian orphans in his account.[68] When the Ittihad government turned on the Armenians in 1915, it drove many of them out to 'Mesopotamia'. Perhaps as many as two-thirds of these Armenians died from disease, starvation, attacks, dehydration and trauma en route to the Euphrates.[69] Some contemporaries thought that Rohrbach was the initiator of the idea of deportation.[70] Hacobian mentioned him directly, believing him to be the first person to suggest the deportation of Armenians in 'agricultural colonies along the Baghdad railway line'.[71] The American Ambassador Henry Morgenthau, whose family originally came from Mannheim in Germany, was even more blunt in his assessment:

> the Armenian proceedings of 1915 and 1916 evidenced an entirely new mentality. This new conception was that of *deportation*. The Turks, in five hundred years, had invented innumerable ways of physically torturing their Christian subjects, yet never before had it occurred to their minds to move them bodily from their homes, where they had lived for many thousands of years, and send them hundreds of miles away into the desert. Where did the Turks get this idea? . . . Admiral Usedom, one of the big German naval experts in Turkey, told me that the Germans had suggested this deportation to the Turks . . . this idea of deporting peoples en masse is, in modern times, exclusively Germanic. Anyone who reads the literature of Pan-Germany constantly meets it.[72]

To speak of the destiny of a people in such sweeping terms clearly inspired later eliminationists. In the autumn of 1941 Adolf Hitler used the idea of deportation as a euphemism for mass murder when talking about European Jews: 'That race of criminals has on its conscience the two million dead of the First World War, and now already hundreds and thousands more. Let nobody tell me that all the same we can't park them in the marshy parts of Russia!'[73]

More recently, Armenian scholars have pointed the finger at German writers. Vakahn Dadrian wrote that 'Rohrbach is . . . suspected to have been the theoretician who implanted in Turkish minds the idea of the expediency of the evacuation of the Armenians from their ancient territories in eastern Turkey and their relocation in Mesopotamia'.[74] In a public lecture in Berlin in February 1914 attended by members of the Turkish Embassy, General von der Goltz is reported to have argued that it was necessary to remove from the Russo-Turkish border-areas, once and for all, the half a million Armenians who inhabited the provinces of Van, Bitlis and Erzerum, which are contiguous to these areas. They should be transported south and resettled in the areas of Aleppo and Mesopotamia. In return, the Arabs of these areas should be resettled along the Russo-Turkish borders.[75] British historian Donald Bloxham takes a rather more nuanced view of Rohrbach's role:

> Contrary to the innuendo of these scholars [Dadrian and Ohandjanian], Rohrbach's concern that the Armenians stayed within the Ottoman sphere did not equate with acquiescence in anything that the Ottomans chose to do with the Armenians. [He] schemed in the economic interests of Germany as a pre-eminent future force in Asia Minor. His

ostensibly fantastic suggestion – though such concepts were common-place in geopolitical thought at the time – involved moving Muslims into eastern Anatolia and transplanting the Anatolian Armenian population to Mesopotamia, where he predicted that they could work fruitfully with and for Germany, for instance on further construction of the Baghdad railway.[76]

During the war, however, Mesopotamia was to become for the Armenians almost what Madagascar was to become for the Jews in 1940: a euphemism for a mass death penalty. Eliminationists often used sweeping and grandiose rhetoric while rarely dwelling on the detail of what the physical consequences of killing so many people would actually be in terms of the disposal of bodies which might spread disease, or even in terms of the psychological impact of mass killing on the perpetrators. But it is as well to remember that the act of genocide involves physical questions about the mechanics of mass death and the disposal of the remains. Christopher Browning notes that the ill-fated Madagascar plan was 'an important psychological step on the road to the Final Solution'.[77] And the euphemism of 'deportation' for women and children might have provided the Ittihad government with a sufficiently plausible script to the effect that, in circumstances of war, they were obeyed by the army and general non-Armenian populace.

Undoubtedly Rohrbach's suggestion about population relocation was largely aimed at building up German economic influence in the region and at trying to break Britain's influence in the Near East and India. Rohrbach was certainly not an enemy of the Armenians in a cultural sense. He regarded them as 'Aryan'[78] and progressive, and, above all, Christian. Thanks to the influence of Rohrbach, Alfred Rosenberg granted official recognition to an Armenian National Council on 15 December 1942. His writings are filled with sympathy for the Armenians after the massacres. He approved of their education by German pastors such as Johannnes Lepsius,[79] so it might be a little unfair to suggest (as did Arnold Toynbee) that Germans were beneficiaries of the destruction of Armenian businesses in Cilicia in 1909.

> [Rohrbach] prophesies that the whole carpet industry of Western Asia, 'from which English and other foreign firms in Smyrna now draw such enormous profits', will soon be concentrated round Urfa in German hands. From Armenia's evil, apparently, springs Germany's good – but in 1911 Dr Rohrbach did not foresee the catastrophe of 1915.[80]

Nevertheless, like many of his contemporaries writing in their most rhetorical vein, he was never one to underestimate the opportunities that chaos and destruction could create. His writing betrays the fact that his geopolitical projec-tions were lacking in overall human considerations when he speaks in abstract terms about 'Menschenmaterial Anatoliens' ('the human material of Anatolia').[81]

As a Baltic German, Rohrbach retained a special interest in the Russian empire. He was sent to Ukraine as an envoy during the Brest-Litovsk negotiations and argued that Germany should take full advantage of a situation of chaos in the region to take control of the territory.[82] After the war, he helped to found the German-Ukrainian society, which influenced leading Nazi and fellow Baltic German Alfred Rosenberg.[83] Their ideas found little favour in the 1920s, but were adapted by Rosenberg in his plans for a 'New Order' in eastern Europe: Ukraine would be bound to Germany yet quasi-independent, and it would counterbalance Russia and Poland.[84] Rohrbach's writings are full of negative evocations of the Russian spirit.[85] It is from Rohrbach that the Nazis probably derived the theory that, if the Soviet Union were attacked, it would fall into segments (like an orange).[86] Germany turning eastwards had already been considered in the imperial period 'in small circles . . . [developing] under the command of Ludendorff when he created the military state of "Oberost" in the Balticum [sic], Poland and later in the Ukraine. It carried clearly racist dimensions against Slavonic people and the Jews . . . This policy was framed around settlement.'[87]

It is rare to find an individual writer who will stand up and advocate mass death as a policy option. Adolf Hitler, Tâlât Paşa and Ion Antonescu – who spoke so rhetorically about mass deaths as if they were as inevitable and natural as plagues or thunders – are the rarities. Self-belief and delusion are clearly part of this equation. Even when the mass destruction of a population is not the point of departure, extremely creative ideas that involve control and then upheaval or massive social change and notions similar to the *Lebensraum* of the Nazis[88] are potentially dangerous when combined with a sense of mission and superiority to other peoples. The states of western Europe had been unified by ruthless ethnic cleansing in the medieval and early modern period. In killing so many Africans, Asians and native Americans in their colonial expansion, Europeans had already crossed a moral Rubicon well before the genocidal crisis of 1912–23. Furthermore, individuals who witnessed or took part in mass killing would have been morally blunted by their experience and found banal exemptions for their behaviour through racist discourse. It is often stated by perpetrators that the first murder is always the hardest one to commit.[89] In this context, the continuity between violent events – not just at the personal level, but as a marker of this epoch – should be re-emphasized.

Notes

1   Jürgen Zimmerer, 'Colonialism and the Holocaust. Towards an Archaeology of Genocide', in A. Dirk Moses (ed.), *Genocide and Settler Society: Frontier Violence and Stolen Indigenous Children in Australian History*, New York/Oxford: Berghahn, 2004, p. 64.
2   Dan Stone, 'The Historiography of Genocide: Beyond "Uniqueness" and Ethnic Competition', *Rethinking History*, vol. 8, no. 1, spring 2004, pp. 134–5.
3   Yehuda Bauer, 'Comparisons with other genocides', in *idem*, *Rethinking the Holocaust*, New Haven, CT: Yale University Press, 2002, p. 67.

4 Hannah Arendt, *The Origins of Totalitarianism*, London: Andre Deutsch, 1986.
5 Mark Levene, *Genocide in the Age of the Nation State: The Rise of the West and the Coming of Genocide*, Vol. 2, London: I. B. Tauris, 2005, p. 84.
6 Evgenii Preobrazhensky and Nikolai Bukharin, with an introduction by Edward Hallett Carr, *The ABC of Communism*, Harmondsworth: Penguin, 1969, p. 189.
7 Philip D. Curtin, 'Epidemiology and the Slave Trade', in Gad J. Heuman and James Walvin (eds), *The Slavery Reader*, London: Routledge, 2003, p. 21.
8 Ho Chi Minh, 'Report on the National and Colonial Questions at the Fifth Congress of the Communist International', in *Selected Writings 1920–1969*, Hanoi: Foreign Languages Publishing House 1977, pp. 35–6.
9 Mike Hawkins, *Social Darwinism in European and American Thought, 1860–1945*, Cambridge: Cambridge University Press, 1997.
10 Christopher Browning, *Ordinary Men: Reserve Police Battalion 101 and the Final Solution in Poland*, London: Penguin, 2001, p. 73.
11 Henry Morgenthau, *Ambassador Morgenthau's Story*, London: Hodder and Stoughton, 1918, p. 375.
12 Mark Twain, *King Leopold's Soliloquy. A Defense of his Congo Rule*, Boston, MA: P.R. Warren, 1905.
13 Arthur Conan Doyle, The *Crime of the Congo*, New York: Doubleday, Page, 1909, p. iii.
14 Edmund Dene Morel, *The Black Man's Burden*, London: National Labour Press, 1920, p. 194.
15 Mark Levene, *Genocide in the Age of the Nation State: The Rise of the West and the Coming of Genocide*, Vol. 1, London: I. B. Tauris, 2005, pp. 178–9.
16 A. Dirk Moses, 'Conceptual Blockages and Definitional Dilemmas in the Racial Century: Genocides of Indigenous Peoples and the Holocaust', *Patterns of Prejudice*, vol. 36, no. 4, 2002, p. 8.
17 Antonio Gramsci, *Cronache Torinesi 1913–1917*, ed. and sel. Sergio Caprioglio, Turin: Einaudi, 1980, pp. 184–6.
18 Djordje Stefanović, 'Seeing the Albanians through Serbian Eyes: The Inventors of the Tradition of Intolerance and their Critics 1804–1939', *European History Quarterly*, vol. 35, no. 3, 2005, pp. 472–3.
19 Aviel Roshwald, *Ethnic Nationalism and the Fall of Empires: Central Europe, Russia and the Middle East, 1914–1923*, New York: Routledge, 2001, p. 49.
20 M. L. Anderson, ' "Down in Turkey, far away": Human Rights, the Armenian Massacres, and Orientalism in Wilhelmine Germany', *Journal of Modern History*, vol. 79, no. 1, 2007, p. 86.
21 Geoff Eley, 'Reviewing the Socialist Tradition', in Christina Lemke and Gary Marks (eds), *The Crisis of Socialism in Europe*, Durham, NC: Duke University Press, 1992, pp. 21–60.
22 Fitzroy Maclean, *Eastern Approaches*, London: Reprint Society, 1951, p. 238.
23 Alfred Andersch, *Sansibar, oder der letze Grund*, Olten: Walter Verlag, 1957.
24 Orlando Figes and Boris Kolonitskii, *Interpreting the Russian Revolution. The Language and Symbols of 1917*, New Haven, CT: Yale University Press, 1999, p. 185.
25 Tim Judah, *The Serbs. History, Myth and the Destruction of Yugoslavia*, New Haven, CT and London: Yale University Press, 1997, p. 75.
26 Viktor Novak, *Magnum Crimen: pola vijeka klerikalizma u Hrvatskoj*, Zagreb: Nakladni Zavod Hrvatske, p. 606.
27 Konfidentenbericht an k.u.k. Ministerium des Äußeren, 27.12.17, quoted in Rolf Hosfeld, *Operation Nemesis. Die Türkei, Deutschland und der Völkermord an den Armeniern*, Köln: Kiepenheuer & Witsch, 2005, p. 261.
28 Johannes Lepsius, *Deutschland und Armenien, 1914–1918: Sammlung diplomatischer Aktenstücke*, Potsdam: Tempelverlag, 1919, pp. 25 and 483.

29 Robert Conquest, *The Harvest of Sorrow: Soviet Collectivization and the Terror-Famine*, Oxford: Oxford University Press, 1986, p. 272.

30 R. J. Rummel, *Death by Government: Genocide and Mass Murder since 1900*, New Brunswick, NJ: Transaction Publishers, 1994, p. 101.

31 'Preface', in Joseph P. Merlino, Marilyn S. Jacobs, Judy Ann Kaplan and K. Lynne Moritz (eds), *Freud at 150: 21st-Century Essays on a Man of Genius*, Plymouth: Rowman & Littlefield, 2008, p. ix.

32 Richard Rorty, 'Human Rights, Rationality and Sentimentality', in *Truth and Progress. Philosophical Papers*, Cambridge: Cambridge University Press, 1998, p. 176.

33 Patrick Henry, 'Banishing the Coercion of Despair: Le Chambon-sur-Lignon and the Holocaust Today', *Shofar: An Interdisciplinary Journal of Jewish Studies*, vol. 20. no. 2, 2002, pp. 74–5.

34 Rosa Luxemburg, 'Einleitung (geschrieben im Strafgefaengnis Breslau im Juli 1918)', in Wladimir Korolenko, *Die Geschichte meines Zeitgenossen*, Berlin: Paul Cassirer, 1919, p. xiii.

35 Lynn Hunt, *Inventing Human Rights: A History*, New York: W.W. Norton, 2007, p. 213.

36 *Kolokol* means 'tocsin' or 'warning bell'.

37 Brian Glyn Williams, 'Hijra and Forced Migration from Nineteenth-Century Russia to the Ottoman Empire', *Cahiers du monde russe*, vol. 41, no. 1, 2000, p. 81.

38 Henri Troyat, *Tolstoy*, Harmondsworth: Penguin, 1970, p. 807.

39 Vladimir I. Lenin, 'Leo Tolstoy as the Mirror of the Russian Revolution', in David Craig (ed.), *Marxists on Literature*, Harmondsworth: Penguin, 1977, p. 347.

40 'The American Mission at Van: Narrative printed privately in the United States by Miss Grace Higley Knapp (1915)', in James Viscount Bryce and Arnold Toynbee, *The Treatment of Armenians in the Ottoman Empire, 1915–1916: Documents Presented to Viscount Grey of Falloden*, Reading: Tadaron Press, in association with the Gormidas Institute, 2000, p. 83.

41 Claire Demesmay and Eddy Fougier, 'Die französische Malaise im Spiegel der Türkei-Debatte', in Angelos Giannakopoulos and Konstadinos Maras (eds), *Die Türkei-Debatte in Europa. Ein Vergleich*, Wiesbaden, VS Verlag für Sozialwissenschaften, 2005, pp. 49–62.

42 Anderson, ' "Down in Turkey, Far Away" ', pp. 84–5.

43 Maud Mandel, *In the Aftermath of Genocide: Armenians and Jews in Twentieth Century France*, Durham, NC: Duke University Press, 2003, p. 26.

44 Jeremy Jennings, 'Of Treason, Blindness and Silence. Dilemmas of the Intellectual in Modern France', in Jeremy Jennings and Anthony Kemp-Welch (eds), *Intellectuals in Politics*, London: Routledge, 1997, p. 69.

45 Simon Goldsworthy, 'English Non-Conformity and the Pioneering of the Modern Newspaper Campaign, Including the Strange Case of W. T. Stead and the Bulgarian Horrors', *Journalism Studies*, vol. 7, no. 3, June 2006, p. 388.

46 Benjamin Madley, 'From Africa to Auschwitz: How German South West Africa Incubated Ideas and Methods Adopted by the Nazis in Eastern Europe', *European History Quarterly*, no. 3, vol. 35, 2005, p. 430.

47 Jürgen Zimmerer, 'Geburt des "Ostlandes" aus dem Geiste des Kolonialismus, die nationalsozialistische Eroberungs- und Beherrschungspolitik in (post-)kolonialer Perspektive', *Sozialgeschichte*, vol. 19, no. 1, 2004, pp. 10–43; Jürgen Zimmerer, *Von Windhuk nach Auschwitz. Beiträge zum Verhältnis von Kolonialismus und Holocaust*, Münster: LIT Verlag, 2007.

48 Dominik Schaller, 'Die Rezeption des Völkermordes an den Armeniern in Deutschland', in Hans-Lukas Kieser and Dominik J. Schaller (eds), *Der Völkermord an den Armeniern und die Shoah*, Zürich: Chronos Verlag, 2002, pp. 517–55.

49 Tacitus, quoted in Marjorie Housepian, *Smyrna 1922: The Destruction of a City*. London: Faber, 1972, p. 39.

50 N. M. Naimark, *Fires of Hatred: Ethnic Cleansing in Twentieth Century Europe*, Cambridge, MA: Harvard University Press, 2001, p. 110.

51 Helmut Walser Smith, *The Continuities of German History. Nation, Religion and Race Across the Long Nineteenth Century*, Cambridge: Cambridge University Press, 2008, p. 201.

52 Schaller, 'Die Rezeption des Völkermordes', p. 520.

53 Munroe Smith, 'German Land Hunger', *Political Science Quarterly*, vol. 32, no. 3, September 1917, p. 462.

54 Gertjan Dijtink, 'Geopolitics as a Social Movement?', *Geopolitics*, vol. 9, no. 2, 2004, p. 466.

55 'Die Theologie ... erschein sie mir als eine Führerin durch die Welt der sozialen Probleme', Paul Rohrbach, *Um des Teufels Handschrift. Zwei Menschenalter erlebter Weltgeschichte*, Hamburg: Hans Dulk, 1953, pp. 15–18.

56 Paul Rohrbach, *Der Deutsche Gedanke in der Welt*, Düsseldorf and Leipzig: Karl Robert Langewiesche, 1912, p. 60.

57 Gottfried Hagan, 'German Heralds of Holy War: Orientalists and Applied Oriental Studies', *Comparative Studies of South Asia, Africa and the Middle East*, vol. 24, no. 2, 2004, p. 147.

58 'Der Deutsche Gedanke, nicht im Sinne politischer Vorherrschaft oder materieller Kolonisation, sondern rein als Weltkulturfaktor', in Rohrbach, *Der Deutsche Gedanke in der Welt*, p. 235.

59 Schaller, 'Die Rezeption des Völkermordes an den Armeniern in Deutschland', p. 520.

60 Michael Mann, *The Dark Side of Democracy. Explaining Ethnic Cleansing*, Cambridge: Cambridge University Press, 2005, pp. 101–2.

61 Paul Rohrbach, 'Koloniale Rassen- und Ehefragen', in *Die Hilfe*, no. 19, from 9/5/1912, p. 291 in Schaller, 'Die Rezeption des Völkermordes an den Armeniern in Deutschland', p. 547, n. 30.

62 Rohrbach, *Der Deutsche Gedanke*, p. 143.

63 Philipp Prein, 'Guns and Top Hats: African Resistance in German South West Africa 1907–1915', *Journal of South African Studies*, vol. 20, no. 1, 1992, p. 107.

64 Paul Rohrbach, *Die Bagdadbahn*, Berlin: Verlag von Wiegandt und Grieben, 1902, pp. 23–47, esp. 26–30.

65 Rohrbach, *Der Deutsche Gedanke*, p. 36.

66 Rohrbach, *Die Bagdadbahn*, p. 18; Rohrbach, *Der Deutsche Gedanke*, p. 166.

67 Rohrbach, *Die Bagdadbahn*, p. 35.

68 Paul Rohrbach, *Vom Kaukasus zum Mittelmeer. Eine Hochzeits- und Studienreise durch Armenien*, Leipzig and Berlin: B. G. Teubner, 1903, pp. 152, 194, 218.

69 Donald Bloxham, *The Great Game of Genocide*, Oxford: Oxford University Press, 2005, p. 1.

70 1915-08-05-DE-002, Scheubner-Richter to Hohenlohe-Langenburg, Erserum, 5 August 1915, in Wolfgang Gust (ed.), *Der Völkermord an den Armeniern 1915/16: Dokumente aus dem Politischen Archiv des deutschen Auswärtigen Amts*, Springe: Zu Klampen, 2005, p. 226.

71 A. P. Hacobian, *L'Arménie et la guerre, Le Point de vue d'un Arménien avec un appel à la Grande-Bretagne et à la prochaine Conférence de paix*, Paris: Hagop Turabian, 1918, p. 67.

72 Henry Morgenthau, *Ambassador Morgenthau's Story*, London: Hodder & Stoughton, 1918, pp. 365–6.

73 Sarah Gordon, *Hitler, Germans and the Jewish Question*, Princeton, NJ: Princeton University Press, 1984, p. 131.

74 Vahakn Dadrian, *The History of the Armenian Genocide. Ethnic Conflict from the Balkans to Anatolia to the Caucasus*, Oxford: Berghahn, 2003, p. 254.
75 Ibid. p. 255.
76 Bloxham, *The Great Game of Genocide*, p. 120.
77 Christopher Browning, with contributions by Jürgen Matthäus, *The Origins of the Final Solution*, Lincoln, NE: University of Nebraska Press, 2004, p. 81.
78 Christopher J. Walker, *Armenia. The Survival of a Nation*, New York: St Martin's Press, 1980, p. 357.
79 Rohrbach, *Die Bagdadbahn*, p. 54.
80 Arnold Joseph Toynbee, *Turkey: A Past and a Future*, New York: George H. Doran, 1917, p. 55.
81 Rohrbach, *Die Bagdadbahn*, p. 19.
82 Henry C. Meyer, 'Rohrbach and his Osteuropa', *Russian Review*, vol. 2, no. 1, autumn 1942, p. 68.
83 Peter Borowsky, 'Paul Rohrbach und die Ukraine: Ein Beitrag zum Kontinuitätsproblem', in Immanuel Geiss and Bernd Jürgen Wendt (eds), *Deutschland in der Weltpolitik des 19. und 20. Jahrhunderts. Fritz Fischer zum 65. Geburtstag*, Düsseldorf: Bertelsmann, 1973, pp. 437–62.
84 Andreas Kappeler, 'Ukrainian History from a German Perspective', *Slavic Review*, vol. 54, no. 3, autumn 1995, pp. 691–701, at 694.
85 Gregory Moore, 'From Buddhism to Bolshevism: Some Orientalist Themes in German Thought', *German Life and Letters*, vol. 56, no. 1, January 2003, p. 38.
86 Paul Rohrbach, cited in Oleksyj Kuraev, 'Der Verband "Freie Ukraine" im Kontext der deutschen Ukraine-Politik des Ersten Weltkriegs', Osteuropa-Institut München: *Mitteilungen*, no. 35, August 2000, pp. 1–47, at 8, n. 10.
87 Helmut Bley, 'Continuities and German Colonialism: Colonial Experience and Metropolitan Developments 1890–1955', paper presented at the Nineteenth International Conference of the Vereinigung von Afrikanisten in Deutschland, Hannover University, 2–5 June 2004.
88 Schaller, 'Die Rezeption des Völkermordes an den Armeniern in Deutschland', pp. 520–1.
89 George Kassimeris, *Warrior's Dishonour: Barbarity, Morality and Torture in Modern Warfare*, Dartmouth: Ashgate, 2006 p. 8.

2

JUDEOPHOBIA AND THE
NAZI IDENTITY

Philippe Burrin

Ever since the Holocaust, scholars have debated the extent to which anti-Semitism played a major role in the Nazi urge to exterminate the Jews of Europe. To be sure, Hitler had railed incessantly against the Jews, Nazi rhetoric in general was replete with anti-Semitism, and the Third Reich ended up devoting substantial energy and resources to identifying, concentrating, and murdering every Jew that came under its rule. But for several decades scholars were engaged in a vehement debate over the causes and mechanisms of the "final solution." On the one side, "intentionalists" such as Eberhard Jäckel and Gerald Fleming asserted that Hitler had always set his sights on eradicating the Jews of Europe and had been the moving force behind the Holocaust; on the other, such "functionalists" as Martin Broszat and Hans Mommsen viewed the Nazi genocide as the outcome of "cumulative radicalization" resulting from a "polycracy," where rival institutions competed over Hitler's favor by opting for the most extreme solutions to the issues they confronted. Presenting Hitler as a weak dictator and totalitarian hegemony as a propagandistic myth, these historians argued that genocide had emerged from the "bottom" as a "practical," if radical solution to logistical difficulties and was only subsequently adopted and systematized by the leadership of the Reich. In other words, whereas the "intentionalists" postulated the primacy of ideology and state control, the "functionalists" insisted on the impact of impersonal structures and practical bureaucrats, in some ways borrowing a page from Hannah Arendt's notion of the "banality of evil." Critics argued that this mechanistic view of genocide left no individual actually responsible for perpetrating it.

These conflicting interpretations came into public view during the German Historians' controversy of the mid-1980s, unleashed by the scholar Ernst Nolte's argument that Nazism and the Holocaust had merely been a response to and a copy of Bolshevism, and that the only original invention of the Nazis were the gas chambers. A decade later, the media hype surrounding the publication of Daniel Jonah Goldhagen's Hitler's Willing Executioners, *which insisted that pre-Nazi Germany had developed a particularly extreme form of "eliminationist" anti-Semitism and that subsequently most Germans wanted to and enjoyed killing Jews, signaled the end of the intentionalist-functionalist debate. Yet the precise balance between prejudice, ideology, and leader-*

ship, on the one hand, and the systemic, faceless functioning of the modern bureaucratic state on the other, remains one of the central questions of scholarship on Nazi Germany and the Holocaust. The eminent historian Ian Kershaw has suggested one of the best formulations for the mechanism that propelled Nazi functionaries, by noting their urge to "work toward the Führer," in an on-going attempt to fulfill the expectations they attributed to him. Since Hitler was both beyond all constraints within the Nazi State, and was known to be the most radical among his followers, working toward him meant choosing extreme solutions.

Reflecting the long-term effects of the intentionalists-functionalist debate, Saul Friedländer, author of the outstanding Nazi Germany and the Jews, has implied a rather different way of understanding Nazi thinking and motivation by proposing the term "redemptive anti-Semitism." This, he suggested, was an amalgamation of long held anti-Jewish prejudices and images, whose roots date deep into medieval Christian Europe, with the new, cutting-edge racial theories that endowed such notions with scientific legitimacy. This strange but effective mélange had the advantage of appealing both to the masses and to the intelligentsia, and of postulating that "removing" the Jews was both necessary according to the laws of nature and imbued with a redemptive quality for those who would be finally liberated of their presence.

In this chapter, Burrin revisits this issue with his own complex and insightful interpretation. He clearly shows that Hitler was personally motivated by fanatical anti-Semitism: whether or not he could envision mass extermination long before the war, there is little doubt that his worldview was predicated on a violent notion of a racial struggle in which the Aryans had to either eradicate the Jews or be themselves wiped out along with the entire universe. Although Hitler's views may have only been shared by a minority, albeit not an insignificant one, in Weimar Germany, once he came into power, this ideology rapidly spread through education, the Hitler Youth, popular media, public speeches, and so forth. Not everyone fully shared these ideas, but many saw the personal benefit to be derived from acquiescing with the regime's anti-Jewish policies, and likely a majority viewed the despised Weimar Republic and the menacing Soviet Union as controlled by the Jews. Burrin concludes that by the late 1930s, as Hitler's popularity neared its peak, and as the Jews became socially almost invisible even as antisemitic rhetoric reached fever pitch, the Führer had largely accomplished his goal of disseminating his racial hatred to wide circles of German society.

Nazism's accession to power in 1933 certainly marked a turning point of the greatest importance. However, there was still a long way to go before Auschwitz, and we now need to examine the problem of how that destination was reached.

The problem can be divided into two questions. The first concerns the dynamics of the persecution that was unleashed as early as 1933 and from then on never ceased to gather momentum. What was the mainspring of that dynamism? Many historians consider it to have been the very way in which the Nazi regime functioned—its polycratic structure and the intrinsic irrationality that allowed it to achieve only negative objectives such as the persecution inflicted upon the Jews. Although this thesis of a "cumulative radicalization," as Hans Mommsen puts it, may contain an element of truth, it discounts the propulsive force of ideology too easily by ascribing to the latter an inconsistency and incoherence that disqualify it as a grid by which to read the world and as a table of orientation for action. We must first check whether it did not, on the contrary, possess considerable coherence and whether a fundamental radicalism was not an inherent part of this.

The second question is one that does not always receive as much attention: What of the German population? The new regime tried hard to imbue it with its own anti-Semitism, and, given that it undoubtedly succeeded, we must identify the means that made this possible. This is an important point, for the absence of any substantial opposition also contributed to the dynamism of the persecution.

It is frequently said of Hitlerian ideology that it contained nothing new and was a potpourri of notions already present in modern anti-Semitism more or less everywhere. This is quite true if one looks no further than the catalogue of its representations and themes: the Jew as an exploiter and a parasite, the Jew as a manipulator and a revolutionary, the Jew as a poisoner and a carrier of infection. All those images had been circulating throughout the continent for several decades, but if we wish to see beyond that inventory, we must seek what it was that fundamentally structured Hitlerian anti-Semitism and, to that end, pay serious attention to the picture that emerges from an attentive reading of *Mein Kampf*.

What do we find there? Above all, a racist ideology—an ideology that considers race to be the explanatory principle of the history of the world. Hitler, a racist thoroughly in agreement with that ideology, postulates the existence of human races as separate from one another as the animal species and arranged in a hierarchy according to how they are evaluated. Positioned at the top of the hierarchy is the Aryan race, the sole creator of culture, as is "proved" by the great empires of antiquity, particularly those of Greece and Rome. Beneath, midway down the hierarchy, are races such as the Japanese, which preserve the fund of culture by assimilating that of the Aryans, particularly their technology, into their own lives. At the bottom of the hierarchy, according to this ideology, are the Jews, who create nothing, have no state or culture of their own, and are parasites living at the expense of the other peoples of the earth, which they inexorably destroy.

According to Hitler, the evolution of the human races established the decisive importance of two "laws of nature" that applied to the entire living world. One was the law of racial purity, racial endogamy, whose violation through interbreeding leads to decadence and eventual extinction. The other was the law of selection, or the elimination of the weak in combat or through a deliberate eugenic policy.

Such an ideology is strictly racist, for it focuses not only upon "aliens"—all those who are defined, by whatever criteria, as not belonging to the superior race—but also upon the members of that superior race itself, only some of whom (the best) must be encouraged to procreate while the rest, "the tainted," must be excluded from reproduction and even from "the banquet of life" itself. Unsurprisingly, Hitler emphatically praised the breeding system for horses and dogs and espoused the social Darwinist idea of a struggle for survival. His morality was of an ancient or, to be more precise, Germanic nature. His constant praise of "toughness" conveyed a desire to destroy the moral barriers of existing civilization, with all its humanitarianism and universalism, and to link up once more with a pre-Christian civilization ruled by ethnic exclusivism and the law of the strongest, which justified the extermination or enslavement of all conquered peoples.

All of this is cast in a biologizing register that testifies to the strength of Hitler's "scientism." But Hitler did not confine himself within this framework, for he also related the so-called "laws of nature" to "the Eternal One," or to "the Lord." He invoked not the personal god of monotheism but a deity confused with Creation, who remains forever mysterious, in contrast to the "laws of nature," which human reason can decipher and which, he recommended, should be observed.

Hitler established a link not only between the "laws of nature" and some kind of transcendence, but also with history, since historical understanding is the means for verifying the validity of all these so-called "laws." He did this when sketching in a history of the Aryans that followed a precise schema. The Aryan peoples, whose supposed superiority stemmed from their being endowed with idealism (a spirit of devotion to the community, reflected in the way they worked and fought), and who respected blood purity and practiced selection: for example, they killed deformed children at birth. In this way, they acquired such power that they were able to conquer peoples far greater numerically and to use them as slaves in the construction of great empires. These empires gave rise to brilliant cultures but then declined, allegedly owing to their eventual interbreeding with the peoples they had conquered.

This historical schema was also a model. Nazism's mission was to restore Germany to a rank of power by curing it of the decadence that afflicted it, thereby enabling it to conquer an empire comparable to those of the past in every respect, including cultural greatness. At the heart of Nazism lay this imperial mission. Through every page of Mein Kampf can be glimpsed a portrait of Hitler imperator.

An anti-Semitic ideology nestles at the heart of this racist framework. The history of the races' battle for survival is immemorial, but for two millennia a struggle had been raging between two races in particular, whose respective characteristics rendered them perfectly antagonistic. The characteristics of the Jews placed them, term for term, as ignoble is opposed to noble, in opposition to the Aryans. They supposedly possessed no idealism and consequently no solidarity, except in situations of danger or in order to lay hold of some prey. They had no religion—only a simple code of practical behavior—no culture other than through imitation, and no state, since they were incapable of organizing one. All they did have, in abundance, was deception, the weapon par excellence that enabled them to live as parasites leeching on other people by getting them to believe that they, the Jews, were assimilable into their nations. On the other hand, they did observe the so-called "laws of nature" and so preserved the purity of their blood. This made them redoubtable in their pursuit of power, as was allegedly illustrated by their project of world domination, which Hitler claimed to be attested by the *Protocols of the Elders of Zion*, a Tsarist forgery that continues, even today, to be circulated by anti-Semites.

This historically determining struggle between Aryans and Jews began when primitive Christianity—proclaimed, of course, by an Aryan and therefore anti-Semitic Christ—was distorted by the Jew Paul, who turned it into a form of universalism that, just like the Bolshevism that it spawned much later, was to encourage the spread of crossbreeding and decadence, thereby greatly profiting the Jews. Ever since, that struggle had become increasingly intense, particularly in the nineteenth century and during World War I. At the time Hitler was writing *Mein Kampf*, he claimed that it was still ongoing, taking two forms that were contradictory only in appearance: one the class warfare propagated by Bolshevism (a supposed Jewish invention), the other the internationalization of economies, brought about by the Jewish financiers of the Anglo-Saxon countries. According to Hitler, the outcome of the struggle, through which the Jews aimed to destroy not only the nations of the world but the very principle of nationalism, would determine the fate of the German people and, indeed, that of the very planet. A Jewish victory would mean not only the end of all culture but, if the Aryan race came to disappear, also the death of the planet. This catastrophe was a theme to which Hitler repeatedly returned. The man's imagination was in thrall to the idea of the extreme situation par excellence—that of annihilation.

The coherence of this ideology hardly requires further corroboration. Although plenty of points, starting with the definition of race, remained vague, there was nothing vague about its construction and articulation. Many of its ideas were already in circulation, but their combination is striking in two respects.

The first is its so-to-speak totalitarian quality. The Hitlerian ideology was cosmic or at least macro-historical. It encompassed the origin of civilizations and even of the planet. It reduced the whole of human history to a handful of determining elements: the observation of racial purity, a struggle between the various races for the possession of rare resources, and the malignant action of the Jews over the previous two thousand years. And, as if to magnify that comprehensiveness at the linguistic level, it consistently intertwined different semantic registers. We have already noted this with regard to biological, religious, and historical registers; to these, those of art and politics should be added.

It would be a mistake to dismiss this interweaving as the result of confused thinking or simply as indicating a half-baked mind seeking to link disparate areas of knowledge into a single system. Fundamentally, it conveys a totalitarian desire to shut down the world of liberal civilization in which social life is divided between a number of autonomous spheres (art, science, religion, politics, economics, and so on) and to do so in order to revert to the holistic universe of the tribe, with all its exclusivism and brutish morality.

The other aspect of Hitlerian ideology that is so striking is the place of prime importance that it assigns to politics. Hitler's thinking was political. He was preoccupied with the means of realizing his ideology and possessed an acute understanding of what was needed for political action to be successful. Pragmatism was his foremost concern. This can be seen from the importance that he ascribed to a highly organized mass party with a modern propaganda apparatus at its disposal, and to the elaboration of not only an external but also an internal strategy. With perfect clarity, he set out the objectives of his foreign policy and also the means of realizing them—namely, a strategy of alliances. In all these respects he had broken with the *völkisch* anti-Semites of both pre-1914 and post-1914. Skillfulness and fanaticism seldom go together, but Hitler possessed both to the highest degree.

How to characterize his anti-Semitism? On one level, it could be said that it was secondary, just a part of his racism. But in truth it was not secondary at all, for it lay at the very heart of his racism. For Hitler, the battle against the Jews possessed an immediacy and intensity unlike any other. What was at stake for him was existential in the strictest sense of the word.

This anti-Semitism of Hitler's combined all the three variants of modern anti-Semitism: Christian anti-Semitism, through Hitler's "Christian rhetoric" ("By defending myself against the Jew, I fight to defend the Lord's work"); national anti-Semitism, through his presentation of a Germany under mortal threat from the foreign presence and antinational behavior of the Jews; and racist anti-Semitism, of course, for this provided the general framework. This was, in short, a particularly successful example of syncretism, capable of branching out in every direction and producing an at least superficial consensus.

More important, this was a radical Semitism, for it represented the Jews as the negative reverse of the Aryan identity. Hitler constructed a relationship of total opposition that implied a total rejection of not only Judaism but also its poisoned fruits, Christianity and all its avatars, which ranged from liberalism to Bolshevism. The "otherness" of the Jews was exaggerated and exalted into an essential "malignancy." The Jews were not only the authors of a two-millennia-old diversion of civilization that was responsible for the decadence of Germany, but they were also the principal adversary now blocking the Nazi path to power.

None of this was new, although the scale and the systematic character of the incrimination were certainly striking. What was new, however, was that the relationship between Aryans and Jews was structured according to an apocalyptic schema. The opposition between the two races was to lead to a final combat of planetary proportions. This was to be a clash between two ambitions for "universal empire": the one attributed to the Jews entirely fantastical, that of the Nazis carefully nurtured.

This apocalyptic schema was derived from the Christian tradition, but it is not hard to see that the latter was reused in a distorted form. The Hitlerian apocalypse accommodated no divine intervention, no eschatology. This battle for racial predominance was a secular one, of a revolutionary nature. The Jews no longer had any place in the divine plan, except perhaps through the anticipation of their conversion at the Last Judgment. They were set up as the enemy at the heart of a battle conceived to be decisive.

By his reuse of an apocalyptic schema, Hitler set himself apart from predecessors who, for their part, had resorted to a Manichean schema. Edouard Drumont, for example, had declared, "When the Jew is on the rise, France declines; when the Jew declines, France rises"—an antagonistic view, to be sure, even a vision of a "final catastrophe" if nothing was done to prevent this, but not an evocation of a battle to the death that would involve the fate of not only France but the entire planet.

Hitlerian anti-Semitism was thus of an apocalyptic-racist variety. The strangeness of the association of those two terms needs to be underlined. The term racism evokes a would-be scientific approach, connoting objectivity and detachment. It suggests the impassivity of the doctor fighting infection and strengthening his patient, the gardener pruning and grafting his plants, or the animal breeder selecting his livestock. Apocalypse, in contrast, conjures up the figure of a prophet, evokes a metaphysical passion, nourishes an existential hatred, the angst of salvation or annihilation (the latter rather than the former being what Nazism cultivated, it must be said).

That association is characterized by the interpenetration of the semantic registers noted earlier: on the one hand that of the "parasitic" Jews, microbes, vermin, and so on, as listed by Eberhard Jäckel; on the other, that elaborated by Claus-Ekkehard Bärsch, featuring the satanic Jew and the Antichrist. Historians tend to emphasize either one or the other. Most associate Hitlerian anti-Semitism with scientism, while a minority link it more with pseudoreligion or a political religion. But it is important to take equal account of both registers for, as already mentioned, they interact fully. To associate them closely in this way is to do justice to the totalitarian aspiration that underlies the confusion. Hitlerian anti-Semitism implacably scours the entire universe, from the microbe to the cosmos. By portraying the Jews as sub-human microbes on the one hand

and, on the other, associating them with the suprahuman devil, it produces an unassailable image of dehumanization.

The association of racism with an apocalypse only operated in reference to the Jews, sparing all the other targets of Hitlerian racism. And, as is not hard to see, it carried with it a limitless potential for violence, for anti-Semitism was further strengthened by being incorporated into a strict racism that not only did not spare its own people but even began by purging them. The virulence of this racist anti-Semitism was then further magnified by its absorbtion into an apocalyptic schema that imbued it with all the fervor that a battle between the principles of good and evil engenders.

We have so far been considering Hitlerian ideology. But what of Nazi ideology? It is fair to say that this manifests a certain pluralism, bounded by two poles: on one represented by the Germano-Nordic and anti-Christian wing of Himmler and Darré, characterized by their vision of the various racially related peoples being brought together within a greater Reich incorporating Germans, Scandinavians, Dutch, and so on; and one represented by Goebbels, who was more concerned with mobilizing the masses around a "socialist" rhetoric. The link between the two sides was provided—as usual, with consummate skill—by Adolf Hitler.

However, a wide consensus did exist among the leadership of the Nazi party. It would have been surprising had it not been so, as Hitler was generally recognized as its theorist and *Mein Kampf* was the regime's bible. It served as a reservoir of maxims that were used in countless school textbooks. The consensus related to four points: (1) the racist idea of the diversity and fundamental inequality of the various human groups; (2) the idea of the regeneration of German society by encouraging the reproduction of its best elements, the purging of those who were flawed, and the expulsion of all aliens; (3) the idea of a special antagonism between the Germans and the Jews, an antagonism portrayed in either Manichean or apocalyptic terms; and finally, (4) the idea of an imperial expansion guaranteed by that prior cleansing of German society.

This amounted to a body of ideas sufficiently consistent to direct political action and incorporating enough agreement for the leader at the head of the party, who held the most radical views, to pull that party in a maximalist direction and if necessary all the way to acceptance of the hypothesis of an extreme solution.

Having noted that the Hitlerian ideology did possess some novel elements, that it was fundamentally radical with a potential for limitless violence, and that it provided the bulk, if not quite all, of Nazi ideology, we must now determine what it was that made it possible for this radical anti-Semitism to root itself so firmly in German society.

Clearly, the crucially important condition was Hitler's appointment to the post of chancellor in 1933. His accession to power was by no means inevitable. It was engineered by a clique of politically shortsighted conservatives at a time when the Nazi wave of popularity was already past its peak. Nor was the consolidation of the new regime a foregone conclusion: the Night of the Long Knives in the summer of 1934, when Röhm's SA was decapitated, shows that Hitler was walking a tightrope. Furthermore, it was not inevitable that he should then, within a relatively short space of time, acquire an autocratic position. Taken all together, these developments, completed by about 1937, were crucial for what followed. They formed the context for the period of peace in which anti-Semitism was progressively diffused throughout German society.

That diffusion, seldom closely examined, needs to be explained. At its peak, the Nazi party had received 44 percent of the poll, and this was at the time of the elections of March 1933, which were marked by the proscription of the Communist Party and the SA's campaign of intimidation in the streets. German society contained sizable subcultures, particularly those of social democracy and the Catholic world, which the Nazi party penetrated only gradually. Even within the Nazi party, the motivation for support varied greatly; anti-Semitism was probably a determining factor for no more than a minority.

Yet, by a few years later, this same society had, at least partially, internalized the regime's anti-Semitism, in its most syncretic version at least, if not its apocalyptic-racist kernel. In other words, it had accepted the idea that there existed a "Jewish question," the solution of which implied at the very least discriminating legislation and possibly the departure of all Jews from Germany.

What is the evidence for this? The regime's police reports indicate so, as do the clandestine records of the socialist opposition, which registered the diffusion of anti-Semitism in circles such as the working class, which had been relatively free of it in the past; also, the weakness of reactions to the Nuremberg laws of 1935, the "Aryanization" of 1938, and the *Kristallnacht* of November 1938 are all indications, although the latter, the brutality of which was exceptional in recent European history, did prompt some mitigated response.

On the whole, the reception of the Nuremberg laws seems most revelatory. These laws demoted Jews from the rank of citizens to that of "people under the jurisdiction of the Reich," thereby introducing into European law a distinction of status that hitherto had characterized only the colonial discrimination between citizens of the metropolis and subjects of the colonies. Yet this considerable change, not to mention the sexual segregation that went with it, gave rise to no serious protests—something that would have been most unlikely only a few years earlier and possibly even in 1933.

It is essential to take this change in people's attitudes into consideration, for without it the genocide could never have been carried out with such efficiency and so little opposition. How can it be explained? One ready-made answer leaps to mind. Once the dictatorship was established, the checks and counterbalances to anti-Semitism disappeared, while, conversely, the new regime benefited from the advantages of legality and legitimacy. Those who had hesitated to allow free rein to their anti-Jewish prejudices under Weimar now felt free to do so, and the rest were intimidated. Furthermore, anti-Semitism was now officially encouraged, whether it involved appropriating Jewish property, seizing Jewish jobs, or simply distancing oneself from Jewish acquaintances. Whatever the circumstances, it was internalized, for people had to find self-justification for what they were doing, and, rather than blame their own cowardice, it was easier to appropriate the "good reasons" provided by the regime. Propaganda was insidiously effective, and the socialization of the young through schools and the *Hitlerjugend*, membership of which became compulsory in 1936, was going full steam ahead.

In such conditions, a society rapidly adapts to exclusion, particularly when those excluded are groups that have long been stigmatized. On this subject the historian Detlev Peukert is probably right when he declares that the "national community" created by Nazism rested above all on the popularity of the measures of exclusion that it had introduced. It is worth adding that those measures constituted the reverse of the efforts at inclusion deployed by the same regime. Both sets of measures were designed to give the German people a new sense of self-esteem.

In any case, it seems clear that the exclusion of the Jews could only function provided it was justified by a whole body of representations in what seemed an acceptable manner. For negative images to be internalized, it was not enough simply for propaganda to purvey them, particularly (and this is the paradox here) when those images related to a population such as the German Jews, which was being progressively marginalized and excluded from any positions that might have afforded it even the slightest power over the society that surrounded it.

Over and above the effects of propaganda and the socialization of the younger generation (although in fact most of those who participated in the genocide were already adult by the mid-thirties), acclimatization to anti-Semitism must have resulted from a more complex, indirect mechanism—namely, an internalization of the Nazi regime's political identity. For it did have an identity, one that involved more than simply negation and rejection. Far from constituting a "nihilism," as disappointed conservatives chose to present it at the time, it incorporated a collection of values that it considered to be "positive" and that oriented its policies. To pick out those values, all we need do is return to the historical schema sketched in by Hitler in relation to the Aryan race, a schema that was, at the same time, a model for the future: Aryan peoples who respected blood purity and practiced selection, and who, as a result, developed such power that they were able to conquer peoples far greater numerically and then use these to construct empires that founded great cultures.

The three key values were health, power, and culture—all three interpreted from a racist point of view and all interconnected. Health was the indispensable condition of power, and it was power that created the culture; power was the main, pivotal value. Unlike the French Republic's triptych, these values were never set up as a slogan by the Nazi leaders, but it is not hard to show that these three values constituted so many polar stars that oriented all their policies. And it is equally easy to show that the Jews, and they alone, represented their exact opposite.

Let us rapidly consider all three values, each one positioned at the center of a network of connected notions. Health is probably the value that may most easily be demonstrated to have oriented the actions of the regime. Health meant on the one hand (racial) purity and cleanliness, on the other industriousness and achievement. The healthy, clean, hardworking, athletic Aryan man, married to a woman of the same race who produced many children for him, was set up as a model and a norm. Anything that deviated from this model was, by contrast, thrown into relief and soon became the object of measures of extirpation: Germans suffering from hereditary diseases (about 400,000 of them) were sterilized; tens of thousands of "asocial" individuals and homosexuals were sent to concentration camps; Gypsies were segregated, and so on.

In this situation, the Jews were one target among many others, and up until 1941 the regime's most radical measures affected other groups, since those suffering from hereditary diseases were already being sterilized, and from 1939 on, the handicapped were murdered. The Jews, however, were directly and strongly affected at the level of how they were perceived. The effect of all the regime's measures in the domain of work and health was to reactivate and reinforce the whole baggage of negative images with which they were connected: images of the Jews as parasites, opposed to productive "German work," or, in the register of hygiene, the ancient association of Jews with filth and the whole recent panoply of metaphors referring to the "Jewish microbe" and the "Jewish cancer" that had invaded anti-Semitic discourse since the end of the preceding century.

Power, as a value, for its part included both the theme of the Reich—the empire—and that of popular unity. The importance that the Nazi regime attached to power is unmistakable. Its propaganda projected the image of a country bent on reconquering the status of a great power, and the first stage in this project was rearmament. The new Wehrmacht was the object of a cult, as was conscription when it was reintroduced in 1935. Both were sources of pride for a people humiliated by Versailles, and were the instruments for creating a new greatness. But the precondition for any external action was internal unity, an objective that was achieved through a mixture of persuasion and terror. This was perfectly illustrated by the Nuremberg rallies: with their theatrical settings, they projected far beyond the boundaries of Germany the impression of a German people welded together around their supreme leader.

If the Jews were one target among others in the case of health, here they were positioned center stage, for the Nazi's desire for power, as if in a mirror image, lent growing importance to the clichés that had been crystallizing around the power of the Jews ever since their emancipation. The power of "Jewish gold" had never ceased to be a successful theme. In politics, the Jews' identification with, first, liberalism, then socialism and communism, had become solidly implanted. The association with Bolshevism had even become the object of renewed propaganda since the outbreak of the Spanish civil war, and it was compounded by the theme of the "Jewish war," a war financed by Jews or fomented by them. This was a theme popularized by the German extreme Right in the immediate aftermath of World War I and later vociferously taken up by the Nazi regime, which propagated an image of Jewish power endeavoring to unite the world against the Reich so as to block the latter's legitimate march toward power. This was the context in which the opposition of those two ambitions for "universal empire" found its strongest expression at the level of representations.

Finally, the value of culture encompassed in the widest sense culture both in the common sense of the term and as religion, both of which served to bind the members of the community together. There is no need to dwell on the Nazi regime's cultural pretensions. They were marked by not only a brutal purging of artistic and intellectual life but also an attempt to encourage conformity with the aspirations of the new masters. The figurative arts and architecture lent themselves particularly well to this end. The importance that Hitler attributed to them is well known. His own plans for the remodeling of the Reich's larger towns testify to his taste for a crushing monumentality that was intended not only to demonstrate the creative capacity of the regime but also to speed the onward march to empire by inspiring the people with confidence and zeal.

The negative reverse of the culture promoted by the regime was, of course, the so-called Jewish culture. In the Nazi mind, "artistic Bolshevism" and Jews were fused, as was shown by the famous 1937 exhibition of "degenerate art," which was a fine example of semantic transition. The works of the avant-garde, identified with the Jews, were assimilated to mental illness by the device of hanging many paintings by mental patients alongside them.

Categorizing religion as a value promoted by the Nazi regime may elicit surprise, but it would be ill-founded. In contrast to its heavy-handed promotion of the values of health and power, the regime in this case tempered the expression of its views with prudence. Hitler remained silent as to his deepest convictions and distanced himself from the anti-Christian wing of the Nazi party, notwithstanding his agreement with it on many issues. On the other hand, he would often resort to "Christian talk," usually (but not invariably) invoking "Providence" rather than "God."

Basically, he tried to adopt a position above both the Protestant and the Catholic confessions and tended to use vaguely Christian references in a bid to plug the gap by which Catholics and Protestants were separated, for, like his *völkisch* predecessors, he regarded this as one of the nation's principal weaknesses. More precisely, he endeavored to encourage the emergence of a religiosity that was superficially Christian but the content of which conformed with a racist canon. Hence his support for the "German Christian" wing, which in 1933 predominated among the Protestants and claimed that its mission was to "dejudaize" Christianity.

Despite rejecting racism on principle, Catholics fell into line with the new regime without much difficulty. Like the Protestants, they were hoping for a re-Christianization of German society. To some extent the Nazi regime responded to that hope with its policy of attacking pornography, prostitution, and homosexuality, not to mention the fact that it had already reduced the defenders of atheism, first and foremost the communists, to silence. Keen observers and ecclesiastical leaders, particularly Catholics, were not fooled but did not have the guts to risk a clash in which their flocks would probably not have followed them.

While Hitler, for his part, indulged in his "Christian talk," he allowed his faithful followers, led by Himmler, to support the diffusion of a Germano-Nordic ethnoreligion that rejected Christianity as being not only infected by the Jewish spirit but also a dire symbol of foreign invasion. By 1939, the *Gottgläubig* movement, to which the supporters of the new religion adhered, had rallied about 5 percent of the German population, a by no means negligible number, particularly as it included most of the members of the SS—a fact that needs to be remembered when one tries to understand their racist and anti-Semitic violence.

In the picture that thus emerges, the Nazi regime appears to have started a widespread religious reinvigoration that ranged in many different directions. The effects of this were bound to be harmful to the Jews, not only because it threw their religious "otherness" into relief, quite apart from the fact that this was increasingly interpreted in racial terms, but also because the Jews had for decades been identified with liberalism, free thinking, atheism, and in general with a "disintegration" and "decomposition" of tradition, including—indeed, above all—religious tradition.

In short, the Nazis' efforts to diffuse an identity designed to become that of the German people as a whole needs to be taken seriously. It is hard to assess the degree to which the regime's values were absorbed by the population and to determine which of those values in particular was the one preferred by most Germans. But there can be no doubt that such an internalization did, at least partially, take place. Otherwise, it is hard to explain the growing popularity that Hitler enjoyed, short of postulating that it could be deliberately dissociated from the policies of the regime that he headed.

It is true that the reception of that Nazi identity was facilitated by a series of factors. In the first place, the successes achieved by Nazi policies both at home (principally the reduction of unemployment) and abroad (the reunion with the Germans of Austria and the Sudetans), both accomplished without unleashing war, seemed to invest that identity with a promising aura. Second, the values of the regime were familiar ones that lent themselves to perfectly benign interpretations as well as to extreme racist ones. Finally, they were soon incorporated into institutions that were directed to apply them in such a way as to strengthen the support for the identity forged by the regime.

Foremost among those institutions was Himmler's specialized apparatus, which combined authority over the police force with the direction of the SS and also became the instrument for executing Hitler's personal wishes. But the role played by many other sectors involved in the realization of the regime's values should not be overlooked. Thus, in the health organizations, the tendencies encouraged by eugenics and racism under the Weimar Republic were by now dominant, as were countless similarly influenced experts in almost every domain: the army—the principal tool for the restoration of power; the business world, which had suffered from the collapse of foreign markets during the depression and now supported an expansionist policy that could bring it the kind of profits likely to accrue from an imperial situation; and the world of culture, particularly the circles that had clashed with the avant-garde movement of the Weimar Republic and also that of the Churches.

Either forthrightly or discreetly, all these sectors involved themselves in the realization of the regime's persecution policy. They did so for a variety of reasons: corporative or personal interests that encouraged them to jostle for advantage in the takeover of Jewish jobs and the spoliation of their possessions; ideological adhesion to the regime; or cynicism pure and simple. As a result, as ideas and practices coagulated at an institutional level, racism and anti-Semitism became more solidly established everywhere.

In the absence of fundamental evidence, it is hard to gauge the relative impact of the various mechanisms involved in the diffusion of anti-Semitism—namely, the openly anti-Jewish propaganda, the racist socialization of the young, and the promotion and acceptance of the regime's "positive" identity. All things considered, the importance of this third factor was considerable. The term-for-term opposition with the Jews that the Nazi identity established either implicitly or explicitly not only made anti-Semitism easier to inculcate, but it also, and above all, made it harder to maintain an attitude of hostility or indifference toward it.

At any rate, the cumulative effect of these mechanisms was to reinforce all variants of Judeophobia: Christian anti-Semitism and religious anti-Semitism generally, as noted earlier; national anti-Semitism, as is clearly shown by the acceptance, without noticeable protest, of the 1935 abrogation of citizenship and the 1941 abrogation of nationality for German Jews; and finally, racist anti-Semitism, which grew increasingly strong and infiltrated the two other variants, although in its apocalyptic form it probably affected no more than a minority of people.

Obviously, the German people were not transformed into a people of radical anti-Semites, for these remained a minority, albeit a powerful one. However, they did become affected by a Judeophobia that assured the regime of a sufficiently wide consensus regarding its policies, as is indicated by the fact that the Germans accepted a whole string of increasingly rigid measures ranging from the 1933 exclusion of Jews from public functions to regulations that banned them from engaging in any form of economic activity, a measure that had reduced them to the state of pariahs by the eve of World War II.

On one point, certainly, the population and the regime appear to have been in perfect agreement: the image of the Weimar Republic. This was now increasingly generally identified with the Jews, and that image became more and more negative as the new regime demonstrated its ability to do better. On every level, whether that of health, power, or culture, the image projected by the defunct regime was one of decadence and failure that now had to be eradicated, if necessary by eradicating the Jews responsible.

In a development unprecedented in the history of modern Europe, Germany had become by the end of the 1930s the laboratory of an experiment designed to create a racist and anti-Semitic society, and the Nazi regime was pressing ahead along this path, strengthened by growing, albeit possibly not homogeneous, popular support. The task that remained was to produce the nucleus of a "geno-cidal community" from within this apartheid society. The war was to make this possible.

3

DEFINING "(UN)WANTED POPULATION ADDITION"

Anthropology, racist ideology, and mass murder in the occupied east

Isabel Heinemann

Even before Hitler came to power, and certainly during his rule, as well as for many years thereafter, a certain image of the typical Nazi was popularized by the regime's political foes and much of the popular media. According to this image, Nazis were uncouth, brutal, sadistic, uneducated louts. And, indeed, some of them were, not least the roughnecks of the SA who fought it out with the communists and vandalized Jewish businesses during the Weimar Republic, and then went on to dismantle the left-wing opposition in the early months following Hitler's "seizure of power." This image was sustained in the postwar period not only by Hollywood but also by such events as the Frankfurt Auschwitz trial of the mid-1960s, where the thugs who had served as concentration and extermination camp guards were popularly perceived as representative of the system as a whole. Yet this view not only let a great many German intellectuals and academics, doctors, and lawyers off the hook; it also created an entirely false image of what Nazism was all about and of the underlying scholarly and seemingly scientific world view that motivated a substantial part of the German elite to provide the intellectual rationale, the organizational framework, and the executive leadership for the Nazi genocidal project. Finally, this misrepresentation of Nazism facilitated not merely the survival of many of its key figures but allowed them to pursue their careers well into the postwar period and to educate new generations of biologists and anthropologists, doctors, and lawyers, as if they had had absolutely nothing to do with the catastrophe in whose unleashing they had been so instrumental.

In more recent years a new generation of scholars has shown the complicity of a whole range of professionals, experts, academics, and intellectuals in legitimizing and facilitating Nazi polices. The role of doctors and lawyers has come under particular scrutiny as historians such as Henry Friedlander and Michael Burleigh demonstrated their involvement in the "euthanasia" campaign against the physically and mentally handicapped that began with mass sterilization and ended up with mass murder, thereby also creating the technological, organizational, and manpower infrastructure that was mobilized for the continent-wide genocide of the Jews. Other scholars, such as

Götz Aly and Susanne Heim, examined the involvement of SS intellectuals in rationalizing and sketching the blueprint for the demographic restructuring of Eastern Europe, in a process that entailed vast population displacements and eventually ethnic cleansing and genocide.

In this chapter, Isabel Heinemann analyzes how university trained "racial experts" became the instruments of implementing Hitler and Himmler's racist ideology. These men were not compelled to work with the regime but rather volunteered their services both because they had long before advocated the "Germanization" of the East and were keen to implement their ideas once a regime willing and able to do so was in power, and because they could quickly accumulate a great deal of influence, not least over life and death. Indeed, their ambitions were vast, just as the damage they inflicted on the populations of Eastern Europe was incalculable. They were so certain of the scientific value and morality of their actions that they continued to have distinguished careers after the war without apparently batting an eyelid, in part because their colleagues' own complicity, distorted notions of academic loyalty, and public ignorance protected them. As Heinemann shows, there were in fact close links between the General Plan East drafted by these anthropologists – postulating the displacement of millions of Poles by ethnic Germans – and the genocide of the Jews, for which this plan provided the necessary context and framework. While the "ethnic reconstruction" of Eastern Europe and Western Russia did not necessitate the outright murder of all the Slavs inhabiting these lands, it did mean the "collateral" death of millions and the enslavement of millions more; and while the Jews were targeted for total eradication without any pretense at "racial selection," their genocide seemed all the more reasonable and necessary when it was presented as part of a vast transformation of Germany's Lebensraum. In the end, argues Heinemann, the Poles, and later also Russians and Ukrainians, would have fared little better than the Jews, though their suffering might have lasted much longer.

Reichsführer-ss Heinrich Himmler used his wartime speeches to outline his specific idea to transform Eastern Europe into a "greater Germanic settlement space." According to Himmler, following military conquest, German authorities—the Schutzstaffel (SS) in particular—were to exploit the land to the benefit of the Reich and German citizens. The indigenous population would be segregated into two groups: a majority of slaves and helots, slowly starving and worked to death, and a minority of carefully selected people considered "fit for Germanization." Along with German and ethnic German settlers, this minority was supposed to form a new kind of elite in the East. In front of a group of the SS and policemen in Ukraine, Himmler declared in September 1942, "This Germanic East up to the Ural needs . . . to be transformed into the plantation of Germanic blood, for in four to five hundred years—if Europe's fate leaves us that much time until a war between the continents will break out—we can rely on five to six hundred million Germanic people [Germanen] instead of one hundred and twenty million."[1] However, only the "racially fit" should have their place in his vision of a Greater Germanic Europe, as Himmler further elaborated: "We will bring together all the good blood, all Germanic blood existing in the world. . . . Every trace of good blood—and this is the first fundamental rule you have to retain—that you encounter anywhere in the East you either have to win to the German cause or to kill it."[2]

These phantasmagorias of conquest and "Germanization" were not confined to an ambitious SS leader, naturally. As early as October 1939, at the end of the Polish campaign, Hitler had informed the German parliament of the planned reorganization of Eastern Europe's ethnographic space (Neuordnung der ethnographischen Verhältnisse), which he considered the primary objective of German occupation policies. What he meant was "a resettlement of nationalities for the sake of better lines of separation than those existing today."[3] Consequently, during the Second World War Himmler's SS expelled and resettled millions of Poles, Russians, ethnic Germans, and people of the Western European countries in the name of a "Greater Germanic Reich."[4] A specific group of perpetrators set up the screening procedure, performed the racial exams, and supervised the expulsions—the SS racial experts from the Race and Settlement Main Office (Rasse-und Siedlungshauptamt, or RuSHA).[5]

One victim of forced expulsion and resettlement was the Polish doctor Josef Rembacz; he had been expelled from his home in the Zamość region of the Lublin District in October 1942. In 1946 he gave the following testimony before a Polish court:

> I, together with other Poles from Skierbiszowo (where I lived and worked as doctor at the local health office), were brought to the camp of Zamość. A commission consisting of several members carried out a racial screening in this camp. . . . The population was divided into four groups. Group I was Nordic (Nordisch) and Group II Phalian, South Dinaric (Fälisch, Süddinarisch). These two groups were brought into the ethnic German settler camp in Łódź for special examination. Group III

consisted of "racially mixed breeds" (*Mischrassen*). This group was turned over to a commission of the labor administration; the families were split up and sent to Germany for work. Group IV was composed of people with hereditary diseases or physical deformations as well as of so-called unwanted races (Jews, Sinti and Roma, Mongols), who were sent to an unknown destination, most likely to Auschwitz. I know that no-one from this group ever returned.[6]

Ascribed to Race Group III, Rembacz was forced to work for the German authorities as a camp doctor in the local expellee camps until the end of 1943. What is striking about this particular statement is the victim's precise description of the racial selection procedure.

Recent years have witnessed much new research on the SS operations in occupied Eastern Europe—especially regarding the implementation of the Final Solution of the Jewish Question.[7] Alongside the motivation of the perpetrators, recent publications have discussed the utilitarian and military objectives of occupation policy, the economic exploitation of the occupied countries, and awareness of the Nazi mass murder of the Jews among ordinary Germans.[8] Comparative analyses of ethnic cleansing during the twentieth century have further placed the Holocaust and Nazi occupation policy within a wider context of genocide.[9] Some scholars, meanwhile, have discussed the Nazi extermination policies as a critical example of biopolitics, drawing on a concept coined by Michel Foucault in the 1970s to describe the crucial link between racism and power in modern societies.[10] Finally, considerable advances have been made in recent years describing how German academics and experts readily contributed to the economic exploitation and ethnic reordering of occupied Europe by providing the regime with background research and detailed planning.[11] Despite scholarly progress since the mid-1990s in explaining the process of mass murder, economic exploitation, and ethnic reconfiguration, we still know relatively little about the racist foundation of occupation policies and its importance for the functioning of the Nazi state in general.[12] Recent attempts to expand the term "ethnic community" (*Volksgemeinschaft*) into an analytical tool have further demonstrated that racist tenets were more than just abstract ideological foundations to many German contemporaries.[13] Consequently, in order to fully understand the deadly effectiveness of the Nazi extermination policies; the motivation of planners, experts, and perpetrators; the attitudes of the German public in the face of mass violence; and the character of the process itself one has to carefully examine not only the concept of Himmler's "new order" of the SS but also the seductive potential of the ideas of "racial purity" and *Lebensraum*.[14]

Accordingly, this chapter argues that forced population transfers (i.e., expulsions, resettlement, and the mass murder of European Jews) not only gained momentum through economic, military, or other utilitarian objectives but mainly pursued racial homogenization of the occupied territories. Following an overview of the racial selection procedure as a product of racial anthropological discourse within German academia, the chapter describes the pattern of expulsion and resettlement in occupied Poland. Next, it examines the plans for ethnic cleansing developed by SS racial experts for other parts of Western and Southeastern Europe. Finally, it explores the causal link between the escalating racial policies and the genesis of the Final Solution of the Jewish Question.

Himmler's visions and German academia: racial anthropologists as prophets

During the interwar period, especially in the Third Reich, anthropology and racial hygiene were considered key sciences. They provided the applied methodology and legitimization for the racist policies of the Nazi state, ranging from forced sterilization and euthanasia to the ethnic restructuring of Eastern Europe and genocide.

Nonetheless, the history of racial science goes at least as far back as the second half of the nineteenth century, gaining momentum after the end of the First World War.[15] Referring to Charles Darwin and Francis Galton but also to social Darwinists like Ernst Haeckel and Wilhelm Schallmayer, German and other Western European scholars described the biological and social disparity of human beings as a natural and thus immutable fact. By defining races as "established entities of human beings living through generations, united in their physical and intellectual qualities," as Alfred Ploetz stated, and referring to Mendel's laws of inheritance, racial anthropologists such as Hans Friedrich Karl Günther propagated the superiority of the Nordic, or Aryan, race.[16] For Günther, the outward appearance, genetic predisposition, and mental qualities of the group members demonstrated the high value of the Nordic race. Therefore, the author of the bestselling book *Rassenkunde des deutschen Volkes* advised the German people and decision makers to decisively prevent "racial mixing" and consecutive "racial degeneration."[17] Like Günther, most racial anthropologists of the 1920s and 1930s conceived of their field as an applied science. During the formative phase of applied genetics (*Erb-und Rassenforschung*) in Germany, scholars from the Universities of Jena, Leipzig, and Munich and from the Kaiser Wilhelm Institute for Human Heredity Sciences and Eugenics in Berlin (Kaiser Wilhelm Institut für Anthropologie, menschliche Erblehre und Eugenik, or KWI-A) all helped to develop racial consciousness and build up scientific networks that persisted beyond 1933. The scholars of the KWI-A (founded by Erwin Baur, one of Germany's leading geneticists in the early twentieth century)—Eugen Fischer, Fritz Lenz, and Otmar Freiherr von Verschuer—prepared the groundwork for the acceptance of the racist paradigm in science and politics in the Third Reich.[18] The Jena "race quadriga"—Hans F. K. Günther, geneticist Karl Astel, and biologists Viktor Franz and Gerhard Herberer—for their part amalgamated current trends in racial biology, anthropology, genetics, and eugenics into an ostensibly modern blend of racial sciences, which they promoted through their contacts in political circles and the SS.[19] In Munich, psychiatrist and eugenicist Ernst Rüdin of the Kaiser Wilhelm Institute

61

for Psychiatry gained an international reputation: in 1932 he succeeded the founder of the American eugenics movement, Charles Davenport, as president of the International Federation of Eugenic Organizations.[20] Another Munich anthropologist, Theodor Mollison, taught racial anthropology, simultaneously acting as one of the editors of the influential journal *Archiv für Rassen-und Gesellschaftsbiologie*. Founded in 1904 by Alfred Ploetz, the journal served as a platform for an elaborate exchange of ideas in the field of racial anthropology. Many of Mollison's students at Munich's Ludwig Maximilian University went on to play roles in shaping SS racial policies. Another key figure in German academic race discourse during the early years of National Socialism was Otto Reche, anthropologist and ethnologist at Leipzig University and director of the Institute for Race Research and Ethnology (Institut für Rassen-und Völkerkunde).[21] Already during the 1930s these scholars enthusiastically welcomed the new research possibilities and funding options offered by the new regime, which made racial sciences one of its top funding priorities.[22] Furthermore, most of the abovementioned scientists lent their expertise to the new regime and eagerly contributed to the fundamental race laws passed during the formative phase of the Nazi state. Thus Rüdin helped to draft the Eugenic Law of July 14, 1933 (Gesetz zur Verhütung erbkranken Nachwuchses), while Fischer and his colleagues at the KWI-A collaborated more indirectly by promoting the benefits of forced sterilization and euthanasia through their scientific writings.[23] Although the notorious Nuremberg Laws were drafted by state officials from the Reich Ministries of Justice, Health, and the Interior, the scholars from the KWI-A as well as individuals such as Reche publicly approved the discriminatory legislation or else assisted by issuing the requested racial-biological hereditary certificates.[24]

However, it was not only anthropologists, geneticists, and biologists who readily accepted and further advanced the new ideological paradigms of Nazi life sciences. Attracted by the hope for national revival, the quest for funding, and a broadened research agenda, ethnographers, population experts, agronomists, and spatial planners embraced the cause of living space and racial purity.[25] Most of them believed that social differences could be explained and ultimately "cured" through the application of biological principles of selection and breeding. These social experts not only explained away the defeat of Germany in the First World War and the economic crisis of the 1930s as a result of the racial degeneration of the German *Volk* but also offered guidelines for political decision making. Beginning in the late 1920s, and especially after 1933, their research in the fields of racial anthropology, agrarian science, and biology received generous funding from the German Science Foundation (Deutsche Forschungsgemeinschaft), thus laying the academic groundwork for the subsequent ethnic cleansing of occupied Eastern Europe.[26]

Once the war began, Himmler and his experts could instantly turn to a circle of scholars willing to collaborate in the implementation of their plans for a large-scale racial purification program. Of special significance in this context is the example of anthropologist Reche, coincidentally a member of the SS.[27] On

September 29, 1939, four weeks after the German invasion of Poland, Reche approached the SS, offering guidelines for the ethnopolitical reconstruction of the East ("Leitsätze zur bevölkerungspolitischen Sicherung des deutschen Ostens"). The opening paragraph of the guidelines read as follows:

> Most of the inhabitants of the newly transferred territory are racially (as well as according to their character, intellect, and physical capacity) completely unsuitable for assimilation into the German *Volk* and body politic [*Volkskörper*]. Above all, the Jews and Jewish mixed breeds [*Judenmischlinge*] living in the respective regions have to be removed as soon as possible. . . . The Polish population must, for the most part, be considered quite an inauspicious, unfavorable mixture of elements of pre-Slavic, East Baltic, and East European races [*prä-slavischen, ostbaltischen und ostischen Rasse*], including particularly strong Mongoloid influences [*mongolische Einschläge*]. . . . Only the racial anthropologist can decide whether, occasionally, parts of the Polish population might be racially suitable [*rassisch brauchbar*].[28]

As we now know from the expulsions and racial screening of non-German civilians during the Second World War and individual cases like that of Josef Rembacz, Reche's proposals did not remain unheard. One of his students, the anthropologist Bruno Kurt Schultz, developed the SS racial screening procedure that served as a model for the later selections. From 1940 the chief of the Race Office of RuSHA, SS-Standartenführer Schultz, assumed a comparatively high position in the SS hierarchy, posing as a leading expert on issues of race. Consequently, in 1942 he was appointed chair of racial anthropology at the newly founded Reich University in Prague.[29] Combining his tasks as a scholar and head of the RuSHA Race Office, he took care of the anthropological training of both university students and SS racial experts. While in Prague, Schultz also coordinated the racial selections of the Protectorate's population.[30] In addition, he drafted plans for the Germanization of occupied Europe. At the beginning of 1942 Schultz, at this time a university professor in Berlin, joined a meeting of race specialists at the Reich Ministry for the Occupied Soviet Territories (Reichsministerium für die besetzten Ostgebiete). Among other participants at the meeting was Eugen Fischer, then head of the KWI-A. During the discussion Schultz declared "that the racially unwanted are to be evacuated to the East, whereas the racially fit shall be accepted into the re-Germanization procedure either in the Old Reich or in the East." Schultz pledged an "accurate, exact racial screening of the population of the Baltic States . . . disguised as sanitary inspection so as to prevent concern among the population."[31]

Besides anthropologists and geneticists, leading agriculturists helped to shape the program of ethnic homogenization introduced by Himmler and his experts. In October 1939 Berlin agronomist Konrad Meyer accepted Himmler's invitation to lead the Planning Office of Himmler's newly created resettlement institution, the

SS Main Office of the Reich commissioner for the strengthening of Germandom (Reichskommissar für die Festigung deutschen Volkstums, or RKF). By this time Meyer had already pursued a successful career as chair of agrarian science at Friedrich-Wilhelm University of Berlin, building up a powerful position as the leading German expert, political adviser, and science manager in the field.[32] An SS member since 1933, Meyer voluntarily chose to become involved with the RKF, ultimately advancing to the rank of SS-Oberführer. Until the end of the war, he and his handpicked fellow scholars in the RKF Main Office worked out detailed plans for the agrarian, economic, ethnographic, and demographic reconstruction of Eastern Europe, financed by the German Science Foundation. Their proposals appeared between 1940 and 1943 in different versions, the most well known of which was Master Plan East (Generalplan Ost) of June 1942.[33] Meyer, like Reche, readily accepted that any "reordering of the ethnographic landscape" of Eastern Europe would include mass expulsions. Thus in 1941 he wrote in a Nazi student newspaper, "We have to bear in mind that we will not succeed in preserving the East for all times as 'German territory' unless we have removed every single drop of 'alien blood' [fremdes Blut] from the German settlement space, which would otherwise endanger the inner coherence of the German Volk [einheitliche Geschlossenheit des grenzdeutschen Volkstums]."[34] In the same year Meyer elaborated how the ethnic homogenization of the newly annexed territories should take place with the help of ethnic Germans, the German peasantry, and especially German youth. In the preface to Landvolk im Werden (Peasants in the making), one of his most influential publications, he thus wrote, "This book mainly addresses the young generation that carries the National Socialist idea of blood and soil in their burning hearts, pushing it forward with all the revolutionary power of the young."[35]

The cases of Reche, Schultz, and Meyer demonstrate that it was scholars from mainstream German academia—and not just those on the radical fringes, as many scholars contended after 1945—who readily set up plans to "purify" the newly colonized territories by means of racial selection and resettlement of ethnic Germans.[36]

Western Poland as "training ground": ethnic reconstruction and racial purification

Following the swift victory over Poland in fall 1939 and the annexation of its western part, Nazi population planners instantly engaged with the question of "Germanization" of a region with a mixed population of Poles, Jews, and Germans. In October 1939 Hitler ordered Himmler to organize the return of ethnic Germans from abroad and the Germanization of the occupied Polish territories. One of the RKF tasks was "the elimination of the harmful influence of alien segments of the population that pose a threat to the Reich and the German ethnic community."[37] Based on his notion of a "Germanic East," Himmler intended a large-scale ethnic reconstruction of Poland "on the basis of the singular and decisive racial worth," to be carried out by the SS.[38] Therefore he ordered the SS racial experts to create a procedure for racial examination that would be performed on the incoming ethnic Germans as well as the local Poles. Sufficiently trained in racial examination techniques (in the form of obligatory racial exams for SS candidates and their spouses that were supposed to guarantee the purity of the new order), RuSHA race specialists enthusiastically accepted this new and challenging task.[39] In response to the considerable boost in competencies, in October 1939 the RuSHA enlarged its staff and created a branch office in Łódź as well as several district offices in the Warthegau and other annexed territories.[40]

The first group of people subjected to racial screening was the ethnic Germans who had followed Hitler's call to return to the Reich ("Heim ins Reich!") since October 1939.[41] Altogether, over 1 million ethnic German settlers were processed by the race experts of the SS during the Second World War. The results of the racial screening determined whether families would receive a "farm in the East," as most of them had hoped to. This privilege would be granted only to people ascribed to Race Group I or II. Persons ascribed to Race Group III were considered to have too much "Polish blood" and therefore were sent to the Old Reich (Altreich) for reeducation. They had to spend their days in settler camps and were obliged to work in factories or as farmhands. Ethnic Germans ascribed to Race Group IV were considered to be "of alien ethnic origin" and "racially unsuitable." During wartime most of them were locked in camps, since logistic difficulties prevented their transportation to their country of origin, as had been originally intended. Sometimes they received permission to move into the Reich, serving as manpower without being recognized as full-blood Germans.

Racial examination was performed by the RuSHA in the transit camps at Poznan or Łódź in the Warthegau as well as by mobile commissions operating in ports of entry for the ethnic Germans.[42] Whereas many ethnic Germans were disappointed when their hopes for a farm in the annexed territories were dashed due to their deficient racial value, in the case of many Poles, like Josef Rembacz, the result of the racial examination proved a matter of life or death. For the latter group, racial selection followed forced expulsion and loss of property as a part of Himmler's settlement plans.

Between five hundred thousand and seven hundred thousand non-Jewish Poles were expelled from the annexed Polish territories in order to provide housing for the incoming German "settlers." The Polish families were routinely rounded up in the early morning hours by security police and SS troops. They had to leave their farms, their cattle, and most of their belongings behind, since only sixty pounds of luggage—excluding valuables and furniture—were allowed per person. In many cases they were not given enough time to pack at all. The expellees were then brought to collection camps where most of them underwent racial screening, as Rembacz had described it.[43] Having lost literally everything, the "racial worth" of the expelled Poles determined whether some of them would be labeled an "wanted population addition" and subsequently dispatched to the Old Reich for "re-Germanization."

The selection procedure was similar in the case of Poles and ethnic Germans. Individuals had to appear naked in front of the screening commission, consisting of at least one racial examiner and one or more assistants. The commission took no less than twenty-one anthropological measurements, which were entered on a special form, the so-called race card (*Rassenkarte*).[44] These race cards used early computer technology (*Hollerith-Verfahren*) to process and store the data thus collected.[45] Josef Rembacz painstakingly described the details of the procedure:

> Examiners considered height, weight, shape of the body, form of the skull, form of the face, color of eyes and hair, thickness of hair, etc. The examination served as a basis for calculating the racial formula. The screening was implemented by racial specialists, the so-called *Eignungsprüfer*. . . . After this examination one had to appear before the main commission. . . . The entire family that had been ascribed high racial value was summoned for a brief examination by the head of the commission. He compared the results of the screening with his own evaluation, and the commission issued its final opinion.[46]

This kind of racial selection was first performed on the Polish population; examination of other ethnic groups followed suit. The "racially fit" were to become Germans—since Nazi racial theory assumed those individuals had German roots—regardless of their ethnicity. A little more than 4 percent of the Polish population were considered a "wanted population addition" (*erwünschter Bevölkerungszuwachs*) and fit for "re-Germanization" (*wiedereindeutschungsfähig*).[47] A majority of those people were dispatched to Germany, where they were expected to undergo transformation into "Germans." In practice, they were exploited as slave labor, even though a formal distinction was made between them and Polish slave laborers. Individuals deemed "racially unfit," and thus an "unwanted population addition," were either brought to special *Rentendörfer* (villages for the children and elderly designed to cause death by starvation) or directly deported to concentration camps—Rembacz had mentioned Auschwitz—where they had to work as slave laborers, slated for imminent destruction.[48] The majority of the population, however, was ascribed to Race Group III. Those people were to perform slave labor in the Old Reich; if they were allowed to stay, then it was only as farmhands on farms that had been given to ethnic Germans. Needless to say, the expellees received no compensation for their confiscated property.[49]

One of the persons deemed an "unwanted population addition" was Ryszard W. The three-year-old boy and his family—his father was a farmer and his mother a schoolteacher—were deported in December 1939 from Kowalew near Jarotschin in the Warthegau, while German settlers took possession of the family's estate. In the General Government (Generalgouvernement), where they arrived by train, they found refuge in Zarnow near Tomaszow. They did not receive any compensation for their property but depended exclusively on the help of a local teacher who let them stay with him.[50]

Significantly, Jews were never considered for racial screening. In contrast to their Polish neighbors, they were deported without undergoing racial selection. For Himmler and his experts, the planned Germanization required the prior annihilation of the Jewish population. Thus the project of Germanization in occupied Eastern Europe generated momentum for the Final Solution of the Jewish Question.[51]

Toward a greater Germanic Europe: attempts at ethnic homogenization in Western and Southeastern Europe

In the course of the Second World War SS experts applied the techniques of racial selection and expulsion throughout occupied Europe, creating RuSHA branch offices along the way. Apart from Poland, Himmler and his race experts focused their attention on the population of Southeastern Europe, opening a RuSHA branch office in Prague in 1941.[52] In addition, during spring and summer 1941 SS experts screened no less than half a million Slovenes in search of "good blood" in occupied Slovenia, specifically in the regions of Lower Styria and Upper Carniola.[53] Although on a smaller scale, the SS also exercised influence on Nazi population policy in Western Europe. In 1942 and 1943 race and settlement experts expelled between twenty thousand and thirty thousand "racially unwanted" French from Alsace and Lorraine to occupied France.[54] People deemed "fit for re-Germanization" were brought to so-called reeducation camps in the Reich, such as the Schelklingen camp in Baden-Württemberg. Marie Louise Zimmermann, a sixteen-year-old girl from the Alsatian village of Bischwiller, was deported along with her parents in winter 1942. The father, a schoolteacher, had been accused of pro-French sentiments. Following racial examination, the family was dispatched to Schelklingen. As Marie Louise recalled years later, the SS commander of the camp told them upon their arrival that they "were to be reintegrated into the German ethnic community [Volksgemeinschaft], depending on our quality as persons deemed fit for re-Germanization [Wiedereindeutschungsfähige]. The camp would be a reeducation camp—effectively a school—where we would have to work in groups on farms, in factories, or within the camp to learn order and discipline."[55]

Further expulsions occurred between November 1942 and spring 1943 during the forced Germanization of the Zamość region in the General Government and in the course of the relocation of ethnic Germans in the Commissariat General Zhitomir in Ukraine.[56] Around the same time, in the area around Himmler's field headquarters, Hegewald, near Zhitomir, settlement experts established so-called settlement pearls (Siedlungsperlen). Their dream of a permanent German settlement in Ukraine was short-lived, however. By November 1943 about thirty thousand ethnic Germans had fled the region, heading for the settler camps farther west.

The objectives of Himmler and his academic planners and the sheer scope of the racial experts' activities strongly suggest that SS population policies were conceived as a European-wide project. The offices of the SS leaders on issues of race and settlement (SS-Führer im Rasse-und Siedlungswesen) attached to the staff of the local higher SS and police leaders sprouted all over Europe, from The Hague and Oslo to Mogilev and Kiev. Whereas these leaders in the Netherlands and Norway mainly screened local women who wanted to marry German SS men, searched for Jews and *Judenmischlinge*, and screened Germanic candidates for the SS, their counterparts in Ukraine and Belorussia had different tasks. They screened prospective members for the local police battalions (*Schutzmannschaften*), engaged in antipartisan warfare, and searched for pure-blood children fit for adoption by German families and for pure-blood maids to be employed in German households.

In search of "Germanic blood": the SS racial expert as a type of perpetrator

When Josef Rembacz appeared in front of the screening commission in Zamość in 1942, SS-Obersturmführer Hans Rihl presided over the session. A member of the RuSHA since 1936 and a member of the Nazi German Student Association since 1935, Rihl had had substantial experience in racial screening. From 1939 to 1941 he had screened Poles in Łódź, in 1941 he directed a screening commission in occupied Slovenia, and after a short intermezzo in the Waffen-SS, he oversaw the racial screening of Poles in the Zamość region.[57] Otherwise, Rihl was a bookseller by profession and had studied anthropology, philosophy, and religion at Munich University.[58] While in Zamość, Rihl wrote monthly reports to the RuSHA Office in Berlin. Among other things, he suggested splitting Polish families of allegedly low racial value—in other words, forcibly separating spouses and taking children away from their parents—in order to secure every drop of "valuable blood" for the Germans. Thus he wrote,

> It should be possible to split families composed of RuS II and RuS IV cases ... Quite often, a man considered suitable for re-Germanization arrives without his family in the camp, or a woman of Race Group II whose husband has fled or disappeared. These people cannot become part of the re-Germanization process, as the whole family will be excluded from the procedure once the missing spouse has turned up. Yet if it were possible to split the families, including a formal divorce, it should be possible to win many individuals of high racial value [*blutlich wertvoll*] to the German cause.[59]

The example of Hans Rihl raises the following question: Who were the men who conceived and implemented racial policy on the ground? During the war some five hundred SS officers occupied leading positions in the Berlin RuSHA Office and its branches throughout occupied Europe.[60] These officers can be considered a specific type of perpetrator who—as highly professional, rational social experts—clearly distinguished themselves from other groups of perpetrators in the Nazi state. According to a definition provided by the German historian Lutz Raphael, an "expert" is a person who possesses "scientific and specialized knowledge" considered crucial for the construction of social systems.[61] This definition fits perfectly with the SS racial specialists, who often referred to themselves as "racial experts" (*Rasseexperten*).

Most of these experts were born between 1900 and 1909, Rihl being one of the youngest. Several qualities distinguished them. First, in contrast to many other perpetrator groups they had a relatively high level of education. A sample of one hundred of these experts reveals that no less than forty of them held university degrees, twenty-one had earned a PhD, and seven had written their *Habilitation* (professorial thesis). Most of them had studied either racial anthropology or agriculture, corresponding to their two main fields of activity—"race and settlement," sometimes rendered as "blood and soil."[62] Second, this group consisted of "rational" men, convinced of the validity of the racist paradigm. Additionally, they considered themselves an ideological elite within the SS elite, thus assuming a specific group identity. Third and most important, they had a double function within Nazi population-policy making: they were planners and practitioners of ethnic homogenization, experts in the literal sense. Simultaneously, they served as "architects of extermination" (to use the original term, *Vordenker der Vernichtung*, coined by German historians Götz Aly and Susanne Heim), while designing far-reaching Germanization plans. Some of them gained considerable influence as RKF planners, for example, Konrad Meyer, author of the different drafts of Master Plan East.[63] At the same time, they implemented racist ideology as members of selection commissions and resettlement commando units supervising racial screening and mass expulsions. Their twofold competence in devising and implementing racial policies characterizes best this specific group of perpetrators.

This observation highlights the connection between racial selection and the character of Nazi resettlement and extermination policy. The implementation of profoundly racist Germanization plans by SS experts was a catalyst for Nazi extermination policy against the Jews and other "unwanted races." The attempts to "reconstruct" entire populations were crucial factors prompting radicalization and eventually mass murder.

First, the results of the racial screening served as the main criterion for the attempted ethnic reordering of the occupied and annexed regions of Europe, evident from the drafts of the Master Plan East that distinguished between "racially valuable" and "less valuable" population groups. For instance, the first draft of the Master Settlement Plan (Generalsiedlungsplan) of December 1942—an expanded version of the Master Plan East that now also encompassed parts of Western and Southeastern Europe—calculated the "Germanization capacity" of the different populations corresponding to the findings of racial experts. The plan gave the following ratios: 5 percent of Poles; 15 of Lithuanians; 30 of Latvians; and 50 of Estonians, Czechs, French, and Slovenes.[64] SS population experts estimated the total population of the territory incorporating Poland, the Baltic States, the Protectorate, Lower Styria and Upper Carniola, and Alsace and Lorraine at approximately 43.5 million. According to the Master Settlement Plan, within a twenty-year period the population of the respective territory should dwindle to 28.4 million, including an additional 5.2 million German settlers. This meant that within the following twenty years about 23.3 million people had to disappear—more than half of the original population. The plan did not specify where these millions of people should go or under what circumstances they should perish. European Jews were not included in this number either. Although none of the plans made it explicit, it is evident that for the racial experts mass death posed a necessary condition for the entire Germanization process.

Second, the racial experts accelerated their activities in step with the radicalization of Nazi extermination policy, including the genesis of the Final Solution. The German victory over Poland constituted the initial phase of radicalization: by trying the techniques of selection and expulsion on millions of civilians, the SS experts assumed far-reaching competencies. The next phase began at the turn of 1941–42 when the Soviet Union and Western Europe became an operating theater for Himmler's race experts and new settlement options emerged. A third and last phase occurred in 1944 as the Soviet advance made the race experts focus on the Old Reich, Austria, and the annexed Polish territories. In those areas they were fighting against the alleged pollution of "German blood" by screening slave laborers who had sexual relations with Germans as well as identifying persons of German-Jewish descent (*Judenmischlinge*).[65] Thus the race experts reapplied their techniques of racial screening and atomization of social groups to the German heartland, introducing forced abortion, deportation, and mass murder.[66]

Finally, the classification of civilians into different race groups, which had the aura of scientific precision, helped to split the Polish people—as well as parts of the population of the Protectorate, Alsace and Lorraine, and Slovenia—into numerous groups that could then be treated differently. The enforced distinction between "ethnic Germans," people "fit for re-Germanization," and "unwanted population additions" made expulsion, expropriation, and exploitation easier to implement. It also advanced the persecution of the European Jews, who were singled out in the course of racial examination.

The number of people screened by the race experts during the Second World War corresponded to the European range of the Germanization plans: at least 2.7 million civilians, made up of 1.2 million ethnic Germans and some 1.5 million non-Germans, went through the hands of the racial examiners.[67] Although Himmler's "plantation of good blood" under the supervision of the SS was never realized, SS racial experts made a significant contribution to an ethnic reconstruction of occupied Europe.

Seduced by abundant research funding and the prospect of swift national revival in the aftermath of defeat in the First World War, many members of the

German scientific establishment enthusiastically contributed to the Nazi cause by laying the academic groundwork for racial screening and ethnic cleansing during the Second World War. In the field of racial anthropology, the scholars of the KWI-A and the Jena "race quadriga," in particular, played an important role in formulating Nazi eugenic and race laws. Whereas some of these scholars engaged in criminal medical experiments—for example, Ernst Rüdin and Otmar Freiherr von Verschuer—in the course of the Second World War, others, like Otto Reche from Leipzig University and Konrad Meyer from Berlin University, resorted to racism when drafting the plans for the reconstruction of occupied Eastern Europe—regardless of human cost. Respected in their academic fields, they were convinced Nazis and members of the SS who shared Himmler's dreams of racial purity and colonial settlement in the East. Along with ruthless SS racial experts like Bruno Kurt Schultz or Hans Rihl, they acted as "architects" of population transfer and mass extermination, thus forming a distinct group of perpetrators. Racist professionals as they were, they both shaped and implemented Nazi population policy. Remarkably, most of them went on to successful careers in West Germany, with their responsibility for contributing to the racial and occupation policies of the Nazi state until recently neither publicly acknowledged nor questioned. For instance, Bruno Kurt Schultz served from 1961 onward as professor emeritus in the Department of Medicine at the University of Münster, while Otto Reche returned to issuing genetic paternity tests. Most prominently, in 1956 Konrad Meyer was appointed chair in landscape design at the Technical University of Hannover, becoming a leading postwar expert in this field.[68]

The SS racial experts succeeded in splitting specific population groups according to their "scientifically proven racial value," making the exploitation and eventual annihilation of individuals easier to implement. Their designed selection procedures, race cards, and plans for the re-Germanization of the occupied territories greatly facilitated this task. The racial parameters that they introduced were conceived as guidelines for a greater Germanic nation to be established after the war by means of resettlement plans such as the Master Settlement Plan.

Obviously, the mass murder of Jews constituted the most extreme element in the attempt to establish a "racially purified" Europe. Still, many other ethnic groups faced expulsion, deprivation of rights, confiscation of property, starvation, and exploitation as slave laborers, depending on their alleged "racial quality" as defined by the racial experts. Consequently, the Final Solution and the "ethnic reconstruction" of occupied Europe through resettlement and expulsion were intertwined processes, both based on the paradigm of racial purity and the quest for a Greater Germanic Empire in the East.

Naturally, the fundamental difference between Nazi racial policies directed against Jews and those against Slavs lies in the extent of implementation. Jews were to perish without exception, whereas the fate of Poles, Ukrainians, and Russians depended on their perceived "racial worth." The mass murder of the European Jews was carried out to the bitter end, while the Germanization plans were only partially put into effect, ultimately postponed until after the (successful) end of the war. Rather tellingly, during the so-called RuSHA Trial (1947–48)—which put RKF officials and SS racial experts in the dock—the prosecution declared the forced population transfers and "Germanization," as experienced by Josef Rembacz from Zamość and millions of other individuals, "techniques of genocide [that were] neither so quick nor perhaps so simple as outright mass extermination . . . [yet] far more cruel and equally effective."[69]

Notes

Abbreviations Used in the Notes

AGK   Archiwum Głównej Komisji Badania Zbrodni przeciwko Narodowi polskiemu (Archives of the Main Commission for the Investigation of Crimes against the Polish People, Warsaw)

BAR   Bundesarchiv Abteilung Deutsches Reich (German Federal Archives, Deutsches Reich Branch, Berlin)

STANU Stadtarchiv Nürnberg (State Archives, Nuremberg)

1 Himmler's speech, 16 September 1942, BAR, NS 19/4006.
2 Himmler's speech, 16 September 1942, BAR, NS 19/4006.
3 Hitler's speech before the Reichstag, 6 October 1939, quoted in Max Domarus, *Hitler: Reden und Proklamationen 1932–1945; Kommentiert von einem deutschen Zeitgenossen*, vol. 2, pt. 1 (Munich: Süddeutscher Verlag, 1973), 1377–93.
4 For a detailed analysis of the Nazi resettlement policies, see Isabel Heinemann, *"Rasse, Siedlung, deutsches Blut": Das Rasse-und Siedlungshauptamt der SS und die rassenpolitische Neuordnung Europas* (Göttingen: Wallstein Verlag, 2003).
5 Isabel Heinemann, "Another Type of Perpetrator: The SS Racial Experts and Forced Population Movements in the Occupied Regions," *Holocaust and Genocide Studies* 15, no. 3 (Winter 2001): 387–411.
6 Testimony of Dr. Josef Rembacz, Łódź, 25 April 1946, STANU, NO-5266.
7 Among recent publications are the following: Peter Klein, *Die "Gettoverwaltung Litzmannstadt" 1940 bis 1944: Eine Dienststelle im Spannungsfeld von Kommunalbürokratie und staatlicher Verfolgungspolitik* (Hamburg: Hamburger Edition 2009); Michael Alberti, *Die Verfolgung und Vernichtung der Juden im Reichsgau Wartheland 1939–1945: Die Anfänge und die Durchführung der Endlösung* (Wiesbaden: Harrassowitz Verlag, 2006); Markus Leniger, *Nationalsozialistische "Volkstumsarbeit" und Umsiedlungspolitik 1933–1945: Von der Minderheitenbetreuung zur Siedlerauslese* (Berlin: Frank & Timme, 2006); Hans-Christian Harten, *Rassenhygiene als Erziehungsideologie des Dritten Reiches: Biobibliographisches Handbuch* (Berlin: Akademie-Verlag, 2006).
8 For recent analyses of the perpetrators' motivation, see Gerhard Paul, ed., *Die Täter der Shoah: Fanatische Nationalsozialisten oder ganz normale Deutsche?* (Göttingen: Wallstein Verlag, 2002); Harald Welzer, *Täter: Wie aus ganz normalen Menschen Massenmörder werden* (Frankfurt: Fischer Verlag, 2005); Michael Wildt, *Generation des Unbedingten: Das Führungskorps des Reichssicherheitshauptamtes* (Hamburg: Hamburger Edition, 2002). See also Christian Gerlach, *Kalkulierte Morde: Die deutsche Wirtschafts-und Vernichtungspolitik in Weissrussland 1941 bis 1944* (Hamburg: Hamburger Edition, 1999); Götz Aly, *Hitlers Volksstaat: Raub, Rassenkrieg und nationaler Sozialismus* (Frankfurt: Fischer Verlag, 2005).
9 Norman M. Naimark, *Fires of Hatred: Ethnic Cleansing in Twentieth-Century Europe* (Cambridge MA: Harvard University Press, 2001); Eric D. Weitz, *A Century of Genocide: Utopias of Race and Nation* (Princeton NJ: Princeton University Press,

2003); Mark Mazower, *Hitler's Empire: Nazi Rule in Occupied Europe* (London: Allen Lane, 2008); Isabel Heinemann and Patrick Wagner, eds., *Wissenschaft, Planung, Vertreibung: Neuordnungskonzepte und Umsiedlungspolitik im 20; Jahrhundert* (Stuttgart: Franz Steiner Verlag, 2006); Donald Bloxham, *The Final Solution: A Genocide* (Oxford: Oxford University Press, 2009).

10 Michael Wildt has recently argued that the Nazi state defined itself as a biopolitical regime displaying a highly selective version of racism. Wildt, "Biopolitik, ethnische Säuberungen und Volkssouveränität. Eine Skizze," *Mittelweg 36*, no. 6 (2006): 87–106. The concept of biopolitics has been applied to the Nazi state by Michel Foucault, in *Verteidigung der Gesellschaft: Vorlesungen am College de France (1975–76)* (Frankfurt: Suhrkamp Verlag, 1999), 300–303; see also Philipp Sarasin, "Zweierlei Rassismus? Die Selektion des Fremden als Problem in Michel Foucaults Verbindung von Biopolitik und Rassismus," in *Biopolitik und Rassismus*, ed. Martin Stingelin (Frankfurt: Suhrkamp Verlag, 2003), 55–79.

11 Götz Aly and Susanne Heim, *Vordenker der Vernichtung: Auschwitz und die deutschen Pläne für eine neue europäische Ordnung* (Frankfurt: Fischer Verlag, 1991); Michael Burleigh, *Germany Turns Eastwards: A Study of Ostforschung in the Third Reich* (Cambridge: Cambridge University Press, 1988); Isabel Heinemann, "Wissenschaft und Homogenisierungsplanungen für Osteuropa, Konrad Meyer, der 'Generalplan Ost' und die DFG," in Heinemann and Wagner, *Wissenschaft, Planung, Vertreibung*, 45–72; Gabriele Metzler and Dirk van Laak, "Die Konkretion der Utopie: Historische Quellen der Planungsutopien der 1920er Jahre," in Heinemann and Wagner, *Wissenschaft, Planung, Vertreibung*, 23–43; Dirk van Laak, "Planung: Geschichte und Gegenwart des Vorgriffs auf die Zukunft," *Geschichte und Gesellschaft* 34, no. 3 (2008): 305–26; Hans-Walter Schmuhl, *Grenzüberschreitungen: Das Kaiser-Wilhelm-Institut für Anthropologie, menschliche Erblehre und Eugenik 1927–1945* (Göttingen: Wallstein-Verlag, 2005); Uwe Hossfeld, *Geschichte der biologischen Anthropologie in Deutschland: Von den Anfängen bis in die Nachkriegszeit* (Stuttgart: Franz Steiner Verlag, 2005).

12 Regarding scholarly progress since the mid-1990s, cf. Dieter Pohl, *Von der "Juden-politik" zum Judenmord: Der Distrikt Lublin des Generalgouvernements 1939–1944* (Frankfurt: Lang, 1993); Pohl, *Nationalsozialistische Judenverfolgung in Ostgalizien 1941–1944: Organisation und Durchführung eines staatliche Massenverbrechens* (Munich: Oldenbourg, 1996); Bogdan Musial, *Deutsche Zivilverwaltung und Judenverfolgung im Generalgouvernement: Eine Fallstudie zum Distrikt Lublin 1939–1944* (Wiesbaden: Harrassowitz Verlag, 1999). Peter Longerich's biography of Himmler defies the trend of lack of knowledge about the racist foundations of occupation policies by focusing especially on the connection between Himmler's ideas of racial purity and German settlement and his role in the implementation of the Final Solution. Longerich, *Heinrich Himmler: Biographie* (Munich: Siedler, 2008). Götz Aly has discussed the mass murder of the European Jews and the ethnic cleansing of occupied Europe as intertwined processes, yet without analyzing the ideological foundation of the Nazi quest for racial purity and *Lebensraum*. Aly, *"Endlösung": Völkerverschiebung und der Mord an den europäischen Juden* (Frankfurt: Fischer Verlag, 1995). In my book I have specifically highlighted the racist component of Nazi occupation policies and its radic-alizing potential toward the Final Solution. Heinemann, *Rasse*.

13 Frank Bajohr and Michael Wildt, eds., *Volksgemeinschaft: Neue Forschungen zur Gesellschaft des Nationalsozialismus* (Frankfurt: Fischer Verlag, 2009). See also the report from the conference "German Society in the Nazi Era: 'Volksgemeinschaft' between Ideological Projection and Social Practice," London, 25–27 March 2010, available online at http://hsozkult.geschichte.hu-berlin.de/tagungsberichte/id=3121, accessed April 8, 2010.

14 Cf. Peter Longerich, *"Davon haben wir nichts gewusst!" Die Deutschen und die Judenverfolgung 1933–1945* (Munich: Siedler Verlag, 2006); Michael Wildt,

Volksgemeinschaft als Selbstermächtigung: Gewalt gegen Juden in der deutschen Provinz 1919 bis 1939 (Hamburg: Hamburger Edition, 2007).

15 For an overview of German traditions of racist thinking, see Ulrich Herbert, "Traditionen des Rassismus," in *Bürgerliche Gesellschaft in Deutschland*, ed. Lutz Niethammer (Frankfurt: Fischer Verlag, 1990), 472–88; Stefan Breuer, *Ordnungen der Ungleichheit: Die europäische Rechte im Widerstreit ihrer Ideen 1871–1945* (Darmstadt: Wissenschaftliche Buchgesellschaft, 2001).

16 Alfred Ploetz, *Die Tüchtigkeit unserer Rasse und der Schutz der Schwachen: Ein Versuch über Rassenhygiene und ihr Verhältnis zu den humanen Idealen, besonders zum Socialismus* (Berlin: Fischer Verlag, 1895); Sabine Schleiermacher, "Grenzüberschreitung der Medizin: Vererbungswissenschaft, Rassenhygiene und Geomedizin an der Charité im Nationalsozialismus," in *Die Charité im Dritten Reich: Zur Dienstbarkeit medizinischer Wissenschaft im Nationalsozialismus*, ed. Sabine Schleiermacher and Udo Schagen (Paderborn, Germany: Schöningh Verlag, 2008), 69–188; Schleiermacher, "Biologie und Gesellschaft: Eugenik und Rassenhygiene im medizinischen Diskurs," in *Biologismus, Rassismus, Rentabilität: Die Ambivalenz der Moderne*, ed. Hanns-Werner Heister (Berlin: Weidler Buchverlag, 2007), 187–201; Peter Weingart et al., *Rasse, Blut und Gene. Geschichte der Eugenik und Rassenhygiene in Deutschland* (Frankfurt: Suhrkamp, 1988); Paul Weindling, *Health, Race and German Politics between National Unification and Nazism, 1870–1945* (Cambridge: Cambridge University Press, 1989).

17 Hans F.K. Günther, *Kleine Rassenkunde des deutschen Volkes* (Munich: Lehmann, 1933); Günther, *Rassenkunde des deutschen Volkes* (Munich: Lehmann, 1933); Günther, *Rassenkunde des jüdischen Volkes* (Munich: Lehmann, 1930); Günther, *Der nordische Gedanke unter den Deutschen* (Munich: Lehmann, 1927).

18 Schmuhl, *Grenzüberschreitungen*; Hans-Walter Schmuhl, ed., *Rassenforschung an Kaiser-Wilhelm-Instituten vor und nach 1933* (Göttingen: Wallstein-Verlag, 2003).

19 Uwe Hossfeld, *Geschichte der biologischen Anthropologie*, esp. 206–66.

20 Sheila F. Weiss, " 'The Sword of Our Science' as a Foreign Policy Weapon: The Political Function of German Geneticists in the International Arena during the Third Reich," in *Ergebnisse: Vorabdrucke aus dem Forschungsprogramm "Geschichte der Kaiser-Wilhelm-Gesellschaft im Nationalsozialismus,"* ed. Carola Sachse and Susanne Heim (Berlin: Forschungsprogramm, 2003); Stefan Kühl, *Die Internationale der Rassisten: Aufstieg und Niedergang der internationalen Bewegung für Eugenik und Rassenhygiene im 20. Jahrhundert* (Frankfurt: Campus, 1997).

21 Katja Geisenhainer, *Rasse ist Schicksal: Otto Reche (1879–1966), ein Leben als Anthropologe und Völkerkundler* (Leipzig: Evangelische Verlagsanstalt, 2002).

22 Anne Cottebrune, *Der planbare Mensch: Die Deutsche Forschungsgemeinschaft und die menschliche Vererbungswissenschaft, 1920–1970* (Stuttgart: Franz Steiner Verlag, 2008), esp. 62–91, 273–82.

23 Schmuhl, *Grenzüberschreitungen*, 280–91.

24 Schmuhl, *Grenzüberschreitungen*, 299–312; Cornelia Essner, *Die "Nürnberger Gesetze" oder die Verwaltung des Rassenwahns 1933–1945* (Paderborn: Schöningh Verlag, 2002).

25 Hansjörg Gutberger, *Bevölkerung, Ungleichheit, Auslese: Perspektiven sozialwissenschaftlicher Bevölkerungsforschung in Deutschland zwischen 1930 und 1960* (Wiesbaden: vs Verlag für Sozialwissenschaften, 2006); Susanne Heim, ed., *Autarkie und Ostexpansion: Pflanzenzucht und Agrarforschung im Nationalsozialismus* (Göttingen: Wallstein-Verlag, 2002); Friedemann Schmoll, *Die Vermessung der Kultur: Der "Atlas der deutschen Volkskunde" und die Deutsche Forschungsgemeinschaft 1928–1980* (Stuttgart: Franz Steiner Verlag, 2009); Willi Oberkrome, *Ordnung und Autarkie: Die Geschichte der deutschen Landbauforschung, Agrarökonomie und ländlichen Sozialwissenschaft im Spiegel von Forschungsdienst und DFG (1920–1970)* (Stuttgart: Franz Steiner Verlag, 2009).

26 Heinemann, "Wissenschaft und Homogenisierungsplanungen," 45–72; Cottebrune, *Der planbare Mensch.*

27 Otto Reche, "Herkunft und Entstehung der Negerrassen," in *Koloniale Völkerkunde, koloniale Sprachforschung, koloniale Rassenforschung: Berichte über die Arbeitstagung im Januar 1943 in Leipzig,* ed. Hermann Baumann (Berlin: Reimer, Andrews & Steiner, 1943), 152–67; Reche, *Verbreitung der Menschenrassen* (Leipzig: List & von Bressendorf, 1938); Geisenhainer, *Rasse ist Schicksal.*

28 Otto Reche, "Leitsätze zu bevölkerungspolitischen Sicherung des deutschen Ostens," in *Der "Generalplan Ost": Hauptlinien der nationalsozialistischen Planungs- und Vernichtungspolitik,* ed. Mechtild Rössler and Sabine Schleiermacher (Berlin: Akademie-Verlag, 1993), 351–55.

29 Charles University was reopened as the German Charles Ferdinand University of Prague. Besides the rather dated book by Teresa Wróblewska—*Die Reichsuniversitäten Posen, Prag und Strassburg als Modelle nationalsozialistischer Hochschulen in den von Deutschland besetzten Gebieten* (1984; repr., Toruń, Poland: Wydawnictwo Adam Marszalek, 2000)—there is no comprehensive history of the German universities in the occupied and annexed territories during the Third Reich.

30 For more information on Schultz, see Heinemann, *Rasse.*

31 Erhard Wetzel's report, 7 February 1942, STANU, NO-2585.

32 Heinemann, "Wissenschaft und Homogenisierungsplanungen"; Robert L. Koehl, RKFDV: *German Settlement and Population Policy; A History of the Reich Commission for the Strengthening of Germandom* (Cambridge MA: Harvard University Press, 1957). Alexa Stiller is currently writing a PhD thesis on the RKF.

33 Summary of the memo on Master Plan East, 28 May 1942, and Ulrich Greifelt to Himmler, 2 June 1942, in *Vom Generalplan Ost zum Generalsiedlungsplan,* ed. Cesław Madajczyk (Munich: Saur, 1994), 85–130.

34 Konrad Meyer, "Siedlungs- und Aufbauarbeit im deutschen Osten," *Die Bewegung* 8 (1941): 7.

35 Konrad Meyer, *Landvolk im Werden* (Berlin: Deutsche Landbuchhandlung, 1942), 3.

36 For a conventional interpretation of Nazi German academia as largely nonpolitical, see Notker Hammerstein, *Die Deutsche Forschungsgemeinschaft in der Weimarer Republik und im Dritten Reich: Wissenschaftspolitik in Republik und Diktatur 1920–1945* (Munich: Beck, 1999). For a more comprehensive analysis proving the deliberate collaboration and individual initiative of relevant parts of the German academic elite, see Karin Orth and Willi Oberkrome, eds., *Die Deutsche Forschungsgemeinschaft 1920–1970: Forschungsförderung im Spannungsfeld von Wissenschaft und Politik* (Stuttgart: Steiner, 2010). See also publications on the history of the Max Planck Society (former Kaiser-Wilhelm Institute) under National Socialism as well as recent studies of German universities in the Third Reich.

37 Hitler's Order on Strengthening the Germandom, 7 October 1939, printed in *Der Prozess gegen die Hauptkriegsverbrecher vor dem Internationalen Militärgerichtshof,* vol. 26 (Nuremberg: IMT, 1947), 255–57.

38 Himmler's speech in Posen, 24 October 1943, quoted in Josef Ackermann, *Heinrich Himmler als Ideologe* (Göttingen: Muster-Schmidt Verlag, 1970), 291–96.

39 Himmler's Marriage Order for the SS, 31 December 1931, BAR, NS 2/174. For the institutional history of the RuSHA, see Heinemann, *Rasse.*

40 Most files of this branch office can be found in the AGK, 167; others are stored in the Russian State Military Archives in Moscow, 1372.

41 This large-scale population transfer had been the result of an agreement between Germany and the Soviet Union, signed shortly before the former's attack on Poland. Further resettlement agreements were ratified, for instance, with the Baltic States.

42 See the files of the Einwandererzentralstelle, BAR, NS 69.

43 See the monthly reports of the RuSHA branch office Zamość to RuSHA in Berlin, AGK, 167/48; report of the Umwandererzentralstelle branch office Zamość, 13 December 1942, BAR, R 75/9.

44 See photos of race cards in Heinemann, *Rasse*, 64–65; original copies in BAR, NS 2/152.

45 Edwin Black, *IBM und der Holocaust: Die Verstrickung des Weltkonzerns in die Verbrechen der Nazis* (Munich: Propyläen Verlag, 2001); Götz Aly and Karl-Heinz Roth, *Die restlose Erfassung: Volkszählen, Identifizieren, Aussondern im Nationalsozialismus* (1984; repr., Frankfurt: Fischer Verlag, 2000).

46 Testimony of Dr. Josef Rembacz, Łódź, 25 August 1946, STANU, NO-5166.

47 In 1944 around thirty-five thousand out of eight hundred thousand Poles were considered a "wanted population addition." Reich Security Main Office to RuSHA and RKF, 19 December 1942, AGK, 167/38; monthly reports of the RuSHA branch office Litzmannstadt, 31 December 1941–30 April 1944, AGK 167/6; monthly reports of the RuSHA branch office Zamość, AGK, 167/48; final report on the Umwandererzentralstelle activities in the Warthegau and the General Government for the year 1943, 12 December 1943, BAR, R 75/3.

48 Final report on the Umwandererzentralstelle activities in the Warthegau and the General Government for the year 1943, 12 December 1943, BAR, R 75/3. See also report on the activities of the Umwandererzentralstelle branch office Zamość from 27 November to 31 December 1942, 13 December 1942, BAR, R 75/9.

49 For the annihilation of the Jewish population in the General Government and the war against the non-Jewish civilian population, see Pohl, *Nationalsozialistische Judenverfolgung*; Bogdan Musial, ed., *"Aktion Reinhard": Der Völkermord an den Juden im Generalgouvernement 1941–1944* (Osnabrück, Germany: Fibre Verlag, 2004); Nils Gutschow, *Ordnungswahn: Architekten planen im "eingedeutschten Osten" 1939–1945* (Gütersloh, Germany: Birkhäuser, 2001); Jacek A. Młynarczek, *Judenmord in Zentralpolen: Der Distrikt Radom im Generalgouvernement 1939–1945* (Darmstadt: Wissenschaftliche Buchgesellschaft, 2007).

50 Attestation by the mayor of Topolice, Tomaszow Mazowiecki District, regarding the resettlement of the Ryszard W. family, 12 December 1940, provided to the author by Ryszard W., October 2006.

51 The Master Plan East and the resettlement carried out in Zamość highlighted the consensus among SS experts that the Jewish population of the territories slated for Germanization had to perish first.

52 Letter of RuSHA head Otto Hofmann to RFSS regarding the racial screening of the Czechs, 17 February 1941, BAB, NS 2/57; letter of the head of the RuSHA branch office in Prague, Ewin Künzel, 17 October 1942, State Central Archives, Prague, 114/25/9. See also Heinemann, *Rasse*, 151–57.

53 For a description of the SS experts' initiatives in Southeastern Europe, see Isabel Heinemann, "Die Rasseexperten der SS und die bevölkerungspolitische Neuordnung Südosteuropas," in *Südostforschung im Schatten des Dritten Reiches. Institutionen-Inhalte-Personen*, ed. Mathias Beer and Gerhard Seewann (Munich: Oldenbourg, 2004), 135–57.

54 Current activities of the Einwandererzentralstelle branch office Litzmannstadt, 30 November 1944, State Archives in Łódź, 204,2/11; Friedrich Brehm to RKF, 25 February 1943, BAR, R 49/79. See also Lothar Kettenacker, *Nationalsozialistische Volkstumspolitik im Elsass* (Stuttgart: Deutsche Verlags-Anstalt, 1973), 267; Dieter Wolfanger, "Die nationalsozialistische Politik in Lothringen (1940–1945)" (PhD diss., University of Saarbrücken, 1977), 173–77.

55 Marie-Louise Roth-Zimmermann, *Denk' ich an Schelklingen . . . Erinnerungen einer Elsässerin an die Zeit im SS-Umsiedlungslager (1942–1945)* (Sankt Ingbert, Germany: Röhrig Universitätsverlag, 2001).

56 Bruno Wasser, "Die 'Germanisierung' im Distrikt Lublin als Generalprobe und erste
    Realisierungsphase des 'Generalplan Ost,'" in Rössler and Schleiermacher, *Der
    "Generalplan Ost,"* 271–93; Bruno Wasser, *Himmlers Raumplanung im Osten: Der
    Generalplan Ost in Polen 1940–1944* (Basel: Birkhäuser, 1993); Wendy Lower, "A
    New Ordering of Space and Race: Nazi Colonial Dreams in Zhytomyr, Ukraine,
    1941–1944," *German Studies Review* 25, no. 2 (May 2002): 227–54; Lower, *Nazi
    Empire-Building and the Holocaust in Ukraine* (Chapel Hill: University of North
    Carolina Press, 2005).
57 SS officer file Hans Rihl, Berlin Document Center.
58 SS officer file Hans Rihl, personal questionnaire, 7 August 1935, Berlin Document
    Center.
59 Monthly report of the SS-Führer im Rasse-und Siedlungswesen head at Zamość,
    Hans Rihl, to the RuSHA branch office Litzmannstadt, 1 January 1943, AGK, 167/48.
60 This number comprises only the high-ranking and midlevel functionaries in RuSHA.
    Otherwise, the total RuSHA membership during the war fluctuated between five and
    ten thousand.
61 Lutz Raphael, "Experten im Sozialstaat," in *Drei Wege deutscher Sozialstaatlichkeit: NS-
    Diktatur, Bundesrepublik und DDR im Vergleich*, ed. Hans-Günther Hockerts (Munich:
    Oldenbourg, 1998), 231–58.
62 For a more comprehensive data analysis, see Heinemann, *Rasse*, 590–91, 601–41.
63 On Konrad Meyer, see Heinemann and Wagner, *Wissenschaft, Planung, Vertreibung*.
64 For the most comprehensive collection of documents on the Master Plan East and
    Master Settlement Plan, see Madajczyk, *Vom Generalplan Ost*, esp. 86–130, 234–55.
65 The entire file, BAR NS 19/1047.
66 See Isabel Heinemann, "'Until the Last Drop of Good Blood': The Kidnapping of
    'Racially Valuable' Children as Another Aspect of Nazi Racial Policy in the Occupied
    East," in *Genocide and Settler Society: Frontier Violence and Stolen Aboriginal Children in
    Australian History*, ed. Dirk Moses (Oxford: Berghahn Books, 2004), 244–66.
67 For a discussion of this data, see Heinemann, *Rasse*, 598–603.
68 Schultz records, Department of Medicine, University of Münster Archives, 52/278;
    Schultz records, Department of Mathematics and Natural Science, University of
    Münster Archives, 92/16.
69 "Opening Statement of the Prosecution," in *Trials of War Criminals before the Nuernberg
    Military Tribunals under Control Council Law No. 10*, vol. 4, pt. 2 (Washington DC: U.S.
    Government Printing Office, 1950), 627.

Part II

IMPLEMENTATION
Normalizing genocide

4

CAMPS AND GHETTOS

Forced labor in the Reich Gau Wartheland, 1939–44

Wolf Gruner

One of the main questions asked when the extent of the Nazi genocidal undertaking against the Jews was revealed, was why would a regime that found itself under increasing military pressure not only devote a great deal of energy to the murder of millions of people who posed no threat to it, but deprive itself of a skilled and willing workforce? As German losses mounted on the Eastern Front, more and more German men had to be pulled out of factories and sent to fight, and the shortage of labor, already felt even before the war began, became especially acute, not least because of the need to produce war materiel at an unprecedented rate and quantity. By the time the German authorities began to think of employing the vast numbers of Red Army soldiers they had taken captive in the early months of the fighting in the Soviet Union, they found that millions of them had died thanks to the Wehrmacht's maltreatment and neglect. It was then, just as it appeared that the "Jewish question" could finally be resolved under the guise of total war and in the remote spaces of the east conquered by Germany that some elements of the regime and the military began to think of the Jews as a valuable resource.

Were the Nazis, then, motivated by a primacy of economics rooted in the urgent need for labor and the burning desire to win the war, or by a primacy of ideology, which viewed the Jews not as innocent victims and useful workers but as the most dangerous enemy of the Reich, which had to be finally exterminated? Historians such as Tim Mason and Ulrich Herbert have discussed this question in previous decades and have concluded that ultimately ideology won out, even at the price of harming the war effort. Recently, however, the historian Adam Tooze has insisted in his massive study, The Wages of Destruction, *that Hitler's chief motivation in launching war was to conquer an economic "living space" of land and resources, especially in the east, without which he believed Germany would never accomplish great power status vis-à-vis the United States. More specifically, the historian Christopher Browning has suggested that in the period of ghettoization, between the victory over Poland in 1939 and the attack on the Soviet Union in 1941, a struggle ensued between German "attritionists," who were glad to see the Jews dying of famine and disease in congested* ghettos, and the "productionists," who claimed that as long as no final solution to the "problem" of the Jews was found and no orders about how to deal with them had arrived from the top, one would do well to make use of their labor, if only in order to produce necessary items for the Wehrmacht (as well as to line the pockets of the Germans overseeing them).

In this chapter, Wolf Gruner demonstrates that in fact the Germans were using Jewish forced labor from the very beginning, first in Germany itself and then in occupied Poland. Focusing on the Warthegau, the part of western Poland that Germany annexed and was planning to empty of its Polish and Jewish populations so as to settle it with ethnic Germans, he shows that the Lodz Ghetto had become, in the words of the city's German mayor, "a large-scale operation sui generis." Fully mobilized for work under the dictatorial rule of its controversial Jewish leader, Chaim Rumkowski (see further in Chapter 9), the ghetto was producing essential items for the military. The implications of this aspect of the Holocaust are complex and disquieting. While the Nazis were happy to use the Jews as slave workers, this also gave them the rationale to murder all those who could not work, the elderly, the sick, and especially the children. And although the Lodz Ghetto survived longer than any other, eventually almost everyone there was murdered, including Rumkowski himself. As for the Germans, even those who saw the insanity of murdering people who were literally working to death for them, in a system that came to be known as "extermination through labor," once the order came down to send the Jews to the gas chambers, none of the Germans showed any hesitation. In this sense, not only did ideology win out, but also first exploiting the victims and eventually killing them when they were no longer of any use made the whole genocidal undertaking appear perfectly rational.

Expulsion plans and forced labor as an intermediate solution

Forced labor had been a basic component of Jewish policy in the Reich before the war, and it was to become an element of war and occupation thinking as well. In September 1939, the Nazi state started the war with Poland. After the quick defeat of the Polish state, it became clear that the forced-labor plans discussed at the end of February could not be implemented as projected in Germany, Austria, or the Protectorate: The Nazi leadership had very hastily made a new, fundamental decision to deport all the Reich's Jews to Poland in the near future. On September 14, 1939, Heydrich announced that Himmler would put forward proposals shortly that "only the Führer could approve because they would have significant implications for foreign policy."[1] On September 19, the Council of Ministers for Reich Defense, including Göring, Heydrich, Frick, and State Secretary Syrup from the Reich Ministry of Labor, conferred on the "population of the future Polish Protectorate and accommodation of the Jews living in Germany."[2]

On September 21, 1939, at a meeting with the Security Police office chiefs and Einsatzgruppe leaders, Heydrich provided an overview of the planned course of events in Poland. The former German provinces were to become German Gaue, and a Gau for speakers of foreign languages would be created on the remaining Polish territory. According to Heydrich, Hitler had authorized the Jews' deportation to the latter Gau. "However, the entire process should be spread over a year. . . . Jewry is to be concentrated in city ghettos to facilitate control and later removal." Summarizing, Heydrich ordered: "1. Jews out of the cities as fast as possible, 2. Jews out of the Reich to Poland, 3. the remaining 30,000 Gypsies to Poland, too, [and] 4. systematic dispatch of Jews out of German territory with freight trains."[3] For the overall plan, Heydrich differentiated between the "final objective" and the "steps for reaching that objective (which would be taken in the short term)." The first step was to deport Jews from the newly annexed territories of Danzig, West Prussia, Posen, and eastern Upper Silesia, as well as to concentrate the Jews in the other occupied territories of Poland in cities along railway lines. Jewish councils of elders were to be established everywhere; they would be responsible for registration of Jews and then for their removal from the countryside or for deportation preparations in the cities. For security reasons, Jews would probably be banned from "certain sectors" of the city or ordered not to leave the ghettos. However, expulsion of the Jews was to "take into consideration the interests of the German economy." That applied not only to support for companies critical to the war effort, but also – with the advent of the newly established German labor offices – to Jewish labor. Copies of this decree went to the SS, the Wehrmacht High Command (OKW), the Reich Interior Ministry, and the chiefs of the civilian administrations of the occupied territories.[4] Heydrich's decree did not refer to the territories east of Krakow because as Heydrich explained in a September 22, 1939, conversation with the Army High Commander, Walther von Brauchitsch, plans called for a "German-administered Jewish state near Krakow."[5]

On October 30, 1939, Himmler again categorically demanded removal of all Jews from "formerly Polish, presently Reich German provinces" by February 1940.[6] However, after a meeting with the General Governor in Krakow, he scaled back the plan. To "cleanse and secure the new German territories," an "initial operation" from mid-November 1939 to the end of February 1940 would first deport 100,000 Jews from the new Reich Gau Wartheland to the area around Lublin and south of Warsaw. The rural *Kreise* (county-size units of government) and the cities of Posen, Gnesen, and Hohensalza would have to be totally cleansed first, while part of the Jewish population (30,000 persons) was to be removed from Lodz (Litzmannstadt).[7] In the part of western Poland annexed to Reich territory and now called the "Warthegau," preparatory measures took effect. For example, the authorities in various cities established the first ghettos in fall 1939. In mid-November, Jews were prohibited from changing residences.[8] On November 14, the newly appointed President of the Kalisch Administrative District, Friedrich Uebelhör, ordered that Jews in the Kalisch district, including Lodz, be marked with yellow armbands and prohibited from leaving their residences between 5:00 p.m. and 8:00 a.m. without special authorization.[9] Then, on December 11, 1939, the Reichsstatthalter of the Warthegau, Arthur Greiser, ordered that all Jews in his territory be marked on the chest and back with a Star of David, the first such measure within the Greater German Reich.[10] But the deportations could not be implemented as quickly and as totally as planned (although by spring 1940 more than 87,000 Jewish and non-Jewish Poles had been removed from the Warthegau), which left room for forced-labor measures.

Various occupation authorities – for example, the civilian administration of the Lodz *Wehrkreis* (military area) commander – already had drafted Jewish men and women for forced labor during the campaign.[11] A general order instituted forced labor for Jews for the first time on October 6 or 7, 1939.[12] In Petrikau, previously Piotrków, Oberbürgermeister Drechsel not only established a ghetto, but also proclaimed on December 1 that the Jewish community would have to provide 1,000 men a day for "mandatory jobs"; the work orders could be picked up at the municipal construction office.[13] As shortly before in Germany, the newly constituted Jewish councils in Warthegau soon had to register all potential workers in card files. The December 1938 decree on segregated labor deployment did not apply to the annexed territories and forced labor for Jews was only instituted officially by the October 1941 order for the entire Reich; consequently, the Warthegau lacked appropriate regulation. However, at this point all the authorities expected rapid deportation of the Jewish population living in the annexed territories.

On December 10, 1939, District President Uebelhör ordered creation of a ghetto in Lodz, where the majority of the Warthegau Jews lived, and specified the following details: A Jewish elder and a community committee were to head the ghetto's self-government. They were to take charge of food, health, security, inhabitants' housing, accounting, and registration. The nutrition office (*Ernährungsamt*) of the Lodz city administration would supply food and fuel to the ghetto's administration. Workers from the ghetto would build a wall to enclose the Jewish residential district. Thus, from the outset the labor potential of the victims was the focus of interest. The instruction states, "When the other city sectors are combed for Jews fit to work and the Jews removed to the ghetto at the time of or shortly after its creation, the Jews fit to work living there are to be taken into custody. They are to be put together in work units, housed in barracks set up by the city administration and the Security Police, and guarded there. These Jews are intended for labor deployment in segregated units [*"für einen geschlossenen Arbeitseinsatz"*]. The work will consist initially in the units razing buildings ready for demolition in the city center." According to the instructions, able-bodied Jews were to be put to work outside the ghetto, and as they lived in the ghetto, they were also to take care of any work there. Uebelhör's order concluded, "I will determine later whether Jews capable of working will be taken from the ghetto and placed in labor barracks. Providing the ghetto is only a temporary measure. . . . The final objective must be in any case to cauterize this plague canker completely."[14] According to the central plan, the entire Warthegau was in the future to be purely German territory "free of Jews" (*judenfrei*). The Lodz ghetto was from the outset a way station before the Jews were shoved across the border. The deportations were repeatedly postponed, however, so in February 1940 construction of the ghetto began, and on May 10, 1940, the ghetto was sealed off from the outside world.[15]

Ghettoization and forced labor

The areas of responsibility for the Lodz ghetto were already clearly defined in April 1940. The municipal administration assumed general supervisory control of the ghetto and was to regulate its internal affairs and economy, while the local police chief (*Polizeipräsident*) was to focus exclusively on keeping the peace and order.[16] The ghetto was thus under the authority of the Oberbürgermeister of Lodz, in the future called Litzmannstadt by the Germans; the Municipal Police, the Gestapo, and the Criminal Police were only responsible for police supervision. Oberbürgermeister Schiffer then transferred limited authority for self-government in the ghetto to the Jewish elder Mordechai Chaim Rumkowski. The liaison office between the ghetto Jewish council and the Litzmannstadt authorities was the city administration's ghetto food and economic office (*Ernährungsund Wirtschaftsamt "Ghetto"*), which was called the "ghetto administration" after October 1940. The Bremen coffee importer Hans Biebow headed this office. His agency, which employed about 400 people, later oversaw labor camps inside the ghetto where its inmates performed forced labor.[17]

Exploitation of Jewish workers thus played a role in planning for persecution in the Warthegau from the outset. In contrast, Christopher Browning believes that in light of the anticipated deadline for total expulsion (summer 1940) there were initially no plans to assign Jews to forced labor, despite initiatives of the ghetto's Jewish elders. Only when deportation plans failed and the ghetto's mortality rates climbed did the German ghetto administration reassess the situation. All efforts for self-preservation were undertaken at this point, including work arrangements.[18] However, registration of workers in the Warthegau, in Lodz, and in the ghetto was a significant factor already in the first planning stages. Thus, the work of building a tailor shop in the ghetto began in May 1940.[19]

Centralization of forced labor and mass transfer of workers

On July 27, 1940, Reichsstatthalter Greiser issued an order that employers in the Warthegau had to pay Jews standard schedule wages. This measure could only mean that previously, because no official regulations existed, large numbers of Jews had been employed as forced laborers and frequently were compensated inadequately or not at all. However, even with the new order, the individual situations of the compulsory employees improved little. Jews only received 35 percent of the schedule wages paid; the other 65 percent flowed into special accounts set up by the district administrators. The Bürgermeister of the Warthegau were ordered to report on their experiences with forced labor, and more specifically, on the relationship between food and performance, the satisfaction level of companies employing Jews, and the support costs for Jews.[20] All these circumstances indicate that forced labor was planned centrally in the Warthegau and that consideration was being given to expanding the program further. In the course of 1940, the first labor camps were constructed for Jews in the Warthegau, in Pabianitz and Löwenstadt, for example.[21]

As the SS leadership was still unable to realize the planned deportations to the General Government to the extent desired in 1940, ghettos were established in the Warthegau's small towns. For example, the non-Jewish Poles were driven out of eighteen villages in Turek Kreis, and 4,000 Jewish Poles were concentrated there.[22] At the same time, exploitation of Jewish labor intensified, because in the meantime tens of thousands of unemployed Jews lived in the Warthegau as the result of all the persecutory measures. Labor shortages continued to grow in the Reich; as a consequence, Fritz Todt received special authorization in October 1940 to use Polish Jews from the Warthegau in constructing the Reich highway system. Beginning at the end of 1940, thousands of Jews were sent from the ghetto to the camps along the Berlin–Frankfurt an der Oder–Posen Autobahn, as we will see in Chapter 7.

A few months later, efforts were initiated to transfer a large number of Jews to the Old Reich. After Reichsstatthalter Greiser had offered workers to the Reich Minister of Labor, both agencies arranged to send 73,000 Polish Jews to the Old Reich in February 1941 for forced labor, believing that the consent of Himmler and Göring was assured.[23] The regional labor offices in Germany and Austria were informed about the undertaking while the Ministry of Labor was still drafting the official instructions for the planned project." At the beginning of March

1941, the Hermann Göring Reichswerke enterprise in Watenstedt was discussing the offer of the Lower Saxony regional labor office to employ 2,000 Polish Jewish forced laborers.[24] Other enterprises also immediately ordered large contingents; the Reich Autobahn directorate (*Reichsautobahn-Direktion*) ordered 8,000, and the Siemens-Schuckert Werke AG, in Berlin, 1,200. The Labor Ministry sent the requests right on to the Reichsstatthalter in Warthegau.[25] On March 14, the ministry informed the regional labor offices of the procedure for directly reserving the workers in Posen and allocated to each district 2,000 Jewish men and 1,500 Jewish women. The ministry demanded that the regional labor offices make available suitable work places in cooperation with all "participating and interested offices and large businesses" and house workers in special labor camps, thereby preventing contact with the general population.[26]

The Reich Ministry of Labor notified the East Prussian regional labor office in Königsberg regarding some special concerns on March 14, 1941. The Army High Command (OKH) had informed the ministry that, despite the withdrawal of 10,000 prisoners of war, the workers required for the so-called Otto Program to expand the railway and street networks in the occupied territories and to prepare for the attack on the Soviet Union still had to be provided. If prisoners of war were no longer available, the ministry asked the regional labor office "to use Jews from the Warthegau if necessary."[27] The ministry wrote much more emphatic comments on a parallel copy of the letter sent to the OKH: "With regard to the situation resulting from withdrawal of large numbers of POWs in Wehrkreis I . . . the projects of the Otto Program must rely on Jews from the Warthegau. I request that possible misgivings be set aside." An additional sentence in the draft says, "The situation regarding the danger of sabotage and separate housing is not significantly different from using prisoners of war."[28] The Brandenburg and Silesian regional labor offices received notification to the same effect.[29] The OKW then informed the homeland transport department (*Heimattransportabteilung*) on March 20, 1941, that Königsberg headquarters I had requested yet another 2,400 prisoners of war for the Otto Program. As prisoners of war could not be brought in from other labor offices, the Ministry of Labor "had already dispatched 7,000 Jewish civilian workers from the Warthegau to Wehrmacht Headquarters I.[30] On March 28, the Reich Ministry of Labor noted that the Reich Ministry of Transportation required yet another 2,000 laborers to lay cable on the stretch from Berlin to Krakow. The regional labor office there reported that the Breslau Reich Railway directorate needed 400 more prisoners of war but rejected Jews "for security reasons."[31] The Ministry of Labor informed the Reich Ministry of Transportation of this situation and pressed for review of doubts about security related to Jews with the argument that the chief of the OKW's transportation planning department also had agreed to the deployment.[32] Likewise on March 28, the Reich Ministry of Labor had supposedly asked the president of the East Prussian regional labor office to assess whether Jews from the Warthegau could be put to work for the railway department.[33] According to East Prussia's April 8, 1941, reply to the

Reich Minister of Labor, the proposal supposedly had been made to the Königsberg (East Prussia) Reich Railway directorate that Jews from the Posen area be employed at the Otto Program's building sites in place of prisoners of war. After several consultations, the Reich railway directorate finally, on April 4, telephoned the regional labor office's president with the number of Jews needed, a total of 1,010. The President of the East Prussian regional labor office had that very day contacted the Reichsstatthalter in Posen and requested trans-fer of another transport of Jews.[34] But the planned transfer of tens of thousands of Jews did not meet with approval. The RSHA objected vigorously, and in April 1941 Hitler himself personally prohibited transfer of Jewish forced laborers out of the Warthegau to the Old Reich.[35]

The Lodz Ghetto – a large-scale operation and legalization of forced labor

Although the Greiser transfer project failed, the exceptional authorization allowing use of Polish Jews in Autobahn construction endured. In spring 1941, Jews were recruited intensively in the Lodz ghetto, which had been declared a permanent facility in October 1940. As hunger and death already held sway over life there, 7,000 people reported for forced labor in the Old Reich.[36] When the terrible circumstances threatened to affect the working inmates in the ghetto, the people in charge changed the rules for supplying food. After July 1941, the rations distributed to working Jews were to be the same as for non-working Poles; rations for non-working Jews would be the same as for Polish prisoners.[37] After all, 40,000 of the 160,000 inmates labored in the ghetto's own workshops. That made the city of Lodz one of the largest enterprises in the Warthegau. Bürgermeister Kar Marder called the ghetto a "large-scale operation sui generis."[38] The inmates' work was organized by the Jewish council but controlled by the municipal ghetto administration. As the ghetto was located within Reich territory, it was hermetically sealed from the outside world. On the one hand, food hardly could be smuggled into the ghetto; on the other – in contrast to the Warsaw ghetto – no private companies managed to penetrate the ghetto walls in order to employ Jews.[39]

In September 1941, after the Nazi leadership's decision about resuming deportations of Jews from the Old Reich, Austria, and the Protectorate, the responsible officials in the Warthegau had to accept that 20,000 Jews would be brought to the overcrowded ghetto. Additionally, in October 1941 Germany issued the first regulations on segregated labor deployment since 1938. The October 3 order defined the relationship of Jews to forced labor; the execution order issued shortly thereafter set down a detailed special labor law. While the former order also took effect in the Warthegau, the special labor law was not introduced in the annexed eastern territories. The Reich Ministry of Labor earlier had agreed directly with the Reichsstatthalter to remove "Jews working in the Jewish residential districts themselves or for businesses in the Jewish residential district from the effective scope of all legally defined social-support regulations." That applied to the ghetto inmates' forced labor. Thus, the Litzmannstadt Jews assigned in 1940–41 to the Frankfurt an der Oder–Posen stretch of Autobahn received only 10 Pfennig per day in pay. As Chapter 7 will describe, 80 percent of the wages left after deducting camp housing, taxes, and fees regularly flowed into a Litzmannstadt ghetto account. The Reich Ministry of Labor wanted to apply the new special law at least to the Polish Jews in the annexed territories employed outside the ghetto in private or public enterprises.[40] At a "heavily attended" meeting in the Berlin ministry, however, the participants agreed at the end of November 1941 that, given the "special circumstances" in the formerly Polish territories annexed to the German Reich, there was no need anywhere to introduce a detailed special labor law for Jews. Agencies' representatives from the Warthegau, Upper Silesia, and Ziechenau administrative districts made it unmistakably clear that the Jews living there had been forced for a long time already to work under much harsher conditions. Introduction of the Old Reich's regulations would thus be a step backwards.[41]

Acceleration of forced labor by the labor offices in late 1941

At this point, the labor administration in the Warthegau intensified the use of forced labor and recruited tens of thousands of Jews for road and improvement projects. Labor shortages were acute in this area. In fall 1941, not enough laborers were available to help with the harvest "despite allocation of prisoners of war, convicts, and several hundred Jews." Overall, however, the labor offices gained hundreds of additional workplaces where Jewish men and women could be put to work in groups. The labor office thus considered the "operation to employ Jews in groups for the first time to be complete." However, planning for further mandatory commitment was already underway.[42] In October 1941, the Warthegau labor offices placed 2,490 Jews, men and women equally, in forced-labor jobs, distributed across the various districts as shown below.

Statistics on new forced laborers recruited by Warthegau labor offices in October 1941[43]

Labor office district	Jewish men	Jewish women
Hohensalza	166	609
Leslau	55	48
Lissa	152	0
Litzmannstadt	0	168
Posen	243	0
Samter	0	63
Schieratz	95	14
Warthbrücken	553	324
Total for October 1941	1,264	1,226

Assignment to forced labor by Warthegau labor offices, 1941–42[46]

Labor utilization	Jewish men	Jewish women	Total
1941			
October	1,264	1,226	2,490
November	1,962	712	2,674
December	509	22	531
1942			
January	242	22	264
February	648	32	680
March	1,062	23	1,085
April	2,299	22	2,321
May	2,983	605	3,588
Total	10,969	2,664	13,633

In November, the Warthegau labor administration recruited an additional 2,674 Jews, and in December, 531.[44] Regarding "utilization of prisoners of war, convicts, and Jews for compulsory labor," a report of the labor administration at the end of 1941 stated, "in Leslau administrative district, all working Jews were housed in camps and therefore taken out of the ghetto. In Gnesen administrative district, the prisoners of war and Jews utilized continued to work despite the weather conditions. The Reich Autobahn employs 1,500 Jews at the moment in Samter administrative district. In Kolmar administrative district, the number of sick among the Jews utilized has increased to twenty per hundred. The Welungen labor office again used Jews for emergency work, so that 603 Jews are now employed there.... In Kutno administrative district, collection of data on work capabilities of Jews is complete; 758 Jews were transferred to labor ["in den Ausgleich vermittelt"]. The Posen labor office reported further demand for prisoners of war and Jews."[45] In spring, allocations were to increase further.

Within eight months the labor offices thus committed far more than 13,000 Polish Jews, mostly men from small cities, to forced labor in the Warthegau. Only in the May 1942 recruitment of over 2,900 men did 2,219 come from the major city Posen alone.[47]

Conflicts between the labor market and persecutory policies

While forced labor of Jews was being expanded throughout the Warthegau, the same process was also in progress in the Lodz ghetto. There, Hans Biebow, the head of the ghetto administration, reported to the Gestapo office on March 4, 1942, that about 53,000 workers were employed in jobs essentially furthering the interests of the war economy. Of course, he continued, there were considerable problems because for a year the rations in the ghetto had been even below the usual dietary allowances for convicts. The mortality rates among the inmates were therefore extremely high. In only four days, 307 people had died of starvation; "Anyone familiar with the conditions in the ghetto knows that workshop employees literally collapse at their work-benches from debilitation." But Biebow immediately qualified this criticism of the Gestapo, with the emphatic statement, "The ghetto administration would never allot more food to the Jews than is absolutely justifiable."[48]

As in other occupied territories, the forced-labor objectives clashed with the interests of persecutory policy. This conflict became especially acute when the anti-Jewish murder program began in the Warthegau, replacing previous deportation plans at the end of 1941. Most of the victims were then killed with gas vans in Kulmhof (Chelmno). The Litzmannstadt State Police office described the mass murder of Polish and non-Polish Jews from the ghetto in June 1942: "On instructions from the Gauleiter, all Jews unable to work were to be evacuated and the persons able to work from the entire Gau concentrated in the Litzmannstadt ghetto. . . . In creating the Gau ghetto, it first proved necessary to make space for the Jews to be settled there. To this end, a large number of the people unable to work were evacuated from the ghetto and taken to the Sonderkommando. Since January 16, 1942, 44,152 Polish Jews have been removed. Ten thousand, nine hundred and ninety-three of the 19,848 Jews sent in October 1941 to the ghetto here from the Old Reich, the Ostmark, and the Protectorate of Bohemia and Moravia were evacuated; thus, space in the ghetto has now been freed up for around 55,000 Jews."[49] So after the ghetto inhabitants from the Greater German Reich had been included in the murder process in May 1942, Polish Jews from rural areas of the Warthegau were moved into the ghetto to replace them.[50] In the course of these deportations from rural Kreise, 60 percent of the forced-labor camps in the Posen area closed during summer 1942.[51]

At this point, about 70,000 of the 103,000 ghetto inmates were still working as laborers and about 15,000 as employees of the Jewish council. To increase productivity, the workers received additional bread rations;[52] intervention of the Wehrmacht offices interested in the inmates' contribution to war production was clearly successful. At the same time, efforts were made to increase the number of forced laborers. The Litzmannstadt Gestapo reported to the inspector of the Secret Police on July 2, 1942, "As the ability of the Jews to resist has waned, their productivity has fallen off. For that reason, the Jewish elder has put all children over ten years old to work."[53] In addition, repressive measures for poor performance became more severe. After a few weeks, there were signs of improvement: "Despite very bad food and nutrition for the Jews – a daily rate of nineteen Pfennig per head – production has risen from the previous month, which can be attributed more or less to the continuous 'pressure' exerted on Jews or individual work leaders."[54]

The new rental system of the labor offices and the situation of forced laborers, 1942–43

While in summer 1942 the SS resumed control of forced labor in the General Government as the mass murder program was progressing, that did not occur in the Warthegau. As in Germany, the labor administration continued to play a decisive role reinforced by the new June 25, 1942, "Order regarding Employment of Jewish Workers in the Wartheland Reich Gau." The labor department of the Reichsstatthalter in Posen emphasized in the order that "employment of Jewish workers ... [was] only allowed with consent of the Reichsstatthalter's labor department"; from that point forward, the same also applied to ghetto inmates. Jews would have to be ordered from the responsible labor office. They were to receive free room and board, but both together were not to exceed one Reich Mark. The forced laborers, who had to work ten hours a day, received no wages, but the employers could pay bonuses up to RM 1.50 per week as an incentive to increase productivity. Every day the amount of RM 0.70 per forced laborer was to be paid to the account of the Oberbürgermeister of the Litzmannstadt ghetto administration at the city savings bank to cover subsistence of "Jews incapable of working." The ghetto was to provide clothing; maintaining the strength to work was absolutely necessary.[55] This order meant that forced laborers in the Warthegau, unlike their counterparts in the Old Reich, no longer even received minimum wages for unskilled labor. The Warthegau labor-office-controlled system for renting out forced laborers used methods resembling those developed in parallel by the SS.

With its order, however, the Reichsstatthalter's labor department also transferred responsibility for maintaining productivity of the borrowed workers to the enterprises and agencies using them. Exploitation of the Jews to the point of total exhaustion had clearly exceeded the level tolerable to the labor administration, which was striving for cost-effective use of Jewish labor. As Jewish forced laborers had no official protection, neither private companies nor public builders felt responsible for them.[56] In spite of the order, the following months brought little change in the victims' situation. At the beginning of October 1942, Altburgund District Commissar in Schubin complained to the municipal administration of the Litzmannstadt ghetto that on June 9 the Hinterwalden camp that he ran received 100 Jews, 86 of whom were incapable of working from the outset. By mid-September, seven forced laborers had died. After a number of requests by the district commissar, the Gestapo had picked up the remaining Jews, who were completely incapable of working, on September 21. For that reason, the district commissar said, he would only pay the rental fee for the laborers capable of working. Referring to the June 1942 order, he requested clothing and footwear for his forced laborers.[57]

At the end of September 1942, the compulsory employees in the Litzmannstadt ghetto were working a twelve-hour day.[58] The head of the ghetto administration had lengthened the work week from fifty-four hours in the beginning to sixty and then to seventy-two hours.[59] Because of its importance for production, the Litzmannstadt ghetto was not closed down, as were so many other Polish ghettos at this point, but instead was declared an ss-controlled labor camp. The Jewish council thus lost its responsibilities, and from that point the Germans exercised direct control over the forced-labor in the ghetto.[60] At year's end, 73,782 people worked in over 90 ghetto factories and workshops, 85 percent of them for the German war economy.[61] In addition to the forced laborers inhabiting the ghetto, at this time 21,000 more forced laborers lived in camps and in other cities. Overall, at New Year's 1943, 95,112 Jewish men and women were performing forced labor in the Warthegau.[62]

Deportations for the purpose of murdering the ghetto inmates continued; the people remaining were mostly forced laborers. Himmler's new plan to relocate the ghetto to Lublin, thereby rendering the Warthegau *judenfrei*, failed.[63] In spring 1943, the ghetto held more forced laborers than ever, 80,000.[64] During the following months, small groups returned from outside deployments. For example, on July 1, fifty totally exhausted men arrived from Jędrzejów labor camp; some of them had to be sent immediately to the ghetto hospital. In August 1943, sixteen Jews in relatively good condition arrived from Klomna labor camp near Lask, where they had worked since 1942.[65] The conditions in the labor camps had not basically changed, despite the previous year's order by the labor administration. Most labor camp inmates suffered from a severe lack of food and clothing, regardless of whether the camps were run by municipal administrations, district administrations, or private enterprises.

In July 1943, Rudolf Lautrich, who operated an engineering and construction enterprise for hydraulic construction and water supply in Hohensalza, wrote to the Oberbürgermeister of Litzmannstadt (ghetto administration) that "the rags" of most of his Jewish forced laborers were "literally falling off their bodies." At his building site, Lautrich employed 211 men and 157 women. He reported to the ghetto administration that he had "succeeded with unrelenting harshness" in converting the men to "halfway decent" workers but that the women were another story. The businessman complained that last winter he had had to pay the "rental fee" for the Jews without actually being able to employ the forced laborers for construction. When the weather got warmer, the Hohensalza district administrator's office had taken most of the Jews away. The same thing had happened in July 1942: The Kreis construction administration had withdrawn thirty Jews who were not sent back until November. Lautrich asked the ghetto administration to officially allocate the Jews to him so that he could conserve his resources for construction measures that he was to undertake for the Reich water resources office in Hohensalza. However, the labor office was still responsible for labor assignments and clearly set other priorities: It had ordered seventeen of Lautrich's forced laborers back to the Litzmannstadt ghetto-labor camp in mid-June 1943.[66]

Forced labor and the last stage of mass murder, mid-1943–44

At the end of August 1943 the Posen Gestapo central office ordered that all municipal Jewish camps in Posen be liquidated. The forced laborers were deported, and the Posen city administration, including its main construction office, lost all of its Jewish forced laborers. In summer and fall 1943, the Security Police closed other labor camps, among them Wolsztyn camp in Posen district. Hundreds of inmates were taken to Auschwitz, and many of them were immediately murdered there.[67] In January 1944, after various new deportations, only 60,000 people lived in the Litzmannstadt ghetto. Of course, 78 percent of the ghetto inmates worked in companies and 17 percent in the ghetto administration; only 5 percent were classified as unemployed ghetto residents. The persecutors were at that point discussing a plan to transform the ghetto/labor camp into a regular concentration camp, the approach taken in a number of SS camps in other Polish areas. But after a long break, the killing facilities in Chelmno were reactivated.[68]

While the murder program intensified, neither local nor central employers wanted to give up their most important forced laborers. According to a March 1944 plan, 1,700 Jews were to be moved from the ghetto to labor camps, for example, to the Jewish camp of Hugo Schneider AG (HASAG), in Częstochowa,[69] today considered one of the worst companies employing forced laborers.[70] At the beginning of June 1944, Himmler personally ordered that the Litzmannstadt ghetto be closed – in other words, that all the inmates be murdered. For economic reasons, however, this order met with the resistance of other parts of the Nazi leadership. Reichsstatthalter Greiser wrote to Himmler on June 9, "The armaments inspection office has undertaken significant countermeasures in opposition to your order to clear the Litzmannstadt ghetto. On June 5, Reich Minister Speer requested figures from the duty officer of the armaments inspection office showing the number of persons employed in the ghetto's various production operations, their weekly work times, and the weekly production of the various branches, ostensibly so that the figures could be presented to the Führer."[71] Himmler still had his way; in June and July transports left the ghetto every three days; each carried 700 people to their deaths in Chelmno.[72] Complete liquidation of the Litzmannstadt ghetto followed, and the remaining inmates were deported to Auschwitz. Two thousand of the people were put in forced labor, and the others were murdered. In the ghetto itself, a horrifying number of people, 43,000, had died of hunger, disease, or debilitation between 1940 and 1944. Seven hundred to 880 Jews remained in Lodz to perform clean-up tasks.[73]

Summary

The comparatively long survival of the Litzmannstadt ghetto, which originally was meant only as a transit station, was primarily the result of the work important to the war performed by the inmates. The ghetto had transformed itself into a significant production factor and was able in that way to hold off liquidation until summer 1944. That was truly impressive because Lodz was in the Warthegau, which as an annex to the Reich was to be Germanized as quickly as possible. Not the ss, but the labor administration (and in the case of the ghettos, the municipal administrations) organized forced labor of the Jews in the Warthegau until the very end. Overall, the work and living conditions of the victims in the annexed Polish territories were much more brutal than in the Old Reich. In practice, social benefits were eliminated and wages reduced in 1941 without any central regulations to that effect. Finally, from mid-1942 on, the labor administration itself officially conducted a rental operation that placed Jews (mostly ghetto residents) with government agencies and private enterprises in the Warthegau; the system functioned in much the same manner as the parallel system introduced by the SS in the General Government at the same time. Because of 1939 plans to deport the Jews rapidly from the Warthegau, the labor administration accelerated use of forced labor here relatively late. Then, when in 1940 a significant labor pool was going to waste, mass transfers were used to remedy situations such as the need for Reich Autobahn construction in the Old Reich.

Notes

1 Quoted in Dieter Pohl, Von der *"Judenpolitik" zum Judenmord. Der Distrikt Lublin des Generalgouvernements 1939–1944* (Frankfurt am Main, Berlin, and Bern, 1993), 26.

2 *Der Prozeß gegen die Hauptkriegsverbrecher vor dem Internationalen Militärgerichtshof (IMT), Nürnberg 14. November 1945–1. Oktober 1946*, Vol. XXXI (Nuremberg, 1948), 231–232, Doc. PS- 2852, Protocol of the meeting on September 19, 1939; see Hans Safrian, *Die Eichmann-Männer* (Vienna and Zurich, 1993), 71. Pohl also reaches the conclusion on the basis of other documents that the decision was made on September 19; Pohl, *Judenpolitik*, 26. For the variants and the difficulties in implementing them – as well as the causal context for resettling ethnic Germans – see Götz Aly, *"Endlösung" – Völkerverschiebung und der Mord an den europäischen Juden* (Frankfurt am Main, 1995).

3 *Europa unterm Hakenkreuz. Die faschistische Okkupationspolitik in Polen (1939–1945)*, document selection and introduction by Werner Röhr with the assistance of Elke Heckert, et al. (Berlin, 1989), 119, Doc. No. 12, RSHA file note, September 27, 1939, regarding the September 21, 1939, meeting.

4 Ibid., 120–122, Doc. No. 13, Commander of the Security Police express letter, September 21, 1939; *Kennzeichnen J. Bilder, Dokumente, Berichte zur Geschichte der Verbrechen des Hitler-faschismus an den deutschen Juden 1933–1945*, edited by Helmut Eschwege (Berlin, 1981), 161–164; and *Eksterminacja Żydów na ziemiach polskich w okresie okupacji hitlerowskiej. Zbiór dokumentów*, edited by Tatiana Berenstein, et al. (Warsaw, 1957), Doc. No. 1, 21–25.

5 Quoted in Safrian, *Die Eichmann-Männer*, 72.

6 *Eksterminacja Żydów*, Doc. No. 2, 29, RFSS Himmler order, October 30, 1939.

7 *Eksterminacja Żydów*, Doc. No. 3, 30–32, HSSPF circular (Koppe), November 12, 1939; reproduced in *Herrschaftsalltag im Dritten Reich. Studien und Texte*, edited by Hans Mommsen and Susanne Willems (Düsseldorf, 1988), 456–457, Doc. No. 18. See also Aly, *Endlösung*, 59–71.

8 For the order to mark the Jews, see Gerald Reitlinger, *Die Endlösung. Hitlers Versuch der Ausrottung der Juden Europas 1939–1945*, 4th reworked and expanded edition (Berlin 1961), 52. For the November 13, 1939, prohibition on changing residence, see Aly, *Endlösung*, 69.

9 *Eksterminacja Żydów*, Doc. No. 30, 72.

10 Florian Freund, Bertrand Perz, and Karl Stuhlpfarrer, "Das Getto in Litzmannstadt (Lódz)," in *"Unser einziger Weg ist Arbeit". Das Getto in Lódz 1940–1944. Eine Ausstellung des Jüdischen Museums in Zusammenarbeit mit Yad Vashem u. a.*, edited by Hanno Loewy and Gerhard Schoenberner (Frankfurt am Main and Vienna, 1990), 17–31, here 18.

11 *Faschismus-Getto-Massenmord. Dokumentation über Ausrottung und Widerstand der Juden in Polen während des zweiten Weltkrieges* (Berlin [GDR], 1960), 199, Doc. No. 147, Letter to the Jewish rabbinate, October 13, 1939.

12 Freund, Perz, and Stuhlpfarrer, "Das Getto in Litzmannstadt," 17–18.

13 *Eksterminacja Żydów*, Doc. No. 32, 75.

14 Document reproduced in *Unser einziger Weg ist Arbeit*, 153–154.

15 Wolfgang Scheffler, "Das Getto Lódz in der nationalsozialistischen Judenpolitik," in *Unser einziger Weg ist Arbeit*, 12–16; Helge Grabitz and Wolfgang Scheffler, *Letzte Spuren. Ghetto Warschau. ss-Arbeitslager Trawniki. Aktion Erntefest. Fotos und Dokumente über Opfer des Endlösungswahns im Spiegel der historischen Ereignisse* (Berlin, 1988), 280–281; Freund, Perz, and Stuhlpfarrer, "Das Getto in Litzmannstadt," 19.

16 Czesław Madajczyk, *Die Okkupationspolitik Nazideutschlands in Polen 1939–1945* (Berlin [GDR], 1987), 156–157.

17 Madajczyk, *Okkupationspolitik*, 156–157; Freund, Perz, and Stuhlpfarrer, "Das Getto in Litzmannstadt," 20–21.

18 Christopher Browning, "Jewish Workers in Poland. Self-Maintenance, Exploitation, Destruction," in *Nazi Policy, Jewish Workers, German Killers* (Cambridge, New York, and Melbourne, 2000), 66.

19 Freund, Perz, and Stuhlpfarrer, "Das Getto in Litzmannstadt," 25.

20 Mentioned in the June 18, 1941, circular order of the district administrator of Kempen and the Litzmannstadt administrative district, reproduced in facsimile in Diemut Majer, *"Fremdvölkische" im Dritten Reich. Ein Beitrag zur nationalsozialistischen Rechtssetzung und Rechtspraxis in Verwaltung und Justiz unter besonderer Berücksichtigung der eingegliederten Ostgebiete und des Generalgouvernements* (Boppard am Rhein, 1981), appended illustrations (English translation published by Johns Hopkins University Press, 2003).

21 Raul Hilberg, *Die Vernichtung der europäischen Juden*, new and expanded edition of the translation into German of 1982 edition, Vol. 1 (Frankfurt am Main, 1990), 265.

22 Madajczyk, *Okkupationspolitik*, 259.

23 On February 4, 1941, Greiser offered Reich Labor Ministry 42,187 male and 30,936 female Jewish workers for the Old Reich; BA Berlin, R 3901 (former R 41) Reich Labor Ministry, No. 193, Fol. 98, March 7, 1941, note of Letzsch as an attachment to the March 14, 1941, decree of the Reich Labor Ministry.

24 Use of Jews was supposed to free up "persons of German blood." The "loyal supporters' leadership, main labor office" (*Gefolgschaftsführung Hauptarbeitseinsatz*), negotiated with the construction and camp service of the enterprise; BA Berlin, 80 Re 15 FC Hermann Göring Reichswerke, Film 44 263, Letter of March 5, 1941 (NI-4283); ibid., Meeting record, March 13, 1941 (NI-4285); see H. G. Adler, *Der verwaltete Mensch. Studien zur Deportation der Juden aus Deutschland* (Tübingen, 1974), 210–211.

25 BA Berlin, R 3901 (former R 41) Reich Labor Ministry, No. 193, Fol. 98, March 7, 1941, note of Letzsch as an attachment to the March 14, 1941, decree of the Reich Labor Ministry.

26 Ibid., Fols. 98 verso – 99 verso, Reich Labor Ministry express letter, March 14, 1941; Nordrheinwestfälisches Staatsarchiv (StA) Münster, Central Presidium (*Oberpräsidium*), No. 5138, Fols. 4 and verso, March 26, 1941, decree of the Rhineland regional labor office; or Paul Sauer (ed.), *Dokumente über die Verfolgung der jüdischen Bürger in Baden-Württemberg durch das nationalsozialistische Regime 1933–1943*, Part II (Stuttgart, 1966), 203–204, Doc. No. 421, March 25, 1941, decree of the southwestern German regional labor office. The Hessian regional labor office intended to use its laborers for improvements. The Hesse-Nassau German Labor Front informed its district administrations regarding the approval of a contingent "from Litzmannstadt" that was not in any case to be employed in the food industry; Hessisches Hauptstaatsarchiv (HHStA) Wiesbaden, Dep. 483, No. 10036, no folio numbers, Frankfurt am Main German Labor Front – Gau circular, March 27, 1941.
27 BA Berlin, R 3901 (former R 41) Reich Labor Ministry, No. 193, Fol. 64, Reich Labor Ministry, Department Va, Labor Utilization, to the East Prussian regional labor office, March 14, 1941.
28 Ibid., Reich Labor Ministry, Department Va, Labor Utilization, to the OKH in Berlin, March 14, 1941.
29 Fol. 64 verso, Reich Labor Ministry, Department Va, Labor Utilization, to the Silesian regional labor office, March 14, 1941; ibid., Fol. 64 verso, Reich Labor Ministry, Department Va, Labor Utilization, to the Brandenburg regional labor office, March 14, 1941.
30 Ibid., Fol. 72, OKW to the home transport department, May 20, 1941.
31 Ibid., Fol. 78 and verso, Note of the Reich Labor Ministry, Department Va, Labor Utilization, March 28, 1941.
32 Ibid., Fol. 78 verso – 79, Reich Labor Ministry, Department Va, Labor Utilization, to the Reich Transportation Ministry (Ministerial councillor Dobmeyer), March 28, 1941, with a handwritten addition.
33 Ibid., Fol. 94, Reich Labor Ministry, Department Va, Labor Utilization, to the East Prussian regional labor office, March 28, 1941.
34 Ibid., Fols. 84 and verso, President of the East Prussian regional labor office to the Reich Labor Ministry (Ministerial Councillor Dr. Richter), April 9, 1941.
35 Ibid., Fol. 97, Reich Labor Ministry express letter of April 7, 1941, rescinding the March 14, 1941, decree. See also Chapter 7.
36 Lucjan Dobroszycki (ed.), *The Chronicle of the Lodz Ghetto 1941–1944* (New Haven and London, 1984), 46, Entry of April 11, 1941.
37 Madajczyk, *Okkupationspolitik*, 370.
38 Quoted in Scheffler, "Das Getto Lódz," 13–14. See Browning, "Jewish Workers," 70.
39 Scheffler, "Das Getto Lódz," 14.
40 *Akten der Parteikanzlei der NSDAP*, Part III, Vol. 4, No. 044775–76, Reich Labor Ministry express letter of October 31, 1941, to Reich Governor in Posen, with an invitation to the November 28, 1941, meeting.
41 Ibid., No. 044778–79, Reich Justice Ministry note regarding the November 28, 1941, meeting; see an excerpt in Kurt Pätzold (ed.), *Verfolgung, Vertreibung, Vernichtung. Dokumente des faschistischen Antisemitismus 1933–1942* (Leipzig, 1983), 322, Doc. No. 300.
42 "Die Lage des Arbeitseinsatzes im Reichsgau Wartheland im Monat Oktober 1941 (The Status of Forced Labor in Reich Gau Wartheland for October 1941)," in "Der Arbeitseinsatz im Reichs-Gau Wartheland, Mitteilungsblatt der Abteilung Arbeit beim Reichsstatthalter in Posen, Fachgebiet Landesarbeitsamt, Posen 1941–42," No. 1, 1 verso to 3 verso.
43 Statistics on managing forced labor by workers for October 1941, in "Der Arbeitseinsatz im Reichs-Gau Wartheland," No. 1, Appendix.

44 Statistics of the Reich Labor Ministry on managing forced labor for November 1941, in "Der Arbeitseinsatz im Reichs-Gau Wartheland," No. 2, Appendix; Statistics of the Reich Labor Ministry on managing forced labor for December 1941, in "Der Arbeitseinsatz im Reichs-Gau Wartheland," No. 3, Appendix.

45 Statistics of the Reich Labor Ministry on managing forced labor for December 1941, in "Der Arbeitseinsatz im Reichs-Gau Wartheland," No. 3, Appendix.

46 Statistics of the Reich Labor Ministry on managing forced labor by labor office for October 1941–May 1942, in "Der Arbeitseinsatz im Reichs-Gau Wartheland," Nos. 1–8, Appendix.

47 Statistics of the Reich Labor Ministry on managing forced labor by labor office for May 1942, in "Der Arbeitseinsatz im Reichs-Gau Wartheland," No. 8, Appendix.

48 *Europa unterm Hakenkreuz: Polen*, 217, Doc. No. 104, Hans Biebow report, March 4, 1942, also reproduced in *Unser einziger Weg ist Arbeit*, 9.

49 *Europa unterm Hakenkreuz: Polen*, 217, Doc. No. 111, Stapo situation report of June 9, 1942.

50 *Unser einziger Weg ist Arbeit*, 200.

51 Madajczyk, *Okkupationspolitik*, 230.

52 Dobroszycki (ed.), *The Chronicle of the Lodz Ghetto*, 195 and 199, Entries of June 2 and 4, 1942.

53 *Faschismus-Getto-Massenmord*, 292.

54 Gestapo situation report of July 27, 1942, in *Unser einziger Weg ist Arbeit*, 87.

55 *Dokumenty i Materialy*, Vol. 1: *Obozy*, edited by Nachman Blumental (Lodz, 1946), 302–303, "Order on Employment of Jewish Workers in the Wartheland Reich Gau," June 26, 1942.

56 See *Dokumenty i Materialy*, Vol. 1, 304–305, Reich Governor, labor department, to the Posen Oberbürgermeister, main construction office, December 21, 1942.

57 *Dokumenty i Materialy*, Vol. 1, 314 and 316, Subdistrict commissar for Altburgund – Rural to the Oberbürgermeister (ghetto administration) of Litzmannstadt, December 5, 10, and 19, 1942.

58 Dobroszycki (ed.), *The Chronicle of the Lodz Ghetto*, 265, Entry of September 30, 1942.

59 Browning, "Jewish Workers," 70.

60 Madajczyk, *Okkupationspolitik*, 158; Dobroszycki (ed.), *The Chronicle of the Lodz Ghetto*, 298, Entry of December 8, 1942.

61 Freund, Perz, and Stuhlpfarrer, "Das Getto in Litzmannstadt," 25.

62 Leo Baeck Institute Archive (LBIA) New York, Microfilms, Wiener Library, 500 Series, No. 526, Inspector for statistics with the RFSS, January 1, 1943 (Korherr Report), 17.

63 Freund, Perz, and Stuhlpfarrer, "Das Getto in Litzmannstadt," 29–30.

64 Browning, "Jewish Workers," 70.

65 Dobroszycki (ed.), *The Chronicle of the Lodz Ghetto*, 352 and 373, Entries of August 1, 7, and 21, 1943.

66 *Dokumenty i Materialy*, Vol. 1, 310–313, Lautrich to the Oberbürgermeister (ghetto administration) of Litzmannstadt, on July 13 and 17, 1943.

67 *Dokumenty i Materialy*, Vol. 1, 319, Posen Oberbürgermeister, main construction office, to the Oberbürgermeister (ghetto administration) of Litzmannstadt, August 31, 1943; and Danuta Czech, *Kalendarium der Ereignisse im Konzentrationslager Auschwitz-Birkenau 1939–1945* (Reinbek near Hamburg, 1989), 513, 585, and 629.

68 Madajczyk, *Okkupationspolitik*, 258; Freund, Perz, and Stuhlpfarrer, "Das Getto in Litzmannstadt," 31; Scheffler, "Das Getto Lódz," 16.

69 Dobroszycki (ed.), *The Chronicle of the Lodz Ghetto*, 466–469, entries of March 4 and 6, 1944.

70 For details, see Felicja Karay, *Death Comes in Yellow. Skarzysko-Kamienna Slave Labor Camp* (Amsterdam, 1996).
71 *Europa unterm Hakenkreuz: Polen*, 300, Doc. No. 179, Greiser to Himmler, June 9, 1944.
72 Dobroszycki (ed.), *The Chronicle of the Lodz Ghetto*, 481–527.
73 Scheffler, "Das Getto Lódz," 16; Freund, Perz, and Stuhlpfarrer, "Das Getto in Litzmannstadt," 31; Czech, *Kalendarium*, 850–851.

5

THE HOLOCAUST AND THE CONCENTRATION CAMPS

Dieter Pohl

For many years after World War II it was assumed that the Holocaust and the Nazi concentration camps were synonymous. This had to do with the fact that the first encounter of especially Western Allied soldiers with the atrocities of National Socialist Germany was when they liberated the camps, where many of the victims they encountered were indeed Jewish. The main killing sites, however, were elsewhere, in territories mostly liberated by the Red Army. But those were far less accessible to Western observers, whereas the Soviet Union was already in the process of denying the specificity of the Jewish genocide.

The association between the concentration camps and the Holocaust made for a great deal of confusion and obfuscation. One example was the influential 1955 film by Alain Resnais, Night and Fog, where no distinction was made between the concentration camps, which for much of the war had little to do with the "final solution," and the extermination camps, where millions of Jews were gassed. The film also made little distinction between people who had been incarcerated in the camps because they had resisted German rule and occupation, and those persecuted and murdered for "biological" or "social" reasons, such as Jews, Roma, and the handicapped. From this perspective, which was already present in part also in the Nuremberg Tribunal of 1945, the misunderstanding of the function of the concentration camps in Nazi Germany played a significant role in obscuring the nature of the Holocaust.

As Dieter Pohl points out in this chapter, prior to 1942 Jews made up a significant proportion of the concentration camp population only in the wake of the November 1938 Kristallnacht pogrom, during which tens of thousands of Jews were incarcerated, about a thousand were murdered, but the majority were released on condition that they leave Germany. Indeed, until 1941, the official policy of the Third Reich was to force the Jews out of German-controlled areas rather than to murder them, although many thousands fell victim to German policies following the invasion of Poland in 1939. The concentration camps were largely used for other categories of people, such as political opponents, homosexuals, and the "work-shy." The rise in the number of Jewish inmates was related to Nazi extermination policies initiated in 1941, first against those unfit for work and then against Soviet prisoners of war identified as Jews.

Yet most of the Jews murdered by the Nazis between the invasion of the USSR in June 1941 and spring 1942 were killed by the Einsatzgruppen and their assistants, largely in mass shootings that took the lives of well over a million men, women, and children. Several more hundreds of thousands died in the ghettos. This was followed by a period in which the "Aktion Reinhardt" extermination camps were used to annihilate the remaining populations in the ghettos and the surrounding countryside, as well as for populations deported from other parts of Europe, altogether about 1.5 million Jews. Finally the Majdanek and Auschwitz camps combined the role of extermination and concentration camps, selecting between those who were killed outright and those who were used for labor, even though the latter were mostly worked to death. Over a million Jews were murdered in Auschwitz-Birkenau alone.

Hence the concentration camp system and the Holocaust had little connection until much of the Jewish population of Europe had already been annihilated. Again, this had a great deal to do with Germany's need for labor, especially in 1943, when forced labor camps were transformed into concentration camps, and new camps were constructed for the purpose of employing Jews in the war industry. Finally, as the Soviets advanced to the west, surviving Jews were taken on horrendous death marches to concentration camps in Germany and Austria, where vast numbers of them died of famine and epidemics as the entire German camp system disintegrated. Throughout this time Jews were invariably treated worse in the camps than other inmates, and consequently had a much higher death toll. The false impression that the concentration camps played a major part in the Holocaust stems from the reality that by the last months of the war most of the surviving Jews still under German rule (with the exception of Budapest) were incarcerated in camps, where well over a million Jews perished, out of a total of close to 6 million victims overall. That so many Jews died in the concentration camps was therefore the result of Germany's labor needs – and thus a temporary concession to the ideological imperative of the "final solution" – and of Germany's evacuation of the eastern territories it had occupied, where most of the Jews had lived and were murdered either in open-air shootings close to their homes or in extermination camps constructed for this purpose.

Prior to 1942, the Nazi concentration camps were much less important for the persecution and murder of European Jewry than had been assumed for decades after the war. Research during the last 25 years has shown that less than half of the victims of the Holocaust were killed in camps; and within this group approximately 1.2 million men, women and children were murdered in concentration camps properly speaking, i.e. those camps subsumed under the Inspection of the Concentration Camps (IKL) and later the SS Business and Administration Main Office (WVHA). The reasons for this lay both in the course of anti-Jewish policy and in the comparatively late expansion of the concentration camps into the massive system they eventually became, which did not begin until the end of 1942.[1]

For a long time the historiography on the subject developed along two separate paths, with camp history on the one side and Holocaust history on the other. Only during the 1990s did it become commonly recognized that Jews were a major element in concentration camp history from 1943 on. Recently the history of Jews in several of the major camps like Gross Rosen, Ravensbrück or Stutthof has been investigated as a separate subject.[2] Current projects for encyclopaedias of the camps enable the historian to trace the history of each satellite camp, where Jews in particular were forced to work.[3] And there is now a growing body of literature on the death marches of 1944/5, which constitute a major part of both concentration camp history and the Holocaust.[4]

Jews in concentration camps, 1933–1940

Jews were among the first victims of Nazi terror when the new regime took over at the beginning of 1933. But the initial wave of terror was not mainly directed against Jews, but predominantly against political opponents of Nazi rule, especially Communists and Social Democrats. It is estimated that in 1933 almost 100,000 persons were imprisoned for some time, almost half of them in the newly established camps, the others in improvised detention centres. Only a tiny minority among them was Jewish, as Jews were usually arrested only if they happened to be prominent political or cultural figures.

In 1934/5 the number of camps and prisoners declined significantly. Nevertheless, Jews continued to constitute part of the prisoner population. Most of them had been criminalized, for example by the new Nuremberg laws which constructed the offence of 'race defilement'. Jewish prisoners ended up in different concentration camps: between 1937 and early 1938, for example, Jewish men were almost exclusively sent to Dachau concentration camp, and a total of 2,500 to 3,000 Jewish prisoners were taken here. Jewish women were deported to the new camp in Ravensbrück when it was opened in 1939; a handful had previously been interned in the women's camps in Moringen and then Lichtenburg.

New prisoners arrived in the late 1930s. The annexations of Austria and the Sudetenland (1938) and Bohemia/Moravia (1939) were accompanied by mass arrests of suspected enemies of the Reich; among them were hundreds of Jews, mostly individuals associated with left wing parties. At the same time, Jews were also hit hard by the new socio-biological strategy of the police. Among the thousands of men arrested as 'asocials' during the wave of arrests in Germany in June 1938 ('Action Workshy Reich'), almost 20 per cent (2,500 men) were of Jewish origin, most of them unemployed or persons with a criminal record; they were sent to the new Buchenwald camp, where they were isolated and treated in an especially inhumane way. During 1938, the Star of David badge was introduced as the marker for Jewish prisoners, in most cases combined with other categories such as 'political', 'asocial' and so on. Jewish prisoners were concentrated in specific huts, which were called the 'Jew Block' (Judenblock) in Dachau and 'Jew Barrack' (Judenbaracke) in Sachsenhausen.[5]

In November 1938, Jews became concentration camp inmates on an unexpected and unprecedented scale. Almost 28,000 Jewish men were arrested and deported to the Buchenwald, Dachau and Sachsenhausen camps. The main purpose of this mass terror was to force Jews to emigrate and hand over most of their belongings to the Reich. Indeed, the great majority of those arrested had been released again by spring 1939 and emigrated. But during the weeks of their imprisonment, Jewish prisoners were treated with outrageous cruelty. They were sent to the worst labour companies and became victims of sadistic games of the SS. Also, the camps had not been prepared for the arrival of so many new prisoners: in Buchenwald 10,000 men were crammed into a special zone without proper housing or rations. An estimated 1,000 Jewish men did not survive their imprisonment in the three camps.[6]

The war years, 1939–1942

Following the German attack on Poland in September 1939, the Gestapo arrested all remaining Jewish men with (former) Polish citizenship living in the Reich. They were either deported to the newly occupied territories or to concentration camps (especially to Buchenwald). Most of them died after a few weeks; some survivors were released by mid-1940.[7] After this date, Jews played only a minor role as inmates of German concentration camps until 1942. For example, around 900 Jews were held at Buchenwald, either in protective custody or as so-called 'asocials'; around 1,600 Jews were deported to Mauthausen in 1941; and, from June 1940, some criminal and political Jewish suspects were deported to the new Auschwitz camp.[8]

Although there was no stated policy of annihilating Jews before autumn 1941, most Jewish inmates during the early war years perished. They were treated as the lowest group in the prisoner hierarchy and were often forced into the worst labour commandos. By April 1941 a new extermination programme was introduced for concentration camp inmates. During the so-called 'Action 14f13', teams of German physicians visited the camps and selected prisoners for transfer to the killing institutions of the Nazi 'euthanasia' programme. The overall aim of these crimes was to kill prisoners considered unfit for work. Jewish inmates were specifically targeted, as they were often in very bad physical shape and were considered as 'undesirable' both by the concentration camp staff and the '14f13' medical experts. Between April 1941 and April 1942 at least ten concentration camps were affected by 'Action 14f13' and at least 10,000 prisoners, probably many more, were deported to the asylum killing-centres at Bernburg, Sonnenstein and Hartheim and murdered. Especially in Buchenwald and Ravensbrück, Jewish inmates constituted a majority of the victims.[9]

New groups of Jewish prisoners entered the concentration camp system from July 1941. During the German military campaign against the Soviet Union, all Jews among captured Red Army soldiers were separated from the other POWs; they were either shot on the spot or sent to isolated zones within the POW camps. From some camps within the Reich, selected POWs – notably Red Army political functionaries, but also Jews – were taken to concentration camps. The first groups were probably transferred in July 1941, from Lamsdorf (Silesia) to Auschwitz.[10] By July/August 1941 it was decided that groups of selected 'undesirable' Soviet POWs were to be transferred to the concentration camps for immediate killing. Thus from September 1941, these men and – to a limited extent – women were killed inside the camps or at nearby execution sites like Dachau-Hebertshausen. It is currently unknown how many Jews were among the (at least) 34,000 victims. Since registration cards for all Soviet POWs in the main German prison of war camps have turned up in Moscow archives during the 1990s, it would now be possible to reconstruct their fate.[11] Overall, very few of the Soviet Jewish POWs who came into the concentration camps survived the war.

The German attack on the Soviet Union was accompanied by the beginning of the systematic murder of Jews, starting on 24 June 1941 in Lithuania. Though historians still debate the process of decision-making for the 'Final Solution', the wholesale murder of European Jewry, there is growing consensus that important steps were taken in September/October 1941. But there is no convincing evidence that the concentration camp system was affected before 1942. In fact, the military crisis of the German army near Moscow and the labour shortages within the Reich at the turn of the year shifted the focus slightly away from mass extermination towards the use of Jewish forced labourers. The main reason for this has to be seen in the utopian 'Peacetime Construction Programme' (Friedenbauprogramm) of the SS, a giant construction scheme for German settlements in the East. Initially, it was envisaged that Soviet POWs would be used as forced labourers for the building programme; but half of the POWs captured in 1941 were dead by early 1942 as a result of starvation, exposure and abuse. Moreover, far fewer Soviet POWs than expected were transferred from the control of the Wehrmacht to that of the SS, and the majority of those deported to the camps were considered unfit for work.

In place of Soviet POWs, the WVHA decided in January 1942 to move Jews from the first deportation wave from central Europe, which had started in October 1941, to the concentration camps. On 25 January 1942 Himmler ordered Richard

Glücks, the head of the concentration camp system, to send 100,000 Jewish men and 50,000 Jewish women to the camps within the following four weeks. This would have tripled the number of concentration camp inmates and was never realized. But in April 1942, Himmler, in a general order, exempted all able-bodied Jews, predominantly men between the ages of 16 and 35, from being murdered and proposed their transfer to concentration camps.[12]

The number of Jews deported to concentration camps had been on the rise since autumn 1941. The construction of the new Majdanek camp near Lublin in particular was mostly undertaken by Jewish labourers from the region.[13] The first SS transports of Jews as part of the 'Final Solution' took place in March 1942. The Reich leadership had negotiated with the Slovak government the deportation of most Slovakian Jews to Poland. While the German negotiators offered to take over 20,000 young and able Jewish men, the Slovak authorities soon pressed for the deportation of entire Jewish families. Between late March and October 1942, around 57,000 Jews were deported, 17,000 to Auschwitz and 40,000 to the Lublin district, of whom 7,000 came to the Majdanek camp. This was by far the largest group of Jews inside the camps since 1938. In addition, the German military administration of Paris organized the deportation of 1,100 Jews from Compiègne to Auschwitz, officially as a reprisal for attacks of the French resistance. Further groups of Polish Jews, all in all about 35,000 persons, were transferred to Auschwitz between March and August 1942 from the forced labour camps of 'Organization Schmelt' (an SS organization of Jewish forced labour in the Katowice area, used for highway construction).[14] Before July 1942 (in Auschwitz) and September 1942 (in Majdanek), Jewish prisoners transported to these two camps were not normally murdered upon arrival, but were registered into the camp as prisoners. But most of them died within weeks as a result of malnourishment and extremely harsh treatment.[15]

Mass murder outside the concentration camp system

The major sites of mass murder in 1942 were the killing fields in the occupied territories of Eastern Poland and the Soviet Union and the extermination camps of 'Action Reinhardt', Bełżec, Sobibór, and Treblinka, which had been established by the regional SS and Police Leader in Lublin, Odilo Globocnik. A further extermination camp existed in Kulmhof (Chełmno) in the Warthegau (part of occupied Poland incorporated into the German Reich), where gas vans were used to murder Jews. Unlike the later practice in Auschwitz and Majdanek, there was almost no selection of Jews in any of these extermination camps. The actual separation of workers and others took place prior to the deportations, during the so-called 'ghetto clearances'.

The ghettos themselves became a major site of the Holocaust. They had been installed in several waves in Poland, especially in 1940 and early 1941, and then from autumn 1941 also in the Baltic States, eastern Poland and in several locations within the occupied Soviet territory. Though living conditions in the ghettos were generally bad, they varied significantly. In the winter of 1940/41, for example, the large ghettos in Łódź and Warsaw became the scene of mass death through starvation and epidemics. In the ghettos established from autumn 1941 onwards, the situation was different, since their establishment was already accompanied by mass murder, especially of poor and physically weak Jews. The ghettos had only minor connections to the concentration camps, since most of them were located in Eastern Europe, far away from the camps. Only the Jewish inhabitants in the cities of Oświęcim and Lublin were affected by the camps early on.

The three extermination camps of Action Reinhardt operated quite differently from the concentration camps. They were not subordinate to the IKL, but had been established by the regional SS and Police leaders in the Lublin and Warsaw districts. And the respective camp sites were comparatively small, with rather more improvised installations. Only around 25 to 30 German functionaries ran each camp, supported by 100–150 so-called 'Trawniki men' (released former Soviet POWs trained in the Trawniki forced labour camp). No more than a hundred Jews were kept alive at any one time to serve as forced labourers in the camp; this means that 99 per cent of the victims were murdered within hours after their arrival, in gas chambers using exhaust fumes. Also, Action Reinhardt extermination camps were shut down comparatively early, starting with Bełżec in December 1942; all corpses of the victims who had been killed by gas earlier on and buried thereafter were disinterred and burnt. In autumn 1943, the Treblinka and Sobibór camps were also closed down and all traces eradicated. In all, approximately 1.5 million Jews were killed in these three camps; only about 150 prisoners survived the war.[16] In the extermination camp at Kulmhof (Chełmno), more than 152,000 Jews from the Warthegau and the Łódź ghetto were killed in a similar fashion.[17]

During the liquidation of most ghettos in Poland in summer and autumn 1942, forced labour camps were established in or near these ghettos, sometimes referred to as 'work ghettos' (*Arbeitsghettos*). Only Jewish workers employed by German firms (often with their families) were allowed to stay in these labour camps, under appalling living conditions; all other Jews from the liquidated ghettos were deported to extermination camps. Germany's allies also established a system of work camps for Jews, notably in Slovakia, Hungary and Yugoslavia. During the second half of 1942, more Jews were confined in these work camps and ghettos than in concentration camps. Most of the forced labour camps in Poland were closed between the end of 1942 and July 1943, following either mass executions or deportations of inmates to extermination camps.[18]

Auschwitz as a centre of the Holocaust from mid-1942

Before July 1942, the concentration camps played no decisive role within the 'Final Solution'. Nevertheless, some mass killings of Jews already took place before then. At the end of the first deportations of the Lublin Jews to Bełżec, as part of Action Reinhardt, some 2,000–3,000 Jews from the city of Lublin were brought to Majdanek on 20 April 1942; with the exception of some selected Jewish labourers, all were shot in the vicinity of the camp.[19] Despite its location in Lublin, Majdanek concentration camp was only indirectly connected to Action Reinhardt (for example, it was included in the statistics of the victims).[20]

Auschwitz and Majdanek emerged as both concentration and extermination camps in 1942. They were integrated into the deportation programme of the Reich Security Main Office (RSHA), which masterminded the 'Final Solution' in all countries, with the exception of the Soviet Union and most of Poland. The Jewish department (*Judenreferat*) in the RSHA organized the deportations, together with the German railway administration (*Reichsbahn*), while the WVHA arranged for their reception in Auschwitz and Majdanek. In contrast to other transports to the camps (predominantly of non-Jews), these deportations were known as RSHA-transports.[21] Mass deportations also changed the prisoner population inside the camps. From mid-1942 onwards, Jews already constituted half of the prisoners in Auschwitz, and at the end of the year a little less; but from 1943 they were in the majority, and ultimately in August 1944 their proportion reached 70 per cent.[22] Thus, unlike in other concentration camps, Jews were represented in all prisoner functionary positions of the Birkenau camp.

Auschwitz became *the* major extermination camp from 1943. But when, exactly, did the camp first become involved in the systematic murder of Jews? This is still an open question among historians. It is clear that mass murder in Auschwitz began on a large scale in August/September 1941, when the toxin Zyklon B was used for the first time to kill Soviet POWs and other non-Jewish inmates. There are some indications that the crematorium for the planned Birkenau sub-camp was conceived with a gas chamber already in October 1941.[23] But the construction of Birkenau was officially commissioned for the imprisonment of more Soviet POWs: no mass transports of Jews to Auschwitz were envisaged at that time.

The mass murder of Jews in Birkenau probably began during the construction of the camp in May 1942. A former farmhouse outside the actual camp area, designated as 'Bunker 1', was sealed off and used as gas chamber. Apparently the first victims came from Upper Silesia. From June/July 1942 on, a second such installation, 'Bunker 2', was also used for the killings.[24] While transports from Upper Silesia and Slovakia were already arriving at Auschwitz in early summer, the general transportation programme from western Europe did not start until 19 July 1942. Now all Jews who arrived by train at the so-called 'old ramp' near Birkenau camp had to undergo selections by the SS camp physicians. Around 20 per cent of the victims were directed to the camp as prisoners; all others were led to the bunkers and killed with Zyklon B. For a limited period, from 26 August to 9 November 1942, the deportation trains stopped before Auschwitz, in Kozle, where Jewish workers were taken away for use by Organisation Schmelt.[25]

It is not quite clear at what stage planning for the big crematoria in Auschwitz-Birkenau (nos. II–V) first included gas chambers. At the latest they were included in the detailed plans of August 1942. It finally took until March 1943 to complete the construction of Crematoria II and IV including their gas chambers, while Crematoria V and III were completed in April and June respectively.[26]

In October 1942, Himmler stepped up the murder of Jews from Germany: all Jewish inmates of concentration camps in Germany and Austria were to be deported to Auschwitz and Majdanek (in the end, all of them came to Auschwitz). Immediately afterwards, the first deportations from the cities of the Reich direct to Auschwitz began. Prior to that, German and Austrian Jews had primarily been deported to the Reichskommissariat Ostland, to Łódź or to the Lublin region with its extermination camps.[27] At first, it was mostly Jews from Berlin, the capital of the Reich, who were deported, but from spring 1943 there were also transports from other German cities.

Almost simultaneously, the deportations of Jews from the Theresienstadt ghetto to Auschwitz started. The RSHA had installed a ghetto in Theresienstadt in Bohemia for Bohemian and older German and Austrian Jews. Since this ghetto served as a camouflage operation to deceive international public opinion, the Jews deported from there to Auschwitz were not immediately killed upon arrival. In autumn 1943, a 'family camp' was installed in Birkenau camp, where all those arriving from Theresienstadt – men, women and children – had to live. They were murdered six months later, in March 1944. The same gap of six months between arrival in Auschwitz and murder apparently also applied to other inmates from Theresienstadt.[28] One of the last national groups deported to Auschwitz came from Greece, as the majority of the Greek Jews under German occupation were deported between March and May 1944, most of them to Auschwitz.[29]

Like all other concentration camps, Auschwitz developed a system of satellite camps – especially in Upper Silesia – from late 1942 onwards. But the Auschwitz satellite camps were different: in contrast to other such camps, the majority of prisoners here (from 1943) were Jewish. Among the biggest of these satellite camps were Blechhammer, Jawischowitz and Neu-Dachs (Jaworzno); some were taken over from Organisation Schmelt. But the most important was the IG Farben plant, which was built in nearby Monowice from March 1941 by predominantly Polish Auschwitz prisoners. From October 1942, a special subdivision of the main camp was established near the construction site, finally named 'Auschwitz III Monowitz' with 11,000 mainly Jewish male prisoners. The other Auschwitz satellite camps were also subordinated to the administration of Auschwitz III. Working conditions in Monowitz were extremely harsh. The camp SS periodically selected weak prisoners and sent them to Birkenau, where they were murdered in the gas chambers. According to existing evidence, more than 7,000 inmates were sent from Monowitz to Birkenau; estimates of the total number of prisoners killed reach 20,000–25,000.[30]

Majdanek was the second concentration camp which, like Auschwitz, simultaneously functioned as an extermination camp. In August 1942 a gas chamber was installed and from October that year Jews arriving in transports were systematically murdered with Zyklon B. Most of these Jews had been deported from the Bialystok area in north-eastern Poland, but from early 1943 transports also arrived from the Warsaw ghetto.[31] New research has established that approximately 59,000 Jews were murdered at Majdanek, making up the majority of all inmates killed in the camp.[32]

New concentration camps for Jews: 1943

By mid-1943, Himmler considered the 'Final Solution' almost complete, as most of the European Jews under German rule had been killed. Nevertheless, due to the unfavourable course of the war since early 1943 and the growing demands on the workforce, the Germans retained a wide range of forced labour camps for Jews as well as one ghetto, in Łódź. Most of the remaining labour camps were situated in central Poland, especially in some of the more industrialized areas. These camps were quite different from concentration camps – they were much smaller, far less organized and generally subordinated to regional SS leaders – and they had almost no connections to the concentration camp system: even the forced labour camps in the Lublin area remained isolated from Majdanek until 1943.

In September/October 1943 Himmler decided to abandon those labour camps located in the more distant eastern regions and to have their inmates killed. During the so-called 'Action Harvest Festival' (*Aktion Erntefest*), 42,000 Jewish forced labourers in the Lublin area where killed within two days (3 and 4 November 1943), including some 8,000 Jewish prisoners from the city of Lublin. The latter were led to the Majdanek camp, where trenches had been prepared, and shot. Jews from the Lwow-Janowska labour camp met the same fate two weeks later.[33] Following these massacres, which killed all Jewish prisoners, most labour camps were transferred to the concentration camp system, Płaszów as an independent camp, and most of the others as sub-camps of Majdanek.

In addition to transforming some labour camps into concentration camps, Himmler also set up additional concentration camps in the nearer regions of Eastern Europe specifically for Jews. Plans to establish further concentration camps had existed since 1942, but they had initially been suspended. It was only during the dissolution of the last major ghettos in spring/summer 1943 that new camps were established in order to imprison the remaining Jewish forced labourers.

The concentration camp in Warsaw represents an exceptional case. In February 1943 Himmler had ordered the establishment of the camp to force some of the local Jews to help with the demolition of the abandoned ghetto after it was cleared. But this plan was thwarted: the Germans faced unexpected and fierce Jewish resistance during the Warsaw ghetto uprising in April 1943. The uprising was brutally put down and the survivors were deported to labour camps in the Lublin region (as planned), sent to Treblinka, or killed on the spot. When the Warsaw camp was finally opened in July 1943, two months after the crushing of the ghetto uprising, its Jewish inmates did not come from Warsaw, but from concentration camps located all over the occupied countries. In all, almost 10,000 Jews were imprisoned in the Warsaw concentration camp. In May 1944, with the Red Army moving closer and prisoner deportations to other concentration camps already underway, the camp was subordinated as a satellite camp to Majdanek. The last remaining 350 prisoners were liberated in August 1944 during the Warsaw Uprising.[34]

In the context of the dissolution of the Warsaw ghetto, Himmler also ordered the liquidation of the last ghettos in the Baltic States and in Minsk. Those inmates not murdered during the ghetto liquidations were to be transported to new concentration camps. In March 1943 the SS started to establish a new camp in the Riga suburb of Kaiserwald (Mezaparks). In August and September 1943 Jewish forced labourers from Riga and Vilnius were deported to this camp. Most of them were Jews from the Reich or the Protektorat, who had been deported to Riga in 1941/42, but they also included Latvian and Hungarian Jews. Including the numerous satellite camps, a total of 16,000 to 19,000 inmates had been held at Riga-Kaiserwald. Several thousands were killed in the camp; the majority were later evacuated to Stutthof.[35]

The camp in Kaunas had also been in planning since 1942, but was officially established only in September 1943. More than 10,000 Jews from the Kaunas ghetto, including children, were brought there. The Kaunas camp had other exceptional features: it was not subordinate to the WVHA, but to its regional branch in Riga (the SS-Wirtschafter Ostland), and it took over some structures of the internal ghetto administration. Nearly all the inmates were either killed or evacuated westwards in July 1944.[36]

Mostly out of economic necessity, the SS also set up new concentration camps in Estonia in 1943, for the purpose of extracting oil shale. The main camp at Vaivara was officially set up in September 1943; most of its inmates came from the Vilnius and Kaunas ghettos. Together with the several satellite camps, about 9,000 prisoners were registered in total. Evacuation already started in February 1944, with prisoners either taken to Stutthof or to satellite camps of Natzweiler in south-west Germany. The last prisoners were shot in September 1944, only days before the Red Army liberated the area.[37]

Among the concentration camps established exclusively for Jews was Bergen-Belsen. Its origins can be traced to the efforts of both the Allied and German governments to exchange prisoners of both sides. As the Nazi leadership was interested in liberating Germans interned in Palestine, it was willing to exchange them against Jews with relatives in Palestine and other countries. Thus, in April 1943, the SS took over a part of the POW camp in Bergen-Belsen and established a 'residence camp' (Aufenthaltslager) for ostensible Jewish exchange prisoners, who lived under much better circumstances than Jews in other camps. Yet most of the exchange projects ultimately failed, and from March 1944 onwards, Bergen-Belsen turned more and more into a reception camp for evacuated prisoners – both Jewish and non-Jewish – from the East. Living conditions deteriorated drastically, especially after the former Auschwitz commandant Josef Kramer took over Bergen-Belsen.[38]

Most of the new camps for Jews established in 1943 were designed to exploit the last surviving Jewish labourers east of the Reich. The SS leadership now sought to concentrate all imprisonment under its WVHA structure in order to pursue its own economic interests, reducing the influence of other agencies and regional SS leaders.

The Jews from greater hungary in the concentration camps

Most Jews arrived in the concentration camp system in 1944, when the majority of Jews under German rule in Europe had already been killed. The greater proportion of them came from Hungary, after the German takeover. The German occupation of Hungary had come unexpectedly. Hitler had always urged the regent Miklos Horthy to hand over the Hungarian Jews to the Germans, but Horthy refused to do so until 1944. When the Germans occupied Hungary in March 1944, in response to the Horthy government's attempt to initiate peace negotiations with the Allies, an RSHA team under Adolf Eichmann, with significant assistance from the Hungarian administration and police, organized the ghettoization and deportation of Jews within a few weeks.[39]

Between 15 May and 6 July 1944 almost 438,000 Jews were deported from Greater Hungary to Auschwitz. Most of them did not come from Trianon Hungary (i.e. Hungary in its 1919 borders) but from the territories annexed by Hungary in 1938/40 (Carpathian Ukraine and northern Transylvania). During the last phase, Jews from Trianon Hungary and even from some parts of Budapest were also deported, before Horthy put a stop to this policy on 6 July. The German occupiers aimed at both murdering and exploiting the local Jews, with Hitler suggesting that more than 100,000 Hungarian Jews should be sent to the German armament industry. In Auschwitz, around 25,000 Hungarian Jews were registered as prisoners, while more than 80,000 were kept in the camp for only one or two weeks and then sent to camps all over occupied Europe, from Belgium to Estonia. But most of the Hungarian Jews arriving in Auschwitz were immediately murdered. In a period of just seven weeks, some 320,000 Hungarian Jews were killed. The camp had to be reorganized, and the former commandant Höß returned from Berlin to supervise the killings, the biggest murder operation in his career.

Another 78,000 Hungarian Jews, predominantly women, were force-marched from Budapest to Austria, were they were either forced to build fortifications (the *Südostwall*) or to proceed to concentration camps in Austria and southern Germany (such as the Kaufering and Mühldorf branches of the Dachau camp).[40] The main purpose of these deportations was to support armaments production for the German air force within the Reich: Jewish men were supposed to build underground installations and Jewish women were supposed to work there.

The last large group of Jews deported to Auschwitz came from the only ghetto which still existed in Poland, Łódź. Here, the local Nazi administration and the Jewish Council had managed to thwart attempts to exterminate all the ghetto inmates in 1943. But after the Red Army summer offensive and advance in 1944, the ghetto was finally liquidated. Between 15 August and 2 September 1944, nearly all of the around 67,000 surviving Jews were transported from Łódź to Auschwitz; only a tiny minority of them, some 3,000 or so, were registered into the camp as prisoners. As in the case of Jews arriving from Hungary, a much larger group of deportees – around 19,000 men and women – did not stay in Auschwitz for long; instead, they were deported as 'transit Jews', kept inside the camp only for a short period, to other concentration camps.[41]

The final period: 1945

In November 1944 Himmler officially stopped the systematic murder of Jews in the concentration camps. The crematoria at Auschwitz were partly destroyed, though there are indications that parts of the installations were to be transferred to the Mauthausen camp complex.[42] Nevertheless, killings of the remaining Jews continued, and even accelerated in 1945.

With the onset of the Soviet offensive in January 1945, most concentration camps started to prepare for evacuation.[43] At this time, around 30–40 per cent of the 718,000 registered concentration camp inmates were of Jewish origin. Jews were likely to be in particularly bad physical shape and had little chance of survival. Some prisoners were further weakened by several consecutive forced marches. During the marches, the guards generally treated Jewish prisoners worse than they had already done in the camps. It is probable that more Jewish prisoners than non-Jewish ones were shot on the roads if they were unable to proceed. During these death marches there were several cases of mass murders of Jewish prisoners. One of the most infamous massacres took place in Palmnicken in the northeastern part of East Prussia, on the Baltic coast. Almost 7,000 Jews, who had been convoyed there from Stutthof camp, were shot by local Nazis on 31 January 1945.[44]

Fewer Jewish prisoners were hit by the second wave of evacuations during April 1945, from Sachsenhausen, Ravensbrück, Neuengamme, Buchenwald and Mittelbau (Dora). Only at the end of April were large numbers of Jews shifted around the system: some at the evacuation of the camps in the south of the Reich, where tens of thousands of Hungarian Jews were imprisoned, and others when the so-called Hungarian camps (*Ungarnlager*) in eastern Austria were evacuated to Mauthausen.[45] These marches were accompanied by outrageous violence against the evacuees. Meanwhile, Bergen-Belsen camp was in an infernal state by April 1945. More and more transports arrived in Bergen-Belsen, and the camp administration no longer supplied the inmates with rations. Between January and mid-April alone 35,000 inmates died from the appalling living conditions; another 14,000 were in such a bad shape that they died immediately after liberation.

The victim statistics of the evacuations are very difficult to establish, as German record-keeping broke down and the death marches during the last weeks of the Third Reich were undertaken under chaotic circumstances, with an enormous number of random killings. New estimates tend to give higher figures than previously, with at least 250,000 prisoners killed during the evacuations, probably half of them Jews.[46]

Jewish inmates and the prisoner population

Prior to the inception of the 'Final Solution' in 1942, Jews always made up a minority among the concentration camp inmates, probably between 5 and 10 per cent (the only exception was the last months of 1938 following the mass imprisonment of Jewish men after the November pogrom). Their absolute numbers even declined between 1940 and 1942, at a time when the camp system was expanding, both with the establishment of new camps and with the arrests of tens of thousands of inhabitants from the occupied countries. This situation changed gradually between 1942 and 1944, when Jews were increasingly sent to the concentration camps; most of them were killed on arrival, with only a minority exploited as forced labourers. Nevertheless, by autumn 1944 Jews probably made up one-third of all concentration camp prisoners. This meant that, at the turn of the year 1944/5, most of the Jews under German control now lived either in concentration camps or in the Budapest ghetto.

Most of the Jewish prisoners in the concentration camps were adult males. The vast majority of Jewish children murdered during the course of the 'Final Solution' had been killed by the end of 1942 because they were not considered 'fit for work'. The perpetrators applied the same reasoning to older persons. And among the Jews of working age, more men than women were selected as forced labourers, as only men were regarded as suitable for certain kinds of work. Thus, the majority of the children, the elderly and women murdered during the Nazi 'Final Solution' were already dead by the time large numbers of Jews entered the concentration camp system. Still, between 30 and 40 per cent of these Jewish prisoners were female; in Auschwitz, for example, there were 82,000 female detainees among the 204,000 registered Jewish prisoners.

Compared with other prisoner groups, Jews always had the worst chance of survival. The primary reason was the extermination of most Jews immediately after their arrival in Auschwitz and Majdanek. But even among registered prisoners, Jews were generally far more likely to die than others. The death rates among Jewish inmates were comparable only to those of Roma prisoners and inmates arrested as 'asocial' during 1942/43. In the concentration camps, a specific policy of anti-Jewish terror prevailed, which led to the deployment of Jewish inmates in the worst working facilities and their selection for the regular mass exterminations. And during the final stage of Nazi terror in 1945, Jewish prisoners had the worst chances of survival during the evacuations, whether in train transports or on death marches.

It is a matter of dispute among historians whether the SS pursued an explicit policy of 'annihilation through labour' against Jews. As far as we know, the term itself was used in the Third Reich only in reference to other murderous measures, such as the forced labour camps of *Durchgangsstrasse IV* (the German supply route for the southern armies in the Soviet Union from Lvov to Dnipropetrovsk) and the transfer of 'asocial' prisoners from the state prisons to concentration camps in 1942/43. Still, Jewish prisoners were worked to death in many camps, for example in Auschwitz-Monowitz. In most cases, the so-called *Muselmann* (the term used in the camps for an emaciated apathetic person) was in most cases a Jewish prisoner in an extreme physical condition, with a life expectancy of a few weeks within the camp. Much more than for other prisoner groups, the treatment of the Jews was primarily dominated by racism; economic expectations were only of secondary importance. From the point of view of the perpetrators, no Jewish prisoners were supposed to survive the war.[47]

Jewish prisoners not only faced the lowest chance of survival, they also had comparatively few opportunities to resist. In general, they were not deployed in the slightly better working facilities within the camp administration and they had very few contacts to the outside world, unlike some ethnic Poles in the camps. Nevertheless, already in 1942/3 individual acts of resistance occurred in the concentration camps, and even right in front of the gas chambers in the death camps. Escapes from the death camps were extremely important for the Jewish communities in Hitler's Europe. The most famous case was the escape of Rudolf Vrba and Alfred Wetzler from Auschwitz in April 1944; they immediately informed the Slovakian Jewish leadership about the extermination camp. Others succeeded in escaping in May and September 1944.[48] Organized Jewish resistance originated in the Special Commandos (*Sonderkommandos*), whose members had to work inside the crematoria. In Treblinka and Sobibór, there were uprisings by the Special Commandos in August and September 1943, and some of the prisoners were able to escape. In Auschwitz-Birkenau, too, a group of prisoners in the Special Commando planned an uprising. Though many of the conspirators were killed before it started, the rest managed to organize a revolt on 7 October 1944, destroying Crematorium IV and escaping to a nearby village, where all of them were killed.[49]

Large numbers of Jewish survivors spent the last months of the war in concentration camps, the only 'legal' way left for them to live under German rule. Probably more Jews survived in the camps than in hiding. Unlike most Jewish victims in Poland, the Baltic states and the Soviet Union, who were shot near their hometowns or murdered during Action Reinhardt, it is possible to establish most of the names of those deported to concentration camps. For most countries of origin, memorial books with lists of names have been published; in other cases, personal data is available via the Internet.[50] For some camps death registers are available.[51]

Conclusion

During the last decade our knowledge about the connection between the Holocaust and the concentration camp system has been considerably broadened. Nevertheless, lacunae remain in the historiography. The foremost task is to reconstruct in detail the role of Auschwitz within the mass murder of Jews, both in the context of the Nazi organization and regarding the Jewish camp prisoners. But the history of Jewish prisoners in other camps and their satellite camps too requires further research, especially in respect of Dachau and Mauthausen. In the long run, the new access to the archives of the International Tracing Service in Arolsen may enable historians to reconstruct most of the deportations to the concentration camps and within the camp system, making it possible to trace movements of Jewish prisoners within Europe.[52]

Overall, around 1.2 million Jewish victims – out of the total of 5.6–5.8 million Jews murdered during the 'Final Solution' – died in the concentration camp system. Most of them were not registered as prisoners, but were killed immediately upon arrival in Auschwitz or Majdanek. More than 400,000 Jews were held as prisoners of German concentration camps in the official sense. This meant that Jews constituted a minority of the prisoners but the majority of those murdered in the concentration camps.

In general, the concentration camps were not designed specifically for Jewish prisoners. From the perspective of the Nazi leadership, Jews were initially to be forced to emigrate (until 1939/41), before policy changed to deportation and ghettoization (1939–1942). From autumn 1941 on, Jews were generally meant to be murdered. But the latter policy was already modified in early 1942, when the value of the Jewish workforce was reconsidered, and a minority of Jews was to be kept alive. The two major concentration camps in Poland, Auschwitz and Majdanek, underwent a change of function. Both were originally established for Polish political prisoners, and then enlarged for Soviet POWs under SS control. In spring and summer 1942, a dual system of exploitation and mass murder was established in both camps. Those considered incapable of working – predominantly children, men and women over the age of 35 and mothers with children – were murdered upon arrival. Only about 10–20 per cent of the new arrivals were initially kept alive as forced labourers; but they, too, soon underwent selection, with all the exhausted prisoners eventually being killed.

It is very difficult to establish the number of Jewish concentration camp inmates who survived the war. Most inmates of RSHA-transports who came to Auschwitz died in the camp, the majority immediately on the arrival; only between 1 and 3 per cent of these prisoners survived the war. Overall, out of more than 200,000 registered Jewish prisoners from all over Europe in Auschwitz, 30,000 survived.[53] The situation was somewhat better for evacuees from the forced labour camps. All in all, approximately 30,000 Polish Jews survived in all concentration camps. Out of the 121,000 Jews from Hungary who were deported to the Reich and survived, a majority had been integrated into the concentration camp system for a while.[54]

The extermination system of Auschwitz developed almost in parallel to Action Reinhardt in spring 1942, and in 1943 grew into the centre of mass murder of European Jewry, culminating in 1944. Most ghetto inhabitants had been killed in 1942, with the surviving labourers kept in forced labour camps built on the former ghetto sites. In 1943, the SS leadership decided to gradually concentrate Jewish forced labour under the control of the WVHA. Thus new camps for Jews were installed in Warsaw, Riga, Kaunas and in Estonia.

During the evacuations from the East in 1944, more and more Jews from the forced labour camps were deported to concentration camps, including Hungarian Jews who either went through Auschwitz or were sent directly to the other camps. As a result, Jews constituted a large proportion of the prisoner population in the concentration camps towards the end of the Second World War; yet many of them did not live to see the liberation of the camps but died during the death marches.

Prior to the Second World War, the concentration camps had served as a testing ground for the mistreatment of Jews. But only after the turn of the year 1941/2 did forced labour and the extermination of deported Jews became an important function of the camps. The concentration camps played a specific role in the 'Final Solution'. Auschwitz more or less succeeded the Aktion Reinhardt camps and Kulmhof as the main centre of extermination. At the same time, Auschwitz gradually became the largest place for Jewish forced labour in Europe besides the Łódź ghetto. And while deportations of Jews to Majdanek stopped in summer 1944, Jewish prisoners later entered all the other concentration camps, from spring 1944 onwards. Not all the victims in the camps were murdered immediately upon their arrival, but all Jewish prisoners were destined for extermination. It was only due to their liberation by the Allies that a minority of Jewish prisoners survived the war.

Notes

1 Cf. J. Matthäus, 'Verfolgung, Ausbeutung, Vernichtung. Jüdische Häftlinge im System der Konzentrationslager', in G. Morsch and S. zur Nieden (eds), *Jüdische Häftlinge im KZ Sachsenhausen 1936–1945*, Berlin: Hentrich, 2004, pp. 64–90; W. Gruner, *Jewish Forced Labor Under the Nazis, 1938–1944: Economic Needs and Racial Aims*, New York: Berghahn, 2006.

2 See L. Apel, *Jüdische Frauen im Konzentrationslager Ravensbrück 1939–1945*, Berlin: Metropol, 2003; D. Drywa, *The Extermination of Jews in Stutthof Concentration Camp*, Gdańsk: Stutthof Muzeum in Sztutowo, 2004; B. Gutterman, *A Narrow Bridge to Life: Jewish Slave Labor and Survival in the Gross-Rosen Camp System, 1940–1945*, New York: Berghahn, 2008.

3 W. Benz and B. Distel (eds), *Der Ort des Terrors. Geschichte der nationalsozialistischen Konzentrationslager*, 8 vols., Munich: Beck 2005–2009; *The United States Holocaust Memorial Encyclopedia of Camps and Ghettos, 1933–1945*, vol. 1. Bloomington, IN: Indiana UP 2009.

4 See Daniel Blatman, 'The Death Marches and the Final Phase of Nazi Genocide', in *Concentration Camps in Nazi Germany*, ed. Jane Caplan et al. (New York: Routledge, 2010), pp. 167–85.

5 Morsch and zur Nieden, *Jüdische Häftlinge im KZ Sachsenhausen*, pp. 117 ff.

6 H. Stein, *Juden in Buchenwald 1937–1942*, Weimar: Weimardruck, 1992.

7 Y. Weiss, *Deutsche und polnische Juden vor dem Holocaust: Jüdische Identität zwischen Staatsbürgerschaft und Ethnizität 1933–1940*, Munich: Oldenbourg, 2000, pp. 212–14.

8 S. Mączka (ed.), *Żydzi polscy w KL Auschwitz. Wykazy imienne*, Warsaw: Żydowski Instytut Historyczny, 2004, pp. 9 ff.

9 H. Friedlander, *The Origins of Nazi Genocide: From Euthanasia to the Final Solution*, Chapel Hill, NC: University of North Carolina Press, 1995, pp. 147–50.

10 J. Brandhuber, 'Die sowjetischen Kriegsgefangenen im Konzentrationslager Auschwitz', *Hefte von Auschwitz* 4, 1961, pp. 5–46.

11 Individual fates mentioned in P. Polian and A. Shneer, *Obrechennye pogibnut. Sudba sovetskikh voennoplennykh-evreev vo Vtoroi Mirovoi voine. Vospominaniia i dokumenty*, Moscow: Novoe Izdatelstvo 2006, pp. 43–4; registration cards are shown on the book cover.

12 J. E. Schulte, *Zwangsarbeit und Vernichtung: Das Wirtschaftsimperium der SS: Oswald Pohl und das SS-Wirtschafts-Verwaltungshauptamt 1933–1945*, Paderborn: Schöningh, 2001. See also order by Gestapo Chief Müller to Kommandeur der Sicherheitspolizei und des SD Litauen, 18.5.1942, in P. Klein (ed.), *Die Einsatzgruppen in der besetzten Sowjetunion 1941/42. Die Tätigkeits- und Lageberichte des Chefs der Sicherheitspolizei und des SD 1941/42*, Berlin: Hentrich, 1997, pp. 410f.

13 B. Schwindt, *Das Konzentrations- und Vernichtungslager Majdanek – Funktionswandel im Kontext der "Endlösung"*, Würzburg: Königshausen & Neumann, 2005.

14 S. Steinbacher, *"Musterstadt" Auschwitz. Germanisierung und Judenmord in Ostoberschlesien*, Munich: Saur, 2000, pp. 277 ff. Contrary to common assumptions in historiography, there is no evidence for a major transport from Organisation Schmelt to Auschwitz prior to March 1942.

15 *Majdanek 1942. Księga zmarłych więźniów*, Lublin: Państwowe Muzeum na Majdanku, 2004.

16 Y. Arad, *Belzec, Sobibor, Treblinka: The Operation Reinhard Death Camps*, Bloomington, IN: Indiana UP, 1987.

17 S. Krakowski, *Das Todeslager Chelmno/Kulmhof. Der Beginn der 'Endlösung'*, Göttingen: Wallstein, 2007; P. Klein, 'Vernichtungslager Kulmhof/Chelmno', in W. Benz and B. Distel (eds), *Der Ort des Terrors. Geschichte der nationalsozialistischen Konzentrationslager*, vol. 8. Munich: Beck, 2008, pp. 301–28.

18 D. Pohl, 'Die großen Zwangsarbeitslager der SS- und Polizeiführer für Juden im Generalgouvernement 1942–1945', in U. Herbert, K. Orth and C. Dieckmann (eds), *Die nationalsozialistischen Konzentrationslager*, Göttingen: Wallstein, 1998, pp. 415–38; cf. C. R. Browning, 'Jewish workers in Poland: Self-maintenance, exploitation, destruction', in his *Nazi Policy, Jewish Workers, German Killers*, Cambridge: Cambridge UP, 2000, pp. 58–88.

19 Schwindt, *Konzentrations- und Vernichtungslager Majdanek*, pp. 101–2.

20 P. Witte and S. Tyas, 'A new document on the deportation and murder of Jews during "Einsatz Reinhardt" 1942', *Holocaust and Genocide Studies* 15, 2001, 468–86; T. Kranz, 'Eksterminacja Żydów na Majdanku i rola obozu w realizacji "Akcji Reinhardt"', *Zeszyty Majdanka* 22, 2003, pp. 7–55. Historians are still debating whether Auschwitz was also connected to 'Aktion Reinhardt', for example in regards to the belongings of the victims; see B. Perz and T. Sandkühler, 'Auschwitz und die "Aktion Reinhard" 1942–45', *Zeitgeschichte* 26, 2000, pp. 283–316.

21 H. Safrian, *Die Eichmann-Männer*, Vienna, Zürich: Europa 1993; Y. Lozowick, *Hitler's Bureaucrats: The Nazi Security Police and the Banality of Evil*, New York: Continuum, 2002.

22 Długoborski and Piper, *Auschwitz*, vol. 2, pp. 46–7; Y. Gutman and S. Krakowski, 'Juden im KL Auschwitz', *Sterbebücher von Auschwitz. Fragmente*, Munich: Saur 1995, vol. 1, pp. 163–94; J. E. Schulte, 'London war informiert. KZ-Expansion und Judenverfolgung. Entschlüsselte KZ-Stärkemeldungen vom Januar 1942 bis zum Januar 1943 in den britischen National Archives in Kew', *Beiträge zur Geschichte des Nationalsozialismus* 22, 2006, pp. 207–27.

23 M. T. Allen, 'The devil in the details: The gas chambers of Birkenau, October 1941', *Holocaust and Genocide Studies* 16, 2002, pp. 189–216. Cf. also the debate on the diverging statements by Auschwitz commander Rudolf Höß: K. Orth, 'Rudolf Höß und die "Endlösung der Judenfrage". Drei Argumente gegen die Datierung auf den Sommer 1941', *Werkstatt Geschichte* 6, 1997, pp. 45–57.

24 D. Czech, *Auschwitz Chronicle, 1939–1945*, New York: Holt, 1990; W. Długoborski and F. Piper (eds), *Auschwitz 1940–1945. Studien zur Geschichte des Konzentrations- und Vernichtungslagers Auschwitz*, 5 vols, Oświęcim: Państwowe Muzeum Auschwitz-Birkenau w Oświęcimiu, 1999, here vol. 2, pp. 158 ff.

25 Steinbacher, *"Musterstadt" Auschwitz*, p. 278.

26 R. J. van Pelt, *The Case for Auschwitz: Evidence from the Irving Trial*, Bloomington, IN: Indiana University Press, 2002; cf. also J. C. Pressac (ed.), *Auschwitz: Technique and Operation of the Gas Chambers*, New York: Beate Klarsfeld Foundation, 1989.

27 A. B. Gottwaldt and D. Schulle, *Die Judendeportationen aus dem deutschen Reich von 1941–1945. Eine kommentierte Chronologie*, Berlin: Marix 2005, pp. 397ff. There were smaller transports from Gliwice already in spring and a transport from Vienna on 17/18 July 1942, the fate of which cannot be determined exactly.

28 T. Brod, M. Kárný and M. Kárný, *Terezínský rodinný tábor v Osvetimi-Birkenau*, Prague: Nadace Terezínská iniciativa – Melantrich, 1994; M. Kárný, 'Das Theresienstädter Familienlager BIIb in Birkenau September 1943–Juli 1944', *Hefte von Auschwitz* 20, 1997, pp. 133–237.

29 H. Fleischer, 'Griechenland', in W. Benz (ed.), *Dimension des Völkermords*. Munich: Oldenbourg, 1991, pp. 241–74.

30 B. C. Wagner, *IG Auschwitz. Zwangsarbeit und Vernichtung von Häftlingen des Lagers Monowitz 1941–1945*, Munich: Saur, 2000; P. Setkiewicz, *Z dziejów obozów IG Farben Werk Auschwitz 1941–1945*, Oświęcim: Państwowe Muzeum Auschwitz-Birkenau w Oświęcimiu, 2006 (with lower figures).

31 T. Mencel, *Majdanek 1941–1944*, Lublin: Wydawnictwo Lubelskie, 1991; T. Mencel and T. Kranz, *Extermination of Jews at the Majdanek Concentration Camp*, Lublin: Państwowe Muzeum na Majdanku, 2007.

32 T. Kranz, 'Bookkeeping of death and prisoner mortality at Majdanek', *Yad Vashem Studies* 35, 2007, no. 1, pp. 81–109.

33 Pohl, 'Zwangsarbeitslager'.

34 B. Kopka, *Konzentrationslager Warschau. Historia i nastepstwa*, Warsaw: Instytut Pamięci Narodowej, 2007; A. Mix, 'Warschau – Stammlager', Benz and Distel (eds), *Der Ort des Terrors*, vol. 8, pp. 91–126.

35 A. Angrick and P. Klein, *Die 'Endlösung' in Riga. Ausbeutung und Vernichtung 1941–1944*, Darmstadt: WBG, 2006, pp. 391 ff.

36 C. Dieckmann, 'Das Ghetto und das Konzentrationslager in Kaunas 1941–1944', in Herbert, Dieckmann and Orth (eds), *Die nationalsozialistischen Konzentrationslager*, vol. 1, pp. 439–71.

37 R. B. Birn, 'Vaivara – Stammlager', in Benz and Distel (eds), *Der Ort des Terrors. Geschichte der nationalsozialistischen Konzentrationslager*, vol. 8, pp. 131–47; M. Dworzecki, *Histoire de camps en Estonie (1941–1944)*, Tel Aviv, 1967.

38 E. Kolb, *Bergen-Belsen 1943–1945. Vom Aufenthaltslager zum Konzentrationslager*, Göttingen: Vandenhoeck & Ruprecht, 2002; A. E. Wenck, *Zwischen Menschenhandel und 'Endlösung'. Das Konzentrationslager Bergen-Belsen*, Paderborn: Schöningh, 2000.

39 R. R. Braham, *The Politics of Genocide: The Holocaust in Hungary*, Washington, DC: Social Science Monographs, 1994; C. Gerlach and G. Aly, *Das letzte Kapitel. Realpolitik, Ideologie und der Mord an den ungarischen Juden 1944/1945*, Munich: DVA, 2002.

40 S. Szita, *Verschleppt, verhungert, vernichtet. Die Deportation von ungarischen Juden auf das Gebiet des annektierten Österreich 1944–1945*, Vienna: Eichbauer, 1999; E. Raim, *Die Dachauer KZ-Außenkommandos Kaufering und Mühldorf. Rüstungsbauten und Zwangsarbeit im letzten Kriegsjahr 1944/45*, Landsberg am Lech: Neumayer, 1992.

41 A. Strzelecki, *The Deportation of Jews from the Łódź Ghetto to KL Auschwitz and their Extermination. A Description of the Events and the Presentation of Historical Sources*, Oświęcim: Auschwitz-Birkenau State Museum, 2006.

42 B. Perz and F. Freund, 'Auschwitz neu? Pläne und Maßnahmen zur Wiedererrichtung der Krematorien von Auschwitz-Birkenau in der Umgebung des KZ Mauthausen im Februar 1945', *Dachauer Hefte* 20, 2004, pp. 58–70.

43 K. Orth, *Das System der nationalsozialistischen Konzentrationslager. Eine politische Organisationsgeschichte*, Hamburg: Hamburger Edition, 1999, pp. 270–336.

44 A. Kossert, 'Endlösung on the "Amber Shore": The massacre in January 1945 on the Baltic seashore: A repressed chapter of East Prussian history', *Leo Baeck Institute Year Book* 49, 2004, 1, pp. 3–19.

45 E. Lappin, 'The death marches of Hungarian Jews through Austria in the Spring of 1945', *Yad Vashem Studies* 28, 2000, pp. 203–42.

46 This figure given by Daniel Blatman in his forthcoming book on the Death Marches; cf. his chapter, cited in note 4 above. Gerlach and Aly, *Das letzte Kapitel*, p. 413, though, suggest that the figures were lower.

47 U. Herbert, 'Labour and extermination: Economic interest and the primacy of Weltanschauung in National Socialism', *Past and Present* 138, 1993, pp. 144–95.

48 M. Gilbert, *Auschwitz and the Allies*, London: Pimlico, 2001; H. Świebocki, *London Has Been Informed . . . Reports by Auschwitz Escapees*, Oświęcim: Auschwitz-Birkenau State Museum, 1997.

49 G. Greif, *We Wept Without Tears. Interviews with Jewish Survivors of the Auschwitz Sonderkommando*, New Haven, CT: Yale University Press 2005 (the author is preparing a greatly enlarged version); *Des voix sous la cendre. Manuscrits des Sonderkommandos d'Auschwitz-Birkenau*, Paris: Calmann-Lévy, 2005.

50 *Die österreichischen Opfer des Holocaust. The Austrian Victims of the Holocaust*. Vienna: Dokumentationsarchiv des österreichischen Widerstandes, 2001 (CD-ROM); S. Klarsfeld and M. Steinberg (eds), *Mémorial de la déportation des Juifs de Belgique*, Brussels, 1982; M. Kárný (ed.), *Terezínská pametní kniha. Zidovské obeti nacistických deportací z Cech a Moravy 1941–1945*, Prague: Nadace Terezínská iniciativa – Melantrich, 1995; S. Klarsfeld, *Memorial to the Jews Deported From France, 1942–1944: Documentation of the Deportation of the Victims of the Final Solution in France*, New York: Beate Klarsfeld Foundation, 1983; *In Memoriam*, The Hague: Sdu Uitgeverij Koninginnegracht, 1995; *Gedenkbuch – Opfer der Verfolgung der Juden unter der nationalsozialistischen Gewaltherrschaft in Deutschland 1933–1945*, 4 vols, Koblenz: Bundesarchiv 2006; A. Recanati, *A Memorial Book of the Deportation of the Greek Jews*, 3 vols, Jerusalem: Erez, 2006; L. P. Fargion, *Il libro della memoria: gli ebrei deportati dall'Italia (1943–1945)*, Milan: Mursia, 1991; http:// www.neveklarsfeld.org/index.shtml (350,000 names of Jews from Greater Hungary).

51 Mączka, *Żydzi polscy w KL Auschwitz*; *Sterbebücher von Auschwitz. Fragmente* (fragments until December 1943; out of the 69,000 inmates contained here 30,000 were Jews. After March 1943, the deaths of Jewish prisoners were not registered

any longer); *Gedenkbuch: Häftlinge des Konzentrationslagers Bergen-Belsen*, Celle: Gedenkstätte Bergen-Belsen, 2005. More databases are available at the camp memorials.

52 Yad Vashem has started a research program on deportations of Jews within Nazi Europe.

53 Y. Gutman and S. Krakowski, 'Juden im KL Auschwitz', p. 194.

54 Józef Adelson, 'W Polsce zwanej Ludowa', *Najnowsze dzieje Żydów w Polsce*, Warsaw: PWN, 1993, pp. 387–477, 398; Gerlach and Aly, *Das letzte Kapitel*, p. 409. Cf. also the Benjamin and Vladka Meed Registry of Jewish Holocaust Survivors at the US Holocaust Memorial Museum, which contains more than 185,000 names of survivors in the United States.

6

DECISION-MAKING IN THE "FINAL SOLUTION"

Peter Longerich

The question of when the Nazi regime actually decided on a concerted policy of outright genocide of all the Jews under its control has exercised historians since the end of the war. But while some information about Nazi extermination policies was already available when the Holocaust was taking place, even today opinions differ as to the timing of the decision or even whether a single definitive instruction for genocide was ever given. No specific order by Hitler to exterminate the Jews of Europe has ever been found, and it is more than likely that such a written directive was never given. Conversely, even before the outbreak of war, Hitler publicly stated his intention to eradicate the Jews. In a speech to the German Reichstag on January 30, 1939, Hitler declared that "if the international Jewish financiers in and outside Europe should succeed in plunging the nations once more into a world war, then the result will not be the Bolshevizing of the earth, and thus the victory of Jewry, but the annihilation of the Jewish race in Europe!"

Similarly, while no paper trail can be reconstructed that provides clear-cut evidence of orders and instructions emanating from the top and being carried out on the ground, there is ample evidence of massive involvement in this vast undertaking. After all, the murder of close to six million people across an entire continent necessitated the engagement of numerous individuals and organizations. Quite apart from the SS and police, as well as the military, a variety of other agencies, such as the railroad administration, economic interests, the foreign ministry, allied and occupied countries, and so forth, all had to be involved in a process whereby men, women, and children, were transported in their thousands to their death. The Holocaust was therefore both a very public event and one whose complex and at times contradictory inner workings are difficult to reconstruct.

In the last couple of decades, the debate over the decision on the "final solution" has been centered on whether it was made in the "euphoria of victory," as Christopher Browning has suggested, sometime in the fall of 1941; or, as Christian Gerlach has argued, only in winter 1941–42, when the Soviet counteroffensive at the gates of Moscow and Germany's declaration of war against the United States meant that from that point on Germany was in fact involved in a world war. Hence Gerlach interprets the Wannsee Conference of January 20, 1942 – in which Reinhard Heydrich, head of the Reich Main Security Office (RSHA), presented his plan for the deportation and eventual murder of 11 million European Jews – as the moment in which Hitler's recent decision was transmitted to the relevant governmental agencies.

In the following chapter, Peter Longerich proposes a more complex model of German policy evolution toward mass murder. For Longerich, Judenpolitik – German Jewish policies – played a central role in Nazi politics from the very beginning, reaching a decisive turning point in 1939, when the regime found itself unable to continue pursuing forced immigration of Jews and began seeking some "final solution" to this self-imposed "problem." With the outbreak of war, the regime identified the Jews as its existential enemy and a main obstacle to German Lebensraum in the East. The solution was the creation of a "Jewish reservation" in the East (or for a while in Madagascar), where Jews would eventually perish. The mass killing of Soviet Jews following the invasion of the USSR, argues Longerich, was similarly perceived as a vast ethnic cleansing operation in preparation for an expanded Germanic living space. But in the fall of 1941 the decision to deport the Jews of Central and Western Europe to the East, and to "make room" for them by murdering indigenous Jews incarcerated in ghettos, led to the construction of the first extermination facilities. Although the notion of mass deportation into Russia in vast forced-labor programs persisted, as partly reflected in the plans outlined at the Wannsee Conference, it appears that with the acceleration of deportations from the west in the spring of 1942 a decision was finally made to murder all Jews indiscriminately. This, notes Longerich, was neither a distraction nor a sideshow for Nazi policymakers; in fact, Germany's Judenpolitik was a major component of its occupation and alliance policy. Most important, for the Nazi regime the genocide of the Jews was never a mere tool of policy but rather at the very core of what it believed to be its existential struggle for survival.

In this study we have made an attempt to interpret the decision-making process leading to the systematic murder of the Jews of Europe within the wider context of German *Judenpolitik*. As a result we have identified four distinct stages of escalation between the start of the war and the summer of 1942, in the course of which the Nazi leadership developed and set in motion a programme for the systematic murder of the European Jews. We have argued that the decisive turning point leading to the 'Final Solution' occurred as early as autumn 1939 and we have shown that the radicalization of *Judenpolitik* occurred within the context of a *Rassenpolitik*, but that no other group was persecuted with the same relentlessness and the same disastrous consequences as the Jews of Europe.

In the years between 1933 and 1939 *Judenpolitik* within the German Reich remained closely associated with the National Socialist seizure and maintenance of power. The 'de-jewification' (*Entjudung*) of German society, in the broader sense the implementation of a racist policy, provided the Nazis with the instrument for gradually penetrating the individual spheres of life in German society and subjecting them to their total claim to power. In the years between 1933 and 1939, not only did this key function of *Judenpolitik* become apparent, but it also became evident that a particular tactic for the phased implementation of the policy was being developed: the regime leadership set general goals and the subordinate organizations utilized the broad scope they were given for the exercise of considerable individual initiative and did so to a degree in competition with one another. But the frictions and tensions that arose could not disguise the fact that the goal of the expulsion of the Jews from German society was based on a broad consensus within the National Socialist movement. The initiation and radicalization of the persecution of the Jews cannot simply be traced back to a chain of decisions taken at the top of the Nazi regime; it would be more accurate to say that a new political field was constituted and developed, in which complex structures and autonomous dynamics then developed, without the leaders of the regime losing control of the overall process of *Judenpolitik*.

This policy was clearly exhausted with the November pogrom and the subsequent legal measures. After the German Jews had been reduced to the status of a plundered minority, completely stripped of its rights, even Nazi propaganda had difficulty evoking dangers that this completely powerless minority could have represented; it was barely possible to supply motives for further anti-Semitic 'actions'.

On the other hand, however, the Nazi regime had not managed to expel all the German Jews. Now it became apparent that, as a result of the plundering of the Jewish minority, a relatively large group of people had been left behind, which was no longer in a position to emigrate. With war on the horizon, the regime set about subjecting this group to total tyranny.

After the November pogrom the Nazi regime proceeded to declare the Jews to be hostages menaced by 'destruction' (*Vernichtung*). Remarkably, Hitler himself, in referring to extermination in his speech of 30 January 1939, did not speak of the German Jews but prophesied—expressly in the instance of a 'global war'—the 'destruction of the Jewish race in Europe'.

However, from the perspective of the National Socialists, the idea of extermination was not a tactically motivated threat but the logical consequence of the notion that dominated the whole of National Socialist policy, that the German people were engaged in a struggle against 'international Jewry' in which their very existence was at stake. The National Socialists saw war as the chance to realize their utopian ideas of an empire ordered along racist lines. From their point of view, war served to legitimate the idea of compensating for the loss of the 'racially valuable' by extirpating the racially 'inferior' in the interests of maintaining 'ethnic biological' equilibrium. It was the emergency of war that produced the opportunity for such an unparalleled break with the humanitarian tradition.

Even during the war against Poland, in mid-September 1939, the German leadership began seriously to address their plans for *Lebensraum* by developing a gigantic resettlement programme for the newly conquered territories. This programme involved the deportation of all Jews living in territory under German control to a 'Jewish reservation' in conquered Poland. These plans were actually set in motion with the so-called 'Nisko Action' in October 1939, but had to be suspended after a short time. In fact, however, the Nazi regime kept to the plan of a 'Jewish reservation' in the district of Lublin and repeated fitful attempts were made to achieve such a mass programme through small-scale deportations.

In fact the plan for a 'Jewish reservation' was aimed at concentrating the Jews from the whole of the German sphere of influence in an area which lacked adequate living conditions, and to cause the death of these more than two million people through undernourishment, epidemics, low birth rates, and so on, possibly over a period of several generations. Plainly such a long-term plan contained the potential to blackmail the Western powers that the leadership of the 'Third Reich' needed in order to construct a *Lebensraum* empire without being disturbed by outside intervention.

The plan for a reservation was thus an initial project for the 'final solution of the Jewish question', a long-term plan involving the deaths of the great majority of Jews living under the control of the Nazi regime. The radical nature of this project becomes fully clear when one views it within the context of the mass murders that the Nazi regime unleashed after the start of the war: the shootings of tens of thousands of Polish civilians (including thousands of Jews), as well as the 'euthanasia' programme, the murder of the sick and the disabled.

Over the next two years, the 'Jewish reservation' project was maintained (in modified form). After the victory over France, the regime concentrated on Madagascar, and early in 1941, as part of the preparations for 'Barbarossa', a plan was developed to deport the Jews under German rule to the territories in the East, which the Germans thought they were about to conquer. Common to all these plans was the prospect of the physical 'Final Solution', even if this was to extend over a long period of time.

Many historians have assumed that a fundamental decision to murder the Jews was taken sometime during the course of 1941 and that therefore one can clearly distinguish an early phase during which 'territorial' solutions were conceived from a later 'final solution phase'. However, this view fails to perceive what was at the core of the plans of National Socialist *Judenpolitik*: the 'territorial solution' was also always conceived as a 'final solution', because in the final analysis its goal was the annihilation of the vast majority of the Jews.

By autumn 1939, then, the point had already been reached at which those involved in *Judenpolitik* began to gear themselves up for the extermination of the European Jews. The measures taken by the regime from 1941 onwards were merely the concrete realization of the extermination already envisaged in 1939. There were only vague ideas of how and over what period of time this extermination was to occur in practice. The 'destruction of the Jewish race in Europe', threatened by Hitler on 30 January 1939, was initially an option, the realization of which was still dependent on certain conditions. From 1941 onwards, when the systematic destruction of the European Jews was actually realized, the idea of what was meant by 'Final Solution' was to be radicalized. General notions of annihilating the Jews within the German sphere of influence over the long term were now developed by the National Socialist leadership into a comprehensive programme of mass murder which was essentially to be implemented even before the end of the war. The abstract concept of 'destruction' (*Vernichtung*) or 'Final Solution' used by the perpetrators allowed them to develop their plans, which since 1939 had been geared towards the death of the European Jews, in stages towards this systematic murder programme. However, since 1939 extermination and 'Final Solution' had equated to millions of deaths.

This radicalization of the process leading to systematic mass murder occurred in the context of the expanding war. For the National Socialists, the racial war for *Lebensraum* included from the outset the prospect of exterminating what they had defined as the Jewish enemy, particularly when the war grew into a world war and the dream of a *Lebensraum* empire was thus endangered.

This link between war and extermination policy does not represent an inevitable automatism, and it would be wrong to imagine that a 'decision' to murder the European Jews was taken around the start of the war. The link was, in fact, the result of National Socialist policy. For the extermination process to be actually set in motion crucial preconditions had first to exist: the 'reservation' had to be definitely determined and established. So long as this had not occurred, extermination remained an intention that could also under certain circumstances be revoked.

In the summer of 1941 the extermination policy reached the second stage of its escalation with the murder of the Soviet Jews. While tens of thousands of Jewish men eligible for military service had been shot during the first few weeks of the war in Russia (and earlier in the mass executions in Poland), from the end of July, but more intensively from August, September, and October 1941, hundreds of thousands of men, women, and children were murdered. This transition from a terroristic modus operandi to a murderous 'ethnic cleansing' cannot be adequately explained by the elation of victory, nor by a change of mood provoked by the failure of the blitzkrieg strategy in autumn/winter 1941.

In fact, in the summer of 1941, the Germans began the 'New Order' (*Neuordnung*) of the conquered *Lebensraum*, precisely as originally planned without waiting for military victory. However, while the war continued the planned reordering of the 'Ostraum' had to be restricted to purely negative measures. The mass murder of the Soviet civilian population, that is those who stood at the lowest level of the Nazis' racist hierarchy, and in their distorted perception formed the chief supports of the Bolshevik system, was from the perspective of the National Socialist leadership an anticipation of the plans discussed before the start of the war, according to which millions of people on Soviet territory were to fall victim to the 'New Order' of the *Lebensraum*.

One factor that may have been crucial to the initiation of genocide in Soviet territory in late summer 1941, which had been planned since the beginning of the same year, was an initiative by Himmler, who wished, through his brutal treatment of the Jewish civilian population, to transfer his competencies as Reichskommissar for the Strengthening of the German Nation to the newly conquered territories, as was also finally sanctioned by Hitler. By ordering in July 1941 the inclusion of elderly men, women, and children in the campaign of extermination through shooting, Himmler was preparing the ground for the 'ethnic cleansing' that was intended to be carried out by the SS and was doing so even while the war was still going on and before the apparatus of the occupying administration could be consolidated. It is plain that in doing this Himmler was anticipating Hitler's intentions; Hitler himself had done everything he could to make sure even before the beginning of the invasion that this war would have the character of a campaign of racist extermination, and he was fully informed about the actions of the *Einsatzgruppen*.

This is not to say, however, that the gradual extension of the murders to the general Jewish civilian population can simply be seen as the result of an order from the Führer or an independent initiative on the part of Himmler which had been authorized by Hitler. The crucial point is that there was from the outset a consensus among the decision makers that the persecution of the Jews should be further and further radicalized in the further course of the war. On the basis of this consensus, general instructions in line with the intuition of the subordinates were issued in certain situations; in this way wider scope was given to independent initiatives. In the end the entire process was coordinated and standardized at the top. The leadership at the centre and the executive organizations on the periphery radicalized one another through a reciprocal process.

The third stage of escalation in the transition to the systematic extermination of the Jews occurred in the autumn of 1941. It consisted of two crucial decisions: on the one hand Hitler's decision made in mid-September 1941 to deport the Jews from the whole of the Reich including the Protectorate of Bohemia and Moravia, if possible that same year, to the incorporated Polish territories, and further eastwards the following spring. If the first step was originally seen as being the deportation of 60,000 Jews to the Lodz ghetto, this intention was soon modified and extended: now 25,000 Jews and Gypsies were to be deported to the ghettos of Riga and Minsk. We know that at this point a third wave of deportations was already planned for the start of the following year. Between September and November, with the marking of the German Jews, the general prohibition on emigration imposed upon Jews throughout the whole of the area under German control, and the withdrawal of citizenship and the remaining property of those deported from Germany, major administrative preparations for the deportation had also been made.

Thus, in September 1941, Hitler set in motion the plan, made early in 1941, to deport the European Jews to the territories of the Soviet Union that were soon to be conquered, although without waiting for the victory over the Red Army. The fact that, although the war was not going to plan, Hitler insisted on the implementation of the final variant of the reservation plan that had been pursued since 1939—with its genocidal consequences—seems to be more significant for the analysis of the decision-making process than any additional factors (the issue of accommodation, repression because of the deportations of the Volga Germans, etc.), which, from the point of view of the Nazi leadership, argued in favour of the instigation of the deportations in autumn 1941. As with the Nisko and Madagascar plans, the Nazi leadership clearly associated the idea of 'hostage-taking' with the first deportations. The United States were to be dissuaded from entering the war through the more or less open threat to liquidate the deported Jews, entirely in the spirit of Hitler's prophecy of 30 January 1939.

The decision that Hitler made in autumn 1941 gradually to deport the Jews under German rule to the East was linked to a second momentous decision (but one which cannot be reconstructed in detail), namely to carry out the mass murder of the indigenous Jews in the provisional reception areas. Now areas 'free of Jews' were also to be created in the occupied Polish territories, as they had been in the Soviet Union since the end of the summer. With the prospect of sending tens of thousands of Central European Jews to the already completely overcrowded ghettos, more radical solutions were demanded of the local authorities.

Reichsstathalter Greiser himself had proposed that the indigenous Jewish population in the Warthegau should be 'reduced' by 100,000 'in compensation for' the reception of Jews from the Reich in Lodz, that is these people were to be killed with gas vans. Further large-scale massacres were carried out until the end of 1941 among the local Jewish population in the other sites destined to receive Jews from the Reich, namely the ghettos of Minsk and Riga. When Einsatzkommando 2 began shooting thousands of Jews deported from the Reich immediately after their arrival in Riga or Kovno (Kaunas), the murder of the

Reich German Jews was suspended by a direct intervention from Himmler. Thus, a distinction was still being made between the Eastern European and Central European Jews.

In the General Government too, particularly in the district of Lublin, preparations for a mass murder of the local Jewish population began in October 1941. Previously, the government of the General Government had been informed that they could not expect to deport any more Jews eastwards from that territory for the foreseeable future. In October preparations began for the construction of the first extermination camp at Bełżec, and at the same time, with the so-called 'Schiessbefehl' (order to shoot on sight) the death penalty was introduced for leaving the ghetto. The goal of these measures was to murder the Jewish population that were 'unfit to work', initially in the district of Lublin. These plans may also have applied to the district of Galicia, which had only been part of the General Government since 1 August and where, like the *Einsatzgruppen* in the other occupied territories, the Security Police had been carrying out similar massacres among the Jewish civilian population since October. References to the construction of an extermination camp in Lemberg (Lvov) are significant in this context. However, the construction of an extermination camp in Bełżec (and possible plans for Lemberg) cannot be seen as specifically intended for the murder of the entire Jewish population of the General Government. The occupying forces initially concentrated on making preparations for those Jews who were 'unfit for work' in the district of Lublin, where a third wave of deportations was expected the following spring. Thus, in autumn 1941 the murder of hundreds of thousands of people had been planned, but not yet of millions. As far as the fate of the remaining Polish and other European Jews was concerned, the older plan of a mass deportation to the Soviet Union (with ultimately genocidal consequences) had not yet been abandoned. At any rate a dynamic of mass murder had now been set in motion, which could only have been halted by a radical change of direction in the regime's *Judenpolitik*.

In the autumn/winter of 1941 facilities for killing with gas were established not only in Bełżec (and possibly in Lemberg) as they had been in Chelmno. Further possible locations have been identified through plans for the installation of such facilities in Riga, and corresponding references to Mogilev (not far from Minsk). There is also the offer that Himmler made to the Slovakian head of state on 20 October, to deport Slovakian Jews to a particularly remote area of the General Government, possibly the basis for the construction of the second extermination camp at Sobibor. The use of gas as a means of killing had thus initially begun in the planned deportation zones. Parallel with this we should consider the events in Serbia, where the Wehrmacht began systematically shooting Jewish men and Gypsies in October. In November the military administration in France also began deliberately to direct their retaliatory measures against Jews, who were to be transported to the East as hostages. In October, November, and December threatening statements by National Socialists also accumulated concerning the deadly fate that awaited the Jews.

As confusing as the overall picture may seem at first sight, it does become clear that, within the space of a few weeks in autumn 1941, German organizations in various occupied territories began to react with remarkable similarity to the new situation in *Judenpolitik* created by Hitler's September decision to deport the German and Czech Jews, by organizing mass shootings (Galicia, Serbia), deploying gas vans (Warthegau) or preparing the construction of extermination camps (district of Lublin, Auschwitz, Riga, possibly Mogilev-Belarus).

If we see these activities in context, it becomes irrefutably clear that the German power holders on the 'periphery' were always acting in the context of an overall policy guided by the 'centre', meaning Hitler and the SS leadership. The centre was always in a position to prevent an escalation of a policy which it found undesirable, as is demonstrated for example by Himmler putting a halt to the murders of Reich German Jews in the Ostland in late November 1941.

However, the centre was only able to guide this process and set it in motion because it knew that impulses issuing from the centre were picked up with great independent initiative by the authorities in the 'periphery'. Just as the extension of the shootings to women and children in the Soviet Union from the summer of 1941 onwards was not simply ordered, the extension of the mass murders to particular regions of occupied Europe in autumn 1941 also required a very complicated interaction between the centre and the executive organizations, involving orders and guidelines from the centre, as well as independent initiatives and intuition on the part of the regional power holders, which were finally channelled and coordinated by the centre, albeit at a much higher level of radicalization.

The Wannsee Conference of 20 January 1942 provides an important insight into the RSHA's policy of consolidating the various approaches for an extension of the murders and thereby designing a comprehensive programme for the impending 'Final Solution'. While, on the one hand, the Germans continued to adhere to the old programme of deporting all Jews to the occupied Eastern territories after the end of the war, they were already engaging with the new prospect of implementing ever larger stages of the 'Final Solution' even during the war, although the murder method was not yet entirely clear. The idea of a gigantic forced labour programme developed by Heydrich, with deadly consequences for those affected, may well in fact have reflected ideas actually held within the RSHA.

From the autumn of 1941 the SS had also developed the perfidious system of 'extermination through work'. Within this system, not only were many people worked to death in a very short time, but it also meant that a hurdle had been erected that those people who were no longer fit for work, or who were not capable of being deployed, were unable to surmount. The perfidious nature of the system of 'extermination through work' was also particularly apparent where there were only a few forced labour projects for Jews, or none at all, as it provided a pretext for marking out those Jews who were 'non-deployable' as 'superfluous'. Jewish 'work deployment' formed an important complementary element in the early phase of the 'Final Solution'.

In the first months of 1942, the deportations were extended in accordance with the declarations of intent made at the Wannsee Conference. In March 1942 Eichmann announced a third wave of deportations involving a total of 55,000 people from the territory of the 'Greater German Reich'. This third wave actually began on 20 March 1942 and lasted until the end of June. Its destination was ghettos in the district of Lublin, the original 'Jewish reservation'.

Now, at the beginning of March 1942, a decision must again have been made to practice mass murder in the reception zone, in the district of Lublin. This decision also applied to the adjacent district of Galicia. In the eyes of the Nazi leadership Galicia represented something like an advance base for the planned New Order of *Lebensraum* in the East and, since the autumn of the previous year, had been already the scene of large-scale mass shootings.

The statement in Goebbels's diaries that the intention was to murder 60 per cent of the Jews living in the two districts is particularly important here. The decision to implement mass murder in the two districts, made early in March, had been prepared since October 1941 by SSPF Globocnik, who was responsible for this mass murder in both districts. The measures taken in the district of Lublin demonstrate important parallels with the mass murder of the Jews in the Warthegau, which was also introduced in autumn 1941, although unlike Greiser Globocnik used stationary gas chambers. As in the Warthegau, and as in Riga and Minsk, the mass murder of the indigenous Jews in the district of Lublin was directly linked to the deportations from the Reich.

With the start of the third wave of deportations to the district of Lublin and the completion of the first extermination camp in the General Government the option of a later resettlement to the East had been definitively abandoned. Most of the people deported to the district of Lublin died miserably in the ghettos after a short time, or were also deported to extermination camps. However the façade of a programme of resettlement and work deployment was maintained. During this third wave of deportations, which occurred between March and June, the RSHA prepared a Europe-wide deportation programme conceived on a much larger scale.

Between 25 March 1942 and the end of June, 50,000 Jews were deported from Slovakia to Auschwitz concentration camp on the basis of the agreements with the Slovakian government. The deportation of hostages from France to Auschwitz also began in March 1942.

It is clear from a remark by Heydrich to Tuka on 10 April that these first deportations from territories outside the 'Greater German Reich' were already part of a Europe-wide programme. According to this, it was planned initially to deport to the East half a million Jews from Slovakia, the Reich, the Protectorate, The Netherlands, Belgium, and France.

This introduced the fourth stage of escalation in the transition to the 'Final Solution'. Now, in spring 1942, the previous scheme for the deportation of

Central European Jews to particular areas in which the indigenous Jews had first been murdered was abandoned. In late April/early May the decision must evidently have been made henceforth to murder Jews indiscriminately.

It can be assumed that in late April or May the Nazi regime made the decision to extend the mass murder of the Jews, which was already in progress in the districts of Lublin and Galicia, to the whole of the General Government. At the same time, the decision must have been made to implement a mass murder among the Jews of annexed Upper Silesia. The systematic mass murder of the Jews in the General Government began in June, but was then interrupted for a few weeks because of the transport ban. The transport ban, introduced because of the offensive in the East, finally had a radicalizing effect on the extermination policy: it accelerated the deportations from the Western territories, and, during this period, the planners of the mass murder clearly had an opportunity to rethink and consolidate their ideas so that the overall programme could resume in July with much more devastating effect. It was during this phase that the SS took over Jewish forced labour in the General Government and thus maintained control over those prisoners who were 'fit for work' and so initially excluded from extermination.

At around the same time as this fundamental decision regarding the Jews in the General Government, at any rate before mid-May, significant decisions must have been made as a result of which the operation of the extermination machinery was further extended. On the one hand, it was decided that the deportations from the territory of the 'Greater German Reich' should be intensified beyond the quota set in March, and on the other the regime now set about murdering either all or almost all of the Jews deported from Central Europe when the transports arrived at their destinations in Eastern Europe. This happened to Jews deported from the Reich in Minsk from mid-May, and from early June in Sobibor to the Jews deported from Slovakia.

It can be assumed that on 17 April 1942 Himmler had already ordered the murder of over 10,000 Central European Jews still living in the Lodz ghetto, who had been deported there in October 1941 and survived the inhuman conditions in the ghetto.

With these decisions, probably made in the second half of April or early May, which came into effect in May/June, the Nazi regime definitively abandoned the idea of a 'reservation' in the eastern area of the General Government or the occupied Eastern territories which had increasingly become a fiction given the mass murder that was already under way. The link between this renewed escalation of the extermination policy and military developments, in other words the preparations for the summer offensive in the East, is just as apparent as the fact that, in view of the mass recruitment of workers from the occupied Soviet Union, in the spring of 1942 the Nazis believed they would soon be able to do without Jewish forced labourers.

At the beginning of June a concrete programme of deportations was established for the West, which according to the plan was to be realized within three months beginning in mid-July. This meant that the 'European' plans first discernible in early April were to be continued and adapted to the conditions set by the transport ban in June/July. In June 1942, however, Himmler went a step further and called for the rapid and complete deportation of all Jews from France.

The transports from Western Europe and—because of the transport ban—also those from Slovakia were now directed to Auschwitz. There, from early June, the great majority of deportees (as before in Minsk and Sobibor) fell victim to the new and more radical variation of the extermination policy: immediately after their arrival they were killed with poison gas, after a 'selection' had taken place on the railway ramp.

In May 1942 the mass murder of the Soviet Jews, which had begun in the summer of 1941, received a new impulse: the murders now resumed on a large scale, before ending in the summer of 1942 in the complete extermination of the indigenous Jewish population.

After the lifting of the transport ban in July 1942, the deportation and murder programme was fully operational, and we know that Himmler insisted on convincing himself of the functioning of the extermination programme by paying an inspection visit. At the end of that inspection, on 19 July he issued the order that the 'resettlement' of the entire Jewish population of the General Government was to finish at the end of 1942.

During the summer of 1942 the first preparations were made to organize larger numbers of deportations from the West and the South-East of those parts of Europe under the control of the 'Third Reich'.

This acceleration and radicalization of the extermination programme in spring and summer 1942 clearly reflected the decision of the Nazi leadership essentially to implement the intended 'Final Solution' during the war. After the USA entered the war the 'Third Reich' faced the necessity of waging a long-term war on several fronts, and this new situation also necessarily altered the status of the systematic mass murder of the Jews. With the extension of this last and most radical stage of *Judenpolitik* to all the territories under German control, the entire German sphere of influence was subjected to the hegemony of racism. The occupied and allied states were drawn into the 'New Order policy' and, for better or worse bound to the German leadership by their participation in an unparalleled crime. The extermination policy thus came to underpin the German policy of occupation and alliance. This central function of the mass murder of the Jews for the maintenance of German rule on the continent also serves to explain the great efforts made by the Nazi leadership to involve more and more countries in the extermination programme by the end of the war.

During the second half of the war *Judenpolitik*—along with efforts to provide political military and police security for the territory under German rule, and alongside the issues of economic and food policy—became a major axis of German occupation and alliance policy. The more the war advanced, the greater the significance that the systematic murder of the Jews assumed, from the point of view of the National Socialist leadership, for the cohesion of the German power block. Because the executive organizations of the mass murders—whether they were German occupying administrations, local auxiliaries, governments willing to collaborate, or allies—were made henchmen and accomplices of the extermination policy, and bound to the engine of that policy, the leadership of Nazi Germany. The altered and more important role given to *Judenpolitik* provides a significant explanation for the fact that the murder of millions in the second half of the war was not only continued but even extended.

During the war something that we have already been able to observe in Germany during the 1930s was repeated on a European scale. Just as it had been impossible to implement a racist policy in a 'positive' way within the German Reich, during the war the Nazi regime was in no position to introduce its planned racist 'reorganization' of Europe through constructive measures. All the measures taken in this direction either failed pitifully or laid bare the absurdity of National Socialist ideas of race.

If the National Socialists did not wish to abandon their aspiration to start the racist reorganization of the European continent even during the war, they were obliged to undertake concrete measures in anticipation of their racist utopia in a negative way. The *Entjudung* of the German sphere of influence—because of the inconsistency and lack of feasibility of a 'positive' racial policy—became the substitute for the unrealizable racial 'New Order'.

There was an additional effect that we have also been able to observe since 1933 with regard to *Judenpolitik* in Germany: the further radicalization of the persecution reinforced the power of the SS and the radical Party forces within the occupying administrations and finally led to an overall gain in importance for these forces within the Nazi system of rule. The total implementation of the *Judenpolitik* within the entire German territory was thus tantamount to the definitive realization of National Socialism's total claim to power. However, from the perspective of the National Socialists, *Judenpolitik* was far more than a mere instrument for the extension of their power: they saw its radical implementation as a matter of their own survival.

Even though all the major decisions concerning the National Socialist Europe-wide 'Final Solution' programme had been made by mid-1942, in the time remaining until the end of the war it turned out that the implementation of the mass murders, because of the central role occupied by the *Judenpolitik* within Germany's occupation and alliance policy, made great additional demands on the Nazi leadership. *Judenpolitik* was not a programme that ran automatically, but a series of systematically organized mass murders that could only be implemented if the National Socialist regime created the appropriate preconditions.

It is possible to identify three further periods during the second half of the war in which the Nazi regime further escalated its *Judenpolitik*: the phase between the Allied landing in North Africa and the Warsaw ghetto uprising, hence the months November 1942 to May 1943, that is the period during which the Axis powers lost the military initiative; autumn 1943, when Italy left the alliance and the German Reich occupied further territories previously controlled by Fascist Italy; finally, the period from spring to summer 1944, during which the German Reich occupied Hungary and Slovakia.

As a consequence of the Allied landing in North Africa which, from the point of view of the German leadership, threatened the whole southern flank of Europe, the Jews of Tunisia and France had found themselves directly in the clutches of the German persecutors, while at the beginning of 1943 the RSHA organized mass deportations in Greece and Bulgaria. The further military successes of the Western Allies, but above all the Warsaw ghetto uprising in April/May 1943, led to a further burst of radicalization of *Judenpolitik*, which can be demonstrated by the intensification of the persecution in Poland, in the occupied Soviet territories, in the Netherlands, in Belgium, in France, in Croatia, and in Slovakia.

After Italy's departure from the Axis alliance *Judenpolitik* was extended to Italian territory under German control as well as to the former Italian zones of occupation in Croatia, Greece, and France. That same period coincides with the attempt to deport the Danish Jews, which can be seen as Germany's reaction to growing resistance in that country.

With the occupation of Hungary and Slovakia and the deportation of the Jews living in those countries, in 1944 the Third Reich attempted to prevent both states leaving their alliance with Germany.

It became apparent, however, that, after the turning point of the war in the winter of 1942/3, it became increasingly difficult to implement the deportations in participation with governments allied or collaborating with Germany. They succeeded in Croatia, to a limited extent in Bulgaria and France; efforts with regard to Hungary and the Italian-occupied territories remained initially ineffective; Romania and Slovakia, which had originally been enthusiastic participants in German *Judenpolitik*, now changed their attitude. However, the Germans did not abandon their policy, since precisely in view of the deteriorating military situation they saw the intensification of the persecution of the Jews and the related compromising of their 'partners' as an important means of securing the German-ruled block.

It was particularly important here that the three states which successfully resisted German *Judenpolitik* during this phase—Italy, Romania, and Bulgaria—managed to leave the alliance with Germany between September 1943 and September 1944 through separate ceasefires. This departure of what Germany saw as its 'philo-Semitic' allies must have looked like confirmation of their policy not to compromise in any way on *Judenpolitik*.

If *Judenpolitik* had originally been one of the chief axes of German occupation and alliance policy, it now entered a phase in which it began to destroy Germany's policy of collaboration and alliance. *Judenpolitik* could only be implemented if a regime of terror was installed in countries where it was completely under the control of the Nazis, and it could only be implemented with the support of indigenous forces.

This policy was to prove horribly efficient in Hungary and Slovakia. It was initially adopted in France and northern Italy, but finally foundered on a lack of support from local forces. All regimes that became collaborators with German *Judenpolitik* in the second half of the war collapsed with the Third Reich: the Vichy regime, the Republic of Salò, the Arrow-Cross regime in Hungary, and the clerical-fascist Slovakian Republic.

The example of Denmark shows that *Judenpolitik* was not feasible without the conditions described: a regime dependent on Germany and support from local forces. The alternative, implementing the deportations with the help of German forces, foundered on a lack of staff resources and the fact that such an action would have destroyed the political basis of the German occupation policy in Denmark.

As far as the mass murders in territories directly under German control were concerned, it has become clear that *Judenpolitik* produced a particularly high percentage of victims in those areas in which a civilian administration was preparing the construction of a 'Greater German Reich' with the support of the SS. This applies to the Reich, including the annexed territories, the Protectorate, Bohemia and Moravia, Poland and the occupied Soviet territories, but particularly also to the Netherlands. The Jews living there only had a chance of survival if they managed to escape before the start of the murders; there were also limited possibilities of surviving by going into hiding, which increased towards the end of the war. But the numbers of victims were also very high in two territories which were controlled by a military administration and were not the target of a Germanization policy: in Greece and Serbia. In Belgium there was a German military administration and the country was also the target of German ideas of Germanization; but the percentage of Jewish victims was—if compared with the Netherlands—considerably lower, which may be down to the lower pressure of persecution, the sluggish Belgian authorities, the more cautious behaviour of the victims, and the helpfulness of the Belgian population. Norway was also considered a 'Germanic' country, and ruled by a civilian administration, but more than half of the small Jewish minority managed to escape the deportations in the autumn of 1942.

This brief survey of the fate of the Jews in the countries occupied by and allied with Germany shows once again that the German persecution of the Jews proceeded in very different ways in the individual territories within the German sphere of influence in the second half of the war. A large number of factors affected *Judenpolitik*, which for these reasons could be accelerated, slowed down, modified, and suspended. It was, among other things, because of this flexibility, the ability to adapt to rapidly changing conditions, that the persecution of the European Jews by the Nazi regime produced such terrible results.

"ONCE AGAIN I'VE GOT TO PLAY GENERAL TO THE JEWS"

From the war diary of Blutordensträger Felix Landau[1]

Ernst Klee, Willi Dressen and Volker Riess

In selecting an appropriate passage from diaries, letters, or testimonies of the perpetrators, one faces a dilemma not unlike that confronted by filmmakers. Claude Lanzmann, for instance, chose not to use any original footage from the Holocaust in making his film Shoah, since that type of material would obviously be contaminated by the Nazi perception of their victims and their will to reduce them to the status of subhumans. Yet by avoiding such documentation altogether one also eschews any attempt to understand the psychology of the killers. This, in turn, leads to a dehumanization of the perpetrators which facilitates avoiding any sense of common human responsibility for their crimes; they become wholly alien and therefore relevant to us only in so far as they may pose a threat to our existence. If we do choose to use filmic or written material by the Nazis, however, the very familiarity with the manner in which they perceived the reality they created can lead viewers or readers to identify with the makers of these images and empathize with their viewpoint. Moreover, these distorted portrayals of the victims may contain the kind of sadistic, pornographic imagery that would turn their audience into voyeurs, thereby making them complicit in the obscenity of mass murder (which is of course their very purpose). We have been exposed to a multitude of dehumanizing, brutalizing images of the victims of Nazism, reprinted over and over again whenever the Holocaust is mentioned, until we think we know what it was like, we almost "remember" it, when in fact all we remember are photographs taken by the killers or scraps of Nazi speeches and propaganda leaflets. They teach us very little either about the killers or about their victims.

It is for this reason that I did not choose one of numerous horrifying accounts of the killing process. Reading such accounts arouses in us empathy neither for those doing the killing nor for the dying; we are too close to the atrocity to feel anything but horror, perhaps shame, possibly curiosity, but hardly any sense of the humanity of either side.

Rather, I chose a far less directly horrifying account, yet one whose ultimate effect appears to me to be far more chilling and more conducive to some understanding of the mind of the perpetrators. For what we see here is the humanity, potential for true affection for another human being, curiosity about different peoples and cultures, devotion to work and duty, capacity for hard work and pleasure at a job well done, along with a deep ideological conviction and powerful prejudices, of a man who is a cog in the mass murder of the Jews. This man is no monster, and his capacity for indifference and compassion is probably not much different from any other average person's. Yet he is one of hundreds of thousands of little people who made the machinery of genocide tick. Had we erased the lines in his diary that mention the brutalization of the Jews, it would not have been very hard to identify with him. What makes his diary so revealing, and so terrifying, is that there is no gradual transition from one to another. It is the very same man who is both just like us, and a mass murderer.

In yet another ironic twist of fate, Landau enlisted the services of Bruno Schulz, a Jewish schoolteacher, artist, and author, now recognized as one of the major modernist voices of the twentieth century in the Polish language. Landau instructed Schulz to paint murals in his son's room. But because Landau had killed a Jew who "belonged" to his colleague, SS Scharführer Karl Günther, the latter avenged the insult by shooting Schulz on the street in November 1942. In 2001 the murals Schulz had created were discovered in Drohobycz. As for Landau, although he was finally arrested and sentenced to life imprisonment in 1963, he was pardoned only a decade later.

On 25 July 1934 members of the 89th SS-Standarte forced their way into the Bundeskanzleramt (the Austrian Chancellor's Office) in Vienna. Although they fatally injured the Chancellor, Engelbert Dollfuss, the coup failed.

One of those arrested was cabinetmaker Felix Landau, who held up the staff of the Chancellor's office at gun point with a sub-machine-gun [see 'Appendix: biographical details' for a detailed biography]. Landau was sent to Wöllersdorf detention camp charged with being an accomplice in the crime. He was released in 1937. He became a naturalized German citizen and obtained a post as a Kriminalassistent. When on 12 March 1938 the German troops marched into Austria he was an SS-Hauptscharführer in a Security Police and SD Einsatzkommando.

Landau was then employed at the Gestapo regional headquarters in Vienna with the responsibility for 'securing' Jewish property. He married and moved into a villa that belonged to a Jew who had fled. In April 1940 he was assigned to KdS (Commander of the Security Police and the SD) in Radom (Polish General-Gouvernement). He was first sent to participate in the fight against scattered Polish units. Afterwards he worked in the records office. On 31 August 1940 his role in the attempted coup in Vienna and his time spent in imprisonment in Austria were recognized and he was awarded the Blutorden of the NSDAP.

At the office in Radom he met a twenty-year-old shorthand typist, Gertrude, who was engaged to a soldier from Vienna but wanted to break off the engagement. Landau learnt that Gertrude – despite her promise to him – was still seeing her fiancé. He thus resolved to break off the relationship. On 30 June 1941, just at the start of the Russian campaign, he reported to an Einsatzkommando (EK). At this point the diary begins.

Lemberg, 3 July 1941

On Monday, 30 June 1941, after a sleepless night I volunteered for a number of reasons to join an EK. By 9 o'clock I had heard that I had been accepted. It was not easy for me to leave. Suddenly everything had changed in me. I almost thought that I would not be able to tear myself from a certain person. I felt acutely how attached one can become to another human being.

As usual our departure was delayed several times but at 17.00 hours we finally left. We stopped one more time and once again I saw the person who has become so dear to me. Then we set off again. At 22.30 we finally reached Cracow. The accommodation was good. No creature comforts whatsoever. You can actually become a soldier in just a few hours if you want to. We then passed through Przemyśl. The town was still burning, on the street we saw shot-up German and Russian tanks. It was the first time I had seen two-tier Russian tanks.

After a short time we set off again towards Millnicze. It was becoming increasingly clear that the troops had recently been through. . . . At 21.30 on 1 July 1941 we arrived in M. We stood around aimlessly without any plan. We quartered ourselves in a Russian military school. It was still burning here too. At 23.00 hours we finally went to bed. I set up my bed and kipped down. Naturally I inquired whether it was possible to send letters but unfortunately it wasn't. On 2 July 1941 we were woken at 6.00 as at the front. There were women and children standing by burning houses and rummaging around in the rubble. During the journey we came across more Ukrainian soldiers. As we got closer and closer to the Russians the smell of decaying corpses got stronger and stronger.

At 4.00 pm on 2 July 1941 we arrived in Lemberg. First impression: Warsaw harmless in comparison. Shortly after our arrival the first Jews were shot by us. As usual a few of the new officers became megalomaniacs, they really enter into the role wholeheartedly. We took over another military school in the Bolshevik quarter. Here the Russians must have been caught in their sleep.

We quickly gathered together the bare essentials. At midnight after the Jews had cleaned the building, we went to bed.

3 July 1941. This morning I found out that we can write and it looks as though the post will actually be dispatched.

So while listening to wildly sensual music I wrote my first letter to my Trude. While I was writing the letter we were ordered to get ready. EK with steel helmets, carbines, thirty rounds of ammunition. We have just come back. Five hundred Jews were lined up ready to be shot. Beforehand we paid our respects to the murdered German airmen and Ukrainians. Eight hundred people were murdered here in Lemberg. The scum did not even draw the line at children. In the children's home they were nailed to the walls. Some of the occupants of a prison nailed to the wall.

Today a rumour went round that we are going to return to Radom. In all honesty I would be happy to see my loved ones again. They mean more to me than I was ever prepared to admit to myself. So far there hasn't been an execution. Today we were on alert all day. It should be happening tonight.

Things are pretty tense. In this confusion I have only written notes. I have little inclination to shoot defenceless people – even if they are only Jews. I would far rather good honest open combat. Now good night, my dear Hasi [bunny].

5 July 1941

It's 11.00 am. Wonderful music, 'Do You Hear My Secret Call' ('Hörst Du mein heimliches Rufen'). How weak can a heart become! My thoughts are so much with the person who caused me to come here. What I wouldn't give to see her even for just ten minutes. I was up all of last night on guard duty, in other words kept watch.

A small incident demonstrated to me the complete fanaticism of these people. One of the Poles tried to put up some resistance. He tried to snatch the carbine out of the hands of one of the men but did not succeed. A few seconds later there was a crack of gunfire and it was all over. A few minutes later after a short interrogation a second one was finished off. I was just taking over the watch when a Kommando reported that just a few streets away from us a guard from the Wehrmacht had been discovered shot dead.

One hour later, at 5 in the morning, a further thirty-two Poles, members of the intelligentsia and Resistance, were shot about two hundred metres from our quarters after they had dug their own grave. One of them simply would not die. The first layer of sand had already been thrown on the first group when a hand emerged from out of the sand, waved and pointed to a place, presumably his heart. A couple more shots rang out, then someone shouted – in fact the Pole himself—'Shoot faster!' What is a human being?

It looks like we'll be getting our first warm meal today. We've all been given 10 RM so that we can buy ourselves a few small necessities. I bought myself a whip costing 2 RM. The stench of corpses is all-pervasive when you pass the burnt-out houses. We pass the time by sleeping.

During the afternoon some three hundred more Jews and Poles were finished off. In the evening we went into town just for an hour. There we saw things that are almost impossible to describe. We drove past a prison. You could already tell from a few streets away that a lot of killing had taken place here. We wanted to go in and visit it but did not have any gas masks with us so it was impossible to enter the rooms in the cellar or the cells. Then we set off back to our quarters. At a street corner we saw some Jews covered in sand from head to foot. We looked at one another. We were all thinking the same thing. These Jews must have crawled out of the grave where the executed are buried. We stopped a Jew who was unsteady on his feet. We were wrong. The Ukrainians had taken some Jews up to the former GPU citadel. These Jews had apparently helped the GPU persecute the Ukrainians and the Germans. They had rounded up 800 Jews there, who were also supposed to be shot by us tomorrow. They had now released them.

We continued going along the road. There were hundreds of Jews walking along the street with blood pouring down their faces, holes in their heads, their hands broken and their eyes hanging out of their sockets. They were covered in blood. Some of them were carrying others who had collapsed. We went to the citadel; there we saw things that few people have ever seen. At the entrance of the citadel there were soldiers standing guard. They were holding clubs as thick as a man's wrist and were lashing out and hitting anyone who crossed their path. The Jews were pouring out of the entrance. There were rows of Jews lying one on top of the other like pigs whimpering horribly. The Jews kept streaming out of the citadel completely covered in blood. We stopped and tried to see who was in charge of the Kommando. 'Nobody.' Someone had let the Jews go. They were just being hit out of rage and hatred.

Nothing against that – only they should not let the Jews walk about in such a state. Finally we learned from the soldiers standing there that they had just visited some comrades of theirs, airmen in fact, in hospital here in Lemberg who had been brutally injured. They'd had their fingernails torn out, ears cut off and also their eyes gouged out. This explained their actions: perfectly understandable.

Our work is over for today. Camaraderie is still good for the time being. Crazy, beautiful, sensuous music playing on the radio again and my longing for you, the person who has hurt me so much, is growing and growing. Our only hope is to get away from here – most would prefer to be back in Radom. I for one – like many of the other men – have been disillusioned with this Einsatz. Too little combat in my view, hence this lousy atmosphere.

Lemberg, 6 July 1941

I had a terrible night last night. How true to life and intense a dream can be! The whole Warsaw affair, the reason why I am here, passed before my eyes so clearly there was nothing more I could wish for.

Once again I am psychologically shattered, just as I was then. I feel as if I won't be able to do it – to see beyond it and forget what I have gone through. If I don't meet T. again very soon I will go and do what I planned to do. No one will stop me. My mood is ghastly. I must get to Radom come what may.

Today I managed to send another letter to my Trude. It wasn't a very lovely letter, it expressed my despair to the full. I couldn't help it. I am now more hopeful that we will see each other again. This afternoon we learned that the Kommando will be going to Radom on Monday, 8 July 1941, after it has been to Drohobycz, an industrial town. We all breathed a sigh of relief. If we'd had to go on indefinitely it would have become impossible for us to continue working together. Four lorries have been taken from our EK. We have found some new telephones and gas masks of Russian origin which we took with us.

Things should start moving at our new post, thank God. Today I am reporting for a dangerous special mission [Sonderaufträge]. If we do have to stay there I will arrange things so that Trude can come.

The reveillé came at 8 o'clock. We sleep a long time so that the days are shorter. Once again work to do. Today I went into town for the nth time to look for a stationery shop. I actually managed to find one. Stationery shops have become my great passion. Naturally I rummaged through everything there and even found something usable. Writing paper, as we know it at home, does not exist here. But I finally have envelopes and now don't have to go round scrounging anymore. I also bought myself a lovely big travelling-bag for 32 roubles/3.80 RM.

So we are finally moving on to Drohobycz tomorrow morning at 8.00. We've been told that the area is partly occupied by the Russians. I am glad we are finally moving on a little. Tomorrow there's another post going to Cracow and Lublin from where it will be forwarded. I can write a quick letter to my little Trude. My feelings for all other women have been dead for a long time. I don't actually know myself how it happened.

This morning there was a special announcement that a further 52,000 Russians had capitulated. I should think there'll be a revolution in Russia in under two weeks. By then Moscow will certainly have fallen. Tonight we are having a social evening with our 'Kameraden' from Cracow.

Drohobycz, 7 July 1941

The social evening ended at 6.30 in the morning. There were no incidents. I picked up my two companions at about half past midnight and then we went together to our room to spend the rest of the night there. Our luggage has grown visibly. Oberführer Schönrad is the head of the EK. Sturmbannführer Röck works at the command post. We should have set off at 8.00. We finally left at 10.00 after a lot of quarrelling.

The people of Cracow are almost without exception complete arse-lickers. We had to go back along quite a stretch of the way we had come. We could already smell the prison where hundreds of people were murdered several streets away. There were hundreds of people standing in front of the shops trying to get hold of food of some kind. On our way two Jews were stopped. They said that they had fled from the Russian army. Their story was fairly unbelievable. Six of our men got out, loaded up and the next minute both were dead. When the order to take aim was given, one of the Jews, an engineer, was still shouting, 'Long live Germany.' Strange, I thought. What on earth had this Jew been hoping for?

At 16.00 we reached our destination. We were divided into several teams, in order to look for quarters for all the men. We found three houses which had been barely lived in. Baths everywhere, former Communist Party functionaries' homes. We were also able to establish that the Ukrainians had done a pretty good job plundering. They had really thought they were the masters for a while. There's going to be an almighty clash here – it's inevitable. Another interesting discovery: although there are very few radio sets here, almost every flat has its own speaker. The speakers can be switched on and off and have an adjustable volume so that means there won't be any need to forbid the men to listen to foreign broadcasts. In this case it won't be necessary.

I have a strong feeling that we will not be going back to Radom. My little Trudchen will thus have to come out here instead. We have occupied a Jewish hotel for a few days. I was ravenously hungry, so I have just 'inspected' the kitchen and managed to find a little something to eat. The quarters are very basic. The place is teeming with bugs. Now I must close because I have to report for guard duty. I'll be relieved at 1.00 tomorrow. My darling Trudchen, good night.

8 July 1941

Today more crazy toing and froing. The Ortskommandant has said that we should not have been here in the first place, since there's no work for us. Marvellous! In the afternoon our Hauptsturmführer went to the Generalkommando to clarify the situation. The explanation: a misunderstanding on the part of the Ortskommandant. Everything now in order. My explanation: no communication and no cooperation with the Wehrmacht. No further comment necessary.

Around midday we moved into new quarters, a former Communist Party military school. I am to work in the financial running of the place and with the horses. In the stable I discovered three small ponies. Actually a whole family: a male, a female and a foal. A small pony cart and also a saddle, and complete harness. People are strange. When I reported for guard duty there were three ugly dirty women, former chambermaids, standing in the lobby gawping at me. An interpreter came up to us and talked to them. One of these women was asking whether I wanted to go to bed with her. These goddamned people are unbelievable. Of course that had the others clamouring round all the more. I thought she'd end up in bed with someone but she didn't, thank God. Otherwise all hell would have been let loose during room inspection.

In the evening we had another comrades' get-together. During supper a couple of the men wanted to take me to the flat with some women – waitresses from the hotel. I refused point blank. They were both very disappointed. I don't want to and can't. My Trude is far too much on my mind. At the social evening I just could not get her out of my thoughts. I am so worried about her. Who knows whether she is still thinking of me. Still not a word from her and I don't even know if she's been receiving my letters.

9 July 1941

Today there were more surprises. In the morning a letter arrived from the Ortskommandantur. In an unfriendly tone we were informed that our work is to be limited merely to checking papers. In addition the letter declared that we were to ask nothing of the Referent for Jewish Affairs. As predicted, an impossible relationship. There was a tremendous amount of work. Once again I have got to play general to the Jews. Today I organized a carriage and harness despite the ban. Today there was beer from the barrel, we could also buy a bottle of Sekt for 1 RM. If only I had post from my Trude. During the day when I am buried in work it is all right but during the night the loneliness and inactivity simply make me despair. Good night Trudchen. Think a little of your Lexi.

10 July 1941

I left the social evening at 2 o'clock in the morning. I poured as much drink down me as I could to lighten my spirits and forget for a short while. Unfortunately to no avail. Ten litres of beer and a few schnapps as well as a litre of red wine still did not have the desired effect. The next day I felt as if I had been hit around the head with a sledgehammer. Today I was called to attend the allocation of assignments. I was working with a colleague from the SD [name illegible – Ed.] Department II Economics, in addition I was officially assigned as 'Judengeneral' ('General to the Jews'). I requisitioned two military vehicles for the department. Others have already done so for their own use.

I have no time for that. The only thing I wanted was a decent apartment. The arguments with the Wehrmacht continue. The Major in charge must be the worst kind of state enemy. I remarked today that I would apply to Berlin for this M. to be put into preventive detention immediately; his actions are a danger to the state. Take his remark that the Jews fall under the protection of the German Wehrmacht. Who could have thought such a thing possible? That's no National Socialist.

14 July 1941[2]

I haven't managed to get round to writing any more in my diary till today. A great many things have happened. New experiences and new impressions.

On 11 July 1941 a vehicle finally left for Radom carrying Dolte, Binder, Gürth and Mireck. Regrettably I could not go with them. At least I was able to give them a letter which I can be sure will arrive. I also have the prospect of hearing from my little Trude to look forward to. Unfortunately I'll be getting other letters as well. Of course, as was to have been expected, our KK [Kriminalkommissar – Ed.] . . . immediately took advantage of Dolte's absence to quench his thirst for action. Barely an hour later his wonderful orders such as 'Get a move on, gentlemen, get that whole pile over here to me' and the like were ringing out. He had arrests and shootings to his heart's desire. The prisoners, mostly Jews but also some Ukrainians, keep on coming. . . . We 'work' right through the night. In the evening a comrade, Urban, and I managed to snatch some time to go and see a cook from whom we can get *Mischlanka*, sour milk and new potatoes. Although the rooms are very small, everything is clean and pleasant. The people were friendly and obliging. There was also a very pretty young Ukrainian girl there. Communication – try as she might – was impossible. The only thing I managed to gather was that she was very interested in me. But my thoughts as ever are still with my Trude. I am not tempted nor do I want to be.

At 11 in the evening we got back to base. A flurry of activity down in the cellar, which I had just cleared up that morning. There were fifty prisoners, two of whom were women. I immediately volunteered to relieve the person who was on guard duty. Almost all of them will be shot tomorrow. Most of the Jews amongst them were from Vienna. Still dreaming of Vienna. I was on duty until three in the morning the next day. Finally went to bed dog tired at 3.30.

12 July 1941

At 6.00 in the morning I was suddenly awoken from a deep sleep. Report for an execution. Fine, so I'll just play executioner and then grave-digger, why not? Isn't it strange, you love battle and then have to shoot defenceless people. Twenty-three had to be shot, amongst them the two above-mentioned women. They are unbelievable. They even refused to accept a glass of water from us. I was detailed as marksman and had to shoot any runaways. We drove one kilometre along the road out of town and then turned right into a wood. There were only six of us at that point and we had to find a suitable spot to shoot and bury them. After a few minutes we found a place. The death candidates assembled with shovels to dig their own graves. Two of them were weeping. The others certainly have incredible courage. What on earth is running through their minds during those moments? I think that each of them harbours a small hope that somehow he won't be shot. The death candidates are organized into three shifts as there are not many shovels. Strange, *I am completely unmoved. No pity, nothing.* That's the way it is and then it's all over. My heart beats just a little faster when involuntarily I recall the feelings and thoughts I had when I was in a similar situation. On 24 July 1934 in the Bundeskanzleramt [Chancellery] when I was confronted with the machine-gun barrels of the Heimwehr [Austrian militia, 1919–38]. Then there were moments when I came close to weakening. I would not have allowed it to show, no, that would have been out of the question with my character. 'So young and now it's all over.' Those were my thoughts, then I pushed these feelings aside and in their place came a sense of defiance and the realization that my death would not have been in vain.

And here I am today, a survivor standing in front of others in order to shoot them. Slowly the hole gets bigger and bigger; two of them are crying continuously. I keep them digging longer and longer; they don't think so much when they're digging. While they're working they are in fact calmer. Valuables, watches and money, are put into a pile. When all of them have been brought to stand next to one another on a stretch of open ground, the two women are lined up at one end of the grave ready to be shot first. Two men had already been shot in the bushes by our KK [Kriminalkommissar] . . . I did not see this as I had to keep my eyes on the others. As the women walked to the grave they were completely composed. They turned round. Six of us had to shoot them. The job was assigned thus: three at the heart, three at the head. I took the heart. The shots were fired and the brains whizzed through the air. Two in the head is too much. They almost tear it off. Almost all of them fell to the ground without a sound. Only with two of them it didn't work. They screamed and whimpered for a long time. Revolvers were no use. The two of us who were shooting together had no failures. The penultimate group had to throw those who had already been shot into the mass grave then line up and fall in themselves. *The last two had to place themselves at the front edge of the grave so that they would fall in at just the right spot.* Then a few bodies were rearranged with a pickaxe and after that then we began the gravedigging work.

I came back dog tired but the work went on. Everything in the building had to be straightened up. And so it went on without respite. In the afternoon the car came back from Radom unexpectedly. Like a small child I couldn't wait to get my post. That was my first question. Unfortunately I didn't get a chance to read all my post, there was so much; no sooner had I begun than the Hauptsturmführer came up to me and asked me to get started on the move to the new offices and set things up there as well.

So I worked until 11 o'clock and had to make myself a plan like a proper little architect. Everyone admired my work.

On Sunday, 13 July 1941, the work started again straight away. I hardly got any sleep. My feet and my head hurt as though I had just been on two pack marches. We also learned that Communists had taken control in the mountainous area behind us. Yet more work. Finally I managed to read all my post. It's strange, my mood completely changed. A lot of what I read gave me great cause for worry. Apart from anything else Trude wrote that she doesn't know whether she can keep her promise and whether she will be strong enough. Why does this have to happen to me with a person I love so much? I have to see her and talk to her, then my little Trude will be strong again. She must come here.

14 July 1941

Attended various meetings. Council of the Jews. Otherwise mostly organized and moved. In the evening found a sheepdog bitch.

20 July 1941

Today is Sunday. Once again I worked until 8 o'clock. It is now 10.00 and I have finally managed to find the time to record in my diary the few events which, in the larger context of what is happening in the world, are so insignificant.

[On] 15 July 1941 I went together with a comrade to the aforementioned Ukrainian family. It was very cosy and also very interesting for someone who is interested in the ways of another people. We talked over just about everything. The only subject I thought it better not to touch upon was religion, as it would be easy for misunderstandings to arise when communication was somewhat limited. We were still talking at 11.00. On the way there – we had gone there in our pony and trap – something very funny happened to us. First we were caught in a downpour, although that did not last long. Then when we turned into a real Russian track we were confronted by potholes over a metre deep. Naturally we were jolted out of our seats on quite a number of occasions. Then we got to a particularly fine spot and my cart bounced backwards slightly while the pony kept on going. All of a sudden I heard a splash and when I turned round I saw my comrade in a pretty deep puddle, with his legs sticking up in the air. Despite the unpleasantness of the situation I couldn't help roaring with laughter. The trip back looked like becoming even more tragic; had the farmer not taken us to the main road we would have certainly ended up, pony, trap and all, in a ditch.

Because of this delightful track we didn't get back until midnight. As we rode through the gate a car was just starting up. Soon I realized that things were pretty lively for this time of night. My first thought was that something was up. Obviously people were worried on our account and thought that something had happened to us. . . . The next morning we were informed that all social intercourse with the Ukrainians was forbidden. He, that is the Hauptsturmführer, had no objections if any of us spent the odd night with an *U-Mädel* [Ukrainian girl] but all other contact was forbidden. Odd attitude. Well as far as I am concerned that is out of the question, since all I wanted was to get to know the people. My small young dog is coming along fine. As each day passes she is becoming more and more devoted but she's still as nervous as ever.

On 16 July 1941 more moving again. My role here is more one of architect than of official. I am now, in addition, responsible for overseeing and conducting the training of 150 Ukrainians. I'm quite happy to play at being master builder and architect, the only thing I wish is that I had workmen and not Jews to carry out the work. Still, that's the way it has to be.

On 17 July 1941 nothing much happened. I messed around with the Jews some more – and that's my work.

18 July 1941. The question of the day is who will travel to Radom. All of a sudden everybody has got to go there. They've all left things they can't do without there. Nobody has a suitcase, nobody has clean laundry. Usually in the military, failure to carry out orders is punished harshly; here, however, it's rewarded with a Sunday excursion to Radom. At midday there was a meeting and yes, as expected, once again I was not amongst those who were to go. I was bursting with rage. Here I am slaving away day and night so that everyone has a nice apartment and is assured every comfort, and then when I make the smallest request others are given preferential treatment.

19 July 1941. The entire day I could not get the thought out of my head that at that very moment I could have been with Trudchen in R. Try as I might to push these thoughts to one side I still imagine my little Trudl there waiting and hoping to see me. What use is my fine apartment fitted out with every comfort if that very thing is missing? Everything is dead in my flat.

19 July 1941. So I was not able to travel to Radom. The way I feel I could kill everyone. I of all people was not permitted to go. I am not very optimistic about my chances next time. Spent the whole day working solidly. How disappointed my little Trude will be when instead of me only a letter arrives. In the evening we had another visit, only a day after the Oberführer arrived without any prior warning. He was very pleased with the rooms and the buildings. As usual others took all the credit. That's the way it will always be given human nature. In the evening as I was lying in bed I was filled with a tremendous yearning, yearning for quiet, peace and love.

21 July 1941

After waiting in vain yesterday for the men to return from Radom, all I could do again today was wait. Every five minutes I asked whether the vehicles had returned from Radom. Again and again my question was in vain. Finally towards midday the car arrived. By that time I no longer needed to ask for they all shouted to me in unison, 'Felix there's a packet for you.' I breathed a sigh of relief. When I read the letter I locked myself in my room. It was short and sketchy. I began to worry and think dark thoughts. Could Trude have been unfaithful after such a short time? I am uneasy. What I would give for Trudchen to be with me. Well, this is how I wanted it, only I thought it would turn out differently. Oh well, ordinary life is far too tame for me. I don't understand Trudchen. She sent me the pictures of my children and my wife. I could understand why she'd send the former, but the latter is beyond me. The men had the day off today, some of them went hunting. I had to work here. Thanks and praise is sure to come my way. The above-mentioned Sturmbannführer went off hunting once again with his five men. The work is going ahead well. I have just been informed by the Hauptsturmführer that I am to take over the training of the militia. Apparently I have the right attitude. Today I answered my wife's letters and sent her 180 RM. Trudchen got a short letter from me.

Another eventful day. In the morning the workers I had ordered failed to appear. Just as I was about to go to the Jewish Committee one of my colleagues from the council came and asked me for my support as the Jews were refusing to work here. I went over. When those arseholes saw me they ran in all directions. Pity I did not have a pistol on me or else I would have shot some of them down. I then went to the Council of Jews and informed them that if 100 Jews did not report for work within an hour I would select 100 of them *not for work but for the firing-squad.* Barely half an hour later 100 Jews arrived together with a further seventeen for those who had run away. I reported the incident and at the same time gave orders for the fugitives to be shot for refusing to work, *which happened precisely twelve hours later. Twenty Jews were finished off.*

Another incident, I sent one of the men off with two Jews to get hold of some material we needed. He took the keys from the usual place and went off. While we were clearing up one of the Ukrainians started pestering the Jews, who were carrying out our orders, naturally with the full agreement of the Germans. Amongst other things he asked the Jews who they thought they were, letting on to the Germans what was in the storeroom. He said he would come and find them in the evening and beat them to death. Well, that really got my blood up. Such people in my opinion are the real enemies of the state, so I had the lad brought in. In my room he received by way of introduction a little bit of my special treatment. After the first beating, blood was spurting. First he tried to deny he had done anything. After the fourth beating however he gave up this tactic. I gave orders for him to be arrested for having an anti-German attitude.

In a village near Drohobycz four released convicts were shot on the spot. This time the Slovaks dug the graves and did the burying.

I am very curious to know how the Council of Jews will take it. They'll all be wailing and gnashing their teeth tomorrow. We also found that No. 13 barracks had been broken into again, and an attempt had been made to steal the rubber tyres from our vehicles. One of the tyres had been sliced right through with a sharp knife. So in the evening I made yet another arrest.

Tomorrow I am going to make a concerted effort to ask about my Trudchen coming here. As a final resort, if I get a refusal I am going to ask for a transfer or obtain one somehow. At the same time I'm also going to sort out the Radom trip. Then tomorrow I'll write a long letter to Trudchen. Good night my dear little rascal, please still love me, think of me and stay true to me. Now I am going to bed, to look at your picture and read your book. When my eyes begin to get tired I shall put the book aside and look at your picture again, give you a big kiss, switch off the light and go to sleep.

23 July 1941

Well, I was not able to put yesterday's plans into action. The reason is simply the unbelievable amount of work. I sometimes wonder how much more I can take of this. At 8 o'clock this morning I should have detailed the Jews for various tasks and drilled the Ukrainian militia at the same time as well. In the afternoon I was given a lot more jobs but I am determined to write the letter to Trudchen. I must see her, speak to her come what may. Today I found quite a few Communist Party banners and weapons. Work is progressing quickly on all the buildings. The new militiamen certainly seem to be finding it difficult to adjust to my tempo and tone. Today ten out of forty men failed to report.

Our chief once again threatened some of the comrades with execution and again for no reason whatsoever. He said to Urban, 'If you don't change your tone with me you will be included in the next execution.' There have already been complaints about him. He has been nicknamed 'Revolver-kommissar' and 'Sonnensoldal' ('Sunshine Soldier'). He is the only one who goes about with a white battle tunic and long trousers. It's now already 23.00 but I must write the letter without fail.

28 July 1941

All of my good intentions – come what may – to write my diary every evening have come to naught. It's midnight and I have finally got round to writing a few lines. I was quite amazed when I discovered on Saturday morning what day it was. I had intended to approach Dolte again on Friday about going to Radom. I was devastated and spent the rest of the day in a frightful frame of mind. I worked until 11 at night. What else can I do? Some of the other men went out at midday and returned towards 7.00 in the evening with some Ukrainian girls whom they took up to their quarters. I was still clearing the place and having carpets laid. On Sunday I worked until 3.00 and then for the first time since my Einsatz I am having a break.

On Friday and Saturday there was an interesting development on the work front. Some Ukrainians brought a report from a neighbouring village which went more or less as follows: Someone had discovered the bodies of twenty-four Ukrainians who had been murdered by the Russians in the woods. The bodies were almost unrecognizable. As this was a murder case the criminal police took it up immediately and went to the place in question. There they were solemnly received by a cleric who told them how pleased he was to see them. The cleric said that it was extremely kind of the Germans to take such an interest in the murder and fate of the Ukrainians. The bodies were solemnly buried and our officials had no choice but to take part. On the way the cleric said to me, 'Do you know, the vilest thing about it is that Jewish passes and papers were put in their pockets.' Now this is unbelievable! These supposed Ukrainians were in fact the very twenty-three Jews plus, I think, two Ukrainians we ourselves had shot! Cheers, bon appetit. The papers on the bodies stank terribly. I had petroleum poured over them, then ordered them to be burnt and buried in the grave. . . .

30 July 1941

I had a wonderful surprise. Post from Trude. I had been waiting for so long! Her post arrived just as I was writing a letter. My mood shot up 100%. What a funny girl my Trude is. In her letter she wrote a philosophical treatise about my love life and marriage, utterly serious as though her life depended on it. Full of intellectual utterances like a wise and experienced woman. There was not a thought or a word about herself. She had excluded herself entirely from the letter. Sometimes there is a slight sense that she wants to convince me of something so that she can be rid of me more easily. But then when I read the letters from the day before and the day after I cannot help smiling at these thoughts, for out of these lines emerges a hot and passionate love, like the one I feel for her. Sometimes I begin to feel afraid, as though in a dream. She has no idea what she has come to mean to me. Also she does not realize what has happened inside me recently. If she, who has come to mean so much to me, disappointed me I would be completely devastated. I think that I would lose my belief in humanity right up to the day I died. Yesterday evening, despite the ridiculous amount of work, I wrote Trudchen another six-page letter. Today I was summoned in confidence to D. who informed me that the GG [General-Gouverneur] will be coming on Saturday. So no trip once again. I am not giving up hope. I sent Trudchen a letter and a small miniature – a baroque love scene.

Today, 31 July 1941, there was a crazy amount of work again. The letter left today with the vehicle for Radom.

1 August 1941

Yesterday I managed to have my much requested conversation with Dolte. This time I refused to let myself be fobbed off. At 8.00 in the evening I went to Dolte's apartment, which is above mine, and asked him whether he had time to see me. He did and asked me to come in and sit down at the table. He had Briese with him. He was just in the middle of reading out a ten-page letter from his girlfriend in Radom to Briese. I was initially slightly embarrassed but in this respect Dolte is as open as I am and does not have any secrets. So much the better for me and my affair. I could not have hit on a better moment. He told me he has not got any further with his divorce and that he has now engaged four lawyers. Then good old Briese left. Dolte offered me some wine and cigarettes and we sat together like old chums. Then I fired away. I no longer had any need to mention what I wanted because it is so widely known and has already been referred to. His position was the following: Every support . . . of course. First of all Trudchen must come here and only then will we take it further. As far as going to Radom was concerned I received a promise that I could travel on Saturday, 9 August 1941. So something is fixed. I was very satisfied with the outcome. My spirits were finally restored after so long. My Ukrainian militia got a 'honeymoon period'. The Jews were 'more considerately' treated. I gave away more cigarettes than usual. You could tell by my whole behaviour that something pleasant had happened to me. However during supper I couldn't avoid getting angry.

A certain Herr Gabriel, a man with an inferiority complex and bulging eyes, became angry because I had dismissed for incompetence a Jewess who was working for me. The gentleman forgets that we have introduced the race law into the National Socialist state. I'd already caught him once tenderly stroking the chin of a Jewess and given him a thorough talking-to. At the time he was pretty discomfited. The gentleman must have already forgotten this.

Once again plenty of work, until 22.00. The General-Gouverneur is due to arrive tomorrow, so my militia have to be properly kitted out. At 7.00 in the evening I went to their barracks and established that out of sixty men only twelve are fully kitted out. About forty tailors had been working for almost three days and could not finish the uniforms. I was furious. Of course, most of the blame lay with the leadership of the militia. I immediately summoned the Council of Elders to me and told them that all the remaining uniforms had to be ready by midday the following day or else I would have five tailors executed for sabotage by firing-squad.

A man was brought before me who wanted to report his sixteen-year-old daughter for whoring. According to his own account his daughter has been on the make since she was thirteen. So now it's up to the police to teach the child how to behave! I gave the father who wanted to put his own flesh and blood in prison such a good clip round the ear that he lost his balance five times. . . .

2 August 1941

Work goes on. This morning we started at 6. The GG is not coming. At 12.00 the Council of Elders reported to me that all the uniforms were ready. *Since I had twenty of its men shot for refusing to work*, everything's been running smoothly. This evening four of the men are off to Radom. So that means a quick letter to my Trude. I also have to send the money, 180 RM, to my wife. I've written the letters and given them to Laufmann. Will Trudchen be pleased? I also sent some toys to my wife for the children. The men left for Radom at 22.00 hours. . . .

5 August 1941

Today we took over four buildings for the women and wives who are due to arrive. Dolte is sometimes too weak, not ruthless enough . . . .

151

6 August 1941

I already know that it is going to take a tough and difficult fight to make her strong enough to get her to assert herself against her parents. She should not simply stumble into a marriage as I did. I will not let her. She is worth more than I am. She is far too good to be thrown away for something which offers her nothing. She will gain far more if she is allowed to love the person who can love her back completely. Today some of the men and I got the Jewish house-maid to roast some chickens for us. We also had new potatoes, cucumber salad and raspberry compote. I contributed the wine. Everything was perfect except for the empty places on my right and left. I looked at both chairs and said to my companions that all that was missing was our sweethearts. Then one of the men talked about his wife and their happy life together. Whether I like it or not I always become dejected and sad during such conversations. There is nothing I can do about it. For the time being there is no happy family life for me. Perhaps somebody will help me to become happy. Good night, Trudchen. Please remain true to me. . . .

Despite the extreme stress, which every single SS and police member had to contend with during these actions, the mood and morale of the men from the first to the last day was exceptionally good and praiseworthy. It was only by a personal sense of duty that every officer and man was able to overcome this pestilence in the shortest space of time.

SS- und Polizeiführer of Galicia, SS-Gruppenführer
Friedrich Katzmann, in a report dated 30th June 1943

---

8 August 1941

. . . My first thought when I awoke and dawn was breaking: tomorrow at this time we could already be leaving for Radom and if all goes well we could be there at 11 or 12 in the morning. Once I had begun to think about this subject naturally I could not go back to sleep. I imagined where I'd meet T., whether she would be able to go with me straight away or if I didn't arrive until the afternoon where I would find her. At her apartment, at the hairdresser's, at the sports centre, at German House, or – I hope not – out with one of my dear comrades. Then I thought about where I would actually be sleeping. If [illegible name – Ed.] is not at my apartment, or rather his apartment, then there. If he's at home then I will ask him to let me borrow my former flat for the night. I have so much to tell T. and I want my Hasi [bunny] to tell me everything on her mind. I fear a lot of unpleasantness. If only she had a quarter of my decisive-ness and strength of will. I would love to give her everything and transfer [some of] my will to her. I still have more than twenty-two hours to wait. I am already more nervous than I have ever been in my entire life. . . .

Appendix: biographical details

Landau, Felix. Born 1910. In 1911 his mother married Landau, a Jew, who gave his name to the child. Following his stepfather's death (1919), Landau attended a boarding-school run by a Catholic lay order. Was expelled from apprentice boarding-school for active recruitment activities for the NS Youth (joined National Socialist Worker Youth in 1925). Apprenticeship as skilled furniture-maker. In 1930 joined Austrian Bundesheer (2. Dragonerschwadron). Joined NSDAP March 1931. May 1931 political leader of a NS-Heeresprengels (army district). June 1933 expulsion from Bundesheer for NS activities. Member of SA from June 1933 to April 1934, after that in SS. Participated in Dollfuss affair 1934. Imprisoned until 1937. Renewed propaganda activities. Because of threat of arrest fled to Germany, where he became a naturalized citizen. Found employment as a police official (Kriminalassistent). In 1938 posted to Vienna Gestapo regional headquarters and married first wife. In 1940 transferred to KdS/SD in Radom (General-Gouvernement) where he met shorthand-typist Gertrude. Reported to an Einsatzkommando in June 1941. From July 1941 in Drohobycz, Lvov district (30,000 inhabitants, half of whom were Jews), where the Einsatzkommando was reorganized into an outpost of the Sicherheitspolizei and SD. Until May 1943 Landau was in charge of organizing Jewish labour. At the end of 1941 he lived with his mistress in an aristocratic villa. After his divorce from his wife in 1942 (his wife was judged the guilty party) married Gertrude in 1943 (divorced 1946). Last rank SS-Hauptscharführer. In 1946 recognized in Linz by a former 'worker Jew' and arrested by the Americans. In August 1947 escaped from Glasenbach prison camp. Lived under the name Rudolf Jaschke, ('design, planning, consultancy, interior decoration, refrigeration equipment') in the Nördlingen district. Was sentenced to life imprisonment by Stuttgart Landesgericht in 1963.

Notes

1 Blutordensträger means Bearer of the Order of the Blood.
2 The first 14 July entry should almost certainly read 11 July, but even then, there are some problems, since that entry mentions 11 July, and ends by saying that he went to bed at 3.30, that is, already on 12 July. Similarly, the 12 July entry includes descriptions of activities on 13 July. Hence one would assume that Landau continued filling in information that went beyond the date he wrote at the top of each entry.

8

KEEPING CALM AND WEATHERING THE STORM

Jewish women's responses to daily life in Nazi Germany

Marion Kaplan

In the past few decades, scholars have increasingly come to understand the importance of distinguishing between the experiences of men and women in the Holocaust. It is of course true that the Nazis targeted Jews as Jews, whatever their gender, age, or background. But the argument, made by the early, predominantly male, scholars of the Holocaust (despite prominent exceptions such as Leni Yahil and Lucy Dawidowicz), that gender made no difference, tended to obscure the specificity of individual and group experience, which was in fact largely determined by one's identity as well as by the perpetrators' perceptions of their victims. Indeed, as early exponents of this view such as Joan Ringelheim and Dalia Ofer have noted, gender, as well as age, class, cultural background, and relationship to religion, which had all been central to people's lives under normal circumstances, also affected them in numerous ways during the Holocaust, at times making the difference between life and death.

Diaries, written and oral testimonies, and memoirs of Holocaust victims and survivors leave no doubt as to the role of gender played in living through and remembering these events. Indeed, to some extent we can say that once historians turned from official documentation and grand reconstruction of the "final solution" to the perspective of the victims and the experience of the event from "below," such distinctions became glaringly clear. To be sure, within each group individual experience was also unique, and there could be great differences between one person and another; yet their sex and age always mattered in coping with the reality to which they were subjected. The most obvious in terms of age was that children were the least likely to survive and the first to be selected for murder (after an initial phase in which men and the "intelligentsia," also predominantly male, were targeted). As for gender, the fact that Jewish boys were circumcised meant that it was easier for girls with an "Aryan" look to pass as non-Jewish; at the same time, girls were targeted for sexual violence more

154

often than boys, even though we have significant evidence of boys and men also being targeted for sexual abuse and exploitation. Men were more likely to be taken to murderous labor; but women, especially when caring for children, were far more often selected for murder, unless they abandoned their children; women might use sex to survive, but were also raped, forced into prostitution, and abused. In other words, all were ultimately victims; but their victimhood was different.

Marion Kaplan examines an earlier period, before mass murder began but when German Jews living under Nazi rule were progressively pushed out of society and condemned to "social death." One extraordinary perspective on this period (as well as on Germany in wartime) can be found in Viktor Klemperer's diary, published in 1995, many years after his death. Klemperer provides a view of German society by the consummate insider, a middle class university professor, who is made into an outsider when the authorities declare him to be a Jew (he had converted to Protestantism many years earlier), deprive him of his position, and marginalize him to a point that he literally vanishes from the sight of his previous professional and social circles. The reason he survives is that he is married to an "Aryan." But while he is not seen, his view, his perspective on German society as it is gradually transformed into a Volksgemeinschaft – a national community from which all undesirable "racial aliens" and other biologically and mentally "unfit" individuals have been removed – is astonishingly perceptive, subtle, and objective. It is, however, the perception of a man and a (childless) husband. As we read Kaplan, we realize that this would have been a very different diary had it been written by a woman.

German Jewish women in prewar Nazi Germany, as Kaplan shows, were faced with a series of challenges that stemmed directly from their gender and the roles assigned to them by society at the time. As their husbands either lost their jobs or were earning much less than before, the women had to enter the job market, often becoming the single wage earners. At the same time they also had to care for the home – frequently without the domestic help they might have previously had – preparing meals, minding the children, and providing a haven for their husbands at a time of anxiety, frustration, and fear. Women also felt the changes in society more keenly than men, because they had more contact with their neighbors, local stores, schools, social gatherings, and so forth. While men might be abused more by the police, and were the primary targets of concentration camp incarcerations after Kristallnacht, women were more likely to stay behind in Germany as their husbands or brothers or sons left. Partly this was because the men set out to prepare the ground for the family, and partly because women more often cared for their parents or had fewer chances of finding positions abroad. This is why by the time immigration was no longer possible, the remaining German Jewish community was disproportionately made up of the elderly and of women. Age and gender mattered, and continued to matter as persecution turned into genocide.

It was through the dozens of daily tasks that ground their lives that most Jews, particularly women, suffered and assessed their situation under the Nazis. Daily life in Nazi Germany consisted not only of the commonplace—activities and beliefs that continued at least until November 1938—but, increasingly, of the unexpected.[1] Lawlessness, ostracism, and a loss of rights took their toll on Jews of all sexes and ages. As Jews tried to make a living, maintain their previously middle-class economic and cultural standards, nurture their families, and succeed at school, they became more and more aware of the growth of hostility and danger around them.

Daily privation

In spite of the apparent ordinariness with which Jewish women continued their daily existence, their internal equilibrium was shattered. Jews became vigilant in public and no longer felt safe even in their homes. They were afraid that the Gestapo would search their houses and find or plant incriminating evidence against them. While the Nazis burned books in public, many Jews burned portions of their libraries and their papers in private. Moreover, Jews could no longer take their homes for granted. Many faced eviction by landlords to whom Jewish tenants had become dangerous or undesirable. Food purchases were also limited, either by decree or by the hostility of shopkeepers. For Orthodox families, the prohibition against kosher butchering, which began as early as April 21, 1933, caused great hardship. Yet, as troublesome as renting and shopping had become, the most important indicator of how the Nazi takeover affected Jewish daily life was the interaction that Jews had with non-Jewish strangers, friends, and neighbors.

Absolute strangers became steadily more hostile toward Jews in public. This coarsening of attitudes was part of a more widespread lack of sympathy toward other purported enemies, such as Communists, Jehovah's Witnesses, and oppositional Social Democrats. In fact, such animosity was characteristic of the everyday behavior of many Germans toward one another. Long before Jews were forced to wear a yellow star in order to facilitate their identification, strangers on trams, in stores, and even on the street targeted those who "looked Jewish" and made their victims feel ill at ease. Some Germans literally used their noses to identify Jews. In particular, Germans drew on their long-standing and still common aversion to garlic, really an aversion to things foreign, to torment Jews. The streetcar seemed to be a favored locus of bad temper and ill will, where "Germans" accused "Jews" of smelling of garlic or simply of smelling "like Jews."[2]

The government intended to isolate Jews completely through intimidation and bribery of the "Aryan" populace. And the Nazis could count on grassroots enthusiasm. Well before the Nazis prohibited friendly contact with Jews, denunciation and gossip discouraged such associations. Historian Robert Gellately found "an extraordinary degree and variety of accommodation . . . to the regime's doctrines on race. Friendships and business relationships going back many years were broken off."[3] Of interest here is not only the fear of the authorities but the often zealous restrictions imposed by Germans themselves. Some exceptional Germans remained loyal, but most either avoided Jews or were hostile toward them.

In my reading of the memoirs and interviews of middle-class Jewish women, I observed that the loss of friends and the decline of sociability in the neighborhood evidently affected Jewish women more than men, because women were more integrated into and dependent upon the community and more accustomed to neighborly exchanges and courtesies. Their lives bridged the gap between family and community. Those who had been active in communal, volunteer, or women's groups suffered when they were ostracized. Moreover, women probably had more frequent contacts with state officials—postal and railroad clerks, social workers, and, for mothers in particular, teachers. Men saw less of neighbors to begin with and had less time to engage in communal or volunteer activities. Also, although men now suffered the loss of even a modicum of courtesy at work, they were more used to competition and a certain degree of conflict in their everyday work life.

Along with social isolation, unemployment began to plague the Jewish community. With the disappearance of many Jewish firms, joblessness became rampant. Even as the German economy improved and German unemployment dropped, Jewish unemployment climbed, emigration notwithstanding. Because more than half of employed Jewish women worked in business and commerce, many lost their jobs as family businesses and shops closed down. Jewish sources estimated that three-quarters of Jewish women in business and trade were affected by the discriminatory laws and the early anti-Jewish boycotts.[4] By April 1938, more than 60 percent of businesses that Jews had owned before 1933 no longer existed, and Jewish social workers were trying to help sixty thousand unemployed Jews.

In spite of their limited options on the job market, many Jewish women who had never worked outside the home suddenly needed employment. While some sought jobs with strangers, many began to work for their husbands, who could no longer afford to pay employees. One article in a Jewish newspaper praised women's flexibility and versatility, commenting that "we find relatively few families in which the wife does not work in some way to earn a living," and women were the sole support for many a family.[5]

Memoirs and statistics indicate that women trained for new jobs and then retrained when they lost newly acquired jobs. One woman took a speed course in becoming a corsetiere. Although Jews could no longer be licensed by the time she finished, she quickly developed private customers and supported herself. Many women trained for several jobs at once. A mother and daughter took courses in Spanish, English, baking, and fine cookery. Then they asked their laundress to accept them as apprentices. This role not only was new for them but was also a reversal of their previous class position.[6]

According to observers, women seemed "more accommodating and adaptable" than men, had "fewer inhibitions," and were willing to enter retraining programs at older ages. Leaders of the Berlin community noted that retraining for women was less costly and also took less time. Women already had some of the skills necessary for new jobs as, for example, seamstresses, milliners, or domestics.[7]

Young people faced particular employment problems. The exclusion of Jews from German universities, vocational schools, and institutions of higher learning restricted future job possibilities. But certain jobs were available for young women. Even though many had lost jobs in commercial fields, women under the age of thirty-five could still find jobs as other Jews began to emigrate. Also, the demand for Jewish help quickly picked up in the expanding Jewish social service sector. In addition, after the Nuremberg Laws were passed, forbidding Jews from hiring female Aryans under the age of forty-five as household help, Jewish households needed help, too. In Berlin, for example, although the majority of Jewish applicants remained jobless, Jewish employment services were more successful in placing women than men.[8]

Private responses

In the face of worsening living conditions, it was women who were supposed to "make things work" in the family. The Nuremberg Laws left Jewish women to their own devices in running a household with greater problems, shopping for food in stores staffed by increasingly unfriendly personnel, and performing all these tasks with ever-shrinking resources. Moreover, they had to soothe frightened children who faced harassment at school and on the streets.

Women's organizations, urging their members to preserve the "moral strength to survive," looked to biblical heroines as role models. But it became increasingly apparent that biblical role models would not suffice to provide Jewish women with the courage or the help they needed. Jewish newspapers began to deal more openly (and perhaps more honestly) with the issues plaguing families, particularly women. Cooking seemed to take a preeminent role among stress-causing issues because of tight budgets, limited household help, and the difficulties of acquiring kosher meat. Articles in Jewish newspapers advised housewives to cook vegetarian menus because they were cheaper and healthier, even if they took longer to prepare. The papers urged housewives to organize, streamline, and cut back on their tasks to lighten their load. Husbands were expected to pitch in only minimally but were requested to limit their expectations: "We demand no sacrifices from husbands—only some consideration and . . . adjusting to the changed circumstances!"[9]

Women frequently took responsibility not only for the greater physical burden but also for the psychological work necessary to raise their family's spirits and tide the family over until better times. Children facing Nazi teachers and hostile classmates at school needed understanding and encouragement.

Husbands facing unaccustomed mistreatment also needed a comforting haven. In sum, women were to be cheerful when gloom was all about. As late as February 1938, one woman titled her article in a Jewish newspaper "Why So Solemn?" Reminding Jewish women that they had traditionally been the ones to light the candles, she urged them once again to brighten their homes with cheer.[10]

Even when women could no longer "light candles" of joy, they often managed a kind of denial about their immediate hardships (while nevertheless pushing for emigration). Although, in some cases, their efforts to distract themselves and their families may have kept the others from realizing the danger sooner, some denial was necessary in order to preserve their own and their family's stability. They accomplished this through what psychologists call the "adoption of temporary frames of security"—for example, by focusing on the practical tasks of cooking or language training.[11] Some women may have even taken solace from their additional burdens, finding safety in the routine of housework. Other women joined voluntary organizations in an effort to help the community and take their minds off the issues plaguing them. Alice Baerwald distracted herself by setting up a Zionist youth emigration program in Danzig. She was so busy with it that she "forgot to dismantle my own life."[12]

Role reversals among Jewish women and men

Jewish families, with their normal middle-class lives and expectations overturned, embarked on new paths and embraced new strategies that they would never have entertained in ordinary times. For women, this meant new roles as partner, breadwinner, family protector, and defender of the business or practice. These roles were often strange to them. Increasingly, women found themselves representing or defending their husbands, fathers, brothers, or sons. Many accounts have been recorded of women who saved family members from the arbitrary demands of the state or from the Gestapo. In these cases, the Jews always assumed that the Nazis would not disrupt gender norms: they might arrest or torture Jewish men but would not harm women. Thus women at first felt that they had greater freedom than men and were able to manipulate the system to some slight extent. Consequently they took on a more assertive role in the public sphere than ever before. In one small town, a Jewish family sent two of its women to the city hall to ask that part of their house not be used as a meeting place for the Nazi party. Other women interceded for family members with German emigration or finance officials. In some cases they not only broke gender barriers but also bypassed normal standards of legality. Many memoirs report that women, quickly recovering from their shock at discovering that Nazi officials had to be bribed, handed them the necessary goods or money without delay.[13]

Some women took responsibility for the entire family's safety. One woman traveled to Palestine to assess the situation there. Her husband, who in other circumstances had been the decision maker, could not leave his practice and simply told her, "If you decide you would like to live in Palestine, I will like it too." She chose to live in Greece, and her husband agreed. Another woman went to England to negotiate her family's emigration with British officials and medical colleagues. Her daughter noted, "It was thanks to her pertinacity and determination that we were able to leave Germany as soon as we did, and it was always to be a great source of pride to her that it was she who obtained the permit allowing us to come to England."[14]

Women often found themselves in threatening situations, in which they exhibited bravery and benefited from luck. Twenty-year-old Ruth Abraham urged her parents to move to Berlin to escape the hostility of their small town and then regularly accompanied her father to Gestapo headquarters for his weekly interrogation. When her uncle was arrested in Düsseldorf, she hurried from jail to jail until she located him. Then she appealed to a judge, who released him.[15]

Women's new roles may have increased stress in some cases, but in general both women and men appreciated the importance of the new behavior. Women forced themselves to behave in "unwomanly" ways, such as putting up a strong front when men could no longer cope. One woman retained her composure for the sake of her children as her husband sank into a deep depression. The testimonies of both men and women emphasize women's calm, dry-eyed state in the midst of turmoil. One woman, remembering how painful it had been to give up prized family heirlooms to the Nazis, reflected on the dignity and self-control of Jews around her: "I was glad that the Jews I saw behaved well, they didn't show any excitement noticeable to strangers."[16] Whether this desire to appear calm was a middle-class reaction against what they perceived as rabble, or an attempt to retain their dignity or their families' equilibrium in the face of persecution, or an assertion of Jewish pride to counter Aryan savagery, or a proclamation of female strength to rebut the stereotype of female frailty, it was noted more by (and in) women than men. Probably, men took this kind of behavior for granted whereas women, previously allowed and encouraged to be the more "emotional" sex, were particularly conscious of their efforts at self-control.

The desire to emigrate

A gender analysis of the *desire* to emigrate highlights women's particular expectations, priorities, and perceptions.[17] Women, whose identity was more family oriented than men's, struggled to preserve what was central to them by fleeing Germany. Men had businesses, clients, patients, political commitments, and, often, their World War I service, all of which tied them to Germany. Moreover, although women were less integrated than men into the work world, they were more integrated into their community. For women, the increasing hostility around them was unmitigated by a promising business prospect or a loyal employee or patient. Women's constant contacts with their own and others' children and with the community probably alerted them to the signals that come through interpersonal relations—and they took those signals seriously. Men's experiences were mediated through newspapers and broadcasts. Politics may have remained more abstract to them, whereas women's "narrower" picture—their neighbors, direct everyday contacts, the minutiae (and significance) of ordinary details—alerted them to danger at home. Summing up, Peter Wyden recalled the debates within his own family and those of other Berlin Jews: "It was not a bit unusual in these go-or-no-go family dilemmas for the women to display more energy and enterprise than the men. . . . They were less status-conscious, less money-oriented. . . . They seemed to be less rigid, less cautious, more confident of their ability to flourish on new turf."[18]

That men and women often *assessed* the dangers differently reflected their different contacts and frames of reference. But *decisions* to remain or to emigrate (in contrast to role reversals in other areas) seem to have been made by husbands—or, later, by circumstances. After the November Pogrom of 1938, some wives broke all family conventions by taking over the decision making when it became clear to them that their husbands' reluctance to leave Germany would result in even worse horrors.

The November Pogrom of 1938

The November Pogrom revealed the radicalization of Nazi persecution. Although the pogrom was called Kristallnacht (Crystal Night), which we understand to signify the broken glass of thousands of Jewish stores, homes, and synagogues, Jewish women's memoirs often focus not on broken glass but on flying feathers—feathers covering the internal space of the home, hallway, and front yard or courtyard. As in pogroms in Russia at the turn of the century, the mobs tore up feather blankets and pillows and shook them into the rooms, out the windows, and down the stairways. Jews were thus bereft of their bedding and the physical and psychological security that it represented. In addition, these items could not be readily replaced because of their expense and because the availability of domestic linens was severely limited in the looming war economy.[19] This image of feathers flying, of a domestic scene gravely disturbed, represents women's primary experience of the pogrom. The marauders beat and arrested Jewish men, sending more than thirty thousand to concentration camps. With brutal exceptions, which are worth noting because they may indicate more violence against women than historians have recognized to date,[20] most women were forced to stand by and watch their homes torn apart and their men abused.

As women cleaned up the wreckage of the pogrom, their most crucial task was to rescue their men. Wives of prisoners were told that their husbands would be released only if they could present emigration papers. Although no statistics are available to indicate their success, these women displayed extraordinary nerve and tenacity in saving a large number of men and in facilitating a mass exodus of married couples in 1939. Women summoned the courage to overcome gender stereotypes of passivity in order to find any means to have husbands and fathers released from camps. They had to organize the papers, decide on the destination, sell property, and organize the departure. One example illuminates the ordeal facing many women. Mally Dienemann, whose sixty-three-year-old husband was deteriorating rapidly in Buchenwald, raced immediately to the Gestapo to prove that the couple were almost ready to emigrate. Next, she traveled to the passport office to obtain their passports, then to the Emigration Office in Frankfurt, the Gestapo, the police, and the Finance Office. She had to send requests to Buchenwald and to the Gestapo in Darmstadt: "Still it took until Tuesday of the third week, before my husband returned. . . . Next came running around for the many papers that one needed for emigration. And while the Gestapo was in a rush, the Finance Office had so much time and so many requests."[21]

Packing for good

After the pogrom those Jews who remained in Germany tried desperately to leave for anywhere—Latin America, Haiti, Cuba, Australia, Shanghai. As is well known, profound obstacles to emigration existed. Even so, Jewish emigration was far from negligible. In September 1939 the number of (racially defined) Jews who remained in Germany was 185,000, but this number diminished to 164,000 by October 1941.[22] Ultimately, about half of those Jews who had lived in Germany in 1933 could save themselves through emigration to safe countries.

When Jews packed, they believed that their departure would be permanent. Without exception, women took charge of the packing. It was so clearly considered women's work that some women stayed behind to do it. Packing was not only a necessity; it quickly became an art as Nazi rulings and red tape made the process into a nightmare. In order to emigrate with one's belongings, one had to obtain a permit from the Finance Department, which became available only after one provided lists of all the items one wished to take. One woman spent an entire week writing "endless lists, in five copies each . . . every item entered, every list neatly typed, and in the end I could only speak and breathe and think in shoes, towels, scissors, soap and scarves." One could not take just anything—only items purchased before 1933 were allowed. After completing the lists, and often with ship or plane tickets in hand, Jews had to await the authorization of the Finance Department. Again, connections and bribes seemed to speed the process, and again, women without much previous experience in the world of officialdom had to seek connections and master the art of bribery.[23]

With the arduous packing completed and papers in hand, many Jewish families sent their belongings in large containers to interim stations, often ports in Holland, to be stored until the owners knew their ultimate destination. The possessions of one family, who landed in Cuba, stayed in Rotterdam until the family arrived in the United States two years later. Some lost their possessions in the German invasion of Holland. Few people could pack all their belongings; the giant containers, and the surcharge that the Nazis demanded for every item, cost too much. Many had to sell most of their belongings. For many, "packing reduced a lifetime of possessions into three suitcases."[24]

Thus, many emigrants, the wealthy and the poor, tried to sell their homes and furnishings for a pittance, while mourning the loss of the haven they had created for themselves. The purchasers were Aryans, many of whom complained of *their* plight. A pastor's wife proclaimed, "We are suffering as much as you are," to which Alice Baerwald retorted, "With the difference that you're buying and I'm selling."[25]

Packing gave some women the opportunity to save valuables and a few mementos from the clutches of the Nazis. What they managed to smuggle out was paltry in comparison with what the Nazis stole from them. Still, it helped their families subsist for a short time when they arrived penniless at their destinations. Some women bribed the officials who came to their home to inspect everything that went into the containers, trunks, and suitcases. A few did this without consulting their husbands, as the women knew full well that their plans would have been vetoed. Other women engaged in even more dangerous schemes, such as smuggling jewelry or money abroad. Alice Baerwald concluded, "So, slowly we were taught how to become criminals, to attempt to circumvent every law."[26] And women were involved in "illegality" not only for personal subsistence or to help family but also to help the community at large. Beate Berger, for example, smuggled money from Berlin to Palestine in order to buy land for a children's home.[27]

Those who stayed behind

Fewer women than men left Germany. Why was this so? There were still compelling reasons to stay, although life was becoming increasingly difficult in the 1930s. First, women, especially young women, could find jobs in Jewish businesses and homes or in Jewish social services.[28] And older, educated single women found a plethora of jobs in cultural and social service fields within the Jewish community. Martha Wertheimer, for example, worked as a journalist prior to 1933. Thereafter she plunged into Jewish welfare work while writing books and plays, contributing to the Jewish press, and tutoring English to earn extra money. She escorted many children's transports to England, advised Jews on emigration and welfare procedures, often worked twelve-hour days without pausing for meals, and took great joy in leading High Holiday services in Neu-Isenburg, at the League of Jewish Women's Home for Wayward Girls, and in organizing continuing education courses for Jewish youth who had been drafted into forced labor. Ultimately, she wrote to a friend in New York that, despite efforts to emigrate, she no longer waited to escape: "It is also worthwhile to be an officer on the sinking ship of Jewish life (*Judenheit*) in Germany, to hold out courageously and to fill the life boats, to the extent that we have some."[29]

Whereas the employment situation of Jewish women helped keep them in Germany, that of men helped them get out. Some men had business connections abroad that facilitated their flight, and others emigrated alone in order to establish themselves before sending for their families. Women's organizations agreed that wives should not "hinder" husbands from emigrating alone if there was no alternative.[30]

Another reason why more women than men remained behind was that before the war, men faced more immediate physical danger than women and were forced to flee promptly. As women feared for their men, they believed that they themselves would be spared serious harm by the Nazis. In retrospect, Ruth Klüger reflected on this kind of thinking and the resulting preponderance of women caught in the trap: "One seemed to ignore what was most obvious, namely how imperiled precisely the weaker and the socially disadvantaged are. That the Nazis would stop at women contradicted their racist identity. Had we, as the result of an absurd, patriarchal short circuit, perhaps counted on their chivalry?"[31]

Further, as more and more sons left, daughters remained as the sole caretakers for elderly parents. One commentator noted the existence of a whole slew of women "who can't think of emigration because they don't know who might care for their elderly mother in the interim, before they could start sending her money. In the same families, the sons went their way." For many, leaving aging parents—again, as statistics indicate, usually the mother—was the most painful act imaginable.[32]

As early as 1936, the League of Jewish Women saw cause for serious concern regarding the more general "problem of the emigration of women which is often partly overlooked and not correctly understood." The league reminded parents of their "responsibility to free their daughters too . . . [even if daughters] feel stronger psychological ties to their families than sons."[33] In 1936–1937, 54 percent of Jewish immigrants to the United States were men. Even as late as January 1938, the Hilfsverein, one of the main emigration organizations, announced, "Up to now, Jewish emigration . . . indicates a severe surplus of men."[34]

Fewer women than men seem to have received support from Jewish organizations in order to emigrate.[35] Moreover, young women and their families were often reluctant to consider Palestine, and the kibbutz, as an alternative for daughters. Total immigration statistics for Palestine compiled by the Jewish Agency indicate that between 1933 and 1942, 27,202 males and 24,977 females entered from Germany. Of these, the children and married people consisted of about equal numbers of males and females. The discrepancy can be seen among the 8,209 bachelors and 5,080 single females.[36]

The disproportion of Jewish women in the German-Jewish population came about partially because, to begin with, there were more Jewish women than men in Germany. In 1933, owing to male casualties during World War I, greater exogamy among Jewish men, and greater longevity among women, 52.3 percent of Jews were women. The slower rate of female emigration meant that the female proportion of the Jewish population rose to 57.5 percent by 1939. In other words, whereas in 1933 the average ratio was 109 Jewish women to 100 Jewish men, by 1939 the ratio had leaped to 136 to 100.[37] In 1939, one woman wrote, "Mostly we were women who had been left to ourselves. In part, our husbands had died from shock [or] ... in a concentration camp and partly some wives who, aware of the greater danger to their husbands, had prevailed upon them to leave at once and alone. They were ready to ... follow their husbands ... but ... it became impossible ... and quite a few ... became martyrs of Hitler."[38]

Elderly women, in particular, remained behind in disproportionate numbers. In 1933 the ratio of Jewish women over the age of sixty-five to Jewish men of the same age group was already 140 to 100. And, because many of the young had emigrated by 1935, the proportion of elderly Jews also increased. By 1937–1938, recipients of the Jewish Winter Relief included a large number of elderly women (as well as, in total, a larger number of women than men).[39] In 1939, there were 6,674 widowers and 28,347 widows in the expanded Reich. When Elisabeth Freund went to the Gestapo for her papers in 1941, she observed "all old people, old women," waiting in line. Freund's was the last train out of Germany. The women she described were trapped. In short, in slightly less than eight years, two-thirds of German Jews emigrated (many to European countries, where they were later caught up in the Nazi net), leaving a disproportionate number of the elderly and of women.[40]

Mary Felstiner has written, "Along the stations toward extinction ... each gender lived its own journey." She is essentially correct. The Nazis attacked Jewish women and men primarily as Jews, and all Jews shared this agony. Yet, Jews were affected by, and reacted to, the Nazi onslaught in gendered ways. Women, focused on the home, saw their role as that of keeping the family together, maintaining a sense of normalcy amid desperation, and protecting their husbands and children. Their gender-based socialization helped them react to the Nazi threat earlier and to press their men to emigrate. And, as a result of gender differences, when the time came to escape, women, in larger numbers than men, were left behind. In referring to the male and female lines at Auschwitz, Felstiner concluded, "The two incommensurate lines on the ramp stretched back decades. Centuries."[41]

Notes

1 For a detailed account of Jewish women and families in Nazi Germany, see Marion Kaplan, *Jewish Life in Nazi Germany: Dignity and Despair* (Oxford: Oxford University Press, 1998).
2 Garlic today in Susan Neiman, *Slow Fire*, chapter entitled "Garlic" (New York: Schocken Books, 1992). "Like Jews" in Baerwald manuscript (by permission of the

Houghton Library, Harvard University, bMS Ger 91, hereafter referred to as "Harvard ms.").

3 Robert Gellately, "The Gestapo and German Society: Political Denunciation in the Gestapo Case Files," *Journal of Modern History* 60, no. 4 (December 1988), pp. 673–674.

4 Erich Rosenthal, "Trends of the Jewish Population in Germany, 1910–1939," *Jewish Social Studies* 6 (1944), p. 262; *Blätter des Jüdischen Frauenbundes* (hereafter BJFB), 1/34, p. 7, and 3/35, p. 2; *Israelitisches Familienblatt* (hereafter IF), no. 8, 2/23/33, p. 9.

5 IF, 1/13/38, pp. 13–14, and 7/14/38, p. 12.

6 Corsetiere in Ruth Abraham, memories, Leo Baeck Institute, N.Y. (hereafter, LBI), p. 2; mother and daughter in Lisa Brauer, memoirs, LBI, p. 53.

7 *Jüdische Wohlfahrtspflege und Sozial Politik* (hereafter JWS) 7 (1937), p. 80.

8 Jobs for women in *JWS* (1933–1934), pp. 118–121.

9 Heroines in *BJFB*, 2/35, p. 12; husbands in IF 5/19/38, p. 19.

10 IF 2/17/38, p. 16.

11 Psychologists in G. W. Allport, J. S. Bruner, and E. M. Jandorf. "Personality under Social Catastrophe: Ninety Life-Histories of the Nazi Revolution," in *Character and Personality: An International Psychological Quarterly* 10, no. 1 (September 1941), p. 14.

12 Alice Baerwald, Harvard ms., p. 65.

13 Defending in Liselotte Kahn, memories, LBI, p. 21; small town in Jacob Ball-Kaduri, memoirs, LBI, p. 30; bribes in Brauer, memoris, LBI, pp. 43, 57.

14 Palestine in Liselotte Kahn, memoirs, LBI, p. 23; England in Ann Lewis, memoirs, LBI, p. 264.

15 Abraham, memoirs, LBI, p. 2.

16 Depression in Hilde Honnet-Sichel, *Sie Durftennicht mehr Deutschesein*, ed. Margarete Limberg and Hubert Rübsaat (Frankfurt, 1990), p. 183; calm in Leo Gompertz memoirs, LBI, p. 10; "glad" in Hanna Bernheim, Harvard ms., p. 56.

17 For a full discussion of emigration, see Marion Kaplan, "Jewish Women in Nazi Germany before the Emigration," in *Between Sorrow and Strength: Women Refugees of the Nazi Period*, ed. Sibylle Quack (Cambridge: Cambridge University Press, 1995).

18 Peter Wyden, *Stella: One Woman's True Tale of Evil, Betrayal, and Survival in Hitler's Germany* (New York: Simon and Schuster, 1992), p. 47.

19 Erna Albersheim, Harvard ms., p. 28; Elsie Axelrath, Harvard ms., p. 43; Baerwald, Harvard ms., p. 72.

20 These exceptions seem to have occurred mostly in small towns (although for examples from Nuremberg and Düsseldorf, see Rita Thalmann and Emmanuel Feinermann, *Crystal Night* [New York: Coward, McCann and Geoghegan, 1972], pp. 70 and 81).

21 Mally Dienemann, Harvard ms., p. 35.

22 Herbert Strauss, "Jewish Emigration from Germany: Nazi Policies and Jewish Responses (I)," *Leo Baeck Year Book* (1980), pp. 317–318.

23 Lists in Brauer, Memoirs, LBI, p. 56; before 1933 in Elisabeth Freund, memoirs, LBI, pp. 144–145; bribes in Brauer, Memoirs, LBI, p. 57.

24 Rotterdam in Lilli Sussmann, memoirs, LBI, p. 5; "three suitcases" in Harold Basser in *We Shall Not Forget! Memories of the Holocaust*, ed. Carole Garbuny Vogel (Lexington, Mass.: Temple Isaiah, 1994), p. 202.

25 Baerwald, Harvard ms., p. 67.

26 Officials in Brauer, memoirs, LBI, p. 54; Freund, memoris, LBI, p. 178; Ruth Glaser, memoirs, LBI, p. 71, and smuggling on p. 38; vetoed in Else Gerstel, memoirs, LBI, pp. 77–79; Baerwald, Harvard ms., p. 73.

27 Regina Scheer, *Ahawah: Das Vergessene Haus* (Berlin and Weimar: Aufbau-Verlag, 1992), p. 265.

28 *JWS* (1937), pp. 7–13, 27, 78–81; Avraham Barkai, "Der wirtschaftliche Existenzkampf der Juden im Dritten Reich, 1933–38," in *The Jews in Nazi Germany, 1933–1945,* ed. Arnold Paucker (Tübingen: J. C. B. Mohr, 1986), p. 163.

29 Hanno Loewy, ed., *In mich ist die grosse dunkle Ruhe gekommen, Martha Wertheimer Briefe an Siegfried Guggenheim* (1939–1941) (Frankfurt: Frankfurter Lern-und Dokumentationszentrum des Holocaust, 1993), pp. 6, 9, 13, 15, 22, 37.

30 *BJFB,* 12/36, p. 5. Among Eastern European Jews who returned east between 1934 and 1937, for example, the majority were male even though almost half of them were married. Maurer, "Ausländische Juden in Deutschland, 1933–39" in Paucker, ed., *The Jews in Nazi Germany,* p. 204.

31 Men beaten in Eisner, *Allein,* p. 8; Nauen (whose father was secretary of the Hilfsverein in Hamburg) interview, p. 15; Ruth Klüger, *weiter leben* (Göttingen, 1992), p. 83.

32 "Sons went" in *BJFB,* 4/37, p. 5. See also Glaser memoirs, LBI, p. 18; Erika Guetermann, "Das Photographien Album," memoirs, LBI. Men, too, felt grief at leaving their parents: see Stein-Pick, memoirs, LBI, p. 46. But more left, nonetheless.

33 "Overlooked" in *BJFB,* 12/36, p. 1; "responsibility" in *BJFB,* 4/37, p. 10; "psychological ties" in *BJFB,* 12/36, p. 1.

34 These statistics referred to 1936–1937, when 59.5 percent of the 11,352 Jewish immigrants to the United States came from Germany. *American Jewish Year Book 5699 (1938–39)* (Philadelphia: American Jewish Committee, 1938), pp. 552–554. Hilfsverein quotation in *Central Verein Zeitung,* January 20, 1938, p. 5.

35 For example, the number of emigrés supported by the emigration section of the Reichsvertretung der Juden in Deutschland broke down to approximately 4,161 men and 3,041 women in 1937. *Informationsblätter* (January-February 1938), pp. 6–7.

36 One survey of graduating classes from several Jewish schools in late 1935 showed that 47 percent of the boys and only 30 percent of the girls considered Palestine as a destination. *JWS* (Berlin, 1935), p. 188. Immigration statistics in "Jewish Immigration from Germany during 1933–1942 (includes Austria since 1938 and Czechoslovakia and Danzig since 1939)," reprint from "The Jewish Immigration and Population," issued by the Department of Statistics of the Jewish Agency.

37 IF, 2/27/36; Sybil Milton, "Women and the Holocaust," in *When Biology Became Destiny,* ed. Renate Bridenthal, Atina Grossmann, and Marion Kaplan (New York: Monthly Review Press, 1984), p. 301. See also Bruno Blau, "The Jewish Population of Germany, 1939–1946," *Jewish Social Studies* 12, no. 2, p. 165.

38 Andreas Lixl-Purcell, *Women of Exile* (Westport, Conn.: Greenwood Press, 1988), p. 92.

39 Data from 1933 in Rosenthal, "Trends," p. 248. In 1939, about 22 percent of Jewish women were widowed. Bruno Blau, "Die Juden in Deutschland von 1939 bis 1945," *Judaica* 7 (1951), p. 271. Of the total number of widows, 16,117 (57 percent) were sixty-five years old or older. Blau, "The Jewish Population of Germany," p. 165. Winter Relief in Vollnhals, "Jüdische Selbsthilfe bis 1938," in *Die Juden in Deutschland, 1933–1945,* ed. Wolfgang Benz (Munich: C. H. Beck, 1988), p. 405; *BJFB,* 10/38, p. 4.

40 Freund, memoirs, LBI, p. 146. See also Richarz, *Jüdisches Leben in Deutschland: Selbstzeugnisse zur Sozialgeschichte, 1918–1945* (Stuttgart: Deutsche Verlags-Anstalt, 1982), p. 61; *JWS* (1937), pp. 96–97 (for statistics on the German Reich); *JWS* (1937), pp. 161–163 (for Hessen-Nassau); and *JWS* (1937), pp. 200–201 (for Koenigsberg).

41 Mary Felstiner, *To Paint Her Life: Charlotte Salomon in the Nazi Era* (New York: Harper-Collins, 1994), pp. 205–206.

9

"GIVE ME YOUR CHILDREN"

Gordon J. Horwitz

On September 4, 1942, the "eldest of the Jews in Litzmannstadt," the Germans' instrument of life and death in the Lodz Ghetto, Mordechai Chaim Rumkowski, made a speech to "his" Jews:

> A grievous blow has struck the ghetto. They are asking us to give up the best we possess – the children and the elderly. I was unworthy of having a child of my own, so I gave the best years of my life to children. I've lived and breathed with children, I never imagined I would be forced to deliver this sacrifice to the altar with my own hands. In my old age, I must stretch out my hands and beg: Brothers and sisters! Hand them over to me! Fathers and mothers: Give me your children!

The Lodz (or Łódź in Polish) Ghetto – the second largest and longest lasting in German-occupied Europe, has come to symbolize the most horrifying choice that humankind can ever face, made under circumstances of unimaginable depravity and sheer, naked evil. For the Germans looking from the outside, the ghetto was a matter of cold, heartless calculation of costs and benefits; for many historians, it is part of the much larger context of the Holocaust. But for the men, women, and children living in that hell, it was a universe that few of us would dare to venture into even in our thoughts. And within that wasteland of famine and disease, imminent threat of death and endless, exhausting, humiliating work and oppression, came the order, given by the Germans, transmitted by the "emperor" of the ghetto Rumkowski, and carried out by the Jewish police (later "helped" by the Gestapo and SS), to give up the weak, the useless mouths to feed, the elderly and especially the children. It is not possible to imagine what this meant to thousands of parents. Perhaps the most that one can do, as Horwitz has chosen, is to depict the event as it happened. And, so as to grasp its fiendish nature, and to realize how two moral universes could have inhabited the same city, simultaneously to paint that canvas of horrors upon the background of a festive, happy and carefree day in the "Aryan" part of the renamed city of Litzmannstadt.

The conundrum of Lodz is not only that the Nazis murdered children, for they murdered them everywhere, some 1.5 million Jewish children in total. Rather, it is that the leader of the ghetto and his henchmen had carried out the Germans' orders and *offered up the children with the hope against hope that the rest of the ghetto might survive (including the policemen's children who were spared so as to motivate them to carry out their grotesque task). But was there no other choice? Can it be that the only choice was to sacrifice one's own children? We cannot accept this, and we should not. But can we lay blame? Can we imagine ourselves in this situation? We cannot. And so we are left with what Primo Levi called the gray zone, in which Rumkowski epitomizes "the fundamental theme of human ambiguity fatally provoked by oppression." It is a zone where all seemingly clear ethical and moral distinctions begin to blur, and inconceivable existential realities drive people to act in ways we cannot grasp from our own sheltered vantage point. Had Rumkowski survived, writes Levi, "no tribunal would have absolved him, nor, certainly, can we absolve him on the moral plane." But "there are extenuating circumstances," of which the "infernal" Nazi order is paramount.*

Rumkowski's hold on power emanated from his ability to implement the fiction that work would keep extermination at bay. This was the Jewish version of the Nazis' cynical concept of "Arbeit macht frei," "work liberates." But whether in Auschwitz or in Lodz, the Nazi concept of Jewish labor was that it liberated only through death, in a process that first deprived people of both their physical and moral humanity, making them eventually into what the Nazis called "life unworthy of life." Yet as long as one was within that process, there was always hope; and that hope entailed, for men such as Rumkowski, working for the enemy: first, by producing essential goods for the German military, even if that forestalled their defeat and thus ensured the death of the Jews; and second, by gradually handing over to the Germans all those who could not, or could no longer work: the sick, the emaciated, the old, and the children.

Driven by an insatiable appetite for power and a talent for both pleasing his masters and bullying his subjects, Rumkowski may have also truly believed that somehow he would save some of the Jews. And, in fact, had the Red Army not stopped its advance a mere sixty miles from Lodz in summer 1944, thousands of Jews might well have survived and Rumkowski would have been remembered differently. Instead, he perished along with the last survivors of that insane universe, that impossible "Jewish State" in the heart of the German empire, to whose creation he had contributed so mightily. Taken with his family in the last transport to Auschwitz, according to persistent rumors, Rumkowski never reached the gas chambers, but was killed in the train car by fellow Jews who could finally wreak revenge on this hated figure.

While war was being made upon the Jewish child, the German child—in the media ever an object of unceasing delight and loving regard, the beauty of its features scrutinized, its athleticism extolled, its wishes indulged, its imagination awakened—was described as if born into a world of splendid welcome, enveloping protection, and satisfaction of all wants. So it was a matter deemed worthy of note that on a day in June, climbing aboard a streetcar on Deutschland Square were young participants in that day's festival sponsored by the organization known as Strength Through Joy. Little girls with "bright dresses and beautifully tied ribbons in their hair" took their seats, while soft-spoken little boys, their hair "combed smooth atop their heads," stood in the aisle at their side. Reaching their stop outside Helenenhof, the youngsters exited the tram and quickly made for the entrance to the park. Live music, performed by local musicians, greeted their arrival. Spectators were on hand to watch as the children, dressed in sportswear, performed athletic routines under the direction of a female gymnastics instructor and later gathered for a round of singing. After speeches and servings of "delicious cakes" offered the "tiny guests" seated at tables decorated with flowers, the festival proceeded to sack and egg races and the playful beating of pots. Storytelling—featured was the "Tale of the Golden Goose"—rounded out the day's activities, culminating in a distribution of prizes by a storybook princess.[1]

Where once, it was said, children had known only dark, hardscrabble courtyards with but the tiniest sliver of sky overhead, now under the new regime German youngsters played in the open, amid greenery, under the watchful eyes of indulgent mothers whom they called to come admire their sandbox creations.[2] At last the world extended its arms to the German child, ever portrayed as the cherished delight of solicitous parents. At a swimming pool in provincial Welungen, where, it was said, experienced swimmers "rise like nymphs from splashing waters[,] . . . our small children look to the unknown 'sea' from a bit of a distance, and only dare approach the shore when mother is near."[3] Was this imagined world of Litzmannstadt and environs, its present so welcoming, its future of such promise, not indeed magical?

Precious though the German child was in this great scheme of renewal, the Jewish child, considered of no use and no value, was for now the chief target for destruction. Utilitarian considerations of the potential for labor among more physically developed Jewish youngsters meant that such targeting largely affected only those deemed too young and tender to be useful. For the purposes of categorizing who among them were to live and who to die, the Germans had drawn a line at the age of ten: those above that age, thought to possess the potential for work (fingers dexterous enough to thread a needle, coordination keen enough to guide a pair of scissors, muscles strong enough to wield a hammer) were spared; those younger, especially the infants—so hungry, so whiny, altogether useless in a workshop—were just additional mouths to feed. Along with the aged and the sick, it was the youngest children—such easy pickings in their delicate size, their defenselessness, their inexperience, so available for seizure—who were taken first. For German administrators relentlessly seeking ways to reduce the expenditures associated with production, children too young to work served no economic purpose. A drain on precious resources, they could make no contribution save through their disappearance and the attendant reduction of costs associated with their upkeep. While cost-cutting considerations lent justification to their removal, the slaughter of the Jewish young proved as well an especially satisfying way of running up the demographic score, the piling up of Jewish dead—and among them their children, their future—being the surest proof of the claim that the Jews who had once peopled the land would soon people it no more. Their disappearance reinforced the assertion of German dominance in all things and gave proof that as a people the Germans were numerically in the ascendant, and that the land was theirs just as the future was theirs, and theirs alone.[4]

Two years into the regime's efforts toward ethnically cleansing the Wartheland of its Jews, the moment of resolution was at hand. For Germans of the Warthegau all doors swung open in an expansive vision of a future of promise coming true. Many indeed were the possibilities that lay before them, and before the city, too, modernizing into the future, a city of flowers, of clean homes to live in, of pure running water available to all, of efficient transport and industry, and above all of demographic increase, its confirmation the free development of the German child.

The official portrait of the city and its people, including its children, remained, as it would until the end, one of ever-increasing beauty, health, and promise. In such a world all German children were fit—or, if unwell, soon on the mend—well dressed, and well fed, the most favored of beings in the most transformed of cities; all that was touched by German hands seemingly turned to blossom and to gold. It was largely a fantasy, of course, but each improvement was touted as offering a glimpse of a time when everything would be in place and all would be just right. The fantasy was built on another, darker one—and this was the one that actually *was* coming true—that of sweeping the city of the presence of Jews.

For the Germans it was a moment of exuberance. The death center, so close, served now as the final destination, the hidden vortex into which a population of Jews deemed superfluous to production was disappearing. Here lay the solution to the demographic problem that from the start had plagued Warthegau and Litzmannstadt officials, frustrated in their desire to expel the Jewish population and realize once and for all their vision of a land free of Jews. Now, one after another, the provincial ghettos were being closed down, their aged, their sick, and their young separated from the remainder of the population and sent to their deaths in Rzuchowski Forest. Those still considered fit were sent on to labor. Even the unwanted Western Jews the authorities had fought unsuccessfully to hold at bay were by now, thanks not only to the physical rigors of life in the ghetto but also to this new solution, reduced to a fraction of their original number.

The enormity of the crime matched the outrageousness of its method. To the Warthegau leadership the accomplishment was satisfying indeed, but inevitably the process, so physically repugnant, demanded further review. For in truth the production of death on so grandiose a scale had left in its wake precisely the kind of mess, evoking the same disgust and the same phobia about the spread of contagious disease, whose elimination had been a principal aim of the enterprise from the start.

Unexpectedly, with the arrival of warm weather, evidence of the massive crime began to surface. In the woods of Precinct 77 the bodies were decomposing in the sun. In the heat of the clearing, the corpses became bloated and the soil over the trenches lifted and bulged; above it a "mist" or "vapor" visibly rose, a pestilential odor filling the air. Forest workers, normally toiling in the vicinity until late in the afternoon, were overwhelmed by the stench and were compelled to break off work by two o'clock.[5] The phenomenon renewed the fear of typhus. In consequence, there followed that summer a halt to killing operations, the arrival of fresh victims pending a means of better disposing of their remains. An initial effort to employ thermal explosives went awry, setting fire to and scorching a patch of woods shielding the clearing from view of the roadway. After this the installation of two outdoor cremation ovens, concrete-lined conical pits dug into the ground, proved a more effective solution. To the Jewish men of the Waldkommando fell the gruesome task of lifting the remains from the newly opened trenches and transferring them to the ovens. Bystanders witnessed the smoke rising from the vicinity.[6] The roasting of the bodies in these twin pits effectively transformed them cleanly to ash. Still, the method, effective as it was, was found to leave behind goodsized chunks of skeletal matter. These bones would have to be refined still further. For this purpose a "bone grinder" was required, and one was found. The mill worked well, reducing the parts to a fine "snow-white" powder. The purified remains were then scattered about the nearby woods and waters.[7] The laundering and cleansing had achieved perfection. Never before had so much living human substance been so systematically and so rapidly compressed to nothingness.

For the Jews of Łódź, a season of growing uncertainty and anxiety had begun. It was clear that new, destructive energies had been unleashed, directly impacting the region and the ghetto. Still, the precise outlines and extent of the damage remained indistinct. Regionally, Łódź lay at the center of events whose scope, from the perspective of the ghetto, was but dimly perceived. The Germans had succeeded in effectively sealing off the ghetto from reliable information. That tens of thousands of persons had recently disappeared without a trace was as much a tribute to the Germans' ability to control information as it was a challenge to the imagination. "Had they been taken abroad, even to the remoteness of the jungles of South America," noted one ghetto observer, "the earth could not have swallowed them as it has done so here, perhaps but several kilometers from Litzmannstadt. For it is a certainty that they have remained within the German sphere of occupation. And that extends but several hundred kilometers to the east."[8]

As the apparent lull in the deportations stretched on into the first weeks of summer, concern over the whereabouts of those previously removed combined with anxiety over the Germans' ultimate intentions, overshadowed life in the ghetto. Worry over the fate of Jewish children was especially grave. It was clear that they had been especially targeted for selection in the provincial ghettos, a matter that understandably raised fears for the lives of the community's own Jewish youngsters in the event of future operations. Unconfirmed reports about the fate of previously deported youngsters circulated with increased frequency. Amid the swirl of plausible rumor, one altogether untrue and misleading conjecture surfaced. On July 9 Shlomo Frank recorded that a report had been picked up from the underground Polish radio station, "Swit,"[9] referring to the destruction of provincial Jewish communities, alleging that a number of Jewish children were being kept alive in labor camps, where their blood was supposedly drawn as a source of "transfusions for wounded German soldiers."[10] Even a tale as ominous as this may have offered some limited hope that the rumored destruction of the children had been less than total. Later in the month, amid menacing pronouncements in the German media about the ghetto's liquidation and the impending total annihilation of the Jews, came the welcome if seemingly contradictory news of a new order for the production of fifty thousand children's beds, necessitating an increase in the labor force in the ghetto carpentry works, a sign of the ghetto's continued usefulness and a reason for its survival. Masking the authorities' true intentions while serving to allay mounting anxieties within the ghetto, a Gestapo agent reportedly explained "that the little beds will be made for Jewish children who are in a special, large camp not far from Lublin."[11]

That reference to the supposed camp sounds similar to another report, recorded in the *Chronicle* on July 26, indicating that people who had disappeared during the spring selections were in fact "alive and well in various camps in the vicinity of Poznań. Exact addresses and some people's serial numbers were even mentioned."[12] Very much in people's thoughts, the deported children were rumored to have been "placed in Poznań itself, in the so-called Judenkinderlager [Camp for Jewish Children] at 5 Rudolfstrasse." But in truth there was "no street in Poznań" by that name. Whether or not the ghetto chroniclers were aware of that salient fact is unknown. Though conceding the "understandable interest" in the rumors, and even the "great calming effect" they were having on the ghetto population, the chroniclers remained deeply skeptical, concluding, "It may be supposed that these rumors, like so many others, are without any foundation whatsoever."[13]

One might have seen in all this the clever machinations of the German security apparatus, eager to spread disinformation. For if the Jews inside the ghetto were carefully watching the Germans, piecing together fragmentary reports about the nature and extent of the harm they intended, the Germans were also observing them. The Criminal Police and the Gestapo were on heightened alert for any signs that their now stepped-up program of extermination had aroused the suspicions of the living. Had the ghetto population gotten wind of the regime's locally escalating murderous deeds? It would have been a logical question to ask. By their own assessment, this much struck the Criminal Police as clear: most of the Jews in the ghetto now realized that ultimately they would not survive. That said, it was imperative to control even more effectively the flow of information to the ghetto from the outside world, and internally to identify and destroy any who might try to exploit the increasing state of deprivation and desperation to make trouble for the authorities. The Kripo were particularly at pains to cut off all contact between the ghetto and those outside. For months there had been a ban on mail. Letters addressed to the inhabitants of the ghetto were without exception destroyed. Arriving aid packages—and they were still being sent—were confiscated and rerouted to military hospitals. Apart from that, the Kripo suggested, in the interest of creating the illusion that no harm had come to the deported, that it might prove useful to pass along to the Jews letters indicating that all was in fact well with their absent brethren.[14]

The Kripo understood the workings of the world, both as it once had been and as it existed now. They had reason to believe that in spite of mounting evidence pointing to their destruction by some recognizable means (by starvation, or even by execution), the Jews could be persuaded that Germany had not crossed some unknown line, implementing a far more outlandish, unimaginable campaign of mechanized killing as efficient as it was thoroughgoing. Fully aware that such a line had indeed been crossed, the German security establishment saw to it that the regime's wider intentions remained hidden, banking on the victims' inability to piece together the truth. In this way the Jews might yet be fooled into believing that although they had been singled out for exceptional punishment, their oppressors were guided by fundamentally rational considerations. All could see that the ghetto was organized for work. It was self-evident: production suited Germany's needs. Insufferable as the conditions were under which they labored, the enterprise they were compelled to serve promoted an understandable purpose. The Germans would exploit this thinking to full advantage, counting on the logic of production to reassure their victims that Germany's plan was consistent with established norms.[15] The Jews might faint at their workstations, they might fall ill and die in the course of their labor, but the Germans did not slaughter them on the floor of the workshops. Rzuchowski Forest did not come to the ghetto. The gas vans did not appear all of a sudden in its streets, rumbling down Łagiewnicka, Franciskańska, or Marysinska, choking the life out of the Jews where they lived. Instead, everything within the ghetto proceeded according to long-established routine. The Gettoverwaltung successfully pursued orders from military and commercial clients, and its highly organized and extensive network of workshops diligently satisfied the demands of its parent organization. All could see that ghetto wares were a necessity and that the Germans had organized the ghetto for their manufacture. That alone was a matter of satisfaction to the Gettoverwaltung, the Gau leadership, and the Security Service, each deeply engaged in the concealed project of murder. In this way the Jews would have reason to discount unconfirmed reports of the worst, still believing that, however cruelly applied, the way of the Germans was the way of work.

It was Rumkowski's way as well. And throughout that terrible season in the aftermath of the year's deportations, he would cling to it more than ever. Early on the evening of May 31, following an extended absence from the rostrum, Rumkowski rose to address a ghetto audience of five thousand listeners assembled in the courtyard of the fire department on Lutomierska Street. "Loudspeakers and a podium had been set up." In addition, "the crowd was calm and orderly, [and] the weather was lovely—sunny and warm." Once again "face to face" with his "brothers and sisters in the ghetto," Rumkowski spoke frankly of recent losses, recalling the 55,000 who had been deported during the previous months. His anger was evident, though it was directed at those who were illicitly dealing in their own rations, in the process "trad[ing] in their own blood and in the blood of their own children," most recently taking advantage of the desperation of German Jews to acquire their possessions on the eve of their departure. On a more positive note, with the ghetto population now consisting of approximately 100,000 souls, he was pleased to state that 70,000 of them were integrated into the labor force, though there was still room for more. "The problem of work ran like a red thread through the Chairman's entire speech," according to the Chronicle, "creating the impression that although the question of resettlement has been averted for the time being, it could crop up again if the labor reserves are not entirely exhausted in the ghetto's workshops." Most important, "he spoke of the creation of new work-shops, of easy work for children and old people, for he would then be able to place those who have registered but have not been assigned, or have not been assigned to suitable positions." Children still too young for work were a particu-lar concern. They were going to have to be kept off the streets and looked after more carefully. Either they would be assigned to day care centers while their parents were out at work, or else the parents would have to work alternate shifts so as to take turns looking after them. Above all, this was not a time to credit irresponsible rumors but a time to keep one's head down and "sit quietly at work," following Rumkowski's own example. "We must work in order to be able to exist. . . . Do your work fully in peace, do not daydream. I stand watch over our common interests," he assured his people, the source of the "only happiness in my life."[16]

The school department, taking the lead in establishing apprentice positions in the workshops for school-age children, was stepping up the pace of its place-ments. By the third week in July some thirteen thousand youngsters were serving in the shops, their apprenticeships supplemented by a model program devoted to the rapid training of the young in tailoring and other trades. In response to the sense of urgency—one observer spoke of the "lightning, American speed" of the undertaking—a program that, in ordinary times, was designed to last for years was compressed into only two months of intense instruction. On the premises of the tailoring works at 29 Franciskańska Street, three hundred apprentices at a time, organized into twelve sections, participated in classes from eight in the morning until four in the afternoon, learning all aspects of the trade, from hand and machine stitching and sewing to cutting and the creation of "technical drawings," as well as knowledge of tailoring machinery, with supplementary training in trade-specific "accounting and mathematics" and a weekly hour of instruction in "occupational hygiene." It was further noted that "for the convenience of the students there is a dining area on the premises where they consume the meals normally provided to working people in the ghetto. The establishment of these educational courses must be acknowledged as an event of far-reaching importance for the future of the children who reside in the ghetto."[17]

Ghetto orphans too were increasingly being integrated into the labor force. By the end of June 1942, out of a total of 589 boarders at institutions, 155 were employed in the workshops, a figure more than double the 75 who had been working at the end of March. And many of the newly employed orphans were noticeably younger, for whereas in March the majority of those employed had been sixteen and older, by this later date nearly all were between the ages of eleven and fifteen.[18] Similarly, by July 31, half of the 1,569 youngsters in ghetto children's colonies, or 784 (454 boys and 330 girls), had taken positions in a variety of workshops. By far the greatest number, 348 (274 of them boys), were occupied in shoemaking, while 139 of the girls specialized in needlework; lesser numbers were employed in "tailoring workshops," "wood wool factories," "corset and brassiere manufacture," and "sorting and recycling departments."[19]

In a society where survival, as all by now surely understood, depended on proving one's usefulness, the elderly were most especially at risk, even more endangered than the very young, who, embodying the future, might count on the community's solicitousness and protection. Their sense of peril found quiet expression. Woefully, on July 12, 1942, in a desperate effort to demonstrate that they too were able to contribute material value to the community, thereby justifying the sums spent on their upkeep and survival, the residents of Old Age Home Number 2 on Gnesenerstraße presented Rumkowski with the gift of "a handmade carpet," asking that he accept their offering "as proof of their devotion and thanks" and a token of their "productive will and capacity," a reminder that "most of the residents are able to carry out craft labor of various and similar type, such as: knitting, darning, stuffing [cushions], sewing, and the like." Their fondest wish was "to demonstrate, through *work*, our right to exist in the ghetto. We appeal to your generosity . . . and ask: Give us the chance of delivering, by way of deed, *the proof* of our ability to work. We are fully conscious of the fact that only *work*—as your motto proclaims as well—can afford the possibility of *alleviating* the food situation for us."[20]

By the end of August, surveying the expanding list of provincial Jewish communities suffering violent uprooting and dissolution, yet having little to go on save the experience of survivors, ghetto observers remained baffled as to the fate of those who had vanished into the unknown. "Jews have arrived here from Pabianice, Bełchatów, Ozorków, Zelów, Wieluń, Stryków, Sieradz, Łask, and, recently, from Zduńska Wola, and the process continues," the *Chronicle* recorded on August 28:

> At the same time, bedding from those small towns has no longer been arriving by truck but by tram dump cars, and this new phenomenon has come to dominate everyone's thoughts. The newcomers tell all sorts of stories about their recent experiences, but the same note of pain and despair runs through all their accounts. Not everyone has arrived here—families have been separated and it is difficult even to determine why some were sent to this ghetto while others had to take another, more dolorous journey. It is difficult to discover any guidelines in all of this, which is precisely what grieves everyone most. Once again a cloud of uncertainty has seized the ghetto; people are shaken by the tales the newcomers tell and by the great unknown, which is worse than the worst reality.[21]

All the same, people had heard enough to know that terrible things were happening to the children out in the provinces. On August 27 Oskar Rosenfeld took note of the murdered children, or "yeladim," of Zduńska Wola, who were "separated from old people and parents," and "ordered to lower" their "head[s]— then shot with [a] revolver."[22]

As best they could, parents kept vigil, watching over their children while they slept. Irena Hauser, a survivor of a transport from Vienna, hard pressed by deplorable material circumstance and fast approaching the limits of her strength, devoted the last of her declining energies to the care of her young son. Lying awake beside him, she watched helplessly as flies circled about her sleeping child's mouth, anxious lest he awake. For what would she do then? Twenty-four hours had passed since either had eaten, and still she had nothing with which to satisfy the child's hunger.[23] Suicidal thoughts invaded her consciousness, and she confided to her diary a wish to throw herself from the window and be done with her anguish, a temptation she abandoned, she wrote, solely out of consideration for her responsibility to her child. She awakened to recall "an interesting dream," its content perhaps reflecting a resurfacing of persistent suicidal thoughts. In the dream she observes "a long train" standing "ready to leave." She is about to climb aboard, sensing that the train will not leave without her. The conductor is watching and "waiting for" her "to give the signal to depart."[24]

Sleep was precious, a ready escape for ghetto inhabitants who found within it temporary relief from unbearable worry. Yet the pressures of daily life and the attendant concern for survival meant that for many, burdened with physical pain and mental suffering, sleep remained an elusive blessing. On a night in late August, while elsewhere in the household his wife and "three grown daughters" slept, a husband and father remained awake, tending with difficulty to a small boy, an orphan he and his family had taken into their care. Hoping gently to ease the child's own journey toward sleep, the man sang to him a variety of familiar songs, to no avail; restless, the boy remained stubbornly awake, crying, screaming, altogether inconsolable. No melody succeeded in calming the child until, at last, the man sang a particular lullaby—a very sad one that told of the death of a king and, in turn, of his unhappy queen, and of the abandonment of the king's vineyard, within which, nesting on the branch of a small tree, had rested a little bird. Upon the death of the king and queen, rousing itself the bird departed, taking flight "like an arrow shot from a bow." Somehow, to this song alone the child proved receptive, even joining in humming the lullaby's refrain, "slumber, slumber, slumber, little child of mine," so that finally, "closing his little eyes," the boy nodded off to sleep. Alone at last, "like a tireless night watchman," the man "lay awake" through the night, pondering the significance of the odd lullaby that, after long hours of restlessness, had brought the child a measure of peace. The key, he concluded, lay in the song's reference to the death of the king, who, as he imagined the child to have recognized, had failed utterly to fulfill his duty to serve as provider and protector to those who needed him most: the children. This was nothing less than a betrayal of trust, resulting in a wound that, until eased by the death of the failed sovereign, offered the child no peace. To this father there could be little doubt that the king to whom the tale alluded was none other than Rumkowski, on whom he heaped his scorn, attributing to the restless child all the anger and bitterness he felt over the failings of a leader who, though looked to as a "protector," had proved nothing of the sort, a sovereign utterly incapable of saving the innocent in his domain from suffering and destruction.[25]

Soon enough the unsettling anxieties of that dreadful summer were to culminate in the terrible realization that the sick, the elderly, and above all the children of the Łódź ghetto were indeed targeted for removal. What had occurred in the Jewish communities in the outlying provinces was to happen here as well. In spite of the growing sense of threat, the blow, when it came, was experienced as a shock of unimagined magnitude, leaving those who survived it forever scarred. All that Rumkowski had staked in attempting to secure his people's survival by diligently serving the Germans, accommodating their perceived economic goals and obediently executing even the most unwelcome of their demands, was to be tested as never before.

At seven o'clock on the morning of Tuesday, September 1, three years to the day since the invasion of Poland and a day similarly beautiful and bright, pedestrians walking past the ghetto hospitals on Łagiewnicka, Drewnowska, and Wesola streets noticed what struck them as the curious if at first unalarming appearance of what were described as military trucks just then driving up to the buildings.[26] Of late, rumors had circulated to the effect that in order to clear space for the creation of additional workshops, the hospitals were soon to be closed, their patients and medical facilities transferred to barracks currently under construction on Krawiecka and Tokarzewski streets.[27] But this work was nowhere near completion, and even more unsettling, it would have been highly unusual for the Germans to send military transports to the ghetto to accomplish the task. Apprehension mounted as observers took note of the unusually heavy presence of Jewish policemen in the vicinity of the hospitals, keeping the growing crowds, increasingly drawn by the strange goings-on, from approaching. That same apprehension quickly turned to panic when they saw the Germans roughly forcing patients out of the buildings, even pushing some children from the windows, and piling them onto the vehicles. Stunned, bystanders soon realized that they were witnessing not just the closure of the hospitals but the beginning of the wholesale deportation of the patients.[28]

Biebow was on the scene, a fact he would acknowledge at his postwar trial in 1947 even while denying in the face of eyewitness testimony that he had approved or participated in such acts of brutality.[29] One of those Jewish eyewitnesses, hiding in a linen closet of the Łagiewnicka Street hospital to avoid being seen, first spied Biebow passing along the corridor in the company of two unidentified "high-ranking" men in uniform. Biebow was speaking of the need to speed the operation. Shortly thereafter, patients at the nearby medical facility on Mickiewicza Street, by now alerted to the threat, began climbing from the windows and taking flight. Biebow rushed to the scene. Rounding the corner at Łagiewnicka Street, quickly assessing the fast-moving events unfolding before his eyes, he reportedly struck a woman and, seizing a man by the hair, dragged him back to the building before hustling down to the corner and shouting for uniformed assistance.[30] Szyja Teitelbaum, who had been passing through the vicinity, remembered noticing Biebow shouting at three young people; he ordered them into a garden and made them turn to face a tree. When Gestapo officers Fuchs and Stromberg arrived, the men "all drew their revolvers and fired. Biebow was standing in the middle. I got a good look," Teitelbaum insisted, "because I was standing at a distance of 6–7 meters from the incident."[31] Hersz Janowski, a ghetto cart driver, also spotted Biebow in the company of these same agents participating in the murder of three youths, aged in his estimation around sixteen to seventeen years old. "Each of the three Germans shot one of the boys from behind," he said, and Biebow was heard crudely joking about it.[32]

Meanwhile, Rumkowski, "in the hospital on Drewnowska Street since early morning," appears to have been attempting, with unspecified success, to intervene, presumably in order to exempt certain individuals from the *Aktion*, as did the director of the Order Service's Special Department, Dawid Gertler, who, taking up position in the main hospital on Łagiewnicka Street, was "surrounded by petitioners of every sort."[33] The Germans were not in the least inclined to let any escapees off the hook. The Jewish Order Service was consequently charged with hunting them down and delivering them for removal with the rest. The Germans demanded a quota of two hundred persons, instructing that should some of the fugitive patients prove unrecoverable, their relatives were to be seized in their stead; also declared eligible for seizure was anyone "who had applied for admittance to the hospital," regardless of whether he or she had been a patient on the morning of September 1. The Order Service complied as instructed.[34]

The following Friday, September 4, was intensely sunny and hot. At two in the afternoon posters went up announcing an assembly set for 3:30 in the fire department square, where at last Rumkowski and other leaders were going to address the ghetto. In advance of the assembly rumors had it that perhaps the children were to be spared after all, or that the *Aktion* was to be put off for another three months. But these were only conjectures. In tears, mothers were already nervously crowding around officials to appeal on behalf of their children. On the main pedestrian bridge over Zgierska Street there was unusually heavy traffic. Rumkowski's carriage had been seen passing at high speed. The atmosphere was feverish. It looked, said one observer, as if "all hell has broken loose." On top of everything else, with the shops and workplaces now to be closed the following day, people were worried about the shortfall in the day's rations. Amid the restlessness of the moment, however, there were pockets of apparent calm. On the grounds of the Church of the Virgin Mary, in the blazing heat the women who stacked and cleaned the featherbedding could be seen lounging atop piles of "eiderdowns and pillows," enjoying their soup. Elsewhere policemen mingled with crowds of anxious ghetto residents, offering reassurances. The routine sound of children hawking sweets could still be heard. But the general mood of the ghetto was tense, if not desperate. Another rumor had it that Polish workers, operating under German supervision, were digging graves on Wolborska Street. Everyone anxiously awaited the promised words of the chairman.[35]

Even in advance of definite news, parents were half crazed over the prospect of losing their children. "Mothers race about in the streets, one shoe on and the other off, half of their hair combed and the rest unkempt," wrote Josef Zelkowicz, "kerchiefs half draped over their shoulders and half dragging on the ground." As yet, however, the worst had not happened. "They still have their children. They can still clutch them fiercely to their shriveled bosoms. They can still kiss their clear eyes. But what will happen afterwards, in another hour, tomorrow? Rumor has it that the children will be removed from their parents today and sent away on Monday. Sent away—where?"[36] But at least "for now, for the moment, every child is still with his mother." In consequence, mothers would lavish small luxuries upon their children: their "last loaf of bread" and, if available at all, some margarine to go with it, even a bit of sugar.[37] "Today, the ghetto has cast aside all thoughts of the future. It is living for the moment, and for the moment every mother is clutching her child." Attended with such unexpected solicitousness, the children could not help but wonder: "Am I ill?" Yet logic led them to ask: "If I am ill, why am I walking about the streets? Why don't they make me stay in bed? Why don't they take me to a doctor?" Zelkowicz knew the truth: "But they are very ill, these wretched Jewish children. They are like baby birds, and like sick birds they are doomed to die."[38] Facing imminent deportation, an elderly person of sixty-five or older might in the end give up, resigned to an unalterable fate, reasoning that "one can't live forever anyway, and what does it matter anymore—to die a few days, a few weeks, even a few years earlier than otherwise?" Again likening the endangered ghetto youngsters to little birds, Zelkowicz could not countenance the same resignation with respect to "the children, who have just poked through their eggshells, whose first glimpse of God's world was through the prism of the ghetto, for whom a cow or a chicken are creatures from the land of fantasy, who have never sensed the fragrance of a flower, the shape of an orange, or the flavor of an apple or pear—is their fate sealed? Must they experience the terror of death at this early juncture[?]"[39]

Time's relentless passage never seemed more acute. No one cheated time. Whether old or young, with each passing day, everyone was one day closer to death. But the inhabitants of the ghetto also knew that for every man, woman, and child there existed in the accounts of the ghetto population registry a second, representational self in which, for administrative purposes, his or her official age was listed. Although time could not be fooled, records were alterable: if only on paper, an elderly person might miraculously be made to appear suddenly more youthful, a little boy or girl instantly more mature. A clean erasure, perhaps, or a precise mark, and at a stroke what was a 3 could be reborn a 13. But the Department of Population Records, under the pressure of the hour, was made off limits. On the night of September 3–4, its bureau was "sealed" to public access.[40]

Meanwhile, at 4 Kościelny Street the Evacuation Committee (the Resettlement Commission referred to in the *Chronicle*) had set up headquarters on a separate floor of the same building as the population registry, where employees were busily compiling lists of candidates for removal from the ghetto.[41] Yet, given the widespread uncertainty over the precise age categories involved, the evacuation bureau was quickly thrown into a state of "chaos, commotion and confusion." Apparently at the start even the chief members of the committee, "Mr. Jakobson, Mr. Blemer, Mr. Rosenblatt, Mr. Neftalin, and Mr. Greenberg," were in the dark with regard to where they were to draw the lines defining the targeted population, and this uncertainty resulted in contending interpretations of the edict. If, as the decree asserted, "the stipulated age was from one to ten," did that not mean that infants under twelve months were excluded and to be left untouched? Or was the measure actually to be "applied to children from the age of one minute up to nine years and three hundred and sixty-five days"? So too there were "similar disagreements about the elderly: did it include those aged sixty-five, or did it begin only after the completion of one's sixty-fifth year?"[42] Nor was it at all clear whether possession of papers might serve to exempt an individual from eligibility for removal.[43] Ghetto inhabitants were only too aware that, however the regulation was interpreted, even those who were healthy, employed, and neither too young nor too old were hardly out of the woods. And should they be spared, they still had to worry about the fate of their children and elderly parents. For word got out, and this time it was true, that together the young children and the elderly, even when all had been seized, would constitute only about thirteen thousand persons, while the demanded quota amounted to some twenty thousand. If so, this meant that others outside the targeted categories would be taken as well. And given the reports that exemptions were to be made for the families of ghetto police and firemen, and workshop managers and other officials as well—a rumor that would also turn out to be true—it was clear that the circle of potential victims would have to widen even further to make up "the difference." As always, those who lacked rank and connections would be the most exposed. Such awareness only spurred the desperation and panic in the streets.[44] Scenes at the remaining food centers still open that day were especially tense. "The shoving and congestion were so terrible that even people who pushed their way through to the distribution yard received their potatoes helter-skelter amid an orgy of fury and madness. Most of the mob, however, after a full day of queuing, went away just as they had come—with empty sacks."[45]

On the afternoon of the fourth, in anticipation of Rumkowski's arrival a crowd estimated at 1,500, among them a large number of concerned parents with children at their side, and many elderly men and women, gathered outside the firehouse at 13 Lutomierska Street to await further news of their fate. In spite of the bright sun and the intense heat of the lengthening afternoon, a cluster of spectators, shunning the patch of shade off to the side, claimed positions close to the speaker's platform. Determined to keep the public at a more comfortable remove so as to control the crowd, the ghetto fire chief, Henryk Kaufman, officiously directed those in front to step aside. Given the evident anxiety gripping those present, Kaufman's brusque demeanor seemed strikingly inconsiderate, and was likely, Zelkowicz thought, a reflection of a lack of concern born of the knowledge that whatever the scope of the impending tragedy, he and his own family would remain unaffected.[46]

Belatedly, at 4:45 Rumkowski appeared, making his way to the podium accompanied by two advisers, Dawid Warszawski, "senior manager of the needleworkers' workshop," and Stanisław-Szaja Jakobson, head judge of the ghetto court and experienced co-coordinator of the year's prior deportations.[47] It was clear at a glance that Rumkowski himself was weak, unsteady; his movements were slow and painful, and he seemed to shuffle forward like "a frail old man who can barely put one foot in front of the other." Rumkowski's crown of "white hair" now appeared noticeably unattended, displaying "unkempt tufts" atop a head that was no longer held erect but was uncharacteristically "stooped, as if he [could] hardly hold it atop his shoulders." As for his mouth, "the tsk-tsk motions of his lips" left no doubt that from them would issue "not even one word of consolation."[48]

Reticent, holding back, Rumkowski came forward only to announce that Warszawski would be the first to address the assembly. Warszawski immediately laid out the details of the decree, forthrightly acknowledging its terrible dimensions while arguing that the ghetto must bow to its demands in full and at all costs. To be sure, he offered a word on Rumkowski's behalf, noting the irony that of all people, this man whose life had been dedicated to the education of children should now be compelled to take upon himself the anguish of directing the forcible removal of young children from the ghetto. Sad as this surely was, Warszawski insisted that for the community there was "no choice" but to submit. "The sentence has been handed down. It is irrevocable. They are demanding sacrifices and sacrifices must be made." By way of justification he invoked the specter of events known to be occurring in Warsaw, where that very summer, in operations still under way, the ghetto was being ruthlessly cleared of nearly its entire population: "There was a decree such as this in Warsaw, too. We all know—it is no secret—how it was carried out." Although his name was not mentioned, in what may have been a veiled allusion to the passive defiance of Adam Czerniaków, head of the Warsaw Jewish Council, who, faced in July with an order to assist in assembling children and others for deportation, had taken his own life, Warszawski, speaking for the Jewish leadership in Łódź, declared that failure to cooperate with the decree would only compel the Germans to use their own forces to do the job. "But we have decided to do it ourselves," he explained, "because we do not want and are unable to transform it into a horrific, terrible disaster." In order to avoid a repetition in their streets of what was happening in Warsaw, there could be no other choice but to cooperate and carry out the evacuation by their own hands, and in this way alone at least ameliorate the effect. "Can I give you any solace? Any comfort?" he said to the crowd. "I can tell you only one thing. It may calm and console you a little: It seems, according to all indications, that we will be able to stay on here uneventfully after the decree."[49] He would be right about that point, but it is doubtful that any who heard it could have followed the weak logic of a final, supposedly consoling thought: Warszawski asked them to consider that, in the conceivable event that Litzmannstadt might be subject to air assault, and inhabitants of the ghetto forced quickly to seek shelter, it would be better if adults were not encumbered by the elderly and the very young. Coming at the end of an otherwise forthright presentation, the idea, to say the least, sounded unconvincing.[50]

Judge Jakobson, next to mount the dais, could only underscore Warszawski's sad revelations, though adding that, of the figure of twenty thousand which his predecessor had noted would constitute the ultimate number of deportees the Germans were demanding, the projected daily quota would be three thousand.[51] More significantly, Jakobson revealed that "to prevent disasters" during the course of the operation the entire ghetto would be subject to a curfew.[52] It was clear, however, in whose interests it was to confine the population to their residences for the duration of the roundup. "Everyone knows that the Evacuation Committee wanted it this way to make its work easier," wrote Zelkowicz. "How simple it is to make everyone wait at home and be ready to be hauled away, obviating the need for a search."[53] All the same, both Warszawski and Jakobson had at least been forthcoming in regard to "the truth about the number of deportees, the types of people to be sent away, and the curfew," an improvement, Zelkowicz thought, over proffering "half-truths, rumors and random conjectures." But the assembled had yet to hear from Rumkowski. It was now his turn to speak.[54]

This time there would be none of his typical bombast, none of his famed self-puffery; today there would be no haughty declarations, no scolding, no admonitions, no threats. The man was obviously troubled, his vaunted ego visibly injured. "The President cries like a little boy," Zelkowicz recorded. "One can see how the agony of the masses has buffeted him, how grievously the decree has hurt him though it applies to him neither directly nor indirectly. These are not crocodile tears. They are Jewish tears, emanating from a Jewish heart."[55] Rumkowski would not dwell on the matter, but in what may have been an effort to evoke from listeners at least a small measure of empathy, even if it was only an expression of self-pity rising to the surface of his awareness, he spoke sorrowfully of his own childlessness, compensated by the many years he had dedicated to the care of children. It was for him a matter of personal anguish to have to bend to a demand that he surrender the young. "I lived and breathed together with the children," he told the crowd. "I never imagined that my own hand would have to bring the sacrifice to the altar."[56] Yet he was careful to concede the greater suffering of parents whose impending loss was immeasurable and crushing. "I understand you, mothers. I see your tears. I also sense the throbbing of your hearts, fathers, who will have to go to work the day after they have taken away your children, when only yesterday you amused yourselves with your beloved offspring. I know and feel all of this."[57] He would not be so presumptuous as to think he could lessen their hardship. "I bear no tidings of consolation today. Neither have I come to calm you today, but rather to expose all of your pain and sorrow. I have come like a thief to deprive you of that which is dearest to your hearts."[58]

Yet he was not going to abandon hope of winning understanding for his position. So unexpected had been the emptying of the hospitals that even he had been unable to prevent harm to his own in-laws. Of course, for some time he had been doing his best to reduce the exposure of young people in the ghetto to new threats. He had endeavored to put more and more of them to work. Touching on the decisive order of the moment affecting the elderly and the young, he indicated that he had not received it until the afternoon of the previous day. He had succeeded, he claimed, in reducing the initial demand from 24,000 victims to 20,000. Though his fervent appeal to exclude nine-year-old children from the general order of deportation had categorically been denied, those aged ten and older had in the end been granted an exemption. Inadequate as this was, he asked the ghetto to take some solace in this small concession. In any case, he wished it known that he had done all that he possibly could; he had even dropped down on his "knees and begged" the Germans to reconsider, "but it was useless."[59] Be that as it may, like his lieutenants, Rumkowski saw no choice but to submit to the edict in exchange for permission to conduct the removal of the young, the elderly, and the ill with the community's own forces. In this way alone might the ghetto avoid the brutality and violence sure to follow should the Germans send in their own troops to carry out the order.[60]

From the start, Rumkowski told his audience, confronted by the edict, he and his trusted associates had been "guided not by the thought 'How many will perish' but 'How many can be saved.' "[61] He reminded them of the fate of the population of the provincial communities, with which they were familiar. "Hardly a thousand Jews reached the ghetto from small towns where seven to eight thousand Jews used to live." The choice facing the Jews of Łódź was as stark as this. "So what's better? What do you want? To leave eighty to ninety thousand people [alive] or to destroy them all, Heaven forfend?" With that, his listeners might have sensed the man finding toward the end of his oration a measure of his familiar dominant bearing. In any event, knowing that in carrying out the order he was a criminal in their eyes, he embraced once more the comparison he knew suited him at this moment only too well. "It takes the heart of a thief to demand what I am demanding of you. But put yourselves in my place, think logically, and draw the conclusion yourselves. I cannot behave otherwise, since those who may be saved far outnumber those whom we are ordered to hand over."[62]

The logic of the argument, cruel as it surely was, was compelling. But given the exhaustion of a last desperate appeal to the Germans to modify their demand, was there truly no alternative to submission and compliance? It is worth noting that Rumkowski remained, as ever, publicly silent about the fate of the deportees. He offered no hope that they were merely being shifted to a new location. His reference to the altar and to sacrifice left little room for conjecture that even the children would survive the journey, though as Zelkowicz and the *Chronicle* attest, speculation to that effect still circulated. But the likelihood of their death—by what means still remained beyond confirmation and beyond imagining—left parents in tears. The members of Rumkowski's audience that afternoon of September 4 were not entirely passive in their grief. At the very moment when he relayed to them the Germans' promise that "if you hand over the sacrifices by yourself, it will be quiet"—that is, compliance would "prevent further sacrifices" and the community would be left in peace— people were heard to shout: " 'We'll all go'; 'Mr. President, don't take only children; take one child from families that have other children!' " Rumkowski responded that he would not accept such "hollow clichés," adding, "I haven't the strength to argue with you."[63]

Apart from the question of substituting youngsters from larger families for those who were their parents' only children—yet another grievous choice implied by the already insane terms of the edict—what if Rumkowski had accepted the logic of those who shouted "We'll all go" and on that Friday afternoon had announced that, at the potential cost of the dissolution of the ghetto, he would not lend his own hand to the destruction of the elderly, the sick, and most especially the young? It would have been a courageous act, and Rumkowski and the ghetto he administered would have been honored for it on that day and on all days of remembrance thereafter. Nevertheless, as Rumkowski knew, it took little imagination to comprehend that such defiance would constitute a direct challenge to a German security establishment whose cruelties both the leaders and the inhabitants of the ghetto had long endured. In all likelihood such an act would have brought the Łódź ghetto to a swift and bloody end. Well before reaching this terrible juncture, Rumkowski knew what to expect from any overt act of defiance. Any Jewish leader who resisted such a decree would have to reckon not just with death but with torture as well. Rumkowski would not have forgotten the fate of the first Beirat and the treatment that preceded their deaths in autumn 1939. And they had done nothing to provoke their torment. But what of a symbolic refusal, one that cheated the Gestapo of the satisfaction of vengeance against a defiant Jewish underling? In his speech Rumkowski had alluded briefly to his own death, if only in the context of wondering if he would live long even after compliantly executing the impending decree. He would have known about Czerniaków's suicide, undertaken in the face of similar pressures, only weeks before in late July. But if the idea of following a similar course crossed his mind now, he dismissed it, whether out of understandable reluctance to take his own life or because Czerniaków's gesture, honorable as it was, had done nothing to prevent the mass deportation that followed. In Warsaw, others had been found to carry out the order.[64] The world would not read of Rumkowski's suicide, or of a courageous ghetto whose people chose, by his word or by his example, to be led away to their deaths rather than offer up with their own hands their aged, their sick, and above all their defenseless young; nor would we hear of those who might have rushed the wooden fence posts and the wires, to die there under fire or, if successful in fleeing the precincts of the ghetto, hunted down and shot in the countryside beyond or, more likely, in the streets of the nearby city.[65]

The words of Warszawski and Jakobson indicate that in advance of addressing the public, internal discussion of how to respond had been going on among a small circle of leaders close to Rumkowski. Others were consulted as well, or at least informed in advance. Speaking of this moment long afterwards Arnold Mostowicz would recall:

> When Rumkowski learned that the Germans had decided to remove all the sick, the elderly, and the children, he called a meeting of doctors. . . . I took part in that meeting. In the course of it ninety percent of the doctors agreed that it had to be done, that the decision must be observed. At the same time they were fully aware that to those deported it meant death. Naturally you can ask me—and it would be a fair question—how did I react? Well, I reacted in the most cowardly way imaginable: I said nothing. I cannot tell you what made me act that way, except one thing which I am sure of now. . . . Personally, I was under no threat; that was one of the reasons for my silence, but it would be too easy to say that it was the only reason. I guess I kept quiet because I was ashamed to say that we should do as the Germans told us, since there was no escape from their decision, but at the same time to admit that it was an utter disgrace.[66]

The speeches ended and evening approached, marking the conclusion of a crushing day. "The sun dips to the west. Dusk has come. As the sun sets, everyone feels the encroachment of impending events," Zelkowicz wrote, groping to express the unrelieved terror of that moment. "No one believes in miracles anymore. All three speakers made it clear that the decree is irreversible—twenty thousand Jews must be deported from the ghetto. Sent away for good. Never to be seen again." Surely "there has never been a sunset like today's." On other days, sunset had brought to the residents of the ghetto the promise of rest. It was the time

> when you returned to your wife after a day at work. After a whole day apart, parents and children gathered for a pitiable dinner. In the courtyard they met with neighbors who declaimed their woes and they breathed musty air into their lungs—musty but, nevertheless, better than the air inside the cramped apartments. Every day, people yearned for sunset. Today, however—how many years of people's lives would they forfeit to keep the sun from setting, to make this day last interminably, to avert the bleak, grotesque morrow forever?[67]

"Once night falls, everyone trembles at the sight of his lengthening shadow." The courtyards are abandoned as people return to their homes to wait out the darkness, or to wait out time's passing:

So the ghetto residents sit in their apartments. Many of them do not even turn on a light. Why bother? For what purpose should people see their own agony and tears in other faces? In other rooms, however, the lights are on. Mostly, these are rooms inhabited by children to whom the hideous decree applies. The best beds have been prepared for these children. Mothers and fathers stand at these beds, not to safeguard the children's slumber or to drive away the ghetto flies, but to contemplate them in their last remaining hours. They can still be together; the parents can still engrave their children's faces into their memory.[68]

A sentence of death hovered over the elderly too. Who, Zelkowicz asked, will watch over them on this night? For them hope is all but extinguished. The old are so obviously useless to the Germans. While death likely also awaited the young, there was at least the sliver of a chance that, under parental protection, children might yet be spared the worst.[69] But as for the elderly, though once their lives had been filled with family, many now were all alone. Zelkowicz thought of them; surely they must "amble along the walls of their rooms, like shadows of stray dogs on a moonlit night in some Godforsaken place." Their fate was grim, their future all but annulled. If any could be sure that this ghetto night was their last on earth, it was they. Their smallest sensory perceptions, momentarily experienced in the vanishing here and now, would be among their last. "So the elderly totter along the walls of the narrow rooms that they now love and cherish so. Even the spider webs and the stains of fleas on the walls have become dear to their hearts." Among them, "who knows what the morrow, and the day after, will look like? Will they have a room at all, or will they share a pit with two hundred, with a thousand people, men, women, children all together—those who have been 'discarded'?" For the last time they enjoyed the comfort of a mattress, a pillow, some sheets, a coverlet: this "bug-infested bedding," uncomfortable as it was, had "suddenly become agreeable" and, in a sense, "their live-in doctor. It allows them to refresh themselves and to relax for a few hours. In their dreams, it reflects the faces of their dear children and grandchildren. How dear this bedding is to an old man in his final hours!" Thus drawn "to that place, to that side of life, to the land of dreams," for one final time an old man might find himself in the company of those who had given a declining life its meaning.[70]

From the outset the ghetto had endured an unsettled relationship with time; ultimately the Jews of Łódź staked all hope on waiting out the Germans until their fortunes failed and the war came to an end. There was always the possibility that through perseverance, through merely holding out, the great remnant might be saved and, once freed, reenter the world. The ghetto would not endure forever. Just as, with all certainty, they knew that at this very moment there existed a world beyond the ghetto, they knew as well that there would be a time to come after it. Whether they might live to experience that future was another matter. Possibly they would. In this hope they could only wish that the intervening time would pass as quickly as possible, that the day of liberation might be near. It was only when a sentence of death drew nearer still that they wanted nothing so much as for time to slow, for the present to be never-ending. But time for them did pass, as time does. Who but a Joshua had the power to delay it?[71] And so the sun set on this day, as on all days before and after, just as surely as it would rise up again and again with each new dawn.

Worry undermined slumber. "Here and there a broken heart issues a groan that emanates from an open window like the sound of an overused violin string, a bleat from a strangled throat like the sound of a slaughtered calf. A child occasionally screams in his restless sleep like the last flickering of a dying candle." But the people knew that nearby existed a kind of peace, the enjoyment of which fed off the misery of the ghetto. It pierced the night with sounds from farther afield. "From that side of life, from the other side of the barbed-wire fence, the ghetto sometimes hears the clatter of a passing streetcar or the screech of a hoarse phonograph record, like the mocking of a drunk nomad who has been placed in charge of the pointless lives of a hundred thousand leprous dogs, that tomorrow or the next day will get their just deserts. 'Cling-clang—one in five to be torn away. Clank-clank—one Jew in five.' "[72]

Night vanished. A new day began. By seven o'clock on the morning of Saturday, September 5, the streets were filled. In anticipation of the curfew, people headed out in the hope of stocking up on any available foodstuffs. "It is utterly impossible to stay at home. Everyone runs out. They literally run—rushing, hustling, as if propelled by someone wielding a whip."[73] For all the commotion there was also an uncharacteristic atmosphere of quiet: "No one converses, it's as if people have left or forgotten their tongues at home. Acquaintances do not offer greetings, as if ashamed of each other. They freeze as they walk. They freeze as they stand in lengthy queues at the distribution points and the vegetable yards. An eerie silence has overtaken the ghetto."[74] Such anxious motion brought to mind a picture of "sinners' souls circulating in the netherworld. This is exactly how they would look: lips buttoned in stubborn silence, eyes filled with a great terror." For Zelkowicz, hellish visions evoked further images of a grotesque metamorphosis: "The three bridges in the ghetto swarm with hundred-headed snakes, an encampment of snakes that moves continually back and forth, hither and yon. The creatures racing about, scurrying in the thick air, are people."[75]

The Jewish police made ready to comply with the tasks ahead, prepared, as on prior occasions, to see to it that orders were carried out. This time they would be assisted by ghetto firefighters, whose cooperation had also been sealed by the promise of safety for their own children and relations and extra servings of bread and sausage to fill their bellies and provide needed energy for the work. Ghetto porters and teamsters, among them men of considerable strength, making up what came to be known unofficially as the White Guard (taking their name from the powdering of "flour, sugar, and rice" that stuck to their garments), were needed as well. These strong men were said to have undertaken preparations to defend their young by mounting guard at the thresholds of their residences "with axes in [their] hands." The display of force proved unnecessary; their cooperation was purchased like that of the police. Their children protected, the transport workers went to work assisting in the operation.[76] Their young children and those of the Jewish police, firemen, and workplace managers—recipients of passes exempting them from resettlement—were brought to a shelter on Łagiewnicka Street, protected for the duration of the Aktion. Removing their small sons and daughters to the shelter when it opened on Sunday, even many of these privileged fathers were anxious, unsure at first that the pledge they had been given would hold.[77]

Even in advance of the curfew, set to begin at 5 PM, the Jewish police started collecting the first of those marked for capture. They began by emptying the old age homes, a relatively effortless undertaking, for the victims were physically weak, isolated from others, certain to be on the premises and there for the taking. In such a place the police could be sure of getting off to a successful start; there they could practice their technique, developing a feel for the Aktion while encountering as little difficulty as possible. "There, as they say, the table's been set. Everything can be taken as is," wrote Zelkowicz. "No need to be selective. Everything is old and fit to be 'thrown on the garbage heap.' "[78] So too "in the old-age homes, the policemen can work in a calm and businesslike way. No one disturbs or annoys them; there are no mistakes. . . . They load the old men and women onto the wagons like pieces of scrap metal."[79]

That would prove the standard procedure, soon to be extended to the ghetto as a whole: those to be removed would climb up onto horse-drawn wagons, guarded by Jewish police and driven by ghetto teamsters to designated assembly points or holding areas established inside the newly cleared hospitals and on the grounds of the ghetto's Czarnieckiego Street prison. From there, in successive transports, they would be loaded onto German trucks that exited the ghetto bound for Chełmno. On that initial weekend morning as well, the first of the carts filled with children were spotted being loaded on Rybna Street. Zelkowicz would record that in stark contrast to grieving parents and other adults nearby, the youngest of the children, apparently oblivious to their fate, were beside themselves with excitement, if also a bit confused. "These children see no reason to cry," he wrote:

> They are quite content: they have been placed on a wagon and they are going for a ride! Since when have children in the ghetto had such an opportunity? If it were not for all those wailing people, if their

mothers and fathers had not screamed so as they placed them in the cart, they would have danced to the cart. After all, they are going for a wagon ride. But all that shouting, noise and crying upset them and disrupted their joy. They jostle in the elongated wagon bed with its high barriers, as if lost, and their bulging eyes ask: What's going on? What do these people want from us? Why don't they let us take a little ride?[80]

Oskar Singer, however, noted that there were also older children, more experienced in ghetto life and its misfortunes, who appeared soberly resigned in the face of what was happening to them.[81] Afterwards—apparently on the evening of September 5—the men of the Jewish Order Service saw to the roundup of the children in the Marysin homes. While some of the estimated 850 youngsters who had been staying there had left in advance of the *Aktion*, Rumkowski, arriving to oversee the removal, made sure that none evaded capture or were left behind.[82]

Confined to their residences, people confronted the knowledge that their own parents, husbands, wives, daughters, sons, sisters, and brothers were potentially targeted for removal, if not already taken, perhaps never to be seen again. The tension and grief, difficult enough to endure by day, became immeasurably worse with the onset of darkness. From the perspective of the following day, Zelkowicz reviewed the distinctive mood prevailing during the nighttime hours of the fifth, wondering: "Who could sleep tonight? Mothers whose children had been taken from them? Men whose wives, their helpmeets, had been taken? People whose ailing loved ones were removed from their beds? . . . The ghetto tosses on its bed and knows no sleep. The aching, enfeebled bones cannot lie still. The ghetto's brain is incurably feverish. All those screams and roars, sighs and groans that split the silence of the night through the open windows and doors have landed on its heart." Sounds of anguish traversed the darkness. For the bereaved, night brought not the least diminution of their suffering: "Hours have passed since these woes, these agonies, were inflicted on those wretched people, but the situation has not calmed down one bit. Mothers have not yet tired of shrieking, fathers' wellsprings of tears have not yet been sealed, and the silence of the night amplifies the reverberations of the screaming and sobbing."[83]

On that same Saturday, September 5, the day that followed Friday's dreadful pronouncement of the irrevocable order for the ghetto to yield up the aged, the sick, and the children of most tender years, an additional camera team from the Ufa studios, recently arrived to continue documenting the city's reconstruction, set up their equipment on location, first at the Telefunken works, and then once more at the site of the newly opened municipal beach and water park in Erzhausen.[84] The filmmakers recorded a charming setting. As the camera rolled, people in bathing suits could be seen diving off a bridge into the

191

water. Panning downstream, the camera found three people seated in a rowboat, another boat overtaking them, passing by. Panning toward the shore, it highlighted two shirtless youngsters seated on a grassy bank. In a sequence lasting only seconds, one of the them, a fair-haired boy, was seen to raise an arm, casually propping it on his knee.[85] In brief, yet another ideal image of a city without Jews, quietly indulging in the pleasures of a lazy, late-summer afternoon. This was but one aspect of the newly emerging city the filmmakers would document as they traveled to numerous sites over the course of what would prove, for the ghetto though decidedly not for the city, a week of unprecedented horror.

But even these images of a relaxed citizenry at play beside gentle waters were but one contrasting facet of the new Litzmannstadt, whose changes were hailed as stunning and whose fast-paced tempo was admired for being precisely what one would expect from a major urban center in the making. Indeed, according to the local press, downtown was jumping, its streets and crossings increasingly crowded, an observation said to have been noted by citizens returning from holidays in the country, as well as by the mayor of Posen, who on a recent visit to the city had commented on the phenomenon as well. To offer a more precise view of just how heavily trafficked the streets were, on September 5 the *Litzmannstädter Zeitung* publicized an informal survey gauging the number of people and vehicles traveling a busy city block, a stretch along Adolf-Hitler-Straße between Meisterhausstraße and Straße des 8. Armee—a distance of some five hundred meters in length—between six and seven o'clock in the evening. The results, published in the paper's Saturday edition, were said to be altogether "startling": during that single evening hour, and along just this one stretch of avenue, had passed no fewer than 3,288 pedestrians, 69 automobiles, 178 streetcars—each loaded with an estimated 100 riders, hence ferrying some 17,800 persons in all at an average rate of three cars per minute—along with 14 trucks, 18 motorcycles, 2 freight trams, 27 horse-drawn cabs, 117 bicycles, and 6 handcarts. The point one was to draw from all this was twofold: Litzmannstadt was indeed a big city, fast-paced and energetic. That said, such a rush of crowds and cars was "synonymous with life and development. In Litzmannstadt life pulses mightily, work is being done, people bestir themselves, they have things to do. Already they are creating today the foundations for the Litzmannstadt of the future."[86]

By dark that evening Litzmannstadt readied for entertainment. As ever, audiences in search of lighter fare that Saturday were invited to stop by the Tabarin cabaret, whose new September lineup included solo dancer Maria Reill, entertainer Jack Barlott imitating a chimpanzee, a team of "comical jugglers" by the name of Waldero and Pifo, the Carinis performing their "Liliput-Trio," as well as the dances of the La-Czarina Ballet, the music of the Kapelle Bojanowsky, and the Trio Nino singing "well-known hits."[87] For audiences in search of more serious entertainment, the Theater an der Moltkestraße was opening its 1942–43 season with a performance of *Kabale und Liebe* by Schiller. Recalling the recent words of Oberbürgermeister Ventzki in stressing the significance of theater to Litzmannstadt, "the easternmost large city of the great German Reich," a correspondent jubilantly proclaimed: "Curtain up! Let the show begin!"[88]

By the following morning, Sunday, September 6, not satisfied that the Jewish police alone could do the job, the Gestapo intervened, sending German forces into the ghetto to oversee the roundup. Far from being relieved of their duties, the men of the Jewish Order Service acted as auxiliaries. As Isaiah Trunk, briefly summarizing the tactics now in force, would note: "Gestapo and SS-men, accompanied by their Jewish helpers, went from house to house, and a very few minutes after hearing the signal (generally a reckless revolver shot), all tenants had to present themselves for the selection. Here everything went at a lightning fast tempo. Fates were determined in a matter of seconds: a glance or a gesture with the hand (left or right)."[89]

Shlomo Frank, himself a Jewish policemen, would recall that in the hours before the Gestapo's arrival, the Jewish police prepared for an escalation in violence. The matter was discussed after midnight, during the course of a conference at Jewish Order Service headquarters on Lutomierska Street. By seven the next morning the word went out to the Order Service rank and file. A Jewish police commander informed his men that the number of people who were going to die in the coming hours was incalculable, but they were ordered to show "no mercy": there could be no disturbances; the ghetto population had to submit.[90] Heading toward Bałuty Market at 7:30 AM, Jewish police encountered a team of Gestapo men, "no more than sixteen" in all, entering the ghetto "on the march" and "with automatic rifles on their shoulders," announcing their presence with an extended volley of gunfire that lasted a good ten minutes. Typically, with a cordon laid down in a targeted sector of neighboring streets, the Gestapo swept in, forcing occupants to assemble in residential courtyards. Children clung to their mothers, begging not to be separated: "Wherever they send you, take me. Together, let's go together."[91] Loaded onto the carts, they cried out for help: "Mama, Mama, save us, do not let us be killed." Some dared to leap from the wagons, attempting to make a break, only to be shot, their blood pooling in the streets. Amid the slaughter, the killers taunted the others, already "frightened to death," cynically asking "if they wanted to jump off the wagons as well."[92] These men were onto the ways of their prey, easily discovering the usual places where parents had hidden children. Other families, attempting to stay one step ahead of the selections, dashed into the streets. But to no avail. They were easily cut down by gunners stationed on rooftops, firing down on fleeing parents and children below.[93] The killers made a sport of the chase; they joked with one another, they teased and taunted their victims, delighting in catching them unawares, shooting them at close range as well as from afar. After pumping a bullet into one victim, a Gestapo official asked, "Taste good?" His colleague was said to have a penchant for tapping Jewish women on the shoulder, telling them to turn around, then shooting them from behind; if his victims were still breathing as they lay in a pool of their own blood, he would stand on top of them until they died.[94] Another "ran about like a wild ox, his nostrils sniffing out places where children were hiding." When he found them, rather than letting them emerge, he opened fire on them where they hid, then ordered neighbors to come and "drag out the filth."[95] On Łagiewnicka Street one of the killers was said to have forced four ten-year-old boys to their knees, ordering them to open their mouths, into which, one by one, he fired. Incredulous, the children were said to have thought he was merely "joking with them."[96]

By mid-morning on that same Sunday, Zelkowicz had succeeded in gathering some initial accounts. They were impossible to bear, though they recorded only the first of many wounds that would be inflicted that week on families throughout the ghetto. Among the very first to suffer such agonies would be a young poet, married, father to a pair of daughters, one no older than eight years of age, another born less than two days before. On Saturday—it was "in the late afternoon"—the first of these daughters, a beautiful child with "golden curls, blue eyes and gleaming white teeth," was taken by the Jewish police; then on Sunday morning the Germans arrived and seized his wife, "ill" and "feverish," still bedridden from having just giving birth. The newborn daughter resting by her side, "a tiny infant with two miniature round fists" and "quiet, motionless eyes," as yet nameless, too weak even to suckle a bit of milk, was taken too. "What miserable, shocking and utterly illogical felicitations come in from the street," wrote Zelkowicz. "The mind does not accept them; the intellect cannot grasp them. Nevertheless they are the absolute truth!"[97] In a courtyard on Zytnia Street, neighbors who had been assembled there witnessed another unfolding crime when a mother, quietly defiant though smiling, remained steely in defying a German ordering her to let go of her four-year-old daughter's hand. Uncharacteristically, the mother was given a few moments to reconsider. "Neighbors standing in the lengthy ranks sneaked a tearful look at the two of them, standing alone and smiling at each other—the girl in contentment for remaining with her mother who clutched her hand, and the mother in contentment for having her daughter next to her and within her." She was told, " 'Face the wall . . .!' Holding even tighter that small hand, she and her child were shot to death from behind."[98]

Residents of another building were witnesses to the fate of another little girl, the only child of a dignified, well-attired German Jewish woman from Danzig whose daily absence from home unleashed in the child fits of sobbing and screaming. Ceaselessly crying for her mother, she "spent whole days mired in tears, unconsolable by anyone but her mother," an odd child, "her head pointed, her face round as a ball, her legs thick and stiff, and her eyes large, black, and almost motionless. She looked more like a clown than a living girl." Early on Saturday her mother, thinking at first the *Aktion* was not yet imminent, had gone to work, only to race back to the residence upon getting word of the impending roundup, retreating to her apartment with the child. Shortly before six that evening, the Jewish Order Service came and took the girl, who, suddenly dignified and silent, a small version of her mother, "walked next to the tall, stiff policeman" while "dressed in a tiny coat and hat, a small girlish pocketbook under her arm," her "round black, expressionless eyes" looking straight ahead. In contrast, her mother's composure was shattered. At the sight of her daughter being led away, she "issued an inhuman scream that resonated throughout the courtyard and on the stairs. . . . She continued to circulate tearfully in the courtyard for hours on end, until late in the evening." Eventually "the neighbors, after strenuous efforts, managed to bring her inside. All that night she lurched from corner to corner in her room," shouting her daughter's name.[99] The sound of screaming filled the air. The despair of parents who had lost their children was immense. One woman "lay on the ground and pounded her head against the pavement." A man ran about, "an ax in his hands," shouting for the return of his child, threatening death to those who would bring it harm.[100]

Meanwhile, only too aware of the perils of displaying outward signs of age, older adults did their best to appear a little younger. Perhaps, they reasoned, it might be possible to fool their would-be captors, given to instant judgment of their features for signs of vitality, of youth, of health, separating the fit from the potential castoffs—the moribund, the decrepit, the sick, the useless—who were their targets. What, after all, did the elderly have to lose by looking well clothed, younger and healthier, fresher, even more attractive in anticipation of that second or two when, at a glance, the captor's eye would glance their way. Hair that was not white, lips and cheeks of a reddened as opposed to a pale or washed-out hue, meant life. One had but an instant to make the right impression. "No one knows what to wear when he or she descends to the courtyard for inspection," wrote Zelkowicz. "If people go as is, without a hat and coat, it may create the impression of disrespect." Or perhaps not. "If you came to the courtyard in ordinary clothes, it showed that you took the matter lightly; if you put on a hat and coat, it meant you were ready for a trip, so why not join the transport?"[101] A man might don a hat or coat, but women could do more. They could "doll up," as Zelkowicz put it. If a woman's lips were pale and she had no lipstick, she had only to bite her lips, forcing the blood to rush to the surface. The same with her cheeks; in the absence of rouge, she had only to pinch them or rub them with a bit of red paper to produce instantly a spot of color. At the very least, gray hair could be tucked away beneath a scarf.[102] Men hoping to achieve a temporarily younger look took to dyeing their hair with coffee.[103]

Others tried more direct means of resisting capture. A fifteen-year-old girl, caught up in a selection and desperate to escape being carted away with the others, repeatedly battled tooth and nail against a Jewish policeman who was determined to foil her efforts to break free and save her life. Ordered onto a wagon full of captives, she begged him to look the other way so she might make a run for safety. Her plea was greeted with brute force. She later recalled the man seizing her arm and pushing her against the already packed vehicle, forcing her aboard. "As I made an attempt to jump down[,] . . . the same Jewish policeman caught me by the hair and pulled me back." When she reached for the side of the transport to make contact with an acquaintance she had spotted on the street below, "the same Jewish policeman caught me, slapped me across the face, and threw me to the floor." On arrival at the collection point on the fenced-in grounds of the hospital on Drewnowska Street, making a break from the others to find a hiding place, she scuffled with yet another Jewish policeman who "screamed as he came running." He took hold of her, tearing her dress, as she "kicked, scratched and struggled" for dear life.[104]

Some children hid in furniture and bedding, others in basements, in heaps of garbage and laundry, or in woodpiles.[105] Parents did whatever they could, concealing their children "in barrels in the attics, in ditches in the field, covered with leaves and branches."[106] One child sought refuge in a tree but was shot dead when discovered.[107] Another, thanks to his father's efforts to fashion an unusual hideout, rode out the danger concealed in a chimney on the roof.[108] Though isolated and abandoned by the time they had been assembled in the collection area, child captives fought and scratched at the walls in a last-ditch effort to resist removal.[109] But these and many other desperate grabs for survival, courageous as they were, were undertaken individually, in an unorganized way, without help from the Jewish authorities, who dared go no further than securing approval to spare the children and elderly relations of the ghetto police, firemen, teamsters, and well-connected officials. The rest, whether children or adults, were on their own and, as far as Rumkowski and the ghetto leadership were concerned, regrettably but necessarily fated to be sacrificed to save the others. Having acquiesced to the Germans' demand, he wanted them to be taken away quickly and with their removal the dirty business finished and put behind him.

One week after commencement of the *Aktion*, on September 12, by "posted" announcement the Gettoverwaltung informed the residents of the ghetto that the curfew was lifted; the terrible roundup came to an end. In the course of these seven days the operation had resulted in the deportation of an estimated 15,859 persons, with "a minimum of 600 shot to death on the spot." Labor, Biebow informed them, was to resume at the beginning of the workweek the following Monday, September 14. "Every manager, worker, and employee is obligated to occupy his workplace punctually if he is concerned to protect himself from the greatest unpleasantness imaginable," he warned, calling upon them "to fulfill their tasks with the greatest diligence and take pains to make up as quickly as possible for the arrears caused by" what he referred to bizarrely as their "rest break."[110]

In the aftermath of the operation, building caretakers and ghetto police inventoried and secured the personal effects left behind in apartments abandoned by the deported. In some of the residences along Marysińska and Marynarska streets, for example, they found jackets, coats, shirts, sweaters, trousers, underpants, skirts, gloves, umbrellas, scarves and handkerchiefs, pillows and pillowcases, blankets, sheets, suitcases, tablecloths, dishware, cutlery, clocks, candlesticks, skullcaps and prayer shawls, rags, and unwashed laundry held in containers or merely lying in a heap.[111]

It was always thought best to have the Jews handle these goods, but the oper-ation being what it was, the Gettoverwaltung had its own tasks of cleanup to perform as well. Appealing to the city Health Department, on September 21 Biebow's deputy, Friedrich Ribbe, requested approval for the provision of addi-tional soap for "around 60 members" of his staff whose tasks brought them "continually in contact with Jews and such things of Jewish origin." It almost went without saying that they were being exposed "to great danger of infec-tion," so it was "perfectly understandable that these people are compelled to wash their hands more often than normal." Approval was granted within seventy-two hours.[112]

Sunday, September 13, would be the final day of shooting for the Ufa film crew; some two hundred meters of footage would be shot that day. After an abbreviated trip to the stadium, they proceeded to the municipal zoo, an institution celebrated for its contribution to the recreational potential of the new city. Litzmannstadt was depicted as a family-oriented, child-friendly city in a filmed sequence that highlighted visitors arriving at the zoo and delighting in its attractions. A small child is seen walking toward the entrance between two men in uniform. Its hands are raised to be held in theirs. A woman, accompanied by a female acquaintance, is pushing a baby carriage. A group proceeds down an outdoor staircase leading onto a wide tree-lined path. A couple—a man in a raincoat and a woman dressed in a lightweight coat, their pace a bit quicker—walk on ahead of the others. The day is bright. The camera pans to take in the image of a gentle stream, a gazebo in the distance, trees reflected on the glassy surface of the still waters. Caged animals come into view: a camel, a tiger, a chimpanzee, a lion cub, a bear.[113]

Summer was coming to an end. One reliable sign of the season had been the daily 7:45 AM departure of the familiar "special" transport from Deutschlandplatz, a regional tram carrying children bound for a government-run day camp in Erzhausen. With the end of the camp's last session approach-ing, the children would have been boarding for their final trips to the city's much-admired recreational district. Based in a home run by the National Socialist Welfare Agency (NSV), the camp, appropriately situated on Sleeping Beauty Street (Dornröschenstraße), lay in a park with lovely wooded surround-ings. All told, some four hundred youngsters, divided into month-long rotating sessions accommodating a hundred campers at a time, got to enjoy the out-of-doors—a published photograph depicts girls in summer dresses joining hands to form a ring—their bodies attended to, cleansed in saltwater baths, and nourished by an ample, healthful diet. Many children had completed their stays "several kilos heavier" than when they arrived. On the third weekend in September a festive farewell Saturday program marked the season's end."[114]

Oblivious to the cruelties to which the elderly and the young had recently been subjected inside the ghetto, writers who served as the public voice of the regime, even in highlighting efforts to promote the welfare of German mothers, proved unable to resist an opportunity to curse the Jews. Evidence of the harm they were alleged to have caused seemed even now, and in spite of their long absence from the city, to keep cropping up, complicating the great tasks of renovation and renewal. That autumn a villa, formerly a Jewish old age home, was being remodeled to accommodate a city training facility for German mothers. A tour of the facilities, beginning with promising impressions of the building's sunny, park-like grounds, from which were heard the delightful sounds of voices singing to "the accompaniment of a flute," occasioned in the mind of a local newspaper correspondent only the brightest of thoughts. Those initial impressions proved altogether at odds with what were described as the horrifying conditions reportedly confronting those whose task it had been to prepare the property for its new occupants. "Even the Polish workmen," thought to be "in this respect used to all sorts of things, were shocked when they discovered the swarm of bugs behind the wallpaper. The filth in this Jewish home was indescribably if authentically Jewish." That past unpleasantness happily overcome, the home was successfully completing conversion, providing facilities for some 225 German mothers at a time to receive instruction in family health, infant care, cooking, sewing, handicrafts, and household decoration. Attractive rooms, including a winter garden, added pleasant touches, and overnight facilities, equipped with showers and baths, were at the disposal of "out-of-town participants" in the courses as well as staff. In brief, the facility was an expression of the party's striving "to enrich the family, and particularly to help make easier the tasks of our women and mothers."[115]

In further material confirmation of the Germans' claim to the land, two weeks after the conclusion of the terrifying roundup inside the ghetto, on the morning of September 26 the city's prehistory museum, located on Deutschlandplatz, was at last ready for the public. An advance tour of its rooms revealed a prominent selection of local archaeological finds: in addition to the usual assortment of iron lances and buckles of gold, silver, and bronze, worthy of special note were relics supposed to offer insight into the practices and belief systems of Nordic settlers dating from as long ago as 1200–500 BC. As an aid to picturing the awesome dimensions of some of the burial sites common to the region, a mockup depicted an impressively long grave, measuring some 130 meters in length. Original artifacts bespeaking practices associated with early Germanic settlement highlighted changing funerary customs, advancing from burial to the burning of the dead. Displayed too were a selection of ash-bearing urns, some with bell-shaped lids and carvings of faces, some bearing the inspiring design of a winged swastika, of local significance because the pattern had been incorporated into the Litzmannstadt city flag. Readers following this account of the exhibition were reminded of previously highlighted finds recovered from a recent excavation in the Erzhausen district. At last citizens would have opportunity to admire in person a selection of these rare finds, among them "a small, twinned vessel" and, perhaps most poignantly, a child's rattle fashioned out of clay that had been discovered inside one of the graves.[116]

At the same time that the archaeological presentation on Deutschlandplatz made available a glimpse into the remote Germanic past, "the first German color film," the Ufa production *Women Make Better Diplomats*, a musical starring Marika Rökk and Willy Fritsch, was playing at the newly renovated Casino cinema. Deemed a historic technical advance comparable to the introduction of sound, the achievement promised to revolutionize the medium, eventually eclipsing black and white. The novelty had been so great as to require an initial period of adjustment for the viewer. The technical reproduction of color, while said to have been, at least in part, astonishingly true, seems to have had a way to go before all colors could be reproduced convincingly. All the same, a feature film of this nature, full of song and dance, was considered ideally suited for showcasing the medium's new potential. Adding a local touch to the premiere, the city's police orchestra was on hand to perform a selection of popular cinematic show tunes.[117]

Walther Genewein, Gettoverwaltung accountant, amateur photographer, and unofficial visual documentarian of the ghetto's administration, might well have taken an interest. For he too had been working in the new medium of color photography, and had by now accumulated a significant and growing collection of images recording the activities of the Biebow administration and ghetto labor.[118] Taking the opportunity to record as well a moment of his own private relaxation and contemplation, in an image dated October 1942 Genewein photographed himself at bedtime, seated at the end of a long, green-cushioned sofa. He wears a red-striped bathrobe and brown slippers, his legs crossed, his head slightly lowered over an open book in his lap: the accountant at leisure, absorbed in his reading, his shadow a dark silhouette cast on the bare wall behind him. A brown or tan throw pillow lies nearby. An oriental carpet fills the space of the floor. On a table to his left, toward which he inclines, sits a substantial wooden box radio, a pair of decorative figurines, and a shaded table lamp with a shiny gold base. Behind them the tiles of what appears to be a tall ceramic oven help create the impression of a cozy niche.[119]

The first days of autumn promised ample opportunity for citizens of the new Reich city to develop their cultural sensibilities. While the opening of the new Museum of Prehistory served to document the Germanic origins

of the region and the culture of its past, modern artists attended to the representations of the moment. Currently on display at the Volksbildungsstätte was
the work of a sculptor, Marta Kronig, a hometown artist since moved to
Munich, again in town for an exhibition of her work. In an interview with
a local reporter, she spoke of giving artistic shape to the depiction of
human emotion, and of the sensibilities most appropriate to creative receptivity
in both artist and viewer. As a contemporary artist, Kronig attended to
the present, declaring: "In my works I want to give shape to the people of
today. . . . Not those of yesterday nor those of tomorrow." On the topic of
suffering, a theme of some prominence in her work, she remarked, "When
I depict suffering . . . I do not give form to suffering that cries out, but to that
suffering which is already beyond the scream, accepting of its fate. And in the
face of suffering one must have reverence." As for future projects, "what she
would most like to create are little fountains. Little in the sense that they are
not meant to be magnificent, but fountains situated in peaceful park locales
seldom visited by anyone and where all is cozy and still, where the splashing of
the fountain waters speak to quiet visitors of fairy tales." To this she added,
"Most of all I would like to create such fairy tale fountains for children's
playgrounds."[120]

Rounding out the season's new offerings on the evening of November 5,
1942, the Städtische Bühnen, expanding into a new realm of performance,
launched its first full season of opera under its own management, selecting
for the occasion a performance of Engelbert Humperdinck's 1890's musical
rendition of the fairy tale classic, *Hansel and Gretel*. Defying not just the
shortage of available musicians and singers but above all the "primitive"
nature of the "technical apparatus," said to have been a legacy of the
abstractly derided "Jewish-Polish want of culture" long dominant on the
local arts scene, the performance had brought forth a masterly rendition.
A critic praised the production for so richly evoking what he termed "a
genuine fairy-tale mood, born of the joy in assuming a childlike perspective on
the world."[121]

On the night of that autumn premiere the audience had been privileged to
enjoy one of the most enduring of tales. Its theme of lost children ultimately
rescued from peril had been well selected to appeal to the sensibilities of
Litzmannstadt operagoers, and appeal it did. Following the performance, the
stage manager, orchestra leader, and cast stepped in front of the curtain to
receive both a warm ovation and the presentation of a gift of flowers. The
municipal orchestra had cleverly arranged key elements of the score. The lighting, so essential to the addition of scenic color, had been magnificent. Actors
and actresses, assisted by a boys' chorus, had succeeded admirably in evoking
the atmosphere and drama of this long-popular tale. It remained an appealing
fable even now, and on that November evening in the city, nightmare had
given way to deliverance. In the final scene the children, held captive on the
grounds of the witch's hideout, were seen to rise miraculously from the ginger-

bread in which they had been imprisoned. Lurking evil had been defeated. Life had been granted them anew. Parents and children, long separated, were united once again.[122]

For the deported children of the ghetto and the parents they left behind, there was no solace. To the parents, details concerning the destination and fate of their young sons and daughters remained shrouded in darkness. This much alone was evident: wherever the Germans had taken the children, there would be no sandman to sprinkle sleep-dust in their eyes, no angels to watch over them as they slumbered in the forest by night, no dewman to awaken them in the morning, no rescue, no release, no reunion with mothers and fathers who, inconsolable, looked into their eyes no more.[123]

Notes

1 S., "Unsere Kleinsten feierten ein Kinderfest: Auf der Spielwiese tummelten sich Mädel und Buben/Manche Überraschung erfreute," *LZ*, 25 June 1942. "So Turnen unsere Kleinen auf der Spielwiese," *LZ*, 26 June 1942.

2 "Fröhliches Kinderglück im Sonnenschein: In den Parks von Litzmannstadt laden viele Plätze unsere Kleinen zum Tummeln ein," *LZ* 15 June 1942.

3 "Badefreuden winken," *LZ*, 8 July 1942.

4 In considering this, I have found Elaine Scarry's commentary on "injuring-as-substantiation" in war, on the body and sacrifice, on the biblical focus on the centrality of numbers in generational increase and decline, and on the importance of laying claim to a land of much interest. Elaine Scarry, *The Body in Pain: The Making and Unmaking of the World* (New York: Oxford University Press, 1985), pp. 137–138, 185–205.

5 Account of Heinz May in K. M. Pospieszalski, "Niemiecki nadleśniczy o zagładzie Żydów w Chełmnie nad Nerem," *Przegląd Zachodni* 18, no. 3 (May–June 1962): 102. See also Łucja Pawlicka-Nowak, ed., *Chelmno Witnesses Speak*, trans. Juliet D. Golden and Arkadiusz Kamiński (Konin: Council for the Protection of Memory of Combat and Martyrdom in Warsaw and District Museum in Konin, 2004), account of H. May, p. 159, and testimony of Andrzej Miszcak, p. 141. Głowna Komisja Badania Zbrodni przeciwko Narodowi Polskiemu—Instytut Pamięci Narodowej, Ob 271, t. III, pp. 208–209: witness statement, Czesław Urbaniak, 5 July 1945.

6 Accounts of May and Misczak in Pawlicka-Nowak, *Chelmno Witnesses Speak*, pp. 158–161, 141. Głowna Komisja, Ob 271, t. I, pp. 70–71: witness statement, Aleksander Wózniak, 16 June 1945; Ob 271, t.II, p. 115: statement of Jozef Czuprynski, 25 June 1945.

7 Account of May in Pawlicka-Nowak, *Chelmno Witnesses Speak*, p. 160. "Testimony by Walter Piller," ibid., p. 185. Affidavit of Rudolf Höss, cited in Richard Rhodes, *Masters of Death: The SS-Einsatzgruppen and the Invention of the Holocaust* (New York: Knopf, 2002), p. 259. The mill's provenance is not altogether certain, but we do know that in the summer of 1942 one was requested from the Łódź ghetto. It is perhaps a mark of the confidence, if not to say the brazenness, of the Gettoverwaltung, accomplice to the crime, that in July 1942 it delivered to Rumkowski a query regarding the availability of such "a bone grinder." The request went so far as to indicate that the mill was being sought for the Sonderkommando Kulmhof (Chełmno). See Ribbe to Eldest of the Jews, Litzmannstadt, 16 July 1942,

in *Dokumeny i materialy do dziejów okupacji niemeickiej w Polsce*, ed. A. Eisenbach, vol. 3, *Getto Lodzkie*, pt. 1 (Warsaw: Centralna żydowska Komisja Historyczna, 1946), p. 279.

8　APL PSZ 1099, p. 124: Oskar Singer, "Der Tag in Fragmenten. Zu Kapiteln von frueher."

9　"Swit ('dawn' in Polish) purported to be broadcasting clandestinely within occupied Poland, but in fact it was a British-sponsored service broadcasting from facilities near London." Robert Moses Shapiro, "Diaries and Memoirs from the Lodz Gheto in Yiddish and Hebrew," in *Holocaust Chronicles: Individualizing the Holocaust through Diaries and Other Contemporaneous Personal Accounts* (Hoboken, N.J.: KTAV Publishing House, 1999), p. 114, n. 31.

10　Shlomo Frank, *Togbukh fun Lodzher geto* (Buenos Aires: Tsentral-farlag fun Poylishe Yidn in Argentine, 1958), entry for 9 July 1942, pp. 289–290.

11　Ibid., entry for 20 July 1942, pp. 292–293.

12　*The Chronicle of the Łódź Ghetto, 1941–1945*, ed. Lucjan Dobroszycki, trans. Richard Lourie, Joachim Neugroschel et al. (New Haven: Yale University Press, 1984), entry for Sunday, 26 July 1942, p. 230.

13　Ibid., and p. 230, n. 76.

14　ZIH Łódź 138: Gettokommissariat, Bericht, Betrifft: Lagerberichteerstattung an den Inspekteur der Sicherheitspolizei und des SD, July 28, 1942, copy. Lagebericht, Gestapo in Litzmannstadt, 2 July 1942, excerpt in Tatania Berenstein, Artur Eisenbach, Bernard Mark, and Adam Rutkowski, *Faschismus—Ghetto—Massenmord: Dokumentation über Ausrottung und Widerstand der Juden in Polen während des zweiten Weltkrieges* (Frankfurt am Main: Röderberg-Verlag, 1960), p. 292.

15　See Dan Diner, *Beyond the Conceivable: Studies on Germany, Nazism, and the Holocaust* (Berkeley: University of California Press, 2000), pp. 133–135.

16　*Chronicle*, entry for 1 June 1942, pp. 194–195. APL PSZ 1091: transcript of speech, dated 31 May 1942.

17　*Chronicle*, entry for Tuesday, 21 July 1942, p. 226, and Thursday, 23 July 1942, p. 228, both credited to B[ernard] O[strowski].

18　USHMM RG-083M, Reel 168, File 867, p. 63: Statistical Tables, "Waisenhaus: Zöglinge nach Alter und Geschlecht I.–VIII. 1942 [January–August 1942]"; "Im Arbeitsressorts beschäftigte Zöglinge nach Alter."

19　USHMM RG-15.083M, Reel 168, File 867, pp. 5[1], 53: Statistical Tables, "Kinderkolonien [,] Bewegung, Kinder anch Jahrgängen und Geschlecht[,] VIII. 1940–IX. 1942 [August 1940–September 1942]"; "Arbeitsstellen der Kinder 31. VII. 1942 [31 July 1942]."

20　USHMM RG-15.083M, Reel 4, File 19, p. 231: Die Insassen des Greisenheims II, Gnesenerstraße 26, to Rumkowski, 12 July 1942. Printed in part in a stylized poster-style format not reproduced here.

21　*Chronicle*, entry for 28 August 1942, pp. 244–245.

22　Oskar Rosenfeld, *In the Beginning Was the Ghetto: Notebooks from Lodz*, ed. Hanno Loewy, trans. Brigitte M. Goldstein (Evanston: Northwestern University Press, 2002), Notebook E, entry for 27 August [1942], p. 118.

23　ZIH File 302/299, pp. 7–8: Dziennik Ireny Hauser, entry for 19 August [1942].

24　ZIH File 302/299, pp. 8, 11–12: Dziennik Ireny Hauser, entries for 19 and 20 August [1942].

25　Janusz Gumkowski, Adam Rutkowski, and Arnfrid Astel, *Briefe aus Litzmannstadt* (Cologne: Friedrich Meddelhauve Verlag, 1967), pp. 72–75.

26　Josef Zelkowicz, *In Those Terrible Days: Notes from the Łódź Ghetto*, trans. Naftali Greenwood (Jerusalem: Yad Vashem, 2002), p. 251. *Chronicle*, entry for 1 September 1942, p. 248, credited to Zelkowicz.

27 *Chronicle*, p. 249. Zelkowicz, *In Those Terrible Days*, entry for 1 September 1942, p. 251.

28 Zelkowicz, *In Those Terrible Days*, pp. 251–254. *Chronicle*, entry for 1 September 1942, pp. 248–249. On the pushing of children from windows, see testimony of Dr. Donat Szmulewicz-Stanisz, in Jerzy Lewiński, *Proces Hansa Biebowa* (Warsaw: PRS, 1999), p. 107, and of Bronyka Szyldwach, in *Preserved Evidence: Ghetto Lodz*, ed. Anna Eilenberg-Eibeshitz, vol. 1 (Haifa: H. Eibeshitz Institute for Holocaust Studies, 1998), pp. 256–257.

29 Note the exchange in Lewiński, *Proces Hansa Biebowa*, p. 67.

30 Testimony of Aleksander Klugman, ibid., pp. 139–140.

31 Testimony of Szyja Teitelbaum, ibid., p. 112.

32 Testimony of Hersz Janowski, ibid., p. 111.

33 *Chronicle*, entry for 1 September 1942, p. 249.

34 *Chronicle*, entry for 2 September 1942, p. 249.

35 Rosenfeld, *In the Beginning*, Notebook E, entry for 4 [September] [1942], p. 121. Oskar Rosenfeld, *Wozu noch Welt: Aufzeichnungen aus dem Getto Lodz*, ed. Hanno Loewy (Frankfurt am Main: Verlag Neue Kritik, 1994), entry for 4 [September] [1942], p. 148.

36 Zelkowicz, *In Those Terrible Days*, p. 264.

37 Ibid., pp. 264–265.

38 Ibid., p. 265.

39 Ibid., p. 266.

40 Ibid., pp. 267–268.

41 Ibid., p. 268. *Chronicle*, pp. 250–251.

42 Zelkowicz, *In Those Terrible Days*, pp. 268–269.

43 Ibid., p. 269.

44 Ibid., pp. 270–271.

45 Ibid., p. 273.

46 Ibid., pp. 274–275.

47 Ibid., p. 276. The account in the *Chronicle* refers to Rumkowski's address as having taken place at 4:00 PM. *Chronicle*, entry for 14 September 1942, p. 250.

48 Zelkowicz, *In Those Terrible Days*, p. 276.

49 Ibid., p. 277.

50 Ibid., pp. 277–278.

51 Ibid., p. 278.

52 Ibid.

53 Ibid., p. 279.

54 Ibid.

55 Ibid., p. 280.

56 Ibid.

57 Ibid., p. 282.

58 Ibid., p. 281.

59 Ibid., pp. 280–283.

60 Ibid., pp. 280–282.

61 Ibid., p. 281.

62 Ibid., p. 283.

63 Ibid., pp. 282–283.

64 In addition, elsewhere the Nazis proved equally capable of carrying out evacuations without engaging the direct cooperation of the councils. See Yehuda Bauer, *Rethinking the Holocaust* (New Haven: Yale University Press, 2001), pp. 77–78.

65 In other ghettos, however, such attempts were made, though with very limited success. See Dov Levin, "The Fighting Leadership of the Judenräte in the Small

Communities of Poland," in *Patterns of Jewish Leadership in Nazi Europe, 1933–1945: Proceedings of the Third Yad Vashem International Historical Conference*, ed. Yisrael Gutman and Cynthia Haft (Jerusalem: Yad Vashem, 1979), pp. 134, 136–142. Leni Yahil, *The Holocaust: The Fate of European Jewry*, trans. Haya Galai (New York: Oxford University Press), pp. 471–472.

66 Quoted in *Fotoamator* (1998), dir. Dariusz Jabłoński, Apple Film Productions, English version trans. Alina Skibińska and Wolfgang Jöhling.

67 Zelkowicz, *In Those Terrible Days*, p. 286.

68 Ibid., p. 287.

69 Ibid., p. 288.

70 Ibid., pp. 288–289.

71 Ibid., p. 286. On the theme of wishful halting of time, see also Bernard-Henry Lévy, *War, Evil, and the End of History* (Hoboken, N.J.: Melville House, 2004), pp. 224–225.

72 Zelkowicz, *In Those Terrible Days*, p. 289.

73 Ibid., p. 300.

74 Ibid., p. 301.

75 Ibid.

76 Testimony of Matithiahu Jakubowicz, cited in Eilenberg-Eibeshitz, *Preserved Evidence*, p. 261.

77 Ibid. Zelkowicz, *In Those Terrible Days*, pp. 349–351.

78 Zelkowicz, *In Those Terrible Days*, p. 302.

79 Ibid., p. 303.

80 Ibid., p. 307.

81 Oskar Singer, *Im Eilschritt durch den Gettotag . . .*, ed. Sascha Feuchert, Erwin Leibfried, Jörg Recke et al. (Berlin: Philo, 2002), p. 137. Zelkowicz, *In Those Terrible Days*, pp. 307–308.

82 Isaiah Trunk, *Łódź Ghetto: A History*, ed. and trans. Robert Moses Shapiro (Bloomington: Indiana University Press, 2006), pp. 244–245. Yakov Nirenberg, "Di geshikhte fun lodsher geto," in *In di yorn fun yidishn khurbn* (New York: Farlag Unser Tsait, 1948), p. 270. Rosenfeld, *In the Beginning*, Notebook H, entry for 12 July [1943], p. 196.

83 Zelkowicz, *In Those Terrible Days*, pp. 343–344.

84 APL Aml GV 28677, p. 256: Betreff: Dokumentarfilm von Litzmannstadt, shooting log for 5 Sept. 1942. The public was also informed of the filmmakers' arrival; see "Der Litzmannstädter Dokumentarfilm," *LZ*, 5 Sept. 1942.

85 Bundesarchiv—Filmarchiv, Berlin, Mag. No. 3578: *Aus Lodz wird Litzmannstadt.*

86 G. K., "Jede Minute verkehren 3 Straßenbahnzüge: Litzmannstadts überaus starker Verkehr/Besondere Disziplin ist sehr notwendig," *LZ*, 5 September 1942.

87 Ilse Schneider, "Litzmannstädter Kleinkunstbühnen," *LZ*, 5 September 1942.

88 G. K., "Nationaltheater des Ostens," *LZ*, 5 September 1942. "Eröffnungsvorstellung im Theater," *LZ*, 5 September 1942.

89 Trunk, *Łódź Ghetto*, pp. 245–246.

90 Frank, *Togbukh*, pp. 308–309.

91 Ibid., p. 309.

92 Ibid., p. 310.

93 Ibid., p. 312.

94 Ibid., p. 317.

95 Ibid., pp. 317–318.

96 Ibid., p. 314.

97 Zelkowicz, *In Those Terrible Days*, pp. 356–358.

98 Ibid., pp. 359–361.

99 Ibid., pp. 375–379.

100 Moshe Pulawer, *Geven iz a geto* (Tel Aviv: Y. L. Peretz-Bibliotek, 1963), p. 19. Dawid Sierakowiak, too, writing on 6 September noted with bitterness: "Laments and shouts, cries and screams have become so commonplace that one pays almost no attention to them. What do I care about another mother's cry when my own mother has been taken from me!? I don't think there can be ample revenge for this." *The Diary of Dawid Sierakowiak: Five Notebooks from the Łódź Ghetto*, ed. Alan Adelson, trans. Kamil Turowski (New York: Oxford University Press, 1996), p. 221.

101 Zelkowicz, *In Those Terrible Days*, p. 348.

102 Ibid., pp. 347–349. Rozka Winogracka, in Eilenberg-Eibeshitz, *Preserved Evidence*, p. 276.

103 Rosenfeld, *In the Beginning*, entry for 12 September [1942], p. 128.

104 Testimony of Rozka Winogrocka, in Eilenberg-Eibeshitz, *Preserved Evidence*, pp. 277–278. She was finally able to break away and survived by hiding inside a mattress (pp. 278–281).

105 Sara Zyskind, *Stolen Years*, trans. Marganit Inbar (Minneapolis: Lerner Publishing, 1981), pp. 94, 103. Testimony of Elchanan Eibeshitz, Etka Krishow, and Irka Schuster, in Eileberg-Eibeshitz, *Preserved Evidence*, pp. 264, 271, 275. See also Trunk, *Łódź Ghetto*, p. 245.

106 Pulawer, *Geven iz a geto*, p. 20.

107 Rozka Winogrocka, in Eilenberg-Eibeshitz, *Preserved Evidence*, p. 279.

108 Pulawer, *Geven iz a geto*, pp. 71–72.

109 Ibid., p. 20.

110 Trunk, *Łódź Ghetto*, pp. 247–248, 287.

111 APL PSZ 465, pp. 16, 30[?], 31, 33, 23, 35, 36: L.DZ.214 G/K/42, Do Referatu Opiekunczego, 15 [17] September 1942, and attached inventories of personal belongings left behind by families and individuals resettled from residences along Marysinska and Marynarska streets.

112 Gettoverwaltung 027/2/Lu/Po, F. W. Ribbe to Städt. Gesundheitsamt, 21 September 1942, and reply of Amtsarzt, Städt. Gesundheitsamt, 24 September 1942, reproduced in Eisenbach, *Dokumenty i materiały*, vol. 3, pt. 1, p. 232.

113 APL Aml GV 28677, pp. 258–259: film log for 13 September [19]42. Bundesarchiv-Filmarchiv Berlin, Mag. No. 3578, *Aus Lodz wird Litzmannstadt*.

114 "Freude und Erholung durch die Partei: Vierhundert Kinder waren Gäste der NS-Volkswohlfahrt im Erzhausen-Tagheim," *LZ*, 20 September 1942.

115 G. K., "Unsere Mütter sind heute ganz auf Draht: Mutterschule des Deutschen Frauenwerks/eine vorbildliche Einrichtung im Werden," *LZ*, 18 October 1942.

116 Adolf Kargel, "Der Hort unserer germanischen Bodenkunde: Ein Gang durch das heute zu eröffende Museum für Vorgeschichte am Deutschlandplatz," *LZ*, 26 September 1942. In June, Kargel had reported on the discovery of these artifacts in Erzhausen, referring to the unearthing of a child's rattle made of clay and bronze. He indicated too that the excavations had drawn crowds of interested spectators. A. K., "Die Ausgrabungen im Stadtteil Erzhausen: Urnengräber aus der Zeit der germanischen Einwanderung in unser Gebiet freigelegt," *LZ*, 20 June 1942.

117 Helmut Lemcke, " 'Frauen sind doch bessere Diplomaten': Erstaufführung des ersten deutschen Farbgroßfilms in Litzmannstadt im 'Casino,' " *LZ*, 26 September 1942. On the recent improvements to the cinema house, see "Litzmannstädter Kulturstätte öffnet wieder: Ufa-Theater 'Casino' spielt nach der Neugestltung am 1. August 'Die große Liebe,' " *LZ*, 1 August 1942; G. K., "Das Lichtspieltheater als eine Kulturstätte: Festliche Wiedereröffnung des wirksam neugestatlteten Ufa-Theaters 'Casino,' " *LZ*, 2 August 1942.

118 On Genewein and his photo series, see Floran Freund, Bertrand Perz, and Karl Stuhlpfarer, "Bildergeschichten—Geschichtsbilder," in *"Unser einziger Weg ist Arbeit,"* ed. Hanno Loewy and Gerhard Schoenberner (Vienna: Löcker Verlag,

1990), pp. 50–58; Frances Guerin, "Reframing the Photographer and His Photographs: *Photographer* (1995)," *Film & History* 32, no. 1 (2002): 43–54.

119 Jüdisches Museum Frankfurt, Farbfotos Genewein, II, 58.

120 Adolf Kargel, " 'Ich will den Menschen von heute gestalten!' Vom Schöpferglück des Kunstschaffenden/'L.Z.'-Besuch bei der Bildhauerin M. Kronig," LZ, 7 October 1942.

121 Dr. Kurt Pfeiffer, "Gelungener Opernstart in Litzmannstadt: Erfolgreicher Aufführung von Humperdincks Märchenoper 'Hänsel und Gretel,' " *LZ*, 7 November 1942.

122 Ibid. See also *Haensel and Gretel: The Story of Humperdinck's Opera*, authorized edition of Metropolitan Opera Guild, Inc., adapted by Robert Lawrence and illustrated by Mildred Boyle (New York: Grosser & Dunlap, 1938), pp. 23–27, 36–37.

123 Ibid.

10

GHETTO DIARY

Janusz Korczak

It is hard to think of a greater contrast between Rumkowski's utilitarian attitude toward the fate of the children in the Lodz Ghetto and Janusz Korczak's dedication to the orphans of the Warsaw Ghetto. Korczak, whose original name was Henryk (Hersz) Goldszmit, was in his early sixties when the orphanage he was directing in the Warsaw Ghetto was ordered to proceed to the train that would take them to the extermination camp of Treblinka. Korczak reportedly told the children to put on their best clothes as they were finally going on a trip to the countryside, after months in the starving, congested, flee- and lice-ridden ghetto. He marched ahead of the column of close to 200 children, and refused any offers to be taken off the transport list. Children, and especially orphans, had been his life's work. He had directed the Dom Sierot, the main Jewish orphanage in Warsaw, for many years, and had written extensively on pedagogy and the needs of children, as well as penning some well known and at the time very popular children's stories. His work had been translated into many languages and he had a significant reputation in Germany. His pedagogical ideas were reflected in the management of his orphanage in Warsaw, which had its own parliament and newspaper, and in such book titles as The Child's Right to Respect and How to Love a Child.

Korczak began writing his diary soon after entering the ghetto. The diary was not meant as a summary of events or a history of the orphanage. Rather, it is a set of ruminations by a man who is struggling to maintain his own and his children's dignity in the face of routine cruelty and inhumanity. He meditates about his interactions with the staff and his "annoying" habit of doing many of the daily chores and interacting more comfortably with the manual workers than with those who keep their hands clean – for even in the ghetto, where eventually everyone was doomed, there was a hierarchy, which Korczak abhorred and detested. He thinks about the daily difficulties of caring for the children, maintaining hygiene, order, discipline. He is aware that everyone is wasting away for lack of food, sanitation, fresh air. But in the midst of all this what shines through is a natural, unforced, intuitive humanity, that no system, no oppression, can diminish. Korczak had the orphanage put up Rabindranath Tagore's play, The Post Office, about a dying boy's dream to emerge from his confined environment into life and liberty, reenacted in a moving scene in Polish director Andrzej Wajda's film Korczak, which is based on the ghetto diary. The very last diary entry is perhaps the clearest, most poignant example of how some people, perhaps few in number but great in spirit, can always perceive – or perhaps imagine – another person's humanity even through the smokescreen of hatred and propaganda, violence and brutality. As he waters the flowers in his window, in a stubborn effort to keep some life in the dying ghetto, he sees a German guard, and even while he knows that the man with the rifle can shoot him with absolute impunity, Korczak recreates him in his mind as a human being, fantasizing his all too mundane, entirely normal life story, refusing to see him merely as an enemy and an assassin.

Primo Levi writes about his encounter with a certain Dr. Pannwitz in Auschwitz, who examines his ability in chemistry. The German chooses him, and thereby his life is saved. But what Levi remembers is the utter lack of mutual human recognition between the "tall, thin, blond" German and himself. Once Pannwitz had written his recommendation, comments Levi, "he raised his eyes and looked at me." What Levi saw horrified him, for

> that look was not one between two men; and if I had known how completely
> to explain the nature of that look, which came as if across the glass window
> of an aquarium between two beings who live in different worlds, I would also
> have explained the essence of the great insanity of the third Germany.

Korczak's gaze rebels against precisely that insanity, embodied not only in Pannwitz's ice-cold glare, but also in Rumkowski's self-pitying lament about his past dedication to the children he could no longer see as anything more than the sacrifice that had to be made to the Nazi Moloch so that healthy adults and men in power might survive a little while longer.

A few hours after gazing at the German guard while watering his flowers, Korczak was marching in front of his children to the train. They were probably all gassed that very day.

July 21, 1942

Tomorrow I shall be sixty-three or sixty-four years old. For some years, my father failed to obtain my birth certificate. I suffered a few difficult moments over that. Mother called it gross negligence: being a lawyer, father should not have delayed in the matter of the birth certificate.

I was named after my grandfather, his name was Hersh (Hirsh). Father had every right to call me Henryk: he himself was given the name Jozef. And to the rest of his children grandfather had given Christian names, too: Maria, Magdalena, Ludwik, Jakub, Karol. Yet he hesitated and procrastinated.

I ought to say a good deal about my father: I pursue in life that which he strove for and for which my grandfather tortured himself for many years.

And my mother. Later about that. I am both mother and father. That helps me to know and understand a great deal.

My great-grandfather was a glazier. I am glad: glass gives warmth and light.

It is a difficult thing to be born and to learn to live. Ahead of me is a much easier task: to die. After death, it may be difficult again, but I am not bothering about that. The last year, month or hour.

I should like to die consciously, in possession of my faculties. I don't know what I should say to the children by way of farewell. I should want to make clear to them only this—that the road is theirs to choose, freely.

Ten o'clock. Shots: two, several, two, one, several. Perhaps it is my own badly blacked out window.

But I do not stop writing.

On the contrary: it sharpens (a single shot) the thought.

July 22, 1942

Everything else has its limits, only brazen shamelessness is limitless.

The authorities have ordered the hospital in Stawki Street to be cleared. And the head doctor, a woman, was told to admit all the bad cases to Zelazna Street.

What do we do? Prompt decision, efficient action.

X and Z have 175 convalescent children. They have decided to place a third of them with me. There are more than fifteen other institutions, but ours is nearby.

And the fact that over a period of six months the lady in question stooped to every conceivable outrage against the patients for the sake of convenience, through obstinacy or stupidity, that she fought with devilish cunning against my humane and simple plan—that goes for nothing [. . .]

While I was out, Mrs. K. agreed to, and Mrs. S. proceeded to put in operation the shameless demand, detrimental in the highest degree, harmful to their children and ours [. . .].

To spit on the floor and clear out. I have long been contemplating it. More—a noose, or lead on the feet.

(It has come out incomprehensibly again. But I am too tired to write more.)

Azrylewicz died this morning. Oh, how hard it is to live, how easy to die!

July 27, 1942. Yesterday's rainbow.

Yesterday's rainbow.

A marvelous big moon over the camp of the homeless pilgrims.

Why can't I calm this unfortunate, insane quarter.

Only one brief communiqué.

The authorities might have allowed it.

Or, at worst, refused it.

Such a lucid plan.

Declare yourself, make your choice. We do not offer a choice of easy roads. No playing bridge for the time being, no sunbathing, no delicious dinners paid for with the blood of the smugglers.

Choose: either get out, or work here on the spot.

If you stay, you must do whatever may be necessary for the resettlers.

The autumn is near. They will need clothes, footwear, underwear, tools.

Anyone trying to wiggle out of it will be caught, anyone wanting to buy himself out—we shall gladly take his jewelry, foreign currency, anything of value. When he has already surrendered all—and fast—then we shall ask him again:

"Here or out there? What have you decided?"

So long as there's no sunbathing on the beaches, no bridge and no pleasant nap after reading the newspaper.

You're a social worker? All right. You can even pretend it for a time and we shall pretend to believe you. In general, we believe as long as it is convenient and whatever is convenient. Excuse me: not convenient. Whatever is in the plan.

We are running a gigantic enterprise. Its name is war. We work in a planned, disciplined manner, methodically. Your petty interests, ambitions, sentiments, whims, claims, resentments, cravings do not concern us.

Of course—a mother, a husband, a child, an old woman, a family heirloom, a favorite dish—they are all very nice, pleasant, touching. But for the present, there are more important things. When there is time to spare, we shall return to such things, too.

Meanwhile, in order not to prolong the matter, things must get a bit rough and painful, and if I may put it that way, without particular precision, elegance or even scrupulousness. Just roughly cut for current expediency.

You yourself are longing to see all this over. So are we. Therefore, don't interfere.

Jews go East. No bargaining. It is no longer the question of a Jewish grandmother but of where you are needed most—your hands, your brain, your time, your life. Grandmother. This was necessary only to hook on to something, a key, a slogan.

You say you cannot go East—you will die there. So choose something else. You are on your own, you must take the risk. For clearly we, to keep up appearances, are obliged to bar the way, to threaten, prosecute and reluctantly to punish.

And you butt in, uninvited, with a fresh wad of bank notes. We have neither time nor desire for that sort of thing. We are not playing at war, we were told to wage it with the greatest possible expedition, efficiently, as honestly as possible.

The job is not clean, or pleasant, or sweet smelling. So for the present we must be indulgent to the workers we need.

One likes vodka, another women, a third likes to boss everyone around while yet another, by contrast, is meek and lacks self-confidence.

We know: they have their vices, shortcomings. But they reported in time while you were philosophizing, procrastinating. Sorry, but the train must run on schedule, according to a timetable prepared in advance.

Here are the railroad tracks.

The Italians, the French, the Roumanians, the Czechs, the Hungarians—this way. The Japanese, the Chinese, even the Solomon Islanders, even the cannibals—the other way. Farmers, highlanders, the middle class and the intelligentsia.

We are Germans. It is not a question of the trademark but of the cost, the destination of the products.

We are the steel roller, the plow, the sickle. So long as it bears fruit. And it will, provided you don't interfere, don't whine, get all upset, poison the air. We may feel sorry for you at times, but we must use the whip, the big stick or the pencil, because there must be order.

A poster.

"Whoever does this or that—will be shot."

"Whoever does not do this or that—we will shoot."

Someone seems to be asking for it. A suicide? Too bad.

Someone else is not afraid. Hail! A hero?

Let his name shine in letters of gold but—now, out of the way since there is no alternative.

A third is afraid—livid with fear, constantly runs to the toilet, dulls himself with tobacco, liquor, women, and obstinately wants his own way. What would you do with him?

The Jews have their merits. They have talent, and Moses, and Christ, and are hard working, and Heine, are an ancient race, and progress, and Spinoza, and yeast and pioneering and generous. All true. But besides the Jews, there are other people, and there are other issues.

The Jews are important, but later—you will understand some day. Yes, we know and remember. An important issue, but not the only one.

We do not blame. It was the same with the Poles and it is the same even now with Poland and Palestine, and Malta, and Martinique, and with the respectable proletarian, and the fair sex and the orphan, with militarism and capitalism. But not all at once. There must be some order of procedure, some priorities.

It's hard for you, it's not easy for us, either. The more so since there is no buffet handy where formerly one could escape from a wearisome discussion.

You must listen my friend, to History's program speech about the new chapter.

Why do I clear the table?

I know that many are dissatisfied at my clearing the table after meals. Even the orderlies seem to dislike it. Surely they can manage. There are enough of them. If there were not, one or two always could be added. Then why the ostentation, the obstinacy, and even maybe I'm nasty enough to pretend to be diligent and so democratic.

Even worse, if anyone comes to see me on important business, I tell him to wait, saying:

"I am occupied now."

What an occupation: picking up soup bowls, spoons and plates.

But worse still is that I do it clumsily, get in the way while the second helping is being passed. I bump against those sitting tightly packed at the tables. Because of me he cannot lick clean his soup plate or the tureen. Someone may even lose his second helping. Several times something fell from the plates carried clumsily. If anyone else had done it, he would be told off and have a case against him. Because of this eccentricity some seem to feel guilty for letting me do it, others feel guilty because somehow they think they are even taking advantage of me.

How is that I myself do not understand or see how it is? How can anyone understand why I do it when right now I am writing that I know, see and understand that instead of being helpful I make a nuisance of myself?

Odd. I sense that everybody thinks I should not pick up the dishes, but nobody has ever asked why I do it. Nobody has approached me: Why do you do it? Why do you get in the way?

But here is my explanation:

When I collect the dishes myself, I can see the cracked plates, the bent spoons, the scratches on the bowls. I expedite the clearing of the tables and the side table used for the little shop, so that the orderlies can tidy up sooner. I can see how the careless diners throw about, partly in a quasi-aristocratic and partly in a churlish manner, the spoons, knives, the salt shakers and cups, instead of putting them in the right place. Sometimes I watch how the extras are distributed or who sits next to whom. And I get some ideas. For if I do something, I never do it thoughtlessly. This waiter's job is of great use to me, it's pleasant and interesting.

But not this is important. It is something quite different. Something that I have spoken and written about many times, that I have been fighting against for the past thirty years, since the inception of the Children's Home, fighting without a hope of victory, without visible effect, but I don't want to and cannot abandon that fight.

My aim is that in the Children's Home there should be no soft work or crude work, no clever or stupid work, no clean or dirty work. No work for nice young ladies or for the mob. In the Children's Home, there should be no purely physical and no purely mental workers.

At the institution at Dzielna Street, run by the City Council, they look at me with shock and disgust when I shake hands with the charwoman, even when she happens to be scrubbing the stairs and her hands are wet. But frequently I forget to shake hands with Dr. K., and I have not been responding to the bows of Drs. M. and B.

I respect honest workers. To me their hands are clean and I hold their opinions in high esteem.

The washerwoman and the janitor at Krochmalna Street used to be invited to join our meetings, not just to please them but in order to take their advice and benefit from their assistance as specialists in matters which would otherwise be left unresolved, i.e. be placed under paragraph 3.[1]

There was a joke in a weekly newspaper of twenty years ago. Actually not a joke but a witty comment.

Josek—I don't remember which one, there were many of them—could not solve a problem in arithmetic. He tried hard and long, and finally said:

"I don't know how to do it. I place it under paragraph three."

No one is better or wiser because he is working in the storeroom rather than pushing the wheelbarrow. No one is better or wiser just because he can wield power. I am not better or wiser for signing the passes, or donation receipts. This brainless work could be done more conscientiously and better by a youngster from third or even second grade.

The collector of money, a rude woman, is a nobody to me. Mr. Lejzor is a fine fellow though he digs in the filth of the sewage pipes and canals. Miss Nacia would deserve respect from me if she peeled potatoes instead of being a typist. And it is not my fault that Miss Irka, the nurse, shifts the inferior jobs onto Mira and that Mrs. Roza Sztokman, whom I also respect, once in a while may not scrub the toilet or the kitchen floor just to have a rest.

In farming, this is called crop rotation. In hygiene and medicine—a change of climate. In church—an act of humility. The Pope is called Holy Father, big men kneel down before him and kiss his slipper. And, once a year, the Pope washes the feet of twelve beggars in the church.

The Jews are conceited and that is why they are despised. I believe this will change, perhaps soon. Meanwhile, please don't get cross with me for collecting the dishes or emptying the buckets in the toilet.

Whoever says, "physical work is dirty work," is lying. Worse still the hypocrite who says, "No one should be ashamed of any work," but picks for himself only clean work, avoids what is described as dirty work and thinks that he should keep out of the way of dirty work.

August 1, 1942

Whenever the stems of potato plants grew excessively, a heavy roller would be dragged over them to crush them so that the fruit in the ground could ripen better.

*

Did Marcus Aurelius read the wisdom of Solomon? How soothing is the effect of his memoirs.

*

I sometimes hate, or perhaps only try to oppose, certain individuals, such as H., or G., more than Germans; from their point of view they work, or rather plan, reasonably and efficiently. They are bound to be angry because people get in their way. Get in their way foolishly.

And I get in their way, too. They are even indulgent. They simply catch you and order you to stand in one place, not to walk about the streets, not to get in the way.

They do me a favor, since roaming about I might be hit by a stray bullet. And this way I am safe standing against the wall, and can calmly and carefully observe and think—spin the web of thoughts.

So I spin the web of thoughts.

*

A blind old Jew remained at the little town of Myszyniec. Leaning on a stick, he walked among the carts, the horses, the Cossacks and the artillery guns. What a cruel thing to leave a blind old man behind.[2]

"They wanted to take him along"—Nastka says. "But he put his foot down and said that he would not go because somebody must stay behind to look after the synagogue."

I struck up an acquaintance with Nastka while trying to help her find a bucket taken by a soldier who had promised to bring it back but didn't.

I am both the blind Jew and Nastka.

*

It's so soft and warm in my bed. It'll be very hard to get up. But today is Saturday, and on Saturdays I weigh the children in the morning before breakfast. Probably for the first time I am not interested in the results for the week. They ought to have put on a bit of weight. (I don't know why raw carrot was given for supper yesterday.)

*

In place of old Azrylewicz, I now have young Julek. There's liquid in his side. He has certain difficulties with breathing, but for a different reason.

Here's the very same manner of groaning, gestures, resentment against me, the same selfish and theatrical desire to attract attention, perhaps even to take revenge on me for not thinking about him.

Today Julek had the first quiet night for a week. So did I.

*

So did I. Now that every day brings so many strange and sinister experiences and sensations I have completely ceased to dream.

The law of equilibrium.

The day torments, the night soothes. A gratifying day, a tormented night.

I could write a monograph on the featherbed.

The peasant and the featherbed.

The proletarian and the featherbed.

*

It's been a long time since I have blessed the world. I tried to tonight. It didn't work.

I don't even know what went wrong. The purifying respirations worked more or less. But the fingers remained feeble, no energy flowing through them.

Do I believe in the effects? I do believe but not in my India! Holy India!

*

The look of this district is changing from day to day.

1 A prison
2 A plague-stricken area
3 A mating ground
4 A lunatic asylum
5 A casino. Monaco. The stake—your head.

*

What matters is that all this did happen.

The destitute beggars suspended between prison and hospital. The slave work: not only the effort of the muscles but the honor and virtue of the girl.

Debased faith, family, motherhood.

The marketing of all spiritual commodities. A stock exchange quoting the weight of conscience. An unsteady market—like onions and life today.

The children are living in constant uncertainty, in fear. "A Jew will take you away." "I'll give you away to a wicked old man." "You'll be put in a bag."

Bereavement.

Old age. Its degradation and moral decrepitude.

(Once upon a time one earned one's old age, it was good to work for it. The same with health. Now the vital forces and the years of life may be purchased. A scoundrel has a good chance of achieving gray hair.)

*

Miss Esterka.

Miss Esterka is not anxious to live either gaily or easily. She wants to live nicely. She dreams of a beautiful life.

She gave us *The Post Office* as a farewell for the time being.[3]

If she does not come back here now, we shall meet later somewhere else. I'm absolutely sure that she will serve others in the meantime in the same way as she used to distribute goodness and make herself useful here.

August 4, 1942

1

I have watered the flowers, the poor orphanage plants, the plants of the Jewish orphanage. The parched soil breathed with relief.

A guard watched me as I worked. Does that peaceful work of mine at six o'clock in the morning annoy him or move him?

He stands looking on, his legs wide apart.

2

All the efforts to get Esterka released have come to nothing. I was not quite sure whether in the event of success I should be doing her a favor or harm her.

"Where did she get caught?" somebody asks.

Perhaps it is not she but we who have gotten caught (having stayed).

3

I have written to the police to send Adzio away: he's mentally underdeveloped and maliciously undisciplined. We cannot afford to expose the house to the danger of his outbursts. (Collective responsibility.)

4

For Dzielna Street—a ton of coal, for the present to Rozia Abramowicz. Someone asks whether the coal will be safe there.

In reply—a smile.

5

A cloudy morning. Five thirty.

Seemingly an ordinary beginning of a day. I say to Hanna:

"Good morning!"

In response, a look of surprise.

I plead:

"Smile."

They are ill, pale, lung-sick smiles.

6

You drank, and plenty, gentlemen officers, you relished your drinking—here's to the blood you've shed—and dancing you jingled your medals to cheer the infamy which you were too blind to see, or rather pretended not to see.

7

My share in the Japanese war. Defeat—disaster.

In the European war—defeat—disaster.

In the World War. . . .

I don't know how and what a soldier of a victorious army feels. . . .

8

The publications to which I contributed were usually closed down, suspended, went bankrupt.

My publisher, ruined, committed suicide.

And all this not because I'm a Jew but because I was born in the East.

It might be a sad consolation that the haughty West also is not well off.

It might be but is not. I never wish anyone ill. I cannot. I don't know how it's done.

9

Our Father who art in heaven. . . .

This prayer was carved out of hunger and misery.

Our daily bread.

Bread.

Why, what I'm experiencing did happen. It happened.

They sold their belongings—for a liter of lamp oil, a kilogram of groats, a glass of vodka.

When a young Pole kindly asked me at the police station how I managed to run the blockade, I asked him whether he could not possibly do "something" for Esterka.

"You know very well I can't."

I said hastily:

"Thanks for the kind word."

This expression of gratitude is the bloodless child of poverty and degradation.

10

I am watering the flowers. My bald head in the window. What a splendid target.

He has a rifle. Why is he standing and looking on calmly?

He has no orders to shoot.

And perhaps he was a village teacher in civilian life, or a notary, a street sweeper in Leipzig, a waiter in Cologne?

What would he do if I nodded to him? Waved my hand in a friendly gesture?

Perhaps he doesn't even know that things are—as they are?

He may have arrived only yesterday, from far away. . . .

Notes

1 Par. 3 of the Home's Code read: "The Court doesn't know how it was in fact, and thus refuses to consider the case."
2 Again recollection of World War I.
3 This is about the tutoress Ester Winogron, a student of natural science at Warsaw University. She helped Korczak in his daily morning medical rounds and dressings. When she was caught by the Germans on the street in the first days of the liquidation of the ghetto, Korczak tried unsuccessfully to get her out of the transport.

As for the play itself, *The Post Office* by Rabindranath Tagore, prohibited by Hitler's censors, was performed on orders from Korczak himself. The direction of Ester Winogron and the performance of the children of the Orphan's Home, especially of Abrasza in the role of the dying Hindu boy, as well as the impact of the play itself, as played in the atmosphere of the dying ghetto, in the climate of its final days—all this produced a staggering impression and an experience not to be repeated.

When after the play someone asked Korczak why he had selected this particular play, he said that, finally, it is necessary to learn to accept serenely the angel of death.

11

"AND IT WAS SOMETHING WE DIDN'T TALK ABOUT"

Rape of Jewish women during the Holocaust

Helene J. Sinnreich

Beyond the question of representing the different experience of women during the Holocaust, which, as we saw, was contested in the early postwar decades, the issue of sexual violence is still considered to be taboo, or at least too contentious to be discussed, by many students of the event. As Helene Sinnreich shows in her chapter, there are many reasons for the combination of extreme caution, discomfort, and, at times, outright rejection of the entire topic in much of the scholarship. And yet, as she powerfully argues, it is high time that we integrate this crucial aspect of the genocide of the Jews into the historiography. As we have learned from the recent genocides in Rwanda and Bosnia, rape constitutes an inherent element of this type of mass violence and has now finally also been recognized as a crime against humanity under international law. But it is also a form of violence that is often denied by the perpetrators, evaded by the victims, and dismissed by the public. The perpetrators deny rape as they will deny their culpability more generally, but especially when rape is used as a form of genocide, such as in impregnating women of one group by members of another; the victims often do not wish to speak of their experiences because of a culturally-induced sense of shame and because of the severe social repercussions such revelations may have on the rest of their lives; the public in general has tended for long to consider rape as a mere sideshow of the more important issue of mass murder and as an understandable aspect of male conduct under conditions of war (as in "boys will be boys"). Indeed the discussion of sexual violence in war and genocide is related to the discussion of rape more generally; as judicial systems and cultures have come to realize the gravity of this offense, so too its importance as a component of organized state violence has been gradually gaining recognition.

In the case of the Holocaust there were many other aspects to the reluctance to touch upon this issue. However incredible it may seem today, in the aftermath of the Holocaust there was a lingering suspicion within communities of survivors and wider Jewish circles, not least in Palestine, that young women who had somehow managed to survive the ordeal had "sold themselves" to the Nazis. This was indeed one root of the illicit but widespread postwar pornographic fascination with sexual violence in the camps, filled with sadomasochistic imagery and role reversals. Linked to this shaming of women was also the shame of men who had not been able to protect their wives, daughters, or sisters from this form of violence. Conversely, as Sinnreich points out, there was and still is a lingering, and quite paradoxical assumption, that because the Nazis had passed racial laws prohibiting sexual contact between Jews and "Aryans," there was no systematic sexual abuse of and violence against women. In other words, that the Nazis' own racism protected Jews from the conventional forms of violence against women in war and genocide. That there was no concerted campaign of mass rape equivalent, for instance, to that waged by the Red Army when it entered German territory in 1945, is true. But it is just as true, and Sinnreich provides many examples out of a host of others that can be found in official archives and especially in personal accounts by survivors, that throughout occupied Europe, and especially in the East, sexual violence against Jewish women was both widespread and in most cases lethal. Any examination of the numerous small towns in Eastern Europe where Jewish communities were murdered either in situ or eventually by being transported to extermination camps, demonstrates the pervasiveness of this violence, in which, one must say, the German-appointed Jewish councils and police were also not infrequently complicit. That this issue has not been thoroughly researched until now is a reflection of the biases and sensibilities of scholars rather than of the historical reality. Thanks to Sinnreich, along with other pioneering researchers on this issue such as Regina Mühlhäuser, Na'ama Shik, and Robert Sommer, we can now begin a more systematic and dispassionate consideration of sexual violence in the Holocaust.

There is a strong connection between rape and genocide. Much of the recent scholarship on rape and genocide has focused on rape as a tool for carrying out genocide.[1] However, rape occurs during genocide not only as a systematic means of attack but also because it places its victims in physically vulnerable positions with limited or non-existent access to redress. Although during the Holocaust the organised rape of Jewish women was not part of official German genocidal policy, the conditions that exposed women to various abuses put them at risk of being raped by a wide range of individuals including perpetrators, bystanders, and fellow victims. This article focuses specifically on rape of Jewish women by German men during the Holocaust – a story that does not fit neatly into the standard narratives of the Final Solution precisely because it contradicted central policy. Just as physical beatings, medical experiments, or other forms of assault need not be part of the means of committing genocide in order to be their byproduct, the rape of Jewish women nevertheless occurred and must be understood as an important part of Jewish women's experience during the Holocaust.[2]

While the sexual abuse and forced prostitution of non-Jews during the Second World War is well known, rape and sexual violence against Jewish women during the Holocaust remains relatively unexplored for a number of reasons.[3] The Laws for the Protection of German Blood and German Honour enacted in September 1935 not only prohibited marriage between Jews and 'subjects of the state of Germany or related blood' but also explicitly forbade extramarital relations. Punishment for either offence was hard labour. Some historians have used these laws to conclude that Germans would not rape Jewish women. Yet the suggestion that a German man would not commit *Rassenschande* by engaging in sexual relations with a Jewish woman is as untenable as any argument which insists that the existence of rules against an action prove that it could not or would not take place. Certainly sexual relations between German men and all women considered racially inferior, including Jews, was against Nazi policy, but these relations persisted nevertheless.[4] Importantly, when the laws were broken, there was little or no punishment. For example, German soldiers who engaged in consensual – or even non-consensual – sexual relations with non-German women were rarely reprimanded. Even when soldiers were disciplined for raping non-German women, it was for the breakdown in military discipline rather than the violation of the woman.[5]

Furthermore, and again related to the question of ideology, the relative lack of scholarship in this area is the product of an illogical belief that Jewish women could not have been raped because they were classed as subhuman and therefore not as sexual beings.[6] Anti-Jewish propaganda such as Fritz Hippler's 1940 film *The Eternal Jew*, in which Jews were transformed from people into rats on screen, has been put forward as evidence that Germans would not rape Jewish women. However, Tutsis who were subjected to mass rape during the Rwandan genocide were dubbed as 'cockroaches' and 'serpents' by propagandists.[7] Following the same logic, the notion that dehumanising Nazi propaganda would create a barrier to rape contradicts numerous theorists who argue that rather than deter rape, the rendering of a victim as sub-human enables a perpetrator. Katharine Derderian has argued, for example, that rape helped the Turks dehumanise the Armenians.[8] Conversely, the dehumanisation of the Armenians made it easier for the Turks to rape them.

To rely on German sexual purity laws and the notion of Jews as sub-human as a way to preclude the very possibility of sexual violence rests on a false premise that equates rape with sex. Forced sex should not be mistaken for violent sex but rather as violence against women perpetrated in a sexual manner.[9] Consequently, one should understand the rape of Jewish women within the context of German men perpetrating violence against Jewish women rather than German men and Jewish women engaging in sexual relations.[10] Moreover, there are clearly strong links between war, violence and sexual aggression.[11] As noted by Copelon, 'War tends to intensify the brutality, repetitiveness, public spectacle, and likelihood of rape. War diminishes sensitivity to human suffering and intensifies men's sense of entitlement, superiority, avidity, and social license to rape.'[12] Similarly, Alexander B. Downes notes that numerous scholars have argued that categorising the enemy as sub-human generates atrocities against them in war.[13] Christoph Schiessl sums up the reasons why soldiers rape during warfare as 'domination and demoralization', noting that, 'in wartime the distinction between killing and other forms of violence gets easily lost. A group power develops which has no comparison in civilian life, enlarging the power of men alone.' In this case, Schiessl argues, sexual violence against women, especially Jewish women, accorded with Nazi goals to 'subjugate and destroy inferior races'.[14]

Historians have also failed to explore the rape of Jewish women because of a broader gender bias in Holocaust scholarship. Despite the fact that Emanuel Ringelblum, writing from within the Warsaw Ghetto, raised the topic of the special place of the Jewish woman during the Holocaust, significant work on the particulars of women's experience during the Holocaust did not appear until the mid and late 1990s. In part this oversight was due to a reticence among some scholars to allow gendered histories to become comparative suffering narratives, which might take the focus away from the victim's Jewishness.[15] As Katrina Koo has put it:

> Ringelheim points to the spectre of the Holocaust as the 'great victim equaliser' and suggests that perspectives on it have erased gender as a category of analysis, claiming that, given the issue's historiography, 'any emphasis on gender can seem irrelevant, even irreverent'. In this sense, women's voices can be silenced by deference to what is considered to be a much greater evil.[16]

Similarly Doerr has noted, 'Traditionally, men have claimed war memories as their possessions ... women's war memories have been neglected and have played no role or at best a secondary role in war-related matters. Until recently, this also applied to the Holocaust.'[17]

This dominance of male voices in Holocaust historiography has had multiple effects. Although Holocaust narratives have focused on a wide variety of experiences including forced labour, ghettoisation, beatings, and starvation, they have not typically included rape. Since women's experiences and especially rape do not fit neatly into the standard Holocaust victimisation narrative, victims do not always share that part of their experience in interviews or memoirs. Zoë Waxman concurs:

> While the observation that rape and sexual assault were relatively rare in the concentration camps is based upon the absence of description of sexual abuse in testimonies, it is possible that such an absence inhibits other witnesses who did experience abuse from including descriptions of it in their testimonies.[18]

The large number of testimonies on rape in the USC Shoah Foundation Institute's Visual History Archive substantiates this notion. Unlike in previous interview projects, interviewees were specifically asked whether or not they had witnessed sexual abuse. In earlier oral history projects, the discussion of rape only arose if a survivor specifically mentioned the incident and some survivors confessed that although their experience of sexual assault continued to haunt them, it did not seem worthy of mention when compared with the mass death that took place.[19]

The notion that rape was a personal experience of suffering and not part of the collective experience of genocide is prominent in cases of rape during warfare. As Katrina Koo notes:

> Women face an international community that has historically preferred to consider rape outside the realm of the political. Thus, women have felt that their testimonies are unwanted. Revelations of their experiences may bring shame, dishonour and embarrassment to themselves and their families and even their nations.[20]

But rape as an experience of Holocaust victims was not just a personal experience because Jewish women were especially vulnerable precisely because of their Jewish identity. Some scholars have also suggested that the suppression of rape narratives was the result in part of a shame on the part of men for not having been able to prevent it, but also the shame and subsequent self-censorship of the victims. Victims were ashamed of their experience and many wanted to hide these events from their family. Lawrence Langer notes that Holocaust victims who underwent physical torture often felt shame at their inability to defend themselves rather than fear of the torture itself. He suggests that some survivors are reluctant to recount their experiences because it was too degrading, citing one survivor who 'was ashamed ... and when I'm ashamed, I don't like to talk about it'.[21]

Rape victims' shame was not limited to their inability to defend themselves against their attackers or modesty about discussing sexual matters: rape was a taboo topic. Although *Eine Frau in Berlin: Tagebuchaufzeichnungen vom 20. April bis 22. Juni 1945* (*A Woman in Berlin: Diary Entries from 20 April to 22 June 1945*) was a diary of a German and not a Jewish woman, its poor reception when it was published in the 1950s was a reflection of this taboo against discussing rape of women during the Second World War.[22] Until very recently, the prevailing myths about rape and the absence of scholarly attention placed additional shame and guilt on the victims. Particularly harmful are those myths which claim that women in some way encouraged or invited the rape or that the experience 'tainted' the rape victim in some way. One reason why the USC Shoah Foundation Institute's Visual History Archive proved particularly fruitful, in addition to the fact that interviewers directly asked about sexual abuse, was the delay in their collection efforts. Since they did not begin collecting material until the 1990s, enough time had passed for women to be forthright about their experiences. In the interim, attitudes towards wartime rape had changed and spouses who may have held some of the views of rape had passed away. Christopher Browning has noted in his work *Collected Memories: Holocaust History and Postwar Testimony* that later testimonies broached sensitive topics with more frequency and candour than earlier ones, and in respect of sensitive topics it was not until the 1990s that survivors were willing to speak out.[23]

The evidence of rape during the Holocaust relies heavily on survivor testimony, but these testimonies are 'often conflicting and contradictory, [and] in some cases clearly mistaken', however, they are useful for the construction of 'a history that otherwise, for lack of evidence, would not exist'.[24] A great deal of the testimony discussed in this article is gathered from the Shoah Foundation Oral Testimony archives. This particular collection of testimonies has also been criticised, in part because it uses a constructed chronological narrative (pre-war, wartime, post-war) in which the sometimes poorly-trained interviewers rely on a set group of questions.[25] Yet while the Shoah Foundation material was at times problematic due to the interviewer's interjection, such interruptions more often than not occurred when the interviewer expressed shock, disbelief, or discomfort at the survivor's admission of having been sexually abused. It also proved a useful source for those exploring the rape of Jewish women because the interviewer asked if the survivor had witnessed sexual abuse. The Shoah Foundation interviews were also conducted after the war in the former Yugoslavia had prompted international recognition of rape as a crime against humanity. In addition to the change in attitudes and the recognition of the connection between rape and genocide, the Shoah Foundation took its testimonies after many of the spouses of the women had passed away which, in some cases, made them less reluctant to talk about such events.

Some survivors explicitly expressed that it was only years later that they could discuss these rapes 'on the record' because their husbands were dead or children grown. Joan Ringleheim has discussed how a number of rape victims have been willing to discuss their experiences with her 'off the record' even as they refused to testify on tape.[26] These emotions, particularly the fear that family members would find out about the rape, are common to other victims of rape.[27] Such fear was in some cases not unfounded. One woman who was raped during the war by a pre-war acquaintance said that she could not talk about it for a long time. When she finally told her husband, he did not support her.[28]

Some victims found that family members did not want to hear about or refused to believe what had happened. One survivor, Sara M. was a very young girl when she was violently raped and beaten at Ravensbrück concentration camp. At the end of her ordeal, she recalled how she had been 'taken back to where my aunt was and it was something we didn't talk about'.[29] Zoë Waxman includes a testimony of a woman who had been raped in front of her husband: 'My aunt told a few members of the family but they didn't believe her – they didn't want to hear or know about it. She never told her children . . .'[30] Here Waxman captures the fact that family members did not want to believe or hear about rape during the Holocaust – even in a case where a male relative, in this case the rape victim's husband witnessed the event. The discomfort of family members with this aspect of Holocaust experience – particularly one that falls outside of the standard narrative – undoubtedly played a role in the underreporting of the experience.

The standard post-war male-dominated Holocaust narrative not only excluded rape but also promoted the idea that it was better to die than to suffer rape. The most famous example of this is the story of the 93 virgins from a girls' religious school (Beis Yakov) in Krakow who, the *New York Times* reported in 1943, committed collective suicide rather than be raped. The story's legitimacy has been questioned but as a propaganda tool it effectively exploited prevailing ideals about how 'proper women' should behave when faced with the possibility of rape.[31] In the case of the Holocaust, a variety of stories and testimonies perpetuate the notion of death as preferable to rape. In the post-war period, survivor Yaakov Rotenberg told the story of a Rabbi from the Lodz Ghetto who,

> arrived in Auschwitz with his beautiful daughter and grandson. The Germans wanted to take his daughter to the house of ill fame . . . The rabbi was not afraid; he understood what the Germans were about to do. He gathered his daughter and grandson and brought them to the section of the camp where people were sent to die, and both were burned. In his speech there he said: 'It is better that I sacrificed my daughter than let her be a prostitute for the Germans.'[32]

Writings of the immediate post-war period were not the only ones that extolled the virtue of suicide in these circumstances. Lawrence Langer writes of a woman Celia K., who was hiding with her sister. One day, their brother, a partisan, delivered a gun and told the girls that they were to kill each other rather than get caught by the Germans because 'of what the Germans are doing to Jewish women caught in that area'.[33] With the prevailing ideals of virtue stating that women died rather than be raped, it is not surprising that many survivors remained silent about their experiences.

Reluctance to discuss rape among survivors was not unique to the Holocaust. Like other rape statistics, one can safely assume that oral and written Holocaust testimonies probably reflect an underreporting of sexual abuse. Nechama Tec, when interviewing women for her book *Resilience and Courage*, noted that when sexual abuse was mentioned, the women were reluctant to share their experiences: 'Judging by the hesitation I encountered among interviewees to recount these coercive sexual experiences, I have to assume that most of these stories will die with the victims.'[34] This is not to say that all other testimonies omitted any mention of rape. However, for a variety of reasons these experiences were not prioritised by many interviewers or scholars as a significant part of the Holocaust narrative. Some dismissed admissions of rape or sexual abuse as lacking credibility due to Nazi anti-miscegenation laws or because it appeared to be an aberration as it deviated from the standard storyline of Holocaust experience. In some of the older scholarship which was written under the shadow of the prevailing rape myths of the period, rape remained a personal, not political experience.

The rape of Jewish women during the Holocaust, however, was created by political conditions and began immediately with German occupation. Jewish women were abducted off the streets and during searches of their homes for valuables. Sometimes forced labour preceded sexual abuse and in some cases, rape was the primary motive for entry into a home. A memorandum from February 1940 written by General Johannes Blaskowitz reported one case:

> On 18 February 1940 in Petrikau, two sentries ... abducted the Jewess Machmanowic (age eighteen) and the Jewess Santowska (age seventeen) at gunpoint from their parents' homes. The soldiers took the girls to the Polish cemetery; there they raped one of them. The other was having her period at the time. The men told her to come back in a few days and promised her 5 zloty.[35]

Although the general German population's access to Jewish women was drastically reduced with internment in ghettos and concentration camps, it did not end the sexual abuse. In *Pamiętnik z Getta Lodzkiego* (*Diary from the Lodz Ghetto*) published in 1960, Jakub Poznanski, a survivor of the Ghetto, wrote of the rape of a Jewish girl by Hans Biebow, the head of the German Ghetto Administration, in a diary entry dated 2 September 1944:

> Ejbuszyc and Blachowski told us about something horrible that happened at 36 Lagiewnicka Street. Dr. Sima Mandels, a pediatrician,

was there with her engineer husband and her two children. The tragedy occurred when Hans Biebow noticed their beautiful 16-year-old daughter. One evening when he was drunk, he grabbed her in the hallway, dragged her into his office, and tried to rape her. The girl tried to defend herself and started screaming. It was then that 'the master of life and death' shot her in the eye. The mother started crying in despair. In order to silence her, Biebow ordered the entire family shipped out immediately. The same happened to the chief physician Dr. Miller, who spoke up for the Mandels family. He was deported with his wife and little son.[36]

Poznanski was not the only person to report the rape of Dr. Mandel's daughter. Evidence of Biebow's crime had been entered into the public record as early as May 1946 at Biebow's post-war trial. Leon Szkier in his affidavit of 31 May 1946 testified that he knew 'that at the time of the deportations, Hans Biebow raped and shot the daughter of Dr. Mandels'.[37] He further reported that Biebow had personally deported the family.[38] Biebow's own affidavit denied the charges, but in the addendum he admitted that while he had indeed shot Dr. Mandels' daughter, her death was accidental.[39]

Taken alone, each of these reports might be dismissed, and it seems that most historians have selected to do just that, preferring instead to present Biebow as a neutral, bureaucratic Nazi.[40] But the rape of Dr. Mandels' daughter was not the only accusation of rape made against Biebow. Esther H. was living in Dresden during the war and there she encountered Biebow. On one occasion he beat her with a rubber whip for failing to carry out an order to his satisfaction.[41] While her proximity to Biebow left her vulnerable to this type of beating, it also enabled her to learn of Rita, a 'beautiful Czech girl' who was raped by both Biebow and another German soldier. Esther testified that Rita was murdered when the prisoners were being evacuated from the camp to escape the advancing front, but not all of Biebow's victims were killed.[42] Bina W. was among those few who were left in the Lodz Ghetto after the final liquidation to clean up the ghetto area. She was roomed in a women's barrack. One night, Hans Biebow dragged her from her bed.[43]

Together these separate reports of Biebow as a rapist lends credibility to each of the survivor's stories, and if Biebow engaged in forced sexual relations with Jewish women, it is possible he also permitted his men to do so. Such a state of affairs would add credibility to Ana C.'s testimony that the Germans took Jewish women from the Lodz Ghetto for forced prostitution.[44] Alternatively, given the late timing of Biebow's rapes – the reported rapes began with the liquidation of the ghetto in 1944 – one could also argue that as this was the end of the war, discipline broke down which allowed Biebow to commit rape or that rape, organised or impulsive, escalated with the violence committed against the Jewish population. Concentration camp guards were noted to have become more violent towards the prisoner populations when Nazi Germany experienced defeat. It seems highly possible that Biebow also vented his frustrations at impending military defeat through violence.

Lodz was not the only ghetto in which sexual abuse was carried out. There were numerous accusations that Jewish women were forced to serve in German brothels. In addition to Jewish women, Slavic women, women marked as 'asocials', and Gypsy women were all also victims of the organised rape camps set up by the Germans. Early in his regime, Hitler positioned himself and the Nazi party as being opposed to prostitution.[45] However, 'by 1936, the Military Supreme Command declared that the construction of military brothels "an urgent necessity" and insisted that health authorities should cooperate'.[46] Brothels were created not only for the military, SS, and civilian population but even for foreign workers.[47] Jewish women served despite proclamations that Jewish women were not supposed to work in brothels servicing Germans.[48] Regulations against Jewish women serving in brothels were made explicit in 1939 when the brothels were first set up but had to be reiterated in another order in March of 1942 suggesting the prohibition was not being observed.[49] In fact, there is sufficient evidence to suggest that despite ideological conflicts, Jewish women were subjected to sexual enslavement in Nazi brothels.

William Samelson reported a request made of the *Judenrat* of Piotrków Trybunalski:

> On the eve of Rosh Hashanah in September 1940, the newly appointed Piotrków mayor, *Oberbuergermeister* Hans Drexel, arrived at the ghetto and the Jewish Council meeting to present his demand for 'hostesses.' He was met with silence. Drexel left the premises with a cynical grin on his face and word of admonishment: 'You Jews had better realize what's good for you. After all, we're here to stay and you must serve our needs.'[50]

Samelson states that this was not the only time that such a demand was made. Rather, in the spring of 1942, following a mass deportation from the ghetto during which a number of Jewish women were raped, the Jewish council was presented with a demand for a large cash payment. In addition,

> the council had to submit a supplementary list of young women considered suitable to serve the needs of the SS garrison stationed in Piotrków. As the Gestapo put it, 'We have in Piotrków a garrison of healthy young men who unfortunately suffer from lack of sexual gratification. On occasions, they find relief with the women of the street. The result is an alarming rise in venereal disease. Your women are known for exemplary cleanliness. They will be properly rewarded for their services.'[51]

Yet the claim here of Gestapo involvement and their reference to the 'exemplary cleanliness' of the Jewish women throws the testimony into doubt. The

Gestapo were responsible for ensuring adherence to political orthodoxy, but the notion of Jewish women being pure was not part of the standard Nazi propaganda. The talk of 'cleanliness' may, however, be an embellishment of testimony on the part of the survivor. Samelson insists that the Jewish council refused to comply and expected reprisals. Whether or not they really refused is unclear, as is the reason that their refusal to comply did not meet with reprisals.

This is, however, not the only testimony to claim that such a demand was made of the Jewish leadership. This second story likewise does not tell of reprisals for refusing the order and similarly names the Gestapo as involved in the organisation of brothels. In an affidavit signed in New York City on 14 January 1940, Dr. Henryk Szoszkies, a former member of the Executive of the Warsaw Jewish Community Council testified that,

> to my own knowledge proposals were made by Nazi officials to the Jewish Community Council to organize houses of prostitution in Nazi-occupied towns, and that Jewish girls be provided for use of the army.
>
> On Thursday, November 2, 1939, Unit Leader Wende, a representative of the German Gestapo, came into the office of the Warsaw Jewish Community Council, where I, as a member of the Executive of the Community had my offices. After asking me to be seated, with no preliminaries of any sort, he declared: 'As you know, we have in Warsaw quite a large garrison of young, healthy men who are suffering from a lack of sexual relations. Casual meetings with women of the streets have already resulted in many cases of venereal diseases. This is a situation which we cannot allow to continue. You are, therefore, in the name of the Gestapo, ordered to indicate to use the persons in your community who will be responsible for the organization of a brothel.' He expressed it in German as a 'puff' to serve the needs of our army.
>
> Incredulous, I asked him 'Are you in earnest, or are you simply making sport of me?'
>
> Wende answered brusquely: 'This is not the time for jokes. You come to the central office of the Gestapo at 23 Szucha Street, room 37 at 3 o'clock on the afternoon of Saturday, November 4 and bring with you the representatives to whom you will entrust the organization of the brothel. As a matter of fact, we will need two brothels; one for the officers and a separate one for privates. We will indicate to your representatives how to assemble and segregate the girls . . .'[52]

Szoszkies goes on to relate that he refused the request and was met with a retort from the officer: 'Don't let the race laws bother you. War is war, and in such a situation all theories die out.' Upon conferring with his superiors, Dr. Szoszkies related that other members of the Jewish Community Council were similarly approached. He noted that they 'decided to tell only two or three of the most prominent members of the Community Council about this demand out of fear that the news might cause a panic among the Jews'.[53] Szoszkies did not show up for the appointed meeting and it was rescheduled for two weeks later by which point he had successfully fled Poland.[54]

Other survivors accused the Germans of utilising Jewish women from the ghetto in brothels. These testimonies have generally been dismissed on the basis that the women had no way of knowing if their destination was the brothel if, as they claimed, they escaped going. For example, Ana C. testified that the Germans took Jewish women from the Lodz Ghetto for prostitution and that she herself was selected for this duty. After the war she found out what happened to the group of girls who were selected with her.[55] She does not explain how she knows what happened to these girls. It is entirely possible that someone read or heard about the testimony in the *New York Times* in 1940 and interpreted Ana C.'s experience to have been the same. Similarly, in her memoir *I was There*, Frances Penney claims that such a list of women was created in the Vilna Ghetto.[56] Another survivor from Lithuania testified that very attractive women were rounded up and selected for 'labour' in the Kaunas ghetto.

Other testimonies provide evidence that German authorities, at least in the General Government, were utilising Jewish women to serve in brothels. Judit Z. was sneaking between the ghetto and the Aryan side of Kaunas. While on the Aryan side, she heard Yiddish cries coming from the windows of the building in which a group of girls were being held.[57] Michael J., who was sent to forced labour in Stanislawów, Poland, testified that one day he and his group were brought to clean an officers' club. It was a four storey building and as they cleaned the top floor, some girls heard them speaking Yiddish and cried out to the boys that they were Jewish girls just there to be raped. Michael started speaking with one of the girls: 'Some of the girls she told me were throwing themselves down the windows . . . from the fourth floor. After that they secured the windows so they could not open anymore and they put a 24 hours guard on duty.'[58]

It was not only Jewish councils that were propositioned to supply Jewish girls for German brothels. Numerous survivors testified that just as the Germans conscripted Jewish men for forced labour, so too Jewish women were rounded up and put into brothels.[59] A.A. Ruzkensky testified in 1941 that Jewish girls were taken from the streets of Lvov and put into a brothel and shot a few days later.[60] Although Ruzkensky does not reveal the source of his knowledge, recruitment into military brothels after being rounded up off the street was a common means of obtaining women for forced sexual slavery and many non-Jewish Slavic women were thus abducted.

Women were also pressed into sexual slavery in the camps. Auschwitz survivor Gerda Northmann-Luner related that Erica, the Kapo at Birkenau, once explained, as they worked side by side in an electrical factory, that her cruelty was due to her own mistreatment in the camp. Erika told Gerda: 'I was made to do all sorts of things there, with German soldiers and what not, and it was all . . . I turned into an animal, from seeing this.'[61] Fela F. testified that two of her friends were taken to the prostitution block where they acquired venereal diseases. She lamented, 'they made from them a mess'.[62] Another second-hand account of forced sexual slavery is provided by Ilse B. who was saved from incarceration in a concentration camp because she was only part Jewish. Ilse testified that Jewish women were military prostitutes. She obtained this knowledge from her Jewish aunt and cousin who had been imprisoned in a concentration camp.[63] While all of these testimonies are second-hand, taken together they all corroborate the notion that Jewish women served Germans in brothels.

The testimonies of Jewish women being forced into sexual slavery call into question the assertion of Doris Bergen that 'the wartime dread that some Jewish women expressed of "girls' battalions" sent east to service the troops may have been a symptom of how much they misunderstood the Nazi genocidal project'.[64] In fact, the mistaken belief in the idea that Germans implemented their genocidal policies with unwavering ideological purity has caused many to turn a blind eye to numerous sources, German and Jewish, which testify to the realities of Jewish experiences during the war.

Some concentration camps were also locations where Jewish women endured all manner of sexual violence. Sexual abuse within the camp was solely the preserve of those in authority. In Skarzysko-Kamienna, a labour camp in Poland to which numerous Lodz and Krakow ghetto inmates were sent, prisoner experienced abuses that deviated from central policy. The leadership of Skarzysko-Kamienna engaged regularly in the rape of the Jewish prisoner population. Survivors testified that numerous German officers took part in the rape of Jewish women, with more than one testimony specifically naming Kurt Krause, Otto Eisenschmidt, and SA member Fritz Bartenschlager.[65] Sexual abuse was so pervasive that it was an acknowledged part of the camp culture. In her book on Skarzysko-Kamienna, Felicja Karay described it as a place where 'the "rites of manhood" were expressed in orgies of drunkenness and gang rapes of Jewish girls'.[66] Most of the men chose newly arrived Jewish women to serve them as room cleaners or meal servers, and then raped and killed them immediately afterwards.[67] At times, the prisoners learned of what was happening from others in the camp. For example, Bronia S. reported that a *Volksdeutsche* at the factory told her that the girls who disappeared were being raped.[68] Sometimes the rapes were perpetrated in full view of the prisoners. Milla D. testified that a girl, Rochma Eisenberg, was raped by five or six Germans in the office in the centre of the factory where she was working. This was but one of many similar incidents.[69] Other prisoners witnessed women being dragged from their beds at night.[70] Luba M. said that one night a few Germans came and took away 20 girls under the age of 15. One of the women was her cousin. The cousin returned covered in blood with a piece of bread and marmalade. A few days later she was taken to the hospital and not seen again. Luba testified that none of the raped girls survived.[71] Tola W. similarly described the nightly raid of the bedchambers by German soldiers.[72]

Also at Skarzysko-Kamienna, Morris K. reported that a Ukrainian guard shot a Jewish girl as she tried to escape. The guard rounded up some Jewish prisoners, of which Morris was one, to bury the body. 'Who wants to fuck her?' the guard asked, before then making the Jewish prisoners spread her legs. Morris K. and two other prisoners had to dig a grave and bury the woman. The woman was around 20 years old.[73] There are numerous testimonies from a variety of camps which discuss women being sexually violated after death.[74] As a way of expressing power over a corpse, this act of necrophilia further desecrated and dehumanised both the deceased and living witnesses.

The Yad Vashem testimonies contain numerous corroborating eyewitness accounts of sexual abuse perpetuated against inmates at Skarzysko-Kamienna. Sexual abuse of women prisoners in other camps might not have been as widespread or as open as at Skarzysko-Kamienna: at some camps, sexual abuse was pervasive; in others, the abuse was more limited to specific circumstances or was carried out by guards without the knowledge of their superiors. However there were German functionaries at concentration camps, not only in Skarzysko-Kamienna, that took advantage of the availability of numerous women, including Jewish women, who were unable to refuse their advances. In some cases it was the commandant himself who organised the abuses. Lya C. was in the Haidari concentration camp in Greece. She noted that every morning the commandant would select the seven most attractive female prisoners – the same seven women. One day, one of the women was sick and he approached Lya. Lya was 14 – she thought the girls were cleaning the rooms; instead she was raped by a young German.[75]

In other camps, rape may have been a product of the general violence and abuse of prisoners. Omer Bartov notes that Wolfgang Sofsky points out in his work *The Order of Terror* that the 'condition of omnipresent murder attracts and breeds sadists'.[76] Within the context of punishment or violence against prisoners, rape appears to have been permitted or at the very least overlooked in some camps. Although rape should not have been permitted according to the racial laws which prohibited sexual conduct, this policy was not always practised.[77] In the case of rape, local German leadership often chose to look the other way. One survivor, Erica B., testified that she was arrested for *Rassenschande* and incarcerated in Dachau. The guards repeatedly raped her in her cell: 'There was sex from morning to night and there was not anything you could do about it . . . Two or three would come in and you had to lie on the floor and that was it.'[78] It is clear from her testimony that she was not the only one subjected to this treatment and that the female guards were aware of what was happening. Rather than intervene or report the male guards for *Rassenschande*, they refused to speak to the women being raped and called them names.[79] It was not only at Dachau that rape as torture or punishment of the prisoners was carried out by the camp guards. Emil G. reported that while he was in Auschwitz-Birkenau, the Germans arranged a 'show' where they took 20 Jewish women prisoners and raped them in front of one of the labour groups. Emil reported that the male prisoners were supposed to stand and applaud. One of the women raped was a woman he knew from his hometown. She survived the war but committed suicide immediately afterwards.[80] Although some may be sceptical of mass rape as a punitive action at Auschwitz, Emil G. seems to be a credible informant. Auschwitz was not the only place where gang rape was reportedly employed as punishment. Survivor Paula N. related an incident that took place in the Bruss-Sophienwalde Concentration camp. A woman in the camp confided in the Commandant that she was pregnant. The Commandant was known to be compassionate, but rather than the sympathetic treatment she expected, he put her on a list to be deported to Stuttgart. The girl hid to avoid deportation but was eventually found. In front of everyone in the camp – mostly young girls – this pregnant woman was gang raped by the guards before being thrown on the truck to Stuttgart.[81]

It is clear from other testimonies, however, that sexual abuse of Jews was not permitted in all the camps. For example, Shari B. was a 14 year old girl in Augsburg when a German man more than twice her age grabbed her under-developed breasts. She felt helpless to prevent his assault and pleaded with him to stop but he did not let go until he saw a female guard coming.[82] Similarly, although sexual abuses were perpetrated at Stutthof, they typically took place when the commandant of the camp was away. Juliana C. reported that five soldiers got drunk and decided to sexually abuse prisoners. Her number was called and she was led to a room where she witnessed a mother raped in front of her own daughter. After the woman was raped the soldiers allowed dogs to attack her and rip off her breasts. Juliana and the woman's daughter saw this happen and neither cried out. Laughing and drinking, the five men raped and sodomised Juliana. When she cried out, an older soldier heard the noise and came in. He said he was going to report them and they better clean up. He told her and the child to come out of the room. Juliana was returned to her sister.[83] As incredible as Juliana's story may appear, hers is not the only report of its type. Sara M., the previously mentioned young girl violently raped and beaten at Ravensbrück had a similar experience of gang rape by drunk and amused guards.[84]

Sometimes single actors perpetrated rape without the knowledge of the local leadership. Krakow ghetto survivor Jan Rozansi described an incident during one of the mass deportations from the Podgorze during which a German SS officer ordered him and his mother to clear a stairwell. At the foot of the stairs they found 'a young girl. She was dead. Her dress lifted and pants torn off her body. She was raped, illegally, and then killed, legally, by the representatives [sic] of the "high race." She was shot directly in the face.'[85]

Rozansi's assertion that the killing of Jewish women was legal but their rape illegal, reveals the central issue of rape as an important experience of Holocaust victims. Even if it was not universally experienced, the power of life and death that the Germans held over Jewish women made the rapes that did occur possible. In this respect, the rape of Jewish women was a specific Holocaust experience because the genocidal conditions and the lack of legal recourse created the women's vulnerability. Jewish women as Jews were placed in situations which made them particularly vulnerable to any type of violence. Being marked as Jews on the streets, in ghettos, in concentration and death camps, in hiding, in medical facilities, or gathered together just before execution were all physically vulnerable situations for Jews. As women without legal recourse, they were vulnerable to sexual abuse. For example, one survivor, Rose A. testified that an old German wanted to have sex with her but she refused. As punishment her brother was undressed and given 25 lashes on his naked body.[86]

Although it is not clear if Sandra Brand is referring specifically to sexual abuse or just abuse, her testimony indicates the vulnerability of Jewish women in the streets during the early days of the occupation.

> We women went shopping, we went to look for food. In some way, we knew that when we went to the store anybody could hit us, anybody could grab us . . . Here and there this did happen . . . You see, if I take the word *hero* loosely, very loosely, during the war every Jewish woman was a hero . . . They exposed themselves to dangers.[87]

The experience of Jewish women during the Holocaust is an important aspect of Holocaust history. Ulrich Herbert in his introduction to *National Socialist Extermination Policies* has noted that one of the weaknesses of German histories of the Holocaust has been the focus on the perpetrators' perspective.[88] This has meant that events which according to the historian Götz Aly would have appeared from the perspective of Holocaust victims to be a 'horrible efficiency of the bureaucracy of death', were judged by the Nazi echelons as disorganised and a failure.[89] Similarly, rape during the Holocaust has been judged outside of Nazi policy and therefore not a central question for historians of the period.

However, it is because it is outside of Nazi policy that rape of Jewish women during the Holocaust is of central importance to those studying perpetrator history. Rape of Jewish women during the Holocaust illustrates that anti-Jewish practice varied based on location and in many cases on local leadership. Historians are constantly grappling with the tension between offering a panoramic view of events without losing sight of the details and exceptional cases. In recent years, regional studies have been employed to get a more detailed and nuanced picture of the Nazi extermination process.[90] Many of these regional studies which have focused on the role of centre–periphery relations concluded that there is often a disconnection between orders and abstract policies from above and the practical experiences, actions and initiatives of those below.[91] In some cases, individuals at the lowest of levels did not follow the policy as dictated by the superiors.[92]

This structure of the central authorities providing guidance in the form of broad directives from above and relying on those at the regional level to carry them out often did not translate as planned. In some cases brutality ensued, while at other times disobedience took the form of saving Jews. Wendy Lower has suggested that it was possible for actions on the periphery to be more brutal as they were under less direct scrutiny. She noted, 'The commissars and regional police forces did not carry out the Nazi goal of genocide in a banal fashion: they fulfilled it barbarically, often encouraging sadistic methods that exceeded the expectations of their superiors, who wanted to maintain order, a measure of control, and secrecy.'[93] However, citing the case of an official who hid Jews during the war, she also pointed out that that same secrecy allowed those at the periphery to carry out actions which were not allowed by Nazi central authorities.[94] Whether due to excess as a result of the overall culture of violence, or a recognition of the humanity of those the regime deemed undeserving of life, it is clear that what took place on the ground during the Holocaust did not always match up to racial policy as directed. This phenomenon meant that the experience of victims during the Holocaust was not always in line with central policies. In some cases, deviations from central policy were reported back to Berlin. In other cases, they were not, and it is only through victim testimony that it is possible to uncover these departures from Nazi orthodoxy.[95]

Acknowledgement

This research would not have been possible without support from Youngstown State University in the form of research funding and leave time. A great deal of work on this project was also accomplished while serving as a Charles H. Revson Foundation Fellow at the Center for Advanced Holocaust Studies at the United States Holocaust Memorial Museum during 2007. Numerous individuals have read and commented on drafts of this manuscript. For this, I would like to thank Christian Gerlach, L. Diane Barnes, Richard Breitman, Monika Flaschka, Galadriel Mehera Gerardo, Susan Grayzel, and Daniel Magilow. I would also like to thank Neil Whitehead and the other members of the Legacies of Violence Research Circle for their support and comments on this paper as it progressed.

Notes

1 For more on the connection between rape and genocide, see Anne Llewellyn Barstow (ed.), *War's Dirty Secret: Rape, Prostitution, and other Crimes Against Women* (Cleveland: Pilgrim Press, 2000); Katharine Derderian, 'Common Fate, Different Experience: Gender Specific Aspects of the Armenian Genocide, 1915–1917', *Holocaust and Genocide Studies* (Spring 2005). pp.1–125; Alexandra Stiglmayer (ed.), *Mass Rape: The War against Women in Bosnia-Herzegovina*, trans. Marion Farber (Lincoln: University of Nebraska Press, 1994); Christoph Schiessl, 'An Element of Genocide: Rape, Total War, and International Law in the Twentieth Century', *Journal of Genocide Research*, Vol.4, No.2 (2002), pp.197–210; Lisa Sharlach, 'Gender and Genocide in Rwanda: Women as Agents and Objects of Genocide', *Journal of Genocide Research*, Vol.1, No.3 (1999), pp.387–99; Roger W. Smith, 'Women and Genocide: Notes on an Unwritten History', *Holocaust and Genocide Studies*,

Vol.8, No.3 (Winter 1994), pp.315–34; Cherif Bassiouni and Marcia McCormick, *Sexual Violence: An Invisible Weapon of War in the Former Yugoslavia* (Chicago: International Human Rights Law Institute, DePaul University, 1996).

2 Ruth Seifert has described rape as a 'violent invasion into the interior of one's body [and] represents the most severe attack imaginable upon the intimate self and the dignity of a human being: by any measure it is a mark of severe torture'. See Todd Salzmann, " 'Rape Camps," Forced Impregnation and Ethnic Cleansing: Religious, Cultural and Ethnical Responses to Rape Victims in the Former Yugoslavia', in Barstow (ed.), *War's Dirty Secret*, p.70.

3 The author defines rape to be the physical invasion of a sexual nature on a person – man, woman or child – under circumstances which are coercive. Sexual violence includes rape but may include acts which do not include physical penetration or even physical contact. This article deals specifically with rape of Jewish women but the Nazi assault on Jewish reproductive abilities in the form of mass sterilisations, genital and reproductive organ mutilations, forced abortions, the murder of newborn children, and ultimately through death may also be considered a form of sexual violence. For more on sexual violence against non-Jewish women during the Second World War, see Birgit Beck's *Wehrmacht und sexuelle Gewalt: Sexualverbrechen vor deutschen Militaergerichten 1939–1945* (Paderborn: Schoeningh, 2004); Baris Alakus, Katharina Kniefacz and Robert Vorberg (eds.), *Sex-Zwangsarbeit in Nationalsozialistischen Konzentrationslagern* (Wien: Mandelbaum, 2006); Wendy Jo Gertjejanssen, 'Victims, Heroes, Survivors: Sexual Violence on the Eastern Front During World War II' (Thesis: University of Minnesota, 2004); Dagmar Herzog (ed.), *Sexuality and German Fascism* (Austin: University of Texas Press, 2002); and Christa Paul, *Zwangsprostitution: Staatlich errichtete Bordelle im Nationalsozialismus* (Berlin: Edition Hentrich, 1995).

4 Similarly, despite strong anti-miscegenation laws, marriages between whites and blacks persisted in places like Virginia where it was a felony offence. See Judy Scales-Trent, 'Racial Purity Laws in the United States and Nazi Germany: The Targeting Process', *Human Rights Quarterly*, Vol.23 (2001), p.273.

5 Birgit Beck, 'Rape: The Military Trials of Sexual Crimes Committed by Soldiers in the Wehrmacht, 1939–1944', in Karen Hagemann and Stefanie Schueler-Springorum (eds.), *Home/Front: the Military, War and Gender in Twentieth Century Germany* (Oxford: Berg, 2002), p.263.

6 See for example, Doris L. Bergen, 'Sex, Blood and Vulnerability: Women Outsiders in Nazi-Occupied Europe', in Robert Gellately and Nathan Stoltzfus (eds.), *Social Outsiders in Nazi Germany* (Princeton, NJ: Princeton University Press, 2001), p.277.

7 Human Rights Watch, 'Rwanda: Women Speak', in Barstow (ed.), *War's Dirty Secret*, p.97.

8 Derderian, 'Common Fate, Different Experience', p.8.

9 See Ruth Seifert, *War and Rape: Analytical Approaches* (Geneva: Women's International League for Peace and Freedom, 1993).

10 Consensual relations between Jewish women and German men also existed during the war but are outside the purview of this article.

11 Madeline Morris, 'In War and Peace: Rape, War and Military Culture', in Barstow (ed.), *War's Dirty Secret*, p.175

12 Rhonda Copelon as quoted in Barstow (ed.), *War's Dirty Secret*, p.8.

13 Alexander B. Downes, 'Desperate Times, Desperate Measures: The Causes of Civilian Victimization in War', *International Security*, Vol.30 No.4 (Spring 2006), p.161.

14 Schiessl, 'An Element of Genocide', pp.197–9.

15 Lawrence L. Langer, *Preempting the Holocaust* (New Haven, CT: Yale University Press, 1998), p.351.

16 Katrina Lee Koo, 'Confronting a Disciplinary Blindness: Women, War and Rape in the International Politics of Security', *Australian Journal of Political Science*, Vol.37, No.3 (2001), p.532.

17 Karin Doerr, 'The Depiction of Auschwitz in an American Novel: Sherri Szeman's *The Kommandant's Mistress*', *Rendezvous: Journal of Arts and Letters*, Vol.34, No.1 (Fall 2000), pp.37–46.

18 Zoë Waxman, *Writing the Holocaust: Identity, Testimony, Representation* (Oxford: Oxford University Press, 2006), p.138.

19 Joan Ringelheim, 'The Split between Gender and the Holocaust', in Dalia Ofer and Lenore J. Weitzman (eds.), *Women in the Holocaust* (New Haven, CT: Yale University Press (1999)), p.343.

20 Koo, 'Confronting a Disciplinary Blindness', p.531.

21 Lawrence Langer, *Holocaust Testimonies: The Ruins of Memory* (New Haven, CT: Yale University Press, 1991), p.88.

22 *A Woman in Berlin: Diary Entries from 20 April to 22 June 1945* (New York: Harcourt, 1954). For a discussion of the book's initial reception, see Elizabeth Heinmann, 'Gender, Sexuality, and Coming to Terms with the Nazi Past', *Central European History*, 2005. Also numerous reviews of the recent republication of the diary following its anonymous author's death discuss the reception of the book when it was first released in Germany in the late 1950s. See for example 'The Rubble Women', *The Observer*, 2 July 2005, and 'Bearing and Recording Degradation', *San Francisco Chronicle*, 7 August 2005.

23 Christopher Browning, *Collected Memories: Holocaust History and Postwar Testimony.* (Madison: University of Wisconsin Press, 2003), p.81.

24 Ibid., p.39.

25 This has manifested itself in multiple ways including interviewers losing interest in a particular storyline or time running out for that specific segment and cutting off the interviewee during the telling of a story, or an interviewer questioning a woman who lived in Krakow who asked her to tell him more about her 'shtetl'. For further discussion on this, see ibid., passim.

26 Private meeting with Dr. Joan Ringleheim at the United States Holocaust Memorial Museum in July of 1995.

27 Anne Llewellyn Barstow, 'Money Can't Buy Our Youth Back; Apology Can't Make up for Our Fate', in Barstow (ed.), *War's Dirty Secret*, p.40.

28 Lillian R. (5990) Shoah Foundation Oral Testimonies Archive. It was not only Jewish women at this time that had partners who could not overcome the prevailing rape myths of the period. In *Eine Frau in Berlin* the woman relates that her beloved abandons her in disgust after he learns of her experience. See Elizabeth Heineman, 'Gender, Sexuality, and Coming to Terms with the Nazi Past', *Central European History*, Vol.38, No.1 (2005), pp.41–74.

29 Sara M. (29016), Shoah Foundation Oral Testimony.

30 Waxman, *Writing the Holocaust*, p.137.

31 The notion that rape and survival should not go together was not new to the Holocaust. It was an older idea that found expression in multiple venues. For example, George Trevelyan in his history of Cawnpore, argued that Eliza Wheeler, a rape survivor, had either 'consented to sex and so was not raped or that she was not a true English women, since a racially 'pure' woman would have died trying to protect her honor or would have committed suicide immediately afterwards.' See Nancy L. Paxton, *Writing Under the Raj: Gender, Race and Rape in the British Colonial Imagination, 1830–1947* (New Brunswick, NJ: Rutgers University Press, 1999), p.11.

32 Gila Flam, *Singing for Survival: Songs of the Lodz Ghetto 1940–1945* (Urbana: University of Illinois Press, 1992), p.51.

33 Langer, *Preempting the Holocaust*, p.10.

34 Nechama Tec, *Resilience and Courage: Women, Men, and the Holocaust* (New Haven, CT: Yale University Press, 2003), p.231.
35 Attachment to report from the Senior Commander, Eastern Division (Oberbefehlsaber Ost), Headquarters Castle Spala, 6 February 1940, in BA-MA Freiburg, RH 53–23/23, p. 28 in file cited in Bergen, 'Sex, Blood and Vulnerability', p.276.
36 Adelson, p.464.
37 USHMM Acc. 1998.A.0249.
38 Ibid.
39 Ibid.; Affidavit of Hans Biebow of 19 August 1946.
40 The exception is Isaiah Trunk who made mention of Biebow's rapes in his work on the Lodz Ghetto. He noted, 'Biebow practiced his sadistic whims here, too (rapes of girls in the women's camp, savage outrages on captured Jews)' (Isaiah Trunk, *Lodz Ghetto: A History*, trans. and ed. Robert Moses Shapiro, intro. Israel Gutman (Bloomington and Indianapolis: Indiana University Press, published in association with the United States Holocaust Memorial Museum, 2006), p.269).
41 Testimony of Esther H. (506), Shoah Foundation Oral Testimonies; Biebow's presence in Dresden during the war is confirmed by his trial records. According to his arrest records, he was there in March of 1945. See USHMM Acc. 1998.A.0249
42 Ibid.; The killing of a camp guard's mistress in his absence was not unique to this case. Moshe Bahir testified that *Scharführer* Paul Grot, the leader of the Ukrainian columns at Sobibor, had a Jewish mistress named Ruth who apparently was murdered the day after Grot was transferred to another death camp. See Miriam Novitch (ed.), *Sobibor: Martydom and Revolt* (New York: Walden Press, 1980), p.151.
43 Testimony of Bina W. (33960), Shoah Foundation Oral Testimonies Archives.
44 Ana C. (864), Shoah Foundation Oral Testimony.
45 Adolf Hitler, *Mein Kampf*, trans. Ralph Manheim (Boston: Houghton Mifflin Co., 1971), p.63.
46 Annette F. Timm, 'The Ambivalent Outsider: Prostitution, Promiscuity, and VD Control in Nazi Berlin', in Robert Gellately and Nathan Stoltzfus (eds.), *Social Outsiders in Nazi Germany* (Princeton, NJ: Princeton University Press, 2001), p.195.
47 Ibid., p.201; Zdeněk Tmej, a Czech forced labourer sent to Wroclaw, photographed a brothel containing prostitutes employed to service the foreign labourers there. Included are pictures of the place where the men paid for the services, the man who ran the brothel with all the women, the women entertaining the men, and portraits of the women in their rooms. A series of portraits of one woman included the following captions, 'This Czech woman was given a choice: brothel or concentration camp . . . Years later I bumped into her in Prague; she was drinking herself to death.' For more of these photographs, see Ana Fárová, Tomáš Jelínek and Blanka Chocholova, *Zdeněk Tmej: Totaleinsatz* (Prague: Torst, 2001). Thank you to Krista Hegberg for pointing out this source to me.
48 Birgit Beck, 'Rape: The Military Trials of Sexual Crimes Committed by Soldiers in the Wehrmacht, 1939–1944', in Karen Hagemann and Stefanie Schueler-Springorum (eds.), *Home/Front: the Military, War and Gender in Twentieth Century Germany* (Oxford: Berg, 2002), p.267.
49 Christa Paul, *Zwangsprostitution: Staatlich errichtete Bordelle im Nationalsozialismus* (Berlin, 1995), pp. 23, 131; Timm 'The Ambivalent Outsider', p.201.
50 William Samelson, 'Piotrków Trybunalski: My Ancestral Home', *Life in the Ghettos During the Holocaust* (Syracuse, NY: Syracuse University Press, 2005), pp. 9 and 10.
51 Ibid., pp.13 and 14; William Samelson describing the round-up of Jews from the Piotrków Trybunalski ghetto by the SS, over two years after the Jews were incarcerated into the ghetto, '[t]he hunters stopped long enough to molest the more attractive women and young girls. Shouts of pain, fear, and anguish resounded throughout the neighborhood as homes were looted and women were violated', p.12.

52 Jacob Apenszlak (ed.), *The Black Book of Polish Jewry: An Account of the Martyrdom of Polish Jewry* (New York, 1943), pp.26, 27. The affidavit was reported to have been published in the *Contemporary Jewish Record* of March-April 1940.

53 Ibid., p.27.

54 Ibid., p.28.

55 Ana C. (864), Shoah Foundation Oral Testimony.

56 Penney recalls that she was on the list but through a fortuitous intervention she had her name removed. Cited in Gertjejanssen, 'Victims, Heroes, Survivors', p.178.

57 Judit Z. (41162), Shoah Foundation Oral Testimony.

58 Michael J. (26142), Shoah Foundation Oral Testimony.

59 Gertjejanssen, 'Victims, Heroes, Survivors', pp.191, 192.

60 Ibid., pp.191, 192.

61 Tec, *Resilience and Courage*, p.173.

62 Fela F. (39064), Shoah Foundation Oral Testimonies.

63 Testimony of Ilse B. in Cynthia Crane, *Divided Lives: the Untold Stories of Jewish-Christian Women in Nazi Germany* (New York: St. Martin's Press, 2000), p.211.

64 Bergen. 'Sex, Blood and Vulnerability', p.278.

65 Testimony mentioning Otto Eisenschmidt: Sonia N. (1832) Shoah Foundation Oral Testimony Archives; Testimonies mentioning Bartenschlager by name: Eva L. (51181) Shoah Foundation Oral Testimony Archives; Sonia N. (1832) Shoah Foundation Oral Testimony Archives.

66 Felicja Karay, *Death Comes in Yellow: Skarzysko-Kamienna Slave Labor Camp* (Amsterdam: Overseas Publishers Association, 1996), p.80.

67 For testimonies on this, see ibid., pp.80, 81. For testimonies on survivors awareness of newly arrived women being taken away and not seen again see Marta C. (2790) Shoah Foundation Oral Testimonies Archive, Pola K. (32812) Shoah Foundation Oral Testimonies Archive, Harry K. (19656)) Shoah Foundation Oral Testimonies Archive, Saul M. (6145)) Shoah Foundation Oral Testimonies Archive.

68 Bronia S. (10747) Shoah Foundation Oral Testimonies Archive.

69 Milla D. (15012) Shoah Foundation Oral Testimonies Archive.

70 It was not only at Skarzysko-Kamienna that women were dragged from their beds at night for sex by the German guards. Rose S. noted that at Glöwen concentration camp, 'at night, the time was ours alone except for some of us – they had to go out and attend the Germans. They just came and picked the girls, whoever they felt like and took them away to their barracks. Sometimes they had to stay overnight.' The women were not given a choice in the matter. See testimony of Rose S. (10119), Shoah Foundation Oral Testimony. Similarly, Paula K. said that when she was in Tschenstochau-Pelzery concentration camp, a Wehrmacht soldier came into the women's barracks and started talking to her and some of her female family members. Four or five weeks later, when they were all asleep, this same soldier, who was very drunk. He came and started to pull the blanket off Paula. One of her family members stood between her and the German and told her to run. Frustrated by his inability to find the first woman he had selected, he grabbed a girl who was sleeping by the entrance to the barrack. He dragged her off and raped her. The girl came back at 4 o'clock in the morning. She was bleeding and screaming and crying. She was taken to the hospital. See testimony of Paula K. (7952), Shoah Foundation Oral Testimony.

71 Luba M. (35267) Shoah Foundation Oral Testimonies Archive.

72 Tola W. (42996) Shoah Foundation Oral Testimonies Archive.

73 Morris K. (3726) Shoah Foundation Oral Testimony Archives; It is unclear if the woman was raped before being shot or if she was truly just shot while running away.

74 For example, see Proces Amona Goetha (trial against Amon Goeth, 1946). USHMM Archives 1998.A.0248.

75 Lya C (450) Shoah Foundation Oral Testimonies Archive.

76 Omer Bartov, *Germany's War and the Holocaust: Disputed Histories* (Ithaca, NY: Cornell University Press, 2003), p.104.

77 Michael Zimmerman, 'The National Socialist "Solution of the Gypsy Question": Central Decisions, Local Initiatives, and Their Interrelation', *Holocaust and Genocide Studies*, Vol.14, No.3 (Winter 2001), p.420.

78 Erica B. (20825) Shoah Foundation Oral Testimonies Archive.

79 Erica B. (20825) Shoah Foundation Oral Testimonies Archive.

80 Emil G. (19178) Shoah Foundation Oral History Testimonies Archives.

81 Paula N. (4788), Shoah Foundation Oral Testimony Archives.

82 Shari B. (1249), Shoah Foundation Oral Testimony.

83 Juliana C. (48403) Shoah Foundation Oral Testimonies Archive.

84 Sara M. (29016), Shoah Foundation Oral Testimony.

85 Jan Rozansi, *In Your Blood I Live*. USHMM RG 02.079*01.

86 Rose A. (25941) Shoah Foundation Oral Testimony Archives.

87 Tec, *Resilience and Courage*, p.34.

88 Ulrich Herbert (ed.), *National Socialist Extermination Policies: Contemporary German Perspectives and Controversies* (New York: Berghahn, 2000), p.17.

89 Götz Aly, *Final Solution: Nazi Population Policy and the Murder of the European Jews* (New York: Arnold, 1999), p.59.

90 Scholars such as Christian Gerlach (*Kalulierte Morde: Die deutsche Wirtschafts- und Vernichtungspolitik in Weissrussland 1941–1944*, Hamburger Edition; Auflage: Studienausgabe, 2000), Dieter Pohl (*Von der Juden politik zum Judenmord. Der Distrikt Lublin des Generalgouvernements 1939–1944*, Franfurt am Main: Peter Lang, 1993), and Bodgan Musial (*Deutsche Zivilverwaltung under Judenverfolgung im Generalgouvernement: Ein Fallstudie zum Distrikt Lublin, 1939–1944* Wiessbaden: Harrassowitz, 1999) have published regional studies. In English, see Herbert (ed.), *National Socialist Extermination Policies*.

91 On the discrepancy between orders from above and the carrying out of actions on the ground in the case of Roma and Sinti, see Zimmerman. 'The National Socialist "Solution of the Gypsy Question' ", p.420.

92 There are many such cases. For example, see Christopher R. Browning, *Nazi Policy, Jewish Workers, German Killers* (Cambridge: Cambridge University Press, 2000), pp.148, 149.

93 Wendy Lower, ' "Anticipatory Obedience" and the Nazi Implementation of the Holocaust in the Ukraine: A Case Study of Central and Peripheral Forces in the Generalbezirk Zhytomyr, 1941–1944', *Holocaust and Genocide Studies*, Vol.16, No.1 (Spring 2002), p.8.

94 Ibid., p.10.

95 Herbert (ed.), *National Socialist Extermination Policies*, p.17.

12

BETWEEN SANITY AND INSANITY

Spheres of everyday life in the Auschwitz-Birkenau *Sonderkommando*

Gideon Greif

In deciding to undertake a continent-wide genocide of millions of people, the Nazis found themselves having to invent a variety of systems that would facilitate mass murder on such an unprecedented scale. The killings began in the most conventional manner, by mass shootings. They were messy, costly, too public, and had undesirable psychological effects on the perpetrators. As Christopher Browning has shown in Ordinary Men, a study of a single police reserve battalion involved in such killings, the perpetrators did become acclimatized to mass murder relatively swiftly. But the repercussions were wrought nerves, heavy drinking, and what the SS, especially Himmler, viewed as unnecessary brutalization and ethical deterioration. New methods had to be invented that would make it possible to kill large numbers of people quickly, and then efficiently dispose of their bodies. Simultaneously, it was deemed necessary to distance the killers as far as possible from their victims, in order to protect them from the disagreeable side effects of carrying out this "most difficult of tasks," as Himmler told his men, and to preserve in them the sense that they had "the moral right" and "duty towards our people, to destroy this people that wanted to destroy us."

Thus the extermination camps came into being. But as it turned out, even there, someone had to perform the "dirty work" of pushing the victims into undressing rooms, relieving them of their valuables and hair, pushing them into the gas chambers, and then, once they had died, disentangling the corpses, pulling out their gold teeth, and finally either burying them in mass graves – which soon turned out to be an environmental hazard in view of the vast numbers and shallow pits – or, in the ultimately perfected Auschwitz-Birkenau complex, incinerating them in cutting-edge crematoria designed by top-notch engineers. Yet all of this still did not resolve the problem of SS-men having to undertake this most unpleasant "job," which would have in fact undermined the entire rationale of the extermination camps as sites geared to minimize contact between the killers and their victims. Therefore the SS came up with the ingenious solution of the Sonderkommando, nicknamed the ravens, and made up of

240

mostly young Jewish men who did the work for the Germans, with the reward of having their lives temporarily spared.

This solution to the self-imposed problem of making vast numbers of human beings disappear without a trace while protecting the murderers from the effects of their deed, created in turn what can be seen as the most perverse, insidious, indeed utterly demonic circumstance in the entire Nazi genocidal apparatus. Here, then, in a situation which, as Greif notes in his chapter, the very essence of Nazism's bottomless evil was exposed, Jewish men were operating a perfected, streamlined, wholly modern machine, designed with the sole purpose of exterminating the Jews of Europe, including these men's own families, communities, and cultures. It was as if, whether they had meant to or not, the Nazis were demonstrating not only that the Jews must and can be eradicated, but that they would voluntarily exterminate themselves, facilitate their own disappearance from the face of the earth, while those who had built and set the machine of death into motion watched from the sidelines, neat, disciplined, and composed, only occasionally making a cynical comment or chuckling from a crass joke.

Greif delves into this forbidden world as no one has before: forbidden because it was the secret core of the extermination apparatus that the Nazis strove to keep hidden from the world. But also forbidden because hitherto, with the partial exception of Primo Levi's The Gray Zone and Tadeusz Borowski's This way for the Gas, Ladies and Gentlemen, most scholars and authors have shied away from stepping into the morally perverse universe of the extermination process and from trying to comprehend its reality. He does so by listening to and reading the testimonies and accounts of the men who were there, and proposing that, as they often articulate it, they had lived in a world suspended between sanity and insanity, a place that had evolved its own logic and routine, even its pleasures and comforts, while being firmly lodged in the lowest chambers of hell. He seeks answers to questions that can ultimately never be resolved: How the men of the Sonderkommando, mostly very young, had endured this reality; how they sought to preserve their humanity; how they interacted with the SS and with the Jews they were sending to their death, and, finally, how those few who survived have lived with these recollections. And he poses a question to us, we who were not there: how can we understand those who were both the instruments and the most wretched victims of the Nazi murder machine; who both collaborated in genocide in the most immediate sense, and yet were the only ones who rose up against this machine, mostly dying in the process; where, in our own understanding of the human condition, do we place these men who preferred to work for the Nazis rather than be killed, yet left behind invaluable diaries, testimonies, and oral accounts, without which we would never have know that very heart of darkness which came to be known as anus mundi.

The killing installations in the concentration and extermination camp at Auschwitz-Birkenau functioned according to the patterns of common industrial plants: machines, production lines, workers, simple managers, senior managers, a general director, and so on. Only two major differences exist between regular factories and Nazi death camps: the raw materials in the Nazi camps were human beings, and the only end product was human ashes. The workers in the death factories were in most cases Jewish prisoners. In Auschwitz-Birkenau they were unofficially called the *Sonderkommando*.

There are various reasons for the creation of a Jewish battalion of death factory workers. The explanation given by Primo Levi in his brilliant book, *The Drowned and the Saved*, stresses one of the crucial motives: "Behind the prag-matic aspect (to economize on able men, to impose on others the most atrocious task) other moral subtle aspects can be perceived. This institution represented an attempt to shift onto others—specifically, the victims—the burden of guilt, so that they were deprived of even the solace of innocence."[1] The Germans decided to create the squads in order to share the burden of responsibility for their crimes with their victims. The Jews not only had to be murdered but also had to become perpetrators in their murder, according to this way of thinking. This explanation reflects the typical distorted Nazi way of thinking and acting toward the Jews: breaking all kinds of existing barriers between perpetrators and victims, between good and evil, between morality and immorality, between civilization and havoc.

They did the "black work of the Holocaust," as Yaakov Gabai, one of the *Sonderkommando* survivors, defined it.[2] The killing action itself, namely, the pouring of the gas crystals inside the gas chamber, was exclusively and always done by the Germans. Such a "profession" has never been practiced by a human being, anywhere, anytime. The six extermination camps had no precedence in human history and can be considered as a purely Nazi invention. The Germans based their confidence that Jewish prisoners would be capable of doing everything needed in the killing installations on the assumption that they had the techniques of breaking the spirits of every human being and could achieve by terror every goal through their slaves. Once confronted with the horrible reality at the killing site, those prisoners would undergo a "shock treatment" and break mentally, and subsequently they would fulfill their tasks obediently. This aim of the Germans was realized. Rudolf Höss states in his memoirs, "[I]t was all done in such a matter-of-course manner that [the *Sonderkommando* prisoners] might themselves have been the exterminators."[3]

Survivors of the *Sonderkommando* remember that the first encounter with the heaps of twisted corpses traumatized them so severely that most of them began to act as "robots" (Gabai) or passive "machines" (Cohen). Some survivors, such as Chazan, for instance, also testify that they "stopped being human by then" (this aspect will be discussed in detail later on). In many sources, including the historical ones written at that time,[4] this kind of characterization of the *Sonderkommando* as emotionless, heartless, rude, beastly, brutal, and apathetic people is very common and widespread: "They are described as crude, repulsive, frightening sights. . . . [They] became even more nauseated at their own condition."[5]

This situation in which an installation for mass killing functions like a regular production facility but in which the workers are more like robots already creates an odd and bizarre atmosphere resembling a science fiction story. While reading the testimonies of the *Sonderkommando*, especially the chilling technical details of the "production line," the reader's impression is of experiencing a nightmare. The two channels—on the one hand the purely technical operation and on the other the extreme crime committed there—scarcely can be combined into one entity.

Naturally, in an environment of daily mass murder, where gas chambers, suffocated cries, corpses, and ashes are omnipresent, it is unrealistic to expect people who work in this place for a long period of time to act as they characteristically would have otherwise. Each had to adapt to the rules of this odd factory if he wanted to survive. Several *Sonderkommando* members worked in the crematoria for more than two years, like the brothers Abraham and Shlomo Dragon, and it is hard to believe that such a long period would pass by without leaving deep scars in the souls of the *Sonderkommando* prisoners. Every member of the unit must have gone through some metamorphosis of the soul because of the nature of the work. The personality of each member must have been reshaped and remodeled to enable the individual to fulfill the day-to-day missions that contradicted the values and laws used and respected by the civilized world.

The goal of this essay is to present the two spheres of the crematoria reality: the sane and the insane. The aim is to test the assumption that all *Sonderkommando* members indeed had turned into living machines who had lost contact with reality and to explain the ability of some to retain their sanity and continue to act as human beings in the midst of the inferno in the crematoria.

The *Sonderkommando* and their environment

Many sources speak about the trauma that was inflicted upon the *Sonderkommando* prisoners as a result of their duties inside the killing centers.[6] The pictures they had seen in the gas chambers and crematoria ovens were unendurable. Yet most of them managed to overcome the first immediate shock and gradually "got used to" the work with the corpses, retaining their job for days, weeks, and even years. The work became routine, the tears dried up over time, the mind grew numb, cries of the murdered were ignored, and the corpses became like pieces of wood. When a new transport arrived, the most significant factor was not its human cargo but the food and possible valuables for exchange that these doomed people would bring into crematorium compounds. Sometimes, when people were called back again to work, the *Kapo* encouraged them by shouting, "A French transport has arrived with nice things from the Champs-Elysées."[7]

Primo Levi correctly defines the invention of the *Sonderkommando* as "the most demonic crime of the NS regime."[8] The *Sonderkommando* represents the most evil and distorted aspect of the National Socialist mind. The Germans intentionally forced the Jewish prisoners to assist them in running the operation that aimed at exterminating all traces of their brethren. The Jewish *Vorarbeiter* (foremen), *Kapos*, and *Oberkapos* gave orders to the hundreds of their subordinates. The killing factory was directed by the victims of the crimes: this indeed was the goal of the real murderers—to put the burden of blame on the Jews. A foreigner who would have come to the crematoria building would have never guessed that all the many workers were merely puppets on a string. In reality they were just slaves, the slaves of the death factory at Auschwitz-Birkenau.

It is painful that the German mind could create a scene in which a Jew had to cremate the body of his wife or child, pull out the corpses of his beloved ones from the gas chamber, and ignore the questions that other Jews posed to him in the undressing room.

The members of the *Sonderkommando* were without choice. Refusing to continue working automatically meant death, while continuing to work was to live in hell. Sanity and insanity could be easily mixed in that atmosphere, intensified by the fact that the *Sonderkommando* was isolated from other prisoners. Its members were doomed to be murdered after they finished their obligations. They knew that they were living on borrowed time. Every day could be decisive for their lives.

The idea and its implementation

The Germans, who tried to create a new world based on new rules and a new ideology, regarded the gas chambers and crematoria ovens as a necessity. The crematorium itself was the peak of the dehumanization process of the victims. In a system whose aim is to wipe out the *Untermenschen* (sub-humans), mass-killing installations are irreplaceable ingredients. The gas Zyklon B fits perfectly into this ideology: in order to get rid of the *Ungeziefer* (vermin), one uses poison. One cleanses the world and liquidates the unwanted parasites. "Race theory" had paved the way to a crime against humanity, endorsed and encouraged by scientists, physicians, biologists, and geneticists.[9]

The Nazi regime introduced patterns of thought, behavior, morality, and culture, which distorted, ruined, and liquidated the already existing values of civilization. In this context we should see the invention of an extermination camp and the *Sonderkommando* as tools through which the revolutionary new ideas of the Nazis could be implemented. In other words, the invention of the death camps and the way in which they were conducted corresponded to the National Socialist *Weltanschauung* (world view).

Apart from the fact that they were considered "bearers of the secret" and were isolated from the other prisoners, other aspects mark the *Sonderkommando* as unique in the context of the death camps. Since the *Sonderkommando* prisoners were involved in the killing process, they were not meant to become *Muselmänner* (people on the verge of death from lack of food and exhaustion), at least not too quickly. Apart from their daily rations, which were similar to those of the other camp inmates, they were allowed to partake of significant amounts of food that the gassed victims had brought into the crematoria compound. This is a part of the insanity: the Jews sentenced to death, who have to kill other Jews sentenced to death, must be fed properly in order to be capable of fulfilling the murderous action. Valuables found in the clothes of the victims gave them opportunities to trade for comparatively high-quality food. In the context of the camp life the area in which more than a million people were murdered also served as a place of commerce and exchange. A kind of a "Persian market" existed in the heart of the killing houses between the gas chambers and crematoria halls.

Between benefits and a death penalty

These aspects of the *Sonderkommando* reflect the duality of the prisoners' daily life: on one level there was the "Final Solution," the full-scale genocide—corpses, ashes, cries, despair; but on another level, life continued in a normal, routine manner. In this reality, the *Sonderkommando* were provided "benefits" that included sufficient nourishment and protection from brutality and bodily punishments. Indeed, one may assume that the *Sonderkommando* prisoners lived a "double life." This world included professional habits, physical work, hours of work, and hours of leisure. The other world was artificial, created by the Germans. In this world the Jews had nothing to say.

The *Sonderkommando*, of course, were victims, too. They can easily be defined as the most miserable of the miserable. The workers of the death factory had to witness day by day the extermination of their own people. There was nothing they could do about it. Their hearts and souls were broken by sorrow and despair. In the undressing room they were forced to be part of the system of deceit and misinformation about the real purpose of the "disinfections." There are testimonies about cases in which *Sonderkommando* prisoners had to push their own families into the furnaces or had to rip gold teeth out of their own mothers' mouths. Any lack of obedience or resistance on their part was immediately punished with death.

Rudolf Höss, the commander of Auschwitz, describes such a situation in his memoirs:

> It often happened that Jews from the *Sonderkommando* discovered close relatives among the bodies and even those who went into the gas chambers. Although they were visibly affected there never was any kind of incident. This incident I witnessed myself: As the bodies were being pulled out of one of the gas chambers, one member of the *Sonderkommando* suddenly stopped and stood for a moment as if

245

thunderstruck. He then pulled the body along, helping his comrades. I asked the *Kapo* what was wrong with him. He found out that the startled Jew had discovered his wife among the bodies. I watched him for awhile after this without noticing anything different about him. He just kept dragging his share of bodies. After awhile I again happened upon this work party. He was sitting with the others and eating as if nothing had happened. Was he really able to hide his feelings so completely or had he become so hardened that something like this didn't bother him?[10]

A mental metamorphosis: from shock to adaptation

When looking more specifically at their mental conditions and responses, one can see that many *Sonderkommando* prisoners went through a kind of meta-morphosis: from shock and paralysis to getting accustomed to the permanent horrors surrounding them, sometimes even enjoying the luxuries donated to them by the crematoria staff. When questioned about their feelings on their first day in the *Sonderkommando*, all survivors describe experiencing an indes-cribable jolt: "How did I react? I was confused. I thought I was going insane. I told myself 'This is the end,' "[11] recalls Joseph Sackar. Leon Cohen says, "What can I tell you? It was terrifying. I can't describe it in words. Just terrible."[12]

These two statements correspond to the memories of Shaul Chazan, also a former member of the *Sonderkommando*, who relates,

> We had a gut feeling that we couldn't identify. We didn't know a thing. On the one hand, I saw the bodies down there; on the other hand, the *Kapo* and the SS men were beating me and cursing at me all that time, to the accompaniment of barking dogs. It was hell on earth. If there's a hell after death, I think it must look like that. It was hell, real hell. There it wasn't a question of whether to believe or not.[13]

A detailed report on the experiences and feelings of the first day in the *Sonderkommando*, on which the "normal" prisoner crossed the line between sanity and insanity by becoming a member of this doomed unit, can be found in the testimony of Eliezer Eisenschmidt:

> They led us into the yard and opened the door of the building that was used as a gas chamber, and we were overwhelmed with grief. We were in absolute shock. We'd never seen anything like this in our worst nightmares. To this day, I can see in my mind's eye what we saw behind the doors as they opened. A dead woman stood there, naked, her body doubled up. We froze. We couldn't grasp what was happening there. We saw the bodies in the gas chamber. When we began to remove the bodies, we saw how they'd become a single mass.[14]

Eisenschmidt belonged to that group that had to load the dead bodies onto the wheelbarrows. When he received this order for the first time, he was "stung to the quick. . . . For a few minutes, I was too revolted to touch a body. Such a thing never happened to me. Obviously I wasn't the only one in the group who felt revulsion. I couldn't work until someone hit me hard on the back with a rod."[15]

Shlomo Dragon, who was just seventeen years old when he was forced to join the *Sonderkommando*, reports similar feelings when he remembers Otto Moll, the crematorium chief, beginning to explain what they were supposed to do: "You have to remove the dead people from the house. There are corpses there, and you have to take them out in wheelbarrows, throw them into these big pits, and incinerate them."[16] Subsequently Moll opened the door. Shlomo Dragon recalls:

> We smelled gas. We saw corpses of both sexes. The whole place was full of naked people on top of each other, falling out . . . almost all of us went into shock. We stared at each other without uttering a sound and fell silent. We were too terrified to make a sound. We were like that for a couple of days and then we pulled ourselves together again. We'd never seen anything like it before.[17]

But despite their inconceivable activity, most of the members of the *Sonderkommando* eventually got used to their work within a short period of time. Yaakov Gabai remembers, "For the first few days, it was just terrible. But I told myself, 'You mustn't lose your sanity.' I knew from then on I'd have to see these sights day in, day out. This would be our job, so we'd better get used to it. A tough job, but get used to it."[18]

Finally, the service for the death industry became partly a technical task, as Lemke Pliszko describes: "Sometimes one could believe it was a common workplace and not a crematorium."[19] He continues:

> We took nothing too seriously. Nothing could move us anymore. When we wanted to eat our bread, then you were sitting on a body and eating the bread. You got used to the place so much, you thought it was always your home. I could see a lot of corpses and nothing moved in my heart. Here in the Kibbutz, where I live [today], when I see a dead person, I'm shivering. Even crying with tears. In the camp when I saw corpses, I thought to myself: "Today the other man is dead. Tomorrow you'll be dead." You get used to everything. We had to sit somewhere when we were eating and the floor was full with bodies. The process of getting used to it was very quick and began immediately. Only one person whom I knew "went to the fence." Only one person. All the others wanted to live. Working in the crematoria I didn't feel as if I were working inside a nightmare. We accepted the

reality as it was. Life was that this is a place where people are killed. That was life. For this reason I could go on working there.[20]

The numbing of the prisoners' feelings and the mental repression were in this context a self-protection mechanism against the horrible reality around them. The process of becoming an "automaton"[21] happened rather quickly—in the case of Leon Cohen it took only two days. To turn the prisoners into puppets, they were taken at the beginning to a pile of corpses that were to be cremated. For young people who have never seen a dead body in their life, this was a real shock. Two or three days later, when the sights of death increased, the prisoners mentally succumbed, becoming paralyzed and numb. The inner change was inevitable.

Becoming accustomed or the only alternative

The mind of every person has its limits, however. The minute that the new *Sonderkommando* prisoners felt the real nature of the work they were forced to do, some of them saw only one outlet: suicide. Shaul Chazan remembers "a Greek Jew from the *Sonderkommando* who jumped into the fire. He saw what was going on and leaped into the pit."[22] Shlomo Dragon also testified on suicides: "There were several cases where people among us would 'run to the fence' in the morning. But not often."[23] This statement accords with Lemke, adding to his remarks above, "After a few days we got used to the situation. Those who got depressed went to the fence [and committed suicide]. Yet there were also those who, even later, never got used to the situation."[24]

For several psychological reasons very few chose to commit suicide. Those who did usually committed suicide in a very early stage of their "service" in the commando.[25] They understood it would be beyond their power to bear the distorted, insane reality to which they had been brought. The shock was too monstrous to be tolerated after just arriving from a relatively "normal" world. The psychological switch that all other members of the *Sonderkommando* must have made to survive and not go crazy must have been tremendous. The minority who decided to put an end to their lives had supposedly comprehended what their expected role in the Nazis' crime was to be.

For the majority that succeeded in getting used to the situation, there was one main principle: the gruesome tasks had to be executed meticulously. The orders, however, did not come directly from the Germans. The Jewish leadership—the *Vorarbeiter* and the *Kapo*—received them from the SS staff and passed them on to their workers. The death plant functioned well even without the presence of the SS men. The Jewish workers were experienced professionals who knew exactly what they were expected to do and worked with efficiency. Each shift arrived on time, and the slight technical problems were not serious enough to sabotage such an important undertaking as the liquidation of the Jewish people.

The common "madhouse" is usually characterized with a bitter sarcasm. The same mood prevailed in the crematoria, a place that the German killers liked. The crime of genocide against the Jewish people was always accompanied by irony, cynicism, humor, and laughter—even when the gas Zyklon B was poured into the chambers. Eliezer Eisenschmidt recalls such a scene:

> After the room filled up with people, the doors were closed. Next, an SS man came over with the Zyklon gas in his hand. He put on a gas mask, opened the canister of gas, and threw the contents in. Shortly after the gas was thrown in, the people began to smell it and then we heard them shout "*Sh'ma Yisrael* ..." from the interior of the gas chamber. The German called out to his comrades scornfully, "They're calling '*schmeiss rein, schmeiss rein*'—'throw it in, throw it in. ...' "[26]

The perpetrators had lost their sense of humanity. But did the same happen to the *Sonderkommando* prisoners? Did all of their emotional and human sentiment vanish, too? A closer look at the testimonies reveals a different aspect of their daily life.

Keeping human mannerisms

The many hundreds of *Sonderkommando* prisoners were not a homogenous group, and many different prisoners displayed very different patterns of behavior. Indeed, many of them lost the capacity for human sensitivity and developed a cold, emotionless attitude. Others were different and tried to retain their former selves. Auschwitz did not create new characters: it strengthened existing character lines and sharpened others. Such were, for instance, religious Jews in the *Sonderkommando*, who became instructors and advisors for many members of the *Sonderkommando* who felt lost and desperate. Leading figures in the commando were ultra-Orthodox Jews such as Zalman Gradowski, Leib Langfuss, Zalman Lewental, and others. Yaakov Silberberg reports on a consultation he once had with one rabbi who did not desist in his spiritual practices even as a prisoner in the camp:

> I had a problem with myself. I was confused, didn't know what to do, how to behave. Personally I had a big problem: I belong to a "Cohen" family, the priests, and at that time, I was religious! I am a priest and, according to the Jewish religion, a "Cohen" has to be outside of the grave, far away the dead, in order not to get impure. ... Shlomo Kirszenbaum told me, that in one of the big crematoria, there was the *Dayan* [religious judge] of Makow, and it was worthwhile talking to him.[27]

Silberberg went to the *Dayan*, who responded: "Don't worry, we are here, in order to fulfill the mission of God. He wants it this way, and we have to act exactly as He orders us to do, this is God's will."[28] Silberberg goes on: "Then he also told me, that what we do here, would be—from his point of view—a *Mitzvah* [commandment], because by this way the Jews received some kind of burial."[29]

Despite the routine and the numbness in the death factory, there are many accounts of how *Sonderkommando* prisoners exhibited respect for the victims, how they mourned the dead around them. One example of their enduring sense of sympathy is found in Zalman Gradowski's unpublished manuscript:

> Here are lying now again two [bodies] . . . young women who once were extremely beautiful. They have filled two complete worlds on this earth. They have given so much happiness and pleasure. Each smile was a comfort, each look was happiness, each word was a heavenly and charming poetry. Everywhere, where they have only put their foot, they have brought with them happiness and contentment. Many hearts loved them. And now the two are lying on a plate made of iron and soon the crater will be opened and within minutes there will be nothing left of them.[30]

The *Sonderkommando* men were tremendously saddened when they realized how many young lives were going to be eliminated:

> No remnant and no memory will be left of all those who are standing here, all those who filled complete cities. They had a place in the world and soon they will be wiped out together with their roots. As if they have never been born. Our hearts are tearing out of pain. We are feeling, we are undergoing in reality their agony of transition from life to death.[31]

The *Sonderkommando* members documented their lives in the crematoria with the intention of leaving evidence for posterity. In fact, many testimonies reveal that a prime factor in their will to survive was the motivation to give evidence and in so doing to take revenge on the Germans. The members of the *Sonderkommando* also assisted other prisoners to escape from the camp in order to disseminate the truth about Birkenau in the free world. There were two pairs of Jewish escapees—Alfred Wetzler and Rudolf Vrba (Walter Rosenberg), as well as Czeslaw Mordowicz and Arnost Rosin—who managed to escape in mid-1944 after having obtained important information from members of the *Sonderkommando*.[32]

Another unique group was the one that founded the underground movement in the *Sonderkommando*. This group initiated the uprising on 7 October 1944, the only armed uprising in the history of Auschwitz, during the course of which they destroyed the crematorium building No. IV, attempted a mass escape, and killed and wounded several SS men.[33] There was a sense of solidarity among the members of the *Sonderkommando*. Cases of betrayal and treason are unknown.

The *Sonderkommando* members acted in different ways in regards to the usage of belongings taken from the murdered: some became greedy and corrupt, while others did not take anything from the luggage of the dead Jews. Joseph Sackar, a Jew from Greece, told this with pride in his testimony.[34] The intention of the Germans to ruin the soul of the *Sonderkommando* prisoners failed—they did not quite succeed in pulling their victims with them into the abyss. In *Reading the Holocaust* Inga Clendinnen rightly points out that the *Sonderkommando* squads of around fifty members were small enough to develop some kind of esprit de corps: "some small sense of community and some recognition of the other as a comrade seems to have bloomed in that unlikely place, and that blooming lightened one corner of the darkness that was Auschwitz."[35]

Undermining the borders—working together in the crematoria

Auschwitz—the site where death, destruction, and extermination reigned supreme—also allowed some space where a pseudo-normal "working relationship" between the SS personnel and the *Sonderkommando* prisoners emerged. One of the most intriguing aspects in this research involves the encounters between the prisoners and their masters.

As mentioned, one aspect peculiar to the *Sonderkommando* was the relative proximity of the prisoners to their SS guards. Typical camp inmates did not necessarily see much of the SS. The SS man was somebody from whom the prisoner ran away, even when the SS man was still at a distance. Whenever an SS guard approached a prisoner it was almost always for torture or punishment.

Prisoner life was, as it is known, largely run and supervised through the system of prisoner functionaries: the *Kapos*, block seniors, and so on. This distance between the SS and most of the inmates was intentional: to prevent any softening effect that encounters with victims might have on SS guards. Distancing was one of the dehumanizing techniques that made the starving and dying people appear like a mass of anonymous *Untermenschen*. The pictorial instruction book of the SS described precisely how far the SS should be kept separate from single prisoners.[36]

In comparison to the whole camp, the situation in the crematoria was special. Only a handful of SS men were usually guarding and supervising the *Sonderkommando* during their work in relative proximity and over prolonged periods of time. More senior SS guards showed up whenever new transports arrived and when people were gassed. Those visits were made for the purposes of robbery and amusement. But for the most part during their shifts the *Sonderkommando* worked in the vicinity of very few SS guards. Hence, in the crematoria compound the distancing effect and the concomitant dehumanization of the prisoners were somewhat reduced. To the SS, the well-fed *Sonderkommando* members in proper clothing must have indeed appeared more like human beings than the emaciated and dying prisoners in the camp, who disgusted and frightened them.

251

In this context it seems worthwhile to shed some light on the range of inter-action between the *Sonderkommando* and their SS oppressors.

Forms of interaction

The same system of prisoner functionaries in the camp also structured life in the *Sonderkommando*. It was mainly the prisoner functionaries, that is, the *Kapos* or the *Vorarbeiter*, who had contact with the SS. They received the orders and passed them on to the *Sonderkommando*.[37] The common *Sonderkommando* worker did not actually interact with any of the SS. Survivors recall that they were mortally afraid of even getting near them. Georg van Ryk, a former member of the *Sonderkommando*, once said, "The SS were like gods. We did not even dare to look at the SS, otherwise they would have started to beat us immediately."[38]

The SS were unsurpassed in their cruelty and sadism. Otto Moll,[39] Friedrich Stiewitz, Walter Quackernack, Johann Gorges, Josef Schillinger, Josef Hustek, Kurschuss, and Scheinmetz (the first names of these two people are unknown) stand among the most despicable murderers who not only executed orders but also took great pleasure in their positions as "gods of the crematoria." They could maltreat, torture, and kill at will. No rules and boundaries restricted the barbarism of these people.

The era of Auschwitz was the "great opportunity" for the people on the lower rungs of German society: the baker, the gardener, the waiter, the little clerk— all of these "nobodies" in normal society suddenly became important, mighty figures who were responsible for life and death in Auschwitz. Their sadistic ideas were translated into practical realities, since the camps allowed the most extreme idea to be practiced, even those ideas that in any normal society before the Nazi time would be considered insane.

Accordingly, the camps were laboratories for the practice of cruelty that knew no bounds. The tendency toward acceptance and adaptation to the most barbarous crimes was widespread. This can be seen in many episodes, described, for instance, in *Seven Departments of Hell* written by Tadeusz Stabholz, a Jewish physician and survivor of three extermination camps: Treblinka, Majdanek, and Auschwitz. Such scenes are, for example, the killing of the prisoner Fink, the cruelty of chief physician Zentkeller, the slaughter of the Jews of Block 7 who tried to defend themselves before being gassed, and the running of the naked Jewish women to the gas chamber.[40] All of these scenes are characterized by beastly cruelty, which was aimed at humiliating the Jews and causing them the utmost suffering.

Moll—the spawn of insanity

The ultimate example of the cruel "Nazi spirit" is that of Otto Moll, the cremat-orium manager, who zealously sought to perfect the killing methods in Birkenau. The obsession with which he undertook the project of digging large pits near crematorium V to accelerate the corpses' burning is typical of the boundless insanity in the camps: the more extreme and cruel the innovation, the more the killers enjoyed it. Moll recruited members of the *Sonderkommando* and accompanied them to the excavation site. As long as his plans were not realized in a perfect manner, he would not be satisfied. The following observation is taken from Filip Müller's memoirs: "Even before work began, Moll paced nervously up and down the site. He inspected the area, going from place to place, consulting a large drawing which he had unfolded and comparing it with smaller drawings of the pits as well as of the rest of the extermination installations."[41]

Indeed, Moll was very excited and wanted the trench to be dug as fast and as well as possible. When the two large pits were finally finished—both forty to fifty meters long, about eight meters wide, and two meters deep—they were not yet ready for use, since "there followed the realization of the refinements thought up by the arch-exterminator's warped ingenuity."[42] Moll took great care with this project: together with his assistant, Eckardt, he climbed down into the pit and marked out a strip to be dug, "running lengthways down the middle from end to end."[43] This channel, which sloped to both sides from the middle, was thought to catch the human fat that would run from the burning corpses into two collecting pans. In his memoirs Müller comments, "The whole concept seemed quite inconceivable: a drain channel to catch human fat which in turn was to be used as fuel in order to obliterate as fast as possible all traces of these murderous deeds."[44]

But Moll was fascinated by this idea, which could mean a paramount improvement considering the effectiveness of one of his main tasks: the burning of the corpses. After all of the refinements were completed, Moll excitedly ordered two buckets of water to test whether the channel would work. But before reaching the collecting pan, the water slopped back and stopped. As Müller recalls, Moll was shocked:

> When he realized that something was wrong with the fall of the channel he grabbed the empty bucket and brought it down to the heads of any prisoners unfortunate enough to be standing within reach. . . . Moll too flung himself on the wretched prisoners in the pit who were cowering together with fright and kicked them viciously, shouting at the top of his voice: "You stupid shits, what's the matter with you, can't you even manage a simple job like that?"[45]

Finally Moll, the manager of the crematoria himself, climbed down into the pit, dressed in blue overalls, and supervised the alterations. Having finished, he ordered again the buckets of water and splashed them. This time the water drained completely. When Moll noticed the success, he relaxed, and as Müller remembers: "His face showed satisfaction and round his lips hovered something like a fleeting smile. He was obviously relieved and convinced that he had taken a big step forward on the road towards a solution of his task."[46] According to Müller, Moll didn't leave the scene immediately. Still standing at the pits he relished his success but, simultaneously, thought about possible problems that could prevent his system from working (e.g., the viscosity of the human fat).

Yaakov Gabai also witnessed Moll enjoying the sphere of insanity. He reports:

A large transport from Lodz came in on 30 August 1944, and that month 250 Polish *"Muselmänner"* were sent from several camps on the outskirts of Auschwitz. By that time, they were unable to move. Right then the commander of the crematorium, Moll of the SS, came and said, "Don't send these ones to the gas." He wanted to butcher them personally. First he beat them with the metal rod that he used to shatter the remaining bones of people who had died. Afterwards, he came down and asked one of the soldiers to give him a rifle and some bullets. He began to shoot. After he shot four or five of them, one of the *"Muselmänner"* called out, "Commander!" and Moll, who was a brutal sadist, answered, "Yes?"

"I've got a request."

"What do you want?"

"As you shoot my friends, I want to sing the Blue Danube Waltz."

"Be my guest! How jolly! It's even better to shoot with musical accompaniment," Moll answered. So the man sang—la-la-la—and Moll shot them all until it was the singer's turn. The last bullet hit him and finished him off.[47]

Scene of amusement and surrealism

The border between sanity and insanity is also demonstrated by the shocking fact that the crematoria building and the gas chambers also served as a site of entertainment and amusement. Senior SS people and high-ranking Nazi officials were attracted by this place. Indeed, the testimonies tell us, from time to time delegations arrived, wishing to be present at the dreadful killing of the Jews. The peephole in the door of the gas chamber enabled the dignified VIP guests to watch "live" how the victims choked and died inside. Actually most guests were pleased and enjoyed the "show." As we see, the killing centers were not only places of painful death but also a scene of circus and theater, like a cabaret stage—an insane mixture of crime, murder, and barbarism with laughter and satisfaction. This contradiction between cruel death and enjoyment is very similar to the bloody fights of the gladiators in the Roman amphitheaters.

Another example of the mixture of sanity and insanity concerning the relationship between the SS men and the prisoners is the existence of some Lithuanian SS men who fluently spoke Yiddish[48]—a language that was not only comprehensible to the German perpetrators, but was also one used by millions of Jews all over Europe; indeed, it was the language in which they expressed their sentiments, sorrows, and dreams. Moreover, the expressions with which these SS men chose to describe their actions denied the humanity of the murdered. They were referred to as *Stuecke* (pieces) and *Dreck* (dirt) that had to be *bearbeitet* (processed). We should keep this in mind as we now attempt to describe the surreal proximity that existed between some *Sonderkommando* and the SS guards in the crematoria.

The meeting of perpetrators and victims

Conversations between SS guards and *Sonderkommando* members were not uncommon. Lemke Pliszko relates that SS men would usually start conversations. There was little time to talk during the hard work, but sometimes during lunch breaks an SS guard would sit with the prisoners.[49] In his testimonies Pliszko describes an atmosphere that is more suggestive of an office environment. If we did not know the identity of this place, we would assume we were dealing with a friendly, polite place of hospitality. Pliszko says:

> We were sitting with the Germans round one table in the crematoria building. We were talking about several topics, including the work we were doing. An especially good mood prevailed when only one German was sitting with us. He himself did not murder Jews. He did not pour the gas inside the chambers. As long as he was alone—he was even friendly. The minute a second German came—he changed his attitude immediately. Being alone he spoke totally differently.[50]

But even though the prisoners used to sit together with the SS men, even at one table, there was always a certain feeling of insecurity: "When they came in the morning, they said 'Good morning!' to us. On the other hand, the same man who said 'Good morning' also could beat us when he was ordered to. Usually we did not get beatings, but sometimes we did get hit with a stick. One of the Germans even sent us to bring the stick to him."[51]

Pliszko recalls one particular SS guard who even emphasized that he would regret what he did, and that he was forced to do it. "Almost everybody said that, at least those that were good, not the evil bastards, of course."[52] This seems like the typical statement from an SS man, heard a thousand times over in the Nuremberg trials, but in the immediate context of the encounter between the prisoner and the SS, such talk—and already the fact that they talked to each other at all, in a relatively normal, human manner—seems surprising. In describing this "humane manner," Lemke Pliszko points out, "Mainly the SS men with lower ranks hinted to the *Sonderkommando* prisoners from time to time that they were dissatisfied."[53]

There are other examples: Morris Kesselman describes that, naturally, he distrusted most of the SS, except for one guard from Holland, with whom he even talked in a more personal manner, about their families, where they came from, and so on. After being bribed with alcohol, this SS man even assisted Morris in smuggling food from the *Sonderkommando* to other camp inmates.[54] Kesselman's statement concurs with Gabai's description illustrating that they interacted with their guards quite well: "They were with us all the time and they were really OK. We had no problems at all with them. One of the guards was from Holland, a good guy, really fine. We always asked ourselves how this Dutchman could possibly be an SS man."[55]

Gabai goes on talking about this specific SS guard: "The SS man from the Netherlands . . . was still a boy—twenty-two, twenty-three at the most. . . . He never said a bad word to anyone. A friend, a buddy . . . he even gave me his weapon and said, 'Take it. You may play with it.' "[56] This Dutch SS man is often mentioned with overtones of appreciation by survivors of the *Sonderkommando*. Such statements also align with those of Miklos Nyiszli, the Jewish doctor who worked in the crematoria and who writes in his memoirs, "Taken individually, any SS guard in the crematorium could be bought."[57] The feeling about the vulnerability of almost every SS man to bribery was an opinion shared by other survivors, too.

Indeed, there was a kind of familiarity between the *Sonderkommando* and the SS, as Nyiszli stresses in a different context: "Three months in the same camp and in the same milieu had created, in spite of everything, a certain intimacy between us [Nyiszli and Muhsfeld, SS-*Oberscharführer*]. Besides, the Germans generally appreciate capable people, and, as long as they need them, respect them to a certain extent, even in the KZ."[58] This "intimacy" even encouraged Nyiszli to ask *Oberscharführer* Muhsfeld to save the life of a young girl who had amazingly survived the gassing in the gas chamber (account follows below).

The special kind of familiarity between the SS guards and the *Sonderkommando* prisoners is also well expressed by Lemke Pliszko, who testified: "The Germans who worked with us knew our first names. . . . The Germans called me Lemke and I called him with his rank. He knew the names of everybody. . . . The relations with the Germans were normal like in normal factories. When one of them wanted to call me, he said: '*Lemke, komm her!*' ['Lemke, come here!']."[59] In this context one should mention that the *Sonderkommando* prisoners actually invented nicknames for the guarding SS men—although Eliezer Eisenschmidt stresses that "giving nicknames didn't mean we felt closer or more confident with them."[60]

The prisoners and the SS men met almost daily, worked physically proximate to each other, and thus knew each other quite well. These nicknames—mostly relating to the physiognomy of the Germans ("The Small One," "The Big One," and "Roiter" because of his red face[61])—were intended to alert fellow prisoners before the appearance of a brutal SS man. As Morris Kesselman explains, it was thereby also possible to speak about the SS men, even behind their backs, without them realizing it. Besides, it was a kind of relaxation from the heavy, constant pressure that ruled over the work in the crematoria. In a way, the nicknames enabled the prisoners to undermine the power and authority of their tormentors. Taking into consideration the fact that a phenomenon typical of social relations between people in normal times was also adapted inside the killing centers leads to the conclusion that giving nicknames was part of a psychological self-defense in order to survive. Even in the darkest areas of the crematoria, the sense of humor did not disappear.

As mentioned above, as long as the low-ranking SS men were alone with the *Sonderkommando*, relationships would seem quite relaxed. The moment other guards or higher-ranking officers showed up the atmosphere changed swiftly. The plane on which this kind of more intimate interaction occurred was brittle and could collapse at any instant. Again Lemke Pliszko describes relatively personal encounters with one SS man from Lithuania: "We [the *Sonderkommando*] did not have any bad intentions, neither did he [the Lithuanian SS]. But we were also careful with those that were not too dangerous to us. Because one slip, one wrong word could still mean your death."[62]

Treading this thin red line—working "together" with the SS men for months or even years, talking to them but also fearing death—illustrates the paradoxical mixture of normality and abnormality that the prisoners experienced in the crematoria. Usually, the members of the *Sonderkommando* were afraid of approaching SS men. Thus they were even more surprised when the SS people then acted in an unexpectedly humane manner. Nyiszli remembers such a situation in the crematoria dormitory after a "social" evening with alcohol and talk, when SS men making rounds stopped and reminded the prisoners it was time to go to bed. Normally such reminding was delivered with punishment. Here it almost seems to be a polite request to switch off the lights.[63] Lemke Pliszko reports on a similar experience: "In 1944 once a German came to our block and he wished us all the best. So the *Blockälteste* [the prisoner supervisor of the block] answered: 'We wish you the same.' "[64]

This "friendly" treatment did not occur by accident. Apart from the constant reign of terror, the SS certainly also had an interest in playing "good guys" vis-à-vis the *Sonderkommando* prisoners so as to be able to enrich themselves on a personal level and more generally to keep the *Sonderkomnando* operations running smoothly without any disturbance. This twisted intention also shines through in the following scenario, mentioned by Yehuda Bacon. He recalls that "prisoners, block seniors, and the SS used to play football and ping-pong together in the Gypsy Camp, when they were offduty on Sundays."[65] Primo Levi also refers to this unusual event:

> Nyiszli tells how during a work break he attended a soccer game between the SS and the *Sonderkommando*, that is to say, between a group representing the SS on guard at the crematorium and a group representing the Special Squad. Other men of the SS and the rest of the Squad are present at the game. They take sides, bet, applaud, urge the players on as if, rather than at the gates of hell, the game were taking place on the village green.[66]

The following scene also illustrates the grotesque coexistence of annihilation and a seemingly normal social interaction between the perpetrators and the victims. Gabai, who was forced to work as a *Heizer* (stoker) and who was accordingly ordered to burn the corpses in the ovens, recalls:

> Once they brought a girl from Hungary who had a two-day-old baby. She knew she was about to be murdered. We had nothing to do that night. We sat around idly and offered her a chair to sit down, some food, and cigarettes. She told us that she was a singer and talked for about half an hour. We sat in front of the furnaces. Next to us sat a Dutch SS man (the one mentioned above), a rather nice, likeable guy. He also listened in. When the story was over, he stood up and said, "Very well, we can't sit here like this forever; now it's death's turn." She was asked what she preferred, that we kill the baby first or her. She said, "Me first. I don't want to see my child dead." Then the Dutchman stood up, brought over the rifle, shot her, and threw her into the furnace. Then he picked up the baby, bang-bang, and that was that.[67]

This horrible story contains the seeds of insanity that prevailed in the undressing rooms and gas chambers. We find in it the quick charge between politeness and bestiality, the ability of the SS man to be human and murderous almost at the same time, the mixture and duality of life and death in one location.

Considering the more exceptional and extreme statements, where *Sonderkommando* survivors talk about a "relaxed" attitude and even show some kind of "solidarity" and understanding vis-à-vis the SS, one should bear in mind that such victims often spoke well of their tormentors in later testimonies. Filip Müller, for example, writes in his memoirs, "We prisoners and [the SS man] Starck were worlds apart. . . . [But] I often wondered how it was possible for this young man, scarcely older than myself, to be so cruel. . . . He was no doubt a *victim* of the Nazi propaganda."[68]

The partial identification with the tormentor, the portrayal of both (oneself and one's tormentor) as victims, all of these are ways to ease the trauma and to make sense of the crime and the suffering. Psychologists have examined such phenomena, referring to them as the "Stockholm syndrome," to mention but one name.[69] Nevertheless, Müller's statement is exceptional—no other *Sonderkommando* survivors share his attempt to find some kind of understanding toward the German perpetrators.

Yet, in depicting instances of human interaction between the SS and the *Sonderkommando*, we intend to point out an apparent paradox. In the very center of the inferno, in the crematorium compound, there also existed a certain margin that helped the prisoners deny and repress to some degree the unimaginably horrible acts in which they were forced to participate.

In fact, this seemingly paradoxical aspect also extends to the ways in which the *Sonderkommando* prisoners related to each other. As mentioned in the beginning of this essay, on the one hand the survivors recall themselves as having acted as human machines, shell-shocked, traumatized, unable to act or do anything about their situation. On the other hand, they also tell of scenes that appear in stark contrast to that of the human robot—moments of friendship and mutual solidarity, evenings with social gatherings and songs, and, of course, the underground activities leading up to the uprising in the *Sonderkommando* in autumn of 1944. We shall now map out these human spaces inside the inferno, which helped the *Sonderkommando* prisoners to retain their sanity, to keep their strength, and, ultimately, to survive.

Relationships within the *Sonderkommando*

Survivors' testimonies about their daily routine in the *Sonderkommando* show the immense pressure exerted on the prisoners during their work shifts. It was sheer physical toil under the most traumatic and gruesome conditions that one can imagine. Yaakov Gabai remembers: "We worked like robots there. I had to stay strong in order to survive and relate everything that had happened in this hell. Reality proves that people are crueler than animals. Yeah, we were animals. We didn't have emotions. Sometimes we doubted whether we were still human."[70]

Chazan recalls the same experience: "I'd stopped being human by then. If I'd been human, I couldn't have endured it for even one minute. We kept going because we'd lost our humanity."[71] Leon Cohen makes a similar argument: "During that time we had no emotions. We were totally drained. We blocked up our hearts; we were dehumanized. We worked like machines. We were human beings devoid of human emotion. We were really animals, not people." Finally Cohen concludes, "We'd become robots."[72]

Yet, time and again their accounts also reveal aspects about everyday life in the crematoria, where the *Sonderkommando* did not quite feel like numb and passive human ghosts. Even when acting like machines and repressing their inner feelings, the death that ruled over the scene was covering all. The pain, sorrow, and grief were certainly penetrating the prisoners' hearts.

Those prisoners on day-shift duty were principally free and could do in their barracks whatever they wanted after the evening roll call. We would expect them to be depressed, broken, and on the edge of insanity. Yet there were also times when they had conversations, when they talked about their past lives, when they sought some consolation in the solidarity that existed among them. They were not totally alone in this horror.

A sense of solidarity and familiarity

Describing the sense of solidarity among the *Sonderkommando* prisoners, Lemke Pliszko recalls: "I knew everyone in our block—we were together like a family."[73] This is illustrated by the fact that prisoners usually addressed each other personally by their names, as Kesselman remembers.[74] The survivors generally confirm that the camaraderie among the *Sonderkommando* prisoners was greater than in other units of the camp because they were so isolated and shared the same fate: the verdict of death.

Prisoners in the *Sonderkommando* gathered in small groups, often being from the same town or area with a similar background. They knew that they could trust each other. Yet the sense of solidarity very much emerged from the feeling that they were all together in this traumatic inferno and also, in a way, from the certainty that none of them would survive—although this awareness was mostly suppressed.

The *Sonderkommando* was, however, not a homogenous unit. Rather, it consisted of people from many different countries and backgrounds. Whenever conflicts occurred, it was usually between such groups, and cases of concrete violence among prisoners are described mainly between Jewish prisoners and the small group of Christian Poles in the *Sonderkommando*, who held the position of *Vorarbeiter*.

Jewish prisoners, although from different countries of origin, could generally speak Yiddish with each other. The only exception was the large group of the Jews from Greece who spoke only Greek or Ladino, with whom the others could initially hardly communicate. The Greeks were a relatively closed group and mostly kept to themselves due to language and cultural differences. Despite such difficulties with communication, the relations between groups from different countries are described as relaxed and friendly. Even with their many different backgrounds, people somehow found their accepted places in the *Sonderkommando*, as Abraham Dragon confirms:

> We got along fine with all the people from different countries. We communicated [with the Greeks] largely by using gestures. They could do as much physically demanding work like us, because they had suffered at home and had become hardened. People from Germany or France could not work as hard, and the *Kapo* arranged for them to work as hair cutters or sorting clothes, things that did not involve hard physical labor.[75]

"Social evenings"

As already mentioned, after work hours the prisoners were mostly so exhausted that they just had something to eat and went to sleep. One would converse mainly with the people in the neighboring bunks. Nevertheless, Joseph Sackar states: "One cannot say [that] we had lived like robots."[76] After having finished work, the *Sonderkommado* prisoners could sit together and talk and think about their situation, their work in the crematoria, their experiences, and what was done to them.[77] There was space to think about what happened to them— and the prisoners indeed reflected on their fate. Those were moments of self-awareness and self-reflection. In an interview Eisenschmidt reports on a feeling of sadness that crept back in when he saw groups walking toward the crematoria building since they reminded him of his family.[78]

The existence of religious life in the killing center also contradicts the picture of passive human machines. Gradowski reports in his secret writings that the religious Jews insisted on continuing the tradition of making a *Minyan* three times a day in one of the crematoria buildings.[79] It seems that the description of the "robot-like" routine would mainly refer to the actual working process, where emotions had to be suppressed to be able to stand the work among all the corpses. In the evening after work some prisoners tried to abandon their "robot behavior."

Sometimes there were also social occasions where prisoners would come together and sing, as Yehuda Bacon recalls, "mainly sentimental songs, about our previous lives and about freedom."[80] Many other survivors highlight the regular singing of the Greek groups in the evenings after work, where even some of the German SS guards were present. Lemke Pliszko, among others, confirms that "the Germans often stood at the door and listened when the Greeks were singing."[81] He goes on recalling: "After duty in our barrack, we were singing Yiddish songs. The Greek prisoners were singing and dancing until late at night. They knew how to sing. They sang for many hours."[82]

Nevertheless, from time to time the members of the *Sonderkommando* who had become accustomed to their work in the crematoria were reminded of their former life, the life outside of the crematoria, when prisoners from other units appeared. Indeed, the link between the "normal" world and that of the *Sonderkommando* is illustrated by the few prisoners who succeeded in entering the barracks of the *Sonderkommando*. Yehuda Bacon, Mordechai Ciechanower, Stanley Glogover, and the other curious, naïve youngsters were mainly interested in the food but also in the human warmth that the *Sonderkommando* prisoners could provide. As Bacon remembers, it was very dangerous for members of the *Sonderkommando* to be in contact with other prisoners, due to their knowledge of every detail of the killing process.[83]

Despite this, contact between the *Sonderkommando* and other prisoners continued. Children working at the nearby "Canada," such as fourteen-year-old Yehuda Bacon, sometimes received permission from the *Sonderkommando* prisoner on duty to enter the *Sonderkommando* block. Although some prisoners were unwilling to speak about their work in the crematoria, Bacon got information about what was going on there. A few people told him about their experiences and even about their feelings at this unique place, where sanity and insanity are so close to each other that it is nearly impossible to distinguish one from the other.

The gap between sanity and insanity is well demonstrated by the astonishing and rare case of a young girl who survived the gas chambers.[84] When the gas pellets were thrown inside the chamber, she fell on the floor and, by chance, was not poisoned. After the gassing, when the *Sonderkommando* prisoners started taking the dead bodies to the ovens, they suddenly discovered that the girl was still breathing. All of the members of the *Sonderkommando* were shocked—this definitely was the first time that something like this had happened. The chief of the gas chamber commando ran to Dr. Miklos Nyiszli, a physician who was both a member of the *Sonderkommando* and simultaneously Mengele's pathological expert. He gave the girl injections and after a few minutes she regained consciousness. Of course she was confused, since she could not grasp what had happened to her. Nyiszli asked her a few questions and learned that she was from Transylvania and was sixteen years old. Immediately the question arose about what to do with her. It was clear that a girl could not stay with the crematorium's *Sonderkommando*. Suddenly SS-*Oberscharführer* Muhsfeld appeared supervising the work and saw the gathering of prisoners. When he entered the room he also noticed the girl. Nyiszli knew there was almost no chance to save the life of the girl, but since he felt respected by Muhsfeld because of his work as a physician, he tried to explain the situation and asked Muhsfeld to do something for the child. When the SS man asked him what he proposed to do, Nyiszli pointed out the possibility of putting her in front of the crematoria gate, where a commando of women always worked. Nyiszli suggested that it would not be hard for her to disappear in the crowd. But Muhsfeld was convinced that a girl of sixteen years would not understand the circumstances of her survival and instead would immediately start telling where she just had come from and what she had experienced in the gas chambers. Finally Muhsfeld concluded: "There's no way of getting round it. The child will have to die."[85] Half an hour later the girl was shot dead.

Epilogue

"It must sound terrible and it's hard to understand how we lived together with our murderers. But anything was possible in Auschwitz."[86] These words of Yaakov Gabai are a concise description of the problem that forms the basis of this article. The extermination camps were sites in which the Nazi spirit flourished and bloomed in its most extreme way: the camps were the essence of the Nazi regime and Nazi ideology and the crimes committed there against Jews and other victims were a compulsory outcome of this ideological belief. The creation of the death factory commandos, the *Sonderkommando*, must be considered one of the worst crimes perpetrated by the Nazis, as Primo Levi justifiably wrote in his famous chapter on "The Gray Zone" in *The Drowned and the Saved*. In the daily activity of those *Sonderkommando* prisoners was a combination of normality and abnormality. The decision to eliminate all Jews in the world was insane in and of itself. The practical way of executing this intention was a direct continuation of this madness. The statements about the seemingly ongoing everyday life in the crematoria, and especially about the relations between some *Sonderkommando* prisoners and the SS, are surprising.

For a deeper understanding of the reality of the *Sonderkommando*, it is important to consider not only the aspects that describe how these innocent people were turned into paralyzed human machines. One should also link this image of the *Sonderkommando* to that of the heroic fighters who organized the uprising in the crematoria, or that of the *Sonderkommando* prisoners who assisted others to escape, or those who wrote down all of the horrors with persistence in order to deliver to the next generations a record of what took place. Survivors frequently claim that those who did not go through the same horror will never be able to understand what they experienced in the camps. The case with the *Sonderkommando* is even more difficult to comprehend. The technical aspect of the death factories is comprehendible, but what lies beyond our empirical abilities of understanding is how the *Sonderkommando* people could persevere. It seems impossible to grasp how a human being could have been able to work for months and even for years in the death factory. Nevertheless, we must make an effort and try to shed light onto each of these unprecedented phenomena that happened in the Shoah. The few survivors of the *Sonderkommando* are unique Auschwitz survivors, and through their testimonies we gain a deeper insight into the Shoah, into ourselves, and into the world in which we live.

Notes

1 Primo Levi, *The Drowned and the Saved*, trans. Raymond Rosenthal (New York: Summit Books, 1988), 53.
2 Gideon Greif, *We Wept Without Tears*, trans. Naftali Greenwood (New Haven, CT: Yale University Press, 2005). See the German edition, *Wir weinten tränenlos . . .: Augenzeugenberichte des jüdisichen "Sonderkommandos" in Auschwitz* (Frankfurt am. Main: Fischer, 1999), 221. Hereafter I cite mainly the page numbers of the German edition.
3 Auschwitz-Birkenau State Museum, *KL Auschwitz Seen by the SS* (Warsaw, 1991), 77.
4 Some members of the *Sonderkommando* wrote clandestine notes, which they buried at Birkenau. Those notes were partly discovered after the war. Among the main chroniclers were Zalman Gradowski, Leib Langfuss, and Zalman Lewental.
5 Ber Mark, *The Scrolls of Auschwitz*, trans. Sharon Neemani (Tel Aviv: Am Oved, 1985), 125.
6 See Wolfgang Sofsky, *Die Ordnung des Terrors—Das Konzentrationslager* (Frankfurt am Main, 1997), 307–10. The English edition is *The Order of Terror: The Concentration Camp*, trans. William Templer (Princeton, NJ: Princeton University Press, 1997). See also Ota Kraus and Erich Kulka, *The Death Factory: Documents on Auschwitz* (New York: Pergamon, 1966).
7 Yehuda Bacon, interview with Gideon Greif (G.G.), Jerusalem, 30 May 2003.
8 Levi, *The Drowned and the Saved*, 53.
9 See Eugen Kogon, Hermann Langbein, and Adelbert Rückerl, eds., *Nazi Mass Murder: A Documentary History of the Use of Poison Gas*, trans. Mary Scott and Caroline Lloyd-Morris (New Haven, CT: Yale University Press, 1994).
10 Rudolf Höss, *Death Dealer: The Memoirs of the SS Kommandant at Auschwitz*, ed. Steven Paskuly and trans. Andrew Pollinger (New York: Da Capo Press, 1996), 160–61.
11 Greif, *Wir weinten tränenlos . . .*, 68.
12 Ibid., 341.
13 Ibid., 303–4.
14 Ibid., 244.

15 Ibid., 245.
16 Ibid., 123.
17 Ibid., 124.
18 Ibid., 196.
19 Interview with G.G., Kibbutz Givat HaShlosha, 21 November 2003.
20 Interview with G.G., 21 May 2004.
21 Greif, *Wir weinten tränenlos* . . ., 353.
22 Ibid., 303.
23 Ibid., 171.
24 Interview with G.G., Kibbutz Givat HaShlosha, 25 July 2000.
25 Greif, *Wir weinten tränenlos* . . ., 197–98.
26 Ibid., 247.
27 Greif, *We Wept Without Tears*, Hebrew edition (Jerusalem: Yad Vashem, 1999), 354.
28 Ibid.
29 Ibid.
30 Ibid., 83–84.
31 Ibid., 58.
32 See, for example, Henryk Swiebocki, *London Has Been Informed: Reports by Auschwitz Escapees* (Oswiecim: Auschwitz-Birkenau State Museum, 1997); Rudolf Vrba, *I Escaped from Auschwitz* (Fort Lee, NJ: Barricade Books, 2002); Erich Kulka, *Escape from Auschwitz* (South Hadley, MA: Bergin and Garvey, 1986).
33 Andreas Kilian, "*Der Sonderkommando-Aufstand in Auschwitz-Birkenau* . . ." ("The Uprising of the *Sonderkommando* in Auschwitz-Birkenau . . ."), published in the bulletin *Lagergemeinschaft Auschwitz—Freundeskreis Auschwitz* (Camp Community Auschwitz—Circle of Friends Auschwitz), 2002–3.
34 Greif, *Wir weinten tränenlos* . . ., 84
35 Inga Clendinnen, *Reading the Holocaust* (Cambridge: Cambridge University Press, 1999), 74.
36 The original is at the Auschwitz-Birkenau Museum archive, MPMAB, section "Höss Trial."
37 On the functionaries in Auschwitz see Hermann Langbein, *People in Auschwitz*, trans. Harry Zohn (Chapel Hill: University of North Carolina Press, 2004).
38 Interview with G.G. and Andreas Kilian, Amsterdam, 8 May 1996.
39 For a biographical sketch see *KL Auschwitz Seen by the SS*, 245–46.
40 Greif, *We Wept Without Tears*, Hebrew edition, 136, 146, 149–50.
41 Filip Müller, *Eyewitness Auschwitz: Three Years in the Gas Chambers*, ed. and trans. Susanne Flatauer (Chicago: Ivan R. Dee, 1999), 129.
42 Ibid., 130.
43 Ibid.
44 Ibid.
45 Ibid., 131.
46 Ibid., 132.
47 Greif, *Wir weinten tränenlos* . . ., 203.
48 Lemke Pliszko, interview with G.G., Kibbutz Givat HaShlosha, 16 December 2003.
49 Ibid.
50 Interview with G.G., 21 May 2004.
51 Ibid.
52 Interview with G.G., Kibbutz Givat HaShlosha, 9 May 2002.
53 Interview with G.G., Kibbutz Givat HaShlosha, 25 July 2000.
54 Morris Kesselman, "Memorials Aren't All in Stone," as told to Arlene Lehto, unpublished manuscript, 124.
55 Greif, *Wir weinten tränenlos* . . ., 217.
56 Ibid., 219–20.

57 Dr. Miklos Nyiszli, *Auschwitz: A Doctor's Eyewitness Account*, trans. Tibère Kremer and Richard Seaver (New York: Arcade Publishing, 1993), 75.
58 Ibid., 117.
59 Interview with G.G., 21 May 2004.
60 Interview with G.G., Givatayim, 12 December 2003.
61 Interview with G.G., Kibbutz Givat HaShlosha, 21 November 2003.
62 Interview with G.G., Kibbutz Givat HaShlosha, 16 December 2003.
63 Nyiszli, *Auschwitz*, 46.
64 Interview with G.G., Kibbutz Givat HaShlosha, 25 July 2000.
65 Interview with G.G., Jerusalem, 19 July 1999.
66 Levi, *The Drowned and the Saved*, 54–55.
67 Greif, *Wir weinten tränenlos . . .*, 204.
68 Müller, *Eyewitness Auschwitz*, 30.
69 Encarta, *World English Dictionary* (1999), 1759.
70 Greif, *Wir weinten tränenlos . . .*, 221.
71 Ibid., 312.
72 Ibid., 356.
73 Interview with G.G., Kibbutz Givat HaShlosha, 16 December 2003.
74 Interview with G.G., Miami Beach, 6 December 1999.
75 Interview with G.G., Ramat Gan, 2 January 2004.
76 Interview with G.G., Holon, 26 December 2003.
77 Eliezer Eisenschmidt, interview with G.G., Givatayim, 12 December 2003.
78 Ibid.
79 Greif, *We Wept Without Tears*, Hebrew edition, 88–91.
80 Interview with G.G., Jerusalem, 30 May 2003.
81 Interview with G.G., Kibbutz Givat HaShlosha, 25 July 2000.
82 Interview with G.G., 21 May 2004.
83 Interview with G.G., Jerusalem, 30 May 2003.
84 Nyiszli, *Auschwitz*, 114–20.
85 Ibid., 120.
86 Greif, *Wir weinten tränenlos . . .*, 220.

Part III

AFTERMATH
Testimony, justice, and continuity

13

WARTIME LIES AND OTHER TESTIMONIES

Jewish-Christian relations in Buczacz, 1939–44

Omer Bartov

Even before the war ended, thousands of Jews who had somehow survived the concerted Nazi attempt to murder them, often with a great deal of local collaboration, sought to bear witness to the ostensibly indescribable events of genocide, to recall the multitudes who had been massacred – not least their own family members – and to put on record the names and actions of the perpetrators. Bearing witness has a long tradition in Jewish history, in many cases related to past events of persecution and destruction. But the Holocaust was an event of such scale and magnitude that its very unprecedented nature made it seem impossible to put into words, and made accounts of it seem insufficient and partial.

There was, then, a vast gap between the urge of survivors to tell what had happened and the ability to encompass the event in individual testimonies, no matter how many. This was compounded by the fact that while the Nazis sought to murder the Jews wherever they found them, the nature of the killing, and the character of the communities that were slaughtered, were very different: the Jews of Salonica or Paris, Eastern Galicia or Norway, Rhodes or Amsterdam, may have all ended up in extermination camps – although many of them, especially in Eastern Europe, were in fact killed close to where they lived; but they had evolved distinct ways of life, cultures, and traditions, which would also be reflected in how survivors of such communities recalled the catastrophe.

Nevertheless, even as the killing was still going on, people tried to write and collect accounts of the events, not least because the goal of the Nazis was not only to murder all the Jews but also to assassinate their memory, to deprive them of their own history and remembrance, so as to be able to either write them out of the past altogether or to rewrite it through the Nazi prism. Hence, testimony became more than telling what happened but rather constituted a form of resistance against total Nazi obliteration and distortion. Yet while these accounts were being collected throughout Europe, and especially in its eastern part, where most of the Jews had lived and were murdered, another factor came into play, which in turn relegated testimonies to a secondary position, if not, indeed, to marginality or irrelevance.

This *factor was historiography, that is, the professional writing by trained and accredited historians of the events of the war and the genocide of the Jews. Historians have an ambivalent attitude toward personal accounts, especially by men, women, and children of lesser rank and importance. On the one hand, such accounts can lend invaluable color and texture to an historical account that may otherwise appear too dry, relying on official documents of a more political and bureaucratic nature. On the other hand, personal accounts can only provide very narrow views of the larger events and, by definition, are subjective, potentially biased, and, especially at a distance of time, may contain many errors of fact and detail, even assuming that they are truthful, which they may not always be. In reconstructing such a complex, continent-wide, and unprecedented case of genocide as the Holocaust, therefore, historians focused for a long time on the official documentation – much of it initially stemming from the vast collection of documents compiled for the Nuremberg Tribunal in 1945 – while perceiving the heartbreaking, but in their judgment, not particularly useful or accurate accounts by individual survivors, as far less pertinent to their scholarship.*

This, however, meant that many of the histories written of World War II and the Holocaust lacked the personal angle, and made little or no use of testimonies, which would have rescued such reconstructions from being told largely from the perspective of the perpetrators, that is, those who produced the allegedly objective official documents historians prefer. This bias toward archival documentation and perpetrator history therefore determined the nature of the historiography. Among the most important repercussions of this tendency was that the nature and significance of genocide on the local level, and what it could tell us about the event as a whole, was largely missed or misunderstood. It also meant that the voices of the surviving victims, who had striven to leave a record, specifically for historians, of their experiences, so that these experiences would be included in and inform the historical record, were in large part ignored and dismissed. As the following chapter shows, once we integrate testimonies into the record, we are not only fulfilling a moral duty that, as historians, we should feel bound to. We can also create a much more complex, nuanced, troubling, and accurate picture of the relationship between perpetrators, victims, and bystanders on the local level in vast swaths of Eastern Europe in which mass murder, gratuitous violence, unbound cruelty, and shameless greed became a routine aspect of everyday life, yet where occasional instances of courage, selflessness, and altruism, also ensured that some people remained to tell the tale, now finally being picked up and retold by historians.

I

The borderlands of Eastern Europe were sites of interaction between a multiplicity of ethnic and religious groups. For city- and town-dwellers, as much as for villagers, living side by side with people who spoke a different language and worshipped God differently was part of their own way of life and that of their ancestors. Ethnicity and religion often also meant a different position within the socioeconomic scale and thus differentiation, bringing with it resentment and envy, status and wealth, poverty and subjugation. As new national narratives began to supplement the old religious and social differentiation between groups, they also provided a new retrospective meaning to the past and a new urgency about mending the present in a manner that would conform to the perceived historical rights and correct former injustices. In the national movements' fantasy, the future belonged to them, or not at all. Past coexistence, which had been the norm, with all its benefits and shortcomings, friction and cooperation, as well as occasional outbursts of violence, came to be seen as unnatural, as a problem to be solved, often by radical social surgery. Cutting off unwanted, seemingly malignant, and allegedly foreign elements would, it was said, enable the newly discovered and supposedly eternal national body to thrive.

It is, however, exceedingly difficult to understand and analyze how this transformation occurred on the ground and how it was perceived by its social protagonists. How was it that zones of coexistence were turned into communities of ethnic cleansing and genocide? To be sure, it was largely external forces, in the shape of occupying states or far-flung national movements, that determined the general course of events and provided the ideological impetus for population policies, mass displacement, and mass murder. But the way such policies and ideas were implemented on the ground had to do not only with the interaction between perpetrators and victims but also with the actions and interactions of the different local groups upon whom these policies were enacted. A close look at what happened in small communities on Europe's eastern borderlands provides us with much insight into the social dynamics of interethnic communities at times of extreme violence. Yet such a view from below of borderland communities also necessitates making use of records of the past often eschewed by historians.

This article makes a case for the integration of personal accounts, or testimonies, into the historical reconstruction of the Holocaust as documents equal in validity to other forms of documentation. By testimonies, I mean all forms of evidence provided by individual protagonists in historical events. These include contemporary accounts and diaries, as well as postwar interviews; written, oral, audio, and videotaped testimonies; courtroom witness accounts; and memoirs. Such testimonies were given by people belonging to all three categories we have come to associate with the Holocaust and other genocides, namely, victims, perpetrators, and bystanders. But to a large extent, one benefit of using materials of this kind is that they largely, though not entirely, undermine this very categorization.

From the point of view of the historian, the single most important benefit of using testimonies is that they bring into history events that would otherwise remain completely unknown, since they are missing from more conventional documentation found in archives and mostly written by the perpetrators or organizers of genocide. Hence personal accounts can at times save events from oblivion. But they also provide a very different perspective on events that *are* known from conventional documentation. This other perspective has in turn two additional advantages. First, it may serve as a factual correction to official accounts; second, it provides the historian with a different vantage point and thereby helps in producing a richer and more complete—in a sense, a three-dimensional—reconstruction of the event as a whole. Finally, by virtue of being personal, or subjective, such testimonies provide insight into the lives and minds of men, women, and children who experienced the events and, thus, tell us much more than any official document about the mental landscape of the period, the psychology of the protagonists, and the views and perceptions of others.

Historians have traditionally been wary of using testimonies as historical evidence. Some have eschewed their use altogether, calling them subjective and therefore unreliable.[1] Others have preferred to use only testimonies offered soon after to the event itself and have largely avoided those given decades later.[2] Others still, most conventionally, have used personal accounts only to illustrate the nature of an historical event whose reconstruction is based on seemingly more reliable documents culled from official archives.[3] This practice, to my mind, has greatly impoverished our understanding of the Holocaust, as it would that of any other historical event. There is no reason to believe that official contemporary documents written by Gestapo, SS, Wehrmacht, or German administrative officials are any more accurate or objective, or any less subjective and biased, than accounts given by those they were trying to kill. Moreover, the use of testimonies only as confirmation of events already known through other documentation condemns to oblivion events only known through testimonies. Finally, the quest to understand the mentality and motivation of the perpetrators, which has already produced a small cottage industry, would have benefited a great deal from knowing what their victims said about them and how these victims described the perpetrators' actions. And of course, testimonies can tell us a great deal about the lives of those subjected to German occupation and the relations between the different ethnic groups that came under German rule.

As noted, some historians have argued that testimonies, if used at all, are more reliable the closer they are given to the time of the event. Those given decades later are said to be suspect both because of the eroding effects of time on memory and because of the cumulative influence of other forms of representation and commemoration that mold the content and form of an individual's recollection. There is of course some truth to this argument. But anyone who has worked with large numbers of testimonies will know that there are two major qualifications to this assertion. First, and especially in the case of those who survived as young teenagers or even children—that is, those most likely to have still been alive six decades later—their experiences in the Holocaust could often be recounted in full only after they reached greater maturity, thanks to the healing effects of time on their traumatized souls, and only long after rebuilding their lives and establishing new families. Second, in some though not all cases, testimonies given decades after the event have all the freshness and vividness of a first account that one may find in some early postwar testimonies. This can be explained not least by the very fact that the memory of the event was kept sealed inside the mind and never exposed to the light of day through telling and retelling, let alone contaminated by the "noise in the system" of external discourse and representation.

These "memory-boxes" were finally unlocked and opened up due to the advancing age of the witnesses and their desire to leave a record of events, whether only to their own children and (especially) to their grandchildren, or more generally to posterity, at a cultural moment more attuned to listening, designated by one scholar "the era of the witness."[4] Such testimonies are also strongly motivated by the urge to recall and inscribe in memory and history the names of the murdered that would otherwise sink into total oblivion with the passing of the witness, and at times also to record the names and actions of long-forgotten perpetrators, collaborators, and especially of rescuers. Hence such testimonies contain much of the clarity and emotional impact of accounts given immediately in the wake of the events.

There has been, of course, a great deal of writing about testimonies as a form of memory, a confrontation with trauma, a literary device, a means to gain insight into the psychology of survivors, or even as a therapeutic tool.[5] But what I am arguing for is that testimonies are also historical documents of invaluable importance that have been grossly underused by historians, especially in the case of the Holocaust, despite the fact that this is a historical event that has produced a vast amount of such materials. Clearly, personal accounts do not tell a single story and are full of contradictions, errors, misjudgments, and untruths, though no less so than any other document. They should be treated with the same care and suspicion as any other piece of evidence pulled out of an archive, but also with the same respect as yet another more or less important piece in the puzzle of the past. That they are concerned with traumatic events should not deter us from using them; quite to the contrary, the nature of those events must indicate to us that we would never be able to fathom them without making full use of the accounts of those who experienced them.

Integrating all these materials into a single text is clearly a difficult and complex undertaking. What one quickly realizes is that apart from such matters as chronology and geography—and not always even then—different protagonists saw and remembered the same event quite differently. Indeed, from the most elementary optical perspective, they did, since they were, so to speak, standing in different places, and because no two individuals can see the same event with precisely the same eyes. But beyond the optical perspective, such differences in views emanate from the fact that each person played a different role in the event. This, in turn, has also determined the manner in which they each remembered it and in which they were willing or able to recall it in words or in writing.

There is, of course, nothing unique in this condition of historical documentation. Herodotus and Thucydides, whose different methods of treating their sources still guide us today, were already aware of this conundrum. The use of testimonies makes it more difficult to say what precisely happened at a given place and time; testimonies tell us more—perhaps more than we would like to know—about what happened, and they tell us that different people experienced, and in some cases remembered and recorded, the same events differently. We may decide to deliver a verdict on what actually happened on the basis of our documentation; or we may prefer to say that we are unable or unwilling to determine precisely what occurred and can simply report several versions or points of view.

Clearly, there are limitations to this kind of documentation. To my mind, testimonies can be most profitably used on two conditions. First, one must collect a critical mass of them, rather than relying on merely a few, if that is at all possible—although I would still argue that even a single testimony that "saves" an event from historical oblivion should and must be used. Second, such testimonies gain immensely from being focused on one locality and a relatively limited span of time and cast of characters. Within such a context, one can much more easily cross-check many testimonies that recount the same events from different perspectives, as well as integrate these individual perspectives into a historical reconstruction that uses all other available kinds of documentation. In the case of the Holocaust, this would mean especially official reports by police, military, and civil administration; as well as documentation of postwar trials; and, finally, scholarly secondary literature.

One last issue cannot be avoided. The use of testimonies of trauma is a very difficult exercise for the historian. It is first of all difficult psychologically because these accounts almost invariably reveal aspects of human nature that one would rather not hear or know about. They are, in that sense, traumatizing. They may also undermine our trust in the historian's craft itself, since it is ultimately based on rationalist and Enlightenment values, on the alleged ability to divine the truth of the past and to identify humanity's progress and improvement. Testimonies also make it very difficult to retain the necessary detachment from the material; in other words, they may hamper the practice of the methods and undermine the philosophical assumptions that have come to be associated with good scholarly writing since the birth of the modern historical profession.

This is possibly the more profound reason for the reluctance of many historians to use testimonies. In other words, historians want to protect their own psychology from the damage they fear might be caused it by, and to protect their profession from the undermining potential of, such testimonies. Yet these accounts are about an event that itself posed the greatest challenge to the values and methods on which the work of historians still bases itself today. These testimonies emanate from the very heart of that historical moment and site of darkness, and because they recount an historical event, they too are part of the historical record, perhaps the most crucial part of all.

Historians cannot escape the event and its implications for them as historians, as individual human beings, and as members of humankind, simply by leaving these accounts to gather dust in crumbling boxes. Historians need to face this challenge and cope with it as best they can. After all, these are accounts by individuals who were determined that what they experienced and saw and remembered would not be forgotten. Historians have largely betrayed these witnesses. By now the vast majority of them are dead. But their recorded accounts can and should still be used, not merely to respect those who left them behind, but to set the historical record straight.

In what follows, I will use testimonies given by residents of the Eastern Galician town of Buczacz and by people who spent some time there during the German occupation in order to explore some aspects of death and survival in an interethnic town in a time of genocide. In this region, the majority of the rural population was Ukrainian, while Poles and Jews constituted the majority of town and city dwellers. Buczacz belonged to Poland in the interwar period, was occupied by the Soviet Union from 1939 to 1941, and was ruled by the Germans from 1941 to 1944. My general argument here is that one of the central questions of historical research on the Holocaust in Eastern Europe—namely, that of the impact of local interethnic relations on the genocide of the Jews—must be analyzed through a close reading of testimonies by the protagonists in these events. I further suggest that this can be accomplished especially by examining a wide range of testimonies from a geographically limited locality.

I also make several more specific points based on these testimonies: first, that much of the gentile population in this region both collaborated in and profited from the genocide of the Jews. Second, I argue that most of the few Jews who survived the genocide in this area were helped by their gentile neighbors for a variety of reasons, which included both greed and altruism. Third, I suggest that the distinction between rescue and denunciation was often blurred and at times nonexistent, as was the distinction between perpetrators and victims; and that the category of bystander in these areas was largely meaningless, since everyone took part in the events, whether he or she suffered or profited from them. Fourth, I note that what we call the Holocaust and associate largely with mass murder facilities and gas chambers was played out more intimately in the form of communal massacres in vast parts of Eastern Europe, where the majority of Jews lived and were murdered. Finally, I point out that crucially important events—such as the otherwise sparsely documented chaotic and extraordinarily violent disintegration of the German occupation of this region in spring and summer 1944—have simply vanished from the historical record because such testimonies have not been used.

I begin with an examination of testimonies on collaboration, betrayal, and denunciation, and then proceed to analyze evidence of rescue and resistance. However, as will become clear, there is both a fair amount of overlap between these categories and a degree of inner contradiction depending on the nature, the timing, and the audience of each eyewitness report.

II

Approximately half of those murdered in the Holocaust perished in ghettos and mass executions at or near their places of residence, in open-air, often public events. Of the five hundred thousand Jews living in Eastern Galicia in 1941, more than 90 percent of whom were murdered, half were deported to the extermination camp of Bełżec and half shot in situ. Even when the shootings were conducted in slightly more isolated forests or cemeteries, the preceding brutal roundups, or Aktionen, which were accompanied by a great deal of gratu-itous violence, took place in public view. Killing sites were frequently close enough for the shots to be heard by other residents. In most cases, locally recruited auxiliary troops and policemen actively participated.

Such spectacles, rarely portrayed in any detail in official documentation or postwar historiography, are amply documented in contemporary diaries, postwar testimonies, courtroom witness accounts, and memoirs. These eyewitness reports shed new light on interethnic coexistence and violence in Eastern Europe and reveal both the peculiarities of the Holocaust and its affinity to other instances of modern genocide. Because the Holocaust in Eastern Europe was often experienced as a communal massacre, it left a deep and lasting imprint on all surviving inhabitants of these areas. In much of Central and Western Europe, the Jews were "simply" deported to the "East," and the few who returned rarely recounted their experiences or found willing listeners for many years thereafter. Conversely, the peoples of Eastern Europe, Jews and gentiles alike, were direct witnesses to and protagonists in a genocide that became an integral, routine, almost "normal" feature of daily life during the war, whether it targeted or spared or was exploited by them.[6]

It bears stressing what this "normality" of communal genocide literally meant. For in Eastern Europe large numbers of Jewish victims were slaughtered in front of family members, friends, and colleagues, in the cemeteries where their ancestors were buried, on the forested hills where they had strolled with lovers or picnicked with children, in the synagogues where they had prayed, in their own homes and farms and cellars.[7] Many postwar inhabitants of former Jewish property retained vivid recollections of the previous owners and the circumstances of their murder. This, too, is a characteristic of communal massacre, which is almost the exact inverse of industrial killing in the extermin-ation camps. Communal massacre devastates lives and warps psyches. It belies the very notion of passive bystanders: everyone becomes a protagonist, hunter and prey, resister and facilitator, loser and profiteer. Often, in the course of events, people come to play several roles. And the resulting sorrow and shame, self-deception and denial, still infuse the way in which people remember, speak, and write about that past.

Nothing demonstrates these aspects of the Holocaust more clearly than testimonies. They expose its intimate, personally devastating effects as much as they reveal the opportunities it presented for greed and violence. Most important, testimonies repeatedly illustrate that even in the midst of the horror there was always a measure of choice, and that such choices could and did save lives and redeem souls. In these conditions, claims of indifference and passivity are meaningless: for what does it mean to remain indifferent to the murder of your classmates under your own windows, or to the sounds of shots and screams from the nearby forest? What is the meaning of passivity when you move into a home vacated by your neighbors whom you have just heard being executed, when you eat with their silverware, when you tear out their floorboards to look for gold, when you sleep in their beds?

Interviewed sixty years after the Holocaust, some non-Jewish residents of Buczacz could still remember the events they witnessed during the war. They recalled seeing "how the Hitlerites committed crimes against the Jews . . . how those people dug their own graves . . . how they buried them alive . . . and how the ground was moving over the people who were still not dead."[8] The Germans, recalled another witness,[9] conducted regular roundups, after which "we could see . . . corpses of women, men and children lying on the road . . . infants . . . [thrown] from balconies onto the paved road . . . lying in the mud with smashed heads and spattered brains. . . . We could hear machine-gun fire" from the nearby killing site.[10] Yet such witnesses also describe relations between local Jews and non-Jews in positive terms. "Our people," says one, "Ukrainians and Poles alike—tried to help them however they could. They made dugouts in the ground, and the Jews hid there. Secretly people would bring food to those dugouts. . . . We pitied those people, for they were beaten, always scared for their lives and never knowing what would happen to them next."[11] Another reported that although "the local people were very careful about associating with the Jews . . . others did help, but very cautiously."[12]

Jewish witnesses interviewed at about the same time provide a different perspective. Stories of local collaboration and denunciation, at times by the very people who had been hiding Jews, are a frequent feature of such accounts. Anne Resnik's family bunker was betrayed by the barber whose shop was over it, and most of her family was murdered. Her sister was shot shortly before the first liberation by "the same people that were pretending to hide" her.[13] Regina Gertner's sister was also denounced by a Polish neighbor and killed just before the end of the occupation.[14] Yitzhak Bauer and other witnesses reported that the Polish dogcatchers Nahajowski and Kowalski specialized in discovering Jews and handing them over to the Germans.[15]

The sense of betrayal runs deep many decades later. John Saunders, who had non-Jewish friends in school, remarked, "During the war you started to discover that they hate your guts . . . they didn't want to help us."[16] Robert Barton also had gentile friends. He assumed a Polish identity during the war. The Germans, he noted, "could not tell who the Jew is and who is a Polack . . . [but] the Polacks . . . used to say . . . you look like a Jew, you talk like a Jew, you walk like a Jew."[17] Jacob Heiss remembered local Ukrainians on horseback chasing and killing Jewish children.[18]

Similar observations can be found in a multitude of Jewish accounts written during the war, in its immediate aftermath, and throughout the following decades. Arie Klonicki wrote in his diary in 1943, "The hatred of the immediate surroundings . . . knows no boundaries. Millions of Jews have been slaughtered and it is not yet satiated!"[19] He and his wife were denounced and murdered shortly thereafter. Joachim Mincer wrote in his diary in 1943 that "executions in the prison yard" were carried out "mainly [by] Ukrainian policemen. . . . The main perpetrator," he wrote, "was an individual by the name of Bandrowski. He liked to shoot Jews on the street." Mincer was also killed soon thereafter.[20] Izio Wachtel recounted that in July 1941, after the Soviets retreated from his town of Czortków and "even before the Germans entered, the Ukrainians arrived at the town with . . . axes and scythes and other instruments and slaughtered and killed and robbed the Jews. With the arrival of the Germans the wild killing ceased and the murder by orders began."[21]

Stories of false rescue are especially striking in this context. Shulamit Aberdam recalled in 1998 that "a Polish woman . . . suggested . . . [to] hide me." Her mother refused. "After the war we heard that the Polish woman had taken another girl, and after getting all the money handed her over to the Germans." Aberdam's family was ejected time and again by rescuers who robbed its members of their last belongings.[22] Fannie Kupitz, who survived as a girl by living with Ukrainians and often posing as one, commented in 1994, "They were good to me but they killed others."[23] As she told me in 2002, her German labor supervisor was fooled into thinking she was Ukrainian and wanted to send her to Germany to his wife.[24] The locals could not easily be fooled, and the thirteen-year-old Fannie "just decided to go on my own. . . . I always was afraid; I only wished I would get a bullet in my back. . . . I . . . used to envy the people that were already dead, I used to envy when I saw a dog that is free and not afraid."[25] When she met a Ukrainian she knew in the forest, "he said to me, 'Oh, you are still alive?'" But his wife took her in for a while. Later her rescuers returned from church citing the priest's words: "Whoever has Jews, let them go, don't keep them!" Shortly afterward she was denounced and fled into the forest.

Girls, especially if they did not look Jewish, had a better chance of surviving than boys. But they were also targets of sexual abuse, a phenomenon that was rarely referred to directly in testimonies. One truck driver took Fannie into the forest. "He says to me, 'You probably had a husband.' And I was so afraid, I was pulling my hair, I was breaking my fingers, I was crying, I said, 'No, I don't have a husband and I am very young,' I said. 'Maybe you have a daughter and somebody would do this to your daughter and what would you do?' " He then left her in the forest and drove away.

Similarly, the 1945 testimony by the thirteen-year-old Rosa Brecher, who was hidden by Polish and Ukrainian women on a farm, reveals sheer terror from her main protector's brother-in-law, Hryń, a drunk and a collaborator: "Hryń came to the attic. . . . He hugged me and . . . [asked if] I was once before in German hands and faced death . . . and whether I was a communist. [He said] he would go to town to take part in the *Aktion*. At that moment I didn't want to live any longer. . . ." On another occasion, "Hryń climbed up to the attic. . . . He was very drunk . . . and he asked who was my father and what organization [my parents] belonged to. . . ." Then again, "At midnight . . . [Hryń] climbed up to the attic and grabbed me by the neck but I managed to scream and began to beg him to let me go. He said give me 1,000 . . . [or] I will denounce you." Rosa recounts that she made "a hole in the roof [of the attic] and . . . looked at the chickens [in the yard] and thought that soon I would be free."[26]

Much of the violence was due to greed. Fannie observed how seven of her relatives were discovered by Ukrainian police: "They knew these people . . . they told them . . . 'We are not going to do nothing to you, just give us whatever you have, and we will let you go.' They gave them everything, [and] when they went out, everyone separately [got] a bullet in the head."[27] Some young Jews tried to prevent this kind of killing or denouncing for profit. Alicia Appleman-Jurman recounted in 1996 how her brother's small resistance group "burned the farmer's barn or beat the farmers up . . . as . . . retaliation, so that . . . people . . . who were hiding Jews should get a message that you can't just betray them" for money. Eventually her brother too "was betrayed by a Polish boy who was . . . helping out" and was hanged in the local police station. Not long after, Alicia herself, who was just twelve years old, was arrested and registered by a Ukrainian police official, "my friend Olga's father . . . who," before the war, "said he loved me like a daughter." On the eve of the liberation, her mother was shot right in front of her after they were denounced by their Polish building supervisor.[28]

Toward the end of the German occupation, the region slipped into total chaos, and the few surviving Jews were at the mercy of greedy peasants, anti-Semitic Ukrainian militias, Nazi murder squads, and local bandits of all descriptions. There is very little reliable official documentation on these last months and weeks of the war in Western Ukraine, but there are many vivid and terrifying testimonies. This is a history that can largely only be told on the basis of these accounts. It has some surprising twists and turns.

One striking account of these days was written in 1947 by the seventeen-year-old Eliasz Chalfen. This testimony implicates the Ukrainian police commander in Buczacz, Volodymyr Kaznovs'kyi, of taking an active part in the first mass execution there as early as 28 August 1941,[29] and goes on to describe many other roundups, in which "the Gestapo, with the help of the Ukrainian police, was trying to find hidden bunkers," and "our neighbors plundered [Jewish homes], taking everything they could," as well as collecting "valuables, gold teeth, etc.," from the thousands of victims of mass executions near the town. By the time of the chaos that preceded the German retreat, reports Chalfen, the "peasants . . . were murdering Jews, taking their belongings and leaving the naked victims in the fields. . . . The Ukrainian bandits . . . would go . . . to the houses that had been pointed out to them as hiding Jews . . . and immediately execute them. . . . Denouncing of Jews at that time," concludes Chalfen, "reached unprecedented levels, and the peasants themselves started murdering and chasing them out" for fear of Ukrainian nationalists.[30]

Ester Grintal testified in 1997 how, as an eighteen-year-old at the time, she tried to survive on a forced-labor farm: "The Ukrainian militia would pass through and . . . we would . . . hide in the toilet and count the shots knowing by that how many people were killed." As the Soviets came closer, "Cossacks and others who had collaborated with the Germans" appeared in the area. "They had never seen so many Jews, so they began murdering them. They did not have enough guns so they hanged people, or killed them with axes, etc. They came to our camp with some collaborators from the village. They locked [us] in an empty barn. . . . They began beating us. . . . They shot a line of people with one bullet . . . but the bullet didn't reach me. Again I was put in a line, and again the bullet didn't kill me. So they began killing people with knives. I was stabbed three times." Even the German military doctor who examined her a few days later said, "What did the Ukrainian swine do to you?"[31]

Yoel Katz, seventeen at the time, recalled in 1995 that when the inmates of his labor camp were struck by a typhus epidemic just before the liberation, the peasants called the police to kill them, surrounded the camp, and shouted, "All the children out, we are going to kill you!" Some were killed with axes; others put in a row and shot with a single bullet. The Ukrainians, he reports, "were very hard . . . the Germans who came from the front protected us from the Ukrainians until the Russians came."[32]

Who would help and who would not was often entirely unpredictable. Joe Perl, who was thirteen years old at the end of the occupation, testified in 1996 that he and his mother were hidden by a Ukrainian nationalist who was actually in charge of killing Jews and Poles.[33] Edzia Spielberg-Flitman, liberated at the age of fourteen, recalled in 1995 how her aunt and cousins were axed to death on the day the Red Army pulled out in July 1941 by a group of Ukrainians who included the children's female teacher. Conversely, her mother was saved from being murdered in a village by her female German friend. They were eventually hidden by a "poor farmer with a wife and four children." The peasant woman said to them, "It doesn't matter how long it takes, we will share our bread and potatoes with you." Yet the peasant who hid Edzia's relatives betrayed them, and they were murdered by Ukrainian policemen.

What is curious about these last months and weeks of the occupation is that according to Jewish testimonies, the Jews often ended up being protected from Ukrainian militias and bandits by German army and administrative officers. Ediza, for instance, worked for a while as a washerwoman for a German army unit with a group of Ukrainian girls. When one of the girls denounced her as a Jew, the local German commander took Edzia, her six-year-old brother, and her mother to safety: "And he left, and he then turned back with his horse one more time and he says, 'I hope you all live well.' " Edzia was "very happy to get away from the Ukrainians because they had pogroms after the war. . . . They were so brutal. I think they were worse than the Germans. . . . They left a big scar upon me. . . . I would say 80 percent [of my family] were killed by the Ukrainians who were our friends."[34]

The much older Mojżesz Szpigiel left a testimony of these events in 1948 at the age of forty-nine. His is a relentless account of mayhem and brutality in the last months of the occupation. When the forced-labor farm where he and his family worked was liquidated in 1943, they hid in the forest, where "we were attacked by peasants. The Ukrainians began to catch people, torture them, take their money." Szpigiel's father and his two nephews were killed by a Ukrainian. Returning to the farm, they found that all inmates who fell ill from the rampant epidemics were killed by the Ukrainian police.

In January 1944, Ukrainian militiamen murdered most of the surviving 120 Jews on the farm, including Szpigiel's fourteen-year-old son. Szpigiel writes, "It is important to state that this killing was not a German action, that it was performed by Ukrainian policemen and bandits." Szpigiel and other survivors protested to the German administrator, but most of the few survivors were butchered with knives and pitchforks in yet another bandit attack just before the liberation. Szpigiel describes "the child orphans . . . stacked up in a pile . . . victims . . . lying with open guts. . . . Everybody," he remarks, "said they would rather die from a German bullet than from a bandit's knife." When the German administrator left, "The Jews earnestly cried." But the new commander, a young German army officer, said to them, "As long as I am here, nothing will happen to you." Indeed, when Ukrainian policemen attacked the last remaining Jews, reports Szpigiel, a German "major . . . went [there] with his aide and hit one policeman on the head with his revolver, threw them out and ordered them to leave immediately."[35]

The fifteen-year-old Izaak Szwarc reported on these same events shortly after the war. He recalled that at the labor camp, "the peasants . . . wanted roundups to take place so that they could rob the Jews. . . . The village head forbade the peasants to give us food. The peasants organized nightly guards around the camp so that the Jews could not escape. . . . The peasants supervised our work, they beat us, did not give us any water . . ." When the camp was liquidated, "the peasants brought out hidden Jews. . . . In the forests Jews were attacked by bandits, and the peasants did not let us in." Under these conditions, the Jews "went to a village where the Germans were. We were safer there from the bandits. . . . We sensed that the peasants intended to remove us as witnesses to their crimes." On the eve of the liberation, as the Hungarian soldiers stationed in his village retreated, "the Vlasov-soldiers [former Soviet troops serving in the Wehrmacht] arrived. . . . They did not have any guns, only cold weapons. They murdered all the Jews they caught. . . . It was impossible to stay in the villages. The peasants organized roundups of Jews, killed them, discovered bunkers. Even those Jews who were hidden in bunkers at peasants' farms were killed by their hosts. The Jews began to gather in Tłusty. The [German commander] . . . promised that the Jews would not be harmed. Three hundred Jews gathered there. . . . On 23 March the Soviets arrived."[36]

Rene Zuroff was only seven years old when she was liberated. In 1995, she recalled roundups in which she and her three-year-old sister would lie in the bunker and hear "the Germans . . . screaming, 'Juden, Juden raus, raus!' and . . . the Ukrainians and the Poles . . . calling 'żyd, żyd!' " and then the "bloodbath in your house, outside the door, in the street, bodies everywhere." Her last recollections of the Holocaust are the most terrifying. She remembers, "We were hiding in the forest and our shelter was a field of tobacco. . . . One night we heard terrible screaming and curses in Ukrainian and running, there was a whole massacre; the Ukrainian militia came at night hunting out the Jews from the woods. . . . [They] were chasing the Jews with dogs and we heard this rampage and started running for our lives . . . we were running blindly . . . and it was the scariest thing I can remember: we saw dismembered bodies, bodies without heads, and we saw death all around us; so that was my nightmare in the tobacco fields and forest."

Rene and her family were rescued by wretchedly poor Polish peasants who by then were also being massacred by Ukrainian nationalists. They hid in a hole in a "barn . . . full of rats and other vermin . . . and when the animals urinated the urine would spill into the hole." But "the old Polish woman was truly a saintly and wonderful human being who risked her life and that of her daughters. She gave us seven . . . pirogi . . . on Sunday, once a week we got food and very little in-between."

When she returned to Buczacz in July 1944, Rene was not given to compassion: "I was a little girl and we would go for our entertainment to the hangings . . . of collaborators . . . in the town square . . . we were totally happy to go to our daily hangings." She came to the United States in 1950, majored in foreign languages, married in 1962, and has two children, one of whom is a rabbi in Israel. She suffers from neuroses, hates the dark, doesn't like to be surrounded by people, and always has to sit near an exit, "for a quick escape." She does not "have a great deal of . . . trust and confidence in people."[37]

III

The testimonies cited above should demonstrate the importance of such materials for reconstructing the typical experience of Jewish victims, especially survivors, in the small towns of Eastern Galicia and, by extension, in much of the rest of Eastern Europe. Such accounts also provide much insight into the psychological conditions that predominated during this period and thus help us understand both patterns of behavior at the time and the long-term effects of these events. In other words, these testimonies are crucial to any analysis of the mental makeup and resilience of those who endured the Holocaust and of the effects of trauma on memory, recollection, and witnessing.[38]

Nonetheless, the picture sketched above remains incomplete without more substantial reference to rescue, resistance, and intracommunal conflict. Relatively rare in the record as a whole, rescue features prominently in testimonies, even as they recount numerous instances of betrayal and denunciation. If rescue was exceptional overall, it was a much more common experience for survivors on whose testimonies we must rely. Indeed, the memories of most protagonists have remained ambivalent on precisely this score: they lay blame and assert humaneness, expose betrayal and recall altruism and sacrifice. Accounts by non-Jews often repress or marginalize Christian complicity and collaboration, while underscoring help and compassion, and in some cases blaming victims for their own fate. Jewish testimonies, quite apart from shifting uneasily between bitterness about the treachery of neighbors and gratitude for rescue by the righteous few, also alternate between repressing evidence of Jewish collaboration and corruption, and expressing profound rage and derision vis-à-vis those identified with the *Judenrat* and the Jewish police. Finally, compassion by Germans, perhaps precisely because of their local omnipotence, appears in such accounts as the strongest evidence for the possibility of choice and the potential for goodness even in the midst of genocide.

Choice constitutes the moral core of any discussion of mass murder; it also retains an underlying psychological dimension for those directly impacted by such events and for later generations.[39] Evidence of choice threatened to expose and shame those whose alibi for complicity was the alleged lack of alternative. But instances of altruism, however few, provide flashes of light in what would have otherwise remained a period of utter darkness. Such glimmers of humanness, faint and far between though they might have been, should not be removed from the historical record. They should be recounted because they occurred; they should be remembered because they give us hope; and they should be contextualized because they serve to highlight the far more prevalent phenomena of glee and greed, complicity and collaboration, violence and cruelty. And there can be no more reliable evidence for gentile help, rescue, and sacrifice during the Holocaust than that derived from the testimonies of Jewish survivors.

Especially for children, survival depended on a combination of luck and the help of others, whether motivated by kindness or prospects of material gain. Safah Prüfer, a little girl from Buczacz interviewed soon after the liberation, recalled that her father "handed me and my little brother to a peasant we knew in our town." But following "a terrible *Aktion* . . . daddy built a hiding-place in the forest. . . . One day the Ukrainian police arrived and shot everybody, only I alone survived. From that day on I began to fight for my existence on my own. I wandered alone for seven months, unable to find any shelter; then finally the Red Army liberated us."[40]

It is inconceivable that such a small girl could have survived the long winter without some help from the locals, however grudging. Non-Jews often claimed that such help was offered quite willingly. A Polish resident of Buczacz related in 2003 that during the war a young woman came running to her with a baby, "crying and exhausted. . . . At my own risk I hid them in the attic of the cowshed. . . . I fed that little girl from my own breast . . . and I shared my own food with that woman." She stressed that this was not "the only case. I tried to help [the Jews] however I could, and my husband never objected."[41]

We do not know what eventually happened to that baby, though in all likelihood it did not survive. Conversely, Emil Skamene, raised as a Christian in Prague, was in fact born to the Kleiner family in Buczacz in 1941, "in a cellar of a Ukrainian peasant, who was hiding my parents." In desperation, Emil's father wrote his sister in Prague, begging her to rescue the baby. She in turn sent Rudolph Steiger, a German with "some function in the SS" who, for a fee, brought the eighteen-month-old baby "in a backpack . . . over two days . . . [on] the train" to Prague. Not long thereafter the peasant murdered Emil's parents as a means to get his hands on their valuables. Emil discovered his true identity only decades later; he subsequently also found out that both his adoptive parents were Jews. As he sees it, he owes his life to the fact that "it was very important for some people that I should survive." Even Steiger, who "originally did it for money," grew attached to the boy, becoming a regular guest at his birthday parties. His goodness paid off, since "as an SS official . . . [he] would have likely been killed by Czechs after the war," had it not been for "an affidavit from my parents." Steiger, concludes Emil, "lived . . . his life basically in exchange for this unbelievable act of heroism."[42]

Some older children adopted a false identity, a precarious choice in a society replete with stereotypes and prejudices. The ten-year-old Genia Weksler testified in 1946 that she spent the last months of the occupation in a Polish village with her mother and sister: "I grazed cattle. . . . In the house they often talked about Jews. 'Jews are cheaters.' . . . The children always played . . . 'manhunt' on Jews . . . we lived as Poles until the liberation. I was often told that I have Jewish eyes, Jewish black hair. I answered that if 'You take a closer look it is possible that I'm completely Jewish.' "[43] Bronia Kahane, who was ten when the Germans invaded in 1941, was initially hidden with her mother by a Ukrainian peasant who felt loyalty to her grandfather, even though his own son was a concentration camp guard. They were also saved from an execution by an Austrian SS man thanks to her mother's excellent German and a $10 bill. But in spring 1944 she lost her entire family and began working as a farmhand. She lived in a house filled with Jewish goods looted by the owner's son and was told by her employer, "You do everything like a Jew." When she returned to Buczacz after the liberation, Bronia "spoke only Ukrainian . . . I forgot everything." She found the few surviving Jews terrified of being attacked: "I never went back to my house . . . because they said . . . 'They're going to kill you.' "[44]

Aliza Golobov, who was fourteen when the Germans invaded, was also first saved by a German soldier, who hid her family during an *Aktion* in 1942. Although she was denounced several times and lost her entire family, Aliza was rescued by a number of Ukrainians and acquaintances of her father's in the town of Stanisławów. The lawyers Dr. Volchuk and Mr. Krochmichek, the latter's father, a priest, and a police inspector provided her with false papers and protected her until the liberation, receiving no compensation and at great risk to their own and their families' lives.[45] Hilda Weitz, who was also fourteen in 1941, was sheltered by a Ukrainian family from Buczacz, despite the fact that "they were . . . very nationalistic" and that "two of the brothers were drafted to German army." She and her younger brother were later hidden by a blacksmith's family in a "very rough anti-Semitic town." The man, his wife, and their child eventually fled the village, "because they were afraid they will come to . . . look for Jews." Hilda and her brother were left alone: "I remember the light looked so beautiful, the sun, the nature, I said, 'Oh my God, life is so beautiful, but we will never see it anymore.' I thought this was our last day. . . ."[46] Shortly thereafter, the Soviets arrived.

In some cases love, passion, and loyalty also played a role. The sixteen-year-old Zofia Pollak jumped off a train headed to the Bełżec extermination camp near the town of Rawa Ruska, only to be arrested by the ethnic German Polish policemen Smola. He said to her: "You are so young . . . and so pretty, you shouldn't be killed." He took care of Zofia for six weeks. "He was really in love with me. . . . But he was a married man. And his wife and two children were on vacation." When his wife returned, Smola sent Zofia back to her father and brother in Buczacz. She survived much of the remainder of the war thanks to the goodwill of a Polish work supervisor on the agricultural farm in which the father, a former estate manager, was employed. Almost murdered by Ukrainian partisans, they ended up in the barn of a poor peasant who had once been helped by Zofia's father. "He said: 'Whatever I have I will share with you. . . .' He covered us with hay. It was very cold. . . . We were there in one position, we couldn't move and this is how we were liberated on February 23, 1944 in that place."[47]

In other cases, youngsters were saved thanks to split-second decisions by strangers. Eighteen-year-old Cyla Sznajder hid in the attic of the German administrative office during the liquidation of the Nagórzanka labor camp near Buczacz in 1942, and "thanks to the cleaner—a Pole, who found me by chance . . . I managed to get out . . . without being seen." During another liquidation action in January 1943, she hid with a friend in the backyard of a farm. The ethnic German peasant who discovered them there "invited us into his hut . . . ordered his wife to prepare warm food . . . fed us . . . [and] found for us some old rags." Later she and a few others were supplied with food by another peasant woman. And at the very end, Cyla and several other Jewish girls hid in the attic of a cloister: "The nuns comforted us that things would not last long, and brought us food."[48]

Rescuers were not all of the same cast, and we have contradictory reports about some of them. In 1946 the twenty-one-year-old Shmuel Rosen testified that he, his two brothers, and their mother had hidden for nine months in a grave where they "built . . . a little apartment . . . with the help of the gravedigger" Mańko Świerszczak, in the Christian cemetery on the slope of the Fedor Hill overlooking the town of Buczacz.[49] In a 1960 testimony, Shmuel described Świerszczak as "an illiterate but a very upright man," who, "in return for a fee," hid "forty Jews in the attic of the cemetery's chapel" during an *Aktion*, refusing to betray them even when the Ukrainian police "beat him up." The Rosens paid Świerszczak "1,000 złoty every month for the supplies" in return for hiding them.[50] Shmuel's older brother Henry depicted Świerszczak in 1997 as "a gorgeous man" and "a Christian. . . . He would say, 'If I will turn you in, then my kids, my grandkids, and their grandchildren will have to pay for my sin.' "[51] But in March 1944, a couple of months after the Rosens moved to "a shelter under the floor" of the mortuary, "a group of German soldiers came into the" house and "the floor collapsed." The brothers managed to escape, "but our poor mother . . . could not run with her sick legs. We saw . . . how our mother was dragged out and shot."[52] Świerszczak later buried her.[53]

The three boys were subsequently hidden by an old Polish acquaintance, the peasant Michał Dutkiewicz,[54] even as some of their relatives were denounced and murdered in the same village.[55] It was thanks to them that Świerszczak's tale of heroism became known, and in 1983 he and his Ukrainian wife Marynka were declared "righteous among the nations" by Yad Vashem in Jerusalem.[56] Yet Yad Vashem's archives also contain an account written in 1947 by Moshe Wizinger, a friend of the Rosens, who had a very different recollection of the undertaker. In June 1943 Wizinger also sought refuge in the cemetery, where he encountered a "very frightened" Świerszczak, followed by his wife, who urged him to leave or to give himself up to the Germans. Shortly thereafter he was captured by Ukrainian fighters, barely managed to escape, and returned to the cemetery. This time Marynka "started to shout at me to run . . . otherwise she herself would call the Germans." Remarkably, at this point Wizinger was taken in by a local Polish resistance group, whose leader, Edek, decided to punish the couple for refusing shelter to a Jew. After beating up Marynka while her husband was hiding under the bed, Edek declared, according to Wizinger, "For what you did to him, I would have killed you like dogs. And only your behavior before that . . . stops me from doing it. Fear of the Germans cannot be an excuse for you . . . we will punish loyalty to German orders with death. Remember this and tell the others."

By the standards of Edek's moral code, then, as reported by Wizinger, according to which Polish honor required saving Jews, whether one liked them or not, Świerszczak did not pass the test. But Edek's group was an uncommon local phenomenon—most nationalist Polish and Ukrainian partisans were at best unfriendly to Jews—and he and most of his fighters were killed. The only record of his heroism is in Wizinger's unread account; consequently he received no recognition by Yad Vashem, and Świerszczak's status was never challenged. This ambiguity of heroism was even more pronounced in the case of Jewish resisters. At the end of his diary, Wizinger scans the handful of Jewish fighters still left on the eve of the liberation and notes that they are "the last of a dying nation."[57] Inquiring who they were and why there were so few of them tells us a great deal about the complexities of the historical reality and the vicissitudes of memory.

An outstanding example is Yitzhak Bauer, eighteen when the Germans invaded and eighty when I interviewed him in 2003. Bauer recalled that "compared to other places the Christian population" of Buczacz "was relatively all right. . . . At least they did not harm us." Saved by a Ukrainian friend during the first *Aktion*, Bauer ended up in a small Jewish resistance group in the nearby forest. While he took action against denouncers, Bauer maintained a nuanced view of Ukrainians, noting, for instance, that even the notorious chief of the local militia, Volodymyr Kaznovs'kyi, refrained from action upon discovering that his own father, a priest, was hiding Jews. Similarly, Bauer's Ukrainian friend Shenko, who provided the group with food, later joined the police, explaining that "the alternative was to enlist for labor in Germany or join the SS Division 'Galicia.'" Not long after, Shenko's house was burned down as punishment for hiding Jews. Bauer also recalled an elderly Ukrainian family friend who invited him and his brother to his home, gave them food, and parted from them saying, "I wish that you manage to survive."[58]

From a deposition he submitted to a West German court in 1968 as evidence for the trial of former Nazi perpetrators in Buczacz, however, it turns out that before becoming a partisan, Bauer had served in the Ordnungsdienst (Jewish police, or OD). He was apparently not the only one who made the transition from collaboration to resistance. Bauer noted that he joined the OD in November 1941. The police, numbering some thirty men, "carried out the orders of the *Judenrat*, but during *Aktionen* . . . we were put at the disposition of . . . the Gestapo or the local gendarmerie." According to Bauer, on 27 November 1942, he "was assigned to participate in the cleanup of the Jewish hospital," which "was overflowing with . . . about 100 . . . sick people . . . The sick who could not move were shot right there and then in their beds. The others were taken out to the railroad station . . . and transported to extermination in Bełżec." Bauer personally witnessed some of the shooting in the hospital, as well as during the *Aktion* of April 1943.[59]

There is no necessary contradiction between Bauer's two accounts; it may be simply a matter of relating different segments of his experiences appropriate to the circumstances in which they were presented. But it is also possible that Bauer could not assimilate the two parts of his story into one psychological and experiential whole: to the German court he asserted his role as an OD man, in order to establish his ability to identify German perpetrators; to me he asserted his role as partisan, thus providing his survival with the more heroic aura befitting the Israeli context. Yet many of those who lived through that period would not share our understanding of the choices made by such men as Bauer or Shenko. Gershon Gross, a tough working-class twenty-four-year-old in 1941, had only contempt for the *Judenrat* and OD: "What was their job? . . . No one wants to talk about it. . . . The Germans would say they need five hundred people. The [Jewish] police went" to seize them. Gershon and his brothers refused to join the police. Of a *Judenrat* member who survived, Gershon noted dispassionately that he "had to hide, like Eichmann. If they found him they would kill him." Jewish collaborators, to his mind, were the worst, since they turned against their own. He had more sympathy for gentiles precisely because his expectations were lower. A Ukrainian policeman, a former classmate, let him go after the OD forced him to bury victims of a mass shooting. When Torah scrolls were "hanged . . . like you hang clothes" from the bridge over the Strypa River in Buczacz, "a Ukrainian priest hid one Torah in the church," retuning it to Gross after the liberation. And when one of his brothers was wounded in a partisan action, a poor Polish peasant sheltered and nursed him back to health. But Gross had no illusions. He knew that "Ukrainian police took" Hungarian and Czech Jewish refugees "to the Dniester River, tied them with wires and threw them alive into the Dniester." Closer to home, his own parents were denounced by a local Polish girl, taken out to their own yard, and shot.[60]

Moshe Wizinger was also harsher toward Jewish collaborators than toward gentile neighbors. He similarly remembered the "harsh protest from the Ukrainian priests," who demanded from "the leader of the Ukrainian bands, Dankowicz . . . to stop desecrating Holy sites," and he noted the initiative of "the head of the Ukrainian Basilian Monastery . . . to carry the scrolls to the monastery where they would be safe." Wizinger distinguished between "German soldiers led by Ukrainian dregs," who in the early days of the occupation "forced their way into Jewish houses and raped young Jewish girls," as well as murdering former communists, including "Jews, Poles and even Ukrainians," and the Ukrainian community leaders who "were helpless" against "the leaders of the formerly secret Ukrainian bands . . . that were ruling now." He also stressed that those "Ukrainian bands" were soon thereafter "appointed as the police forces" that constituted the main local component of future mass killings. But it was about the Jewish leadership that Wizinger wrote most contemptuously, deriding the manner in which "the countless demands by the Germans or Ukrainians were fulfilled immediately" by the *Judenrat*. The OD, for its part, "robbed the Jews of furniture, bed linen, and clothing," so that even "in those terrible times" Jewish officials "were able to lead a very good life and to amass large sums of money," while "Jews who were trying to hide their belongings were mercilessly beaten" by them. When Jews from neighboring smaller towns and villages were expelled to Buczacz, not only were they "attacked and robbed by the peasants," but once they arrived the Jewish police targeted them: "The OD are robbing, killing, worse than the Germans."

Some Jewish leaders did try to set a different moral standard. Thus, when the Germans demanded 150 Jews for work in a forced labor camp, the head of the *Judenrat*, Dr. Engelberg, "announced that he would under no condition take part in selecting the people." But his assistants, Dr. "Seifer and Kramer Baruch ... proposed to exchange those unable to work with healthy and young workers" and "supported their proposal with presents." As a result, "the names taken off the list belonged to those who could pay more," while Seifer and Kramer "made a great deal of money ... and did not refuse to accept jewelry as well." There were some moments of heroism. Jankiel Ebenstein, "who during his few months of work at the *Judenrat* became hated by everyone," and "was called an agent of the Gestapo ... was ordered to help ... looking for hidden bunkers." He initially "tried to convince the Chief of the Gestapo that no Jews were hiding in" a certain house. But "when ... they started pulling Jews out of there," he "grabbed a hatchet and tried to hit the Gestapo soldier," only to be immediately shot down. As Wizinger wrote, "that's how the man ... died a hero's death. That day he was forgiven everything."[61]

The effect of German rule on intraethnic and interethnic relations is noted in many testimonies. Zofia Pollak "had very close ... gentile friends" but "after the Germans occupied our city they wouldn't even look at me because I was Jewish." As for the ghetto, "the *Judenrat* was very mean and the Jewish police was very mean. They thought that by being very obedient to the Germans, they will save their own lives. So the very nice people became very ugly." But, Pollack concluded, "at the end everybody was killed."[62] Shmuel Rosen recalled that "the two hundred richest Jewish families found their way to the labor camp," considered the last safe site in Buczacz, by paying the *Judenrat* exorbitant sums.[63] Soon thereafter the labor camp was also liquidated. Yet Rosen did think that wealth and corruption made a difference in survival rate. Of up to one thousand Jews who came out of hiding following the first liberation of Buczacz in March 1944, "next to a handful of upright people, only dubious characters survived—denouncers, militiamen." To be sure, most of them were murdered when the Germans recaptured the town a few days later. Only a few managed to escape, and some became partisans. The Rosen brothers, for their part, joined the Red Army. By the second liberation in July 1944, less than one hundred Jews were still alive in Buczacz.[64]

Survivors have often been reluctant to speak about internal Jewish corruption and complicity, invoking the phrase, "one does not speak ill of the dead." Yet this was a crucial component of life during the Holocaust and of its subsequent memory. Witnesses from Buczacz also observed that the Jewish leadership opposed and hindered the creation of armed resistance. In 2002, Shmuel Rosen recalled overhearing a conversation between *Judenrat* leaders and a man called Zuhler, who "served in the Polish army before the war. ... He said to them, 'We want to create partisan groups and to go to the forest ... but we have no money for weapons.' ... So they said, 'Sir ... we will not agree to this.' And he left, and that was that."[65]

Rosen speculated that Jewish leaders "were scared," and that while "some in the *Judenrat* . . . wanted" to organize resistance, others "were together with the Germans. Excuse me for saying that, to our regret, Dr. Seifer was one." By this Rosen meant that Seifer preferred collaboration to resistance, and his willingness to name the man must have also had to do with the fact that of all the *Judenrat* members, it was only Seifer who survived: "They say he is in Australia." Zeev Anderman, another survivor, who was also present at the interview with Rosen, suggested, "Let's get off this subject, gentlemen, it is too painful. . . ." But Rosen insisted: "Look, they have to know this. . . . There were bad things in the *Judenrat* . . . they would seize a young man for work and they would exchange him [for another]. Who would [serve for the] exchange?" Now Anderman gave way: "One of the poor boys." And Rosen concluded, "Exactly, they would get the poor kids, [in exchange for] those of the rich. . . ." And Anderman added, "My uncle, they got him. . . ."[66]

These are fraught and agonizing issues. Ultimately, in conditions of communal genocide, no one remained entirely apart from the events. A passing remark by Shmuel Rosen revealed that, in fact, he too had worked in the *Judenrat*, if only in the position of a "helper" ("I made tea, coffee"). Zeev Anderman spoke with pride about his brother Janek's death in April 1943, when he pulled out a pistol and shot a Ukrainian policeman, only to be beaten, dragged to the town square, and burned alive.[67] Yet some sources suggest that Janek had a pistol because he was or had been an OD man. Perhaps, just like Ebenstein, his heroic end made up for his past actions in the police.[68]

IV

Personal accounts of genocide, by their very nature, do not allow for the creation of a single, uniform narrative of events. Rather, they offer a multitude of perspectives, some complementary, others contradictory, which, when put together, can provide an imperfect yet multidimensional picture of past reality. At times, this may be a contentious or opaque portrait, all the more so considering the extreme circumstances of World War II and the Holocaust. Yet listening closely to the witnesses allows us greater depth and nuance than can be derived from the tendentious obfuscation of official accounts. Individual, personal perspectives are all the more important in reconstructing events on the ethnically mixed borderlands of Eastern Europe.

Indeed, certain internal contradictions within individual accounts carry special significance for collective memory and historiography. Generalizing statements by witnesses on the conduct of entire ethnic groups tend to conform to conventional views, which are in part reflected in the overall course of events. Yet the same witnesses often cite specific cases of individual actions that belie the generalizations and, not least importantly, were vital to the witnesses' own survival. Such instances of atypical but crucial behavior provide a corrective to widespread prejudices and undermine deterministic views of the past by introducing an element of choice.

The gap between conventional generalizations and unique individual experience makes for ambivalence. This reaction comes into particularly sharp relief in extreme situations such as genocide. Jewish accounts contain a large measure of mixed feelings about Christian neighbors, reflecting a general impression of universal betrayal and individual experiences of rescue. Precisely because denunciation and murder were so pervasive, rare instances of mercy and altruism stand out all the more. And of course, witness accounts disproportionately represent gentile rescue, since survival was so heavily dependent on such acts.

But testimonies also tell us that just as perpetrators occasionally showed pity or compassion, rescuers were not always altruistic, as motivations for action ranged from pure goodness to cynical exploitation. While a few men with blood on their hands occasionally chose to save someone, others masqueraded as rescuers only to rob and betray those they sheltered; while many upstanding citizens became complicit in plunder and murder, some wretchedly poor peasants shared their last crumbs with the desperate remnants of destroyed communities. Some sought a postwar alibi, others paid back moral debts; generalizing about motivation is futile. Habitual killers may have acted kindly only once; others might have been transformed by that first pang of conscience. Some began with good intentions and then turned to denunciation; others acted out of greed but became attached to those they rescued. Ambivalence was hardly restricted to survivors.

Observing the dynamics of communal genocide from a local perspective reveals that not a few of those who perpetrated violence at one point became its victims at another. Ukrainian nationalists collaborated with the Germans in killing Jews and massacring Poles; they were in turn targeted by the prewar Polish state, by the Soviet authorities, and eventually also by the Germans. Poles benefited from their prewar state's discriminatory anti-Jewish and anti-Ukrainian policies; in turn, they were subjected to Soviet deportations and Ukrainian ethnic cleansing. Jewish community leaders and educated youths tried to save themselves by becoming complicit in the victimization of poorer and weaker fellow Jews, only to have their illusions of power and security dispelled as they too were murdered. Some saw this turning of tables as a kind of justice, but ultimately this merely resulted from the dynamics of unbound, unrestricted violence on a hitherto unimaginable scale.

And yet many testimonies also contain a mélange of unspoken gratitude for the rescuers and inarticulate remorse for having failed to recognize and thank them for so long. The pervasive atmosphere of mayhem and violence, betrayal and abandonment, might have made such acts of mercy stand out all the more. Instead, they often receded into the background as survivors mourned the dead and tried to build a new life. But the testimonies tell a different story. The multitudes of the drowned have left precious little behind, yet the few who were saved have given us a detailed record of these events—of which their rescuers constituted a vital component. This is of course an unbalanced historical record. But it has the benefit of enriching our understanding of the Holocaust and its aftermath. Ultimately, beyond saving their lives, acts of rescue also saved the souls of the survivors. After all, it is astonishing that men, women, and children who lived though that era had the inner resources to rebuild their lives; and yet many of them did just that. This is testimony to their strength and resilience. But I would argue that what contributed no less to their determination to raise new families, and to their ability to instill in their children trust and humanness, was the memory of those who had selflessly saved them.

This memory remained deeply etched in the souls of the survivors. But it did not find public expression for decades, providing just enough sustenance to go on living but never completely resurfacing, perhaps because of the hardships of life after the catastrophe, or because allowing it to emerge would have brought back all the other horrors and betrayals and losses. When it did return, decades later, it came after lives had been lived, children and grandchildren had been born, and one could face the approaching inevitable end with more equanimity and sense of fulfillment. And with the memory of rescue came a recognition that those who had chosen to act then had done more than save lives and, unbeknownst to themselves perhaps, had rescued the very concept of a shared humanity—precisely that which the Nazis had set out to eradicate—by recognizing the human spark in those who were hunted down like animals.

What the witnesses I have cited here experienced hardly provides a single, one-sided lesson on human nature, or on history, or even on the events of the Holocaust. But these accounts, fraught and painful and contradictory as they are, constitute a crucial component of the past—in Buczacz and, by extension, in many other sites of communal genocide, most especially in the borderlands of Eastern Europe.[69] Ignoring them, setting them aside, using them merely to illustrate some point or thesis unrelated to their deeper meaning not only constitutes abuse of these records of human experience; it also distorts and ultimately falsifies the historical record itself. No history should be written without listening to its protagonists, least of all the history of an event whose main goal was to silence these voices, and especially because the few who survived the disaster hoped more than anything else to transmit the memory of the events they experienced to posterity and thereby to save the multitudes of the dead from complete oblivion, statistical abstraction, and mass burial in the voluminous footnotes of scholarly publications.

Notes

1 For a forceful statement on the need for an objective and value-free use of documents, see David Engel, *Facing a Holocaust: The Polish Government-in-Exile and the Jews, 1943–1945* (Chapel Hill: University of North Carolina Press, 1993), 1–14; at several scholarly meetings, Engel has expressed strong reservations about the use of testimonies.

2 For interesting comments on sources along these lines, see Dieter Pohl, *Nationalsozialistische Judenverfolgung in Ostgalizien 1941–1944: Organisation und Durchführung eines staatlichen Massenverbrechens* (Munich: Oldenbourg, 1996), 17–21, who also writes, "Research of Jewish history under German occupation in East Galicia would have demanded knowledge of Yiddish and Hebrew, which I lack. This limitation is painful, but unavoidable" (ibid., 15). See also Thomas Sandkühler, *"Endlösung" in Galizien: Der Judenmord in Ostpolen und die Rettungsinitiativen von Berthold Beitz, 1941–1944* (Bonn: Dietz, 1996), 15–9. Skepticism over the use of diaries is expressed in Raul Hilberg, *Sources of Holocaust Research: An Analysis* (Chicago, IL: Ivan R. Dee, 2001), 141–2, 155–9, 161–2. For a more sympathetic view that stresses the chronological proximity of accounts, see Saul Friedländer, *The Years of Extermination: Nazi Germany and the Jews, 1939–1945* (New York, NY: HarperCollins, 2007), xxiv–xxvi.

3 This is ultimately the case even in Friedländer, *Years of Extermination*. A good example is Debórah Dwork and Robert Jan van Pelt, *The Holocaust: A History* (New York, NY: Norton, 2002). A much more sophisticated discussion can be found in Alexandra Garbarini, *Numbered Days: Diaries and the Holocaust* (New Haven, CT: Yale University Press, 2006); and Simone Gigliotti, *The Train Journey: Transit, Captivity, and Witnessing in the Holocaust* (New York, NY: Berghahn Books, 2009).

4 Annette Wieviorka, *The Era of the Witness*, trans. Jared Stark (Ithaca, NY: Cornell University Press, 2006).

5 A few examples: Lawrence L. Langer, *Holocaust Testimonies: The Ruins of Memory* (New Haven, CT: Yale University Press, 1991); Cathy Caruth, ed., *Trauma: Explorations in Memory* (Baltimore, MD: Johns Hopkins University Press, 1995); Shoshana Felman and Dori Laub, *Testimony: Crises of Witnessing in Literature, Psychoanalysis, and History* (New York, NY: Routledge, 1992); Kenneth Jacobson, *Embattled Selves: An Investigation into the Nature of Identity through Oral Histories of Holocaust Survival* (New York, NY: Atlantic Monthly Press, 1994); and Efraim Sicher, ed., *Breaking Crystal: Writing and Memory after Auschwitz* (Urbana, IL: University of Chicago Press, 1998). An early exception is Terrence Des Pres, *The Survivor: An Anatomy of Life in the Death Camps* (New York, NY: Oxford University Press, 1976).

6 Among the most harrowing texts on this "return," see Charlotte Delbo, *None of Us Will Return*, trans. John Githens (New York, NY: Grove, 1968); and Primo Levi, *The Reawakening*, trans. Stuart Woolf (New York, NY: Simon & Schuster, 1995).

7 For a detailed account of one such public massacre in an East Galician town, known as "The bloody Sunday of Stanisławów" (now the city of Ivano-Frankivs'k in Western Ukraine), from various perspectives, see Pohl, *Judenverfolgung*, 144–7; Sandkühler, *Endlösung*, 150–2; Elisabeth Freundlich, *Die Ermordung einer Stadt namens Stanislau: NS-Vernichtungspolitik in Polen 1939–1945* (Vienna: Österreichischer Bundesverlag, 1986), 154–64; and Avraham Liebesman, *Im Yehudei Stanislavov bi-yemei klayah* [*With the Jews of Stanisławów in the Holocaust*] (Tel Aviv: Hakibbutz Hameuchad, 1980, in Hebrew), 22–31.

8 Julija Mykhailivna Trembach, written on her behalf by her daughter, Roma Nestorivna Kryvenchuk, in 2003, collected by Mykola Kozak, translated from Ukrainian by Sofia Grachova.

9 Maria Mykhailivna Khvostenko (née Dovhanchuk), interview with Mykola Kozak, 2003, translated from Ukrainian by Sofia Grachova.

10 Ibid.

11 Trembach, 2003.

12 Tetiana Pavlyshyn, "The Holocaust in Buczacz," *Nova Doba* 48 (1 December 2000), collected by Mykola Kozak, translated by Sofia Grachova.

13 Anne H. Resnik (née Herzog), telephone interview with me, 11 September 2002.

14 Regina Gertner, telephone interview with me, 31 July 2002.

15 Yitzhak Bauer, interview with me, Tel Aviv, November 2003, in Hebrew.

16 John Saunders, telephone interview with me, 30 July 2002.

17 Robert Barton (Bertisz), telephone interview with me, 5 July 2002.

18 Jacob Heiss, telephone interview with me, 5 July 2003, and meeting in New York City, December 2002.

19 Arie Klonicki-Klonymus, *Yoman Avi Adam* [*The Diary of Adam's Father*] (Jerusalem: Hakibbutz Hameuchad, 1969, in Hebrew), 47.

20 *Przeżycia i rozporządzenie Joachima Mincere* [*The Life and Testament of Joachim Mincer*], probably written in 1943, Yad Vashem, in Polish, translated by Eva Lutkiewicz.

21 Undated account by Yitzhak Shalev, formerly Izio Wachtel, sent to me by his son, Ziki Slav, on 25 February 2007.

22 Shulamit Aberdam (Freiberg), Shoah Foundation videotaped testimony, 28 April 1998, Haifa, Israel, in Hebrew.

23 Fannie Kupitz (Feldman), Shoah Foundation videotaped testimony, 25 April 1994, Forest Hills, New York.

24 Salomon and Fania Kupitz, interview with me in New York City, 10 October 2002.

25 This and all subsequent citations of this witness are taken from Kupitz, Shoah Foundation video.

26 Rózia Brecher, "Recollections from the City of Buczacz," Yad Vashem Archives Division: 033, File: 765, E/32–3–, translation from Polish original with help from Joanna Michlic; Rosa Brecher, "Protocol, Taken Down in the Refugee House, Bucharest, Calea Mosilor 128, on 20 May 1945," ZIH 301/4911, translation of German original.

27 Ibid.

28 Alicia Appleman-Jurman, Shoah Foundation videotaped testimony, 29 January 1996, La Habra, California.

29 See the extraordinary apologetic accounts of this man's career, in Yefrem Hasai, "Under Police Uniform There Beat the Heart of a Ukrainian Patriot," *Nova Doba* 16:8065 (23 April 2004); Mykhailo Kheifetz, *Ukrayinski syluety* (Kharkiv: Folio, 2000), available at Kharkiv Group for Human Rights Protection: http://www.khpg.org/index.php?r=14, both translated by Sofia Grachova. And see records of Kaznovsk'kyi's 1957 trial in Ternopil', Branch State Archive of the Security Service of Ukraine (Haluzevyi derzhavnyi arkhiv Sluzhby bezpeky Ukraïny): HDA SBU, m. Ternopil', spr. 30466, 26874, 14050-P, 736, 3713, 14340-P, 9859-P, 8540-P, 8973-P, 14320-P, multiple documents, in Russian and Ukrainian.

30 Eliasz Chalfen, Yad Vashem Testimony, M1/E 1559, translated from Polish by Eva Lutkiewicz.

31 Ester Grintal (Nachtigal), Shoah Foundation videotaped testimony, 21 September 1997, Netanyah, Israel, in Hebrew.

32 Yoel Katz, Shoah Foundation videotaped testimony, 11 December 1995, Netanyah, Israel, in Hebrew.

33 Joe (Yekhezkiel, Jechezkiel, Olszy) Perl, Shoah Foundation videotaped testimony, 14 October 1996, Los Angeles, California.

34 Edzia Spielberg-Flitman, Shoah Foundation videotaped testimony, 14 March 1995, Skokie, Illinois, transcribed by Joshua Tobias.

35 Mojżesz Szpigiel, USHMM, reel 37 301/3492, łódż, 10 March 1948, translated from Polish by Evelyn Zegenhagen.

36 Izaak Szwarc, USHMM, RG-15.084 Acc.1997 A.0125, Reel 5, testimony 327, ZIH 301/327, translated from Polish by Evelyn Zegenhagen.

37 Rene Zuroff (Tabak), Shoah Foundation videotaped testimony, 31 August 1995, Bellmore, New York.

38 This has been discussed especially well by Lawrence L. Langer, *Holocaust Testimonies: The Ruins of Memory*; and Wieviorka, *The Era of the Witness*.

39 Rafael Moses, ed., *Persistent Shadows of the Holocaust: The Meaning to Those Not Directly Affected* (Madison, CT: International Universities Press, 1993); Dan Bar-On, *Legacy of Silence: Encounters with Children of the Third Reich* (Cambridge, MA: Harvard University Press, 1989); and Dan Bar-On, *Fear and Hope: Three Generations of the Holocaust* (Cambridge, MA: Harvard University Press, 1995).

40 Safah Prüfer, USHMM, reel 49, from ZIH 301/4581, trans. Evelyn Zegenhagen, probably written in 1945–46.

41 Trembach, 2003.

42 Emil Skamene (Kleiner), Shoah Foundation videotaped testimony, 3 February 1998, Quebec, Canada, transcribed by Rachel Hoffman.

43 Genia Weksler, USHMM, RG-15.084 Acc.1997 A.0125, Reel 19, Testimony 1865, ZIH 301/1865, sometime in 1946 in Wrocław, translated from Polish by Evelyn Zegenhagen.

44 Bronia Kahane, Shoah Foundation videotaped testimony, 8 August 1995, South Fallsburg, New York, transcribed by Josh Tobias.

45 Aliza Golobov (Bernfeld), Division 0.3, Yad Vashem Testimonies, File # 10241, cassette # 033C/5361, recorded on 29 April 1997, in Hebrew.

46 Hilda Weitz, Shoah Foundation Videotaped testimony, 4 November 1998, Fort Lee, New Jersey, transcribed by Rachel Hoffman.

47 Zofia Pollak (Zonka Berkowicz), Shoah Foundation videotaped testimony, 23 August 1995, Brooklyn, New York, transcribed by Rachel Hoffman.

48 Cyla Sznajder (Huss), Jewish Historical Institute, Warsaw (ZIH) 301/5699, Wrocław, 25 January 1960.

49 Samuel (Shmuel) Rosen, USHMM, translated from the Polish by Evelyn Zegenhagen, reel 20, *testimony 1935*, from ZIH (Jewish Historical Institute, Warsaw), 301/1935, given on 6 August 1946, in Kraków.

50 Samuel (Shmuel) Rosen, Yad Vashem, 03/2055, Tel Aviv, 20 December 1960, in file M-49/1935, translated from Polish by Frank Grelka.

51 Henry Rosen, Shoah Foundation videotaped testimony, 10 November 1997, Chicago, transcribed by James T. Stever. A gist of Henry Rosen's story can also be found in Mordecai Paldiel, *The Path of the Righteous: Gentile Rescuers of Jews during the Holocaust* (Hoboken, NJ: Ktav, 1993), 191–3, along with a photo of Świerszczak.

52 S. Rosen, Yad Vashem, 1960.

53 Omer Bartov interview with Shmuel (Samuel) Rosen and Zev Anderman, Tel Aviv, 12 March 2002, transcribed by Raz Bartov.

54 S. Rosen, Yad Vashem, 1960.

55 H. Rosen, Shoah Foundation videotaped testimony, 1997.

56 The Holocaust Martyrs' and Heroes' Remembrance Authority, The Righteous among the Nations Department, Righteous among the Nations Honored by Yad Vashem by 1 January 2010, www.yadvashem. org, http://www1.yadvashem.org/righteous_new/vwall.html.

57 Wizinger, Moshe, Yad Vashem, 03/3799. The account was written in Cyprus in 1947. Wizinger was a radio technician from Buczacz. Translated from Polish by Eva Lutkiewicz.

58 Bauer, 2003.

59 Bundesarchiv B 162/5182: "Aufklärung von NS-Verbrechen im Kreis Czortków/ Distrikt Galizien, 1941–1944, Sammelverfahren gg. Brettschneider u.a.," deposition taken on 10 January 1968, pp. 6212–4.

60 George (Gershon) Gross, Shoah Foundation Videotaped testimony, 17 June 1996, Deerfield Beach, Florida.

61 Wizinger, Yad Vashem, 03/3799.
62 Pollak, Shoah Foundation videotaped testimony.
63 S. Rosen, Yad Vashem, 1960.
64 Ibid.
65 Members of the Zuhler family in Buczacz included Prof. Zuhler, who taught German at the gymnasium in 1939 and is said to have survived the war; Herzas Zuhler, who was a prominent prewar merchant; and Regina Zuhler, born in 1907, who testified at a German trial in 1965. Stanisław J. Kowalski, *Powiat Buczacki i jego zabytki* (Biały Dunajec-Ostróg: Ośrodek "Wołanie z Wołynia," 2005), 89; Adam Żarnowski, ed., *Kresy Wschodnie II Rzeczypospolitej: Buczacz* (Kraków: Wydanie Własne [privately published], 1992), 9; *Aufklärung von NS-Verbrechen im Kreis Czortków/Distrikt Galizien 1941–1944: Sammelverfahren gg. Brettschneider u.a.*, Bundersarchiv, B 162/5163, pp. 492–3.
66 Bartov interview with Rosen and Anderman, 2002.
67 Yisrael Kohen, ed., *Sefer Buchach* [*The Book of Buczacz*] (Tel Aviv: Am Oved, 1956, in Hebrew), 246, 288.
68 Szwarc, ZIH 301/327. Another account mentions an Abraham Anderman, who is said to have shot a policeman during an *Aktion* in July (more likely June) 1943: Zakhar Gerber, Shoah Foundation video-taped testimony, 28 November 1996, Akko, Israel, in Russian, translated by Jane Zolot-Gassko; similarly, Moshe Wizinger mentions a certain A. Anderman who shot and killed a Ukrainian policeman in June 1943 and then escaped: Wizinger, Yad Vashem, 03/3799; and Yitzhak Bauer's above-cited 1968 deposition speaks of "Max Andermann, a former member of the OD, [who] was killed in May 1944": Bundesarchiv B 162/5182. But Dr. Max Anderman, born in Buczacz in 1907, made a deposition in Israel to a German court in 1965. According to this document, he worked in the Jewish hospital until May 1942, after which he was in hiding until the liberation: Bundesarchiv B 162/5169, *Aufklärung von NS-Verbrechen im Kreis Czortków/Distrikt Galizien, 1941–1944, Sammelverfahren gg. Brettschneider u.a.*, deposition taken on 27 December 1965, pp. 1977–8.
69 For an effective use of oral histories in reconstructing interethnic violence in another part of the world, see Vazira Fazila-Yacoobali Zamindar, *The Long Partition and the Making of Modern South Asia: Refugees, Boundaries, Histories* (New York, NY: Columbia University Press, 2007).

14

KHURBN FORSHUNG

Jewish historical commissions in Europe, 1943–49

Laura Jockusch

It had long been argued that in the immediate aftermath of the Holocaust there was a general silence over the genocide of the Jews. Following an early sense of horror, induced by the discovery of the camps and the news media's horrifying reports and footage of emaciated survivors and mounds of corpses, and after the flurry of interest evoked by the Nuremberg Tribunal, the public put all this aside and moved on to rebuild the ruined cities, indulge in the "economic miracle" of the 1950s, and focus on the new threat of the Cold War. The survivors, it was argued, were reluctant to talk about what had happened to them, and, whether they returned to their original places of abode or built new lives elsewhere, their surrounding societies were even more disinclined to listen. Save for a few early exceptions, the main scholarship on the Holocaust began appearing only in the 1960s and gathered momentum in the 1970s and 1980s, accompanied by a renewed public discussion, which gradually shifted the position of the Holocaust from a marginal event in the history of World War II to what is now seen as a major catastrophe in the heart of Europe.

This picture is not entirely false, but needs to be modified and nuanced. Notably, the trajectory of public discourse over the genocide of the Jews has moved in the opposite direction to that of World War II and Nazism more generally. While scholarship about the latter accumulated in the early postwar decades, not least thanks to the German archives falling into allied hands, it had little to say on the extermination of the Jews. Conversely, early writings on the Holocaust (mostly by survivors, and subsequently also in the State of Israel), focused largely on the victims of the genocide. This writing did not enter into the mainstream of scholarship even when historians began turning their attention to the "final solution," since it was seen as related more to a Zionist politics of memory, a Jewish tradition of lamentation, or an understandable but historically irrelevant mythicization of a national catastrophe. Hence, while World War II was becoming history, the Holocaust was perceived as being transformed into memory.

The larger context of this trend was that European historians had long seen Jewish history as located largely outside their sphere of interest. Modern Jewish historians, dating back to Simon Dubnow at the end of the nineteenth century, had argued for the integration of the Jews into European history more generally, reflecting their centuries-long interaction with Christians on the continent. Dubnow and his followers, not least Emanuel Ringelblum, later founder of the Oyneg Shabes archive in the Warsaw Ghetto, sought to facilitate that integration by modernizing the writing of Jewish history. Both men, and countless others engaged in this undertaking, were murdered by the Nazis. Their loss, and the trauma of the Holocaust deeply undermined this project, and the history of the Jews, not least that of the Holocaust, remained for a long time separate from the history of Europe and World War II.

Ironically, the shift from memory to history in writing on the Holocaust came just as Europe became increasingly interested in memory, epitomized in the "rediscovery" of the sociologist Maurice Halbwachs' writings on "collective memory," and the vast project of mapping Europe's "sites of memory" led by the historian Pierre Nora. And yet, at the same time, such historians as Martin Broszat were arguing that whereas German scholars were producing a "scientific" history of Nazism, Jewish historians were engaged in writing the Holocaust as memory and myth. From this perspective, while Europe could now finally move from documenting history to remembering the past, the alleged Jewish obsession with the memory of past was blocking it from engaging with its history.

To be sure, in the last decades there has been a growing integration of the historiography of World War II and the Holocaust, as well as of the perspectives of perpetrators and victims in the course of the genocide itself, although there is still a long way to go. Similarly, the old project of integrating the Jewish past into European history has progressed but is still largely in its infancy. Yet in all this debate about the relationship between history and memory, what has largely been ignored, forgotten, or dismissed, is that in the immediate wake of the war, and in many cases even before the fighting had ended, groups of Jewish survivors, scholars, amateurs, and intellectuals, in Poland, France, and the displaced persons camps in Germany, Austria, and Italy, began collecting documentary and testimonial evidence in order to provide precisely that crucial basis for writing the history of the Holocaust. This was an immense undertaking under the most challenging conditions conceivable, in a devastated continent, where the divisions between East and West were growing by the day, by men and women who had had just emerged from the most horrendous mass murder in European history. The goals of those involved were in fact to realize the late Dubnow's objective, that is, to record and to write the history of the event. For that purpose they created a vast archive that has indeed served as an invaluable source for subsequent histories of the event. But their own undertaking was largely forgotten: in part, because they were seen as mostly amateur historians, even though their ranks included several major scholars; and in part, because they were conflicted between the goal of writing history and the desire to use their sources for prosecuting the perpetrators; and possibly most important, because of lack of funds, vast logistical difficulties, and the changing international priorities with the onset of the Cold War and the struggle over the State of

Israel. But their endeavor, now salvaged from oblivion by Laura Jockusch, demonstrates that from the very beginning, an important core of survivors had striven to write the Holocaust not as memory and myth but as a historical event, whose reconstruction, based both on official documents and survivors' testimonies, they saw as their commitment to the victims and contribution to posterity.

Introduction

Contrary to the popular assumption that historical research on the Holocaust began in the early 1960s, the systematic study of the mass murder of European Jews started at least one and a half decades earlier.[1] While the Eichmann trial played a seminal role in moving the Holocaust into the center of the historiography on the Nazi regime, it cannot be ignored, however, that Jews throughout Europe had already begun comprehensive research on the destruction of European Jewry as early as 1943: they founded historical commissions, documentation centers, and documentation projects for the purpose of gathering extensive collections of Nazi documents, several thousand eyewitness testimonies and questionnaires, Jewish folklore, photographs, and film material along with museum artifacts.[2] These collections served as proof in claims for restitution and provided vital evidence in the principal war crime trials in the late 1940s and early 1950s. The numerous publications, yet another result of these early initiatives, included a great variety of memoirs, compilations of annotated documents, anthologies of ghetto and camp literature, historical periodicals, and large numbers of meticulous local studies covering the political, socioeconomic, and cultural aspects of the persecution of the Jews in a great array of towns, cities, and regions. Furthermore, the archival collections compiled in the early postwar years laid the basis for the major Holocaust archives, museums, and research institutions in Europe and Israel, such as the Mémorial de la Shoah in Paris, the Jewish Historical Institute in Warsaw, and Yad Vashem in Jerusalem. Even though most of these historical commissions were short-lived, their work proved crucial in raising important questions regarding the decision-making and implementation of the "Final Solution," the Jewish responses to persecution at different stages, the possibilities and constraints for rescue, and the relations between Jews and their non-Jewish neighbors in the face of Nazi occupation. The work of these historical commissions and documentation centers thus serves as a call for a reevaluation of the supposed silence and speechlessness of the survivors in the early postwar years.

Why did these early initiatives to document the Holocaust methodically and comprehensively during and after the war not receive the credit they deserved, and why have their numerous historical publications figured so little in the historiography of the Holocaust? There appear to be several reasons for this historiographic silence. For one, these commissions and documentation centers were by and large proto-professional, grassroots initiatives by people untrained in the methods of academic historical scholarship who acted out of the conviction that their survival of the catastrophe made bearing witness an imperative, and that their experiences qualified them to document the recent past. Only a few professional historians – those who had careers before the war like Philip Friedman or those who made careers as historians after the war such as Léon Poliakov, Nachman Blumental, Josef Kermisz, Isiah Trunk, and Josef Wulf – received any recognition among historians who were not survivors themselves.

The fact that amateur historians constituted the backbone of the historical commissions and documentation centers devalued their work in the eyes of most professional historians.

Another reason for the lack of recognition of these early endeavors of writing the history of the destruction of European Jewry has less to do with the commissions themselves than with the nature of the academic historiography of the Holocaust in Europe and the United States. Until recently, this scholarship has focused mainly on the perpetrators and their sources while it has given only marginal attention to the victims' experiences. Since the works of these early Jewish documentation projects centered on the experiences of the victims, and to a large extent on survivor testimonies collected in the early postwar years, their approach now appears ahead of its time.[3]

The lack of recognition might also have been due to the fact that the work of the historical commissions and documentation centers by and large did not exceed the level of collecting primary sources, documenting and chronicling the events and only rarely reached a more analytical and synthetic level of historiography which academic historians might have appreciated.

These limitations should not take away from the important fact that these historical commissions and documentation centers pioneered in developing a blueprint for the field of Holocaust historiography from a Jewish perspective, which in many ways prefigured later research questions. Through their indefatigable efforts in retrieving any documentation pertaining to the persecution of European Jews left behind by the Germans and their collaborating governments, these initiatives laid the basis for later research into the functioning of those regimes as well as their treatment of European Jews.

This essay analyzes the history of the Jewish historical commissions and documentation centers where they were largest and most significant in implementing their goals: in France and Poland, and in the Jewish Displaced Persons (DP) camps in Germany, Austria, and Italy.[4] After a brief overview of the genesis of the respective institutions, this study explores three questions. Who were the people involved in the historical commissions and documentation centers and what did they hope to gain from the meticulous study of their traumatic past? What methodological tools did they develop to research this European-wide catastrophe in the immediate wake of the event? How was this early documentation work received among the larger public of the *She'erit Hapletah* – the "surviving remnant" – in the respective countries? Concluding remarks discuss the wider significance of the early postwar documentation projects.

"Why historical commissions?" – Foundations and motivations

In the countries in question, two different types of historical commissions and documentation centers emerged: those whose main goal was to assemble documentary evidence for historical scholarship and those which aimed at using the data toward political ends such as the prosecution of war criminals, the fight for material compensation, and against anti-Semitism.

The cases of Poland, Germany, and Italy are of the former type. In Poland, a group of five Holocaust survivors founded a historical commission – *Historishe Komisye* – in Lublin on August 29, 1944, five weeks after the Red Army liberated Eastern Poland from Nazi rule in late July. The commission, headed by the Communist Marek Bitter with the writers Szabse Klugman and Dawid Kupferberg as co-workers, aimed at collecting testimonies from the survivors who flocked the city in search for material and moral support from a newly founded Jewish Committee, the first representative body of the *She'erit Hapletah* in the liberated areas. Due to a lack of personnel and financial means and the difficult conditions of a population of traumatized survivors in a country devastated by war, these efforts had little success and the commission disbanded in early November 1944, less than two and a half months after it was formed.[5] However, on December 28, 1944, the historian Philip Friedman[6] who had gained a reputation as a historian of Polish Jewry before the war and who had recently come to Lublin from Lvov where he had survived the war in hiding, founded a new commission. The Central Jewish Historical Commission (*Centralna Żydowska Komisja Historyczna*, CŻKH), as this institution was named, continued the documentation work of its predecessor on a larger and more professionalized scale while its financial expenses were covered by the newly founded Central Committee of Polish Jews and the Union of Jewish Writers, Journalists, and Artists. The CŻKH, now joined by Nachman Blumental, Josef Kermisz, Mejlech Bakalczuk, and Noe Grüss, and briefly also by the poet Abba Kovner, aimed at

> "researching and illuminating the German murders committed against the Jews of Poland. For that purpose any kind of printed matter, manuscripts, pictures, illustrations will be collected, and oral testimonies of people who suffered and witnessed the Hitler barbarities are written down [. . .]. The commission also has the task of editing the material in [. . .] brochures, monographs and larger publications which will be able to provide a picture of the tremendous atrocities [. . .], the annihilation of the Jewish population, both in terms of the physical extermination, as well as the systematic destruction of the material and cultural treasures of Polish Jewry. The works of the commission will also bring to light the ingenious and sadistic methods used for the first time in world history. Through lectures and publications [the commission will] popularize the results of its research and make it accessible to larger circles of the Jewish and non-Jewish population."[7]

After Poland was completely liberated in spring 1945, the CŻKH established up to twenty-five branches throughout the country, with Regional Historical Commissions in Kraków, Wrocław, Warsaw, Białystok, and Katowice, and transferred its headquarters to Łódź. The branches of Kraków, under the auspices of Michał Borwicz, Josef Wulf, and Nella Thon-Rost, and Warsaw, headed by Hersz Wasser, played a particularly active role.

In Allied-occupied Germany, historical commissions operated among the Jewish Displaced Persons (DP) population in the American and the British Zones. In the British Zone, a historical commission crystallized in the DP camp Belsen on October 10, 1945, in the framework of the cultural office of the Central Committee of Liberated Jews in the British Zone.[8] The initiators – among them the Polish-born journalists Paul Trepman, Dovid Rosental, and Rafael Olewski along with the actor Sami Feder – aimed at recording the recent catastrophe by collecting "pictures, photographs, all kinds of publications, songs and stories in all languages, clothing and uniforms, urns of the dead and burnt, lists of people resettled, murdered, witnesses, prisoners; books and Torah scrolls – everything, relating to the Hitler era."[9] Initially, the commission meant to function as an archival department of the Central Committee collecting documents on the recent cataclysm on behalf of the YIVO Institute for Jewish Research in New York. It maintained correspondents in Celle, Bremen, and Göttingen and soon adopted the name Central Historical Commission at the Central Committee of Liberated Jews in the British Zone (*Tsentrale historishe komisye baym tsentral komitet fun di bafrayte yidn in der Britisher zone*). In May 1947, the Polish-born Cwi Horowic[10] established the Jewish Historical Commission for Lower-Saxonia (*Jüdische Historische Kommission für Niedersachsen*) in Göttingen as a regional branch of the commission in Belsen.

In the U.S. Zone of Germany, on November 28, 1945, Israel Kaplan, a Byelorussian-born journalist and history teacher, and Moyshe Yosef Feigenbaum, a Polish-born accountant and former CŻKH co-worker, founded a historical commission (*historishe komisye*) in Munich, as a sub-division of the cultural office of the Central Committee of Liberated Jews in Bavaria.[11] They intended to prepare "materials for the future historian that would enable him to fathom the reason why liberalism turned into Hitlerism in Germany."[12] The group planned to collect both German documents and eyewitness accounts of the survivors and to place it at the disposal of the Jewish Agency for Palestine, in the hope that this way, the documentation material would not only be of value for the writing of Jewish history but would also serve "in the fight for our rights in the international arena."[13] Within several months, the commission turned into the Central Historical Commission (*Tsentrale Historishe Komisye*) supervising over fifty departments in the entire U.S. Zone.

In Italy, the organization of former Jewish partisans *Pakhakh* (acronym for the Yiddish *partizaner, khayolim un khalutsim* – Partisans, Soldiers, and Pioneers) established historical commissions in Milan and Rome in fall 1945 under the leadership of the Lithuanian-born journalist Moyshe Kaganowicz.[14] The *Pakhakh* movement had originated in Poland in spring 1945 when former Jewish partisans maintained their organizational structures for the purpose of mutual aid and preparation for immigration to Palestine.[15] Although a historical commission had been set up in Poland with the goal of "collecting auto-biographic tales and documents of surviving partisans, their comrades in arms, their way of life in the woods and steppes, their battles and methods of fight against the Nazis,"[16] this effort bore little fruit as those involved chose to leave Poland as a result of their Zionist agenda. However, because of the difficulties in accessing Palestine even by means of illegal immigration, the majority of the *Pakhakh* members stayed in the DP camps of Austria, Germany, and Italy. As the most convenient point of embarkation for Palestine, Italy became the center of the movement and its historical commissions and the historical commission in Rome soon became *Pakhakh*'s Central Historical Commission (*Tsentale Historishe Komisye bay Pakhakh*) for all Italy.[17]

The cases of France and Austria are of the second type of historical commissions and documentation centers whose primary goal was to use the data they collected toward political ends. In France, the documentation work had already begun during the war when, on April 28, 1943, the Russian-born industrialist Isaac Schneersohn[18] gathered a group of forty representatives of various official and underground Jewish organizations to form a documentation center (*centre de documentation*) in Grenoble which was then under the relatively benign Italian occupation. The group hoped to document the persecution of the Jews of France in order to provide those who would survive with evidence to buttress their legal and material claims in the postwar era. As an early mission statement asserted,

> "[a]bove all, we want to write the Great Book of the Martyrdom of French Judaism. Therefore we must unite large-scale documentation of what is going on in the two zones [. . .]. Assess the scale of [. . .] Aryanized Jewish property; portray the suffering of internees, deportees, of Jewish hostages shot dead; make the heroism of Jewish fighters visible [. . .] register the attitudes of governments, the adminis-tration, the various levels of public opinion; note the reactions of the intellectuals, the middle and working classes, [. . .] the [. . .] churches . . . In short, we maintain that everything having a favorable or unfa-vorable effect on the Jewish world of France must be brought to light in a strictly objective manner. [. . .] We must prepare the [juridical] demands of the Jews of France [. . .]. Thus, [. . .] the goal we suggest is to work together in compiling a vast documentation [. . .] which will eventually serve our representatives at the League of Nations."[19]

Little was achieved, however, before the liberation of France. The actual work began when Schneersohn reconstituted the documentation center in Paris in fall 1944 and renamed it Center of Contemporary Jewish Documentation (*Centre de Documentation Juive Contemporaine*, CDJC).

In Allied-occupied Austria, the Polish-born teacher and former CŻKH affiliate Mejlech Bakalczuk[20] established a Jewish Historical Commission (*Jüdische*

Historische Kommission) in Linz in early 1946. In summer 1946, the Jewish Central Committee for the American Zone of Austria in Linz incorporated the commission in its cultural office and placed it under the leadership of the Galician-born engineer Simon Wiesenthal. The Jewish Historical Documentation (*Jüdische Historische Dokumentation*), as Wiesenthal renamed the commission in January 1947, aimed at "fighting for Jewish rights in the world [. . .] and for the expiation of the crimes of the war years, as well as securing historical material for future generations."[21] In Vienna, the Polish-born Towia (Tadek) Frydman[22] took a parallel initiative in July 1946 for the purpose of collecting evidence against war criminals in Austria.[23] The commissions in Vienna and Linz, both named Jewish Historical Documentation, collaborated closely, establishing a network of correspondents in the DP camps of Austria.

Despite their tendencies to place different emphases on historical research on the one hand and the fight for justice on the other – a separation which was not clear-cut and tended to shift in the course of their work[24] – the survivors active in the commissions shared a set of common characteristics in terms of their organizational structures, motivations for the documentation work as well as in their social makeup.

Even though some of the initiatives referred to themselves as "commissions," others as "documentation" or "documentation project," they all shared the organizational structure of *commissions* in the sense that they were provisional bodies of between less than a dozen and one hundred people who charged themselves with the task of documenting and researching the catastrophe according to certain principles and methods they had agreed upon. Usually the group was guided by a central branch, headed by a board of directors, and maintained several correspondents or sub-commissions in different DP camps, cities, or regions.

In all the countries in question, the commission activists were motivated by a strong conviction that their survival made bearing witness a moral imperative for every single survivor, a "holy duty" (*heyliker khoyv*) toward the dead and the generations to come. This sense of duty was a common theme of the calls which the commissions issued in the Jewish press for the purpose of encouraging the larger public of survivors to join the historical work. For example, an appeal of the CŻKH in Łódź of October 1946 argued:

> "Remember what Amalek did to thee! *With a burning call* the Central Jewish Historical Commission in Poland is urging all of those, who under the German occupation were in the ghettos, camps, lived on the Aryan side, hid in the woods or fought in partisan units [. . .] to hand over to the historical commission the accounts of your personal experiences as well as of others in the dreadful time of the German rule. [. . .] *The blood of our martyrs, of our relatives is still fresh, it screams and calls upon us not to forget!* The Jews of every town and village [. . .] who stayed alive are obliged to report all details of the events.

The surviving Jews are obliged to give to the historical commission pictures, documents, community registers [*pinkeysim*], diaries and other items in their possession. *This is a holy duty for every individual.* We hope that everyone understands the importance of this and fulfills his duty toward Jewish history."[25]

As indicated in this call, the survivors active in these commissions regarded historical documentation as a way of mourning and commemorating the dead. The act of collecting and recording in itself had the function of a symbolic "gravestone," "memorial," or "monument" for those who had been murdered. Given that their graves were unknown and that the majority of the victims did not have graves, the commission workers regarded their historical project as the epitaph which the survivors actually could erect for eternalizing the memory of their dead. For example, an undated call from the U.S. Zone of Germany stated:

"Brothers! Remember that not a single detail of our life before, during and after the war must be forgotten! Do not forget that every document, picture, song, legend is the only gravestone which we can place on the unknown graves of our parents, siblings, and children! Therefore help the historical commission in its work! Describe the economic, social, and cultural life of the destroyed Jewish community from which you come. Describe the activity of the society or organization you used to be a member of before the war. Eternalize how the Jews lived, fought, and were murdered under the Nazi regime. Eternalize all expressions, legends, and stories from the bygone tragic days. Write down the songs sung in ghettos, camps, and among the partisans during the Nazi era. Hand the material over to the historical commission which collects and preserves this material for the generations to come! Do not refuse your help when the historical commission turns to you!"[26]

Apart from eternalizing the memory of the dead and the culture and way of life that had been destroyed, the symbolic historical epitaph would also have the function of reminding the perpetrators of their deeds and of the fact "that we, the survivors, will never forget and never forgive!"[27] as a call from Łódź put it.

Yet the survivors felt equally obliged toward future generations of Jews. Those who had not witnessed the cataclysm themselves needed to be provided with an accurate and comprehensive account of the tragic events or else future generations would not know what European Jews had endured and the memory of the dead would not be perpetuated. For example, a call from the U.S. Zone of Germany urged: "Brother Jew! Fulfill your duty toward the generation to come. Report to the historical commission about your survival of the concentration camps, in hiding, and about partisan life, so that your children will know your path of martyrdom."[28] The commission activists believed that this "holy duty" toward the dead and the generations to come could only be fulfilled if documenting become a communal project joined by every single survivor. Not only did they regard every testimony, document, poem, or photograph as a symbolic "stone" added to the "monument" they endeavored to build, but they regarded every survivor "as a piece of history"[29] worthy of being preserved. Moreover, the historical truth exposed in the documentation was the most powerful charge against the perpetrators and the most poignant appeal to the "conscience of the world"[30] to buttress the material and moral claims of the survivors in the postwar world. For the commission activists, historical documentation was a necessary pre-condition for the rebuilding of Jewish life because it helped them to fulfill their moral obligations toward the dead and the generations to come.

In all countries, both in Western and Eastern Europe, the drive to document was spurred by activists who were survivors of Eastern European, predominantly Polish, backgrounds. With few exceptions, most commission affiliates had no training in history but were accountants, engineers, lawyers, writers, journalists, teachers, merchants, and medical doctors among other.[31] This dichotomy between professional historians and so-called amateurs led to deep tensions among the researchers.[32] This was further complicated by the fact that many of the younger co-workers were without higher education as a result of the persecution. The heads of the commissions, however, often nonetheless took pride in the diversity of their co-workers including not only diversity in social, religious, and educational backgrounds but also in age as well as gender.[33] At times, female commission workers seem to have prevailed. For example, in November 1945, twenty out of the thirty co-workers of the headquarters of CŻKH in Łódź were women and its regional and local branches had fifty employees, men and women in equal parts.[34] While it is most difficult to ascertain the exact number of the commission workers because of the high fluctuation in personnel and the lack of statistics, an estimated 500–800 people seem to have worked for the commissions in France, Poland, Germany, Austria, and Italy in the years 1944–1949.[35] In most cases, it is virtually impossible to know the biographical and social backgrounds of the employees, not to mention their motivations for engaging in the historical work. Although rare, there is some evidence of what the historical commissions meant to some of the workers. For example, Zelig Pacanowski, a 38-year-old survivor of the Łódź ghetto and the Birkenau extermination camp, where he had lost his wife and child, wrote to the CŻKH in Łódź in May 1946: "When Mrs. Hirsz visited us in the hospital she invited me to work for the Jewish historical commission. This invitation is the most beautiful present I have received these days. This work will give my life a purpose."[36] A young woman by the name of Gesja Grynwald, who had survived on "Aryan papers" in a Polish village together with her two small children, wrote to the CŻKH in Łódź after it had called

307

upon the Jewish population to provide information on Jewish mass graves in Poland in July 1946:

"I am very pleased that finally there is an organization interested in knowing where our brothers and sisters lie [. . .]. Back then, I often thought if I survive, I will do much for those who have so tragically perished. Yet, now I am simply ashamed in front of the dead because we, the survivors, have forgotten so quickly. [. . .] When I read [about your project], I cried with joy because finally people are taking an interest."[37]

Such revelations among the lower echelons of commission workers are very rare, however.

Among the leaders of the commissions there was a tendency to see themselves as part of an Eastern European Jewish tradition according to which history writing was a communal project and a form of self-defense against persecution equaling armed resistance in its honorability and significance.[38] In fact, many saw themselves as continuing documentation projects which had originated during the war. For example, the historical commissions in Göttingen and Munich understood their work as a continuation of the *Oyneg Shabes* (Yiddish, "joy of the Sabbath") archive directed by the Polish Jewish historian Emmanuel Ringelblum in the underground of the Warsaw ghetto in the years 1940–1943.[39] In Poland, there was a direct link between the CŻKH and *Oyneg Shabes* because the only survivors of Ringelblum's staff, the writer Rachel Auerbach and the former secretary of the underground archive, Hersz Wasser, became active in CŻKH's Warsaw branch and helped to unearth portions of the archives under the rubble of the ghetto in September 1946 and December 1950. In Italy, Yitskhok Kvintman, secretary of the Central Historical Commission in Rome, asserted that *Pakhakh's* historical commissions worked toward fulfilling "the last will of the famous Jewish historian, Professor Dubnow, who shouted on his last way: 'Jews, write, record, and tell this to the future generations'."[40]

At times the commission leaders expressed their own sense of superiority over Western European Jews who did not share this Jewish cultural heritage in which historical documentation equaled resistance. At least this must have been Feigenbaum's rationale when he rebuked German Jewish survivors for neither founding historical commissions of their own nor supporting the commissions initiated by Jewish DPs of Eastern European backgrounds in occupied Germany.[41] He explained the apparent disinterest of the German Jews in the historical work and the absence of secret Jewish archives in Germany, arguing that German Jews lacked the "dynamics of the Jewish communities in Eastern Europe," were "brought up in discipline" and therefore "far from revolutionary and conspirational deeds."[42] While Feigenbaum certainly oversimplified the nature of the encounter between the German and Eastern European survivors in the realm of historical documentation in postwar Germany, comparable popular grassroots initiatives to document the recent catastrophe were virtually absent among Western European survivors.[43]

"Sewage workers" of holocaust research

Just as many commission activists shared a sense of acting in a distinct tradition of history writing they also had a sense that they were "pioneers of a new science that is being born,"[44] as Michał Borwicz,[45] director of CŻKH's Kraków branch formulated it – or, to use the less idealizing words of a CDJC co-worker, the commissions were doing the work of "sewerage workers"[46] for a new field of Jewish historiography. To be precise, the unique difficulty lay in the unprecedented nature of the destruction of European Jews in terms of its numbers of victims, geographic scope, and the method and planning which had exceeded all previous catastrophes of the Jewish past.[47] The quality of the atrocities seemed to render conventional methods of historical inquiry defective and even the language appeared inadequate to describe what had occurred.[48] The new field of research – khurbn forshung (destruction research, also Churbnforschung, études churbaniques)[49] in Philip Friedman's nomenclature – needed to draw from an eclectic methodology combining history and sociology and using a broad array of historical sources. Among these were questionnaires, folklore, photograph and film material, sound recordings, museum artifacts, statistical and legal records.[50]

In establishing a methodology for the new field, the commissions returned to and reinvigorated the social science-oriented approach to studying Jewish society both in the past and present developed by the YIVO Institute for Jewish Research in interwar Poland. Many commission workers had been affiliated with YIVO before the war or were at least familiar with YIVO's works and the commissions stood in close contact with YIVO in New York which assumed an advisory function.[51] Although the commission workers saw themselves in the Eastern European Jewish tradition of history writing and used research methods developed already in the interwar period, they nevertheless had a sense that they needed to build a new field of research in which "neither we nor anyone else in the world had had any experience"[52] and that this was a process of "self-education" as the teacher Noe Grüss admitted in his first annual report on the work of the CŻKH in early 1946.[53]

Early on in this process, the commissions placed different emphases on historical sources, some giving greater credence to perpetrators, others to victims. The CDJC focused almost exclusively on collecting perpetrator sources because, as Léon Poliakov,[54] the CDJC's research director explained, the CDJC's research was based on the assumption that the Nazi mass murder of European Jews was the result of a grand scheme whose origins and implementation could only be understood through the "confessions of the perpetrators"[55] which allowed the researcher "to penetrate the laboratory where the Nazi venom was distilled."[56] Consequently, the CDJC did not collect survivor testimonies and its publications were virtually all based on German and Vichy documentation.

The commission activists in Poland, Germany, Austria, and Italy shared a fundamental skepticism as to the value of perpetrator sources for the description of the Jewish cataclysm. They had realized that Nazi documents intentionally concealed the regime's actual treatment of the Jews. For example, Michał Borwicz observed that "all German documents are false, not in terms of their authenticity, but in terms of their content. First of all, they are full of pseudonyms or euphemisms. The murder is never indicated as such, the cremation is never named."[57] In fact, Borwicz believed "the German system was based [. . .] on a double accountancy of the murders in inversed proportionality to the actual importance of the events. Of the most dreadful acts very little traces were left while on the less significant issues there is extensive communication."[58] Apart from their faulty nature, German sources did not give an adequate description of the victims' experiences and responses to the persecution at various stages. For example, Philip Friedman argued,

> "as worthy as the administrative documents might be, they are not capable of giving a thorough and truthful description of the most difficult, saddest chapters of our martyrdom. The administrative German documents have rarely reflected the atrocities of the *Aktionen* and concentration camps; on the contrary, these German documents were meant to conceal these atrocities through a camouflaging jargon of criminals."[59]

Consequently, Nazi documents could only be used if they complemented with Jewish sources. To that end, the commissions in Poland, Germany, and Austria concentrated on collecting both German and Jewish sources. However, the activists were aware of the dilemma that as a result of the annihilation process sources pertaining to the victims' experiences virtually did not exist and the survivors were "left with empty hands."[60] Certainly, the remnants of Emmanuel Ringelblum's secret ghetto archive soon assumed an iconic position among the commission workers also outside of Poland as the ideal Jewish source, because it was not produced after the fact but captured the Jewish experience of German occupation as the events unfolded.[61] However, it was clear that *Oyneg Shabes* had been the notable exception to a devastating rule: together with the human beings, Nazi genocidal policies had targeted Jewish cultural treasures. Consequently, the survivors were deprived of "traditional" historical sources, such as institutional and administrative records, which had been destroyed along with Jewish archives, libraries, museums, organizations, and communal and cultural institutions.[62]

The commissions in Poland, Germany, Austria, and Italy therefore saw their main task in creating new, "non-traditional," historical records drawn from the memories of the survivors, mainly in the form of eyewitness testimonies and questionnaires. In Poland and in the U.S. Zone of Germany, the commission leaders designed various kinds of questionnaires, either as guidelines for the commission workers who interviewed survivors to take their testimonies (as was the case in Poland), or as fill-in-questionnaires completed by the commission workers or the survivors themselves (as was the case in Germany). These questionnaires interrogated the survivors on a great variety of wartime experiences, among them ghettos, labor, concentration and extermination camps, bunkers, hiding places, life in partisan units, and on living with false papers among the non-Jewish populations – on the so-called "Aryan side." The questions concentrated not on the physical persecution alone but on the socio-economic, cultural, and political effects of persecution on Jewish society and the relations between Jews and non-Jews.[63]

In their quest to map out the new field of research, the commission workers often debated whether or not they – as survivors and Jews – could be at all "objective" or "scholarly" historians given their painful emotional ties with the subject matter of their research. As Philip Friedman described this dilemma in September 1945:

"The task of a historian – a Jew – regarding the recent past is particularly difficult. Writing history requires the guidance of reason and not that of emotions which creates numerous problems. In writing the history of the six years of German occupation, one cannot merely be a scholar having purely scholarly goals in mind, because a large role is played by factors of an emotional nature, such as personal experiences and personal loss."[64]

Friedman's colleague Noe Grüss was more radical in admitting that "scholarly objectivity" was virtually impossible for the survivors when he stated:

"We are not 'objective' and cold scientists. We approach the material of our work not like a professor approaches a body in a morgue. Our historical material are the dead bodies of our children and parents, the bodies of our dishonored wives and sisters, the memories of the partisans and ghetto fighters, the courageous hearts and burning love for [our] people and the disdain for our tormentors."[65]

Given these emotional constraints, many survivors questioned whether the time was ripe for historical research on the recent catastrophe.[66] Yet in spite of its being a subject of heated debates, this question was a rhetorical one for most commission associates. In essence, they were convinced that they should not lose time under any circumstances because time was working against them; they needed to act immediately to seize memory while it was "fresh" and while documents were still available. Not only in the sense that memory would become less reliable as time went by, but also in the sense that once the survivors had adjusted to their new lives, testimony taking would become even more difficult. This imperative for immediate action was especially strong among those commission activists operating among the DP population, where large numbers of survivors being held "captive" made their interrogation relatively easy.[67] Another reason why the commission activists believed that it was not too early to begin to research the recent past was the fact that despite its proximity to the present, the *khurbn* was a clear-cut event with a well-defined subject matter and it was already more thoroughly documented than other historical events in the more remote Jewish past.[68]

For some commission workers, the question of whether it might be too early for historical research on the recent catastrophe was irrelevant because they did not see themselves as historians. Instead, they saw their task in preparing the tools for future historians who would analyze this material from a greater distance.[69] Others, most notably Philip Friedman, argued that personal experience as such did not necessarily prevent objectivity. Since all historical writing was a matter of interpretation, Friedman maintained, there was "no such thing as uncolored historiography."[70] What made any historian a good historian was "a clearly defined philosophical framework, within which he [sic] remains loyal to the documentary sources [and] does not let passionate, political or personal considerations influence him in his work of analysis and interpretation."[71] In the context of *khurbn forshung*, this meant refraining from hyperbole and over-sentimentalizing and withstanding the tendency to indulge in accusatory or idealizing descriptions – especially in the context of the Jewish leadership in the ghettos or Jewish resistance and heroism.[72] Although natural from a psychological point of view, tendentiousness and emotionality were counterproductive for the endeavor of the *khurbn forshers* whose historical record could only convince through a factual description of the events, leaving the accusation to attorneys and judges.[73] Ultimately, only an awareness of the shortcomings and weaknesses of their endeavor, an open methodological discourse, and careful training of their co-workers could lead to qualitative results.

As early as 1947, many commission activists believed that the time had come to move beyond simple documentation and use the material compiled in creating a "great synthesis" on the presumably broader, deeper, and inclusive level of a more analytical and far-seeing historiography.[74] Friedman encouraged his colleagues not to shy away from such a synthesis, since it constituted a mere starting point in establishing the new field:

> "No synthesis is perfect, none is eternal. All are subject to being revised, recast, modified in the course of centuries. This is one of the fundamental laws of the human spirit and of all spiritual creation. Our synthetic works will certainly not represent the last word in Jewish historical scholarship on this subject, but they must constitute a beginning."[75]

The precondition for such a "synthesis" was the close collaboration of all historical commissions and documentation centers on a European level, for the geographic scope of the Holocaust necessitated a comparative perspective. After all, as Friedman argued,

"no Josephus Flavius would be capable of covering the full extent of the recent catastrophe on his own. [. . .] Such work can only be done by a collective of scholars."[76]

Therefore, in December 1947, the CDJC hosted the First European Conference of Jewish Historical Commissions and Documentation Centers for the purpose of coordinating the research efforts. Thirty-two delegates from thirteen countries founded a "European Coordination Committee" for the purpose of exchanging documents, standardizing research methods, and publishing a scholarly journal.[77] Despite the fact that the delegates shared a sense of unity as a "community of victims," they were divided on various issues which caused the efforts at coordinating their research to fail. For example, there was a latent competition over leadership within the "community of victims": Polish Jews felt entitled because the Polish Jewish community had suffered such extraordinary losses whereas French Jews claimed leadership on the basis of the republican and humanitarian values that France represented in postwar Europe. The delegates were divided on whether they saw the ultimate purpose of the documentation work in terms of Jewish historical scholarship as an end in itself or as a tool in the political fight against anti-Semitism, fascism, and reaction and in the struggle for bringing the perpetrators to justice. Furthermore, the delegates disagreed on the language and intended audience of the commissions' publications. Some maintained that the studies on the Holocaust had to be in the language of the "Jewish masses," Yiddish, to reach a Jewish audience throughout the world, while others opted for French and English to reach a broader, predominantly non-Jewish audience. A latent conflict among the delegates also arose from the general problem that a minority of professional historians and committed laypeople who saw historical scholarship as the main goal of their endeavors confronted a majority of amateurs who were primarily interested in the practical use of the documentation material the commissions had collected to date. These ideological divisions were further complicated by the burgeoning Cold War which made the interaction of the commissions in Eastern and Western Europe increasingly difficult. The European Coordination Committee also suffered from a chronic lack of funding which rendered it defunct before it could begin its work.[78] The tragedy of this was that despite the European-wide scope of the Holocaust itself and of the documentation projects among the *She' erit Hapletah* in Europe, no European-wide collaboration emerged among the various commissions because this well-intended and deeply committed group of *khurbn forshers* remained divided by country of origin, language, approach, and even the ultimate goals of their efforts.

313

What this intended "synthesis" would have looked like, had it been realized, remains opaque. Several oblique references by some of the commission activists, most notably Philip Friedman, suggest that the envisioned "synthesis" would have included comparative studies of Nazi polices against the Jews as well as of the instruments and institutions the Germans and their collaborating governments had created to implement these policies. "Synthetic" works would have been less localized and documentary, that is to say, they would not have been limited to annotated primary sources, but have given more of a historical narrative covering not only towns or cities but entire countries, or even Nazi-occupied Europe at large. They would also have considered the behavior of the Germans, the response of the Jews to persecution, and the role of non-Jews in and outside of the Nazi orbit in either assisting the Jews or collaborating with the Germans. Last but not least, "synthetic" works might have integrated both official sources of the Germans and their collaborators as well as Jewish sources from during and after the war.[79]

The historical commissions in the "Jewish street" of postwar Europe

Most survivors in the respective countries were ambivalent toward the historical commissions, even though both commission activists and outside observers of the She'erit Hapletah noted, the survivors had a great urge to speak and write about their recent past, an urge sometimes described by activists and observers as being pathologic and obsessive.[80] Philip Friedman interpreted this sudden interest in history writing among the survivors as a "dynamic tension comparable to the messianic movements which followed our earlier national catastrophes."[81] He further observed: "Today we have hundreds of Nathan Neta Hanovers, who feel a need to write down their exceptional experiences. Hundreds and hundreds of people, who in their entire lives have never mustered any interest in historical research, now out of an inner, irresistible urge, grab a pen to write."[82] By referring to the seventeenth-century chronicler of the Chmelnicki pogroms, Friedman indicated that he deemed the masses of antiquarians and chroniclers among the She'erit Hapletah inadequate for twentieth-century khurbn forshung. In fact, Friedman and other commission workers saw a certain danger in this sudden and amateurish interest in history writing because it might turn into "graphomania and a people's plague"[83] and a "psychosis of publicity"[84] which could result in a "flood of publications by people without scholarly responsibility."[85] However, despite the fact that the recent past was omnipresent in the lives of the survivors and was the subject of popular writing, cultural events, and commemorative celebrations, when the commissions asked the survivors to engage in systematic documentation and methodical research in the form of testimonies and questionnaires, the majority showed indifference or even reluctance.

There appear to be several reasons for this paradox. Of course there were different levels of involvement with the commissions, from either a one-time donation of a testimony or questionnaire to permanent work as a *zamler* (collector) of historical material. On the level of one-time cooperation, many survivors were apparently reluctant to submit their experiences to the historical commission as an institution with co-workers who might ask questions and raise issues which the survivors did not want to talk about.[86] It was less burdensome if the survivors could choose what they would write about rather than have a commission worker follow a complex questionnaire touching on a comprehensive array of subjects. The official appearance and scholarly behavior of the commission workers, the official stationery, that the testimonies received a stamp and were signed by the witness and the protocol writer, and were often verified by another witness, might have intimidated some survivors from cooperating with the commissions.[87] Many survivors neither seem to have understood what the commissions were looking for nor grasped the significance of methodical historical work.[88] As time went by, commission workers noted a growing "passivity" and "forgetfulness" among the survivors, which seemed to prevent people from following the commissions' invitations to give testimonies.[89] They believed that survivors had been most responsive immediately after the liberation while their willingness to testify declined as their lives resumed normalcy.[90] In the DP camps – despite the obvious already stated advantage of having so many survivors so close at hand – the historical commissions had to compete for the attention of the survivors against political parties, educational facilities, and entertainment as well as the urge of many to concentrate on the future through founding families.[91]

As far as the recruiting of permanent workers was concerned, the psychological burden of the historical work seems to have been the greatest obstacle, perhaps even greater than the fact that the research was time-consuming and paid poorly. Working for the historical commissions on a daily basis meant literally "going back into the graves," as Feigenbaum described it.[92] Similarly, Noe Grüss of the CŻKH in Łódź noted:

> "A person who engages in the monotonous work of the historical commission is depressed. Every document is a tragedy, every file is a murder. Tragedies of individuals and families, murders of entire generations. You look at photographs of people hanged or of those who were candidates for the ovens, you read reports on the amount of fuel used to burn people. There is no word which can possibly describe the state of mind in which we work – 'graveyard atmosphere,' 'mood of the grave' – all these do not express the experiences and thoughts evoked by our work."[93]

This kind of work-related depression also affected the most committed of the commission workers.[94] Permanent workers could not allow themselves the luxury of the "healthy symptom" (*a gezunder symptom*)[95] of forgetting. With a good portion of self-irony Feigenbaum remarked that it required no small amount of insanity and stubbornness for a survivor to work for the commissions voluntarily.[96] Only the conviction of the ultimate necessity to document the atrocities for the sake of the dead and the generations to come and for the historical truth could compensate the commission workers for the agonizing effects of the work itself.

An integral part of the commissions' public relations work thus focused on convincing the survivors that methodical historical documentation would benefit their postwar lives and on harnessing the general interest in the recent past for the systematic documentation work pursued by the historical commissions. To that end, the commissions launched an indefatigable and multifaceted "propaganda work" (propagande arbet) which used publications,[97] appeals and posters,[98] historical exhibitions,[99] and essay writing contests[100] and sent commission workers to establish personal contacts with the survivors.[101] In France and Poland, "Societies of the Friends" were established to raise funds, sell commission publications, and enhance public awareness among the larger Jewish community.[102] This way the commissions persuaded several thousand survivors to make one-time or short-term contributions.

In the years 1944–1949, they collected around 16,000 testimonies and questionnaires.[103] As a comparison, when Steven Spielberg's Shoah Visual History Foundation began its work in 1994, it planned to have interviewed 300,000 survivors by the year 2000. By spring 1998, the foundation had collected only close to 40,000 interviews, although it had a staff of 240 full-time employees and a 60 million dollar budget for the years 1995–1998.[104] The Fortunoff Video Archive for Holocaust Testimonies at Yale University gathered 34,000 testimonies between 1981 and 1995.[105] Bearing in mind that the Jewish historical commissions worked at a time of extreme material shortages in countries devastated by war, with interviewers and interviewees who were not only traumatized by their experiences but also worried about their most basic needs, such as food, housing, and physical safety, their achievements are extraordinary.

Conclusion

The case of the historical commissions and documentation centers shows that immediately after the liberation, Holocaust survivors began to document the recent cataclysm because they believed that historical documentation was crucial in the reconstruction process, since it best served the present and future political, material, and moral needs of the survivors: chronicling the tragedy was a way to commemorate the dead and assure that the account of the events be passed on to posterity. The activists also believed that the data collected would serve the prosecution of perpetrators, buttress claims for restitution, and facilitate the fight for Jewish rights and would further constitute the basis for future historical research.

While the commissions differed in their emphases on history writing on the one hand, and the fight for justice on the other, they also differed in their larger self-perceptions. For the commission workers in the DP camps in Germany, Austria, and Italy, it was clear from the beginning that their stay in Europe was temporary and that they planned on continuing their work outside of Europe, preferably in the framework of an independent Jewish state. Documenting the atrocities provided a justification for the otherwise involuntary and prolonged sojourn on the "cursed soil" of Europe, of Germany in particular, and it was a vibrant affirmation of Jewish survival. The DP commissions dissolved in the late 1940s and early 1950s and handed their collections to what would become Yad Vashem in Jerusalem.[106] However, apart from contributing the nucleus of the Yad Vashem archives, the work of the DP commissions did not find its continuation in Israel. This was due to the fact that the Yad Vashem leadership, most notably its first director, the historian Benzion Dinur, rejected the former DP commission activists as amateurs and did not want them to participate in Holocaust research in Israel which Dinur sought to establish as an academic field under the auspices of the Hebrew University of Jerusalem.[107] As a committed Zionist, Dinur saw the Holocaust as the outcome of the archetypical antipathy of non-Jews toward Jews, which was inherent in the exilic Jewish existence. Therefore, he conceptualized research on the Holocaust within a broad framework of *galut* study and the history of anti-Semitism rather than focusing on the specific history and development of the Holocaust as had been the concern of the historical commissions in the DP camps.[108]

In France, those who had initiated the CDJC's documentation work, predominantly Jews of Eastern European backgrounds who had come to France prior to the First World War or in the interwar period, strongly identified with France's culture and republican values. While the CDJC activists had initially aimed at collecting evidence in order to bring the perpetrators to justice, reclaim legal equality, and gain reparations for despoiled Jewish property, they increasingly came to focus on historical research. However, the CDJC never abandoned its pursuit of postwar justice and provided the French delegation at the Nuremberg Trials and other local French tribunals with documentary evidence from its archives. The CDJC's research methods differed from those applied elsewhere in that they did not use the help of non-professional *zamlers* and did not rely on testimonies but used institutional records of the Germans and the Vichy regime. For the CDJC activists, narrating the story of wartime Jewish suffering – and Jewish participation in the *Résistance*, as they increasingly emphasized – was a means of integrating the Jewish narrative into the general French narrative of wartime suffering and resistance. It was also a means of reintegrating the survivors into their surrounding society. For the CDJC activists it was beyond question that they would continue their research in France, for they saw themselves primarily as Frenchmen while their Jewish identity was secondary. In 1956, a memorial and museum (*Tombeau du Martyr Juif Inconnu*, today *Mémorial de la Shoah*) was added to the documentation center and even though it initially did not meet the support of the French Jewish community, it gradually became a central *lieu de mémoire* for the French Jewry's commemoration of the Holocaust.[109]

In Poland, the CŻKH activists understood the murder of over three million Polish Jews as a national Jewish catastrophe which had exceeded the suffering of non-Jewish Poles. However, because they conceived themselves as a national minority in Poland, they deemed the Jewish tragedy an integral part of the history of Poland under German occupation. From the outset of its work, the CŻKH had placed major emphasis on scholarship, continuing the social science-oriented approach to the study of the Jewish past developed by YIVO in interwar Poland, using the help of non-professional *zamlers* from all echelons of the Jewish community. In addition, the commission in Łódź pursued the fight for justice. To that end, it closely collaborated with the High Commission for Research on German Crimes in Poland (*Główna Komisja Badania Zbrodni Niemieckich w Polsce*), established by the Polish Ministry of Justice in March 1945 to research German war crimes, and some of its co-workers testified at Polish trials against German war criminals. In the summer of 1947, the Łódź-based headquarters of the CŻKH moved to Warsaw and as of October that year, the historical commission was replaced by the Jewish Historical Institute (*Żydowski Instytut Historyczny*, ŻIH) Warsaw. Until 1949, the Institute maintained branches in Łódź, Kraków, Wrocław, Katowice, Białystok, Szczecin, and Wałbrzych and as of April 1948, the Institute also housed a Jewish museum in addition to its archives and research facilities.[110] The growing repression of the Communist regime and the shrinking autonomy granted to the Jewish minority in Poland caused most of the former commission workers, especially those who were committed to scholarship and unwilling to compromise their scholarly standards by political agitation, to leave the country. By the early 1950s, most of the original staff of the CŻKH had emigrated. Some found employment at Yad Vashem: Josef Kermisz as director of the archives, Nachman Blumental as researcher and editor, and Rachel Auerbach as head of the testimony division. Others continued their research in France, as Michał Borwicz and Noe Grüss, in Germany, as Josef Wulf, and the United States as Philip Friedman, Isiah Trunk, and Hersz Wasser. The Institute in Warsaw was tolerated by the Communist authorities on the condition that it followed the general line of the state ideology. It widened the scope of its research and, rather than exclusively focusing on the Holocaust, its research covered the history of the millennium-long Jewish presence in Poland.[111]

Despite the fact that the commission activists had a clear notion that documenting the destruction of European Jews required the close collaboration of the Jewish documentation projects on a European-wide level, they did not manage to step beyond their local and national contexts. Given the instability of some of the research institutions – especially those in the DP camps – and the migration of most of the commission affiliates in Germany, Austria, Italy, and Poland, the first generation of *khurbn forshers* remained scattered over Europe, Israel, and the United Stated and those who continued their work beyond the 1950s worked in isolation from each other.

In the long run, Israeli Holocaust research adopted approaches to studying the Jewish catastrophe which were similar to those of the *khurbn forshung* developed by the commissions and documentation centers in the immediate wake of the war. Unlike Holocaust research in Europe and the United States, which mainly concentrated on the perpetrators and their sources, Israeli Holocaust research focused on an internal Jewish perspective on the Nazi onslaught. It explored the Jewish responses to persecution and mass murder, studying in particular the behavior of the official Jewish leadership and the resistance activities of the Jewish underground, integrating both Jewish sources, such as testimonies and memoirs, as well as sources of the perpetrators. However, this was less the result of continuity in the work of former commission workers in Israel and their connections with Israeli researchers, but more a product of developments in Israeli society in the 1960s and 1970s. Initially, Benzion Dinur and his colleagues in Yad Vashem were extremely skeptical of the value of Rachel Auerbach's testimony division and testimonies did not play an important role in Yad Vashem's research.[112] Only in the 1960s did "oral documentation" (*ti'ud be 'al peh*) become valued by academic historians in Israel. This change occurred under the impact of the Eichmann trial, which raised public awareness of the role of the witness and the potential value of oral testimony in presenting the history of the Holocaust.[113]

Thus, ultimately, the most significant legacy of the early postwar documentation projects in France, Poland, Germany, Austria, and Italy were their collections of Nazi documents which still constitute the archival basis for the academic field of Holocaust studies in Europe and Israel. The thousands of compiled survivor testimonies, their research questions and agendas formulated in the early postwar years, as well as their numerous publications have yet to be fully delved into and analyzed by historians and scholars of literature, cultural studies, and psychology.

Notes

1 On the claim that serious, comprehensive, and methodical research on the Holocaust began only in the 1960s, see, for example, Michael R. Marrus, The Holocaust in History, New York 1987, 2 and 4 and Moishe Postone/Eric Santner (eds.), Catastrophe and Meaning. The Holocaust and the Twentieth Century, Chicago/London 2003, 3.

2 The countries in which such documentation projects crystallized included Austria, Bulgaria, Czechoslovakia, France, Germany, Great Britain, Greece, Hungary, Italy, Poland, Rumania, Sweden, Switzerland, and the Soviet Union. For an overview on the different initiatives, see: Philip Friedman, European Jewish Research on the Holocaust, in: idem, The Roads to Extinction. Essays on the Holocaust, ed. by Ada June Friedman, New York/Philadelphia 1980, 500–524, and Shmuel Krakowski, Memorial Projects and Memorial Institutions Initiated by She'erit Hapletah, in: Yisrael Gutman/Avital Saf (eds.), She'erit Hapletah 1944–1948. Rehabilitation and Political Struggle, Jerusalem 1990, 388–398.

3 On the debate over the idea that the victims' sources are relegated to the realm of "memory" while the sources of the perpetrators pertain to "history" and are thus eligible for "historiography," see: Saul Friedländer/Martin Broszat, Um die

"Historisierung des Nationalsozialismus." Ein Briefwechsel, in: Vierteljahreshefte für Zeitgeschichte 36 (1988), 339–372 and Martin Broszat/Saul Friedländer, A Controversy about the Historicisation of National Socialism, in: Yad Vashem Studies 19 (1988), 1–47. This debate began in the 1950s, cf. Nicolas Berg, Der Holocaust und die westdeutschen Historiker. Erforschung und Erinnerung, Göttingen 2003, 343–345. While in the 1980s and 1990s oral testimonies of contemporaries gained popularity, only recently have studies on the Third Reich begun to integrate testimonies and other sources of the victims and sources of the perpetrators into the historical narrative. See, for example, Saul Friedänder, Nazi Germany and the Jews, vol. 1: The Years of Persecution, 1933–1939, New York 1997, and vol. 2: The Years of Extermination, 1939–1945, New York 2007.

4 Criteria for choosing these cases over others included to focus on initiatives taken a) by the survivors themselves not under the auspices of the World Jewish Congress or the Jewish Agency, b) by Jews who survived under Nazi occupation not by Jewish émigrés, c) by groups not individuals, and d) by institutions which had not existed before the war but which were founded toward the end of the war and in its aftermath for the sole purpose of documenting the cataclysm.

5 See the protocols of the commission, August 29, 1944 through November 5, 1944, Archives of the Jewish Historical Institute in Warsaw, Central Jewish Historical Commission Collection (hereafter AŻIH CŻKH) 303/XX folder 10, 1–21 (Yiddish). Please note: In 2006, the Jewish Historical Institute in Warsaw changed the cataloguing system for the collection of the Central Jewish Historical Commission, CŻKH. Part of the present research had been undertaken before this change. Since it has not been possible to track the old archival call numbers into the new system, both systems are being used. The citation "AŻIH CKŻP KH" (Archives of the Jewish Historical Institute, Central Committee of Polish Jews Collection, sub-division of the Jewish Historical Commission) refers to the old call number. The citation "AŻIH CŻKH 303/XX" (Archives of the Jewish Historical Institute in Warsaw, Central Jewish Historical Commission Collection) refers to the new call number.

6 Philip Friedman (1901–1960), born in Lvov, received a doctorate in modern history from the University of Vienna. Prior to the Second World War he taught Jewish history in Jewish schools and lectured at the Institute for Jewish Studies in Warsaw. He survived the war in hiding in Lvov. In 1946, he left Poland and served as head of Education and Culture Department of the American Joint Distribution Committee in the U.S. Zone of Germany. In 1948, he left Germany for the United States where he became a lecturer in Jewish History at Columbia University. Cf. Congress for Jewish Culture (ed.), Leksikon fun der nayer yidisher literatur [Dictionary of Modern Yiddish Literature], New York 1968, vol. 7, 485–489.

7 AŻIH CKŻP, KH, folder 1, 178, YPO Bulletin [Jewish Press Agency Bulletin], no. 6(16), January 19, 1945, 3. – Translation of the present and all following quotations by L.J.

8 Yad Vashem Archives Jerusalem (hereafter YV) O70 folder 30, frame 19, Arkhiv fun der oysrotungs tekufe funem eyropeyshn yidntum baym yidishn tsentral komitet in bergnbelzn [Archives of the Time of Annihilation of European Jewry at the Jewish Central Committee in Bergen Belsen], November 1, 1945.

9 YIVO Archives New York Displaced Persons Camps Germany Collection, RG 294.2 (hereafter YIVO DPG), reel 114, frame 0354, work report of the cultural office of the Central Committee of Liberated Jews in the British Zone, June 1946 (Yiddish).

10 Born in 1899 in Kraków, Horowic began to learn the furrier's trade, and then tried his hand in tailoring, millinery, plumbing. He never practiced any of them, instead living the life of a little-known writer. In the interwar years, he briefly immigrated to Palestine but because of his left-wing political activities the British Mandatory powers forced him to return to Poland. He survived the Second World War in the

Soviet Union, returned to Poland after the war, but left for the British Zone of Germany in 1947. Two years later, he immigrated to Israel. See S. Sh. Noam's introduction to the Hebrew edition of Horowic's novel, Mishpahat Horovits. Ha-Nefilah ha-Gedolah [The Horovitz Family. The Great Decline], Kiryat Tiv' on 1973, 14.

11 Moyshe Yosef Feigenbaum, born 1908 in Biała-Podlaska, Poland, survived several ghettos, escaped from execution and deportation to Treblinka. In 1945 he left Poland for Germany, four years later he immigrated to Israel. Israel Kaplan, born 1902 in Volozhin, Byelorussia, a graduate of Kovno University, survived the Riga ghetto and the concentration camps Kaiserwald and Dachau. In 1949 he migrated to Israel where he died in 2003. Cf. Leksikon fun der nayer yidisher literatur, vol. 7, 342, and vol. 8, 94, and Lucy Dawidowicz, From that Time and Place. A Memoir 1938–1947, New York 1991, 304f.

12 YV M1P, folder 2, p. 9, protocol of the founding meeting of the historical commission in Munich, November 28, 1945 (Yiddish).

13 Ibid.

14 Moses Kaganowicz, born 1909 in Ivia, Byelorussia, a journalist for the Yiddish press in Vilna and Warsaw before the Second World War, he survived the war as a partisan in the Soviet Union. In 1945 he left Poland for Italy, four years later he immigrated to Israel. See Leksikon fun der nayer yidisher literatur, vol. 8, 26.

15 F. Falk, Tsvey yor Pakhakh [Two years of Pakhakh], in: Farn Folk [For the People], no. 20, November 30, 1947, 4. On the history of Pakhakh, see Yehuda Bauer, Flight and Rescue, Brichah. The Organized Escape of Jewish Survivors of Eastern Europe, 1944–1948, New York 1970, 24f.; David Engel, Between Liberation and Flight. Holocaust Survivors in Poland and the Struggle for Leadership, 1944–1946, Tel Aviv 1996, 87, 198 f. (Hebrew); Zeev Mankowitz, Life Between Memory and Hope. The Survivors of the Holocaust in Occupied Germany, Cambridge 2002, 158–160, and Itzhak Zuckerman, A Surplus of Memory. Chronicle of the Warsaw Ghetto Uprising, Berkeley 1993, 571, 585, 607–610, 637–640.

16 Yitskhok Kvintman, Tsvey yor tetikeyt fun der historisher komisye bey Pachach [Two Years of Work of Pakhakh's Historical Commission], in: Farn Folk, no. 20, November 30, 1947, 18.

17 YIVO Displaced Persons Camps Italy Collection RG 294.3 (hereafter YIVO DPI), reel 26, folder 351, frame 0467, Informatsye Byuletin [Information bulletin], no. 1, November 25, 1945.

18 Isaac Schneersohn (1881–1969), born in Kamenets-Podolski to the Hassidic family of Lubavitch rabbis, trained as a rabbi and active as a communal leader, left for France in 1920 and became a successful industrialist; he survived the Second World War in hiding in the South of France. Cf. Leksikon fun der nayer yidisher literatur, vol. 8, 755, and Isaac Pougatch, Isaac Schneersohn, un grand seigneur hassidique, in: idem, Figures Juives de Théodore Herzl à Ida Nudel, Paris 1984, 107–141.

19 Archives of the Alliance Israélite Universelle, Paris, Archives of the Consistoire Central during the Second World War (Maurice Moch Collection), microfilm reel 1, folder 4, Voici quelques mots en ce que nous voulons [1943]. There is virtually no documentation on the CDJC's pre-liberation activity; see Renée Poznanski, La création du centre de Documentation Juive Contemporaine en France (Avril 1943), in: Vingtième Siècle 63 (July–September 1999), 51–63.

20 Mejlech Bakalczuk, born in 1896 in Sernik, Polesia, studied at the University of Kiev and prior to the Second World War worked as a Hebrew teacher in Jewish schools; he survived the war as a partisan in the Soviet Union. He returned to Poland in 1945 and left for Austria later that year. In 1947 he left for Palestine, the following year he immigrated to South Africa. Cf. Leksikon fun der nayer yidisher literatur, vol. 1, 230f. See also his autobiography, Zikhroynes fun a yidishn partizan [Memories of a Jewish partisan], Buenos Aires 1958.

21 YIVO Displaced Persons Camps Austria Collection RG 294.4 (hereafter YIVO DPA), reel 4, frame 0962f, Simon Wiesenthal, Die Rolle der Jüdischen Historischen Dokumentation bei der Verfolgung und Bestrafung der Kriegsverbrecher (Beispiel Österreich), November 25, 1947. In its statutes the organization emphasized historical research as its main goal which seems to have been a means to appease the Austrian authorities. Cf. YV M9, folder 36, 1–3, 1, statutes of Jewish Historical Documentation in Linz, January 14, 1947 (German).

22 Towia Frydman, born 1922 in Radom, survived the ghetto of Radom and as a partisan, left Poland for Austria in spring 1946 and went to Israel in 1952 where he opened a documentation center in Haifa. Cf. Leksikon fun der nayer yidisher literatur, vol. 7, 476. See also his autobiography, The Hunter, ed. and trans. by David C. Gross, London 1961.

23 YV 05, folder 2, work report of the Jewish Historical Documentation in Vienna, May 16, 1947 (German).

24 For example, even though the CDJC had begun in pursuit of political goals, historical research became its major focus when Léon Poliakov joined the CDJC staff in fall 1944. However, the CDJC also supplied documentation to the French delegation at the International Military Tribunal at Nuremberg. Likewise, CŻKH provided the Polish war crimes tribunals with documentation and some of its employees testified as experts in various war crimes trials, most notably the trials of Rudolf Höss and Hans Biebow in 1947, even though its major focus was the writing of Jewish history. The Central Historical Commission in Munich mainly focused on historical research, yet it also hoped to serve a general concept of "fighting for Jewish rights." The Jewish Historical Documentations in Linz and Vienna named historical research as their official goal even though they focused almost exclusively on the prosecution of the perpetrators and only began to pursue historical research toward the end of the 1940s as they grew exasperated over the increasing leniency of the Allied and Austrian authorities in the prosecution of Austrian war criminals.

25 AŻIH CKŻP KH 330/folder 28, 17, Zkhor et 'Asher 'Asah lekha 'Amalek! [Remember what Amalek did to Thee!], October 30, 1946; emphasis in original (Yiddish).

26 YV M1P-N digital image M1P 789 for U.S. Zone of Germany. For the gravestone and memorial motive, see also YV M1P, folder 38, report on the first conference of historical commissions in the U.S. Zone of Germany, May 11–12, 1947, 10; AŻIH CKŻP KH, folder 31, 23f. Tsu ale yidn in Poyln! [To all Jews in Poland!]; YV AM.1, folder 126, frame 0554, Fun der historisher komisye tsu ale partizaner! [From the Historical Commission to All Partisans!], July 20, 1947 and Yitskhok Kvintman, A denkmol dem umbakantn yidishn partizan un geto-kemfer [A Memorial to the Unknown Partisan and Ghetto Fighter], in: Farn Folk, no. 27, October 12, 1948, 10.

27 AŻIH CKŻP KH 303/XX folder 195, 11–13, Yisker leksikon [Memorial Encyclopedia] [1946].

28 YV M1P folder 61, frame 27, Yid! [Brother Jew!].

29 CŻKH (ed.), Metodologishe onveyzungen tsum oysforshn dem khurbn fun poylishn yidntum [Methodological Instructions for Research on the Destruction of Polish Jewry], Łódź 1945, iv and AŻIH CKŻP KH, folder 31, 23, Tsu ale yidn in Poyln!

30 On the moral weight of historical documentation in the fight for the prosecution of the perpetrators see Wiesenthal, Die Rolle der Jüdischen Historischen Dokumentation, YIVO DPA, reel 4, frame 0962 f. The argument of the historical truth being the best case against the perpetrators was a dominant theme also in Poland. Cf. AŻIH CKŻP KH, folder 31, 23f., Tsu ale yidn in Poyln! See also the protocols of the meetings of the Society of the Friends of the Central Jewish Historical Commission (Towarzystwo Przyjaciół Centralnej Żydowskiej Komisji

Historycznej) in Łódź, AŻIH CKŻP KH, folder 15, 1, November 23, 1945, and folder 13, 11, November 29, 1945.

31 Archives of the Centre de Documentation Juive Contemporaine, Paris (hereafter CDJC), box 5, Moyshe Yosef Feigenbaum, Work Report of the Central Historical Commission in Munich, November 1945 through November 1947, dated March 15, 1948, 1 (Yiddish). Please note: The administrative archives of the CDJC have not been catalogued to date; the box numbers refer to a provisional numbering in the order in which the boxes were consulted for this study.

32 See, for example, Philip Friedman, The European Jewish Research on the Recent Jewish Catastrophe in 1939–1945, in: American Academy for Jewish Research Proceedings 18 (1948–1949), 179–211, here 197, 200f., 203.

33 Moyshe Yosef Feigenbaum, Barikhtn tetikeyt [Work Report], in: Fun Letstn Khurbn [Of the Latest Destruction], vol. 5, May 1947, 102. Feigenbaum mentioned the particular involvement of women among the 70–100 employees in the U.S. Zone of Germany at the time.

34 Cf. AŻIH CKŻP KH, folder 85, 88, Philip Friedman to Raphael Mahler in New York, November 2 [1945] (Yiddish).

35 An average of 80–100 people worked for the commissions in Poland and the U.S. Zone of Germany while between 30 and 50 people worked for the commissions in France, Austria, and Italy while the British Zone of Germany had less than a dozen commission workers not differentiating between temporary and permanent workers.

36 AŻIH CKŻP KH, folder 93, 67 68, May 30, 1946 (Yiddish).

37 AŻIH CKŻP KH, folder 93, 168, July 1, 1946 (Yiddish).

38 The concept that documenting anti-Jewish violence provided a way for Jews to defend themselves because it had the potential of influencing world public opinion in favor of the victims, bringing the perpetrators to justice, and buttressing claims for material compensation was not entirely new in the wake of the Second World War. It had already crystallized among Eastern European Jews under the impact of several cases of mass violence in the twentieth century prior to the Holocaust and was a result of the Eastern European approach to the writing of Jewish history as it was developed by Simon Dubnow in the late nineteenth century. Dubnow had advocated Jewish historical writing as a national Jewish endeavor that was based on the popular support of large segments of Jewish society and strengthened the national cohesion, especially in times of crisis. Not only were "ordinary Jews" to carry out the research but Jewish society was also the recipient and subject of the research itself. See Simon Dubnow, Nahpesah we-Nahkorah Kol Koreh 'el ha-Nevunim ba- 'Am ha-Mitnadvim La 'asof Homer le-Binyan Bnei Yisra'el be-Polin we-Rusia [Let Us Search and Research! A Call to the Erudites Among our People to Collect Material to Build of the Edifice of the History of the Jews in Russia and Poland], in: Pardes 1 (Odessa 1891), 221–242. See David Engel, History Writing as a National Mission. The Jews of Poland and Their Historiographical Traditions, in: Yisrael Gutman (ed.), Emmanuel Ringelblum. The Man and the Historian, Jerusalem 2006, 109–130 (Hebrew), esp. 118–120.

39 On Emmanuel Ringelblum's concept of documentation equaling armed resistance, see Emmanuel Ringelblum, O. Sh., in: idem, Ksovim fun geto [Writings From the Ghetto], Warsaw 1963, vol.2, 102. For comprehensive analysis of Ringelblum's endeavors see, for example, Samuel Kassow, Who Will Write Our History? Emanuel Ringelblum, the Warsaw Ghetto, and the Oyneg Shabes Archive, Bloomington/ Indianapolis 2007. On the claim of some commission activists that their work was a continuation of Ringelblum's efforts, see: Stadtarchiv Göttingen, Records of the Cultural Office of the Municipality of Göttingen, file no. 475, Report by Cwi Horowic on the Activities of the Historical Commission in Göttingen [1947], (German); CDJC box 4, Protocols of the Conference of Jewish Historical

Commissions and Documentation Centers in Paris, December 1947; Michał Borwicz, Protocol of the Third Day of the Conference, Paris, December 3, 1947 morning session, 11, and Moyshe Yosef Feigenbaum, Protocol of the Fifth Day of the Conference, December 7, 1947, morning session, 2. The CDJC emphasized that its work was part of the *Résistance* and gradually made Schneersohn the "Ringelblum of France," cf. Marcel Livian, Le Centre de Documentation Contemporaine à Quatre Ans, in: *Le Monde Juif*, May–June 1947, nos. 9–10, 20; Message André Spire, in: Le Monde Juif, March–April 1953, 25; Michel Mazor, Historique du CDJC, in: Le Monde Juif, nos. 34–35 (1963), 43f. See also Poznanski, La création du centre de Documentation Juive Contemporaine en France, 52–54.

40 Kvintman, A denkmol dem umbakantn yidishn partizan,10. Simon Dubnow is said to have exclaimed before he was murdered in the Riga Ghetto in December 1941: "Good people – do not forget, good people – tell, good people write." Cf. Sofia Dubnov-Ehrlich, The Life and Work of S.M. Dubnov, ed. by Jeffrey Shandler, Bloomington/Indianapolis 1991, 247.

41 Barikhtn tetikeyt, in: Fun Letstn Khurbn, vol. 10, December 1948, 169.

42 Ibid., 163.

43 While there were a number of survivors in Western and Central Europe who began research on an individual level, most importantly H.G. Adler, commissions of the type discussed in this essay were absent in Western Europe, and if they existed, they were usually initiatives taken by Eastern European Jews. No commission existed in the Netherlands and Belgium; in Sweden, a historical commission was founded by the World Jewish Congress but run by Polish Jews formerly affiliated with the CŻKH; in Great Britain, Alfred Wiener and other German Jewish emigrants had set up the Central Jewish Information Office, or Wiener Library, in 1939 (originally founded 1934 in Amsterdam), which collected information for the fight against Nazism and anti-Semitism and took a different perspective than the commissions in question. On the idea that the commissions were the result of a specifically Eastern European Jewish tradition of history writing, see Boaz Cohen, Holocaust Survivors and the Genesis of Holocaust Research, in: Johannes-Dieter Steinert/Inge Weber-Newth (eds.), Beyond Camps and Forced Labor. Current International Research on Survivors of Nazi Persecution, Osnabrück 2005, 290–300.

44 Cf. CDJC (ed.), Les Juifs en Europe (1939–1945). Rapports présentés à la première conférence européenne des commissions historiques et des centres de documentation juifs, Paris 1949, 174.

45 Michał Maksimilian Borwicz (Boruchowicz) born 1911 in Kraków, studied history and history of literature at the University of Kraków, worked as a writer and journalist before the Second World War, and was affiliated with the Poale Zion movement in interwar Poland. He survived the Janowska camp and fought among Polish Socialist partisan units. He left Poland for France in 1947, where, together with Josef Wulf, he established a documentation center for the history of Polish Jews *Centre d'étude d'histoire des Juifs Polonais* in Paris. In 1953, he earned a doctorate in sociology from the Sorbonne. He died in 1987 in Paris. Cf. Leksikon fun der nayer yidisher literatur, vol. 1, 245 f.

46 CDJC box 10, Procès-verbal de la Réunion de la Commission de Presse, February 26, 1945, 6. The notion of the commission workers being "sewage workers" – *égoutiers* – came from the Russian Jewish writer Don Aminado, then a co-worker of the CDJC.

47 The characteristics distinguishing this catastrophe from previous ones were frequently discussed in the commissions and it was also a topic of debate at the occasion of the first conference of historical commissions in Paris in December 1947. Léon Poliakov, Technique et buts de la recherche historique, in: CDJC DCCXIV 714, 1. Philip Friedman, Les problèmes de la recherche scientifique sur notre dernière catastrophe, in: Les Juifs en Europe (1939–1945), 72–80, here 72. Mayer Halevy,

Pour une lexicographie du 'Churban,' in: Les Juifs en Europe (1939–1945), 161–164, here 161f.

48 On the perception among the commission workers that the conventional language was inadequate to describe the cataclysm, see for example, Zentralarchiv zur Erforschung der Geschichte der Juden in Deutschland, Heidelberg, B.2/1.c, No. 527, Nella Thon-Rostowa, Badanie zbrodni, która nigdy nie przeminie [Research on Crimes that Will Never Wither], 3. On the perception of the inadequacy of "traditional methods" of historical inquiry, see Michał Borwicz, Les tâches de la nouvelle historiographie juive, in: Les Juifs en Europe (1939–1945), 93–96, here 93, and CDJC box 4, Protocol of the Third Day, December 3, 1947, morning session, 11.

49 For Philip Friedman's use of the term see, for example, Philip Friedman, Die grundsätzlichen Probleme unserer Churbnforschung (Kurzer Inhalt eines Vortrags gehalten in Paris auf der europäischen Konferenz der historischen Kommissionen), CDJC, box 13, 1 (German). Friedman conceived this field as a new sub-discipline of Jewish historiography (cf. Friedman, Les problèmes de la recherche scientifique, 74) while Borwicz spoke of a "new Jewish historiography" (cf. Bowicz, Les tâches de la nouvelle historiographie juive, 93). The term *khurbn* is the Yiddish version of the Hebrew *hurban*, "destruction." Originally referring to the destruction of the First and Second Temple, the term became a synonym for catastrophe in the Jewish past in general and it became the term which Yiddish-speaking survivors used for the destruction of European Jews.

50 On this concept of historical sources cf. Friedman, Les problèmes de la recherche scientifique, 75, and Poliakov, Technique et buts de la recherche historique, 4.

51 On YIVO's concept of Jewish scholarship see Cecile Kuznitz, The Origins of Yiddish Scholarship and the YIVO Institute for Jewish Research, Ph.D. dissertation Stanford University 2000; Lucjan Dobroszycki, YIVO in Interwar Poland. Work in the Historical Sciences, in: Yisrael Gutman et al. (eds.), The Jews of Poland Between Two World Wars, London 1989, 494–518, and Michael Brenner, Propheten des Vergangenen. Jüdische Geschichtsschreibung im 19. und 20. Jahrhundert, Munich 2006, 150–155.

52 Noe Grüss, Rok pracy Centralnej Żydowskiej Komisji Historycznej [One year of work of the Central Jewish Historical Commission], Łódź 1946, 9. Noe Shloyme Grüss (1902–1985), born in Kiełków, Poland, was educated as a teacher at the University of Kraków, and worked as a history teacher and Yiddish journalist before the Second World War. He survived the war in exile in the Soviet Union but returned to Poland in 1944. In 1947 he immigrated to Israel but left in 1952 to settle in Paris where he worked as head of the Hebrew and Yiddish section of the National Library. Cf. Berl Kagan, Leksikon fun Yiddish Shraybers [Lexicon of Yiddish Writers], New York 1986, 182.

53 Grüss, Rok pracy Centralnej Żydowskiej Komisji Historycznej, 10.

54 Léon Poliakov (1910–1997), born in St. Petersburg, migrated to France in 1920 where he was trained as a lawyer but worked as a journalist. He survived the war in the Southern Zone of France and joined the CDJC staff in 1944. In 1952 he left the CDJC for the Centre National de la Recherche Scientifique; see his autobiography, Léon Poliakov, Mémoires, ed. by Gilles Firmin, Paris 1999.

55 Poliakov, Technique et buts de la recherche historique, 1.

56 Ibid., 2f.

57 Borwicz, Les tâches de la nouvelle historiographie juive, 93.

58 Ibid.

59 Philip Friedman, Die Probleme der wissenschaftlichen Erforschung unserer letzten Katastrophe, (October 13, 1947), CDJC box 13, 8f. See also Meyshe Yosef Feigenbaum, Tsu vos historishe komisyes? [Why Historical Commissions?], in: Fun Letstn Khurbn, vol. 1, August 1946, 2.

60 Moyshe Yosef Feigenbaum's comment, CDJC box 4, Protocol of the Sixth Day, December 8, 1947, morning session, 3.
61 Borwicz, Les tâches de la nouvelle historiographie juive, 95; Poliakov, Technique et buts de la recherche historique, 3 f.
62 Feigenbaum, Tsu vos historishe komisyes?, 2.
63 As early as summer 1945 the CŻKH published three separate questionnaires for *zamlers* (collectors) of historical material and folklore, and interviewers of child survivors. Josef Kermisz (ed.), Instrukcje dla zbierania materiałów historycznych z okresu okupacji niemieckiej [Instructions for Collectors of Historical Material From the Time of the German Occupation], Łódź 1945; Nachman Blumental (eds.), Instrukcje dla zbierania materiałów etnograficznych w okresie okupacji niemieckiej [Instructions for Collectors of Ethnographical Material From the Time of the German Occupation], Łódź 1945; Noe Grüss/Genia Silkes (ed.), Instrukcje dla badania przeżyć dzieci Żydowskich w okresie okupacji niemieckiej [Instructions for Research on the Life of Jewish Children at the Time of the German Occupation], Łódź 1945. In addition, a Yiddish version of all three questionnaires appeared: CŻKH (ed.), Metodologishe onveyzungen tsum oysforshn dem khurbn fun poylishn yidntum [Methodological Instructions for Research on the Destruction of Polish Jewry], Łódź 1945. In Germany, the Central Historical Commission in Munich modeled several questionnaires upon the Polish examples. It used a "statistical questionnaire" inquiring into the experiences of individuals, a "historical questionnaire" interrogating the survivors on the history of the places they had been during the war, and a questionnaire for collectors of folklore materials. In addition, the Central Historical Commission in Munich used a "questionnaire for postwar experiences" and one interrogating German officials on the fate of the Jewish population in their towns and districts.
64 AŻIH CKŻP KH, folder 29, 4, Philip Friedman, Der tsushtand un di oyfgabe fun undzer historiografye in itstikn moment [The State and Task of Our Historiography in the Present Moment], September 19, 1945.
65 AŻIH, CKŻP, KH, folder 7, 41, Noe Grüss, undated speech on the activities of the commission (Yiddish).
66 Friedman, Les problèmes de la recherche scientifique, 75 f.
67 YIVO DPG, reel 13, frame 0154f. See also YV O-37 folder 8, frame 18, Vendung num. 1 [circular letter], January 27, 1947, and YIVO RG 294.2, reel 116, folder 1644, frame 1225, work report of the regional historical commission [in Frankfurt am Main] October 1946 through February 1947 (Yiddish).
68 Friedman, Les problèmes de la recherche scientifique, 73 f., 76.
69 CDJC box 4, Protocol, Sixth Day of the Conference, December 8, 1947, morning session, 2.
70 Friedman, Les problèmes de la recherche scientifique, 77.
71 Ibid.
72 Ibid., 78f.
73 Ibid., 77–79.
74 CDJC box 4, Protocol of the Third Day, December 3, 1947, morning session, 11, and Poliakov, Technique et buts de la recherche historique, 5.
75 Friedman, Les problèmes de la recherche scientifique, 80.
76 Friedman, Die Probleme der wissenschaftlichen Erforschung, 4.
77 See the resolutions adopted by the delegates of the conference: Textes des resolutions adoptées par la conférence, structure de l'organisation centrale, in: Les Juifs en Europe (1939–1945), 185–190.
78 This is the general picture gained from the presentations and debates of the delegates, cf. the conference volume *Les Juifs en Europe (1939–1945)* and the protocols of the conference in CDJC box 4. The delegates hoped for the support of the AJDC

which had been the major funding institution of all historical commissions under discussion here. However, by 1948 when the European Coordination Committee began its work, the AJDC's funding priorities had shifted from Europe to the Middle East. Cf. Isaac Schneersohn to Philip Friedman, February 17, 1948, YIVO RG 1258, box 6, folder 296.

79 The only attempts at such synthetic works include: Philip Friedman's essay Zagłada Żydów polskich 1939–1945 [The Destruction of Polish Jews 1939–1945], published in Biuletyn Głównej Komisji Badania Zbrodni Hitlerowskich w Polsce 1 (1946), 163–208, which gave an overview of the Holocaust in all of Poland; and Léon Poliakov's La Bréviaire de la haine (1951), which was the first study to discuss the "Final Solution" on a European-wide level, making the case for a tradition of racial hatred as the root of the German mass murder of European Jews. In September 1950, on the occasion of an international conference hosted by the Netherlands Institute of War Documentation in Amsterdam on "World War II in the West," Philip Friedman presented a paper entitled "Outline of Program on Holocaust Research." He envisioned Holocaust research to cover six major fields: the origins of Nazi ideology of annihilating European Jews (considering the Second Reich and the Weimar Republic as precursors of the Nazi regime); legislation and economic actions against the Jews of Europe 1939–1945; acts of terrorism and extermination; the impact of Nazi persecution on Jewish life; the behavior of the "outside world" (including the Allies, international relief organizations, and the governments of German satellite countries); and the relations between Jews and non-Jews in German-occupied countries. Cf. Friedman, The Roads to Extinction, 571–576. See also Friedman's later essay, Problems of the Research on the European Jewish Catastrophe, in: Yad Vashem Studies 3 (1959), 25–39.

80 For example, AJDC workers who visited the DP camps of Germany noted a "compulsion to speak" about the recent past among the survivors, cf. Koppel S. Pinson, Jewish Life in Liberated Germany, in: Jewish Social Studies 9 (1947), no. 2, 108 f., and Dawidowicz, From that Time and Place, 303 f.

81 Friedman, Die Probleme der wissenschaftlichen Erforschung, 7.

82 Ibid., 5.

83 Ibid.

84 Moyshe Yosef Feigenbaum's speech on the occasion of the first European conference of historical commissions and documentation centers in Paris, December 8, 1947, YV AM. 1, folder 128, frame 0641.

85 CDJC box 4, Protocol of The Sixth Day, December 8, 1947, morning session, Borwicz' comment 2 and Friedman's comment, 4. See also Feigenbaum in: Les Juifs en Europe (1939–1945), 175.

86 Barikhtn tetikeyt, in: Fun Letstn Khurbn, vol. 10, December 1948, 163.

87 Feigenbaum observed an "inferiority complex of the man in the street" toward the historical commissions, cf. Les Juifs en Europe (1939–1945), 175. See also CDJC box 4, Protocol of the Sixth Day, December 8, 1947, morning session, 3.

88 YV M1P, folder 1, frames 8 and 10, Tetikeyts berikht fun der historisher komisye [Work Report of the Historical Commission] [1947], and Farn Folk, no. 8, February 10, 1947, 5.

89 See the letters by co-worker Helen Fuchsman to Simon Wiesenthal reporting on her difficulties in collecting survivor testimonies which she attributed to "a certain passivity, a negligence and a decrease in the feelings of revenge among the former Jewish inmates toward their tormentors and murderers," cf. YIVO DPA, reel 5, folder 153, frames 1000 and 1016, February 17, 1948 and March 12, 1948, and YV M9, folder 49, 271 f. (April 17, 1948) and 334 (May 31, 1948) (German).

90 Kvintman, A denkmol dem umbakantn yidishn partizan, 10. In the U.S. Zone of Germany, 2,540 testimonies were collected between December 1945 and December

1948. 1,500 testimonies were collected in the course of the first eleven months while only a little less than 1,000 were collected in the following 25 months. This might indicate that the willingness of the survivors had waned but it might also be due to the fact that as of early 1947, the majority of the DPs in the U.S. Zone were Polish Jews who had survived in the Soviet Union, an experience which was not addressed in the questionnaires of the commission.

91 For an analysis of the multifaceted activities of the survivors in the DP camps of Germany, see, for example, Mankowitz, Life between Memory and Hope, and Hagit Lavsky, New Beginnings. Holocaust Survivors in Bergen-Belsen and the British Zone in Germany, 1945–1950, Detroit 2002, and Atina Grossmann, Trauma, Memory, and Motherhood. Germans and Jewish Displaced Persons in Post-Nazi Germany, 1945–1949, in: Richard Bessel/Dirk Schumann (eds.), Life After Death. Approaches to a Cultural and Social History of Europe During the 1940s and 1950s, Cambridge 2003, 93–127.

92 YIVO DPG, reel 13, frame 0195, A yor tsentrale historishe komisye in der amerikaner zone, daytshland [One year of Work of the Central Historical Commission in the U.S. Zone], January 1, 1947. YV M1P, folder 38, 6, report on the first conference of historical commissions in the U.S. Zone (Yiddish).

93 AŻIH CKŻP, KH, folder 7, 44f., Noe Grüss, Dokumenty wrodzonej szlachetności [Documents of Congenital Nobleness].

94 "Vu es vert gezamlt [. . .] a geshprekh mitn leyter fun der tsentraler historisher komisye in minkhn M.Y. Feygnboym" [Where things are being collected [. . .] an interview with the director of the Central Historical Commission in Munich, M.Y. Feigenbaum], in: Undzer Veg [Our Path], no. 57, December 6, 1946.

95 YIVO DPG, reel 116, folder 1644, frame 1225, Work Report of the Regional Historical Commission [in Frankfurt]. See also YIVO DPG, reel 13, frame 0195, A yor tsentrale historishe komisye, January 1, 1947.

96 YV M1P, folder 38, 2, report on the first conference of historical commissions in the U.S. Zone (Yiddish).

97 Most notable are the commissions' own periodicals Fun Letstn Khurbn published by the Central Historical Commission in Munich and Le Monde Juif published by the CDJC. The Jewish Historical Institute in Warsaw, which replaced the Central Jewish Historical Commission as of October 1, 1947, published Bleter far Geshikhte (Pages for History, as of 1948) and Biuletyn Żydowskiego Instytutu Historycznego (Bulletin of the Jewish Historical Institute, as of 1950). In addition to the periodicals the commissions in France, Poland, Germany and Italy engaged in a multifaceted and comprehensive publication project of memoirs, local studies, collections of documents and photographs, the most productive being France with 20 and Poland with 40 publications until 1949.

98 This was most common in the DP camps and in Poland. These appeals usually called upon the survivors from specific villages, cities, regions, ghettos or camps as well as on people who could testify on certain criminals of war to give their testimonies at the historical commission in their vicinity. Or they made a general case for the duty of the survivors to give their testimonies for the sake of documenting the recent catastrophe. See, for example, YV M1P folder 2, frame 34, Bakantmakhung [Announcement]; YIVO DPA, reel 5, folder 148, frame 0799; YV M1P, folder 9, 11, Achtung! Bensheimer Jdn! [Attention! Jews of Bensheim!]; YV AM.1, folder 126, frame 0554, dated July 20, 1947, Fun der historisher komisye tsu ale partizaner! [From the Historical Commission to All Partisans!]; YIVO DPA, reel 5, frame 0968, Toyte klogn on – lebendike zogn eydes! [The Dead Accuse – The Living Give Testimonies!]. The commissions in Germany and Poland also used colored posters, cf. YV M1P folder 2, frames 36 and 37, and M1P-N as digital copies of the originals, see figure.

99 For example, on the occasion of the First Congress of the She'erit Hapletah on January 27, 1946, the Central Historical Commission prepared a historical exhibition for the delegates; see YV M1P folder 71, frame 8, Di Centrale historisze komisje [The Central Historical Commission], September 3, 1946 (Yiddish with Latin characters). In the British Zone, the commissions in Belsen and Göttingen followed suit in July 1947, see Undzer veg in di freyheyt (barikht fun der oyzshtelung) [Our Path to Freedom. Report on the Exhibition], in: Undzer Shtime [Our Voice], vol.22, August 20, 1947, 3–6.

100 This was mainly aimed at recording testimonies of children and youth. For example, the Central Historical Commission in Munich urged teachers in the Jewish schools of the U.S. Zone to support the historical commissions by assigning the students written exercises on the topic "My experiences of the Nazi occupation" (cf. YIVO DPG, reel 69, frame 1366). Likewise, the Central Historical Commission directed its efforts to adolescents in vocational training schools and youth groups and *kibbutzim* in the U.S. Zone and opened essay writing contests for children and youth. Cf. YIVO DPG reel 13, frame 0211 and VY O37, folder 8. Kurce instrukcjes far naj ensztanene Historisze Komisjes [Short Instructions for Newly Founded Historical Commissions] (Yiddish with Latin characters); YV M1P, file 71, frame 15, work report for July 1946, August 27, 1946 (Yiddish). YV M1P folder 10 II, frame 15, Tsu ale kibbutzim in der amerikaner zone [To All Kibbutzim in the American Zone], and YV M1P, folder 9, frame 3, September 17 [1947].

101 In the DP camps, the commissions saw it as their mission to have their co-workers address the larger public by touring the DP camps in a car provided by the AJDC, see, for example, YV M1P, folder 2, frame 14, Protocol of the Second Meeting of the Historical Commission in Munich, December 3, 1945 (Yiddish); YV M1P, folder 6II, frame 16, Arbets-in-struktsyes far historishe komisyes [Instructions for Historical Commissions], January 27, 1947, 2, and YIVO DPG, reel 13, frame 0189, A yor tsentrale historishe komisye, January 1, 1947.

102 The "Society of the Friends" was modeled upon YIVO. In France, historical research was less dependent on the support of the French Jewish community because the CDJC did not collect survivor testimonies; however, the CDJC staff faced the problem that French Jews did not read the historical works it published. In 1950, Schneersohn sought to improve the situation by adding a memorial and museum to the documentation center which was not well received by the community, mainly because under the impact of postwar anti-Semitism many French Jews wanted to keep a low profile as Jews in public.

103 A rough estimate: 5,000 testimonies in Poland, 2,540 in Germany, 800 in Italy, 7,000 questionnaires roughly, 15,400 testimonies and questionnaires between 1944 and 1949. According to Philip Friedman, Holocaust survivors in Europe collected a total of 18,000 testimonies until the end of the 1950s. Cf. Raul Hilberg, "I Was Not There," in: Berel Lang (ed.), Writing and the Holocaust, New York 1988, 7–25, here 18.

104 Annette Wieviorka, The Era of the Witness, Ithaca/London 2006, 96–144, esp. 107–118.

105 Geoffrey Hartman, The Longest Shadow. In the Aftermath of the Holocaust, New York 1996, 133.

106 In Germany, the commissions dissolved in the year 1949. While it is unclear where the collection of the British Zone went, the Central Historical Commission transferred its collection to Yad Vashem. Kaganowicz left Italy for Israel in 1949 and transferred his collection to Yad Vashem as well. Towia Frydman left Austria in 1952 and opened a documentation center in Haifa, giving parts of his collection to Yad Vashem. Simon Wiesenthal closed his documentation center in Linz in 1954 and gave his material to the Yad Vashem archives.

107 Boaz Cohen, The Birth Pangs of Holocaust Research in Israel, in: Yad Vashem Studies 33 (2005), 203–243, here 205.

108 David Engel, On Studying Jewish History in the Light of the Holocaust, Maurice and Corinne Greenberg Inaugural Lecture, United States Holocaust Memorial Museum, Washington D.C., 2003, 8–13, and Roni Stauber, Lesson for this Generation. Holocaust and Heroism in Israeli Public Discourse in the 1950s, Jerusalem 2000, 82–95 and 171–181 (Hebrew).

109 Annette Wieviorka, Jewish Identity in the First Accounts by Extermination Camp Survivors from France, in: Yale French Studies 85 (1994), 135–151, esp. 149–151, and idem, Un lieu de mémoire et d'histoire. Le Mémorial du Martyr juif inconnu, in: Revue de l'Université de Bruxelles 1–2 (1987), 107–132.

110 Archives of the AJDC New York, AR 45/54 file 729, Jewish Historical Institute in 1948, Report by the Polish Research and Information Service, New York, December 1948.

111 For an analysis of the CŻKH and the Institute's works in the larger context of Holocaust historiography in Poland, see Natalia Aleksiun, Polish Historiography of the Holocaust. Between Silence and Public Debate, in: German History 22 (2004), 406–432. On this widening of the research scope, see Josef Kermisz, Trois années d'activité de la Commission Centrale Historique et du l'Institut Historique Juif auprès du Comité Central des Juifs en Pologne, in: CDJC (ed.), Les Juifs en Europe (1939–1945), 140–144, here 144.

112 On the history of Yad Vashem's testimony division and Rachel Auerbach's work see Boaz Cohen, Rachel Auerbach, Vad Vashem, and Israeli History, unpublished manuscript (to be published in *Polin*), 2–6, and on the criticism of Auerbach's work by Benzion Dinur, see Orna Kenan, Between History and Memory. Israeli Historiography of the Holocaust. The Period of 'Gestation' from the Mid-1940s to the Eichmann Trial in 1961, Ph.D. dissertation, University of California Los Angeles, 2000, 166–168.

113 On the general developments of Holocaust research in Israel in the 1960s and 1970s see Boaz Cohen, Holocaust Research in Israel 1945–1980. Characteristics, Trends, Developments, Ph.D. dissertation, Bar-Ilan University, 2004, 241–328 (Hebrew).

15

SEMANTICS OF EXTERMINATION

The use of the new term of genocide in the Nuremberg trials and the genesis of a master narrative

Alexa Stiller

The end of the war and the revelations about the massive crimes of the Third Reich brought about an attempt to create a new international regime that would prevent, and if necessary punish states involved in, wars of aggression and crimes against humanity. Conversations about an international tribunal had begun during the war, and the Allies issued warnings to Germany and its collaborators to expect retribution for their crimes. Meanwhile the Polish-Jewish lawyer Raphael Lemkin, having escaped to the United States, had formulated the new term "genocide" in 1944, meant to describe policies intended to destroy groups of human beings as such. Even before the United Nations Resolution on Genocide in 1948, various interpretations of this term were available to the International Military Tribunal (IMT) of 1945–46, and the United States Nuremberg Military Tribunals (NMT) of 1946–49, as well as other trials by additional occupying countries.

Although the need for justice seemed urgent, both the tribunals and the term genocide turned out to be highly controversial. One difficulty had to do with the international character of the tribunal, which meant that each of the four countries involved – the United States, Britain, France, and the Soviet Union – brought to bear its distinct legal concepts and traditions, as well political interests, ideology, and wartime experiences. The German public, for its part, saw the tribunal very much as meting "victors' justice." And indeed, while there was no doubt as to the scale and depravity of Nazi crimes, the absence of any mention of Allied war crimes was jarring to many. Finally, a new judicial language had to be crafted in order to find individuals guilty of actions deemed legal at the time they had been ordered by a higher authority, and to charge others with murder although they had never actually pulled the trigger.

As Alexa Stiller demonstrates in her chapter, another important issue raised at Nuremberg concerned whether the term genocide should be applied exclusively to the extermination of the Jews, or would encompass the larger complex of German policies associated with the attempt to create a "living space" for "Aryans" in Eastern Europe and Russia. Based on the General Plan East (GPO), this policy entailed the expulsion or murder of millions of Slavs, Romani, and Jews, and biological policies curtailing the reproductive abilities of "undesirable" groups and the kidnapping of children deemed racially valuable. According to Stiller, at Nuremberg the meaning of genocide shifted from "a broad analytical concept of oppression, persecution, and extermination, to a crime of mass murder." This had to do not only with legal and definitional issues but also with politics: with the start of the Cold War it appeared necessary to restrict the numbers of Germans indicted for genocide in order to be able to include the new Federal Republic in a Western coalition against the communist block. And once genocide came to mean the "final solution" rather than the GPO, the definition of perpetrators could also be restricted only to the SS and security police.

Simultaneously, also largely for political reasons, the UN definition of genocide in 1948, whilst retaining the possibility of including not only physical destruction of a group but also the cultural, excluded political and social categories and focused on the extermination of national, ethnic, racial and religious groups. This also appeared to coincide more closely with the mass murder of the Jews and similar future genocides targeting ethnic and religious groups with the intent of entirely or partially destroying them. And, indeed, there have been numerous genocides since the Holocaust. This may indicate that the efforts made in the late 1940s to prevent such future events failed. Whether this was because of a narrower definition of genocide or because of the international community's unwillingness or inability to intervene in such cases is debatable. But as Stiller sees it, the narrower definition applied by the Nuremberg tribunals made for a false understanding of the crimes of the Third Reich and obscured the larger context of the mass murder of the Jews within the vast ambition of creating a Germanic "living space." It is indeed striking that already at such an early stage, American judicial teams had understood the demographic and colonial ambitions of the Nazi regime, a finding substantiated by historians only decades later. But perhaps we should also pay heed to these jurists' other insight, cited by Stiller, that the motivation for the Nazi "crimes of genocide" had been racial ideology; and that while "the Jews were only one of the peoples marked for extermination in the Nazi program," it was also the case that "anti-Semitism was a cardinal point of Nazi ideology," and that the war presented the regime with "a golden opportunity to carry out these doctrines to their logical and terrible conclusion – the extermination of all Jews in Germany and in the countries overrun by the Wehrmacht."

This chapter could also be entitled: "Genocide: from a broad analytical concept of oppression, persecution, and extermination, to a crime of mass murder," as this is exactly what happened to the new term between 1944 and 1949. Some scholars have already shown that Lemkin's original concept of genocide, which he published in 1944,[1] had been more comprehensive than that adopted by the United Nations Convention on the Prevention and Punishment of the Crime of Genocide.[2] The same can be observed in the Nuremberg trials in which the crime of genocide was not consistently seen as congruent with the Holocaust, i.e., the mass murder of the European Jews. Instead, the prosecutors and some judges defined genocide much more broadly and conceived Nazi occupation policies during World War II as genocide against people. Raphael Lemkin's book, *Axis Rule in Occupied Europe*, had a bearing on the usage of the term in the Nuremberg trials.

Significantly, Lemkin's concept of genocide was most prominent in a trial on the Nazi population, settlement, and Germanization policy in occupied territories, mainly Poland. The Race and Settlement case of the United States against Ulrich Greifelt et al., known also as "RuSHA case" or *Volkstumsprozess*, was explicitly conceptualized as a "genocide trial." Consequently, the Race and Settlement case stands in the center of the present analysis on the usage of the word genocide and its definition within the Nuremberg trials.

The trial's framing was immediately apparent from the *New York Times* headline "Fourteen Germans Listed in Genocide Case" on the first day.[3] And on March 11, 1948, another article on the same case concluded that eight defendants were found "guilty of directing the mass extermination of people in twelve 'inferior' nations." The main defendant, Greifelt, was described as, "the driving force of the genocide program."[4] Furthermore, the United Nations War Crimes Commission (UNWCC) stated in 1949 that this trial has been of "fundamental importance, examining with particular reference to Poland . . . the crime of genocide."[5] And when the American series on the *Trials of War Criminals before the Nuremberg Military Tribunals* was published in 1953, a short description of the trials claimed that a "systematic program of genocide" had been charged in the Race and Settlement case.[6] Genocide, then, was the term used to name the extermination of nations.

But neither of the two important document series on the war crimes trials employed this phrase for any other Nuremberg trial. This implies that neither the *Einsatzgruppen* case, in which former SS officers were charged with mass shootings mainly of Jews but also of other people in the occupied Eastern territories, nor the Ministries case, in which the Wannsee conference played a decisive role and therefore defendants were charged with knowledge of and contribution to the mass murder of the European Jews, were explicitly considered as "genocide trials." The *New York Times* did not label the *Einsatzgruppen* case a genocide trial. Instead its blunt headline of 1947 stated that "SS Officers are indicted in the Murder of Million Persons."[7] The *Einsatzgruppen* case was universally regarded as "the biggest murder trial in history."[8]

Obviously, in the years between 1945 and the 1960s, genocide was conceptualized differently from that on which most contemporary Holocaust and genocide scholars would agree, that is the definition of the Genocide Convention. The Nazi extermination of the European Jews is often considered as a synonym of genocide, as the prototype or "ideal type" of genocide, while some scholars insist that the Holocaust is a unique phenomenon, other cases of destruction and extermination of peoples are still strongly controversial.[9] In a contrasting trend, research in genocide studies places mass violence in a broader historical and sociological framework.[10] The mass murder of the European Jews, it will be argued, should therefore be seen and can only be fully analyzed in the context of the entire Nazi persecution and extermination policy.[11]

It is less important to list how many times the protagonists in the Nuremberg trials used the word genocide than to examine how the prosecution and the judges interpreted the aims and conduct of the Nazi persecution and extermination policy in general. William A. Schabas and Frank Selbmann have examined the Nuremberg trials' usage of the charge of genocide but, perhaps due to their legal perspective, they have erroneously identified the contemporary use of the term genocide with the later definition of the Genocide Convention.[12] As Lemkin's original concept was not limited to the mass murder of Jews, this analysis is neither a study of Lemkin's thoughts about the Holocaust[13] nor of the definition and documentation of the Holocaust within the Nuremberg trials.[14] This chapter will show that the new term genocide was not applied exclusively to Nazi crimes against the Jews in the trial against major war criminals before the International Military Tribunal (IMT) and in several of the twelve subsequent proceedings before the Nuernberg Military Tribunals (NMT).

This chapter will proceed by tracing the theoretical unfolding of the new term from its first appearance in Lemkin's book to the Genocide Convention in 1948 and, at the same time, by showing the practical application of the new term and the transformation of the meanings of genocide from the IMT to the NMT trials. Particular attention will be paid to the Race and Settlement case and a brief excursion will tackle the early Polish trials against war criminals.

Lemkin's original concept

Raphael Lemkin coined the new term genocide on the basis of a comprehensive analysis of Nazi occupation policy in the World War II. Explaining the need for "new conceptions for destructions of nations," he did not claim that the crime as such was new, but simply that it required "new terms."[15] Lemkin regarded genocide (the German translation of the word means *Völkermord*[16]) not exclusively as a crime of mass murder of entire national, racial, or religious groups. His initial concept was based on the assumption of Nazis' having waged a "war against people."[17]

The simultaneity of denationalization, destruction of the local population and their institutions in the occupied territories by political, economic, social, cultural, and moral methods was at the heart of Lemkin's notion of genocide. In considering a term for these policies, Lemkin rejected the older term of denationalization because it did not include biological and physical methods of exterminating certain peoples. Nor did it include the aims of the oppressors which Lemkin saw as imposing their own "national pattern"—in the Nazi case this was the biologically motivated policy of Germanization and settlement.[18]

Lemkin's thoughts clearly arose out of the idea of the protection of minorities which had been at the core of legal discussions in interwar Europe.[19] Sharing the contemporary view that ethnic groups, as well as nations, were primordial, it was obvious to him that minorities required special protection.[20] The forced assimilation and forced migration of specific groups led to the destruction of culture which appeared as extermination of a minority group per se. Like Lemkin, Josef L. Kunz, an Austrian-American legal scholar and expert in the field of minority rights, put the Nazi persecution and extermination policy in the context of minority politics. Kunz identified four different methods that the Nazis, as well as other nation-states in the interwar period, had used in order to destroy ethnic minorities: first, forced denationalization (resp. assimilation), secondly, annexations of territories (irredentism), thirdly, a "voluntary" or compulsory exchange of population and other forms of forced migrations; and, fourthly, the physical extermination of national or ethnic minorities.[21]

Lemkin's new concept of genocide incorporated a whole set of different "techniques": denationalization and Germanization as methods of forced cultural assimilation *and* biological extermination; destruction of political and social institutions as methods of oppression but closely connected with plundering and compulsory labor as economic *and* biological methods of enslavement *and* extermination; forced emigrations, deportations, and replacements as physical methods for achieving an economic, cultural, *and* biological usurpation of the soil; decrease of nutrition and health service—as well as mass killings—as economically *and* biologically motivated methods for achieving the extermination of certain peoples while simultaneously strengthening the own people and other specific groups selected for assimilation.[22]

It is crucially important to keep in mind that the main aim of Lemkin's study was the documentation of the legal basis of the crimes committed under Axis rule,[23] and he created the new term genocide from this empirical analysis of Nazi occupation policy. He did not mean that the Nazis committed one, two, or many genocides—the entire occupation policy was a program of genocide with two phases: "one, destruction of the national pattern of the oppressed group; the other, the imposition of the national pattern of the oppressor."[24] Both sides of this Nazi genocide policy—also known as racial population policy—were inextricably intertwined with one another.[25] And by seeing this nexus of the Nazis' persecution and extermination policy on the one hand, and Germanization and settlement policy on the other, Lemkin was able to extract the motivation and objectives of the Nazis—territorial expansion, Germanization of the conquered countries, and economic exploitation intertwined with an extermination of all "undesired" groups of populations.[26]

Genocide in the inter-allied trial before the IMT

Lemkin's ideas had a tangible presence at Nuremberg, both through his work and his person. As a member of the US delegation and, later on, one of the legal advisors to the US chief prosecutor Jackson, Lemkin played a part in the formulation of the IMT indictment. He also corresponded with some of the prosecutors on genocide, and his book *Axis Rule* was widely read and discussed by the members of the different delegations.[27] Under count 3, war crimes, the indictment argued that the defendants had "conducted deliberate and systematic genocide, viz., the extermination of racial and national groups, against the civilian populations of certain occupied territories in order to destroy particular races and classes of people and national, racial, or religious groups, particularly Jews, Poles, and Gypsies and others."[28] For the first time the concept of genocide was applied in a court case. Furthermore, the indictment mentioned the extermination of "persons whose political belief or spiritual aspirations were deemed to be in conflict with the aims of the Nazis."[29] Genocide was defined as the annihilation and destruction of national, racial, religious, political, or social groups of people. However, the indictment did not clarify if the term "extermination" signified plain murder or if it implied a broader concept of genocide.

During the actual proceedings, the new term was not elaborated, although most of the prosecutors referred to genocide in their closing statements. The British chief prosecutor, Hartley Shawcross, listed additional aspects which had been part of the Nazi "policy of genocide": the annihilation of the mentally and physically disabled,[30] the slow death measures the Nazis had imposed on forced laborers from foreign countries,[31] and those policies aimed at reducing the birthrate in the occupied territories by sterilization, abortion, and separating men from women.[32] This physical and biological extermination of certain groups of people, particularly in the occupied territories but also in Germany, had not been an aim in itself. Shawcross advanced a sophisticated interpretation of the motivations of the Nazis that manifestly built on Lemkin's assumption of denationalization and Germanization as the core of the Nazi policy of genocide:

> Their aims went beyond mere Germanization, the imposition of the German cultural pattern upon other peoples. Hitler was resolved to expel non-Germans from the soil he required but that they owned, and colonize it by Germans . . . Such were the plans for the Soviet Union, for Poland and for Czechoslovakia. Genocide was not restricted to extermination of the Jewish people or of the gypsies. It was applied in different forms to Yugoslavia, to the non-German inhabitants of Alsace-Lorraine, to the people of the Low Countries and of Norway.

The technique varied from nation to nation, from people to people. The long-term aim was the same in all cases.[33]

Shawcross drew attention to the Nazi program of conquering "Lebensraum" for settlement reasons. This main tenet had led the German occupants to establish a regime based on Germanization on the one hand and on persecution and extermination on the other.

The French chief prosecutor concurred with Shawcross's opinion: "The conquest of living space, that is, of territories emptied of their population by every means including extermination—that was the great idea of the Party, the system, the state."[34] Auguste Champetier de Ribes named this strategy "the greatest crime of all, genocide, the extermination of the races or people at whose expense they intended to conquer the living space they held necessary for the so-called Germanic race."[35] At first glance, it seems as if both Shawcross and Champetier de Ribes shared the same opinion. But the French prosecutor already meant mass murder when he resorted to the terms extermination and genocide.[36]

Meanwhile, the Soviet chief prosecutor, General Roman Andreyevich Rudenko, introduced a third point of view. He attached more importance to the Nazi ideology. This "fascist racial ideology"[37] had implied murder, plunder, destruction of culture, and the extermination of people. Rudenko elucidated cultural and economic aspects. Thus, the Nazi extermination policy had hit different groups alike, political opponents of the Nazi regime, prisoners of war, forced laborers, concentration camp inmates, Jews, and other inhabitants of the occupied territories.[38] The aims of Nazi policy had not only been "world domination" but also "enslavement and genocide" per se.[39] This interpretation, which centered around the belief that the Nazi ideology had been based not so much on the strengthening of their own as on the sheer destruction of other peoples, clearly differed markedly from the British prosecutor's perspective, and owed much to the vastly different wartime experiences of the Allies but also to the Soviet interest to link genocide closely to fascism.[40]

Finally, the American chief prosecutor Robert H. Jackson hardly dealt with the concept of genocide at all. The focal point of his closing statement was not genocide but the conspiracy to overthrow the Treaty of Versailles through a war of aggression.[41] The application of the new term genocide did not figure prominently on Jackson's agenda and certainly no more than the "individual barbarities and perversions" upon which he touched fleetingly. His concern was the overarching, all-embracing "Nazi master plan."[42] Still, Jackson did not omit the policy of extermination in his closing statement: "The Nazi movement will be of evil memory in history because of its persecution of the Jews, the most far-flung and terrible racial persecution of all time."[43] None of the other Allied prosecutors had restricted the Nazi extermination program to the mass murder of the Jews as the worst of the Nazi crimes. Jackson's final emphasis was probably rooted in the same experience Telford Taylor retrospectively recalled: the

sheer dimension of the mass murder of the European Jews came to full awareness only during the IMT's proceedings.[44]

In their verdict, the four Allied judges found that the main aim of the
Nazis, i.e., the conquest of living space, had been amply proven by the prosecution. Therefore, they viewed the atrocities committed during the war as
consequences rather than ends—but did not refer to these policies as a program
of genocide:

> The evidence shows that at any rate in the East, the mass murders and
> cruelties were not committed solely for the purpose of stamping out
> opposition or resistance to the German occupying forces. In Poland
> and the Soviet Union these crimes were part of a plan to get rid of
> whole native populations by expulsion and annihilation, in order that
> their territory could be used for colonization by Germans.[45]

This statement shows that the tribunal referred to another method of destruction which Lemkin had mentioned in his original account: the technique of
forced displacement of populations. The four judges stressed in their judgment
that "civilian populations ... of the Soviet Union and Poland" had fallen
victim to systematic starvation, torture, slave labor, plunder, expulsion, and
mass shootings.[46] At the same time, they elucidated the Nazi program of the
Final Solution directed exclusively against the European Jews.[47] In the event,
although the court adumbrated the various policies highlighted by Lemkin,
neither the whole Nazi program of extermination in the occupied territories for
settlement purposes, nor the mass murder of the European Jews, was explicitly
labeled "genocide" in the IMT judgment. In this respect, the trial of major war
criminals did not establish a precedent.

On the whole, the new term of genocide carried diverse meanings in the
course of the IMT's proceedings. Genocide was used to characterize a broad
policy program, composed of a set of crimes and of various "techniques" directed
against several victim groups, and with the broad aim of gaining new "living
space" for the purpose of colonization rather than being exclusively defined as a
deliberate crime targeting an entire extermination of one single ethnic group.
Predominantly, the prosecutors and the judges did not interpret the mass
murder of Europe's Jews as being exclusively congruent with genocide in
general, but understood the persecution and extermination of the Jews as part of
the aggressive war and not only fueled by antisemitism.[48]

The Polish genocide trials

If Lemkin's concept of genocide was marginal and its meaning unstable in the
Nuremburg trials, it proved to be of great importance in some of the Polish war
crimes trials. The Supreme National Tribunal of Poland (Najwyższy Trybunał
Narodowy, NTN) was established to try the main Nazi perpetrators who had

committed crimes in occupied Poland.[49] In particular, three cases are interesting in view of the definition and application of the term genocide in early war crimes trials: the cases against Arthur Greiser, *Gauleiter* of the Wartheland (June–July 1946), the case against Amon Leopold Göth, commandant of the concentration camp in Płaszów (August–September 1946), and the trial against Rudolf Höß, commandant of the Auschwitz concentration camp (March 1947). As the trials against Greiser and Göth had already been completed before the verdict of the IMT was handed down, the Polish judgments were the first to use the term genocide. While the trial against Greiser elucidated the main strands of Nazi occupation policy in the Wartheland, the trials against Göth and Höß focused on murder, torture, and ill-treatment of concentration camp inmates (Jews, Poles, and Soviet prisoners of war), as well as on forced labor and medical experiments.

Greiser was charged with the following offences: mass murder, ill-treatment and persecution of, and causing bodily harm to civilians and prisoners of war, "systematic destruction of Polish culture, robbery of Polish cultural treasures and Germanization of the Polish country and population, and illegal seizure of public [and private] property."[50] Additional accusations concerned the establishment of the ghetto of Łódź, and of the extermination camp at Chełmo, and various deportations of Poles and Jews to the so-called *Generalgouvernement*, as forced laborers to Germany, and of Polish children for the purpose of Germanization, and so forth. When the judges pronounced the sentence, they stated: "There were three ways of arriving at such a Germanization of the [Wartheland] ...: by deportation of adult Poles and Jews, Germanization of Polish children racially suited to it, the new method of mass extermination of the Polish and Jewish population, and complete destruction of Polish culture and political thought, in other words by physical and spiritual genocide."[51] Interestingly, the Polish judges classified not only mass murder but also deportations as physical genocide. In addition, they included the aspects of cultural, political, and moral techniques in the Nazi program of persecution and extermination of the Polish and Jewish population.

In the trial against Göth, the prosecution claimed that genocide was a *crimen laesae humanitatis* (crime against humanity) and therefore *eo ipso* part of international criminal law.[52] The judges adopted the new term and declared: "This criminal organization did not reject any means of furthering their aim at destroying the Jewish nation. The wholesale extermination of Jews and also of Poles had all the characteristics of genocide in the biological meaning of this term, and embraced in addition the destruction of the cultural life of these nations."[53] Here, physical and biological extermination were blended, although the original aspect of cultural destruction played a prominent role. In the trial against Höß, neither the prosecution nor the judges employed Lemkin's term.[54] Even so, all three trials were classified as "genocide trials" by the UN War Crimes Commission, attesting to the broader definition of genocide favored by the Commission. Significantly, the UNWCC grouped yet another tribunal along with the said Polish trials: the case against Ulrich Greifelt before the Nuernberg Military Tribunal I.[55]

The concept of genocide in the race and settlement case

The Office of Chief of Counsel for War Crimes (OCCWC) under the direction of Telford Taylor clearly devised their prosecution strategy in the light of the IMT's outcome—but also modeled it on Lemkin's concept of genocide. Lemkin himself remained an active force behind the scenes, writing scores of memoranda to Taylor's staff advising the use of the term genocide in various planned trials and suggesting taking up other, specific trials.[56] The prosecutors used the new term genocide in several indictments and in the opening and closing statements of the trial series: in the Medical case, the Pohl case, the *Einsatzgruppen* case, the Ministries case, the High Command case, and most extensively in the Race and Settlement case.

In the so-called RuSHA trial, all fourteen defendants were officials of various SS organizations responsible for implementing the "new order" in Eastern Europe: the Main Office of the Reich Commissioner for the Strengthening of Germandom (*Stabshauptamt des Reichskommissars für die Festigung deutschen Volkstums*, RKF), the Race and Settlement Main Office of the SS (*Rasse- und Siedlungshauptamt der SS*, RuSHA), the Ethnic German Liaison Office (*Volksdeutsche Mittelstelle*, VoMi), and the *Lebensborn* society.[57] The prosecution subsumed about a dozen crimes under the counts of crimes against humanity and war crimes, such as kidnapping of "racially valuable" children, forcing "racially undesirable" pregnant women to undergo abortions, hampering reproduction of foreign nationals, sending persons who had had "interracial" sexual relationships to concentration camps, deporting foreign populations and resettling ethnic Germans (*Volksdeutsche*) on such lands, plundering of property, and for general participation in the persecution and extermination of the Jewish population.[58] The mere list of offenses attests to the significance attributed to Nazi racial population policy (*Volkstumspolitik*[59]) as a component on the persecution and extermination policy. The prosecutors stated that the object of the "systematic program of genocide" had been "to strengthen the German nation and the so-called 'Aryan' race at the expense of such other nations and groups by imposing Nazi and German characteristics upon individuals selected therefrom (such imposition being hereinafter called 'Germanization'), and by the extermination of 'undesirable' racial elements."[60]

In their Opening Statement on October 20, 1947, the prosecution offered their definition of genocide: "This program of genocide was part of the Nazi doctrine of total warfare, war waged against populations rather than against states and armed forces."[61] The foundations of the Nazi program of genocide had been laid by "theories of race and Lebensraum," the chief prosecutor James McHaney explained. Therefore the "General Plan East" (*General Plan Ost*, GPO) drafted by the defendant Konrad Meyer(-Hetling) on behalf of Himmler in 1942 played a decisive role in the prosecution's strategy. That plan of an ethnic reconstruction of Eastern Europe had been based upon displacement, expulsion, and mass killings of millions of Poles, Lithuanians, Belarusians, Russians, Ukrainians, and the entire Jewish populace in order to resettle ethnic Germans for "germanizing of the soil." The prosecutors identified the GPO as the core of the Nazi program of genocide: "It was a coordinated plan aimed at the destruction of the essential foundations of the life of national groups."[62] The prosecutors did not merely rely on Lemkin's original conceptualization of genocide; they quoted him directly and at some length:

> This destruction can be and was accomplished with the help of these defendants by a number of different means, which may be broadly classified as physical, political, biological, and cultural. They sought the "disintegration of the political and social institutions of culture, language, national feelings, religion, and the economic existence of national groups, and the destruction of the personal security, liberty, health, dignity, and even the lives of the individuals belonging to such groups."[63]

The RuSHA trial's prosecutors also reflected on the divergent notions of the term employed in Nuremberg and distinguished between their own use and that of the prosecutors in the *Einsatzgruppen* trial:

> In another courtroom of this same building, 23 leaders of the notorious Einsatzgruppen of the Security Police and SD are being tried for the mass annihilation of Jews and Russians. While a number of the defendants in this dock also participated in those very same crimes and others of similar nature, their main efforts were devoted to the destruction of national groups by other methods. The technique of these defendants was the mass deportation of oppressed peoples, the deprivation of their means of livelihood by the wholesale confiscation of property, the forced Germanization of citizens of occupied countries, and the destruction of their national culture, folkways, and educational facilities, the creation of conditions which increased the mortality rate and prevented increase of the population, and the kidnapping of children.[64]

In this case, the prosecutors assessed the annihilation of the Jews as a major crime but only as one crime amongst several that together constituted the "program of genocide" which in turn had resulted from the superordinated "master plan."[65] To that extent, they did not differ significantly from the predominant concept established in the IMT. Like that of Shawcross, the prosecutors' legal approach in Case 8 was marked by a succinctly moral emphasis reflecting Lemkin's philosophy: "These techniques of genocide, while neither so quick nor perhaps so simple as outright mass extermination, are by

341

the very nature of things far more cruel and equally effective. If crimes such as these are allowed to go unpunished, the future of humanity is in far more danger than if an occasional murderer goes free. It is the enormity and far-reaching effects of these crimes that give this case its significance."[66]

In the closing statement, the prosecution team referred to other Nuremberg trials that had dealt with the Nazi program of genocide. Despite these parallels, the prosecutors identified a distinctive trait of the Race and Settlement case. Whereas the Medical, Pohl, and *Einsatzgruppen* cases had elucidated "primarily the negative side," the extermination of peoples, the Race and Settlement case unveiled "the entire program of Germanization and genocide with all its ramifications."[67] The prosecutors emphasized that the Nazi policy of "strengthening Germanism" (or *Volkstumspolitik*) also had been a program of genocide, composed of two intertwined elements:

> Genocide, as practiced by the Nazis, was a two-edged sword, both aspects of which were equally criminal. The positive side, according to the German concept, was the Germanization program by which they sought to strengthen themselves by adding to their population large groups of people selected from among the populations of the conquered territories, and by forcing the German language, culture, citizenship, and ideals upon those so selected. The negative side of this program, through which the so-called positive side was in equal measure accomplished, was the deliberate extermination and enslavement of the remaining population of these conquered territories. Thus, Germany would be strengthened by adding to its population, and its neighbors would be weakened by subtracting from their population, and the strength of Germany would thereby be proportionately increased.[68]

Predictably, the German defense counsels rejected all allegations that defendants had participated in a systematic program of genocide. What is more, the defense strategy built on the assertion that there was no such thing as a crime of genocide in international law. Carl Haensel, Greifelt's counsel, advanced the following argument: "An individual cannot murder an entire people. If one wants to arrive at this legal construction, one has to start out from the premise that a people can only be murdered by a people. Since, however, any penal guilt is the guilt of an individual and thus the collective guilt cannot lead to punishment of an individual, the individual cannot become guilty of genocide by leading his people to genocide."[69] Moreover, the defense lawyers argued that the use of the term genocide lacked any positive legal basis and that, therefore, the prosecution's charges contradicted the established maxim of *nullum crimen sine lege, nulla poena sine lege*.[70] Finally, the defense attorneys questioned whether relocation of population was a crime, because past resettlements had allegedly been legal in most cases.[71] To back up their argument, the German lawyers referred both to international agreements like the population transfer between

Greece and Turkey in the 1920s, and to the ongoing expulsions of Germans from the Eastern territories, Poland, Czechoslovakia, and Hungary at that time.[72] These points were quite obviously *tu quoque* ("You, too") arguments, but on the other hand they were not completely beside the point.

While the judges turned down all *tu quoque* arguments of the defense, they indirectly agreed that the crime of genocide was not part of the international law by refusing to integrate the term into their verdict. The Nazi "genocide program," as the prosecution had called it, was reduced to a "Germanization program." The judges, however, were convinced of the existence of a common plan of total Germanization and Nazi domination in the occupied territories. They pointed out that the program, which had been actively supported by the defendants, had been based on the following foundation: "The two-fold object-ive of weakening and eventually destroying other nations while at the same time strengthening Germany, territorially and biologically, at the expense of conquered nations."[73] The tribunal recognized the significance of the double character of the Nazi policy, i.e., the inseparability of the "positive" and "negat-ive" measures and motifs.[74]

The Main Office of the RKF was seen as the "directing head of the Germanization program,"[75] while its leader Ulrich Greifelt had been, "with the exception of Himmler, the main driving force in the entire Germanization program" and "criminally responsible" for the "kidnapping of alien children; hampering the reproduction of enemy nationals; forced evacuations and reset-tlement of populations; forced Germanization of enemy nationals; the utiliza-tion of enemy nationals as slave labor; and the plunder of public and private property."[76] Other defendants were found equally guilty of committing these crimes. Undoubtedly, the judges viewed these crimes as parts of the Nazi extermination program: "the solution of the question of dealing with the so-called 'racially inferior' population was solved not so much by deportation as by the adoption of extermination measures, thus bringing about a speedier elimina-tion of undesirable foreign elements by death."[77] The verdict mentioned not only physical but also biological extermination: "As a part of the gigantic program of strengthening Germany while weakening, and ultimately destroying, enemy nations, measures were taken to hamper and impede the reproduction of enemy nationals. These took the form of various decrees, all aimed at one purpose—to greatly reduce the birth rate among enemy nationals and thereby gradually bring about the destruction of the entire national group."[78] Later, these crimes would be included in the Genocide Convention, but the judges did not refer to the UN Resolution on Genocide from December 1946.

The count of the persecution and extermination of the Jews was subordinated to the other elements of the cases, such as punishments for sexual intercourse with Germans, the plundering of property, and the evacuations of enemy nationals. The judges stated: "Persecution upon racial grounds were directed particularly toward the Poles and Jews, and both the Poles and Jews were the victims of similar measures, as we have heretofore shown in this judgment."[79]

This evaluation of the Nazi extermination policy clearly followed the notion of the prosecution, which had already described the destruction of the Jews as an aspect of the Nazi plan of conquering new living space. The judgment emphasized that the General Plan East had been "a drastic plan which in all its cruel aspects sought the reconversion of the East into a Germanic stronghold practically overnight."[80] The judges assumed that Konrad Meyer, the scientist who had drawn up the plan, was not guilty, but an executive tool. Instead, they held Himmler responsible for the murderous outcome of the "General Plan East" which resulted in a harsh extermination policy towards the native people.[81]

Genocide in other cases before the Nuernberg military tribunals

Initially, Telford Taylor intended to follow Jackson's tracks and continue the conspiracy and aggressive war theory line of argument against the German defendants. Taylor did indeed regard this endeavor to link the waging of aggressive war, including the Nazi persecution and extermination policy, with militarism and the German industry as the heart of the matter at Nuremberg. Therefore, he focused on military leaders, state bureaucracy, and German business leaders for their support of the Nazis before and after the assumption of power.[82] Atrocities were mostly seen as products of aggression, war, and occupation. However, he also pursued a second, both more conventional and more straightforward approach to Nazi persecution and extermination policy, namely to convict perpetrators of atrocities.[83] This consideration was less concerned with re-educating German society or strengthening international law than with punishment. But if achieving convictions was a primary objective, then the individual's guilt would have to be proven beyond reasonable doubt, i.e., it had to be proven and to withstand scrutiny in international tribunals as well as in national criminal courts. That was the reason why the *Einsatzgruppen* case (and not the trial against the Reich Security Main Office, as planned in an early stage[84]) was implemented, because evidence of individual participation in crimes was abundant and unequivocal.[85]

In the Medical case, the prosecution team linked the crimes of human experiments, sterilization, castration, and "euthanasia" committed by German physicians in concentration camps and sanitariums to the broader Nazi policy of extermination and called these medical crimes "techniques of genocide."[86] The prosecutors tried to prove that these crimes had been testing grounds and predecessors of the mass-scale persecution and extermination policy in the occupied territories during World War II: "The thanatological knowledge [the science of producing death], derived in part from these [human] experiments, supplied the techniques for genocide, a policy of the Third Reich, exemplified in the 'euthanasia' program in the widespread slaughter of Jews, Gypsies, Poles, and Russians."[87] The prosecution similarly used the concept of genocide for the crime of sterilization: "They [the Nazis] were developing a new branch of medical

344

science which would give them the scientific tools for the planning and practice of genocide. The primary purpose was to discover an inexpensive, unobtrusive, and rapid method of sterilization which could be used to wipe out Russians, Poles, Jews, and other people."[88] Strikingly, the prosecution team of chief prosecutor James M. McHaney strongly emphasized the heterogeneity of the affected people. In the Medical case judgment, experiments and sterilizations were prominently marked as integral parts of a broader Nazi program, although this program was not labeled genocide.[89]

The extermination of diverse groups by means of physical and biological techniques was likewise confirmed in the indictment of the Justice case: "The Ministry of Justice participated in the Nazi program of racial purity pursuant to which sterilization and castration laws were perverted for the extermination of Jews, 'asocials,' and certain nationals of the occupied territories. In the course of the program thousands of Jews were sterilized. Insane, aged people, and sick nationals of occupied territories, the so-called 'useless eaters,' were systematically murdered."[90] Curiously, the judgment made no mention either of sterilization and "euthanasia" or of the murder of disabled people and so-called asocials. Nevertheless, it was in the Justice case that the new term genocide made its first appearance in a judgment formulated by any of the Nuremberg tribunals, even referring to the genocide resolution adopted by the General Assembly of the United Nations.[91] The judges of Case 3 defined genocide as Nazi racial persecution and extermination policy against Jews and Poles alike.[92]

McHaney had not only been chief prosecutor in the Medical but also in the three SS trials. Highlighting the instability of genocide's meaning, his interpretation of the Nazi persecution and extermination policy underwent slight but significant changes from case to case as he adapted the definition to suit the respective facts. In the Pohl case on the SS business and concentration camp system, the prosecution held the view that the Nazi extermination policy targeted different "groups considered racially inferior, such as the Poles, but the Jew was especially marked for destruction."[93] The American lawyers called the annihilation of the Jews, the deportations of thousands of people to concentration camps, the use of slave labor, and the confiscation of property a "war waged against populations" and therefore, a "crime of genocide."[94] But the Nazi policy towards the Jews had been somewhat special, the prosecution expounded: "The systematic and relentless annihilation of the Jewish people by the Nazis constitutes one of the blackest pages in the history of the civilized world."[95] Medical experiments, sterilization, "euthanasia", ill-treatment of the concentration camp prisoners (Jewish and others) and the extermination of the Jews were closely connected, the judges stated in their opinion.[96]

For all that, the verdict did not mention genocide. But Judge Michael A. Musmanno did in his concurring opinion, and set forth a definition of the new term, which differed from that of the three judges in the Justice case. In his concurring opinion, he described the extermination camps as absolute killing institutions and as manifestation of "the trend of modernity toward mechanization and assembly line method," ultimately leading to "genocide—a business so novel that a new name had to be coined for it. Genocide, the scientific extermination of a race."[97] Paraphrasing Lemkin, genocide in Musmanno's conceptualization stands for industrial mass killings of European Jewry.

The prosecution in the *Einsatzgruppen* case had charged the defendants with a "plan of genocide" that the Nazis had constantly enlarged during the war: "They [the *Einsatzgruppen*] were to destroy all those denominated Jew, political official, gypsy, and those other thousands called 'asocial' by the self-styled Nazi superman."[98] The motivation for this "crime of genocide" by the Nazis had been their racial ideology, and "the Jews were only one of the peoples marked for extermination in the Nazi program," the prosecution propounded.[99] In the closing statement, the prosecutors adhered to this opinion but added a further aspect: "It is only too well known that antisemitism was a cardinal point of Nazi ideology . . . The war presented Himmler and Heydrich with what, to them, was a golden opportunity to carry these doctrines to their logical and terrible conclusion—the extermination of all Jews in Germany and in the countries overrun by the Wehrmacht."[100] The twofold narrative that the Nazi persecution and extermination policy had been directed against a range of groups of people, denominated "undesirables," but that the Jews had been especially affected,[101] had already gained acceptance in the course of the American Military Tribunals in 1947.[102]

As in the Pohl case, the *Einsatzgruppen* trial focused on the fact that first and foremost Jews had been killed, but also kept one eye on the murder of other victims: partisans, communist leaders, Romanies, mentally disordered, and so-called "Asiatic inferiors,"[103] as well as the killing of prisoners of war.[104] In principle, the judges declared, the charge in this case was murder.[105] Building on this premise, Military Tribunal II stated that the way in which the *Einsatzgruppen* had perpetrated "their homicidal duties, it appears that the Einsatz authorities now even set up a school in this new development of the fine art of genocide."[106] Musmanno and his colleagues called this particular method of mass murder "ultra-modern executions"[107] and saw them as a technique of genocide. They also identified especially the annihilation of the Jews in no uncertain terms as a "genocide program."[108] Judge Musmanno seems to have played an important role in emphasizing the special case of the Nazi mass murder of the European Jews and in referring to it as "industrialized" or engineered killing—a misleading trope, which historians would seize upon later.[109]

Yet another narrative became prevalent in 1948—not by chance in the aftermath of the Pohl and *Einsatzgruppen* cases. In the High Command and the Ministries cases, the two last trials before the NMT, the prosecutors and the judges adhered to the assumption that the "program of genocide and extermination" had mostly been perpetrated by the Security Police and SS. Genocide was therefore reduced to the extermination of the European Jews. During 1948, the broader definition of genocide as a policy composed of different techniques, directed against many groups of people, perpetrated by various agencies and layers of society, aiming not only at exclusion (extermination) but also at inclusion (Germanization), and acquisition of soil for settlement reasons, vanished. The Race and Settlement case did not displace this interpretation. Instead, the results of the other SS trials suited the political consensus of a re-emerging German society that gladly adopted the notion of the genocidal SS as an "alibi of the nation."[110]

The prosecutors in the High Command case denounced the *Einsatzgruppen* more than the Wehrmacht for being responsible for the coordinated mass murder: "The triggermen in this gigantic program of slaughter were, for the most part, the members of the so-called *Einsatzgruppen* of the SS . . . The chief victims of this genocidal program were the Jews, and it can be conservatively estimated that nearly one million Russian Jews were slaughtered by the *Einsatzgruppen*."[111] The judges did not convict the Wehrmacht generals in total for committing genocide or participating in the Nazi extermination policy; they convicted single defendants solely for their knowledge of the mass murder of Soviet Jewry in the occupied territories.[112]

In the last of the twelve NMT, the Ministries case (starting in January 1948 and ending in April 1949), OCCWC lumped all remaining accused war criminals under investigation together in one trial. Initially, Taylor's team had planned individual cases against the Foreign Office members, against the bankers, against Gottlob Berger and Walter Darré, as well as against other ministers and undersecretaries. But time pressure and financial problems forced OCCWC to bring the war crimes trial program to an end.[113] Dirk Pöppmann has recently shown that the Ministries case started as a trial of the Nazi ministerial bureaucracy but ended as an SS trial.[114] The same gap between the interpretations of the prosecutors and the judges can be found in several of the NMT. However, the strategy of the prosecution itself changed in the course of the proceedings. While the team organized by chief prosecutor Robert M.W. Kempner stated in the indictment that all defendants had participated in a

> systematic program of genocide, aimed at the destruction of nations and ethnic groups within the German sphere of influence, in part by murderous extermination, and in part by elimination and suppression of national characteristics. The object of this program was to strengthen the German nation and the alleged "Aryan" race at the expense of such other nations and groups, by imposing Nazi and German characteristics upon individuals selected therefrom (such imposition being hereinafter called "Germanization") and by the extermination of "undesirable racial elements"[115]

at the end of 1947, when the indictment was filed, the prosecutors defined genocide as consisting of both Germanization *and* extermination. The detailed indictment comprised eight counts and seventy-five single elements of crimes, so that Nazi persecution and extermination policy against opponents of the occupation was dissociated from the "program for the extermination of all surviving European Jews."[116] In the Opening Statement, the Final Solution played a prominent role and all defendants were charged with taking part in this annihilation program.[117] Nevertheless, in their closing statement the prosecutors mentioned the "genocidal policy of the Third Reich" only once— and here they implied the extermination of the Jews alone and the special participation of Schellenberg and Berger in this program.[118]

Consequently, the judges did not use the new term genocide at all in their opinion. Moreover, they did not link the Germanization and resettlement program to the persecution and extermination policy. A process of decontextualizing the mass murder of the European Jews from the grand picture of Nazi policy in the occupied territories was thus well under way. Jews, Poles, Russians, Romanies, and other victims in the occupied territories were no longer perceived of as having been affected in similar ways. Instead, the persecution and extermination of the Jews was explained as an aim in itself: "Hitler made the Jewish persecution one of the primary subjects of his policy to gain and retain power."[119] A new analysis of the Nazi policy was now evolving and emanating from Nuremberg. The judges came to the conclusion that the members of the German Foreign Office had had only some knowledge of the extermination program by the Einsatzgruppen but "no jurisdiction or power to intervene." Event though the tribunal found that the diplomats had "played an essential part" in the deportation of Jews as slave labor and/or to the extermination camps, the judges cleared the diplomats of guilt at the Wannsee Conference and of planning the Final Solution: they "neither originated it, gave it enthusiastic support, nor in their hearts approved of it."[120]

According to the judges, the SS had had the greatest share in the extermination program. As a consequence, Berger, one of the highest-ranking SS officers in the Third Reich occupied center stage when the "mass murder charge" was brought up. He was convicted for his role in the destruction of the European Jews and sentenced to twenty-five years in prison.[121] Judge Powers elaborated on this issue in his dissenting opinion: "The handling of the so-called Jewish question was vested by Hitler exclusively in Himmler and his SS."[122] Additionally, he alleged: "The evidence by those who were on the inside of this terrible extermination program strongly tends to show that not over 100 people in all were informed about the matter."[123] Although a single man's opinion, Powers' elucidation positively represented an increasingly discernible tendency in the Nuremberg trials to restrict the meaning of genocide to the murder of the European Jews and to identify the SS as the main perpetrator. This new narrative would have major consequences in the respective realms of both history and the law.

The Genocide Convention

Lemkin was not only involved in the American war crimes trials program, he also played a major part in the elaboration of the convention on genocide adopted by the United Nations.[124] In Lemkin's eyes, the Nuremberg trials could not have been a substitute for a universal, legally binding convention on genocide.[125] For different reasons, the definition of genocide in the eventual Genocide Convention was a reflection of the original concept rather than anything else. In fact, the prolonged process of drafting the convention mirrored the Nuremberg precedent insofar as the concept of genocide was significantly curtailed in successive steps. This development had started as early as December 1946 when the UN Resolution 96(I) had declared, "genocide is a denial of the right of existence of entire human groups, as homicide is the denial of the right to live of individual human beings." While this had clearly connoted mass murder, the resolution had also stated: "such denial of the right of existence . . . results in great losses to humanity in the form of cultural and other contributions represented by these human groups."[126] The "denial of the right to existence" was used as a variable phrase for extermination but also differed from the interpretation of mass killings up to cultural destruction of "racial, religious, political and other groups . . . entirely or in part." It had been Lemkin though who had drafted the first version of that resolution.[127] However, the General Assembly had implied that genocide was the murder of an entire human group (after specific criteria). While still keeping an eye on cultural destruction, the definition omitted the intention of denationalization as a state policy with all its political and socio-economic implications.[128]

Two years later the UN Convention on the Prevention and Punishment of the Crime of Genocide defined genocide in Article II:

> genocide means any of the following acts committed with intent to destroy, in whole or in part, a national, ethnical, racial, or religious group, as such: (a) Killing members of the group; (b) Causing serious bodily or mental harm to members of the group; (c) Deliberately inflicting on the group conditions of life calculated to bring about its physical destruction in whole or in part; (d) Imposing measures intended to prevent births within the group; (e) Forcibly transferring children of the group to another group.[129]

There is an ongoing debate between scholars from the legal and political sciences whether this definition is too narrow or too broad. From a historical perspective, though, it is of far greater interest to examine which parts of the original, broader concept were missing, and to ask which political interests were the reasons for this deliberate omission.

Prima facie, extermination was defined as biological or physical destruction. Culturally intended oppression or destruction of certain groups, for example prohibiting the use of native language, forced assimilation, destruction of cultural monuments and achievements—the complex of cultural genocide—was omitted.[130] But not completely: rendering the compulsory transfer of children illegal acknowledged that such policies did not only aim at the biological extermination of people but also at their cultural assimilation.[131]

Another major complex of the original empirical analysis on the Nazi "genocide" was absent—the relocation of population: forced emigration, deportation for forced labor purposes, deportation to ghettos and camps, resettlement and expulsion. The Nazi policy of relocating millions of people definitely caused "serious bodily harm," or even death as the Nazis had usually no regard for the plight of their victims. On the transports, in the camps, in segregated residential areas, the Nazis inflicted on these relocated people "conditions of life calculated to bring about [their] physical destruction" and associated with this they often "intended to prevent births." Paragraphs (b) to (d) of the Genocide Convention could surely also be intended measures in general and they were in the case of the Nazi policy of persecution and extermination without deportations and relocations, e.g. as a form of segregation policy in times of peace (conceivably also in a colonial setting) and as a form of occupation policy in times of war. However, without a designation of an actual act (deportation, segregation), paras (b) to (d) had little practical relevance.[132]

Lemkin's original concept had stated that such actions (or crimes) were based not only on racial ideology but also on concrete socio-economic interests: the Nazis sought to exterminate "undesired" groups of people *and* rob their property and possessions *and* partially exploit their manpower. Furthermore, Nazi persecution and extermination policy aimed at gaining new living space by annexing territories, making them "German," imposing National Socialist and German cultural patterns on these populations, deporting and murdering the native populace, and colonizing these regions with Germans. This means, the emphasis on genocide in the UN Convention, the reduction of "destruction" to mass killings "in whole or in part, [of] a national, ethnical, racial, or religious group," led to an—initially unintended—focus on just one single motivation, the intent to murder a group "as such." However, from a historian's perspective, the claim of an alleged, universally valid intent of genocides does not stand up to empirical examination.[133] But from a jurist's perspective, this specific intent distinguishes genocide from common murder.

The question why the negotiations of the Genocide Convention led to this inapplicable definition cannot be discussed at length here. The drafts of the Convention included several more measures aimed at the destruction of national and ethnic groups in addition to the obvious methods of killing.[134] It certainly requires little speculation to argue that a broader definition of "extermination" of certain groups of people would have put a lot of governments into serious trouble. Besides the Soviet Union, which achieved the exclusion of the protection of political groups,[135] a range of countries and regimes pursued vested interests in obstructing a more far-reaching convention: colonial powers, apartheid states, democratic states with an indigenous minority "problem," and newly decolonized states with the objective of building a homogeneous nation all had obvious motives to discourage any move that would have made cultural, political, and socioeconomic discrimination or the destruction of minorities (including forcible population transfers and forced assimilation) an internationally criminal and punishable act.[136]

Instead of strengthening minority (or group) rights, the UN General Assembly decided to issue the Universal Declaration of Human Rights. The Genocide Convention and the Universal Declaration belong together and the latter explains to a certain extent why cultural genocide was left out of the former.[137] There were attempts to include minority rights in the Universal Declaration but finally, when the last version was promulgated, group rights were ignored. The idea of international protection of human rights and non-discrimination of individual persons differed very much from the interwar notion of the protection of minorities (in East Central and Southeast Europe). But the notion of international and global protection of minorities was ultimately dropped after World War II. The Genocide Convention—by all means a law for the protection of minorities—theoretically offered protection only to certain groups, i.e., none defined along political, social, or economic lines, from annihilation.[138] The shift from minority rights to individual human rights after 1945 "represented a considerable weakening of international will compared with the interwar League [of Nations]," as Mark Mazower has assessed the value of the Universal Declaration, because it "had no binding legal force."[139]

Scholars, apart from Lemkin, who were concerned with the protection of minorities by international law in future times, could see very clearly that these nationality conflicts or minority "problems" had not faded away in the aftermath of the war. Their claim for general principles sorted ill with the continuing population transfers in East Central and Southeast Europe[140] and the massive population exchanges between India and Pakistan—both forced migration processes—were accompanied by massive violence. But for Lemkin the coming into force of the Genocide Convention on January 12, 1951 was definitely a personal and institutional success.[141] In his unpublished manuscripts, though, he stuck to his original opinion that the Nazi genocide had been a broader policy with different techniques and victims groups. Lemkin noted: "The Nazi plan of Genocide was related to many people, races, and religions and it is only because Hitler succeeded in wiping out six million Jews, that it became known predominantly as a Jewish case."[142] Ultimately, Lemkin's thoughts and his actions seemed inconsistent,[143] although he just might have been very pragmatic.[144]

Conclusion

The Nuremberg trials established several interpretations of the Nazi regime. Most ominous from today's perspective was that, during the years of the trial program, the planning of the Nazi persecution and extermination policy were reduced to a conspiracy of Hitler, Himmler, and Heydrich, and that perpetrators were effectively narrowed down to the SS. Equally crucial was that the mass murder of the European Jews was singled out from other Nazi mass violence. Institutional networks between the Nazi party and the state bureaucracy, economic interests of German industry, the cooperation between the Wehrmacht and the SS (Waffen-SS, Security Police and SD, as well as the regular police force) were poorly highlighted. Thus, connections between the persecution and extermination of the Jews and mass killings and ill-treatment of other people, forced labor, malnutrition and anti-guerilla warfare, Germanization, population and settlement policy, eugenics, racial policy, and antisemitism were insufficiently linked with one another.

Among historians in particular, the de-contextualization of the annihilation of the Jews from the larger framework of Nazi policy turned out to be efficacious, if misguided. Only a few studies professing an interest in the persecution and extermination of European Jewry were published between the end of the Nuremberg trials and Adolf Eichmann's trial in Israel, which would mark a turning-point in the Holocaust's rise to prominence in public memory.[145] Undoubtedly, these books, which all relied heavily on the Nuremberg evidence, were (and still are) all of great importance.[146] Although these studies concentrated on the Nazi policy toward the European Jews, the authors did not conceal that Nazi mass violence targeted also other groups of people. Nevertheless, their focus on the Jewish case considerably eased the triumph of the narrative of the Holocaust as *the* Nazi genocide, indeed, it helped construct this narrative.

Simultaneously, historical research on the Nazi policy in the annexed and occupied territories of Poland and the Soviet Union implicitly negated any connection between the population, Germanization and settlement policy, the destruction of Poles and other Slavic people on one hand and the extermination of the Jews on the other.[147] In addition, these studies drastically diminished the role of the German scientists,[148] the state bureaucracy, and the organization of the Reich Commissioner for the Strengthening of Germandom within the Nazi extermination policy.[149] At that time Polish historians entertained a broader perspective on the Nazi genocide. To them, the destruction of the Jews, the Poles, and the Germanization aims of the Nazi had all been intertwined.[150] It was not until the 1990s that historical research started to reassess Nazi population and settlement policies and re-connect these with the extermination policy, sparked by the studies of Götz Aly and Susanne Heim.[151]

The use of Lemkin's new term genocide within the Nuremberg trials varied and underwent massive changes between 1945 and 1949. Even in the IMT trial, the Allied prosecutors defined genocide in different ways. Shawcross followed Lemkin's original concept and interpreted the Nazi occupation policy as consisting of physical, biological, cultural, political, and economical persecution and extermination of populations. Jackson, by contrast, explicitly stressed the annihilation of the Jewish people and called the Nazi persecution of the Jews the most terrible racial crime in history. Two diverging interpretations of genocide thus were shaped in and emerged from the IMT arena.

Taylor's staff resorted to the concept of genocide in several of the NMT trials but with shifting implications. In the Medical, Pohl, *Einsatzgruppen*, and High

Command cases, the American prosecutors focused on biological and physical methods of genocide, whereas in the Justice and Ministries cases genocide was conceptualized in a *temporally* broader manner. Here, the prosecution included the racial, political, and economical persecution of the Jews in Germany before 1939. At the same time, this interpretation was narrower because, *materially*, it focused exclusively on the Jewish case. Only in the Race and Settlement case did OCCWC's prosecutors apply genocide within a broader historical and sociological framework of oppression, persecution, and extermination of minorities and populations in occupied territories. Therefore, two interpretations of genocide came into existence during the NMT trials: one considered genocide as an overall policy of persecution and destruction of various groups of people, by various techniques, based not only on racial ideology but also on a plan of gaining living space. The other restricted genocide to the Nazi extermination policy towards the European Jews—one group of victims, one main group of perpetrators—the SS, and one ideological intent. These two, principally antagonistic lines of interpretation had already been formed during the IMT trial (even if that had not been clearly recognizable at the time) but were fully established during the NMT. Obviously, the dynamic development of these diverging interpretations followed the logic that arose from the chronology of the trials: after the Pohl, RuSHA, and *Einsatzgruppen* cases, the narrative that, above all, the SS had been the collective agent of genocide, was ultimately established. Coincidentally, such an interpretation fostered analyses and narratives that focused dominantly if not exclusively on the persecution and extermination of the European Jews.

The broader use of the term genocide mainly in the Race and Settlement case, the interpretation of genocide as a whole set of Nazi crimes not limited to mass killings, would have been impossible after the official codification of the definition of genocide in the Genocide Convention. A reduction of Lemkin's broad concept and a decontextualization from the specific Nazi crimes to transform it into a legal institution with universal force could be seen as a normal case of legislative evolution. At the same time, this process forecast the future problems historical analyses of phenomena of mass violence would face when dealing with this definition. The reason why the Genocide Convention defined genocide in a much narrower sense than Lemkin's original definition depended only partly on the perception of the persecution and mass murdering of the European Jews as the worst crime in history, because this perception had just slowly emerged in the course of the Nuremberg trials. The limitation of the concept of genocide to mass killings (and some other alleged subordinated elements of crimes) was by and large based on the both divergent and coalescing political interests of the members of the United Nations at that time.

The narrowing of the spectrum of Nazi atrocities in the Nuremberg trials and the legal formulation of the crime of genocide by reducing the original definition of the concept had a common denominator—the emerging Cold War. The diminishing scope of the term "genocide" in the course of "Nuremberg" was to a certain degree related to the changing interests of the American occupation policy in Western Germany. Although this development hardly affected the use of the genocide concept by the prosecution, the judges proved to be more concerned with historical and political changes.[152] West Germany's integration in the Western hemisphere, an important political tenet of US policy in the late 1940s, would have been much more difficult if the public service, the military elite, and the German industrialists had been convicted on charges of large-scale mass murder. The focus on the SS as the main perpetrator thus prevailed at an opportune moment.

Notes

1 Raphael Lemkin, Axis Rule in Occupied Europe: Laws of Occupation, Analysis of Government, Proposals for Redress (Washington, DC, 1944), 79–95.
2 See Johannes Morsink, "Cultural Genocide, the Universal Declaration, and Minority Rights," Human Rights Quarterly 21 (1999): 1009–60; William A. Schabas, Genozid im Völkerrecht (Hamburg, 2003), 237; A. Dirk Moses, "The Holocaust and Genocide," in The Historiography of the Holocaust, ed. Dan Stone (New York, 2005), 533–55, here 535; Martin Shaw, What is Genocide? (Cambridge, 2007), 33–36; Bartolomé Clavero, Genocide or Ethnocide, 1933–2007. How to Make, Unmake, and Remake Law with Words (Milano, 2008), 57.
3 New York Times, July 2, 1947, 2.
4 New York Times, March 11, 1948, 10.
5 Law Reports of Trials of War Criminals. Selected and Prepared by the United Nations War Crimes Commission [LRTWC], 15 vols (London, 1947–1949), here XIII, ix.
6 Trials of War Criminals before the Nuremberg Military Tribunals under Control Council Law No. 10 [TWC], 15 vols (Washington, DC, 1950–1953), here XV, 1184–85; Introduction, RuSHA case, TWC, IV, 599.
7 New York Times, July 4, 1947, 4.
8 Preface, TWC, IV, iii–iv.
9 For an excellent summary on recent research on genocide, see Birthe Kundrus and Henning Strotbeck, "Genozid. Grenzen und Möglichkeiten eines Forschungsbegriffs—ein Literaturbericht," Neue Politische Literatur 51 (2006): 397–423. See also Donald Bloxham and A. Dirk Moses, "Changing Themes in the Study of Genocide," in The Oxford Handbook of Genocide Studies, eds. Bloxham and Moses (Oxford, 2010), 1–15.
10 Cf. Mark Levene, "Why Is the Twentieth Century the Century of Genocide?," Journal of World History 11 (2000): 305–36; A. Dirk Moses, "Conceptual Blockages and Definitional Dilemmas in the 'Racial Century': Genocide of Indigenous Peoples and the Holocaust," Patterns of Prejudice 36 (2002): 7–36; Christian Gerlach, "Extremely Violent Societies: an Alternative to the Concept of Genocide," Journal of Genocide Research 8 (2006): 455–71; Donald Bloxham, The Final Solution: A Genocide (Oxford, 2009).
11 Cf. Sybil Milton, "The Context of the Holocaust," German Studies Review 13 (1990): 269–83; Henry Friedlander, The Origins of Nazi Genocide: From Euthanasia to the Final Solution (Chapel Hill, 1995); Christian Gerlach, Kalkulierte Morde. Die deutsche Wirtschafts- und Vernichtungspolitik in Weißrußland 1941–1944 (Hamburg, 1999); Götz Aly, "Final solution:" Nazi Population Policy and the Murder of the European Jews (New York, 1999); National Socialist Extermination Policies: Contemporary German Perspectives and Controversies, ed. Ulrich Herbert (New York, 2000); Michael Wildt,

Generation des Unbedingten. Das Führungskorps des Reichssicherheitshauptamt (Hamburg, 2002); Götz Aly and Susanne Heim, *Architects of Annihilation: Auschwitz and the Logic of Destruction* (Princeton, 2003); Isabel Heinemann, *"Rasse, Siedlung, deutsches Blut": Das Rasse- und Siedlungshauptamt der SS und die rassenpolitische Neuordnung Europas* (Göttingen, 2003); *German Scholars and Ethnic Cleansing, 1919–1945*, eds. Michael Fahlbusch and Ingo Haar (New York, 2004); Wendy Lower, *Nazi-empire Building and the Holocaust in Ukraine* (Chapel Hill, 2005); Phillip T. Rutherfort, *Prelude to the Final Solution. The Nazi Program for Deporting Ethnic Poles, 1939–1941* (Lawrence, KS, 2007); Peter Longerich, *Heinrich Himmler. Biographie* (Munich, 2008).

12 See Schabas, *Genozid im Völkerrecht*, 71–74; Frank Selbmann, *Der Tatbestand des Genozids im Völkerstrafrecht* (Leipzig, 2003), 41–44.

13 See Dan Stone, "Raphael Lemkin on the Holocaust," *Journal of Genocide Research* 7 (2005): 539–50.

14 Other scholars have already analyzed how the Nuremberg trials dealt with the extermination of the European Jews and have, interestingly, come to different conclusions. Whereas Marrus considers that the IMT established the fact that the extermination of the European Jewry is "of great historical importance," Bloxham finds Nuremberg's legacy in this regard to be distorting rather than clarifying. See Michael R. Marrus, "The Holocaust at Nuremberg," Yad Vashem Studies 26 (1998): 5–41, here 40–41; Donald Bloxham, *Genocide on Trial. War Crimes Trials and the Formation of Holocaust History and Memory* (New York, 2001), 221–27.

15 Lemkin, *Axis Rule*, 79.

16 Actually, Lemkin did not coin the word but translated it into English or rather into a Greco-Latin derivative. The first mention of the word *Völkermord*, as far as it is known, was made by a German, August Graf von Platen, in his *Polish Songs* from 1831, which were a critique of the second division of Poland. To use the word *Völkermord* became quite prominent amongst the early German democrats in the mid-nineteenth century, whenever they denounced the oppression of the Polish nation. See *Geflügelte Worte: Zitate, Sentenzen und Begriffe in ihrem geschichtlichen Zusammenhang*, eds. Kurt Böttcher, Karl Heinz Berger, Kurt Krolop, Christa Zimmermann (Leipzig, 1981), 466.

17 Lemkin, *Axis Rule*, 81.

18 Ibid., 79–81.

19 Claudia Kraft, "Völkermorde im 20. Jahrhundert: Rafael Lemkin und die Ahndung des Genozids durch das internationale Strafrecht," in *Finis mundi: Endzeiten und Weltenden im östlichen Europa*, eds. Joachim Hösler and Wolfgang Kessler (Stuttgart, 1998), 91–110, here 101; John Cooper, *Raphael Lemkin and the Struggle for the Genocide Convention* (Basingstoke, 2008), 14–25; Stone, "Raphael Lemkin," 539. On the protection of minorities in Europe, see: Mark Mazower, *Dark Continent: Europe's Twentieth Century* (London, 1998), 41–75; Martin Scheuermann, *Minderheitenschutz contra Konfliktverhütung? Die Minderheitenpolitik des Völkerbundes in den zwanziger Jahren* (Marburg, 2000); Carole Fink, *Defending the Rights of Others: The Great Powers, the Jews, and International Minority Protection, 1878–1938* (Cambridge, 2004).

20 A. Dirk Moses, "Lemkin, Culture, and the Concept of Genocide," in *The Oxford Handbook of Genocide Studies*, eds. Bloxham and Moses (Oxford, 2010), 19–41, here 22–25.

21 Josef L. Kunz, "The Future of the International Law for the Protection of National Minorities," *American Journal of International Law* 39 (1945), 89–95.

22 See Lemkin, *Axis Rule*, 82–90.

23 Daniel Marc Segesser and Myriam Gessler, "Raphael Lemkin and the International Debate on the Punishment of War Crimes (1919–1948)," *Journal of Genocide Research* 7 (2005), 453–68, here 461.

24 Lemkin, *Axis Rule*, 79.

25 See Stone, "Raphael Lemkin," 545.

26 After the Nuremberg trials and the declaration of the Genocide Convention, Lemkin still stuck with this opinion. In an unfinished manuscript on the Nazi crimes he discussed this Nazi driving force in a chapter entitled "Intent to Kill." See *Raphael Lemkin's Thoughts on Nazi Genocide. Not Guilty?*, ed. Steven L. Jacobs (Lewiston, 1992), 159–71.

27 See Segesser and Gessler, "Raphael Lemkin," 463; Jonathan Bush, " 'The Supreme . . . Crime' and Its Origins: The Lost Legislative History of the Crime of Aggressive War," *Columbia Law Review* 120 (2002), 2324–424, here 2368; Anson Rabinbach, "The Challenge of the Unprecedented—Raphael Lemkin and the Concept of Genocide," *Simon Dubnow Institute Yearbook* 4 (2005): 397–420, here 410; Cooper, *Raphael Lemkin*, 62–75.

28 Indictment, *Trial of the Major War Criminals before the International Military Tribunal [IMT]*, 42 vols (Nuremberg, 1947–49), here I, 43–44.

29 Ibid., 66–67.

30 Closing Statement of the British Prosecution, Hartley Shawcross, July 27, 1946, IMT, XIX, 509.

31 Ibid., 514–15.

32 Ibid., 498.

33 Ibid., 496–97. Lemkin's cited this passage of Shawcross's closing statement in length in his unfinished manuscript. This citation and the discussion about the motivation of the Nazis is part of the chapter "Intent to Kill." See *Raphael Lemkin's Thoughts*, 171. Dan Stone erroneously attributed Shawcross's citation to Lemkin; see Stone, "Raphael Lemkin," 544.

34 Closing Statement of the French Prosecution, M. Auguste Champetier de Ribes, July 29, 1946, IMT, XIX, 543.

35 Ibid., 561–62.

36 Ibid., 531.

37 Closing Statement of the Soviet Prosecution, Gen. Rudenko, July 29, 1946, IMT, XIX, 600.

38 Ibid., 574.

39 Ibid., 570.

40 This reading was not too dissimilar from Hannah Arendt's theoretical analysis of the Nazi totalitarian movement which, though, also applied to Stalin's Soviet Union. See particularly her chapter on the concentration camps: Hannah Arendt, *The Origins of Totalitarianism* (New York, 1951).

41 See, for example, Closing Statement of the American Prosecution, Robert Jackson, July 26, 1946, IMT, XIX, 406.

42 *Report of Robert H. Jackson, United States Representative to the International Conference on Military Trials, London 1945* (Washington, DC, 1949), 48. Cf. Bradley F. Smith, *The Road to Nuremberg* (New York, 1981); Marrus, "Holocaust at Nuremberg," 14.

43 Closing Statement Jackson, IMT, XIX, 404.

44 Telford Taylor, *Anatomy of the Nuremberg Trials: A Personal Memoir* (New York, 1992), xi.

45 Judgment, September 30, 1946, IMT, XXII, 480.

46 Ibid., 477–78, 484–85.

47 Ibid., 491–96. Cf. Marrus, "Holocaust at Nuremberg," 38.

48 Lawrence Douglas, "Film as Witness: Screening Nazi Concentration Camps before the Nuremberg Trials," *Yale Law Journal* 105 (1995): 477; Marrus, "Holocaust at Nuremberg," 39–40.

49 On the NTN trials, see Tadeusz Cyprian and Jerzy Sawicki, *Siedem procesów przed Najwyższym Trybunałem Narodowym* (Poznań, 1962); Janusz Gumkowski and Tadeusz Kułakowski, *Zbrodniarze hitlerowscy przed Najwyższym Trybunałem Narodowym* (Warsaw,

1965); Alexander V. Prusin, "Poland's Nuremberg; The Seven Court Cases of the Supreme National Tribunal, 1946–1948," *Holocaust and Genocide Studies* 24 (2010): 1–25. Excerpts of some NTN trials are published in English translation in the UNWCC's series, see *LRTWC*, VII, XIII, and XIV.

50 Trial of Artur [sic] Greiser, *LRTWC*, XIII, 71.

51 Judgment of the NTN, Trial of Greiser, *LRTWC*, XIII, 114.

52 Trial of Amon Leopold Goeth, *LRTWC*, VII, 7.

53 Judgment of the NTN, Trial of Goeth, *LRTWC*, VII, 9.

54 Trial of Rudolf Franz Ferdinand Hoess [Höß], *LRTWC*, VII, 11–26.

55 Foreword by Robert Wright, *LRTWC*, XIII, vii–ix. On the history of the UNWCC, see Robert Wright, *The History of the United War Crimes Commission and the Development of the Laws of War* (London, 1948); Arieh Kochavi, "Britain and the Establishment of the United Nations War Crimes Commission," *English Historical Review* 107 (1992): 323–49.

56 In January 1947, after the UN General Assembly had adopted the Resolution on the crime of genocide in December 1946, Lemkin wrote three memoranda on the crime of genocide and how it could be charged in the NMT trials, and sent them to OCCWC: "The Importance of the Genocide Concept for the Doctors Case," "The Participation of German Industrialists and Bankers in Genocide," and "Planning of a Special Trial on Abduction of Women into Prostitution." See Paul Weindling, *Nazi Medicine and the Nuremberg Trials: From Medical War Crimes to Informed Consent* (Basingstoke, 2004), 227–28, 230–31; Jonathan A. Bush, "The Prehistory of Corporations and Conspiracy in International Criminal Law: What Nuremberg Really Said," *Columbia Law Review* 109 (2009): 1094–262, here 1178–81 and 1258. See also Paul Weindling, "Victims, Witnesses and the Ethical Legacy of the Nuremberg Medical Trial," in *Reassessing the Nuremberg Military Tribunals: Transitional Justice, Trial Narratives, and Historiography*, eds. Kim C. Priemel and Alexa Stiller (New York: Berghahn Books, 2012), chap 3.

57 For more details on the RuSHA case, about the individual defendants, and the strategies of the prosecution and defense, see: Heinemann, "*Rasse, Siedlung, deutsches Blut*," 565–80; Alexa Stiller, "Die Volkstumspolitik der SS vor Gericht: Strategien der Anklage und Verteidigung im Nürnberger RuSHA-Prozess, 1947–1948," in *Leipzig—Nürnberg—Den Haag: Neue Fragestellungen und Forschungen zum Verhältnis von Menschenrechtsverbrechen, justizieller Säuberung und Völkerstrafrecht*, ed. Helia-Verena Daubach (Düsseldorf, 2008), 66–86.

58 RuSHA case, Indictment, July 1, 1947, *TWC*, IV, 609–10.

59 The Nazi term *Volkstumspolitik* is literally translated as "ethnicity policy," but it was actually a racial population and settlement policy intertwined with the Nazi persecution and extermination policy. See: Alexa Stiller, "Grenzen des 'Deutschen': Nationalsozialistische Volkstumspolitik in Polen, Frankreich und Slowenien während des Zweiten Weltkrieges," in *Deutschsein als Grenzerfahrung: Minderheitenpolitik in Europa zwischen 1914 und 1950*, eds. Mathias Beer, Dietrich Beyrau, and Cornelia Rauh (Essen, 2009), 61–84.

60 RuSHA case, Indictment, July 1, 1947, *TWC*, IV, 610.

61 RuSHA case, Opening Statement of the Prosecution, October 20, 1947, *TWC*, IV, 622.

62 Ibid., 626.

63 Ibid., 626.

64 Ibid., 627. In fact, when two former staff members of the OCCWC compiled the trial materials for publication, they put the RuSHA and the *Einsatzgruppen* cases together in one volume because, from their point of view, these two trials belonged together and had shown two different aspects of the Nazi genocide program. See: 3rd Draft of the Preface, RuSHA case, Green Series, December 15, 1948, National Archives and Records Administration (NARA), RG 238, NM-70, Entry 159, Box 2, Folder 2.

65 RuSHA case, Opening Statement of the Prosecution, October 20, 1947, *TWC*, IV, 634, 637, 663, 687, 693–94. Interestingly, the passage on the persecution of the Jews in the Opening Statement is literally identical with one in the Opening Statement in the Pohl case. See Ibid., 666; Pohl case, Opening Statement of the Prosecution, April 8, 1947, *TWC*, V, 250–51. But this identical passage is hardly surprising because both prosecution teams were headed by James M. McHaney, Chief of the SS Division, Chief Prosecutor, and later Deputy Chief of Counsel in the Medical, the Pohl, the RuSHA, the Hostages, the *Einsatzgruppen*, and the High Command cases. Hans Froehlich and Daniel J. Shiller were also active in the preparation of the Pohl and RuSHA cases for trial and respective members of the prosecution counsel.

66 RuSHA case, Opening Statement of the Prosecution, October 20, 1947, *TWC*, IV, 626–27.

67 RuSHA case, Closing Statement of the Prosecution, February 13, 1948, *TWC*, V, 31.

68 Ibid.

69 RuSHA case, Opening Statement for Defendant Greifelt, Dr. Carl Haensel, November 20, 1947, *TWC*, IV, 701–702.

70 Carl Haensel (Greifelt's attorney), RuSHA Trial transcript, German translation, 1194–95; Karl Dötzer (Brückner's attorney), ibid., 1257; Kurt Behling (Meyer's attorney), ibid., 1295.

71 Werner Schubert (Lorenz' attorney), ibid., 1267.

72 Haensel, ibid., 1186, 1196; Dötzer, ibid., 1258.

73 RuSHA case, Opinion and Judgment, March 10, 1948, *TWC*, V, 90.

74 Ibid., 96.

75 Ibid., 100–2.

76 Ibid., 154–55.

77 Ibid., 97.

78 Ibid., 121.

79 Ibid., 152.

80 Ibid., 156.

81 Mechthild Rössler, "Konrad Meyer und der 'Generalplan Ost' in der Beurteilung der Nürnberger Prozesse," in *Der 'Generalplan Ost.' Hauptlinien der nationalsozialistischen Planungs- und Vernichtungspolitik*, eds. Mechthild Rössler and Sabine Schleiermacher (Berlin, 1993), 356–68.

82 See Kim C. Priemel, "Tales of Totalitarianism. Conflicting Narratives in the Industrialist Cases at Nuremberg," in *Reassessing the Nuremberg Military Tribunals: Transitional Justice, Trial Narratives, and Historiography*, eds. Kim C. Priemel and Alexa Stiller (New York: Berghahn Books, 2012), Chapter 6.

83 The Medical and the *Einsatzgruppen* cases were primarily murder trials. See Weindling, *Nazi Medicine*, 170; Hilary Earl, *The Nuremberg SS-Einsatzgruppen Trial, 1945–1958. Atrocity, Law, and History* (New York, 2009), 81–82.

84 Ferencz recommended a concentration on Ohlendorf, the *Einsatzgruppen*, and the SD. See Intra-Office Memorandum from Ferencz to Section Chiefs, February 5, 1947, NARA, RG 238, NM-70, Entry 202, Box 3, Folder 1. Cf. Memorandum from Taylor to Ervin and others, February 6, 1947, printed in Bush, "Prehistory," 1262.

85 Bloxham, *Genocide on Trial*, 189–94; Earl, *SS-Einsatzgruppen Trial*, 76–82, 95.

86 Raphael Lemkin, "Genocide as a Crime under International Law," *The American Journal of International Law* 41 (1947): 145–51, here 147, footnote 6; Michael R. Marrus, "The Doctor's Trial in Historical Context," *Bulletin of the History of Medicine* 73 (1999): 106–23, here 116; Weindling, *Nazi Medicine*, 170, 179–87, 225–32.

87 Medical case, Opening Statement of the Prosecution, December 9, 1946, in *TWC*, I, 38.

88 Ibid., 48.

89 Medical case, Opinion and Judgment, August 19, 1947, *TWC*, II, 181, 183, 197, 278.
90 Justice case, Indictment, January 4, 1947, *TWC*, III, 20–21.
91 Justice case, Opinion and Judgment, December 3–4, 1947, *TWC*, III, 983.
92 Ibid., 1063–64, 1128, 1142, 1146, 1156.
93 Pohl case, Opening Statement of the Prosecution, April 8, 1947, *TWC*, V, 250–51.
94 Ibid., 250–51, 253, see also 232–33.
95 Ibid., 250–51.
96 Pohl case, Opinion and judgment, November 3, 1947, *TWC*, V, 971–80.
97 Pohl case, Concurring opinion by Judge Musmanno, November 3, 1947, *TWC*, V, 1135.
98 *Einsatzgruppen* case, Opening Statement of the Prosecution, September 29, 1947, *TWC*, IV, 30–31.
99 Ibid., 32–33.
100 Ibid., 369–70.
101 On the presupposition of intent in the *Einsatzgruppen* case, see Bloxham, *Genocide on Trial*, 204–6; Earl, SS-*Einsatzgruppen Trial*, 211–16.
102 Further work on this issue needs to be done.
103 *Einsatzgruppen* case, Opinion and Judgment, April 8–9, 1948, *TWC*, IV, 415–16.
104 "The extermination program on racial and political grounds also extended to prisoners of war." Ibid., 441.
105 Ibid., 411.
106 Ibid., 450.
107 Ibid., 450.
108 Ibid., 469–70.
109 On Musmanno, see the chapter by Earl in this book.
110 This phrase goes back to Gerald Reitlinger, *The SS: Alibi of a Nation 1922–1945* (Melbourne, 1956). See Jan Erik Schulte, "The SS as the 'Alibi of a Nation'? Narrative Continuities from the Nuremberg Trials to the 1960s," in *Reassessing the Nuremberg Military Tribunals*, Chapter 6.
111 High Command case, Opening Statement of the Prosecution, February 5, 1948, *TWC*, X, 138–39. Cf. also High Command case, Closing Statement of the Prosecution, August 10, 1948, *TWC*, XI, 347, 353, 364. On the High Command case in general, see Valerie G. Hebert, *Hitler's Generals on Trial. The Last War Crimes Tribunal at Nuremberg* (Lawrence, KS, 2010).
112 High Command case, Judgment, October 27–28, 1948, *TWC*, XI, 462–697, in particular 547–49.
113 Telford Taylor, *Final Report to the Secretary of the Army on the Nuernberg War Crimes Trials under Control Council Law No. 100* (Washington, DC, 1949), 76. For a general overview, see Frank Buscher, *The U.S. War Crimes Trial Program in Germany, 1946–1955* (New York, 1989).
114 Dirk Pöppmann, "Der Wilhelmstraßenprozess—ein Ministerial- oder SS-Verfahren?," paper presented at the conference "Negotiating the Past: German-American Perspectives in the U.S. War Crimes Trials in Nuremberg, 1946–1949," at the European University Viadrina, Frankfurt, April 23–25, 2009.
115 Ministries case, Indictment, November 4, 1947, *TWC*, XII, 44.
116 Ibid., 45–49.
117 Ministries case, Opening Statement of the Prosecution, January 6, 1948, *TWC*, XII, 176, 204, 219, 232.
118 Ministries case, Closing Statement of the Prosecution, November 9, 1948, *TWC*, XIV, 41.
119 Ministries case, Judgment, April 11–13, 1949, *TWC*, XIV, 470.
120 Ibid., 472–78.

121 Ibid., 541, 48, 666–67.
122 Ministries case, Dissenting Opinion of Judge Powers, April 13, 1949, *TWC*, XIV, 910–11.
123 Ibid., 910. For that reason, Powers found von Weizsäcker, Woermann, Steengracht von Moyland, Veesenmayer, Dietrich, Schwerin von Krosigk, and Puhl not guilty of taking part in the extermination of the Jews. See ibid., 909–31.
124 Cooper, *Raphael Lemkin.*
125 Weindling, *Nazi Medicine*, 228.
126 United Nations Resolution 96 (I). The Crime of Genocide, December 11, 1946, http:// www.un.org/documents/ga/res/1/ares1.htm (May 2010).
127 Lemkin, "Genocide as a Crime," 148–50.
128 Shaw, *What is Genocide?*, 27, 33–36; Clavero, *Genocide or Ethnocide*, 39, 45.
129 Convention on the Prevention and Punishment of the Crime of Genocide, adopted by Resolution 260 (III) A of the UN General Assembly on December 9, 1948, Entry into force: January 12, 1951, *United Nations Bulletin* 5 (1948): 1012–15.
130 Josef L. Kunz, "The United Nations Convention on Genocide," *The American Journal of International Law* 43 (1949): 738–46, here 742.
131 Clavero, *Genocide or Ethnocide*, 53–56. Cf. Robert van Krieken, "The Barbarism of Civilization: Cultural Genocide and the 'Stolen Generations' ", *British Journal of Sociology* 52 (1999): 295–313; *Genocide and Settler Society: Frontier Violence and Stolen Indigenous Children in Australian History*, ed. A. Dirk Moses (New York, 2004); Ward Churchill, *Kill the Indian, Save the Man: The Genocidal Impact of American Indian Residential Schools* (San Francisco, 2004).
132 The original concept of Lemkin's "genocide" covered what has become known as "ethnic cleansing" since the 1990s. However, the Genocide Convention does not include population relocations in any way. Nowadays scholars differentiate between both acts by referring to the intent: while the intention of genocide is the total physical and biological destruction of a group of people, ethnical cleansing intends "only" the expulsion of a supposedly ethnically homogeneous population. See Schabas, *Genozid im Völkerrecht*, 265; Norman M. Naimark, *Flammender Hass. Ethnische Säuberungen im 20. Jahrhundert* (Munich, 2004), 12. The question remains if this difference is not only theoretically construed for legal reasons but historically hard to detect for both acts occur simultaneously and are often intertwined. Or, as Lemkin suggested in *Axis Rule*, what we call genocide and ethnic cleansing principally pursue an identical intention.
133 On the problematic issue of the decision-making process to commit genocide within historical analyses, see Birthe Kundrus, "Entscheidung für den Völkermord? Einleitende Überlegungen zu einem historiographischen Problem," *Mittelweg 36*, 6 (2006): 4–17.
134 First Draft of the Genocide Convention by the UN Secretariat, [May] 1947 (UN Doc. E/447), and Second Draft of the Genocide Convention, Ad Hoc Committee of the Economic and Social Council (ECOSOC), April 5, 1948 and May 10, 1948 (UN Doc. E/AC.25/SR.1 to 28), http://www.preventgenocide.org/law/convention/drafts/ (May 2010). For more details, see: Kunz, "UN Convention on Genocide," 738–46; Morsink, "Cultural Genocide;" Schabas, *Genozid im Völkerrecht*, 75–137; Matthew Lippman, "A Road Map to the 1948 Convention on the Prevention and Punishment of Genocide," *Journal of Genocide Research* 4 (2002): 177–95.
135 On the other hand, the communist delegations favored a cultural genocide paragraph. See Morsink, "Cultural Genocide."
136 Some authors hint to these diverse political interests. Cf. Morsink, "Cultural Genocide;" Schabas, *Genozid im Völkerrecht*, 239–45, 258–60; Anson Rabinbach, "Challenge of the Unprecedented," 402; Calvero, *Genocide and Ethnocide*, 54–55. It should also be noted that Pakistan brought up the charge of genocide against India,

because of India's mistreatment towards Moslems, before the Security Council several times in 1948. See Cooper, *Raphael Lemkin*, 127.

137 Morsink, "Cultural Genocide;" Johannes Morsink, *The Universal Declaration of Human Rights: Origins, Drafting, and Intent* (Philadelphia, 1999).

138 Joseph B. Schechtman, "Decline of the International Protection of Minority Rights," *The Western Political Quarterly* 4 (1951): 1–11; Josef L. Kunz, "The Present Status of the International Law for the Protection of Minorities," *American Journal of International Law* 48 (1954): 282–87, here 284.

139 Mark Mazower, "The Strange Triumph of Human Rights, 1933–1950," *Historical Journal* 47 (2004): 379–98.

140 Kunz, "Future of the International Law," 94–95; Hans Rothfels, "Frontiers and Mass Migration in Eastern Central Europe," *Review of Politics* 8 (1946): 37–67.

141 On Lemkin's campaign for ratification of the Genocide Convention, see Cooper, *Raphael Lemkin*, 173–88.

142 Lemkin's draft on "The Hitler Case", n.d., cited in Rabinbach, "Challenge of the Unprecedented," 408; Stone, "Raphael Lemkin," 546.

143 On Lemkin's inconsistencies, see Clavero, *Genocide or Ethnocide*, 57.

144 Moses, "Lemkin, Culture, and the Concept of Genocide," 37–38.

145 On the development of Holocaust memory in American Society, see: Peter Novick, *The Holocaust in American Life* (Boston, 1999), 103–24; Lawrence Baron, "The Holocaust and American Public Memory, 1945–1960," *Holocaust and Genocide Studies* 17 (2003): 62–88.

146 See: Léon Poliakov, *Bréviaire de la haine: Le IIIe Reich et les juifs* (Paris, 1951) [*Harvest of Hate: The Nazi Program for the Destruction of the Jews of Europe* (Syracuse, 1954)]; Gerald Reitlinger, *The Final Solution: the Attempt to Exterminate the Jews of Europe 1939–1945* (London, 1953); *Das Dritte Reich und die Juden: Dokumente und Aufsätze*, eds. Léon Poliakov and Joseph Wulf (Berlin, 1955); Wolfgang Scheffler, *Judenverfolgung im Dritten Reich: 1933–1945* (Berlin, 1960); Gerhard Schoenberner, *Der gelbe Stern: die Judenverfolgung in Europa 1933 bis 1945* (Hamburg, 1960) [*The Holocaust: The Nazi Destruction of Europe's Jews* (Edmonton, 1969)]; Raul Hilberg, *The Destruction of the European Jews* (New York, 1961).

147 Robert L. Koehl, *RKFDV: German Resettlement and Population Policy 1939–1945. A History of the Reich Commission for the Strengthening of Germandom* (Cambridge, 1957). In contrast, see Ihor Kamentsky, *Secret Nazi Plans for East Europe. A Study of Lebensraum Policies* (New York, 1961).

148 Helmut Heiber, "Der Generalplan Ost," *Vierteljahreshefte für Zeitgeschichte* 6 (1958): 281–325.

149 Hans Buchheim, "Rechtsstellung und Organisation des Reichskommissars für die Festigung deutschen Volkstums," in *Gutachten des Instituts für Zeitgeschichte* (Munich, 1958), 239–79; Martin Broszat, *Nationalsozialistische Polenpolitik 1939–1945* (Stuttgart, 1961).

150 Tadeusz Cyprian and Jerzy Sawicki, *Nazi Rule in Poland 1939–1945* (Warsaw, 1961); Janusz Gumkowski and Kazimierz Leszczyński, *Poland under Nazi Occupation* (Warsaw, 1961); *Genocide 1939–1945. War Crimes in Poland*, eds. Szymon Datner, Janusz Gumkowski and Kasimierz Leszezyński (Poznań, 1962).

151 Aly and Heim, *Architects of Annihilation*; Aly, "Final Solution."

152 Jonathan Friedman, "Law and Politics in the Subsequent Nuremberg Trials, 1946–1949," in *Atrocities on Trial. Historical Perspectives on the Politics of Prosecuting War Crimes*, eds. Patricia Heberer and Jürgen Matthäus (Lincoln, NE, 2008), 75–101, here 92f.

16

THEORIZING DESTRUCTION

Reflections on the state of comparative genocide theory

Maureen S. Hiebert

Since the 1980s a new field of studies has emerged: the study of genocide. Although the term was coined toward the end of World War II, was employed at the Nuremberg tribunals, and was then enshrined in the 1948 UN Convention on Genocide, the phenomenon as such was not studied much over the next few decades, even as events of mass murder and crimes against humanity proliferated. A major reason for this was that under the shadow of the Cold War most violent events in the world were classified through the lens of East versus West, democracy versus communism. Meanwhile the study of the Holocaust, seen by many as the paradigmatic genocide, and by others as a unique case that could not be subsumed entirely under this rubric, picked up pace as of the 1960s. By the time the Soviet Union and communism in Eastern Europe had collapsed, and the Cold War finally ended, there was a substantial body of Holocaust research available to scholars interested in other cases of genocide and the ways in which they might be studied.

Thus, the new scholarship on genocide, beginning with such pioneering works as Leo Kuper's 1980 comparative study, was clearly influenced by interpretations and methodologies developed in research on the "final solution" in the preceding decades. By the 1990s, even as the end of the Cold War led to the opening of numerous previously inaccessible archives as well as to thinking about violence outside the ideological framework of that long-drawn conflict, the world was confronted with a series of new genocidal events that greatly enhanced interest in the phenomenon as a whole. The mass killings that accompanied the wars in the former Yugoslavia, where national identity, ethnicity, and religion played a prominent part, the reappearance of concentration camps, mass rape, massacres of civilians, torture and dehumanization, were all eerily reminiscent of the events of World War II, which no one had believed would ever recur on European soil. One difference was that the violence in the former Yugoslavia was extensively covered by the media; and yet, despite all the pledges and vows made after 1945, hundreds of thousands of people were to die before military intervention finally put an end to the killing. In Rwanda in 1994, within the space of ten weeks, approximately 800,000 people, mostly Tutsi, were murdered by their Hutu neighbors using light weapons, machetes, and fire, in what turned out to be the fastest genocide in history. This event, too, was initially not only well covered, but also occurred at the doorstep of a UN contingent which, instead of being reinforced and sent to put a halt to the violence, was drastically reduced in size and barred from intervention. As half-hearted talks and negotiations went on, almost the entire Tutsi population of Rwanda was murdered. The genocide was finally stopped not by an international effort but by an invading Tutsi army.

From this context, genocide studies could draw two lessons. On the one hand, the rich scholarship on the Holocaust provided a model for the study of other genocides; on the other, it was shown that neither the rhetoric of "never again," nor the creation of international legal and political mechanism meant to prevent such events, had any meaning as long as states, or the international community as a whole, could not muster the political will to act. Hence genocide studies, as an outgrowth of research on the Holocaust and of the political realities of our time, is both a field of study and an undertaking with real political investment and potential ramifications.

Perhaps because of this double genesis, genocide studies has also been at times somewhat plagued by a sense of competition with Holocaust historiography. Arguments have been made that the insistence of some scholars, by now an extremely small minority, and a far more pervasive public and political discourse about the so-called uniqueness of the Holocaust, has had a detrimental effect on the study of other genocides and may have even played a role in preventing the world from paying sufficient attention to cases of mass murder that seemed not "as bad" as the Holocaust. Indeed, some western politicians wishing to avoid involvement in risky intervention, and some Israeli leaders trying to divert attention from their own illegal occupation policies, have invoked the Holocaust as either worse than subsequent genocides or as giving license for clearly illegitimate policies by the descendants of its victims.

But the abuse of memory and the cheapening of catastrophe for political ends should not distract students of the Holocaust and other genocides from the crucial effort to reconstruct their histories, understand their causes, and, thereby, seek ways to prevent their recurrences; not through empty rhetoric and ceremonious pledges, but through education, humanitarian work, and, when necessary, robust intervention and swift but fair punishment. The tools for all this are in fact mostly already there, and the growing body of knowledge, as clearly and systematically laid out in Hiebert's chapter, is available and can be brought to bear. Thinking back to the genocide of the Jews seven decades ago, one may indeed despair at the thought that the killing still goes on. For many survivors such as Primo Levi and Jean Améry, it was precisely the realization that we had learned nothing, and forgotten nothing, that was the most difficult to accept. And it is for this reason that any student of the Holocaust cannot and must not restrict himself or herself to studying that past but must commit to fighting the on-going murder of innocents in our own time.

Introduction

Comparative genocide studies is a young discipline that seeks to understand an "old scourge." As the post-Holocaust plea "never again" consistently went ignored in the latter half of the twentieth century, scholars in the social sciences and humanities began to examine the origins and processes of what is arguably the worst form of collective human behavior and to try to answer the vexing question of why human beings do such terrible things to each other "again and again." Much of what we now call "genocide studies" began with single case studies of individual genocides, but in the 1980s a small group of scholars began to engage in the comparative analysis of multiple cases of geno-cide, in the hope of uncovering the underlying logic of this terrible crime. Given the very real human suffering attached to the subject, comparative geno-cide studies has evolved not only into an academic discipline concerned with understanding and explaining past genocides but also into a goal-oriented research project aimed at preventing the perpetration of genocidal violence in the present and future.

This article focuses on the current state of comparative genocide theory,[1] specifically the creation of theories intended to account for the causes of geno-cide and the processes of genocidal destruction. It does not cover the consider-able body of literature concerning the definition of the concept of genocide and what cases of mass atrocities ought to be considered as such. The state of the genocide literature in this respect has been well rehearsed elsewhere and, there-fore, need not be further rehearsed here. More importantly, however, the issue of definition is omitted from the current discussion because the fixation among genocide scholars on how to define genocide has diverted needed attention away from the creation and testing of theories. Of course, defining core concepts is a central and necessary part of the theorizing process, but it is not a substitute for theory or theorizing itself. The obsession with definitional debates has arguably left comparative genocides studies undertheorized relative to other disciplines in the social sciences and humanities.[2]

What this article does do is attempt to categorize and critically evaluate the most prominent theoretical approaches used to explain the origins and processes of genocide. The list of approaches and authors considered is, admit-tedly, far from exhaustive. Reviewing the theoretical literature on genocide is somewhat difficult, given the interdisciplinary nature of the field and the lack of a unified theoretical or methodological approach, an agreed-upon set of cases, or a preferred level or unit of analysis.[3] The lack of theoretical and methodological coherence in the field is not necessarily a problem, however. Genocide is not only a horrible phenomenon, it is also an exceedingly complex one that occurs across a wide variety of times and places and involves different kinds of collective actors (perpetrators, victims, bystanders, collaborators, rescuers, etc.) and a number of different variables, structures, and processes that do not fit neatly into simple, generalizable explanatory models. The heterogeneity of theoretical and disciplinary approaches we find in genocide studies may be entirely appropriate for a discipline that studies one of the most convoluted and seemingly unfathomable forms of human activity. The failure of past grand theories in the social sciences to predict many of the seismic changes of the past century should also serve as a cautionary tale to comparative genocide scholars.

The review that follows does not divide the literature into disciplinary approaches, in order to allow us to consider the evolution of theorizing in the field as a whole. Instead, for the sake of clarity, the literature is categorized according to the relative weight given to individual or group agency, structural factors, or processes of identity construction in accounting for the origins and unfolding of genocidal destruction. This approach allows us to concentrate on what individual authors and approaches suggest is the initial source of the complex web of events, individual and collective actions, and processes that produces genocide. Admittedly, this way of categorizing the literature imposes on it a somewhat artificial structure, since many approaches either imply or explicitly state a reciprocal or mutually constitutive relationship between human agency, structure, and process. Nonetheless, the initial discussion of agency-oriented approaches focuses on theories that suggest that genocide is driven, in terms of decision making or perpetration, by elite perpetrators, front-line perpetrators, or societal behavior. Next, structural approaches are considered; in this section the literature is divided according to whether the theories espoused stress the importance of culture, institutional organizations, societal cleavages, structural crises, regime type, modernity, or ideology. The final set of approaches considers processes of collective identity construction, namely the conception of the victim group as the "other," as subhuman, and as a threat.

Theories of genocide

Agency-oriented approaches

Elites

One way in which scholars have tried to explain genocide is to look at the role played by elite decision makers. For some authors who use this approach, analysis focuses on the role played by specific individual leaders, from Hitler to Stalin to Pol Pot and others, in the genocidal process. Here the argument is that the most senior decision makers, for reasons of personal psychology, life and leadership experience, or ideological beliefs, make the decision to exterminate whole groups of people, which makes these individual leaders the ultimate source of genocidal policies. Some works, such as Gerald Fleming's *Hitler and the Final Solution*,[4] were written explicitly to counter the claims of genocide deniers and minimizers that specific elites, in this case Hitler, did not sanction the killing, were lied to about it by their subordinates who were really to blame, or simply were not aware of what was happening to the victims. Other works are not specifically about a genocide at all but, rather, are biographical histories that shed light on several aspects of an individual leader's life, public and private, including his role in committing genocide.[5] As largely ideographic (i.e., single-case-study) historical works, these explanations tell us in great detail the role played by specific historical figures in the initiation and perpetration of genocide, but they also raise a more general comparative question: Are genocides primarily the result of the actions of individual leaders? Would the Holocaust have happened without Hitler, or the "killing fields" without Pol Pot? Is there a not-so-great-man theory of genocide? The answer to this question is that we simply do not know. Although senior political elites are central to the genocidal decision-making process, we cannot turn back the clock and factor out individual leaders from the equation to see whether a given genocide would have happened without them. As a basis for comparison, it is counterproductive to extrapolate from single case studies of individual leaders the idea that these leaders are the only significant actors in the genocidal process. The role of individual elites in a particular genocide may be highly idiosyncratic and, therefore, not comparable to those of other elites in other cases.

Leaving the influence of specific historical figures aside but maintaining the focus on elite agency, recent works by Benjamin Valentino and Manus Midlarsky, for example, have adopted a *strategic actor* model to account for the conditions under which elite actors make the decision to commit genocide.[6] Valentino sees genocide, or what he calls "mass killing," as a barbaric, immoral, and seemingly illogical act but one that is the product of a rational choice made by elites to achieve specific policy goals. For Valentino, genocide is not an end in itself but a strategic means to achieve an end. In the pursuit of radical policy goals, perpetrator elites commit genocidal violence against a target group in order to force its members to do something they would otherwise not do but which is required for the realization of specific policy goals. The decision to commit genocide is made only when elites have concluded that other, less violent forms of repression or concessions to the target group for achieving their ends have failed or are impractical.[7]

Similarly, Daniel Chirot and Clark McCauley argue that, for elite perpetrators, mass murder is the "cheapest" way to overcome resistance to policies favored by the perpetrators or simply to dispose of groups that are perceived to be "in the way" of the realization of desired policies. Chirot and McCauley suggest that indigenous populations are most often the targets of genocide based on these kinds of strategic calculations because their presence on a given piece of territory is "troublesome," decreasing the strategic and/or economic value of that territory. When elite perpetrators calculate that the population "cannot be controlled or dispersed," genocide becomes the policy option.[8] In the *Killing Trap*, Midlarsky also links the strategic choice to commit genocide to policy failure, but he suggests that genocide is a response to external, particularly territorial, losses. For Midlarsky, genocide is motivated by elite decision makers' desire for "loss compensation."

Whether one accepts a strategic actor explanation (particularly of the Valentino variety) as a useful basis for explanation and comparison hinges in part on one's position concerning the status of genocide as a means to an end or as an end in itself. Scholars who see genocide as a policy goal in and of itself will be at odds with the foundational premises of this approach, but those who take the opposite view may find it useful for understanding how and under what circumstances political elites make the policy choice to exterminate groups of people. As a broadly comparative theory of genocide in general, however, a strictly elite decision-making model leaves out the crucial role played by societal actors in the total process of destruction. If it takes a village to raise a child, it takes the state *and* society to perpetrate a genocide.

Frontline killers

In taking up the actors missing from elite-centered approaches, other genocide scholars who adopt an agency-centered approach have attempted to explain the behavior of the state and societal actors who actually carry out the order to commit genocide. Here the focus is still on explaining how human agency drives the genocidal process, not in terms of why the decision is made to pursue genocidal policies but in terms of how ordinary people can follow the brutal orders of their political and military superiors and slaughter their fellow human beings in great numbers.

Early attempts at this kind of explanation by psychologists and social psychologists assumed that the low-level perpetrators of genocide and other atrocities were outside the psychological norm because their actions were so beyond the pale of "normal" human experience. Theodor Adorno and his colleagues, for example, tried to identify among Nazi perpetrators a specific "authoritarian personality" that allowed these individuals to carry out genocidal policies.[9] But research into individual and group responses to authority and organizational structures, including the infamous Zimbardo prison experiments at Stanford University, as well as later social psychological research based in part on these experiments and on other research, has determined that genocidal killing is perpetrated by quite ordinary people. One of the first scholars to make this profoundly disturbing observation, historian Christopher Browning, demonstrates in *Ordinary Men: Reserve Police Battalion 101 and the Final Solution in Poland* that the low-level perpetrators in this specific case were neither psychologically extraordinary nor highly ideological or fanatical believers in Nazi racial policies. Recent works by Chirot and McCauley, James Waller, and Alex Alvarez confirm Browning's observations through their respective explorations of the role of normal human psychology under extreme conditions and within particular military/security and bureaucratic organizational contexts.[10]

Chirot and McCauley's work concentrates on the central role of psychological needs, goals, and emotions in motivating not only elites but, more importantly, ordinary people to become killers. "Political killing," as Chirot and McCauley call it, is motivated by four often mutually reinforcing motivations. The first motivation, convenience, is in fact a strategic motivation that involves the same strategic calculation made by elites, as noted above, to simply "get rid of" groups that are in the way. The remaining three—revenge, "simple" fear (including fear of retribution by the victim group and fear of extermination), and fear of pollution—are psychological motivations that elites may feel but which they also manipulate in society at large.[11] The "psychological foundations" for ordinary people's actual participation in mass killing lie in the confluence of a separate set of human emotions (again, often manipulated by elites), appeals to a "sense of duty," and the routinization of killing, training, "and good organization"[12] that foster obedience and provide incentives that "undermine personal responsibility."[13] Chirot and McCauley cite some very basic human emotions in their explanation, including fear, anger, love, hate, shame, and humiliation, although they suggest that fear is the "key emotion for understanding genocide."[14] The authors also include in their explanation the human tendency toward what they call "essentializing others" and "double essentializing," described as a "battle of good and evil, of two incompatible essences in which love of the good [one's own group] means necessarily hate for the threatening out-group."[15]

What Waller calls his "four-pronged" process model of "extraordinary human evil" concentrates on the psychological and organizational contextual foundations of individual and collective behavior. Underpinning human behavior (extraordinarily evil or otherwise) is the first prong, our "ancestral shadow" that shapes our responses to authority (ethnocentrism, xenophobia, and the desire for social dominance) and is held in common by all human beings across time and space. The second prong identifies three forces that "mold the identity" of frontline killers: cultural belief systems that determine how one evaluates "controlling influences on one's life," "moral disengagement of the perpetrator from [the] victim" (facilitated by the use of moral justifications, euphemism, and "exonerating comparisons"), and individual rational self-interest. The third prong concentrates on the "immediate social context of the culture of cruelty" and how this influences the way individuals "think, feel, and behave." Here Waller cites three central factors: the role of professional socialization into military and security organizations, the binding factors of the group that "reinforce commitment to the group and its activities," and the "merger of role and person," that is, how "evil-doing organizations change the people within them." Finally, Waller's fourth prong, to be considered later, deals with the construction of the collective identity of the victim group, a process that leads to the "social death" of the victims.[16]

Drawing on criminological approaches to explaining youth delinquency, Alvarez disputes the idea that humans are naturally aggressive and prone to violence. For Alvarez, the real question is not "Why do they kill?" but "How do ordinary people overcome internalized norms against violence and become the executioners of genocidal regimes?" Alvarez argues that, like delinquent youths, low-level perpetrators defer, repress, or neglect personal beliefs and feelings[17] so that their actions are reframed as acceptable to themselves and others through several "neutralization" techniques. These techniques include "denial of responsibility," in which the perpetrator claims that he or she was following orders or was otherwise coerced into killing and, therefore, does not bear responsibility for killing; "denial of injury" through the use of euphemistic language that cognitively sanitizes killing and brutality as "special treatment," "purification," "cleansing," and the like; "denial of [the] victim" such that killing becomes an act of self-defense against a threatening enemy and not the wanton destruction of innocent and defenseless men, women, and children; "condemning the condemners," whereby the perpetrator attempts to neutralize external criticism by arguing that similar acts have been perpetrated throughout history, even by the critics themselves; "appeals to higher loyalties" that characterize genocidal killing as a distasteful but necessary activity carried out not for personal gain, or based on personal motives, but for the greater good of the nation, race, or revolution; and "denial of humanity" through the dehumanization of the victim group and the deliberate creation of conditions of life that turn the victims into little more than animals, thus confirming the perpetrator's conception of the victims as subhuman.[18]

The great strength of Waller's analysis is his careful attention to the results of individual and social psychological research, which he uses to great effect to debunk any notion that, at least with respect to adult perpetrators, genocidal killers are psychologically abnormal or that their actions can be explained by the effects of indoctrination (i.e., "brainwashing") or socialization (e.g., Daniel Goldhagen's notion of a particularistic "eliminationist" anti-Semitism in Germany). Waller, Chirot and McCauley, and Alvarez[19] also all effectively spell out the complex interrelationship between human agency based on psychological characteristics and emotions, on the one hand, and the influence of organizational structures, particularly military and bureaucratic organizations, on the other. Although human psychology is key to Waller's and Chirot and McCauley's explanations and remains ontologically prior, these authors, particularly Waller, carefully demonstrate that institutional structures shape and reshape, sometimes permanently, human behavior under extreme conditions. Where Waller's argument is less convincing is in his insistence that there is a hard-and-fast human nature shared by all human beings, regardless of culture, historical experiences, and the like. The evidence he presents to substantiate this point involves a high degree of inference from rather sketchy theories of early human development. The inferences he draws from these theories may not be warranted, since theories on their own do not constitute evidence. Moreover,

Waller's references to experimental research on human subjects seems to confirm his main theses, but the research to which he refers involves, as far as the reader can tell, adult subjects only. With the advent of the Khmer Rouge in Cambodia, the Interahamwe in Rwanda, and the use of child soldiers in a large number of atrocity-laden conflicts in parts of Africa and Asia, the perpetrators of what Waller calls "extraordinary human evil" are now often children and teenagers. Such young, vulnerable, and likely impressionable killers may in fact be motivated to kill by indoctrination, abuse, and alcohol and drug use inflicted on them by their adult masters. Further research is required to determine whether Waller's conclusions about adults hold for child perpetrators as well or whether the behavior of child perpetrators is explained by other exogenous factors.

Like Waller's, Chirot and McCauley's model is rich in variables and, to a greater extent than Waller, these authors include references to a wide variety of cases of genocide to substantiate their claims. Leaving aside criticisms that could be leveled based on Chirot and McCauley's and Waller's use of broad dependent variables such as "political killing" and "extraordinary human evil" instead of the narrower variable of genocide, Chirot and McCauley's reliance on such a large number of independent and intervening variables and their use of mostly emotive variables makes comparative testing of their claims somewhat problematic. Since we are dealing with human emotions such as anger, hate, love, and revenge, it is not clear how one is to go about operationalizing these emotions into variables that can actually be measured and compared across cases, in stable comparisons by which the researcher can be confident that he or she is measuring and comparing the same thing. How does one measure human emotions, particularly in historical cases? The authors do not give us much methodological guidance, and their very general and often brief references to historical case studies similarly does not show us in a convincing way how emotions of the kind they believe are significant can accurately be gleaned from historical sources. Survey- and interview-based research into perpetrator behavior in more recent cases of genocide may be a preferable way to tap the variables the authors find important, but, again, this kind of research would have to include an extended discussion of how the survey was constructed in order to accurately measure the existence and the precise effect of the emotional variable(s) under investigation.

Further, because emotions like anger, hate, fear, and revenge are commonly held by ordinary people and are often manipulated for instrumental reasons by political and other elites, under all sorts of circumstances and for all sorts of different reasons, one can question whether the explanation of political killing offered by Chirot and McCauley might also just as effectively explain other phenomena, such as terrorism, civil war, or ethnic conflict. To develop a comparative theory of genocide, we need to highlight the variables that lead specifically to genocide and not to other dependent variables.

Society

Agency-centered approaches also focus on a third collective actor in genocide—society, namely the role ordinary people play as bystanders who, through their acquiescence or tacit consent, allow genocide to happen. Early attempts to explain societal behavior argued that societies that have gone on to experience genocide are psychologically predisposed toward the victimization of specific marginal groups. Such predispositions are said to be linked to aspects of early childhood development such as authoritarian parenting or to commonly held psychological characteristics in what some analysts have labeled "national character."[20] Rejecting the assertion that certain societies have the same psychological make-up or are socialized into exactly the same cognitive orientation toward a specific victim group, Ervin Staub compares different societies in which genocide has occurred and suggests that many members of societies that experience genocide become psychologically distressed as a result of severe crises and are therefore willing to accept the victimization of marginal groups. These same societies also have a history of antipathetic relationships with what are perceived to be marginal groups. Once crises take hold, members of the society project their own frustrations and hardships onto these groups. Crises are perceived by ordinary people as events that create "winners" and "losers"; marginal groups are identified as the "winners," while the members of the majority group see themselves as the "losers" who are suffering at the hands of a distrusted minority. As crises deepen, and as the state begins to use repression and violence against the victim group, the wider society gradually becomes psychologically disposed to accept the victimization of the group and, in the case of some individuals, ripe for recruitment into the genocidal process as low-level killers.[21]

By employing an explicitly comparative approach, Staub avoids the central problem of the Goldhagen study: the labeling of specific societies and specific groups of people as "natural born killers," so to speak. Staub is more interested in the general conditions under which ordinary people are willing to accept the perpetration of genocidal violence against members of their own society and in the social psychological orientation toward the victim group that is required for a population to become bystanders to genocide. But, like that of Chirot and McCauley, Staub's work lacks explicitly stated methodological guidelines that would leave the reader confident that his research, which—again like Chirot and McCauley's—is quite general in many cases, is based on the operationalization and comparison of equivalent variables and sound inferences.

In sum, agency-oriented approaches, mostly focused on psychology, offered by scholars in recent years give us a foundation upon which we can try to understand and explain elite, individual, and societal behavior in genocide. But they cannot account for what the structural explanations give us—the macro cultural, social, economic, political, security, and ideational contexts that also shape genocidal policies and behaviors.

Structural approaches

Culture

Culture can be seen as a necessary but not sufficient condition to explain genocide. Cited by some scholars as an important background condition, culture is regarded, depending on the author, as either a macro- or a micro-level variable. While culture is an important variable, its use in explaining genocide is fraught with difficulties, both because culture is hard to define and measure and because of the problem of over-generalization, particularly at the macro level when the culture variable concerns the culture of a whole society. Nonetheless, the idea of trying to find which long-standing beliefs, norms, attitudes, and practices underpin genocide continues to be an attractive, if partial, approach in the literature.

At the macro level, perhaps the most ambitious and controversial use of the culture variable is that of Daniel Goldhagen in *Hitler's Willing Executioners*. In this book Goldhagen attributes the Nazi genocide of European Jews to the thorough cultural indoctrination of Germans into what he calls "eliminationist anti-Semitism."[22] Goldhagen's thesis is a study in what can go wrong in an overly simplistic culture-based argument, namely the uncritical assertion, backed by insufficient or distorted evidence, that all Germans were socialized or indoctrinated into exactly the same form of anti-Semitism and that the eliminationist anti-Semitism of Germany was unique to that country and its people. Goldhagen's analysis has been widely criticized on a number of grounds, not the least of which is his tendency to essentialize the identity of the perpetrators.

A much more effective use of culture is Alex Hinton's examination of the importance of local cultural influences on how low-level perpetrators in Cambodia were able to turn with such brutality against not only the country's ethnic minorities but other Khmers from the cities and inward against suspect cadres within the Khmer Rouge itself.[23] Hinton shows that the Khmer Rouge leadership was able to skillfully employ culturally salient language and appeal to cultural practices to motivate ordinary Khmers to commit genocidal violence. He argues, for example, that one enduring cultural practice called *kum*—a long-standing grudge as a result of real injury or a public loss of face—has often led historically to the meting out of *karsangsoek*, or "disproportionate revenge."[24] Hinton suggests that the cultural model of disproportionate revenge is a "form of knowledge which most Cambodians have internalized and may be inclined to enact in given circumstances"—usually in the aftermath of individual or collective injury or loss of face. The "cultural knowledge" of disproportionate revenge "constitutes a crucial site upon which genocidal regimes can work," with perpetrator elites "us[ing] these highly salient cultural models to motivate individuals to commit violent atrocities."[25]

The importance of local culture and genocidal violence has also been noted by Christopher C. Taylor in his examination of mass participation in the

Rwandan Genocide. For Taylor, the perpetrators in Rwanda conceptualized the victim group, and the threat they were believed to pose to the Hutu majority, along culturally specific lines that referred to commonly held beliefs in the deleterious effects of "obstructions" in the body that interrupted the proper "flow" of bodily fluids. The Tutsis were characterized, according to Taylor, as "sacrificial victims" in a "mass ritual purification, a ritual intended to purge the nation of obstructing beings." This conceptualization of the threat posed by the victim group was "imagined through a Rwandan ontology that situates the body politic in analogical relations to the individual human body."[26] These culturally specific reference points not only motivated the killing but informed the manner in which the killing was manifested in the Rwandan case, which included dumping victims (dead or alive) into latrines or rivers.

From a historical perspective, Omer Bartov also calls for a detailed examination of local contexts so that we can understand "much of the reality of genocide" that occurs at the local level, including "the interaction between friends and neighbors" and "encounters with reception of forces [tasked with committing the genocide] arriving from outside the community." Bartov continues that "the conduct of the community is often crucial to the success or failure of state-organized genocide in a given area."[27] Jan Gross's study of the destruction of almost the entire Jewish community in the Polish village of Jedwabne by their non-Jewish neighbors on a single day of bloodletting in 1941 is a leading example of this kind of micro-level history.[28]

Although Hinton's, Taylor's, and Gross's studies are ideographic examinations of the role of culture, appeals to culturally significant language and practices, and local historical contexts in three specific cases, we need not rule out the search for cultural or local comparisons across cases. Such comparisons can be made at the societal or the local level, provided that attention is paid to establishing with sufficient evidence the relationship between cultural beliefs and practices, on the one hand, and genocidal behavior, on the other, both within and across cases, and that equivalent (not identical) beliefs and practices can be found in other cases upon which we can base reliable comparisons.

One way to further develop comparative cultural approaches at the macro level is to focus on the role of political culture specifically as a precursor to genocide. Two dimensions of the pre-genocide political culture lay the ideational foundation for later genocidal policies: beliefs and attitudes concerning membership in the political community and elite political cultural perceptions of the meaning of conflicts in society and the state's response to conflict. The first, purely attitudinal, dimension taps how members of the dominant society and political elites conceptualize membership in the political community. Societies that have historically maintained a restrictive conception of who constitutes "genuine" or "authentic" membership, even in the face of formal legal recognition of membership, may be more likely (though by no means certain) to commit genocide against "inauthentic" marginalized members who are later redefined as completely alien and a serious threat to the survival of the community. The second dimension shifts the analysis toward an examination of historical elite conceptualizations of real and perceived conflicts, either within society or within the state, as zero-sum struggles that cannot be solved through dialogue or compromise but only through the exercise of state power, possibly including the use of force.

In sum, although cultural explanations of this or any other kind fill in part of the genocidal puzzle, they cannot, on their own, explain why genocide happens. Values, beliefs, norms, and practices at the macro and micro levels can, under the right conditions (see the discussion of crisis below), set the stage for genocide and, once the killing begins, shape the course and character of the genocidal process at the state, societal, and local levels.

Divided societies

Another structural approach found in the literature suggests that societies riven by ethnic, religious, socioeconomic, or other cleavages are particularly vulnerable to genocide. One of the first comparative genocide scholars, Leo Kuper, took the prior existence of what he labeled "plural societies" as the "structural base for genocide."[29] As a necessary condition, but one that does not make genocide inevitable, Kuper argued that plural societies in which cleavages are particularly "persistent and pervasive" are more likely to experience genocide, especially when political or economic inequality is "superimposed" on ethnic, religious, racial, or socioeconomic "differentiation." This kind of social structure, in turn, "aggregate[s] the population into distinctive sections, thereby facilitating crimes against collectivities. The divisions being so pervasive, and relatively consistent in so many spheres, issues of conflict may move rapidly from one sector to another, until almost the entire society is polarized."[30] Applying a similar argument to the Armenian Genocide, Richard Hovanissian argues that the existence of a plural society "with clearly defined racial, religious, and cultural differences" in Ottoman Turkey was one of the preconditions for the genocide of 1915.[31] Kuper cautions, however, that simply because a society is characterized by moderate or even extreme pluralism, it does not follow that it will automatically fall victim to genocidal violence. Genocide is unlikely if a plural society does not experience "the subjective reactions and opportunities to sustain a destructive conflict" that mark genocidal violence.[32]

Hinton argues that societies that go on to experience genocide are marked by severe "social divisions" that arise because of "segregation and differential legal, sociocultural, political, educational, and economic opportunities afforded to social groups."[33] Helen Fein also notes that societies that are marked by "ethnic stratification" are more likely to be predisposed to ethnic, racial, or religiously based genocides[34] but that political revolutionary or anti-revolutionary genocides, such as those in Cambodia or in Indonesia during Suharto's attack on the Indonesian Communist Party in 1965, are the product of other factors (legitimacy problems, moral exclusion, blaming the victim, "tolerance" of an international patron for a regime's genocidal policies, social unrest due to economic conditions, and the onset of war).[35]

Critics of the "divided society" approach contend that large-N, mostly quantitative empirical evidence shows that not all plural societies go genocidal and that some societies that do experience genocide, such as Cambodia's, are not characterized by deep ethnic, religious, or socioeconomic cleavages.[36] While the first observation is accurate, scholars who cite societal cleavages as an important variable do not argue that such cleavages directly cause genocide, or that they do so alone. Rather, such divisions create the potential for genocidal violence, but only in concert with other intervening variables such as severe destabilizing crises or radical eliminationist ideologies espoused by equally radical genocidal elites.

No matter what the source of societal cleavages, the important contribution of this approach is the recognition that divided societies are fragmented societies in which there is a relative lack of solidarity, trust, and, sometimes, tolerance between groups.[37] Just as political scientist Robert Putnam feared for the health of American democracy because Americans were "bowling alone," genocidal societies are often (but not always) societies whose members tend to "bowl with their own kind." Genocidal elites skillfully play on and exploit these divisions, while groups within society are unable or unwilling to rally together to resist such entreaties and to protect targeted members of their own community.

Crises, revolution, and war

The fact that serious political, economic, or security crises have frequently preceded genocide, at least in the modern era, has not been lost on many genocide scholars. While it is recognized in the literature that most societies that endure destabilizing crises of one kind or another do not go on to perpetrate genocide, there is a strong sense among some genocide scholars that there is a connection between crises, revolutionary upheavals, warfare, and genocide.

In her pioneering work *Accounting for Genocide*, Helen Fein lists reduction of a state's "rank" as a consequence of defeat in war or of internal strife as one of several "predisposing conditions" that can propel a state toward a "crisis of national identity" in which elites become more likely to "adopt a new political formula to justify the nation's domination and/or expansion" as well as "idealizing the singular rights of the dominant group."[38] For Fein, crises, and elite responses to them, do not directly cause genocide; rather, crises are part of a longer process that can, under certain circumstances, culminate in genocide. In his analysis of elite responses to crises, Midlarsky argues that political elites make the strategic decision to commit genocide in the face of a loss of territory and other external security crises as a form of "loss compensation."[39] Approaching the effects of crises in a more general way, Florence Mazian identifies in another early work in the field the role of "internal strife" as a "social condition" that may contribute to the "value added process" that results in genocide, since internal strife—including "real or threatened deprivations," various economic shocks, real or imagined or anticipated frustration, and what Mazian calls "normative upheavals" such as rapid social and institutional change or modernization—can "heighten social cleavages such as ethnic, political, class, and religious divisions."[40] With respect to ordinary members of society, Staub suggests that crises create psychologically "difficult life conditions" that induce feelings of distress and frustration, which are then projected onto a marginalized group, particularly any such group that has recently enjoyed a greater degree of socioeconomic success.[41] For Hinton, crises create a "hot" and "volatile" context in which genocidal processes are more likely to be "set off." Socioeconomic, political, and security upheavals produce "anxiety, hunger, a loss of meaning, the break-down of existing social mechanisms," and often presage a "struggle for power."[42] Barbara Harff's large multi-case quantitative analysis of genocides and politicides since 1955 confirms that political upheaval and a prior history of genocide or politicide are strongly predictive of similar atrocities.[43]

Conceptualizing crises as opportunities that are seized by elite actors, Chirot and McCauley suggest that crises create the conditions under which genocide and mass killing are more likely to occur. A crisis is a disruptive event during which moral inhibitions against killing are loosened, especially when political elites manipulate the crisis. As such, crises give rise to "the potential for mass killing" that can quickly reach "genocidal proportions."[44] In this argument, elite responses to crises are largely instrumental, in that crises are opportunities that elites grab to mobilize support for their own destructive policies. Another crisis-as-opportunity argument suggests that crises allow radical political elites both to come to power and to implement previously developed genocidal policies against a target group. In this case crises are what Sidney Tarrow calls, in another context, a "political opportunity structure."[45] Lucy Dawidowicz's "intentionalist" thesis that Hitler's Nazis developed their plan to exterminate European Jewry during the turbulent interwar years before their rise to power, used the upheavals of that period to come to power, and initiated a continentwide war to realize their pre-existing genocidal policies stands as a prime example of a political opportunity approach.[46]

We can see, then, that authors who link crises to genocide do not generally suggest that destabilizing crises necessarily lead to genocide. Rather, crises are conceptualized as an intervening variable, as a precursor that acts as a trigger for genocide. What is important about crises is not so much the specific nature of the crises themselves but how they are perceived by ordinary people and elites: Why did they happened, who is to blame, and, most importantly, how can the state and society be protected from similar events in the future? To borrow Alexander Wendt's phrase about anarchy in the international system, crisis is what elites and society "make of it."[47] What elites and society "make" of crises rests, at least to some degree, on prevailing cleavages, attitudes, beliefs, and practices. In genocidal situations, crises are interpreted as illustrating an ongoing struggle between the political community, on the one hand, and a specific group, on the other. This group is seen to be responsible for the current situation and to benefit from it. Taken together, crises and elite (and popular) reactions to them serve to animate the more virulent anti-group features of the pregenocide political cultural norms, attitudes, and practices, turning what were hitherto relatively benign manifestations of exclusionary beliefs and authoritarian political practices into an extremist construction of the identity, interests, and potential actions of the target group. This reconstruction of the victim group culminates in the formation and implementation of genocidal policies designed to bring about the physical or biological destruction of the target group.

Opportunities for genocide can also arise in the form of revolutions. While noting the central importance of revolutionary ideology (see below) and political myth in explaining genocide, Robert Melson also argues that a key structural condition for the revolutionary recasting of society and the "total domestic genocides" that resulted in Ottoman Turkey, Bolshevik Russia, Nazi Germany, and Khmer Rouge Cambodia was the collapse of the old regimes and their fragile successors—the collapse not only of the state's political institutions but also of its legitimacy. Key crises for Melson are military defeat and domestic political and economic upheavals.[48]

In a more recent book, however, Edward Kissi notes that not all revolutions give way to genocide and that while revolution turned genocidal in Cambodia, it did not in socialist revolutionary Ethiopia. In Kissi's view, revolutions turn genocidal only under very specific conditions: when the targets of mass political killing are fragmented and atomized to such an extent that they cannot defend themselves against an aggressive state; when the state is able to successfully dominate society; and when the state targets for liquidation ethnic, religious, socioeconomic, and inactive or already defeated political groups, not political groups that genuinely and actively resist a revolutionary regime. In Ethiopia, which Kissi believes experienced "politicide" (as defined by Barbara Harff) and not genocide, revolution gave way to severe repression, political violence, and terror directed at the many armed opposition groups (but not at ethnic or religious groups) and their supporters.[49]

Wars, as other scholars have argued, can also act as a structural condition that can lead to, and facilitate, the perpetration of genocidal violence. Eric Markusen and David Kopf, for example, have argued that while total war and genocide are not identical phenomena, they nonetheless share a number of characteristics. Total wars and genocides are pursued by political elites to protect national security, are underpinned by ideologies that dehumanize the targets of violence, are bureaucratically organized, and are perpetrated with sophisticated technologies that kill large numbers of people easily and efficiently in a manner that insulates the killers from the suffering of their victims.[50] Aside from these commonalities, Markusen and Kopf also suggest that war, as a form of extreme security crisis, creates social and psychological conditions "conducive to the outbreak of genocide and genocidal killing." By exposing societies to severe crises and threats to national survival, wars

> create the potential for pre-existing inter-group tensions in a culturally or racially diverse society to flare into violence directed by the majority against members of a minority group. The threat of disruption is not only blamed on the external enemy but can also be directed at members of a minority group within the society.[51]

Further, war can give governments the tools to commit genocide and to cover its tracks. Markusen and Kopf thus note that governments engaged in total war "tend to become more centralized, secret, and powerful" and tend to use dehumanizing propaganda to vilify their enemies. "The result can be diminished popular awareness of, and resistance to, ruthless governmental actions against both external and internal enemies."[52] Governments at war also have at their disposal combat-ready soldiers in the field who can be diverted to perpetrate genocide. Meanwhile, the conditions of war leave victim groups isolated and vulnerable and perpetrators and bystanders psychologically desensitized to violence as a result of their exposure to the violence of war.[53] Similarly, Scott Straus argues that in Rwanda the renewed civil war in 1994 helped drive the genocide because the war was constructed by the perpetrators as a security crisis in which violence had to be used to overcome a threat; all Tutsis were constructed as "enemies" along with the Rwandan Patriotic Front. The civil war also created a circumstance of uncertainty and insecurity within which mass violence was legitimized and "specialists in violence" such as soldiers, gendarmes, and militias could be mobilized for genocidal killing.[54]

Omer Bartov, focusing on the construction of the meaning of war, notes that defeat in war can lead not only to the search for, and punishment of, internal "enemies" responsible for the catastrophe but also to the conceptualization of combat in modern industrialized total war as a necessary and glorious form of destruction in which the "destruction of others" is believed to bring about one's own "resurrection."[55] In the German case, "the Great War's new fields of glory were the breeding ground of fascism and Nazism, of human degradation and extermination, and from them sprang the storm troops of dictatorships and the demagogues of racial purity and exclusion."[56] When war came again on a much wider and more horrific scale, German soldiers

> expressed pride and satisfaction in finally being able to destroy their enemies, be they soldiers, prisoners, civilians, or provoking the greatest glee, Jewish men, women, and children. It was at this point that massacre and glory became synonymous.[57]

For scholars like Markusen and Kopf, Kuper, and, more recently, Martin Shaw, war not only sets the stage, and acts as a cover, for genocide but can devolve into genocidal violence. Genocide, for Shaw, is in fact a distinctive form of war against civilians and is intertwined with other forms of war, particularly what he calls "degenerate war." Degenerate war involves "the deliberate and systematic extension of war against an organized armed enemy [what Shaw identifies as legitimate or "real war"] to war against a largely unarmed civilian population"[58] in conflicts such as guerrilla wars, counter-insurgencies, or wars that involve the aerial bombardment of civilian populations. Although Shaw defines genocide as "the destruction by an organized armed force of a large unarmed civilian group (or groups)" in which civilians are regarded as enemies "in themselves" and not "through their relationship to an armed enemy," genocide, because of its "definition of civilian groups as enemies to be destroyed," utilizes the logic of war and is, therefore, an extension of degenerate war. Genocides are often perpetrated, Shaw notes, within the context of military (war) and political (revolutionary and counter-revolutionary) struggles and are frequently ended by war.[59] War, and the preparation for it, can also help, in Shaw's view, to turn the corner from degenerate and other forms of war to genocide. Perpetrator states are often militarized states that have experienced war in the recent past and consequently have in place the military and paramilitary institutions and a militaristic ideology that legitimizes the use of military force against defined enemies.[60] Because Shaw sees genocide as a form of war, he claims that genocides, wars, and revolutions are all forms of conflict defined by two commonly held characteristics: that "opposing sides aim to destroy each other's power" and that each side is "prepared to engage in mass killing of the enemy in order to achieve their goal."[61] Like war, genocide is a form of conflict in which the perpetrator aims to "destroy" the "social power" (economic, cultural, and political power) of a group and their ability to fight back.[62] While the conflict usually begins as an unequal struggle in which the victim group (a term Shaw conspicuously does not use) is initially unarmed, it evolves into a more balanced confrontation once the victims begin to resist and find more powerful domestic or international allies. Shaw offers the fact that wars fought by internal forces (e.g., the Rwandan Patriotic Front) or by external forces (e.g., the Allies in World War II) frequently end genocide as evidence of this position.

As the literature shows, revolution and war are the extremist contexts within which modern genocides are often perpetrated. But it would be a mistake to equate or conflate genocide with either. Both revolutions and wars occur without going genocidal; some genocides occur *after* a war is over (e.g., in Cambodia) or do not occur during warfare at all (e.g., the Stalinist purges of the 1930s—assuming, of course, that one classifies the latter as genocide). Shaw's contention that genocide is a form of war because "opposing sides aim to destroy each other's power" and each side is "prepared to engage in mass killing of the enemy in order to achieve their goal"[63] conflates genocide with something it clearly is not: a contest between two opposing forces that possess the intention to defeat each other in a struggle over something concrete (economic, political, and cultural sources of "social power" as Shaw puts it) fought by two opponents with actually existing offensive and defensive power capabilities.

Part of the problem with Shaw's thesis is the confusion over the status of the perpetrators' and victims' intentions. The UN Convention on the Prevention and Punishment of the Crime of Genocide and many genocide scholars argue that genocide is defined by the "intent to destroy, in whole or in part" the victim group "as such."[64] This is an intention that is held only by the perpetrators, not the victims, which is precisely why the two main collective actors in genocide are referred to not as "combatants" but as "victims" and "perpetrators." Physical and/or biological destruction of the members of the victim group is the policy goal of genocidal regimes, not simply the stripping of the group of it power capabilities, which could be accomplished by all sorts of other policies that fall short of genocide. On the other side of the ledger, confronting a regime as an opposing force bent on depriving the state of its power capabilities, possibly through resort to "mass killing," was not the intention of the Ottoman Armenians, European Jews, the various victims of the Khmer Rouge, or Rwandan Tutsis (save members of the Rwandan Patriotic Front).

As for the use and deployment of force by the victim group, the victims of genocide are victims of this particular crime precisely because of their helplessness and the lack of real (as opposed to perceived) threat and opposition they pose to the perpetrators. In her definition of genocide, Helen Fein tells us that genocide is a

> sustained purposeful action by a perpetrator to physically destroy a collectivity directly or indirectly, through interdiction of the biological and social reproduction of group members, sustained *regardless of the surrender or lack of threat offered by the victim.*[65]

For Frank Chalk and Kurt Jonassohn, genocide is a "form of *one-sided mass killing* in which a state or other authority intends to destroy a group";[66] Israel Charny, in what he calls his "generic" definition of genocide, similarly notes that genocide is characterized by the

> mass killing of substantial numbers of human beings, *when not in the course of military action* against the military forces of an avowed enemy, under conditions of the *essential defenselessness and helplessness of the victims.*[67]

Whether we argue that genocide and war are distinct phenomena or that genocide is in fact a form of warfare, we must recognize that the victims of genocide are just that: victims who do not pose a real threat to their tormentors, who are not combatants in an equal or even an unequal contest with a state or other authority, and who do not possess actually existing power capabilities that they can deploy to defend themselves and fight their enemies. The fact that small numbers of victims may actively resist their destruction, sometimes through force of arms, neither transforms these people into regular combatants nor turns the attempted destruction of their own group by a predatory state into a two-sided conflict.

Regime type

Other structural explanations focus on how the structure of political regimes determines the adoption (or not) of genocidal policies. One of the earliest comparative explanations of genocide, offered by Irving Horowitz, argues that genocide is inherent to totalitarian political systems. Because totalitarian regimes attempt to exert total political, economic, and social control over all aspects of life and over all members of society, such regimes inexorably end up liquidating whole groups of people who are deemed to be outside of, or hostile to, the totalitarian order.[68] Similarly, for Hannah Arendt (although her work predates Horowitz and does not deal explicitly with genocide but with totalitarianism) the fullest expression of totalitarianism—that practiced by the Nazi and Stalinist regimes—was the exercise of "total domination" in the death camps, in which "everything," including the extermination of superfluous peoples, became possible.[69]

The main weakness of the totalitarian regime thesis is that it is overly deterministic. As we will see below, although the ideologies that animate what have been labeled totalitarian regimes[70]—namely, Communist regimes and Nazi Germany—were radical and highly exclusionary, not all totalitarian regimes have perpetrated genocide against segments of their own population. Pol Pot's Democratic Kampuchea certainly did so, but other so-called totalitarian regimes, such as unified socialist Vietnam, did not single out whole groups of people for destruction, although the first decade of Communist rule after Vietnam's unification in 1975 was marked by repression and serious human-rights abuses against elements of the former regime. Given the different experiences of totalitarian regimes in the twentieth century with respect to the perpetration, or not, of genocide, we cannot definitively argue that the structures and processes of totalitarianism invariably result in the genocidal killing of specific groups.

Looking at the opposite side of the political spectrum, Rudolph Rummel links regime type to genocide and other forms of mass violence by suggesting that while democratic regimes are liable to inflict violent death on citizens of other states through combat operations, bombings, or isolated atrocities, they are very unlikely to target their own citizens for mass repression or killing. Based on a detailed statistical examination of deaths caused by governments, Rummel argues, according to what he calls the "power principle," that

> the more power a government has, the more it can act arbitrarily according to the whims and desires of the elite, and the more it will make

war on others and murder its foreign and domestic subjects. The more constrained the power of governments, the less it will aggress on others.[71]

Taking Rummel's analysis further, Harff's statistical analysis shows that failed authoritarian states are three and a half times more likely to lead to genocide or politicide than state failure in democratic regimes.[72]

As Rummel's empirical investigation tells us, regime type, at least for twentieth-century genocides, is related to whether a regime is more or less likely to commit genocide. Non-democratic regimes have a higher incidence of committing atrocities, including genocide, against their own people, than democratic regimes, which in the past century have not perpetrated genocides against their own people. But because there is also a large number of authoritarian regimes, historical and current, that have not perpetrated genocide, Rummel's study tells us only that there is a correlation between authoritarian regimes and genocidal policies, not that there is a causal connection between the two phenomena. The most we can say, then, is that non-democratic states are more likely than democracies to commit genocide. This is so not simply because a state is authoritarian but because states that go on to commit genocide historically have used authoritarian methods, such as repression and sometimes violence, to manage domestic conflicts and confront real and perceived enemies. Elites' strategy of habitually using confrontational or violent methods of conflict management is underpinned by a long-standing elite political culture that frames conflicts as zero-sum struggles in which the state must win or be completely defeated.[73] This history of authoritarian practices and perceptions, in turn, creates an ideational and experiential context that sets the stage, during genocide, for the targets of destruction to be perceived as a mortal threat by elites. Following historical and political cultural precedent, the victims are dealt with not through concessions or lesser forms of repression but through violent processes of extermination intended to secure the survival of the state and the majority society.

Modernity, the modern state, and modern exclusionary ideologies

The final group of structural arguments links the onset of genocide to broad processes of modernization, particularly the rise of the modern bureaucratized nation-state, as well as to the creation of radical exclusionary nationalist, racist, or revolutionary ideologies. The former argument suggests that it is the material structure of the modern nation-state that facilitates genocide, while the latter argument concentrates on ideology as an ideational structure that produces genocidal behavior.

Zygmunt Bauman argues in his analysis of the structural foundations of the Holocaust that the increased division and specialization of bureaucratic functions within the modern nation-state and society allows the thousands of people involved in genocidal programs to remove themselves conceptually from any moral responsibility for their small and specialized part in the extermination process.[74] Thus the killing of whole groups of innocent human beings has become conceptually, psychologically, and morally unproblematic in the modern age.

Influenced by modern conceptions of inferior and superior races or exploited and exploiting classes, coupled with a proclivity for powerful, centralized, bureaucratic states to conceive of grand projects of social engineering and their capacity to implement such policies, modern states have the potential to become genocidal "gardener states," according to Bauman. For the gardener state, genocide is not a policy of destruction but a grand project of construction. Recalling Arendt's totalitarian everything-is-possible thesis, Bauman argues that the gardener state seeks to construct new social, economic, demographic, or political orders as a landscaper plants and tends a garden. Just as gardens inevitably grow weeds that do not belong in a meticulously designed garden, so new racial, national, or revolutionary systems contain human beings who do not belong in the new order. As weeds are pulled by a gardener to maintain the intended design and composition of the garden, groups of human beings who do not belong to the new order must be exterminated by the gardener state.[75]

Although Bauman offers a compelling metaphor congruent with the spirit of many radical ideologies and genocidal elites' desire to construct completely new societies, his analysis does not tell us why the pulling of human weeds—that is, the removal of certain groups who do not belong to the new order—necessarily involves physical extermination. Simply understanding a group as misfits who upset the composition of the new order cannot explain why genocide becomes a policy option for some elites, rather than apartheid-like segregation and repression, internal deportation, or expulsion. The latter policies accomplish exactly what Bauman suggests the gardener state wants to do: the removal of groups of people who are thought to deviate in some way from the rest of the newly constructed order. His metaphor is not irrelevant, but it is too benign. We must remember why gardeners get rid of the weeds in their gardens. It is not just because weeds do not look right, or were not in the flat of flowers the gardener planted; it is because, if left unchecked, they will choke off and kill the garden. That is why gardeners do not just pull off the tops of weeds, or replant them somewhere else, but instead are careful to thoroughly dig weeds out by their roots or use herbicide to ensure that the weeds can never grow again.

Alvarez also focuses on the role of the state and state institutions as the principal perpetrators of genocide, but without explicitly linking this role to the consequences of modernity itself. For Alvarez, genocide is a form of "state criminality" that is underpinned by two "constructs of belief," sovereignty and nationalism.[76] Because sovereignty rests on the principle of non-interference by states in the domestic affairs of other states, and because there is no higher authority in the international system above and beyond the state, states encounter few, if any, restrictions on their domestic policies and are unlikely to be faced with intervention by other states.[77] Nationalism, meanwhile, is the ideological mechanism that "assures loyalty to and belief in the state."[78] Alvarez acknowledges that nationalism exists in a variety of forms and that it is the most extreme forms of ethnic nationalism, particularly in multiethnic states, that fuel state-sponsored genocide. Citing Michael Ignatieff, he contends that ethnic nationalism "exacerbates perceived differences among people, and transforms divisions into all-important definitions of identity."[79] Alvarez's account of why states perpetrate genocide extends beyond these two foundational conceptions, however, to include the connection between genocide and war (in a manner similar to that discussed above) and the law, which he identifies as a "set of resources" that the state mobilizes and uses as a tool to translate its power into genocidal policies.[80] Expanding on Bauman's analysis, Alvarez also discusses in detail the role of state institutions, both military/security and civilian bureaucratic, in the perpetration of genocide. For Alvarez, state institutions are perpetrators of genocide, because their role is to implement specific genocidal policies. Once genocide begins, the members of these institutions engage in criminal activity (i.e., genocide) not as individuals but as members of what have essentially become criminal organizations. Members of military, paramilitary, and state security organizations perpetrate genocidal killing because "their training is geared toward providing recruits with the technical skills of violence and socializing them into a value system that supports fierceness, aggression, and solidarity with their comrades."[81] Civilian state bureaucracies, with their emphasis on technical efficiency, depersonalization, and the strict application of rules and procedures, produce desk killers who faithfully apply the "rules" of genocide to unseen depersonalized "units" without having to think about or witness the very real consequences of their small, often specialized, but entirely lethal actions.[82]

Bauman's and Alvarez's insights into bureaucratic specialization and the moral distancing of perpetrators from the genocidal process do help explain how it was that large numbers of public and private employees, managers, and administrators in Nazi Germany could continue to play their own small but deadly parts in keeping the machinery of destruction in motion, unmolested by moral qualms about the program's outcome. This kind of argument, however, cannot explain other genocides, such as those in Cambodia and Rwanda, where the killing was not bureaucratized but instead involved face-to-face public killing, albeit directed by the state,[83] sometimes by ordinary people who were not members of a state security organization. Nor can the modern bureaucratic state thesis explain why political elites decide to perpetrate genocide in the first place, only how it was that a modern Western state like Nazi Germany, with desks full of killers like Adolf Eichmann, had the capacity to execute genocidal policies.

Other genocide scholars suggest that the main product of modernity that has produced the genocides of the twentieth century and beyond is not the modern state itself but modern revolutionary ideologies that are inherently genocidal.[84] These ideologies rest, Eric Weitz argues, on modern conceptions of the world as naturally divided into races and nations, or on Marxist notions of class conflict between exploiting and exploited classes,[85] or, as Hinton contends, on a more general turn toward an "emphasis on the individual, empiricism, secularism, rationality, progress," and the potential of science. For Hinton, the latter can produce genocidal processes of social engineering in which "human societies, like nature, could be mastered, reconstructed, and improved."[86] In modern societies, our innate capacity to identify differences between peoples becomes "reified" in a world in which modern nation-states "covet homogeneity." Modernity also gives rise to the crafting of hierarchical scientific typologies that identify groups as inherently inferior or superior, to the use of science as the "legitimating rationale for slavery, exploitation, and ultimately genocide," and to conceptions of progress that are used as a standard against which peoples are judged or can be manipulated or even exterminated "to achieve [a] desired end."[87]

In his account of twentieth-century genocides, Weitz concentrates specifically on the evolution of, and appropriation into, radical eliminationist ideologies of a number of specifically modern concepts. Influenced by Johann Gottlieb Fichte's and Johann Gottfried von Herder's conception of nations as primordial entities with a common language, culture, and history, nationalism by the nineteenth century, according to Weitz, morphed into a racialized understanding of nationhood as an ethnic and racial community and not simply a locus of political rights.[88] Primordial and exclusionary understandings of race and nation gained particular prominence in Germany and elsewhere on the European continent by the latter half of the nineteenth century. Weitz further argues that the rise of race thinking and ethnic nationalism coincided with the rapid expansion of European imperialism and the resulting exposure of increasing numbers of Westerners to indigenous and other peoples who were physiologically and culturally different from themselves. These encounters only seemed to confirm the idea that some races, namely white Europeans, were superior to others, namely Africans, Asians, and the indigenous peoples of the Americas already colonized by European settlers in previous centuries.[89] The felling of Western colonists by tropical diseases and the simultaneous rise in support for eugenics and the "theory" of social Darwinism (the struggle for the survival of the fittest races) culminated in a conception of society as

> analogous to the body and race as a biological organism, whose health needed constant attention, whose vitality was continually in danger of being sapped by killer bacteria borne by the weaker members and by those of completely alien races.[90]

When added to the dehumanization of the enemy during World War I, all of these ideational factors produced, according to Weitz in the case of the Holocaust, the idea that the Jewish "disease" in Germany weakened the German "body" and should be removed through radical eugenicist measures in order to preserve the racial purity of Aryans.[91] Similar revolutionary ideas that societies are divided based on the ownership of the means of production into classes, and the inevitability of class conflict, inspired genocidal revolutionary movements and regimes that identified certain classes as exploiters and counter-revolutionaries who did not fit into the new revolutionary system and, therefore, had to be eliminated in genocidal purges in states such as the Stalinist Soviet Union and Democratic Kampuchea.

Ideological explanations are not always tied to modernity or the ideologically driven creation of radically new societies, however. Ben Kiernan's treatment of ideology suggests that while certain elements such as race thinking and the homogenization of populations on newly acquired or desired territories are modernist parts of the radical ideologies that underpin genocide, other elements of genocidal ideology are fundamentally anti-modern. For Kiernan, many genocidal regimes conceptualize the peasantry as the most "authentic" members of the political community, while cosmopolitan urban areas and their populations are considered to be "contaminated with foreign and decadent elements."[92] The goal for these genocidal elites is to recreate a glorious rural past through the genocidal destruction of peoples who are supposedly contaminating the pure peasantry and the countryside.

Ideology-based explanations point to the importance of ideas in the genocidal process as well as to the propensity for genocidal elites to categorize groups in society and to conceptualize their victims as alien and hostile to new or old revolutionary systems that must be purified of all deviant behavior, thought, or unworthy or inferior human beings. More than other explanations of genocide, the ideology approach also picks up the central role of threat perception, namely that genocidal elites come to see their victims not just as inferiors or misfits but as dangerous "enemies within." But, as with the modern state approach, the ideology variable cannot on its own account for why genocide, and not some other policy of repression or violence, occurs. Weitz, for example, lays out in great detail the conceptual origins of Nazi and radical Communist thought, but then, when it comes to the case studies of individual genocides, does not really account for why genocide was perpetrated against some groups and not others. In the case of the Holocaust, Weitz ties the Nazis' racist, social Darwinist ideology to the T4 eugenics program that targeted physically and mentally ill patients in Germany; the harsh treatment meted out against Poles, who were slated to became a vast pool of slave labor for the Nazis in the new German East during and after the war; and the Jews, who from the summer of 1941 onward were the objects of total extermination. Thus, in his analysis, the same ideology explains three different policy outcomes.

Process explanations: identity construction

While the approaches discussed thus far do at times refer to the processes by which genocide comes to be perpetrated, theories that concentrate on identity construction as the main explanatory variable are much more explicitly process-oriented approaches. When discussing the identity construction of the victim group by the perpetrators of genocide, the literature tends to group a number of different constructions under one generic label, such as "dehumanization" or "demonization." If we look carefully we can, in fact, identify three distinct yet interrelated processes of identity construction that scholars suggest lead to genocide: conceptions of the victims as an "alien" other; as sub- or non-humans; and as threatening "enemies within."

Victims as other

From a social psychological perspective, Chirot and McCauley argue that human beings have the capacity to "single out for genocide any kind of self-reproducing social category."[93] Humans categorize other human groups as "others" because we naturally divide the world into in-groups and out-groups characterized by their own distinct "essences." These essences, either one's own or another's, are regarded as "an unchanging quality that makes a group what it is."[94] For the authors, this dynamic of essentializing the identity of the other as different or foreign is a necessary part of the process of identity construction that leads to genocide, but it is not a sufficient condition on its own. Developing a similar social psychological approach, Waller notes the innate capacity of humans to divide the world into "us" and "them," which, under the right contextual and institutional conditions, helps lead to what he calls the "social death" of the victim, whereby the victim group is psychologically removed from the wider society. One of the features (along with dehumanization and blaming the victim) of the social death of the victims is the persistence of "us–them thinking."[95] Waller also cites moderate, rather than radical or ideologically driven, feelings of antipathy toward the victim group and a "lack of emotional connection" with the victims as part of a dynamic that, in genocide, neutralizes popular aversion to authoritarian politics in general and the genocidal destruction of other groups in particular.[96]

In a frequently cited reference, Fein argues that one of the key preconditions for genocidal destruction is the removal of the victim group from the "sanctified universe of obligation." Referring specifically to the Armenians and Jews, Fein continues that the universe of obligations from which these groups were excluded was traditionally constituted by "that circle of people with reciprocal obligations to protect each other whose bonds arose from their relationship to a deity." The historical exclusion of the Armenians and Jews based on religious criteria set the precedent for the later secular conception of these groups as "strangers."[97] Fein's sociological analysis is significant because it points to two important dynamics. First, the exclusion of groups from society and their definition as aliens is not ahistorical but, rather, flows from already existing exclusionary practices and beliefs in society, although the exact content of these practices and beliefs may change over time. Second, the emphasis on reciprocity goes beyond inquiring into the tendency of human beings to see other human groups as simply different and imbeds the meaning of that conception of difference in a wider social context in which those who are deemed to belong are extended rights and mutual support while, as Herbert Hirsch and Roger W. Smith point out,[98] those who are not are stripped of any protection, formal or informal, that membership in the community provides against a predatory state. The definition of the victim group as outsider, therefore, allows us to understand why bystanders wash their hands of a group to whom they believe they owe nothing and why perpetrators come to believe they can pursue their genocidal policies unopposed.

Taking the analysis further, Hirsch and Smith argue that defining the out-group through the use of myths not only marks one group off as different from other groups and apart from the wider society but also involves the dehumanization of the members of the group and culminates in calls for concrete action to bring about the group's extermination.[99] For Waller, defining the victim group as other produces the "moral disengagement" of bystanders and perpetrators from the victims. This process entails an "active but gradual process of detachment" from the victims that exceeds mere moral indifference or invisibility and instead leads to the conceptual placing of the victim group "outside the boundary in which moral values, rules, and considerations of fairness apply."[100] As in Fein's analysis, this conception of the victim group leaves it cut off from society and thus vulnerable to all manner of abuses.

Victims as sub- or non-human

Categorizing groups into "us" and "them," or even into the more normative "us" versus "foreigner" or "stranger," is insufficient in and of itself to account for genocide. To understand why the physical destruction of the group becomes necessary from the perspective of the perpetrators, scholars who focus on identity construction look further, to conceptions of the victim groups as non-human. Once the victims are so conceived, the perpetrators can do anything to them, because the victims are seen to stand not only outside a particular political, national, ethnic, or racial community but outside of humanity itself.

In his pioneering work on the psychology of genocide, Israel Charny defines dehumanization as the act of redefining the victims of genocide as "not being part of the human species."[101] For Chirot and McCauley, the perceptions of the different "essences" that mark off groups from one another can further give rise to more malevolent conceptions of the victim group as "not quite human." Conceptualized as non-human, the victims can thus be "used, abused, and eliminated as if they were another species of animal."[102] In his "eight stages of genocide" early-warning taxonomy, Gregory Stanton identifies dehumanization as integral to the genocidal process because the conception of the victim group as non human not only "denies the humanity of the other group" but also performs the crucial function of overcoming "the normal human revulsion against murder."[103] As for which groups are most likely to be the target of dehumanization, Waller argues that the dehumanization of victim groups is most easily projected onto people belonging to different racial, ethnic, religious, or even political groups who are "regarded as inferior or threatening."[104] Chalk and Jonassohn similarly contend that genocide cannot happen to people who are regarded by their tormentors as equal to themselves or as fully human. The tendency to see outgroups as non-human is most apparent when "the differences between the people and some other society [are] particularly large." The tragic consequence of conceptualizing particular groups as "less than fully human," as "pagans, savages, or even animals," is the consequent understanding that the "values and the standards of the people" are not applicable to the out-group.[105]

The dehumanization of the victim group is likewise a necessary step in the genocidal process, for Waller, because it facilitates the "moral disengagement" of the perpetrator from the victim. This process involves not just indifference to the plight of the victims but "an active [. . .] gradual, process of detachment by which some individuals or groups are placed outside the boundary in which moral values, rules, and considerations of fairness apply."[106] Charny similarly argues that dehumanization "aims at a redefinition of the other person as not deserving the protection due members of our species. Hence, anything and everything that is destructive of the other person, even killing, does not violate nature's design." Charny considers dehumanization to be both the "ideological justification" for genocidal killing and its ultimate "rationale."[107] With respect to the perpetration of violence against the victims, Herbert Kelman contends that dehumanization is one of the processes by which the "usual moral inhibitions against violence become weakened," which, in turn, creates a context in which moral principles are believed to no longer apply to the victim,[108] thus facilitating smooth and guilt-free killing.

Victims as threat

Finally, the identity construction literature focuses on perpetrators' conceptions of the victim group as a source of danger or threat that the perpetrators believe they must counter through the physical destruction of the victims. For strategic choice theorists like Valentino, the victims of genocide are conceptualized as a threat because they are seen to stand in the way of the realization of radical policy goals. For scholars who focus on identity construction specifically, perceptions of the threat believed to be posed by the victim group are said to be manifested in fear of the victim group, including fear of death in general and fear of lethal contamination and extermination in particular.

Charny argues that genocidal killing is an extreme but logical product of an all-too-human process of projecting onto others that which we fear most. In genocide, the overwhelming fear of death itself is projected by the perpetrators onto the victims. The perpetrator thus kills his or her victims because "he believes he is justified in sparing himself death" by causing the death of others.[109] Sharpening Charney's rather general explanation, Chirot and McCauley suggest that genocidal killers are motivated by specific fears that grow out of a more general fear of death. For these authors, fear of "pollution" is the "most extreme reason" for genocidal and mass killing and for other policies such as deportation. Here the victim group is seen to represent a "mortal danger" that must be removed from society in some way. This fear of pollution stems historically from concerns with religious purity, and in the twentieth century from concerns with racial and class purity.[110]

Perceptions of threat can also, according to Chirot and McCauley, produce other powerful emotions such as hatred of the victim group. Because the victim group is seen to be possessed of a "bad essence" (see above), that essence produces a hatred of the victim group grounded in a conception of the group as so "fundamentally flawed" that it "cannot be fixed."[111] As noted earlier, Chirot and McCauley point to a dynamic they call "double essentializing," in which a "battle" ensues between "good and evil," between the "two incompatible essences" of the perpetrators and the victims, in which the love for members of the in-group necessarily engenders hate for the threatening out-group. For Chirot and McCauley, the double essentializing dynamic is at the heart of the most extreme genocides.[112]

The conception of victims as threat is amplified by the perception of the victims as a powerful force bent on the extermination of the perpetrators, the state, society, the nation, the race, or a new revolutionary order. Given what is perceived to be the very real possibility of one's own extermination at the hands of the victim group, the latter must be exterminated first. Psychologist Robert Jay Lifton, for example, concludes his study of Nazi doctors at Auschwitz by suggesting that "[w]here the threat is so absolute and so ultimate [. . .] genocide becomes not only appropriate but an urgent necessity."[113] Lifton continues,

> thus perceived as an absolute threat to the continuous life of one's own people, the victim group is seen as the bearer of death and therefore the embodiment of evil. More than merely non-human or heathen, it is dangerously anti-man and anti-God. Its disease takes the form of infecting others with death taint and deadly weakness. [. . .] Only genocide, total elimination of the disease will protect one from that weakness.

The victim group "threatens one's own people with extinction so one must absolutely extinguish [them] first."[114] Chirot and McCauley argue that genocidal killers are motivated by the short-term fear that "failure to enforce vengeance will ultimately allow the enemy to regain strength and inflict further punishment" and by long-term fears of collective extermination at the hands of the victim group.[115]

The literature on identity construction contributes to our overall understanding of why and how genocide happens by demonstrating that perceptions of the victim group matter. Elites and ordinary people base their actions toward the victim group on how they perceive the identity of the victim group, because the interests and actions (past, present, and future) of the victim group are believed to rest on the group's collective identity. The existing literature, while promising, needs to be developed further to flesh out the exact relationship between collective identity construction, on the one hand, and the initiation and acceptance of genocidal policies, on the other. As it is, how exactly perceptions of the victim group lead to genocide, and not some other form of repression and violence, is treated in a rather general way. One possible avenue of inquiry is to explore the proposition that the relationship between collective identity construction, interests, and actions is a linear one whereby perpetrators believe that the identity of the victim group determines the group's interests, which, in turn, determines its actions. This perceived relationship between identity, interests, and actions could be what links perceptions of difference, non-humanness, and threat to the initiation, implementation, and acceptance of genocidal policies.

The identity construction literature also needs to consider more carefully how the identities of the victim group are constructed in the first place and how this construction can change over time. The works of Fein and of Hirsch and Smith serve as a starting point for exploring how the historic relationship between groups and perceptions of the nature of that relationship, particularly exclusionary attitudes toward the eventual victims of genocide, underpin later, more malevolent constructions of the victims as foreigners, enemies, threats, and subhuman vermin. We must also search for the triggers that turn generalized long-standing anti-group feelings, attitudes, and practices into the specific kinds of identity construction that are linked to genocide. Crises and the rise to power of highly ideological radical political elites are likely candidates for the transformation of the eventual victims of genocide from marginal insiders seen in a negative light to pernicious, threatening "enemies within" requiring extermination.

Finally, the literature sometimes appears to conflate what are in fact different but interrelated conceptions of the victim group. This conflation obscures our understanding of the specific functions that each of these conceptions plays in the genocidal process. Although this review groups the literature into three categories of identity construction (victims as outsiders, victims as non-humans, and victims as threat), genocidal scholars have a tendency to refer to disparate conceptions simultaneously, in an undifferentiated list of labels, as if they were all one and the same. Hirsch and Smith, for example, begin their stimulating analysis of language, myth, and genocide by suggesting that the first function of exclusionary language and myths is "defining the out-group." The label "defining the out-group" would seem to suggest a specific conception of the victim group as outsiders or foreigners, but the section begins with language that defines the victims not just as other or foreign but as "vermin, infidels, traitors, heretics, enemies of the people," all of which are said to loosen inhibitions against mass killing.[116] Chalk and Jonassohn likewise argue that one of the key precursors to genocide is the perception that the victim group is not equal to, and fundamentally different from, the wider community. The conceptions of the victim group in the authors' analysis subsequently include references to the victims as "less than fully human" ("pagans, savages, and even animals"), "worthless, outside the web of mutual obligations, a threat to the people, immoral sinners, and/or sub/human."[117] If we look at Hirsch and Smith and Chalk and Jonassohn's lists of conceptions of the victim group, we find that some of the conceptions are rather different from others. Some of them conceptualize the victims as outsider ("infidels," "heretics," "outside the web of mutual obligations"), some as sub- or non-human ("vermin," "less than fully human," "pagans," "savages," "animals," "worthless," "sub-human"), and some as threats ("enemies of the people," "a threat to the people").

Drawing distinctions among different perceptions of the victim group rather than treating them as different names for the same perception is important if, as suggested earlier, we argue that perceptions of identity determine perceptions of interests and future actions. Victims who are defined by the perpetrator group as outsiders or foreigners are seen to have fundamental interests that do not fit with those of the wider community. Victims who are defined as subhuman or as animals are seen to be so base as to be completely expendable. Victims who are conceptualized as threats are seen as powerful forces, as mortally imperiling the survival of the entire political community. It is this latter conception of the victim group that motivates genocide, not the dehumanization of the victims or seeing the victims as outsiders and foreigners. The last two conceptions are a necessary part of the genocidal process because they facilitate killing and because they separate the victims from the rest of society, respectively. But neither of these conceptions serves as the motivator for genocide, because they are too benign: non-humans are so low as to be nothing and, therefore, cannot constitute an overwhelming threat; groups conceived of as only outsiders or foreigners are believed to be non-members of the community and, therefore, are not owed rights or obligations, but this conception on its own does not threaten the community and does not require a genocidal response. Only the "mortal threat" conception of the victim group leads elites to initiate, and society to accept, genocidal policies, because only this conception requires elites and society to act to protect themselves from a threat whose continued existence is perceived to portend their own destruction if it is not first neutralized through genocidal policies.

The way forward

Comparative genocide theorizing has flourished over the last twenty years. Scholars from a variety of disciplines have produced theories to explain the genocidal behavior of elite and societal actors and have identified the big and small structures and processes that lead to genocide. What we need to do now is concentrate on how we theorize, specifically how we create comparative theories and how we test those theories using the comparative method.

As the review above has shown, many genocide scholars have already begun to generate theories in which the exact variables at play in the genocidal process are spelled out in great detail. We must continue this trend, and we must think very carefully, as we theorize, not just about the variables we think are associated with genocide but about precisely what the relationship is between the variables we think are important and under what conditions these variables produce genocidal policies or behavior. In doing so, we should clearly state whether we are making deterministic claims (A, B, and C cause D) or whether we are making probabilistic claims (D is more likely to occur when A, B, and C occur under a specific set of circumstances). Once the relevant variables and the relationship between them are identified, we should further indicate precisely what empirical indicators we will use to illustrate each variable and to measure the effect of each variable. Here we need to demonstrate what evidence in each case will be used as a measure of a given variable and why we think that evidence is comparable to evidence measuring the same variable in other cases. If we do this, scholars and readers can be more confident that the evidence cited really does measure the variables under investigation and that we are making valid and stable comparisons across cases, rather than telling general narratives in support of theoretical claims.

Methodological discussions, to date, have tended to revolve for the most part around which cases we can compare based on a specific definition and which cases we cannot compare because they do not constitute genocide. This is always an important, albeit divisive, part of the comparative process and needs to continue. Beyond this, however, we need to begin to evaluate the comparison of cases based on other, more strictly comparative methodological criteria. Scholars need to explicitly consider the relative merits and limitations of ideographic (single-case-study) versus nomothetic (multiple-case-study) theorizing and comparisons. Ideographic studies can still be comparative, so long as the theories they generate and test can be generalized, at least to a certain degree, to explain similar cases. Nomothetic comparisons, of which we are seeing more and more, should contemplate the relative advantages and disadvantages of intensive comparisons (a small number of cases and a large number of variables) versus extensive comparisons (a large number of cases and a small number of variables). The former approach currently represents most genocide case comparisons. These sorts of comparisons allow for the "thick" description and analysis of a small number of cases using theories that include a number of variables designed to explain the vast complexity of the cases; this approach, however, is limited in terms of generalizability. The latter approach, adopted by Barbara Harff, for example, eschews "thick" description in favor of relatively parsimonious theories of genocide and politicide tested against a very large number of cases in order to construct and test much more general theories of genocide and politicide. Whichever approach scholars use, we need to justify why we have taken the approach we have and why we think it contributes to our knowledge of genocide.

Finally, when we choose our cases, we should state whether we are engaging in what Adam Przeworski and Henry Teune call "most similar systems" or "most different systems" comparisons.[118] As Przeworski and Teune tell us, *most similar* comparisons are the most effective and reliable comparisons, because they control for a wide number of variables, allowing the researcher to test the effect of variation in only a small number of variables. *Most different* comparisons, on the other hand, are comparisons in which there is a number of differences across each case but where a few key variables are the same. This kind of comparison also tests how much variation across cases of genocide a theory can explain. Like ideographic versus nomothetic comparisons, most similar and most different comparisons have their pros and cons. It is up to genocide scholars to decide which approach is most appropriate and, again, to justify why a most-similar or most-different approach is amenable to each scholar's research question, theoretical approach, and available evidence. Manus Midlarsky's *The Killing Trap* (a nomothetic study) and Scott Straus's *The Order of Genocide* (an ideographic study) are leading examples of the ways in which genocidal scholars in the social sciences should be thinking through comparative theoretical and methodological issues and problems when creating and testing comparative theories.

Sound theory, methodology, and research in comparative genocide studies are of value as an academic enterprise, but they should also be an important foundation for the formulation of effective strategies for genocide prevention and reconciliation after genocide. As a goal-oriented project, genocide studies must find a way to bridge the gap between abstract theorizing, on the one hand, and concrete policy making and implementation, on the other. Although our theories may tell us that factors such as human social psychology, societal fragmentation, various forms of crises, radical exclusionary ideologies, and conceptions of collective identity lead to genocide, how to turn this knowledge into concrete workable policies in real life and real time is not entirely obvious. Generalizability, while a desirable goal for comparative research, is not necessarily the goal with respect to crafting policies for prevention and, when required, intervention. Grand schemes to remake societies at greater risk of genocidal violence will be futile if they are one-size-fits-all policies or if they envision massive and sustained intervention in the domestic affairs of sovereign states by other states, intergovernmental organizations, or non-governmental organizations. No matter how passionate genocide scholars are about finding ways to prevent genocide, prescriptions for prevention that fail to take into account the realities of sovereignty, the cold hard realpolitik of international relations, and the real economic costs (not to mention the question of who will pay those costs) are not worth the effort. Genocide scholars, activists, and policy makers may also have to confront the very real possibility that regimes bent on waging "final solutions" against their perceived enemies may not be swayed by what the outside world thinks or does.

Similarly, strategies for fostering reconciliation in societies that have experienced genocide must avoid totalizing approaches that fail to recognize the particularities of individual cases. Approaches to reconciliation must, of course, take into account what we know in general about group dynamics in genocidal situations in order to move beyond them, but our prescriptions must first and foremost focus on culturally and situationally specific conditions and the concrete reality of individual and group dynamics on the ground. We must also take a good hard look at what reconciliation strategies have and have not worked, why they have or have not worked, where they have been successful and not, who has benefited and who has not. As in the case of prevention, crafting strategies for reconciliation is not the exclusive purview of genocide scholars. Prevention and reconciliation are collaborative projects that, by necessity, involve policy makers, activists, professionals, survivors, victims' families and communities, and the perpetrators or would-be perpetrators.

In sum, comparative genocide theory has come a long way in a short time. As in all disciplines and subjects in the social sciences and humanities, there is more work to do. But we should never forget that comparative genocide studies is far more than the scholarly pursuit of theory, testing, and generalization. We must remember the harsh reality of what it is we are really trying to do: to discover, bit by bit, why humanity continues to perpetrate this terrible crime, and why it is that innocent men, women, and children, simply because they continue to exist, fall victim to this "old scourge."

Notes

1 For a review essay on the state of comparative genocide research see Scott Straus, "Second Generation Comparative Research on Genocide," *World Politics* 59 (2007): 476–501.

2 This article also leaves aside discussions of typologies in the literature, again because they have been discussed elsewhere, but also because typologies are primarily an exercise in categorization. While typologies do hold some important explanatory power, they are, like definitions of concepts, a foundation upon which theories are constructed, not theories in and of themselves.

3 This characterization of comparative genocide studies is based on David Laitin's similar observation on the current state of comparative politics: David D. Laitin, "Toward a Political Science Discipline: Authority Patterns Revisited," *Comparative Political Studies* 13 (1998): 423–43.

4 Gerald Fleming, *Hitler and the Final Solution* (Berkeley: University of California Press, 1982).

5 See, e.g., David P. Chandler, *Brother Number One: A Political Biography of Pol Pot*, rev. ed. (Boulder, CO: Westview Press, 1999); Ian Kershaw, *Hitler 1936–1945: Nemesis* (London: Allen Lane/Penguin, 2000).

6 Benjamin A. Valentino, *Final Solutions: Mass Killing and Genocide in the 20th Century* (Ithaca, NY: Cornell University Press, 2004); Manus I. Midlarsky, *The Killing Trap: Genocide in the Twentieth Century* (Cambridge: Cambridge University Press, 2005).

7 Valentino, *Final Solutions*, 4, 72–73.

8 Daniel Chirot and Clark McCauley, *Why Not Kill Them All?: The Logic and Prevention of Mass Murder* (Princeton, NJ: Princeton University Press, 2006), 20, 2.

9 Theodor W. Adorno, Else Frenkel, and Daniel J. Levinsons, *The Authoritarian Personality: Studies in Prejudice*, abridged ed. (New York: W.W. Norton, 1993).

10 Chirot and McCauley, *Why Not Kill Them All?*; James Waller, *Becoming Evil: How Ordinary People Commit Genocide and Mass Murder* (Oxford: Oxford University Press, 2002); Alex Alvarez, *Governments, Citizens, and Genocide: A Comparative and Interdisciplinary Approach* (Bloomington: Indiana University Press, 2001).

11 Chirot and McCauley, *Why Not Kill Them All?*, 20–44.

12 Ibid., 52.

13 Ibid., 90.

14 Ibid., 61.

15 Ibid., 86.

16 Waller, *Becoming Evil*, 19–20.

17 Alvarez, *Governments, Citizens, and Genocide*, 110.

18 Ibid., 114–28.

19 Because Alvarez takes a structural rather than an agency-centered approach with respect to institutions, the review of his analysis of the modern state and state institutions as principal perpetrators of genocide is covered below, in the section on structural theories.

20 See Adorno et al., *The Authoritarian Personality*.

21 See, e.g., Ervin Staub, *The Roots of Evil: The Psychological and Cultural Origins of Genocide and Other Forms of Group Violence* (Cambridge: Cambridge University Press, 1989).

22 Daniel Jonah Goldhagen, *Hitler's Willing Executioners: Ordinary Germans and the Holocaust* (New York: Vintage Books, 1997).

23 Alexander Laban Hinton, *Why Did They Kill? Cambodia in the Shadow of Genocide* (Berkeley: University of California Press, 2005).

24 Alexander Laban Hinton, "A Head for an Eye: Revenge in the Cambodian Genocide," *American Ethnologist* 25 (1998): 352–77, 353.

25 Ibid., 353.

26 Christopher C. Taylor, "The Cultural Face of Terror in the Rwandan Genocide of 1994," in *Annihilating Difference: The Anthropology of Genocide*, ed. Alexander Laban Hinton, 137–78 (Berkeley: University of California Press, 2002), 139.

27 Omer Bartov, "Seeking the Roots of Modern Genocide: On the Macro and Microhistory of Mass Murder," in *The Specter of Genocide: Mass Murder in Historical Perspective*, ed. Robert Gellately and Ben Kiernan, 75–96 (Cambridge: Cambridge University Press, 2003), 85.

28 Jan Tomasz Gross, *Neighbors: The Destruction of the Jewish Community in Jedwabne, Poland*, (Princeton, NJ: Princeton University Press, 2001).

29 Leo Kuper, *Genocide* (New Haven: Yale University Press, 1981), 57.

30 Ibid., 58.

31 Richard G. Hovannisian, "Etiology and Sequelae of the Armenian Genocide," in *Genocide: Conceptual and Historical Dimensions*, ed. George J. Andreopoulos, 111–40 (Philadelphia: University of Pennsylvania Press, 1994), 112.

32 Kuper, *Genocide*, 59.

33 Alexander Laban Hinton, "The Dark Side of Modernity: Toward an Anthropology of Genocide," in *Annihilating Difference: The Anthropology of Genocide*, ed. Alexander Laban Hinton, 1–42 (Berkeley: University of California Press, 2002), 29.

34 Helen Fein, "Accounting for Genocide after 1945: Theories and Some Findings," *International Journal on Group Rights* 1 (1993): 88–92.

35 Helen Fein, "Revolutionary and Anti-revolutionary Genocides: A Comparison of State Murders in Democratic Kampuchea, 1975 to 1979, and in Indonesia, 1965 to 1966," *Comparative Studies in Society and History* 35 (1993): 796–823.

36 See, e.g., Valentino, *Final Solutions*, 16–22. Valentino cites large-scale quantitative studies including James D. Fearson and David D. Laitin, "Ethnicity, Insurgency and Civil War," *American Political Science Review* 97 (2003): 75–90; Matthew Krain,

"State Sponsored Mass Murder: The Onset and Severity of Genocides and Politicides," *Journal of Conflict Resolution* 41 (1997): 331–60; Barbara Harff, "No Lessons Learned from the Holocaust? Assessing Risks of Genocide and Political Mass Murder Since 1955," *American Political Science Review* 97 (2003): 67–68. While these kinds of studies are useful, they attempt to control for, and, therefore, factor out as much as possible, the effect of contextual factors. They are also much more vulnerable to coding errors because of the sheer number of cases and the lack of specific expertise by the researcher(s) in most of the cases in the comparison.

37 This argument is the inverse of Robert Putnam's thesis that democratic institutions work best in an environment of "civic engagement" characterized by a high degree of solidarity, trust, and tolerance between groups in society and a rich associational life that cuts across communal cleavages. Robert D. Putnam, *Making Democracy Work: Civic Traditions in Modern Italy* (Princeton, NJ: Princeton University Press, 1993), 167–76.

38 Helen Fein, *Accounting for Genocide: National Responses and Jewish Victimization During the Holocaust* (Chicago: University of Chicago Press, 1979), 9.

39 Midlarsky, *The Killing Trap*, 103–7.

40 Florence Mazian, *Why Genocide: The Armenian and Jewish Experiences in Perspective* (Ames: Iowa University Press, 1990), 145, 21–42, 145–56.

41 Staub, *The Roots of Evil*, 107–10.

42 Hinton, "The Dark Side of Modernity," 29.

43 Harff, "No Lessons Learned," 66.

44 Chirot and McCauley, *Why Not Kill Them All?*, 94.

45 Tarrow developed this concept to account for the rise and timing of social movements. Sidney Tarrow, *Power in Movement: Social Movement, Collective Action, and Politics* (Cambridge: Cambridge University Press, 1994).

46 Lucy S. Dawidowicz, *The War Against the Jews: 1933–1945* (New York: Bantam Books, 1975).

47 Alexander Wendt, "Anarchy Is What States Make of It: The Social Construction of Power Politics," *International Organization* 46 (1992): 391–425.

48 Robert F. Melson, *Revolution and Genocide: On the Origins of the Armenian Genocide and the Holocaust* (Chicago: University of Chicago Press, 1992), 260, 267.

49 Edward Kissi, *Revolution and Genocide in Ethiopia and Cambodia* (Lanham, MD: Lexington Books, 2006), 79–120.

50 Eric Markusen, "Genocide and Total War: A Preliminary Comparison," in *Genocide and the Modern Age: Etiology and Case Studies of Mass Death*, ed. Isidor Wallimann and Michael N. Dobkowski, 97–123 (Syracuse, NY: Syracuse University Press, 1987); Eric Markusen and David Kopf, *The Holocaust and Strategic Bombing: Genocide and Total War in the Twentieth Century* (Boulder, CO: Westview Press, 1995), 55–92.

51 Markusen and Kopf, *The Holocaust and Strategic Bombing*, 64.

52 Ibid.

53 Ibid., 65.

54 Scott Straus, *The Order of Genocide: Race, Power, and War in Rwanda* (Ithaca, NY: Cornell University Press, 2006), 7.

55 Omer Bartov, *Mirrors of Destruction: War, Genocide, and Modern Identity* (Oxford: Oxford University Press, 2000), 18.

56 Ibid., 12.

57 Ibid., 29.

58 Martin Shaw, *War and Genocide: Organized Killing in Modern Society* (Cambridge: Polity Press, 2003), 5.

59 Ibid., 27.

60 Ibid., 44–45.

61 Ibid., 28.

62 Ibid., 46.

63 Ibid., 28.

64 *Convention on the Prevention and Punishment of the Crime of Genocide*, 9 December 1948, 78 U.N.T.S. 277, http://www.unhchr.ch/html/menu3/b/p_genoci.htm (accessed 18 September 2008), art. 2.

65 Helen Fein, *Genocide: A Sociological Perspective* (London: Sage, 1993), × (emphasis added).

66 Frank Chalk and Kurt Jonassohn, *The History and Sociology of Genocide: Analyses and Case Studies* (New Haven: Yale, 1990), 23 (emphasis added).

67 Israel W. Charny, "Toward a Generic Definition of Genocide," in *Genocide: Conceptual and Historical Dimensions*, ed. George J. Andreopoulos, 64–94 (Philadelphia: University of Pennsylvania Press, 1994), 75 (emphasis added).

68 Irving Horowitz, *Taking Lives: Genocide and State Power*, 4th ed. (New Brunswick, NJ: Transaction Publishers, 1997).

69 Hannah Arendt, *Origins of Totalitarianism* (New York: Harcourt Brace, 1979), 437–59.

70 The label "totalitarian," as distinct from authoritarianism, has always been controversial, as it has not always been clear that actually existing regimes usually labeled totalitarian, such as Nazi Germany or Stalinist Russia, really achieved the total penetration of all aspects of life suggested by prevailing theories of totalitarianism.

71 Rudolph J. Rummel, *Death by Government* (New Brunswick, NJ: Transaction Publishers, 1994), 1–2.

72 Harff, "No Lessons Learned," 66.

73 In one of his early works, Robert Putnam refers to these kinds of elites as "conflict-oriented politicians" for whom conflict is highly salient. They are likely to be "fragmented and paralyzed, for their cognitive lenses magnify conflicting interests and minimize mutual interest." The interpersonal orientation of these elites is riven by "personal and partisan antagonism," a "culture of conspiracy, mutual suspicion and cynicism." Robert Putnam, *The Comparative Study of Political Elites* (Englewood Cliffs, NJ: Prentice Hall, 1976), 86.

74 Zygmunt Bauman, *Modernity and the Holocaust* (Ithaca, NY: Cornell University Press, 1989), 98–111.

75 Ibid., 66–76.

76 Alvarez, *Governments, Citizens, and Genocide*, 57, 59.

77 Ibid., 59.

78 Ibid.

79 Ibid., 63.

80 Ibid., 71–78.

81 Ibid., 93, 94–97.

82 Ibid., 97–100.

83 See, e.g., Straus, *The Order of Genocide*.

84 Chalk and Jonassohn, *The History and Sociology of Genocide*, 37–40; Helen Fein, "Revolution and Anti-Revolutionary Genocides: A Comparison of State Murders in Democratic Kampuchea, 1975–1979 and in Indonesia, 1965–1966," *Comparative Studies in Society and History* 35 (1993): 796–823; Peter du Preez, *Genocide: The Psychology of Mass Murder* (London: Boyars/Bowerdean, 1994), 28–47.

85 Eric D. Weitz, *A Century of Genocide: Utopias of Race and Nation* (Princeton, NJ: Princeton University Press, 2003).

86 Hinton, "Toward an Anthropology of Genocide," 8.

87 Ibid., 12–13.

88 Weitz, *A Century of Genocide*, 17–31.

89 Ibid., 45–46.

90 Ibid., 39.

91 Ibid., 47.
92 Ben Kiernan, "Twentieth Century Genocides: Underlying Ideological Themes from Armenia to East Timor," *The Specter of Genocide: Mass Murder in Historical Perspective*, ed. Robert Gellately and Ben Kiernan, 29–52 (Cambridge: Cambridge University Press, 2003), 29, 33, 40–45. Also see Ben Kiernan, *Blood and Soil: A World History of Genocide and Extermination from Sparta to Darfur* (New Haven, CT: Yale University Press, 2007).
93 Chirot and McCauley, *Why Not Kill Them All?*, 82.
94 Ibid., 82.
95 Waller, *Becoming Evil*, 19–20.
96 Ibid., 43.
97 Fein, *Accounting for Genocide*, 4–5.
98 Herbert Hirsch and Roger W. Smith, "The Language of Extermination in Genocide," in *Genocide: A Critical Bibliographic Review*, vol. 2, ed. Israel W. Charny, 386–403 (London: Mansell Publishing, 1991), 387.
99 Ibid., 388–91.
100 Waller, *Becoming Evil*, 186.
101 Israel W. Charny, *How Can We Commit the Unthinkable? Genocide: The Human Cancer* (Boulder, CO: Westview Press, 1982), 207.
102 Chirot and McCauley, *Why Not Kill Them All?*, 84–85.
103 Gregory H. Stanton, "The 8 Stages of Genocide," Genocide Watch (1998), http://www. genocidewatch.org/aboutgenocide/8stages.htm (accessed 18 September 2008).
104 Waller, *Becoming Evil*, 20, 245.
105 Chalk and Jonassohn, *The History and Sociology of Genocide*, 28.
106 Waller, *Becoming Evil*, 20.
107 Charny, How Can We Commit the Unthinkable?, 206–7.
108 Herbert C. Kelman, "Violence Without Moral Restraint: Reflection on the Dehumanization of Victims by Victimizers," *Journal of Social Issues* 29 4 (1973): 25–61. 48–49.
109 Charny, *How Can We Commit the Unthinkable?*, 186, 192.
110 Chirot and McCauley, *Why Not Kill Them All?*, 36–42.
111 Ibid., 72–73.
112 Ibid., 86.
113 Robert Jay Lifton, *The Nazi Doctors: Medical Killing and the Psychology of Genocide* (New York: Basic Books, 1986), 477.
114 Ibid., 479.
115 Chirot and McCauley, *Why Not Kill Them All?*, 31–32.
116 Hirsch and Smith, "The Language of Extermination in Genocide," 388.
117 Chalk and Jonassohn, *The History and Sociology of Genocide*, 28.
118 Adam Przeworski and Henry Teune, *The Logic of Comparative Social Inquiry* (New York: Wiley, 1970), 31–46.

APPENDICES
GEOGRAPHICAL MAPS

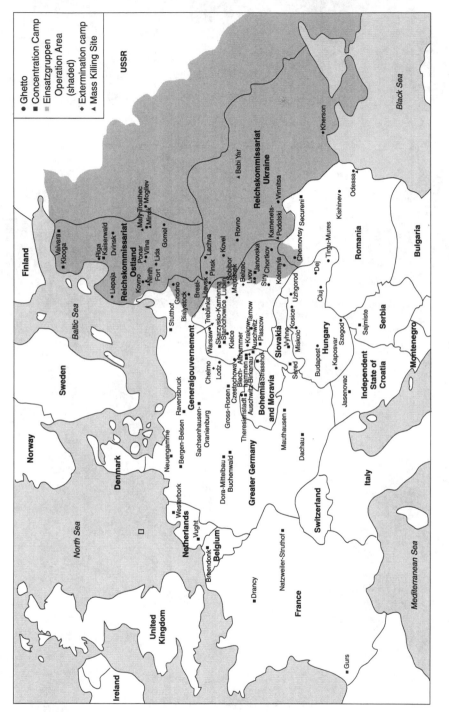

Map 1 – Main ghettos, concentration camps, extermination camps, and mass killing sites in German-occupied Europe.

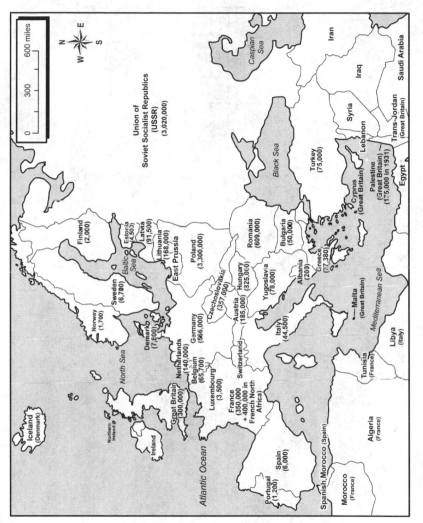

Map 2 – Estimated Jewish populations in pre-World War II Europe. Adapted from a map by Becky L. Eden, Arizona Geographic Alliance, Arizona State University.

Note: Boundaries are approximate as they were constantly changing during this period

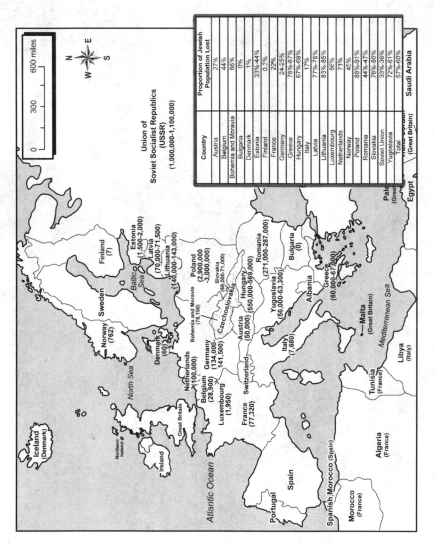

Map 3 – Jewish victims in the Holocaust, totalling 5,860,129–5,969,029.

Adapted from a map by Becky L. Eden, Arizona Geographic Alliance, Arizona State University.

Note: Boundaries are approximate as they were constantly changing during this period.

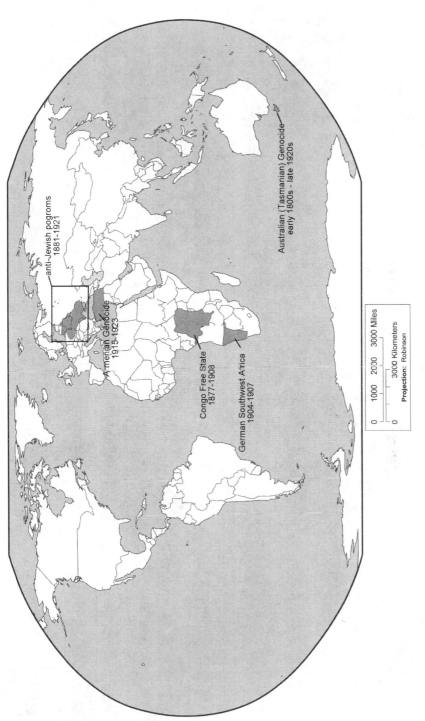

Map 4 – Colonial-imperial genocides and other mass killings between the late nineteenth century and World War II. Adapted from a map by Terry Dorschied, Arizona Geographic Alliance, Arizona State University.

The following labels appear on the map:

anti-Jewish pogroms
1881-1921

Armenian Genocide
1915-1923

Congo Free State
1877-1908

German Southwest Africa
1904-1907

Australian (Tasmanian) Genocide
early 1800s - late 1920s

0   1000   2000   3000 Miles

0   3000 Kilometers

Projection: Robinson

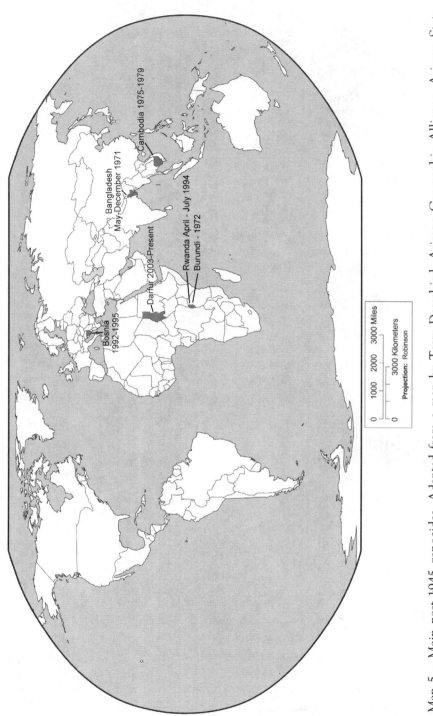

Map 5 – Main post-1945 genocides. Adapted from a map by Terry Dorschied, Arizona Geographic Alliance, Arizona State University.

CHRONOLOGY

1850   German composer Richard Wagner publishes *Das Judenthum in der Musik* (*Judaism in Music*), denouncing the influence of Jews on culture.

1853–55   French diplomat and writer Arthur de Gobineau publishes *Essai sur l'inégalité des races humaines* (*Essay on the Inequality of the Human Races*), asserting the superiority of the white race.

1859   British scientist Charles Darwin publishes *On the Origin of Species*, proposing and documenting his theory of evolution.

1866   German biologist Ernst Haeckel publishes *Generelle Morphologie der Organismen* (*General Morphology of Organisms*), introducing his notion of evolutionary racism and the need to preserve German racial purity.

1879   German journalist Wilhelm Marr publishes *Der Sieg des Judenthums über das Germanenthum* (*The Victory of Jewry over Germandom*) and establishes the League of Antisemites, thereby popularizing the term anti-Semitism throughout Europe.

1880   German historian Heinrich von Treitschke publishes *Ein Wort über unser Judenthum* (*A Word about Our Jews*), coining the phrase "the Jews are our misfortune," later used as the motto of the Nazi rag *Der Stürmer*.

1881   German philosopher and economist Eugen Karl Dühring publishes *Die Judenfrage als Racen-, Sitten- and Culturfrage* (*The Jewish Question as a Racial, Moral, and Cultural Question*), presenting the Jews as corrupting their environment and proposing their isolation, internment, and deportation (later calling for their annihilation).

407

1881–84　Following the assassination of Russian Tsar Alexander II, a wave of pogroms against Jews, primarily in Ukraine, results in scores of deaths, hundreds of rapes, and massive property damage and looting, sparking mass Jewish immigration.

1885–1908　Belgian King Leopold's rule over the Congo Free State, using forced labor for the extraction of ivory and rubber, results in the death of approximately ten million Africans.

1886　French journalist Édouard Drumont publishes *La France Juive* (*Jewish France*), calling to prevent the Jews' alleged takeover and destruction of France by forcing them out of public life.

1894–1906　The conviction on false charges of Jewish French army captain Alfred Dreyfus of treason sparks a protracted debate in France pitting proponents of anti-Semitism against the opponents of prejudice and racism.

1895　German physician Alfred Ploetz begins publishing his *Grundlinien eine Rassen-Hygiene* (*Basics of a Race Hygiene*) calling to eliminate medical care for "weak" races; in 1905 he founds the German Society for Racial Hygiene.

1903　Publication of *The Protocols of the Elders of Zion*, a widely distributed forgery produced by the Russian secret police, allegedly documenting a plot by the Jews to destroy Christian civilization and achieve world domination.

1904–7　Sparked by the Russo-Japanese War and the 1905 revolution, another wave of pogroms claims some 3,000 Jewish lives, with over 17,000 wounded, mass rapes, and widespread plunder and destruction mostly in Russia's southern regions.

1904–7　In response to an uprising against the settlers of German Southwest Africa, the German military commander orders the extermination of the Nama and Herero peoples, thereby unleashing the first genocide of the twentieth century, in which up to 110,000 Africans are murdered.

1915–16　Under the cover of World War I, the Ottoman Empire systematically murders up to 1.5 million Armenians, combining deportations, death marches, concentration camps, and mass shootings, in the first ever instance of a modern genocidal campaign.

1917–19　A third wave of pogroms during the Russian Civil War claims up to 100,000 Jewish victims and the destruction of whole communities, primarily in Ukraine.

1918–19	World War I ends with Germany's surrender. The emperor abdicates and the Weimar Republic is established, accepting the harsh terms of the peace Treaty of Versailles.
1920	German jurist Karl Binding and psychiatrist Alfred Hoche publish *Die Freigabe der Vernichtung lebensunwerten Lebens* (*Allowing the Destruction of Life Unworthy of Life*), calling for the "mercy killing" of the mentally and physically disabled.
1920	The Nazi Party (*Nationalsozialistische Deutsche Arbeiterpartei*, National Socialist German Workers Party, NSDAP) is established.
1921	Adolf Hitler becomes leader of the NSDAP.
1923	Hitler's attempt to seize power in Munich in the "Beer Hall Putsch" fails. Hitler is tried and imprisoned but released after only 9 months.
1925	Publication of Hitler's violently anti-Semitic pamphlet *Mein Kampf* (*My Struggle*), presenting history as a ruthless racial war for existence and advocating German conquest of "living space."
1929–30	Growing unemployment in Germany as a result of the Great Depression.
1930	Massive electoral victory for the NSDAP makes it the second largest party in Germany.
1932	The NSDAP become the largest party in Germany with over 37 percent of the vote.
January 30, 1933	Hitler is appointed Reich Chancellor.
March 23, 1933	Passage of the Enabling Act, allowing the government to pass laws without parliamentary consent.
July 14, 1933	The NSDAP is declared the only legal political party in Germany; the *Gesetz zur Verhütung erbkranken Nachwuchses* (Law for the Prevention of Genetically Diseased Offspring) is passed, resulting in the sterilization of 400,000 German citizens over the next few years.
1933–34	A series of racial laws drastically restrict Jewish participation in public life, including state service, the military, schools and universities, and the professions.
June 30, 1934	Hitler employs the army and Heinrich Himmler's SS to murder the leaders of the Storm Troops (SA) and other perceived opponents, thereby launching Himmler's rise as the regime's chief police and race enforcer.

August 2, 1934   President Paul von Hindenburg dies and Hitler is declared Führer and Reich Chancellor of Germany.

September 15, 1935   The Nuremberg Laws are declared, revoking Jewish German citizenship, criminalizing sexual relations with Aryans, depriving Jews of numerous civil rights, and subsequently defining Jews by ancestry.

November 9–10, 1938   *Kristallnacht* (night of broken glass), a state-organized, country-wide pogrom, in which hundreds of synagogues and 7,500 Jewish businesses, homes, and schools are destroyed, 91 Jews murdered, and 28,000 Jewish men taken to concentration camps, about 1,000 of whom die.

September 1, 1939   World War II begins with Germany's invasion of Poland.

October 1939   Beginning of the "euthanasia" or T-4 program, in which 200,000 mentally and physically handicapped German citizens are murdered, often in gassing facilities that provide a model for the later extermination camps.

1939–41   Expulsions of Polish and Jewish inhabitants of western Polish territories annexed by Germany in order to facilitate resettlement by ethnic Germans as part of the General Plan East, aimed at radically transforming Eastern Europe's demography.

1940–41   Concentration of Polish Jews in often walled-off ghettos, the largest of which are Warsaw, Lodz, Krakow, Lublin, and Czestochowa, and later also Kovno, Minsk, Bialystok, Vilna, and Lviv. Hundreds of thousands of residents die from famine, epidemics, and direct killings.

June 22, 1941   The Wehrmacht's invasion of the Soviet Union unleashes a "war of extermination" against "Judeo-Bolshevism" claiming the lives of up to 30 million Soviet citizens and soldiers, including over three million prisoners of war and hundreds of thousands of political commissars shot without trial.

July 1941 – summer 1943   Four *Einsatzgruppen* (mobile killing units) made up of police and SS personnel follow the Wehrmacht into the USSR, murdering over a million Jews and other perceived biological and political enemies. In a single mass shooting in Babi Yar near Kiev in September 1941, 33,000 Jews are murdered in two days.

Late 1941 – November 1944   Establishment and operation of the six extermination camps Chelmno, Bełżec, Sobibor, Treblinka, Majdanek, and Auschwitz, where 3–3.5 million Jews, deported from across Europe, are murdered in gassing facilities.

March – October 1944	Following the German invasion of Hungary close to 438,000 Hungarian Jews are deported to Auschwitz. Altogether about 565,000 Hungarian Jews are murdered by the Nazis and local fascists.
Summer 1944 – May 1945	Himmler orders the evacuation of camp inmates to the west in a series of death marches in which tens of thousands are shot or die of hunger, disease, and exhaustion.
July 1944 – mid-April 1945	Discovery of death camps and liberation of concentration camps by the Red Army and the Western Allies, where many of the inmates continue to die of malnutrition and disease.
April 30, 1945	Hitler commits suicide in his Berlin bunker.
May 7, 1945	Germany signs the Instrument of Surrender.
August 1945 – October 1946	The International Military Tribunal (IMT) against 22 major Nazi war criminals held in Nuremberg.
1946–49	The Nuremberg Military Tribunals (NMT), a United States-led complex of 12 group trials of doctors, judges, industrialists, Einsatzgruppen commanders, the Wehrmacht's high command, and others.
November 29, 1947	The United Nations adopts a resolution recommending partition of Mandatory Palestine into an Arab State and a Jewish State. The plan is accepted by the Jewish leadership in Palestine but rejected by the Arab States.
May 14, 1948	The termination of the British Mandate in Palestine is followed by the declaration of the State of Israel, which absorbs some 650,000 Holocaust survivors and refugees from Arab lands within 18 months, thereby doubling its population.
May 15, 1948 – March 10, 1949	Attacked by neighboring Arab countries, Israel expands its territories beyond the UN partition plan. About 700,000 Palestinian Arabs are either expelled or flee from their homes and are barred from returning.
December 9, 1948	The United Nations Convention for the Prevention and Punishment of the Crime of Genocide, defined as "a crime under international law … committed with intent to destroy, in whole or in part, a national, ethnical, racial or religious group, as such."
December 10, 1948	The United Nations Universal Declaration of Human Rights, recognizing that "All human beings are born free and equal in dignity and rights," have "the right to life, liberty and security of person," and will not "be held in slavery or servitude" or "torture or to cruel, inhuman or degrading treatment or punishment."

May 1949	The creation of the Federal Republic of Germany (FRG) in the zone occupied by the Western Allies.
September 10, 1952	The Reparations Agreement between the FRG and Israel offers compensation for the suffering and material damage caused to European Jewry by the Nazi regime.
1961–63	Adolf Eichmann, former senior functionary in the Holocaust, is tried, convicted, and hanged in Israel, in the first judicial event focused entirely on the "final solution" including numerous survivor testimonies, but criticized by others as a politically-motivated show trial.
May – December 1971	In the course of a national liberation war in Bangladesh the Pakistani military murders anywhere between 300,000 and 3 million people; up to 200,000 women are raped, and 10 million become refugees.
1972	The Tutsi-led government of Burundi responds to a rebellion by Hutu insurgents with a mass murder of between 80,000–200,000 Hutu citizens.
1975–79	The communist Khmer Rouge regime in Cambodia, which it renames Kampuchea, murders 1.7 million people (over twenty per cent of the county's population), through displacement, forced labor, internal purges, and mass executions, targeting Buddhists, ethnic minorities, and "new citizens" (intellectuals and city-dwellers).
1992–95	Following Bosnia's declaration of independence local Serbs assisted by Belgrade attempt to "ethnically cleanse" the Muslims: some 100,000 are killed, two million displaced, thousands raped, and entire towns devastated. On July 13, 1995, approximately 8,000 Bosnian Muslim men and boys are executed in Srebrenica, Europe's single largest massacre since the Holocaust.
April – July 1994	The Hutu regime of Rwanda unleashes a deliberate and systematic genocide, led by the extremist Interahamwe militia. Within 100 days anywhere between 500,000 and a million Tutsis along with many moderate Hutu are murdered, mostly with light arms, machetes, and fire, in the fastest genocide of the modern era, in which vast numbers of women are also often first raped and about a million people become refugees.
2003 to the present	A local rebellion in Darfur against the Sudanese authorities spurs systematic mass killings, mass rape, eradication of entire villages, and scorched-earth actions by government forces and its *Janjaweed* militia, with an estimated 300,000–400,000 victims and a massive outpouring of refugees.

INDEX

Page numbers followed by "n" indicate notes: page numbers in italics indicate figures.